Educational
Ideologies

EDUCATIONAL IDEOLOGIES

Contemporary Expressions of Educational Philosophy

William F. O'Neill

University of Southern California

Goodyear Publishing Company, Inc.   Santa Monica, California

Library of Congress Cataloging in Publication Data

O'Neill, William F
    Educational ideologies.

    Includes bibliographical references and index.
    1. Education—Philosophy.   I. Title.
LB1025.2.053   370'.1   80-27816
ISBN 0-8302-2305-3

Copyright © 1981 by Goodyear Publishing Company, Inc.
Santa Monica, California 90401

Current printing (last digit):

10 9 8 7 6 5 4 3 2 1

ISBN: 0-8302-2305-3

Production Editor and Copy Editor: Susan Caney-Peterson
Text and Cover Designer: Linda M. Robertson
Proofreader and Indexer: Sonsie Carbonara Conroy
Typesetter: Composition Type
Page Layout: Valerie Takatani
Artist: Etc. Graphics
Printed in the United States of America

To Beverly Lewis O'Neill

He knoweth nothing as he ought to know, who thinks that he knoweth anything without seeing its place and the manner how it relateth to God, angels and men, and to all the creatures in earth, heaven and hell, time and eternity.

Thomas Traherne, Centuries of Meditation

$A = bh$ over 2.
  3.14 is π.
But I'd forgotten, if I ever knew,
  What R's divided by.
Though I knew once, I'd forgotten clean
  What a girl must study to reach fifteen—
How V is Volume and M's for Mass,
  And the hearts of the young are brittle as glass.

I had forgotten, and half with pride,
  Fifteen's no field of clover.
So here I sit at Annabelle's side,
  Learning my lessons over.
For help is something you have to give
  When daughters are faced with the Ablative
Or first encounter in any school
  Immutable gender's mortal rule.

Day after day for a weary spell,
  When the dusk has pitched its tents,
I sit with a book and Annabelle
  At the hour of confidence
And rummage for lore I had long consigned
  To cobwebby attics of my mind,
Like: For the Radius, write down R,
  The Volga's a river, Vega's a star,
Brazil's in the Tropic of Capricorn,
  And heart is a burden that has to be borne.

Oh, high is the price of parenthood,
  And daughters may cost you double.
You dare not forget, as you thought you could
  That youth is a plague and trouble.
N times 7 is $7n$—
Here I go learning it all again:
The climates of continents tend to vary,
The verb "to love" 's not auxiliary,
Tomorrow will come and today will pass,
But the hearts of the young are brittle as glass,

Phyllis McGinley, "Homework for Annabelle"

Contents

APPENDIX II:
MANUAL FOR THE EDUCATIONAL IDEOLOGIES
INVENTORY

GLOSSARY

INDEX

List of Figures

Preface

This book emerged out of an attempt to find a new way of thinking about the traditional approaches to the educational philosophies. It was originally designed as an outline taxonomy to accompany a collection of selected readings that would offer first-hand examples of the various ideological positions. In response to critical readings by students and colleagues, it grew, through several drafts, into a manuscript far too extensive to serve merely as a conceptual structure for an anthology, and is presented instead as an independent work.

THE FOCUS

This book is aimed primarily at pre-service and in-service students, largely upper-division or graduate, who are enrolled in professional education curricula at the college and university level. It is intended to be used in courses dealing with the philosophical foundations of education or in courses (such as the standard "Introduction to Education") that are largely devoted to providing some kind of basic overview of teaching and learning in America. The focus throughout is on contemporary public education in the United States, and, while historical developments are occasionally considered, and essentially non-American points of view (such as fascism and naziism) are discussed, they are included only because they relate to the basic philosophical options currently confronting public schooling in this country. Questions relating to the origins and intellectual history of the various ideologies, or to expressions of the major ideological positions that have occurred in different cultures at different points in history, exceed the scope of this study and are therefore deferred for a later work.

The book is organized in such a way as to move from the more conservative and traditional educational ideologies to those which are more liberal and unconventional. As in any philosophical enterprise, the model of educational ideologies developed here is essentially oversimplified and conceptual in nature. It is, in other words, a cognitive classification of different theories; and does not purport to be an accurate description of any particular philosophical position within education or to provide a definitive listing of all conceivable theoretical differences with respect to the nature and functions of education. Rather it attempts to provide a synthetic overview of the most significant ideological options in educational philosophy as they currently exist in our own culture.

SOME NECESSARY LIMITATIONS

No book can attempt to do everything, and this one is certainly no exception. The focus, throughout, has been intentionally restricted to a descriptive analysis of the various ideologies; and, while all of them are compared and contrasted in the final section, no attempt has been made to perform a philosophical critique of any or all of these orientations. This course of action has been followed for several reasons. First, a certain degree of evaluation is implicit in any attempt at defining philosophical positions. All perception is necessarily selective, and no attempt at designing a philosophical taxonomy can ever hope to be totally neutral or objective. Second, a critique of philosophical positions that goes beyond such matters as semantic clarification and purely logical analysis (which are incorporated as aspects of this work) is implicitly based on philosophical convictions that necessarily relate to one or more of the ideologies being discussed. As a result, such critiques tend to become ideological arguments in and of themselves.

Any sort of classification scheme with respect to complicated social phenomena is bound to fall short of its necessarily somewhat presumptuous intentions. As Abraham Kaplan states in his book *The Conduct of Inquiry*:

> ... we are caught up in a paradox ... which might be called *the paradox of conceptualization*. The proper concepts are needed to formulate a good theory, but we need a good theory to arrive at the proper concepts. . . . Every taxonomy is a provisional and implicit theory (or family of theories). . . . Like all existential dilemmas in science, of which this is an instance, the paradox is resolved by a process of approximation: the better our concepts, the better theory we can formulate with them, and, in turn, the better the concepts available for the next "successive definition." It is only through such successions that the scientist can hope ultimately to achieve success.[1]

> There is always something else to be explained, but it is surely not true that we understand nothing until we understand everything. Explanations, like concepts and laws, have a certain openness; in particular, every explanation is "intermediate," in the sense that it explains elements which are to be explained in turn.[2]

As Whitehead once counseled, it is necessary to "seek simplicity and distrust it," and as the Jain religion of ancient India states in its doctrine of *syadvada*, every proposition is true only up to a point or in certain respects. The taxonomy presented here is, to use Abraham Kaplan's terminology, both a *pattern model* of explanation, which shows the reason for something by fitting it into a known pattern, and, a *deductive model* of explanation, which shows how reasons can be deduced from other known truths.[4] Going along with Gunnar Myrdal, I have accepted the scale of radicalism-conservatism as "the master scale of biases" affecting both the perception and the solution of virtually all problems concerning human conduct.[6]

TREATMENT AND ORGANIZATION

With respect to the materials that follow, three preliminary comments are necessary.

First, while I have attempted to be objective, no special attempt has been made to give equal time to the various ideological positions. Because the theoretical foundations of educational fundamentalism and educational conservatism have been largely neglected in the literature concerned with educational philosophy, I have spent slightly more time on these positions than on some of the others that have been more frequently and explicitly discussed, and therefore tend to be better understood. In a similar sense, because religion in recent years has been treated as either irrelevant to educational philosophy or as something essentially nonphilosophical in nature, I have given more attention to the generally neglected religious expressions of the various educational ideologies—and particularly the more conservative ideologies, where specific religious doctrines frequently play a central role—than might otherwise have been the case.

Second, in the organization of the book I have altered the format of the chapters rather radically between Part II, which deals with the Conservative educational ideologies, and Part III, which deals with the Liberal educational ideologies. In dealing with the Conservative ideologies, the political and economic theories fundamental to the educational positions (as well as their secular and religious variations) are discussed in the same chapters as the educational positions themselves. Conversely, the section pertaining to the Liberal educational ideologies begins with a special chapter entitled ''The Liberal Ideologies,'' which gives extended consideration to the political and economic theories underlying these positions as well as to the secular and religious traditions that feed into them. The specific educational positions espoused by each of the three ideologies are considered in separate and much shorter chapters.

I have followed this procedure for two basic reasons: (1) The differences between the religious expressions of the Liberal ideologies, as well as that between the religious and secular expressions of the same ideologies within the Liberal spectrum, are far less important than is the case with the Conservative ideologies. This overview chapter provides an opportunity to discuss (and largely downgrade) the significance of this distinction as it relates to the Liberal orientations. (2) The Liberal ideologies tend to present more of a theoretical continuum with respect to political and economic beliefs, featuring largely differences in degree rather than kind, than do the Conservative ideologies, and this overview chapter provides an opportunity to discuss the entire range of Liberal traditions and the interrelationship that exists between them.

An additional variation between Part II (the Conservative ideologies) and Part III (the Liberal ideologies) occurs with the inclusion in Part III of John Dewey's brief manifesto of educational beliefs called *My Pedagogic Creed.* This selection (first published in 1897) was included as a central aspect of the text rather than in a special appendix for several reasons. Dewey is, almost without doubt, the central figure in the liberal (progressive) reform of American education during the twentieth century, and he was also the formative figure in the development of mainstream educational liberationism. (More specifically, this is the type of educational liberationism that I shall later discuss as *radical liberationism,* which is closely akin to the position which is frequently referred to as *social reconstructionism* in contemporary educational philosophy.) This selection represents perhaps the best and most succinct statement of Dewey's fully developed educational theory, written during a formative era in his intellectual development. It provides an excellent summary of his educational liberalism as well as a clear and definitive statement of his radical liberationist views. As such, it provides a more complete exposition of the two basic Liberal ideologies of educational liberalism and educational liberationism, serving to somewhat counterbalance the lengthier explanations required by the less frequently discussed ideologies which constitute the Conservative points of view.

Terminology and Meaning

Third, and finally, it is necessary to guard against a virtually unavoidable semantic problem that arises in a work of this sort. The special sense of certain terms is difficult to convey solely in the written word. Thus, where special usage or special philosophical or theological meaning is intended, terms have been placed in single quotes. In addition, there is the problem associated with the fact that, short of constructing a totally new vocabulary, the same terms have frequently had to be used to describe similar ideas, such as *political liberalism* and *educational liberalism,* or the same ideas as they relate to different levels of theoretical abstraction (such as philosophical conservatism, political conservatism and educational conservatism). For the sake of simplicity, and because the focus of this study is educational philosophy, I have used the terms employed to describe the six basic educational ideologies (educational fundamentalism, educational intellectualism, educational conservatism, educational liberalism, educational liberationism, and educational anarchism) as generic terms that encompass the more profound political and philosophical positions. These positions are, however, actually more basic, and would normally assume logical priority over their more specifically educational expressions.

To use a specific example, in the chapter dealing with educational conservatism, the term *educational conservatism* is used to include social conservatism (as a political philosophy) as well as the conservative social ethic (or moral philosophy). This is not to deny that there is a real and important difference between a social ethic, a political philosophy, and an educational ideology, but once this difference has been identified and discussed, I have tended to disregard it in subsequent discussions of the various ideologies in order to reduce terminological confusion.

I have also generally used the labels attached to the various educational ideologies as a short-hand reference to the underlying philosophical and political positions associated with these views. To reduce confusion, I have capitalized the terms *Conservatism* and *Liberalism* whenever I have used them in reference to overall orientations in moral and political philosophy (and where the usage was not clear in context), and I have not capitalized the same terms when they were used in reference to the specifically educational ideologies of educational conservatism and educational liberalism.

THE MODEL AS A TAXONOMY

There are many things which this book does not do, and which it was not intended to do. For one thing, the organization of this book is explicitly and intentionally structural. It is intended to establish a taxonomy of educational ideologies, of the most significant options currently available with respect to the nature and conduct of education in contemporary Western society. It is not meant to explore the intellectual history of these ideologies nor to describe all of the various ways in which such ideologies have been expressed either in our own culture or elsewhere in the world. When necessary for clarity, concrete examples and illustrations have been identified and, in some cases, explored at some length. In general, however, examples have been cited rather than analyzed.

This approach has been used for several reasons. First, it ensures that the present volume will not grow out of proportion in an attempt to go beyond the discussion of an ideal-type model into a discursive analysis of all the various applications and implications of such general positions to specific instances or particular social conditions. Second, since the educational ideologies are *philosophical* categories, and therefore necessarily address themselves categorically to very general questions rather than offering specific prescriptions for particular conditions, it was thought advisable to restrict the discussion to broad points of view. Educational philosophy is only one—if a central one—of several factors (economic, social, psychological, and such) that govern responses toward specific and important problems, such as school integration or affirmative action.

Because the educational ideologies are essentially philosophical orientations, they encompass exceedingly abstract considerations and consist of statements at very high levels of generalization. Thus, the educational principles associated with the various ideologies are more trustworthy at the higher levels of abstraction—for example, with respect to the goals of education, the objectives of the school, and the nature of the child as learner—than at the lower levels which relate to considerations more contingent upon special circumstances, such as course content, methodology, and discipline. In other words, the more philosophical (and therefore abstract) the statements, the more warrantable they are likely to be.

Accordingly, generalizations about the various educational ideologies become less valid as they become more specific. Virtually all educational philosophies have both an ideal, or utopian, position (*If* I were able to define the situation, *tnen* I would do X); and a more realistic, or practical, position (*However* I am not in control, *hence* the best way to improve things in terms of what I consider to be ideal is to do Y). Ironically, whenever a person addresses himself to immediate and impending educational problems, he tends to go away from the ideal (what one would do, other things being equal) and toward the practical (what one would do to improve a less than totally desirable situation), because his decision is generally contingent on a whole series of specific conditions over which he has little or no control.

Thus, many of the central educational questions in our own society at the present time—school integration (particularly busing), the educational treatment of ethnic or racial minorities, teacher rights, "tracking" of students, and such—do not easily reduce into ideological terms. There are a vast number of social and personal variables that contribute to decisions in these areas—whether or not one has school-age children, white flight from the central city, the rate of illegal immigration from Mexico, and such—which have little or nothing to do with educational philosophy as such, but are centrally involved in any kind of full and intelligent consideration of the problems at hand.

The Relationship between Principles and Practice

This book is primarily concerned with tracing the logical relationships which flow from philosophical convictions to educational principles and practices; rather than with discussing the interplay of influences which operate in the reverse direction between practice and theory, or between different levels and dimensions of theory. Not all schooling is based on theoretical preconceptions, but this book is concerned with those elements which *are* or, at the very least, *can be* (under certain conditions). Philosophy is seldom sufficient to account for all that goes on in classrooms, but it is one of the more important considerations necessary for any full understanding of contemporary educational issues.

The pages that follow are concerned primarily with the effects caused by (or at least generally correlated with) certain ideological approaches to education. The assumption is that ideological differences do (or at least can) make a difference, and that these differences warrant serious consideration. Since the intent of the book is to discuss the necessary (structural) relationship between abstract convictions and educational practices, the materials are organized in the direction ranging from philosophical (and particularly moral and political) convictions to educational practices. This perspective was taken with the full awareness that, in the case of circular relationships, the line of argument could well have started with some other, essentially nonphilosophical, consideration. In effect, this book is based on the premise that:

a) *If* a person has a conscious philosophical orientation, encompassing moral and political convictions

b) other things being equal

c) he will think and act in predictable ways which merit special attention when it comes to educational questions.

None of the components of this premise should go unchallenged. In all probability, only a minority of educators have a conscious and coherent educational ideology, even of the most eclectic sort. Other things very seldom are equal, and therefore knowing about a person's educational ideology is unlikely to be sufficient to inform you about his probable course of action. Conflicts between beliefs, or conflicts between theoretical convictions and practical considerations, may very well cause a person to act in ways that ostensibly contradict his basic philosophical beliefs. Certainly, philosophical convictions are only one basis for predicting what a person will do when confronted with educational problems.

Empirical Analysis

Several of my friends and colleagues who were kind enough to critique this book prior to publication urged me to subject the various ideological positions to some sort of empirical analysis. In essence, they suggested making it quite explicit that certain of the ideologies are essentially prescientific (or even nonscientific) and therefore refuted by either the conventional wisdom of contemporary science, or more often, by recent discoveries in the contemporary social and behavioral sciences, particularly psychology.

I have resisted this suggestion for several reasons. First, my intention in writing this book was to describe the various intellectual options currently available with respect to the nature and objectives of education. My purpose was not to subject these options to searching critical scrutiny—a commendable but far lengthier task that I prefer to defer to some later date.

Second, it seems clear to me that the assumptions upon which contemporary science operates are themselves based upon philosophical preconceptions that cannot be viewed as independent of ideological considerations. I am personally predisposed toward empirical and experimental modes of thinking, but to critique the traditional rationalism of the educational intellectualist on the basis that it fails empirical tests which are not compatible with the rationalist's own assumptions about the way basic knowledge is ultimately and properly determined, strikes me as a rather futile and somewhat dubious enterprise. In a similar sense, to critique the characteristic antiintellectualism of the educational fundamentalist because he rejects the conventional notion that intellectual (reasoned) answers are best is equally pointless. For the fundamentalist, intellectual answers are subordinate to answers grounded in "common sense," intuition, or faith; and any criticism directed at this belief is a way of tacitly objecting to the basic worldview of fundamentalism itself.

Third, while an objective critical analysis of the various ideologies from the point of view of one particular set of beliefs, such as those encompassed in contemporary science, might be valuable, one of my intentions in writing this book was to explicate the fact that different philosophical positions have radically different conceptions of what constitutes an *objective* analysis. It is an exceedingly naive, if widespread, idea to believe that virtually everyone accepts the notion that the standard scientific criteria for verification are the only, let alone the best or most objective, standards for evidence with respect to notions about the good, the beautiful and the true. Unfortunately—or at least for those who adhere to the liberal enthusiasm for experimental verification— probably most of the people in the world today do not subscribe to this idea. And, while they may be willing to accept scientific explanations for most mundane phenomena, they are far less likely to be congenial to the idea that science is the ultimate authority for defining basic religious and philosophical convictions. These convictions are centrally important when it comes to discussing social, political, economic and educational matters.

THE PARTS OF THE BOOK

This book consists of four basic sections. Part I begins with the Educational Ideologies Inventory, a diagnostic test for pre-test and post-test purposes that was derived from the conceptual model of the six basic educational ideologies. Part I also discusses the relationship between philosophy and education, defines certain key terms, and presents a general overview of the various educational ideologies. Part II identifies and defines the three essentially conservative educational ideologies: educational fundamentalism, educational intellectualism, and educational conservatism. Part III identifies and defines the three liberal educational ideologies: educational liberalism, educational liberationism, and educational anarchism. Part IV presents an outline summary which compares and contrasts the six basic educational ideologies in terms of the positions which they characteristically assume with respect to certain basic educational questions. The Appendices contain (1) a section entitled "Judaism and Jewish

Education'' (see footnote 6); and (2) the Manual for the Educational Ideologies Inventory, which assists in interpreting the inventory scores. A glossary of key terms follows Appendix 2.

The pages that immediately follow contain the Educational Ideologies Inventory. This Inventory is placed at the very beginning of the book so that each person can determine the nature of his own educational ideology (or, more properly, his own ideological *profile*) prior to considering the various ideologies themselves. A second set of answer columns is designed to serve as a post-test, with the reader covering the pre-test answers while taking the test again upon finishing the book. This should determine whatever changes (if any) may have occurred as a consequence of becommming familiarized with the various ideological positions. Hopefully, this pre-test/post-test format will be both interesting and informative, providing some information about where one's educational commitments reside both before and after studying educational philosophy.

ventory. Undoubtedly, everyone will end up with a profile which reflects a special combination of different kinds, degrees, and combinations of beliefs. As the Manual for the Inventory indicates, eclecticism (some mixture of convictions and commitments ranging across the various ideological positions) is the norm. It is the total profile which is revealing. For an interpretation of test scores and the test profile, see Appendix 2.

NOTES

1. Abraham Kaplan, *The Conduct of Inquiry: Methodology for Behavioral Science*. (San Francisco: Chandler Publishing Company, 1964), pp. 53–54. Used by permission of Harper & Row.

2. Ibid., p. 340.

3. Ibid., p. 332.

4. Ibid.,

5. Gunnar Myrdal, ''Methodological Note on Facts and Valuations in Social Science,'' in his *An American Dilemma* (New York: 1944), pp. 1027–64; quoted in Kaplan, *Conduct of Inquiry*, p. 376.

6. A section of the book which might well have been included in Part II, since it relates primarily to educational intellectualism, appears instead as one of the appendices. This is the section entitled ''Judaism and Jewish Education.'' This section of the book was included because it was clear that Jewish religion and philosophy are too important in contemporary America to be either neglected or relegated to the status of occasional reference. At the same time, it is clear that the various traditions within Judaism and their approaches to education pose a very large topic and could not be handled as merely one aspect of an already extended chapter without throwing the entire treatment of the various educational ideologies out of balance. My compromise was to treat Judaism and Jewish education—which is an extremely controversial topic even within the Jewish community—at some length, but to include this section as a special appendix rather than as an integral part of the basic text itself. Hopefully, this compromise recognizes the extreme importance of Jewish thought in the American tradition but avoids a disproportionate emphasis on Judaism/Jewishness as a special tradition.

Acknowledgments

I would like to express my appreciation and gratitude to my various friends and colleagues who have provided valuable criticism at various stages in the preparation of this book: Robert L. Brackenbury, Mahroo Navai-Gastaldi, and Karen Drinkard, all of the University of Southern California, Robert McLaren and Jacque Weiss of the California State University at Fullerton, Tom Grundner of Case Western Reserve University, and John C. Carpenter of Florida International University. Not least to those who have assisted in the arduous tasks of manuscript preparation and typing: my very good friend and secretary, Ilda Bonar, as well as my secretaries at USC, Isabel Mahoney and Debbie Hamilton.

I am especially indebted to Robert Ellwood of the Department of Religion at the University of Southern California who graciously allowed me permission to quote extensively from his excellent book on some of the more recent developments in evangelical Christianity, *One Way: The Jesus Movement and Its Meaning* (Englewood Cliffs, New Jersey: Prentice-Hall, Inc., 1973); and to Joseph L. Blau, Professor of Religion at Columbia University, for permitting me to borrow liberally from his equally trenchant book *Modern Varieties of Judaism* (New York: Columbia University Press, 1966).

I would also like to express my gratitude to Chris Jennison of Goodyear Publishing Company for his encouragement and patience. Finally—and most emphatically—I would like to recognize the contributions of the editor who worked so closely with me in the final stages of manuscript preparation, Susan Caney-Peterson. Susan is one of those rare individuals who can see the forest as well as the trees. Her wisdom, taste, and judgment are substantially reflected throughout this book.

Educational Ideologies Inventory

DIRECTIONS

This test is designed to determine your basic educational philosophy.* You are asked to respond to each of the 104 statements by making an appropriate mark in one of the five response-categories which appear to the right of the statement. These indicate the *nature* of your response (whether it is positive, negative or undecided) and the *degree* (strongly agree, agree, undecided, disagree, strongly disagree). The two sets of answer columns enable you to take the test both before and after reading the text. You may wish to cover your Pre-test answers while taking the Post-test.

This Inventory is diagnostic in nature and not evaluative. It is not a test of your knowledge about the various philosophical positions, and there are no right or wrong answers. There is no time limit, but it is probably best to respond to each statement rather immediately and without a great deal of reflection, since it is your overall response pattern on all of the questions rather than any specific answer or answers which is most informative about your basic educational orientation.

The statements which comprise this Inventory are not intended as simple descriptions of the way things actually are (although they may occasionally be this as well). Consequently, an indication of agreement or disagreement with any particular statement should *not* be based on whether or not you consider the statement to be an accurate representation of prevailing belief or behavior. Rather the statements included in the Inventory should be viewed as essentially *philosophical* in nature—that is, as constituting either descriptions of the unchanging nature of reality or general prescriptions for changes which can and should be instituted in order to make the world a better place.

There are five possible responses to each of the statements: SA (strongly agree), A (agree), U (undecided, uncertain, or neutral), D (disagree), and SD (strongly disagree). When you decide upon your response to a statement, make an appropriate mark in the corresponding space in that column.

---

*See Appendix II of this book (Manual for the Educational Ideologies Inventory) for information about obtaining additional copies of this diagnostic test.

If you *strongly agree* with the statement, make an appropriate mark in space

	SA	A	U	D	SD
	(X)	( )	( )	( )	( )

If you *disagree* with the statement, make an appropriate mark in space

	SA	A	U	D	SD
	( )	( )	( )	(X)	( )

And so on.

The Inventory may be scored by hand or by machine. A Scoring Key is provided to facilitate hand scoring. If machine scoring is desired, a standard IBM answer sheet designed for five-item multiple-choice tests can be readily adapted to the scoring of the Inventory. In such cases those taking the test should be instructed to rekey the answer sheets in such a way that Number 1 in the answer column corresponds to *Strongly Agree* and is assigned a value of +2, 2 to *Agree* (+1), 3 to *Uncertain* or *Undecided* (0), 4 to *Disagree* (-1), and 5 to *Strongly Disagree* (-2).

	PRE-TEST	POST-TEST
	SA A U D SD	SA A U D SD
1. The teacher should be more concerned with motivating, with stimulating an interest in learning, than with conveying knowledge.	( ) ( ) ( ) ( ) ( )	( ) ( ) ( ) ( ) ( )
2. The most valuable type of knowledge is that which involves symbolism and abstract thinking.	( ) ( ) ( ) ( ) ( )	( ) ( ) ( ) ( ) ( )
3. Open and nonauthoritarian schools give rise to open and nonauthoritarian people.	( ) ( ) ( ) ( ) ( )	( ) ( ) ( ) ( ) ( )
4. In the final analysis, human happiness derives from adapting oneself to prevailing standards of belief and behavior.	( ) ( ) ( ) ( ) ( )	( ) ( ) ( ) ( ) ( )
5. The schools should shape moral character; they should place their major emphasis on helping students develop proper personal values.	( ) ( ) ( ) ( ) ( )	( ) ( ) ( ) ( ) ( )
6. Individual differences (physical, psychological, and social) are so significant that they dictate against the wisdom of prescribing the same or similar educational experiences for all people.	( ) ( ) ( ) ( ) ( )	( ) ( ) ( ) ( ) ( )

	PRE-TEST	POST-TEST
	SA A U D SD	SA A U D SD
7. The elementary school child is not sufficiently mature in most cases to make responsible decisions about the proper course of his own education.	( ) ( ) ( ) ( ) ( )	( ) ( ) ( ) ( ) ( )
8. Behavior problems in the classroom generally indicate that the students are insufficiently motivated.	( ) ( ) ( ) ( ) ( )	( ) ( ) ( ) ( ) ( )
9. Traditional classroom procedures, such as lectures, recitations, and highly-structured group discussions, promote good moral character by teaching students self-restraint and respect for authority.	( ) ( ) ( ) ( ) ( )	( ) ( ) ( ) ( ) ( )
10. Students should be expected to adhere to absolute and enduring moral standards which are based upon absolute and enduring intellectual convictions.	( ) ( ) ( ) ( ) ( )	( ) ( ) ( ) ( ) ( )
11. Generally speaking, the school-age child should be the judge of whatever education, if any, is best suited to his own personal needs.	( ) ( ) ( ) ( ) ( )	( ) ( ) ( ) ( ) ( )
12. The school should encourage an appreciation for time-tested cultural institutions, traditions, and processes.	( ) ( ) ( ) ( ) ( )	( ) ( ) ( ) ( ) ( )
13. The school should focus on individual and group problem-solving procedures.	( ) ( ) ( ) ( ) ( )	( ) ( ) ( ) ( ) ( )
14. Secondary education should provide the student with an orientation to life in general. emphasizing his role as a human being rather than training him for any particular social role or position.	( ) ( ) ( ) ( ) ( )	( ) ( ) ( ) ( ) ( )
15. Public school teachers should be free to criticize whatever social conditions block the fullest realization of individual potentialities.	( ) ( ) ( ) ( ) ( )	( ) ( ) ( ) ( ) ( )
16. A person defines himself, both to himself and to others, through his actions.	( ) ( ) ( ) ( ) ( )	( ) ( ) ( ) ( ) ( )

	PRE-TEST	POST-TEST
	SA A U D SD	SA A U D SD
17. Education requires the restoration of more traditional principles and practices.	( ) ( ) ( ) ( ) ( )	( ) ( ) ( ) ( ) ( )
18. Science must be supplemented by a more authoritative system of knowledge, such as religion or traditional philosophy, if it is to serve as a satisfactory basis for human values.	( ) ( ) ( ) ( ) ( )	( ) ( ) ( ) ( ) ( )
19. The teacher should be a model of both moral and academic excellence.	( ) ( ) ( ) ( ) ( )	( ) ( ) ( ) ( ) ( )
20. The school should work to develop the sort of students who will be capable of operating effectively in a society which will no longer require compulsory schooling or most other formal constraints on individual freedom.	( ) ( ) ( ) ( ) ( )	( ) ( ) ( ) ( ) ( )
21. The best society is a democratic socialism which seeks the maximum degree of social justice for all.	( ) ( ) ( ) ( ) ( )	( ) ( ) ( ) ( ) ( )
22. A deep respect for law and order is the fundamental basis for constructive social change.	( ) ( ) ( ) ( ) ( )	( ) ( ) ( ) ( ) ( )
23. The schools should place their basic emphasis on *man as man;* that is, on the sort of abiding human nature which all individuals share.	( ) ( ) ( ) ( ) ( )	( ) ( ) ( ) ( ) ( )
24. Education is essentially its own end; it *is* life, and is only incidentally a preparation for some future course of action.	( ) ( ) ( ) ( ) ( )	( ) ( ) ( ) ( ) ( )
25. The elementary school should properly stress memorization and drill.	( ) ( ) ( ) ( ) ( )	( ) ( ) ( ) ( ) ( )
26. The schools should promote a certain kind of reasoned conformity, relying on the best answers that have emerged out of the past as the most reliable guide to effective action in the present and future.	( ) ( ) ( ) ( ) ( )	( ) ( ) ( ) ( ) ( )

	PRE-TEST SA A U D SD	POST-TEST SA A U D SD
27. The schools should emphasize those changes in the present social system that are required in order to bring about a more humanistic and humanizing society.	( ) ( ) ( ) ( ) ( )	( ) ( ) ( ) ( ) ( )
28. The school should emphasize the utopian vision of a world in which it will be possible for people to function as self-regulating moral beings.	( ) ( ) ( ) ( ) ( )	( ) ( ) ( ) ( ) ( )
29. Democracy must be supplemented by some more abiding system of moral standards if it is to be effective as a means for directing education.	( ) ( ) ( ) ( ) ( )	( ) ( ) ( ) ( ) ( )
30. The highest good is to live in accordance with natural and/or cosmic law.	( ) ( ) ( ) ( ) ( )	( ) ( ) ( ) ( ) ( )
31. Thinking and learning are basically collective undertakings which ordinarily occur in various sorts of group interactions.	( ) ( ) ( ) ( ) ( )	( ) ( ) ( ) ( ) ( )
32. Education should be conducted with a full awareness of the fact that virtually all personal belief is ultimately determined by the sort of socioeconomic conditions that prevail within a given culture.	( ) ( ) ( ) ( ) ( )	( ) ( ) ( ) ( ) ( )
33. Too much learning and thinking frequently undermines and interferes with a person's underlying common sense.	( ) ( ) ( ) ( ) ( )	( ) ( ) ( ) ( ) ( )
34. The school should exist primarily to transmit the information and skills that children will find necessary in order to survive and succeed within the existing social order.	( ) ( ) ( ) ( ) ( )	( ) ( ) ( ) ( ) ( )
35. The democratic (majority rule) method is the best means of resolving interpersonal differences which do not lend themselves to clear-cut intellectual resolution on rational-scientific grounds.	( ) ( ) ( ) ( ) ( )	( ) ( ) ( ) ( ) ( )

	PRE-TEST	POST-TEST
	SA A U D SD	SA A U D SD
36. Under present conditions, control over education should be invested in an enlightened minority of responsible intellectuals who are capable of implementing required social changes through the schools.	( ) ( ) ( ) ( ) ( )	( ) ( ) ( ) ( ) ( )
37. The study of philosophy is a very important aspect of proper education.	( ) ( ) ( ) ( ) ( )	( ) ( ) ( ) ( ) ( )
38. The school should be community-centered; it should reflect the needs and interests of the locality in which it resides.	( ) ( ) ( ) ( ) ( )	( ) ( ) ( ) ( ) ( )
39. Conventional teaching ordinarily subverts the child's capacity for self-learning.	( ) ( ) ( ) ( ) ( )	( ) ( ) ( ) ( ) ( )
40. All learning involves feeling, the emotions.	( ) ( ) ( ) ( ) ( )	( ) ( ) ( ) ( ) ( )
41. The overriding goal of education should be to help students identify, preserve, and transmit Truth, the objective meaning of life.	( ) ( ) ( ) ( ) ( )	( ) ( ) ( ) ( ) ( )
42. America is in danger of losing the organic structure of ideas, values, and beliefs that constitutes a faith common to Americans as Americans.	( ) ( ) ( ) ( ) ( )	( ) ( ) ( ) ( ) ( )
43. Learning *how* to think is generally more important than *what* one thinks.	( ) ( ) ( ) ( ) ( )	( ) ( ) ( ) ( ) ( )
44. There are certain constant elements in human experience which help us to understand the present and to anticipate the future.	( ) ( ) ( ) ( ) ( )	( ) ( ) ( ) ( ) ( )
45. Problems associated with student control and discipline are frequently caused by a society which blocks the development of personal responsibility by overcontrolling everyone, including students.	( ) ( ) ( ) ( ) ( )	( ) ( ) ( ) ( ) ( )

	PRE-TEST	POST-TEST
	SA A U D SD	SA A U D SD
46. The basic value of knowledge is its contemporary social utility; knowledge is primarily a means of adapting successfully within the existing social order.	( ) ( ) ( ) ( ) ( )	( ) ( ) ( ) ( ) ( )
47. The *best* act in any particular situation is ultimately the most *intelligent* act in that situation.	( ) ( ) ( ) ( ) ( )	( ) ( ) ( ) ( ) ( )
48. The school should restrict itself, insofar as possible, to cultivating the intellect, leaving other important aspects of individual development to other social institutions, such as the church and the family.	( ) ( ) ( ) ( ) ( )	( ) ( ) ( ) ( ) ( )
49. The psychological is an aspect of the biological, the mental of the physical.	( ) ( ) ( ) ( ) ( )	( ) ( ) ( ) ( ) ( )
50. The best way for a person to satisfy his future needs is to learn how to resolve his present needs satisfactorily.	( ) ( ) ( ) ( ) ( )	( ) ( ) ( ) ( ) ( )
51. Psychotherapy conducted under the auspices of the school is generally a disguised form of social control and conformity-training.	( ) ( ) ( ) ( ) ( )	( ) ( ) ( ) ( ) ( )
52. Education must necessarily be based upon certain implicit and unresolvable assumptions about the nature of truth and value.	( ) ( ) ( ) ( ) ( )	( ) ( ) ( ) ( ) ( )
53. Knowledge is ultimately a tool, a means to be used in solving the problems of everyday living.	( ) ( ) ( ) ( ) ( )	( ) ( ) ( ) ( ) ( )
54. Formal education is basically unnecessary and contributes little or nothing to the vast sum of human experience.	( ) ( ) ( ) ( ) ( )	( ) ( ) ( ) ( ) ( )
55. The school should emphasize the present rather than the historical past or the anticipated future.	( ) ( ) ( ) ( ) ( )	( ) ( ) ( ) ( ) ( )

	PRE-TEST	POST-TEST
	SA A U D SD	SA A U D SD
56. The schools should emphasize the unique personality of each child, adapting themselves to the specific nature of each individual.	( ) ( ) ( ) ( ) ( )	( ) ( ) ( ) ( ) ( )
57. The teacher should be a model of intellectual excellence.	( ) ( ) ( ) ( ) ( )	( ) ( ) ( ) ( ) ( )
58. The elementary teacher should attempt to cover a specified curriculum in a systematic and comprehensive way.	( ) ( ) ( ) ( ) ( )	( ) ( ) ( ) ( ) ( )
59. The secondary schools should stress controversial social problems and issues, emphasizing the identification and analysis of underlying values and assumptions.	( ) ( ) ( ) ( ) ( )	( ) ( ) ( ) ( ) ( )
60. Schooling must necessarily attend to all aspects of the child's experience, the interpersonal, the emotional, and the physical as well as the cognitive.	( ) ( ) ( ) ( ) ( )	( ) ( ) ( ) ( ) ( )
61. Since truth, value, and human nature are relatively unchanging, the curriculum should not ordinarily vary to any significant extent.	( ) ( ) ( ) ( ) ( )	( ) ( ) ( ) ( ) ( )
62. The history of this nation is preeminently a spiritual history, guided by Providence.	( ) ( ) ( ) ( ) ( )	( ) ( ) ( ) ( ) ( )
63. Decisions about the nature and conduct of schooling should be arrived at primarily by means of reflective reason (logical analysis) rather than by popular opinion or professional expertise.	( ) ( ) ( ) ( ) ( )	( ) ( ) ( ) ( ) ( )
64. Intelligent action in pursuit of social justice is the most important characteristic of an educated person.	( ) ( ) ( ) ( ) ( )	( ) ( ) ( ) ( ) ( )
65. In formal education, the cognitive properly takes priority over the affective.	( ) ( ) ( ) ( ) ( )	( ) ( ) ( ) ( ) ( )

	PRE-TEST	POST-TEST
	SA A U D SD	SA A U D SD
66. Compulsory instruction should be replaced by free but unforced access to educational opportunities for all people.	( ) ( ) ( ) ( ) ( )	( ) ( ) ( ) ( ) ( )
67. We should seize upon the child's own needs and interests as they occur, using them as the basis for modifying instructional programs and practices.	( ) ( ) ( ) ( ) ( )	( ) ( ) ( ) ( ) ( )
68. Control over education should be invested in mature and responsible educators who have a deep respect for due process and who are sufficiently prudent to avoid sudden changes in response to popular demand.	( ) ( ) ( ) ( ) ( )	( ) ( ) ( ) ( ) ( )
69. The teacher should be a model of intellectual commitment and social involvement.	( ) ( ) ( ) ( ) ( )	( ) ( ) ( ) ( ) ( )
70. The best government is the least government.	( ) ( ) ( ) ( ) ( )	( ) ( ) ( ) ( ) ( )
71. Patriotism should be fostered by introducing children to a set of more or less sacred persons, events, beliefs, rituals, and symbols.	( ) ( ) ( ) ( ) ( )	( ) ( ) ( ) ( ) ( )
72. Students should be trained to be good citizens in terms of prevailing cultural views about the nature of good citizenship and proper conduct.	( ) ( ) ( ) ( ) ( )	( ) ( ) ( ) ( ) ( )
73. Complete objectivity is not possible.	( ) ( ) ( ) ( ) ( )	( ) ( ) ( ) ( ) ( )
74. Education should be based on certain clearly recognized philosophical certainties and on the sort of conduct which is logically implied by such certainties.	( ) ( ) ( ) ( ) ( )	( ) ( ) ( ) ( ) ( )
75. At all levels, the school should be primarily concerned with the child's ability to solve his own personal problems successfully.	( ) ( ) ( ) ( ) ( )	( ) ( ) ( ) ( ) ( )

	PRE-TEST SA A U D SD	POST-TEST SA A U D SD
76. The secondary school should provide most students with occupational training which makes them adept at some socially useful trade or skill.	( ) ( ) ( ) ( ) ( )	( ) ( ) ( ) ( ) ( )
77. The teacher should be basically an organizer and expediter of learning activities and experiences.	( ) ( ) ( ) ( ) ( )	( ) ( ) ( ) ( ) ( )
78. The child is predisposed toward error and antisocial behavior unless he receives firm guidance and sound instruction.	( ) ( ) ( ) ( ) ( )	( ) ( ) ( ) ( ) ( )
79. Children should be encouraged to apply relevant classroom learnings to the solution of real out-of-school problems by involving themselves in community improvement projects, social action movements, and so on.	( ) ( ) ( ) ( ) ( )	( ) ( ) ( ) ( ) ( )
80. Learning, in the traditional sense of acquiring academic information and skills, is not important for everyone.	( ) ( ) ( ) ( ) ( )	( ) ( ) ( ) ( ) ( )
81. Education should stress prudent and responsible action directed toward the preservation of existing social institutions.	( ) ( ) ( ) ( ) ( )	( ) ( ) ( ) ( ) ( )
82. Science is capable of providing a viable system of human values.	( ) ( ) ( ) ( ) ( )	( ) ( ) ( ) ( ) ( )
83. Schools should be run in a manner consistent with the conventional wisdom (the common sense beliefs) of society at large.	( ) ( ) ( ) ( ) ( )	( ) ( ) ( ) ( ) ( )
84. The schools should stress the critical analysis and evaluation of prevailing social beliefs and behavior.	( ) ( ) ( ) ( ) ( )	( ) ( ) ( ) ( ) ( )
85. Effective thinking should be the natural byproduct of effective living in a society reorganized along truly enlightened and humanistic lines.	( ) ( ) ( ) ( ) ( )	( ) ( ) ( ) ( ) ( )

	PRE-TEST		POST-TEST	
	SA A U D SD		SA A U D SD	

86. The students' immediate interests should be properly subordinated to the long-range requirements of society.

( ) ( ) ( ) ( ) ( )   ( ) ( ) ( ) ( ) ( )

87. A central purpose of education should be to revive and reaffirm an almost religious commitment to certain profound national goals.

( ) ( ) ( ) ( ) ( )   ( ) ( ) ( ) ( ) ( )

88. Time-tested ideas and practices are a more reliable guide to educational activities than those which are grounded in intellectual speculation.

( ) ( ) ( ) ( ) ( )   ( ) ( ) ( ) ( ) ( )

89. Individual differences (physical, psychological, and social) are generally more important than individual similarities, and they should be given priority in determining educational programs.

( ) ( ) ( ) ( ) ( )   ( ) ( ) ( ) ( ) ( )

90. The school should encourage a return to the simple and straightforward virtues of an earlier day, to the older and better ways.

( ) ( ) ( ) ( ) ( )   ( ) ( ) ( ) ( ) ( )

91. The ability to choose freely is more important than the nature of the choices made.

( ) ( ) ( ) ( ) ( )   ( ) ( ) ( ) ( ) ( )

92. The best government is a representative democracy founded upon a system of free and unhampered economic enterprise.

( ) ( ) ( ) ( ) ( )   ( ) ( ) ( ) ( ) ( )

93. Education should concentrate on the "generative" subjects, like mathematics and language, which create the sort of intellectual potential which allows the student to deal more effectively with increasingly more difficult realms of experience.

( ) ( ) ( ) ( ) ( )   ( ) ( ) ( ) ( ) ( )

	PRE-TEST	POST-TEST
	SA A U D SD	SA A U D SD
94. Individual similarities (physical, psychological, and social) tend to be more important than individual differences, and should therefore be given priority in determining appropriate educational programs.	( ) ( ) ( ) ( ) ( )	( ) ( ) ( ) ( ) ( )
95. The fullest realization of human happiness requires the development of new and more person-centered social institutions.	( ) ( ) ( ) ( ) ( )	( ) ( ) ( ) ( ) ( )
96. Education should stress creative individuality rather than group conformity.	( ) ( ) ( ) ( ) ( )	( ) ( ) ( ) ( ) ( )
97. The individual finds his greatest fulfillment in a voluntary subordination to the ends of the State.	( ) ( ) ( ) ( ) ( )	( ) ( ) ( ) ( ) ( )
98. The curriculum should be continuously adapted to the changing needs of both the students and the community.	( ) ( ) ( ) ( ) ( )	( ) ( ) ( ) ( ) ( )
99. The schools should encourage students to recognize and respond to the need for particular kinds of liberalizing social reforms.	( ) ( ) ( ) ( ) ( )	( ) ( ) ( ) ( ) ( )
100. At the secondary level, general evaluations of intellectual ability (as in essay-type examinations) are ordinarily better than those which stress factual content (as in objective-type examinations).	( ) ( ) ( ) ( ) ( )	( ) ( ) ( ) ( ) ( )
101. The schools should emphasize the virtues of the historical past as a way of correcting the existing overemphasis on the present and the future.	( ) ( ) ( ) ( ) ( )	( ) ( ) ( ) ( ) ( )
102. Man is essentially a product of his culture who is shaped by the norms and standards of the society in which he lives.	( ) ( ) ( ) ( ) ( )	( ) ( ) ( ) ( ) ( )
103. The present system of schools should be replaced by voluntary and self-directed learnings.	( ) ( ) ( ) ( ) ( )	( ) ( ) ( ) ( ) ( )

	PRE-TEST	POST-TEST
	SA A U D SD	SA A U D SD
104. The schools should emphasize cultural stability over the need for change; they should encourage only changes which are basically compatible with the established social order.	( ) ( ) ( ) ( ) ( )	( ) ( ) ( ) ( ) ( )

Scoring

To score the test it is necessary (1) to identify the educational ideologies represented by the various items and (2) to determine the numerical weight of the responses assigned to the various items. (For a fuller interpretation of the Inventory, see Appendix 2, Manual for the Educational Ideologies Inventory.)

Scoring Key (Educational Ideologies)

Educational Fundamentalism	F
Educational Intellectualism	I
Educational Conservatism	C
Educational Liberalism	LL
Educational Liberationism	LB
Educational Anarchism	A
General Conservatism	GC
General Liberalism	GL

Scoring Key (Numerical Scores)

Strongly Agree	+2
Agree	+1
Undecided	0
Disagree	−1
Strongly Disagree	−2

F	I	C	LL	LB	A	GC	GL
5. __	2. __	4. __	1. __	3. __	6. __	7. __	16. __
17. __	10. __	12. __	8. __	15. __	11. __	9. __	40. __
19. __	14. __	22. __	13. __	21. __	20. __	18. __	47. __
25. __	23. __	34. __	24. __	27. __	28. __	26. __	49. __
33. __	37. __	46. __	31. __	32. __	39. __	29. __	60. __
42. __	41. __	55. __	35. __	36. __	45. __	30. __	73. __
52. __	48. __	68. __	38. __	51. __	54. __	44. __	82. __
62. __	57. __	72. __	43. __	59. __	66. __	58. __	89. __
71. __	61. __	76. __	50. __	64. __	70. __	86. __	98. __
78. __	63. __	81. __	53. __	69. __	80. __	94. __	102. __
87. __	65. __	83. __	56. __	79. __	85. __		
90. __	74. __	88. __	67. __	84. __	91. __		
97. __	93. __	92. __	75. __	95. __	96. __		
101. __	100. __	104. __	77. __	99. __	103. __		

Score

F ____ I ____ C ____ LL ____ LB ____ A ____ GC ____ GL ____

EDUCATIONAL IDEOLOGIES PROFILE

	FUNDAMENTALISM (F)	INTELLECTUALISM (I)	CONSERVATISM (C)	LIBERALISM (LL)	LIBERATIONISM (LB)	ANARCHISM (A)
Raw score						
Mean score	−6	−1	0	12	7	4
Standard Deviation	8	6	8	6	6	7

GENERAL CONSERVATISM

GENERAL LIBERALISM

F 12 8 4 0 −6 −12 −16 −20 −24
SA A N D SD

I 12 8 3 −1 −5 −10 −14

C 18 14 10 6 0 −6 −10 −14 −18

LL 25 21 16 12 8 3 −1

LB 20 16 11 7 3 −2 −6

A 19 14 9 4 −1 −6 −11

9 8 7 6 5 4 3 2 1
mean

100% 96% 89% 77% 60% 50% 40% 23% 11% 4% 0%

GENERAL IDEOLOGICAL ORIENTATIONS

	General Conservatism (GC)	General Liberalism (GL)
Raw score		
Mean score	0	7
Standard Deviation	6	4

PART ONE

PHILOSOPHIES, IDEOLOGIES AND EDUCATION

Chapter I

Introduction

Virtually everyone today has heard of "future shock." It is, in the words of Alvin Toffler, who first coined the term, "the shattering stress and disorientation that we induce in individuals by subjecting them to too much change in too short a time."[1]

Whether we like it or not, the world today is increasingly characterized by radical discontinuity, and future shock has assumed critical proportions throughout society. Acceleration, transience, novelty, the heightened tempo of everyday existence, all conspire to make us experience the world and ourselves differently. In so doing, they push the very limits of human and institutional adaptability. One result of this massive, continuous, and universal process of wholesale change has been to bring us to the brink of a new society that shows every indication of being radically different from that to which most of us have grown accustomed.

In a sense, of course, the large-scale changes that have been occurring in our thinking about teaching and learning are merely one aspect of these much larger changes within American society, changes that are still far from complete. "I was not born," Margaret Mead once commented, "in the world in which I live, and I do not live in the world in which I shall die."[2]

What is true of society in general is no less true of its schools. The very meaning of the term *education* has become increasingly controversial. More and more, time-honored educational convictions are being subjected to rigorous and searching reconsideration. In recent years, the very legitimacy of schools, special institutions offering formalized instruction, has been called into serious question. Teaching, which was once what Margaret Mead has described as a *downward vertical* transmission, in which learning descended from adults to children, is more and more becoming a *horizontal* transmission, in which those who possess relevant information pass it on to others who require it, with little or no concern for the traditional proprieties of age. In some respects we even seem to be evolving toward an *upward vertical* transmission of knowledge, in which the more up-to-date younger generation will reeducate its elders periodically with respect to the kind of understanding and skills required by a rapidly changing world.[3]

All of these changes have had a tremendous impact upon contemporary educational thinking. It has become increasingly obvious to informed observers that Peter Drucker is quite right. There is a significant difference between efficiency — doing things right — and effectivenesss — doing the right thing.[4] Our schools have frequently become victims of what Callahan has popularized as the "cult of efficiency,"[5] too often sacrificing educational convictions at the altar of administrative expediency.

In his book *Crisis in the Classroom,* Charles Silberman states that contemporary American schools frequently suffer from too much unquestioned behavior and from too many unexamined assumptions. The problem with teacher education, notes Silberman, is not that it is overly practical but "that it fails to provide teachers with a sense of purpose, with a philosophy of education."[6] "Skill without insight is dangerous, because skills tend to be repetitive while insight allows for growth."[7]

> The preoccupation with order and control, the slavish adherence to the timetable and lesson plan, the obsession with routine, the absence of noise and movement, the joylessness and repression, the universality of the formal lecturer or teacher-dominated "discussion" in which the teacher instructs an entire class as a unit, the emphasis on the verbal and the de-emphasis of the concrete, the inability of students to work on their own, the dichotomy between work and play — none of these are necessary; all can be eliminated.[8]

While it remains unrecognized by many, then, it is becoming increasingly • evident to others that our society has undergone wholesale changes, and that the kind of education it requires has also changed radically. One result of this explosion of change has been a very significant downgrading of the value of informal *experience* as compared with formal and explicit *knowledge.* Even the traditional distinction between "training" and "education" is becoming increasingly vague, for "the qualities essential to employability and productivity are coming closer and closer to the characteristics that have long been attributed to the educated person."[9]

In a more specific sense, and as economist and management consultant Peter Drucker indicates in his book *The Age of Discontinuity,* the American economy itself has become preeminently a "knowledge economy."

> . . . every one of the new emerging industries is squarely based on knowledge. Not a single one is based on experience.
>
> Every single technology and with it every industry before 1850 was based on experience. Knowledge, that is, systematic, purposeful, organized information, had almost nothing to do with any of them. Even the so-called modern industries which came into being in the second half of the nineteenth century and which still dominate our economic and industrial life today, were largely experience-based rather than knowledge-based. Science had almost no part to play in the birth of automobile or airplane, not even the auxiliary role of godmother, let alone that of midwife. These technologies were still experience-based. And so was the electrical industry in a large part; Edison, for instance, was much more traditional craftsman than modern researcher. Only in the chemical industry were there inventors with university training in their science. Otherwise, in the "heroic age of inventions," that is, in the sixty or seventy years before World War I, university-trained inventors were conspicuous by their almost total absence.
>
> The new emerging industries ... embody a new economic reality: knowledge has become the central economic resource. The systematic acquisition of knowledge, that is, organized formal education, has replaced

experience—acquired traditionally through apprenticeship—as the foundation for productive capacity and performance.[10]

*　　　*　　　*

Ninety percent of all scientists and technologists who ever lived are alive and at work today. In the first five hundred years since Gutenberg, from 1450 to 1950, some thirty million printed books were published in the world. In the last twenty-five years alone an equal number has appeared. Thirty years ago, on the eve of World War II, semiskilled machine operators, the men on the assembly line, were the center of the American work force. Today the center is the knowledge worker, the man or woman who applies to productive work ideas, concepts, and information rather than manual skill or brawn. Our largest single occupation is teaching, that is, the systematic supply of knowledge and systematic training in applying it.

In 1900 the largest single group, indeed still the majority, of the American people, were rural and made a living on the farm. By 1940, the largest single group by far, were industrial workers, especially semiskilled (in fact, essentially unskilled) machine operators. By 1960, the largest single group were what the census called "professional managerial, and technical people," that is, knowledge workers.... At the latest by 1980, this group will embrace the majority of Americans at work in the civilian labor force.[11]

While education is central to constructive change in the contemporary world, however, educational institutions remain notoriously difficult to reform. It is, someone once remarked, easier to reform a cemetery than a university. Much the same sort of observation might be made about schooling in general. "A curious quality of education," the then Dean of the Harvard Graduate School of Education, Theodore R. Sizer, once observed, "is that, while most persons experience it intimately, few study it in any serious way at all."[12]

It is too easy, though, merely to follow traditional practice and to dismiss the real or imaginary failings of the schools as a vague conspiracy of a nefarious educational mafia—a self-perpetuating educationalist "establishment" of public school teachers and administrators, education professors, state departments of education, and national and regional accreditation agencies—which is intent upon imposing its own educational ideology upon the schools. Rather, and as Silberman aptly remarks, it is not collusion and conspiracy but "banality" and "mindlessness"—the failure "to think deeply and seriously about the purposes and consequences of education"[13]—which lies at the heart of the problem.

> ... by and large, teachers, principals, and superintendents are decent, intelligent, and caring people who try to do their best by their lights. If they make a botch of it, and an uncomfortably large number do, it is because it simply never occurs to more than a handful to ask *why* they are doing what they are doing — to think seriously or deeply about the purposes or conseqences of education.

*　　　*　　　*

If mindlessness is the central problem, the solution must lie in infusing the various educating institutions with purpose, more important, with thought about purpose, and about the ways in which techniques, content, and organization fulfill or alter purpose. And given the tendency of institutions to confuse day-to-day routine with purpose, to transform the means into the end itself, the infusion cannot be a one-shot affair.[14]

One of the things that makes our schools so fascinating today is precisely the fact that they mirror on a smaller scale the various intellectual and moral conflicts within the larger culture. Ironically, the question of what education *is* and *ought to be* has become the central concern of contemporary education. The schools have become *self*-conscious. Like so many of the students within them, they find themselves confronted with an identity crisis. As a result, the debate over the larger purposes of education is no longer a peripheral matter that warrants only incidental consideration. It has become a priority item that belongs where it properly should have been from the very beginning, at the very heart of the curriculum.

NOTES

1. Alvin Toffler, *Future Shock* (New York: Random House, 1972), p. 4.
2. Margaret Mead, "Thinking Ahead," *Harvard Business Review,* XXXVI (November–December 1958), p. 34.
3. Margaret Mead, *Culture and Commitment: A Study of the Generation Gap* (Garden City, New York: Natural History Press of the American Museum of Natural History, 1970), *passim.*
4. Peter F. Drucker, *The Age of Discontinuity: Guidelines to Our Changing Society* (New York: Harper & Row, 1969), p. 198.
5. Raymond E. Callahan, *Education and the Cult of Efficiency: A Study of the Social Forces That Have Shaped the Administration of the Public Schools* (Chicago: University of Chicago Press, 1962).
6. Charles E. Silberman, *Crisis in the Classroom* (New York: Random House, 1970), p. 472.
7. Ibid., p. 491.
8. Ibid., pp. 207–8.
9. Francis Chase, Dean of the Graduate School of Education at the University of Chicago, quoted in Silberman, *Crisis in the Classroom*, p. 114.
10. Drucker, *Age of Discontinuity,* pp. 39–40.
11. Ibid., pp. 263–4.
12. Theodore R. Sizer, Foreword to *The Graduate Study of Education: Report of the Harvard Committee*, Cambridge, Mass.: Harvard University Press, 1966.
13. Silberman, *Crisis in the Classroom*, p. 11.
14. Ibid.

Chapter II

Educational Philosophies and Educational Ideologies

"If," John Dewey once stated, "we are willing to conceive of education as the process of forming fundamental dispositions, intellectual and emotional, toward nature and fellow men, philosophy may be defined as *the general theory of education.*"[1] Accordingly, continued Dewey, "there is nothing that education is subordinate to save more education."[2]

> There is no better way to realize what philosophy is about when it is living, not antiquarian, than to ask ourselves what criteria and aims and ideals should control our educational policies and undertakings. Such a question, if it is systematically followed out, will bring to light things that are morally and intellectually fundamental in the direction of human affairs....[3]

THE THREE APPROACHES TO EDUCATIONAL PHILOSOPHY

It has become increasingly apparent over the years that there is much truth in what Dewey had to say. If the ability to formulate a philosophy—a set of coherent generalizations at the highest level of meaningful abstraction, the sort of generalizations which allow a person to organize his overall behavior both systematically and with a minimum of inconsistency and self-contradiction—is the highest and most systematic development of man's reason, then educational philosophy *is* vitally important. On the other hand, educational philosophy is a very difficult topic to discuss. No small part of this stems from the fact that it has traditionally been approached in at least three basic ways: (1) as an active process of 'educational philosophizing,' using the *problems analysis*, or analytical, approach; (2) as a *formal systems* approach in which basic systems of philosophy, such as realism and idealism, are applied to education; and (3) in the guise of more or less self-contained *educational philosophies*.

Problems Analysis

In the so-called problems analysis approach, no attempt is ordinarily made to formulate any particular philosophy of education. Instead, the emphasis is placed upon "doing philosophy"[4] with respect to some specific educational problem (usually some theoretical situation with respect to the aims of education, the nature of the curriculum, or methods of teaching and learning) that lends itself to penetrating intellectual analysis. In most cases, this sort of philosophical analysis involves itself with one or more of three basic approaches: (1) a *semantic analysis,* in which the attempt is primarily to clarify the meaning of certain terms or statements employed in educational discourse; (2) *rational analysis,* in which the effort is primarily directed toward determining whether a particular line of reasoning is logical and coherent; or (3) *empirical analysis,* in which the effort is essentially directed at determining whether a statement can be proved factual on the basis of some accepted protocol for experimental verification, usually the scientific method. Examples of work in educational philosophy that use the problems analysis, or analytical, approach are such books as *Ethics and Education* by R. S. Peters, *Conditions of Knowledge* by Israel Scheffler, and *An Introduction to the Analysis of Educational Concepts* by Jonas Soltis.[5]

Many philosophers take the position that the problems analysis approach is essentially neutral (or at least more objective) than the more systematic approaches to the philosophy of education, because the analyst uses merely internal criteria (such things as linguistic clarity and logical consistency) which are acceptable to virtually all of the different philosophical positions regardless of more specific differences. This is true in part, but it is also somewhat misleading. In at least two senses the philosophical analyst does more than merely philosophize about existing problems. First, he invariably analyzes a selected statement or idea which he has already identified as being both relevant and problematic—a step which itself involves significant philosophical assumptions. Second, if he does more than merely clarify linguistic and logical meanings, becoming in any sense involved with evaluating the *truth* of a statement, the analyst must invariably do so on the basis of his own assumptions about what constitutes necessary evidence. Even when this entails no more than a demand for the scientific verification of knowledge-claims, it implies a tacit commitment to some specific set of philosophical beliefs about *what* is capable of being known and *how* such knowing is possible.

The Formal Systems Approach[6]

The second, and perhaps the most prevalent manner in which educational philosophy is treated, is through the formal systems (or "systems of philosophy as applied to education") approach. In this method (exemplified in J. Donald Butler's *Four Philosophies and Their Practice in Education and Religion*) traditionally accepted systems of philosophy (such as idealism, realism, existentialism, and pragmatism) are identified and defined, and their implications for the organization and conduct of education are systematically developed.[7]

This approach ordinarily involves three steps: (1) the identification of basic philosophical systems (such as *realism* or *idealism*); (2) the exemplification of such systems, usually by presenting the particular philosophy of one or more prominent spokesmen for each (such as the philosophy of Aristotle as an example of classical realism); and (3) the presentation of the educational philosophy that is either implied by or encompassed within these various philosophical systems (as, for example, in discussing the educational 'perennialism' normally associated with the classical realist).

In his book *Four Philosophies and Their Application for Education of Religion,* for example, J. Donald Butler takes a rather representative position when he summarizes the idealist position with respect to educational philosophy in the following words:

1. The teacher is the creator of the educational environment of the child and the chief source of his inspiration.
2. One important and valuable means by which student response is given birth is imitative activity, especially when given direction by worthy models of creative work and a noble teacher personality.
3. Another valuable stepping stone to student response is interest. Preferably, interest should permeate the greatest majority of student activities. Sometimes, of course, it will need to be supplemented by the student's own effortful application. And on occasion this latter may need reinforcing by the pressure of external discipline.
4. Throughout all teacher activities the result sought is the active response of the learner. It is only when the self of the pupil becomes attached to activities by its own initiative that real growth and development of self get started.
5. As to curriculum, there must be much objective content and much book learning if there is to be solidity in education and students are to have a rugged mental diet. But lest education be no more than impartation of knowledge, the curriculum must go beyond books and subject matter to include direct experiential relation with actualities.
6. Teaching methods should be used that create a slight feeling of suspense for the student—suspense to be resolved only by his own decision or active effort. Questioning and discussion lend themselves admirably to this purpose, but there is also much place for solid instruction, as in lecturing, and for pupil activity, as in projects employing constructive and creative work.[8]

Others who prefer the formal systems approach tend to favor a more indirect relationship between the various philosophical systems and educational theory. This method, which is perhaps the most popular among those who currently use the formal systems approach, attempts to find correspondences between the various systems of philosophy, on the one hand, and the much more delimited theories termed 'educational philosophies' (which are themselves viewed as having far more specific implications for educational practice at a far less abstract level) on the other. This approach assumes that coherent philosophical systems, encompassing a full consideration of metaphysical, epistemological and axiological questions, logically terminate in certain identifiable convictions pertaining to the more central questions regarding education.

It is, for example, frequently maintained that conservative philosophies—that is, absolutistic systems of belief based upon metaphysical assumptions, such as classical realism and idealism—logically terminate in certain kinds of educational beliefs. Thus, for many educational philosophers, virtually all idealists (and frequently realists of the Aristotelian and Thomist sorts as well) tend to be viewed as *educational perennialists* (a position similar to, but not synonymous with, the *educational intellectualist* position employed in the conceptual model which will be developed here). Most contemporary, or 'scientific,' realists (unless very traditional in their orientations) have tended to be viewed as *educational essentialists* (a position which corresponds in many respects to the ideology of *educational conservatism*). Pragmatists have been presented as *educa-*

tional progressives or, if politically radical, as *social reconstructionists*. Existentialists—except where the term has been used to describe a specific educational philosophy as well as a system of general philosophy—have tended to be viewed as either progressives, reconstructionists, or both.[9]

Preliminary Definitions of Terms. Some of the terms used in the last few paragraphs are somewhat elliptical. They are defined briefly at a later point in this chapter, and some of them are discussed at some length in later chapters. The term *metaphysical* is frequently used in two basic senses in philosophy. First, and as discussed below, it refers to one of the basic questions or topics treated by systematic philosophy as it has been traditionally defined—the question of what is ultimately *real* or *true*. It is, on the other hand, also used on occasion to describe a metaphilosophical position under which a number of different formal systems of philosophy can be subsumed. In the latter case, a metaphysical system of philosophy is generally viewed as one which is based on the primary assumption that *essence precedes and determines existence*—that some kind of absolute meaning (whether transcendent or immanent) exists before, and gives rise to, all personal experience (and therefore to all personal knowledge). The term *metaphysical* has become rather controversial in philosophical circles for a variety of reasons, but perhaps primarily because (1) many contemporary philosophers reject the notion that ultimate (that is, final or absolute) truths exist; and (2) most of these would therefore reject metaphysical philosophies (in either of the senses of the term) as illegitimate approaches to meaning. Most relativistic philosophies, which are ordinarily based on the overriding empirical proposition that *existence precedes and determines essence*—that personal experience comes before, and gives rise to, all knowledge whatsoever (which is the logical contrary of the metaphysical position)—are not overly fond of having their absolute rejection of metaphysical knowledge described as a metaphysical principle. Going along with Bertrand Russell's theory of types, they hold that an absolute commitment to relativism is not an *absolute* (except on a semantic level), because it defines the boundaries of legitimate discourse in strictly relativistic terms and therefore constitutes a nonappellate limit which bars any further (and necessarily paradoxical) description of relativism as a subset of absolutism (viewed as a larger and more encompassing category).

There have been two basic consequences of this dispute about the legitimacy of metaphysical assertions. First, some philosophers have abandoned the attempt to talk about formal systems of philosophy altogether, and have focused increasingly on the problems analysis approach. Second, some have begun to use a more generalized term, *ontology,* to describe any probing inquiry into the basic nature of knowing and the known, including valuing, in place of the more conventional designations of *metaphysics* (What is ultimately knowable?), *epistemology* (How can we ultimately come to know it?), and *axiology* (What is the ultimate nature of value?). This has the advantage of providing a special label for the kind of speculation into the ultimate nature of reality that: (1) does not suggest that knowing, knowledge, and valuing can be approached as separate and/or separable questions and (2) does not etymologically connote (*meta,* ''beyond'') that it is possible to arrive at conclusions that exist in some sense beyond personal experience (or, at least, beyond personal experience viewed, as it is conventionally by modern science, as an essentially psychobiological phenomenon). On those rare occasions when I venture into speculative philosophy (as in the discussion of *synergism* in the latter part of this chapter) I have opted for the term *ontology* (*ontos,* "being," and *logos,* "study of") over the more controversial *metaphysics,* and I have generally used the more conventional designations of *metaphysics, epistemology* and *axiology* as useful, if somewhat arbitrary, divisions within the essentially indivisible realm of ontological speculation.

Developed and Undeveloped Philosophies.   The more developed, definitive, and comprehensive a philosophy is, the more likely it will be to imply clear-cut educational policies. On the other hand, it is almost impossible to describe, explain, or predict specific educational practices on the basis of a general system of philosophy like realism or existentialism. This is true because what makes such positions general systems in the first place is precisely the fact that they fail to make definitive statements about particular problems (by defining particular moral policies) and that they therefore fail to develop many of the areas of intermediate theory (such as moral and political philosophy) which are central for the development of an effective philosophy of education. For this reason, the educational implications of general philosophical systems are probably better exemplified through the ideas of particular representatives of such systems (such as Aristotle in the area of traditional realism or John Dewey in the area of experimentalism) than by extrapolating on the basis of fundamental agreements between individuals sharing a common philosophical orientation at a very high level of abstraction.

Educational Philosophies

A third approach to the philosophies of education holds that it is possible to identify and define educational philosophies that exist substantially apart from other types of philosophy and that can be looked upon as at least conceptually separable from the traditional formal systems of philosophical thought. Phrased somewhat differently, if the formal systems approach, which is still very important within educational philosophy, tends to begin with the ultimate philosophical generalities and to move toward educational specifics on the basis of rational inference, the educational philosophies approach tends to alter this procedure. It begins with more specific proposals, usually in the realm of social ethics, that are more directly related to the basic problems of schooling, and subsequently organizes these principles and policies into a coherent and logical system of ideas about the nature and purposes of education. The term *social ethics* encompasses the areas normally described as moral and political philosophy. It refers both to ethics, in the sense of general theory of interpersonal responsibility, and to the practical implications and/or applications of particular ethical positions for social action. The terms *ethics* and *moral philosophy* are used interchangeably in this book to encompass both questions of personal, or psychological, value and questions of social value (i.e., interpersonal obligation). In this approach, very little effort is made to trace these specific 'educational philosophies' back to more fundamental differences in the area of traditional philosophical first principles.[10]

The educational philosophies approach differs in two basic respects from the approach that focuses on the educational implications of established philosophical systems. First, the educational philosophies are not true philosophies in the usual sense of the word. They do not begin with a coherent system of general beliefs directed toward the basic philosophical questions of knowing and the known; but rather, commence with intermediate theory, generally in the area of social ethics, using these somewhat less abstract considerations as the basis for establishing an overall approach to the problems of schooling. In other words, rather than starting with a system of fundamental philosophical principles and systematically developing their applications and implications for schooling, the educational philosophies approach tends to operate at a less exalted level, focusing on the educational expressions of the major contemporary social philosophies. Only secondarily (if at all) do they become involved with the truly basic philosophical first principles that are frequently assumed to underlie such points of view.

Second, the educational philosophies approach tends to focus upon two basic educational questions: (a) What should be the basic relationship between the school and society? (How should educational goals relate to overall social purposes?); and (b) What does this relationship imply with respect to the nature and organization of instruction? (What are the goals of education, and how should these goals be implemented by curricula and instructional procedures?)

THEODORE BRAMELD'S CLASSIFICATION OF EDUCATIONAL PHILOSOPHIES

An educational theorist of the first rank who has developed a particularly important expression of the educational philosophies approach is the well-known educational philosopher Theodore Brameld. Brameld, a very prolific writer and an influential figure in American educational philosophy for well over a generation, has formulated his ideas in a number of books, but perhaps most effectively in his works *Philosophies of Education in Cultural Perspective* and *Toward a Reconstructed Philosophy of Education,* published respectively in 1955 and 1956.[11] Brameld, like Butler, distinguishes four basic systems of education. Brameld, however, uses a fundamentally different classification of philosophical systems from Butler, distinguishing between (1) the classical tradition of philosophy which emanates from the theories of Plato, Aristotle, and Saint Thomas Aquinas; (2) the more modern expressions of traditional realism and idealism; (3) pragmatism; and (4) what is perhaps best regarded as the "sociology of knowledge" point of view which is most often associated with the ideas of Karl Marx and Karl Mannheim.*

---

*The origins of sociological epistemology are difficult to trace. Brameld's point of view does not appear to emerge out of the sociology of knowledge approaches of Marx and Mannheim, but it probably approximates this point of view more closely than any other. Brameld is not, however, a Marxist, and it would be misleading to suggest that his reconstructionism is explicitly geared to Marxist assumptions about the nature of reality.

Closely related to these four fundamental approaches to philosophy, as Brameld sees it, are four basic educational philosophies, which he terms *perennialism, essentialism, progressivism* and *reconstructionism.*[12]

Perennialism, states Brameld, is basically the point of view which holds that the proper goal of education is "possession of everlasting, timeless and spaceless principles of reality, truth and value."[13] It is rooted in the philosophical tradition associated with Plato, Aristotle, and Saint Thomas Aquinas, and it posits the existence of changeless, universal patterns that underlie and determine all actual objects and events. Profoundly regressive in its overall cultural outlook, perennialism seeks to restore the kind of absolute standards that governed the ancient and medieval world, and is intrinsically opposed to genuine democracy.

Essentialism, on the other hand, holds to the central proposition "that the universe and all of its elements are governed by encompassing law and preestablished order, and that therefore the chief task of men is to understand this law and order so that we may appreciate and adjust to it."[14] For the essentialist, the central aim of the school is to acquaint students with the basic character of this orderly universe by introducing them to their cultural heritage. Philosophically, essentialism is grounded in the classic principles of modern realism and idealism. Its ontology is either "objective realism, which maintains that reality is a material substance, or objective idealism, which maintains that reality is a spiritual substance."[15] Its epistemology is ultimately the "correspondence theory of knowledge," which holds that truth re-presents (or corresponds to) objective facts. As an overall social philosophy, essentialism presents "a contemporary policy and program of cultural conservation"[16] that reflects the classical humanism that originated during the Renaissance and reached its peak during the mid-nineteenth century.

In the case of educational *progressivism* the central purpose of the school is to improve practical intelligence, to make the child more effective in solving the problems presented within the context of normal experience. Characteristically, "this-worldly, exploratory, active, evolutionary,"[17] the educational progressive is primarily oriented to "an interpretation of the liberal way of life in American culture."[18] Philosophically, progressivism is supported by the philosophy of pragmatism. It envisions no final answers and validates its conclusions through the consequences of behavior.

Finally, *reconstructionism* holds that the school should be "dedicated to the attainment of a worldwide democratic order."[19] Philosophically, the reconstructionist maintains that theory is ultimately inseparable from its social setting in a particular historical era. Thinking, then, is the product of living in a particular society at a particular time.

The Difficulties with Brameld's Classification Scheme

Brameld's approach to educational philosophy—taken in conjunction with the many variations of his basic orientation that have emerged over recent years—is perhaps the best known and the most influential in contemporary American education. Compared with most of the other conceptual models that purport to relate underlying systems of philosophy to established educational outlooks, it possesses certain distinct advantages. It presents a simple and systematic overview of available theories that address themselves to the underlying nature and purposes of education. It attempts to relate specifically educational ideas to more basic philosophical orientations. Finally, because of its popularity and widespread acceptance, Brameld's classification scheme has frequently provided precisely the sort of commonly understood concepts that are invaluable in any attempt to come to grips with basic educational problems. Indeed, it testifies to Brameld's influence in the area of educational theory that his critics have frequently been reduced to using his terminology even when they were intent upon attacking his basic ideas.

Unfortunately, Brameld's model, while it has done much to further the consideration of important educational ideas for well over a generation, also suffers from certain severe deficiencies. First, Brameld's distinctions, while they were suitable in many respects for the less complicated ideological arena of the forties and fifties, do not adequately represent the variety and complexity of educational philosophies that are available today. Certainly additional educational philosophies have emerged in the last two decades—the *revolutionary liberationism* of the more radical wing of the Students for a Democratic Society during the sixties or of the more recent New World Liberation Front, as well as the extreme *educational anarchism* of Ivan Illich are excellent examples— which did not exist in any significant sense when Brameld's classification scheme was first developed, and which are not properly represented within it.

Second, Brameld's model tends to oversimplify the richness and variety within contemporary educational philosophy. It provides important distinctions, but, viewed from the vantage point of the early eighties, it also glosses over many significant differences that warrant equally serious consideration. Certainly, contemporary educational philosophy is much more varied and complicated than Brameld's original scheme suggests, and some of this complexity must be recognized at the risk of imposing an overly superficial order on underlying confusion. Brameld, as one of the founding fathers of educational reconstructionism, is quite correct in perceiving that one of the central philosophical issues affecting contemporary American education is that associated with the demand that the school assume the primary responsibility for initiating a constructive and humanistic social order. He is less acute, however, when he brackets the involved and complicated subvarieties of social dissent which would opt to use the schools as agents of social reform under the single rubric "reconstructionism." Indeed, what has normally been termed *educational reconstructionism* is a very mixed bag of cats. The differences between the moderate (and generally non-Marxist), methods-oriented, and school-focused reconstructionism of the *educational liberal,* the far more radical (and frequently Marxist or quasi-Marxist) reconstructionism of what is called here the *educational liberationist,* and the extreme and virtually revolutionary iconoclasm of the *educational anarchist,* while they may be differences of degree in one sense, are sufficiently drastic differences to warrant being recognized as essentially differences in kind as well.

Third, and despite its occasional usefulness, Brameld's conceptual scheme fails to be fundamentally coherent, because it is not always based on comparable concepts. Perennialism, essentialism and progressivism are parallel ideas. They all address themselves to the same basic questions: What is the underlying purpose of education? and What should be taught? Reconstructionism, on the other hand, asks an entirely different, and perhaps even more basic, kind of question: What is the proper relationship between the school and society?

This has led to understandable confusion on the part of many who have tried to comprehend educational philosophy on the basis of Brameld's model. Phrased somewhat differently, very real questions inevitably occur in conjunction with Brameld's point of view. For example: Is reconstructionism a left-wing social-activist variation of progressivism? Is it possible for an essentialist to be a reconstructionist? Much of this confusion is not easily resolved, however, because it comes down to a question of relating theories that address themselves to substantially different questions. Reconstructionism, for better or worse, asks essentially an *external* question: How should the school as a particular social institution relate to society in general? The other three positions ask what are fundamentally *internal* questions: What is the overriding value of the school as an institution? What should be taught within the school? and, to a certain extent, How? To look upon the four educational philosophies as merely providing different answers to the same questions is to confuse the political with the purely pedagogical.[20]

Finally, and perhaps most importantly, Brameld's explanation of the formal, or causal, relationship between educational philosophy and the more basic *systems* of philosophy, such as realism, idealism, and pragmatism, is open to serious question. Not all modern realists—and Bertrand Russell, for example, certainly viewed himself as a realist—are either social conservatives or educational essentialists. In a similar sense, not all pragmatists are necessarily either experimentalists (in the sense that they adhere to the scientific method as the best way of solving problems) or political liberals. Strictly speaking, in our culture at this time, most are, it is true. But a correlation does not establish a causal relationship; and, as will be discussed more fully in the pages that follow, it is seriously misleading to suggest a necessary alliance where there is none.

IDEOLOGY AND EDUCATION

All of the basic approaches to educational philosophy have their advantages, and, obviously, some work better for certain purposes and under certain conditions than others. In general, however, of the three basic approaches to educational philosophy, the educational philosophies approach has probably been applied most productively by professional educators. This is true for several reasons.

For one thing, the educational philosophies approach does not demand a high level of philosophical sophistication or an extensive familiarity with traditional philosophical ideas. It addresses itself primarily to theoretical problems that exist in and around formal education and does not become preoccupied with determining the practical implications emanating from more profound philosophical disputes at the most exalted reaches of intellectual discourse. It is estimated that only about six percent of the graduates of American colleges and universities have ever taken a course in general philosophy,[21] and, regrettable though this situation may be, it remains a fact. The instructor who maintains that before he can teach *educational* philosophy, he must first teach *general* philosophy in order to subsequently apply it to education, generally discovers that he has little time left for applications.

In addition, and at least as compared with the educational philosophizing approach, the educational philosophies format has the advantage of presenting an organized and coherent conceptual model of basic educational approaches. For better or worse, most people seem predisposed toward some kind of conceptual schema; not only because it satisfies their natural inclination toward intellectual closure, but also because it provides them with a readily accessible tool for subsequently dealing with problems concerning the nature and purposes of education. The dangers of misconceiving educational differences through poorly conceived classification schemes are great; but the danger of relegating these differences to intellectual limbo by refusing to develop any sort of general categories that will allow them to be explicitly examined, is probably even greater.

Finally, and as compared with the formal systems orientation, the educational philosophies approach has the advantage of being able to start at the practical beginning of educational philosophy, where it emerges out of social ethics, rather than having to regress back to the extremely rarified realm of philosophical first principles. Basic metaphysical, epistemological, and axiological ideas are profoundly important in determining educational purposes; but, in a more immediate sense, they are frequently far *less* important than more substantive and specific ideas in the areas of moral and political philosophy that exist at a significantly less abstract level of discourse.

This is not to derogate the importance of studying the basic philosophical questions or of relating the formal systems of philosophy to education. These are both productive ways of approaching educational philosophy, and they are probably necessary steps for anyone who plans to have anything approximating a complete understanding of the relationship between philosophy and education. On the other hand, if a course in educational philosophy is not going to serve as a ''remedial'' liberal arts course in introductory philosophy for students who have never been exposed to the discipline (in which case, the educational implications of the various systems frequently become merely ancillary considerations tacked onto an already impossible intellectual agenda), it is probably better to deal with *educational* philosophy than to try and rectify the oversights of previous education by attempting to take the student all the way through the entire discipline of philosophy in order to examine the basic propositions underlying education.

PHILOSOPHY AND IDEOLOGY

In the pages that follow, a substantially new model of what are ordinarily referred to as the 'educational philosophies' is presented. This classification scheme is admittedly eclectic. In a sense, it involves educational philosophizing, because it is the product of a serious philosophical analysis of the more significant intellectual options that are currently available in American education. On the other hand, its ultimate intent is clearly less to philosophize about this or that particular problem within education than to develop a fundamental taxonomy of the basic alternatives that are available in the entire area of educational philosophy. It differs from the more traditional ''systems of philosophy as applied to education'' approach in that it is only incidentally concerned with relating overall educational theories to fundamental differences between rival philosophical systems. In this sense, the model presented is probably closer to what has been called the educational philosophies approach than to the problems analysis or formal systems orientations.

PHILOSOPHY

Philosophy is by definition general. It aims at universality. ''To describe a man's philosophy,'' notes American philosopher Abraham Kaplan, ''is to say how he orients himself to the world of his experience, what meanings he finds in events, what values he aspires to, what standards guide his choices in all he does.''[22] Philosophy is concerned primarily with the general and not with the particular, with *meaning* and not with *fact*.[23] ''Philosophy,'' remarks Susanne Langer, is ''the continual pursuit of meanings—wider, clearer, more negotiable, more articulate meanings.''[24]

Until recently, the problem of defining philosophy was somewhat minimized by adopting the expedient of subdefining philosophy to encompass a study of four basic topics, and regarding any body of thought that addressed itself to these topics with sufficient rigor and profundity as being essentially 'philosophical.' These four topics were ordinarily identified as (1) *metaphysics* (What is ultimately *real*?); (2) *epistemology* (What is ultimately *knowable*?); (3) *axiology* (What is ultimately *good*?); and (4) *aesthetics* (What is *beauty*?).

In some cases *formal logic* (the theory of the structure and relationship of truth-propositions) was included as a fifth branch of philosophy or even as the fourth branch replacing aesthetics, which was occasionally subsumed under axiology. Today logic is generally included as a subcategory under the general topic of epistemology, just as *ethics* (as the theory of interpersonal responsibility, that is, goodness and badness with respect to one's relationship to other people) tends to be regarded as a subtopic within the more general area of axiology. To be more specific, the traditional classification of philosophy might be outlined (in very simple form) as shown in Figure 2–1.

For better or worse, we know a great deal more about the world than we did when these original subclassifications of philosophy were established. Among other things, we know that reality (whatever it may be) is a great deal more subtle and complicated than this traditional breakdown would suggest. For one thing, recent advances in human knowledge make it quite obvious that one cannot probe into what is *real* (metaphysics) without also becoming unavoidably entangled with the question of what is *knowable* (epistemology). In addition, one of the central problems in modern philosophy calls into question the fundamental distinction which has traditionally been made between *truth* and *value*. Many contemporary philosophers reject the notion that there is any meaningful distinction between a ''truth'' and a ''value,'' and many—including virtually all experimental (including psychological) behaviorists—would go so far as to say that all truth-propositions are indirectly value-propositions as well. Finally, whole new areas of philosophical speculation, such as *value theory* (which is actually a sort of *axiological epistemology*), simply fail to fit the old rubrics and necessitate new ways of talking about philosophy.[25]

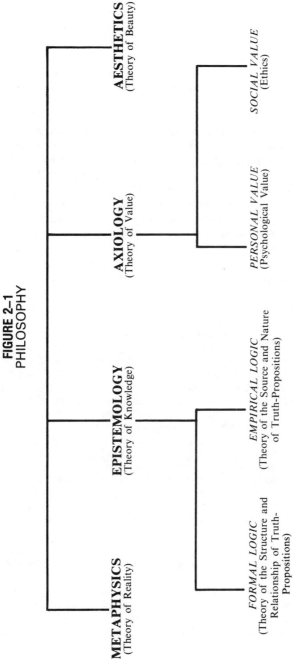

FIGURE 2–1
PHILOSOPHY

IDEOLOGY

The term *ideology* is most frequently associated with two major thinkers, Karl Marx and Karl Mannheim. For Marx *ideologies* are basically interrelated systems of false ideas, false consciousness produced by a person's membership in a particular social class. Accordingly, political ideologies are for the most part *ex post facto* justifications for the existing material or economic organization of society. Mannheim's concept of a total ideology (as opposed to his concept of a particular ideology) is essentially the same as Marx's; and, in his book *Ideology and Utopia,* he calls attention to the fact that ideology can best be understood in the unfolding historical process.

More recently, an "end-of-ideology" thesis has been advanced by such leading social theorists as Edward Shils, Daniel Bell, and Seymour Martin Lipset.[26] The central message of this proposition is that, in the advanced industrial societies of the West, ideology (in the traditional Marxian sense of the term) is at an end because fundamental social conflict is at an end, conflicting ideological interests having been domesticated within the welfare state. Needless to say, this explanation arouses little enthusiasm in Marxian circles where the end-of-ideology thesis is itself viewed as profoundly ideological since it obviates the necessity for social revolution anywhere except in the underdeveloped countries of the world.

For present purposes, the term *ideology* is used rather loosely, but is generally oriented to Alastair C. MacIntyre's view that an ideology always has three key features.

The first is that it attempts to delineate certain general characteristics of nature or society or both, characteristics which do not belong only to particular features of the changing world which can be investigated only by empirical inquiry. . . . The second central feature of any ideology is an account of the relationship between what is the case and how we ought to act, between the nature of the world and that of morals, politics, and other guides to conduct. That is to say . . . a defining property of an ideology [is] that it does not merely tell us how the world is and how we ought to act, but is concerned with the bearing of the one upon the other. This involves a concern, explicit or implicit, with the status of statements of moral rules and the statements expressing evaluations. . . . the third defining property of an ideology is that it is not merely believed by the members of a given social group, but believed in such a way that it at least partially defines for them their social existence. . . . its concepts are embodied in, and its beliefs presupposed by, some of these actions and transactions, the performance of which is characteristic of the social life of that group.[27]

Or, as Sargent indicates in his book *Contemporary Political Ideologies,*

. . . an ideology is a value or belief system that is accepted as fact or truth by some group. It is composed of sets of attitudes toward various institutions and processes of society. It provides the believer with a picture of the world both as it is and as it should be, and, in so doing, it organizes the tremendous complexities of the world into something fairly simple and

understandable. The degree of organization and the simplicity of the resulting picture vary considerably from ideology to ideology, and the ever-
increasing complexity of the world tends to blur all the pictures. At the
same time, the basic picture provided by the ideologies seem to remain
fairly constant.[28]

EDUCATIONAL IDEOLOGIES

The term *educational ideologies* is used in preference to the more traditional
educational philosophies for several reasons. First, in a very practical sense,
the use of *ideologies* serves to separate the concepts formulated here from all of
the related concepts, such as essentialism, perennialism, and progressivism,
which have been conventionally associated with the term *educational
philosophies*. In a more basic sense, however, the term *educational ideologies*
also captures a more profound difference in basic approach. The term *ideology*
is somehow less academic and abstract than *philosophy*. It suggests not an inert
body of knowledge, but a somewhat more specific and dynamic pattern of
general ideas which serves to direct social action.

The most unfortunate thing about the term *ideology* is that it generally connotes intransigence and—to some extent—suggests a tendency toward pros-
elytization and propaganda. Intransigence is to some extent a characteristic of
all basic belief systems, since any overarching set of convictions tends to serve
to some degree as a self-fulfilling prophecy (see pages 38–43 and 78–102).
However, *closed systems* of belief, which are based upon an encompassing set
of substantive convictions about the specific meaning of reality, tend to be far
more rigid than *open systems,* which restrict their convictions to exceedingly
general assumptions about the nature of reality at very high levels of abstraction, or which focus on methods of verifying knowledge claims based upon
such highly abstract assumptions. All philosophies that can be defined at all are
based on limits (categorical assumptions or 'absolutes') in some sense; but open
philosophies, which tend to absolutize processes and procedures rather than
more specific representations of reality defined in terms of certain particular
and identifiable types of 'meaning,' tend to have very broad, flexible, and
somewhat ambiguous limits which allow far greater latitude for the individual
to determine his own specific view of reality within very general parameters.
Such philosophies tend to focus on protocols for inquiry and not on specific
doctrines of belief.

In a similar respect, there is a sense in which all belief systems tend to
proselyte, to persuade others. At basis, all behavior is at least a tacit conviction, and a person necessarily 'witnesses' nonverbally for his beliefs whenever he
lives them in front of others. Again, however, philosophers differ markedly in
how, and to what extent, they tend to impose their ideas on others. Not even all
closed systems of religious belief are evangelical, and some, such as Judaism,
tend to be very reluctant to seek converts at all. In an even more basic sense,
the individual who is committed to individualism and cultural pluralism (as
most political and educational liberals tend to be) may actively proselyte for
diversity—which is scarcely what the average person would view as indoctrination.

The educational ideologies employed in this book are related to philosophical systems, but they differ from the usual systems of philosophy in four basic respects:

1. They are more specific systems of general ideas than most philosophies tend to be.
2. They are immediately rooted in social ethics (that is, in moral and political philosophy) and only distantly rooted in the more abstract systems of philosophy, like realism, idealism and pragmatism.
3. They are intended primarily to direct social action and not merely to clarify or order knowledge.
4. They are both a cause and an effect of fundamental social change.[29]

In order to achieve some sort of clarity and some basis for organized comparisons, the vast array of actual ideological differences has been restricted to six basic points of view. It is, however, important to bear in mind that none of the educational ideologies are monolithic. They all include a variety of factions and disagreements within themselves. In order to reduce the length and complexity of the classification scheme, these intraideological differences have frequently been disregarded in the various charts and outlines that accompany the text, but they are explored at some length in the text itself.

RELATING PHILOSOPHY TO EDUCATION

Regardless of how philosophical points of view are identified and defined, there are a number of basic difficulties inherent in virtually any attempt to formulate philosophical generalizations about education. In general these can be summarized in ten points:

Philosophical Inconsistencies in Some Philosophers

1. Some philosophers have two or more different philosophies of education.

Most philosophers do not change their basic philosophical point of view significantly during the course of their lives, but several have altered their political philosophies—that is, their concepts of how their moral philosophies should be applied in the light of existing conditions—as they have grown older. Such variations in political philosophies have frequently led to significant modifications in educational philosophies as well. Both Plato and Rousseau, for example, present two basically different philosophies of education. In the case of Plato, the radical, utopian vision of a pure intellectual meritocracy presented in *The Republic* is replaced in his later years by the far more conservative and traditional views contained within *The Laws*. Similarly, in the case of Rousseau, the romantic naturalism of *Émile* is followed after several years by the much more conservative position expressed in *Considerations on the Government of Poland*.

Prescriptive and Descriptive Points of View

2. With respect to the real or apparent inconsistency that may occasionally occur between the ideas of the same thinker, writing at different times during his life, it is necessary to distinguish between a philosopher's proposals for education under *ideal* conditions and his proposals for education under *existing* conditions.

In contrast to those who fail to develop *any* educational theories, some philosophers have put forth two essentially different proposals with respect to education: an *ideal* scheme, which is essentially a utopian vision of what education should be in a different sort of society reconstructed along proper philosophical lines; and a *practical* scheme, which is essentially a compromise within the situation as it is, a strategy for making education as effective as possible under existing, and necessarily imperfect, conditions. In the case of both Plato and Rousseau, for example, it can legitimately be questioned whether they propose two different and fundamentally inconsistent philosophies of education or whether they propose two applications of one educational point of view. One could be regarded as an *if-then* proposal (*if* we create a perfect society, *then* we should educate in a certain way), and one which might be called an *however-hence* proposal (*however,* in our culture at this time, perfect education is impossible; *hence* we should modify the existing practices to make them as good as possible in view of the circumstances that prevail).

The Circumstantial Context of Philosophy

3. The way in which any philosophy applies to schooling necessarily depends upon a variety of conditions quite apart from philosophical theory as such: the nature of the situation confronted, the physical and psychological nature of the individual responding to it (his sensory acuity, intellectual level, temperament, knowledgeability, and such), the individual's psychological response to the situation, and so on. Philosophy, as philosophy, is an integrated system of very general ideas to enable a person to intellectually organize his experience. Practical behavior—in the classroom or elsewhere—is always a compromise between the perfect and the possible; and this compromise is affected by a large number of variables quite apart from personal philosophy as such. Philosophy may affect the way a person *construes* his circumstances or the priorities he attaches to certain courses of action within them, but it does not necessarily play the dominant role in *creating* the circumstances which he so construes and evaluates.

In other words, the educational ideologies *are* important in determining what individuals will do with respect to educational matters, but they are not all-informing. Many other considerations also affect their responses. Some are theoretical, such as the individual's knowledge of the situation or his particular religious convictions, and some are practical, such as the number of students to be taught, the availability of trained teachers, or the amount of money available for instructional materials. In the final analysis, all behavior is multimotivated and tends to be the outgrowth of a number of different determining factors in continuous interaction.

On the other hand, while wars, famines, per capita income, social mobility and racial imbalance may all be centrally important to how education is organized and handled at any particular time, they are essentially circumstantial considerations which affect how and to what extent a particular philosophy will be expressed. Phrased somewhat differently, a philosophy may originate in culture and be a cultural phenomenon, but it is so pervasive in its effects that it actually describes different options for acculturation. These options are qualitatively larger than any of the particular cultural phenomena that occur within any particular philosophical frame of reference. In short, even if one were to view the various ideologies, in line with most thinking in the social and behavioral sciences today, as merely products of differential cultural conditioning; nevertheless they would be qualitatively different kinds of cultural phenomena than most others. They would constitute a directive sort of cultural orientation—a supra-orientation, or Weltanschauung—which serves to determine the way in which virtually all other cultural experiences are perceived and evaluated.[30]

Any generalization about the educational implications of a more basic philosophical position is necessarily tempered by the implicit qualification "other things being equal." The traditional philosophies assume the fundamental stability of all things (that is, that other things *are* generally equal, that variability and change tend to be the exception rather than the rule), and thus tend to provide a more explicit and definitive basis for educational system-making than do the open-ended, process-oriented philosophies, which characteristically stress relativity, subjectivity, and individual differences. However, this is not to say that the empirical, or process, philosophies such as experimentalism, which take personal experience as their point of departure, are less capable of generating effective approaches to education. It is that the moral and political principles associated with these positions tend to incorporate variability and change as absolutes and that they are therefore far less likely to absolutize particular *types* of belief and behavior than are the more traditional philosophical systems.

Ethnocentrism and Ideology

4. Some of the educational ideologies are more culture-free (in the sense of being less bound to specific cultural circumstances at a specific time) than others. Educational intellectualism is, for example, founded on the notion that knowledge of absolute and invariable truth can be realized through one absolute and invariable method (trained reason). Historically, it can be argued that both the end (the truth to be attained) and the method employed (rationalism) are the product of a particular culture (Western civilization) at a particular time (from approximately the sixth century B.C. through the Renaissance). The point is, however, that the intellectualist point of view, *once established,* becomes less of a rigid determinant with respect to subsequent cultural experience than many of the other ideologies because it is based on very broad assumptions common to Western culture in general more than it is based on the particular beliefs of specific societies within Western culture as they exist (or existed) at any particular point in history.

In the case of educational fundamentalism, on the other hand, much the contrary is true. Once the fundamentalist has identified and defined his vision of the utopian past, and his goals of education have been focused around the need to restore such an era, cultural change tends to become subordinate to a substantive set of beliefs peculiar to a particular society at a particular time. Indeed, this is one of the reasons why it is so difficult to speak categorically, or cross-culturally, about fundamentalism, or virtually any of the other educational ideologies except for educational intellectualism. Different cultures invariably have different ideas with respect to the sort of society that should be revived. The Wagnerian vision of Nazi Germany differs radically from the romantic vision of the American frontier presented by many contemporary American fundamentalists.

In a similar sense, conservatism, liberalism, liberationism, and anarchism all tend to express themselves somewhat differently in different cultural settings. This is particularly true when one is attempting to compare and contrast any of these ideological orientations as it expresses itself in nations which share entirely different cultural traditions. For example, cultural milieux must be considered in attempting to contrast political or educational liberalism in Tanzania with the same orientation in Denmark.

Direct and Indirect Educational Philosophies

5. Not all philosophers address themselves explicitly to education; therefore much philosophy of education is necessarily a matter of inference and extrapolation based upon relatively "pure" philosophy that makes little explicit mention of teaching and learning.

What makes inferences from basic philosophical assumptions to specific educational practices possible in many instances is the fact that educational philosophy is implicit in most fully developed philosophical systems. (Although the contrary is not necessarily true—it is quite possible to "rationalize" philosophical reasons for justifying educational practices which have emerged primarily through expediency.) This relationship might be summarized as follows:

a) What is ultimately *good* is ultimately *right* (in the sense that it serves as the criterion for justifying subsequent behavior) and should therefore be done.
b) That which a society deems right (morally preferable), when viewed in terms of existing conditions, provides the basis for specific *moral policies*.
c) Specific moral policies, construed in the light of existing conditions, give rise to recommendations for particular *moral practices* as well as to recommendations for the sort of *conditions* (including social institutions such as schools) which are designed to preserve and promote such moral practices.

Phrased in somewhat different terms, then, philosophy, when interpreted in the light of existing social conditions, generates prescriptive rules which imply the necessity for certain social controls. *Political philosophy* is ultimately *applied moral philosophy,* an ideological rationale for using power to guarantee the establishment and survival of good (moral) behavior within society at large. In this sense, government consists of that system of social controls that exists in order to guarantee the fullest realization of some overriding concept of the general good. Our schools, as merely one institution within government, are both a product of society and its values and, at the same time, a determinant of society and its values. Like all social institutions, however, the school is basically an agent for social control that exists in order to modify personal behavior. It employs socially sanctioned power in behalf of socially sanctioned purposes.

Put still differently, then, formal education is one of the conditions (institutions) necessary for effective political control. It acts to shape social behavior at the most basic level of all, by determining whether the next generation will possess the ability and inclination to behave in a manner consonant with dominant political (and therefore moral) purposes. The relationship between moral philosophy, political philosophy and educational philosophy might be outlined as shown in Figure 2–2.

FIGURE 2–2
THE RELATIONSHIP BETWEEN SOCIAL ETHICS AND EDUCATIONAL PHILOSOPHY

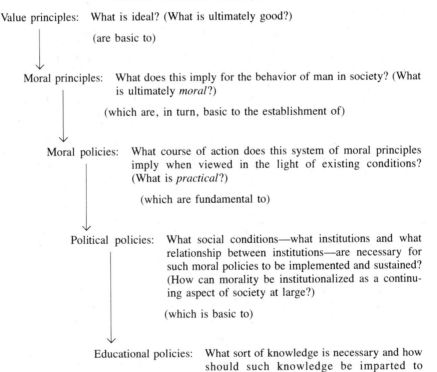

Value principles: What is ideal? (What is ultimately good?)

(are basic to)

Moral principles: What does this imply for the behavior of man in society? (What is ultimately *moral*?)

(which are, in turn, basic to the establishment of)

Moral policies: What course of action does this system of moral principles imply when viewed in the light of existing conditions? (What is *practical*?)

(which are fundamental to)

Political policies: What social conditions—what institutions and what relationship between institutions—are necessary for such moral policies to be implemented and sustained? (How can morality be institutionalized as a continuing aspect of society at large?)

(which is basic to)

Educational policies: What sort of knowledge is necessary and how should such knowledge be imparted to others?

Figure 2–2 is an ideal-type model, focused on theoretical 'oughtness' and not (necessarily) on practical 'isness.' The relationship between the school and society is not a one-way linear process but is reciprocal and interaffecting. The entire process occasionally "rationalizes backward" in the sense that educational policies justify and confirm political policies, which generate moral policies as after-the-fact legitimizations, and so on. The real or potential circularity of the process, as well as the interpenetration (or essential unity) of all of the elements which constitute the whole are discussed in Chapter II, pages 38–43 and in Chapter III, pages 78–102. The point, as noted earlier, is that this diagram represents a formal (and prescriptive) model which addresses itself to the potential relationship between theory and practice, and not a simple descriptive model of how events actually occur in the real world.

In a similar sense, the same descending level of abstraction can, as indicated earlier, be observed in the relationship between general philosophy and educational philosophy. This relationship might be outlined as in Figure 2–3.

FIGURE 2–3
THE RELATIONSHIP BETWEEN PHILOSOPHY AND PHILOSOPHY OF EDUCATION

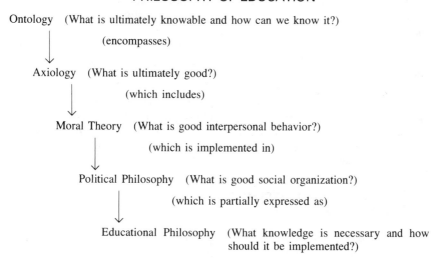

Ontology   (What is ultimately knowable and how can we know it?)

           (encompasses)

Axiology   (What is ultimately good?)

           (which includes)

Moral Theory   (What is good interpersonal behavior?)

           (which is implemented in)

Political Philosophy   (What is good social organization?)

           (which is partially expressed as)

Educational Philosophy   (What knowledge is necessary and how should it be implemented?)

The term *ontology* in Figure 2–3 is used to encompass any profound and systematic speculation about first principles relating to knowing (epistemology), the known (metaphysics) and the nature of value (axiology). *Axiology* is used primarily to cover considerations of personal (or psychological) value. (What is the nature of personal value and how can it be attained?) Some theorists would hold that *psychological* value and *social* value (interpersonal morality) are inseparable, even in a developmental sense, and would include both of these under the general rubric *axiology*. The distinction is not essential to the basic line of reasoning presented here, so, for all practical purposes, the terms used appear to be adequate. In a similar sense, *philosophy of law* might be interposed between *moral theory* and *political philosophy,* but the essential relationship would remain the same.

Again, it should be stressed that this discussion, as well as the various figures that accompany it, apply to educational ideologies (as well as related philosophies and social theories) of the ideal type—that is, if-then philosophies and not however-hence philosophies, as was discussed in point number 2. Nothing here should be construed as indicating a naïve faith in either the rationality or the morality of actual educational systems as they exist in specific societies at the present time. Books on logic are not written on the assumption that people are always necessarily logical, and models of the *logical* relationship between social ethics, political theory and educational philosophy are not meant to convey the notion that the real world invariably operates in this manner.

On the other hand, two basic assumptions are made throughout this book. First, it is assumed that (1) generally speaking, it is better to act on the basis of intellectual conviction than to act unreflectively, and (2) a good portion of the behavior that occurs in schools is based upon such convictions and is not merely predicated on the unreflective "practice of practice." Second, the assumption is made that the study of the various educational ideologies will enhance sensitivity to ideological differences and therefore generate a higher degree of concern for educational theory; thereby making educators more inclined to think carefully about some of the more central questions and issues confronting contemporary education.

In all events, political theory is not the same thing as realpolitik; the ideal does not always represent the real. It is quite true, as is discussed at some length in pages 37–41, that political philosophy probably provides an a posteriori rationalization for the existing distribution of power within society as often as it provides a basis for determining what sort of authority should be vested in whom.

Overgeneral and Overspecific Philosophies

6. Particular philosophies or systems of philosophy may be either too general or too specific to provide a satisfactory basis for a truly effective philosophy of education.

There are two basic difficulties that can occur in the attempt to trace the educational implications associated with more basic philosophical points of view. One difficulty arises in those cases where there is a clear-cut political philosophy but where this political philosophy is not coherently related to any explicit set of underlying philosophical (and particularly ethical) precepts. In such a case, it is not difficult to draw reasonable inferences about the general sort of education needed on the basis of overall political requirements, but neither the political nor the related educational prescriptions are effectively grounded in any convincing philosophical rationale. In such cases, and while political philosophy is a *necessary* basis for educational theory, the political philosophy itself does not provide a *sufficient* foundation for establishing a really compelling set of educational principles.

The other fundamental difficulty arises in the opposite case, where there is a convincing philosophical base, but where this highly abstract worldview is not sufficiently spelled out to encompass a full consideration of specifically political questions. In this instance—as frequently occurs in existentialism and Zen—the problem arises primarily from the fact that the philosophy is too abstract, and therefore too vague, to be applied directly to the particular questions of education. In this case it is necessary to make preliminary inferences about the nature of the political philosophy that is implied by the overall philosophical point of view, and then to use the political inferences as a basis for even more extended speculations about schooling. Again, the difficulty is primarily one of ambiguity. Basic philosophical theory is necessary, but, without additional intermediate theory in the area of politics, it is scarcely sufficient for establishing an effective philosophy of education. The sort of inferences that are necessary in order to build a philosophy of education are simply too extended to be convincing.

The Problem of Elliptical Relationships

7. There is no one-to-one relationship between general philosophy (that is, general 'philosophical systems,' such as realism or experimentalism) and specific educational practices. The same or similar ethical and social systems occasionally stem from significantly different philosophical first principles. It is therefore in the realm of social ethics, and particularly in the area of political philosophy, which is the first step toward the formation of specific social action from the more abstract considerations of ethics, that fundamental differences in educational philosophies—the so-called educational ideologies—emerge.

The translation from social philosophy to educational philosophy, while predictable, is restricted almost entirely to the more generalized realm of *educational policies* and does not ordinarily extend to specific *educational practices*. Phrased somewhat differently, *philosophical principles* (even at the intermediate level of abstraction represented in social ethics) do carry over into more specific and issues-oriented educational policies; but there is a vast difference between educational policies, which serve to channel broad categories of behavior across a wide range of the same and similar situations, and specific educational practices, which describe what is actually done in response to particular problems. It is, for example, virtually impossible to specify how a person will respond to such problems as class size or administrative style merely on the basis of his commitment to this or that set of overall educational policies (assuming, of course, that these sorts of things are not *defined* as "policy considerations" in the first place). Policies are simply neither that explicit nor that inclusive, and many other variables of an essentially nonphilosophical nature also intervene to affect practical responses to specific school situations.

Truth from Value: The Practice of Practice

8. Not all education—whether one is talking about specific educational practices or more generalized educational policies—is based upon a coherent philosophy of education.

Contrary to the intellectual's traditional retort that all practice is the practice of some theory, most practice is not based upon "theory" at all. Instead, most practice—educational or otherwise—is merely an extension of prior practice. For better or worse, most people generally practice *practice* and not *theory;* and most people generally behave according to habit, custom, or impulse, rather than on the basis of serious intellectual convictions. This is not necessarily to deny that man is a rational animal. On the other hand, this statement refers primarily to man's potentiality for rational action and not to his customary mode of operations. Quantitatively, very little human behavior appears to be actually motivated by ideological preconsiderations.

A central element of confusion here stems from a tendency to equate two significantly different ideas. The idea "All practice is the practice of some theory" is not true. On the other hand, the idea "All practice can be interpreted on the *basis* of some theory"—that is, "All behavior can be theorized, or philosophized, *about*"—is true, but it conveys an entirely different sort of meaning. The latter statement differs from the former in one basic respect: It does not assume that "rational" behavior is necessarily "reasoned" behavior; that is, it does not hold that all behavior that can be explained in terms of abstract ideas is necessarily motivated by a conscious commitment to the realization of such ideas. It does not deny the possibility of ideological, or theory-motivated, behavior. It does, however, deny that *all* behavior is *necessarily* ideological.

Translated over to the province of educational practices, what this means can be summarized as follows: All educational practices can be subjected to intellectual analysis and construed in terms of theoretical precepts. On the other hand, not all educational practice is theoretical in the sense of being based upon explicit ideological presuppositions or of being motivated by conscious ideological intent.

In this regard, it is important to bear in mind that there is a significant difference between an educator who is consciously and intentionally committed to some particular educational philosophy and one whose educational practices are construed by others to reflect such a commitment. Interpretations on the basis of observed behavior can be notoriously misleading. The Marxist who teaches in a Catholic school so that he can afford to spend his weekends writing tracts against Christianity is not a "Thomist" regardless of his superficial conformity to Catholic doctrine in the classroom. A student radical who actively promotes repressive procedures on the part of the high school principal as a tactic for fomenting a campus revolt on behalf of student rights is not an "educational conservative" despite certain appearances to the contrary.

One point of view which causes a great deal of confusion in this general area is that which holds that, since all education is purposive, and since all purposes are based upon philosophical assumptions about the ultimate nature of value, all education is necessarily "philosophical." This position, which is actually a variation of the position already discussed, makes two fundamental errors.

First, as previously indicated, it confuses theory (in the sense of the assumptions that can be analyzed out of behavior) with the internal dynamic, or psychological motive, which gives rise to such behavior in the first place.

Second, it mistakenly assumes that all purposes are based upon assumptions about the abstract nature of value. That is, it confuses the *conative* (preconscious but implicitly purposive behavior), the volitional (consciously willful behavior), and the normative (behavior based upon consciously recognized abstract ideas about value).

The Conative, the Volitional and the Normative. This latter point is a particularly difficult one to deal with, because the three terms, *conative, volitional* and *normative,* are frequently confused. *Conative behavior* is behavior which is implicitly purposive but not consciously so. The newborn's behavior is implicitly intentional, because he seeks the satisfaction of needs and therefore the realization of goals, which he is not yet capable of comprehending. He engages in a process very similar to what psychologist Carl Rogers refers to as *organismic cognition.*[31] If and when the child comes to understand the meaning implicit in his own behavior, his conative behavior becomes conscious (explicit) and therefore volitional. *Volitional behavior* is conscious (explicit) conative behavior in which the individual actually "has a purpose in mind." *Normative behavior* is behavior that is either implicitly or explicitly directed by some idea (some abstract concept or point of view) with respect to what is generally good or desirable.

In a sense, all behavior is originally conative. Some conative behavior becomes conscious (explicitly intentional) and therefore volitional. Some volitional behavior is based on higher cognition involving abstract notions of what is good and bad, right and wrong, and is therefore normative. In the course of psychological development, the child is conative before he is volitional, and he is volitional before he is normative. Ultimately his behavior comes to reflect a combination of all three. In the final analysis, however, conative behavior is the broader and more encompassing category: All normative behavior emerges out of the volitional, and all volitional behavior develops from the conative. Developmentally, the volitional is, in this sense, a subset of the conative; and the normative is, in turn, a subset of the volitional. The basic relationship might be viewed as shown in Figure 2–4.

Belief and Behavior. An individual's beliefs and his behavior correspond to the extent that his professions of belief are corroborated by appropriate types of behavior. In the final analysis, however, *behavior verifies belief:* a person is what he does and not what he says he does. This is true for three basic reasons.

a) Belief is ultimately a facet of behavior. Behavior is a far broader category which encompasses belief as but one of its aspects. Only a small part of behavior is directed by conscious awareness, let alone by explicit ideas and theories. In short, belief is a subset of behavior, which is used to explain and direct additional types of behavior.

b) All belief is a product of behavior. Belief evolves out of behavior. At basis, our beliefs describe the meaning inherent within the experience generated by our past behavior.

c) The purpose of belief is to direct behavior.[32]

Developmentally—and without considering the complicated feedback loops and circularities which enter into the system—the relationship between behavior and belief might be summarized as in Figure 2–5.

FIGURE 2–4
CONATIVE, VOLITIONAL, AND NORMATIVE BEHAVIOR

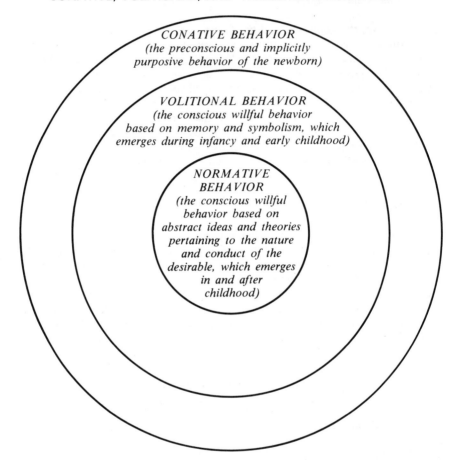

CONATIVE BEHAVIOR
(the preconscious and implicitly
purposive behavior of the newborn)

VOLITIONAL BEHAVIOR
(the conscious willful behavior
based on memory and symbolism, which
emerges during infancy and early childhood)

NORMATIVE
BEHAVIOR
(the conscious willful
behavior based on
abstract ideas and theories
pertaining to the nature
and conduct of the
desirable, which emerges
in and after
childhood)

Or, in more philosophical terms, what occurs can also be expressed in the basic worldview of empirical behaviorism as in Figure 2–6.

Some Qualifications. Figures 2–5 and 2–6 require some qualification, because much more than the preceding pages, they are highly influenced by a particular philosophical point of view. In descending order of abstraction, this point of view is empirical, behavioristic, pragmatic, experimental, and generally oriented to the findings of contemporary scientific psychology. Most of these philosophical orientations and associated theoretical positions are discussed at length in Chapter VII, but, in order to be as objective as possible, I would like to be quite specific about any biases that may unavoidably intrude. Since the intellectual subculture in America today is generally predisposed to accept most of these philosophical assumptions—which are, after all, implicit

FIGURE 2–5
THE EMERGENCE OF VALUES

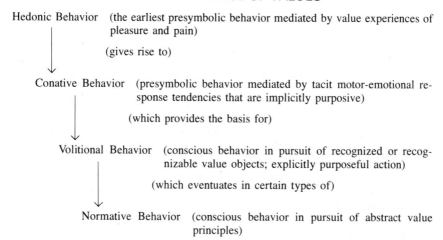

Hedonic Behavior (the earliest presymbolic behavior mediated by value experiences of pleasure and pain)

(gives rise to)

Conative Behavior (presymbolic behavior mediated by tacit motor-emotional response tendencies that are implicitly purposive)

(which provides the basis for)

Volitional Behavior (conscious behavior in pursuit of recognized or recognizable value objects; explicitly purposeful action)

(which eventuates in certain types of)

Normative Behavior (conscious behavior in pursuit of abstract value principles)

FIGURE 2–6
BEHAVIOR AND KNOWLEDGE

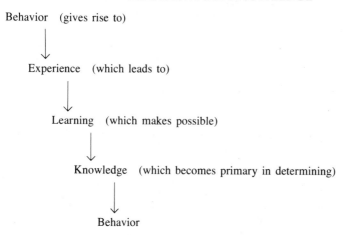

Behavior (gives rise to)

Experience (which leads to)

Learning (which makes possible)

Knowledge (which becomes primary in determining)

Behavior

within the contemporary scientific point of view—the statements made here may strike many people as simply an extrapolation of 'conventional wisdom.' In a sense this is true, but, in another sense, modern 'scientific psychology' is not neutral. It is based upon quite definite philosophical assumptions that not everyone is inclined to accept (see Chapter III, pages 103–109). Thus, a caveat: Since I am talking here about the relationship between theory and practice at the psychological (descriptive) level, there may appear to be a contradiction between the description of behavior offered here and the prescriptive model offered earlier, in which the linear flow was essentially logical rather than psychological, moving from theory to practice. The contradiction is merely ostensible, however. The 'fact' that the child becomes rational on physiological and psychological bases through a sequence of essentially 'prerational' events does not mean that he cannot psychologically adapt to intellective criteria for action once they have emerged developmentally. The *logical* may emerge *psychologically;* nevertheless it may become functionally autonomous of its origins, and is potentially capable of becoming a central determinant of subsequent behavior under certain conditions.

Three particular qualifications should be appended to this line of reasoning reflected in Figures 2–5 and 2–6. First, these generalizations apply to empirical behaviorism *as a philosophy.* They are necessarily based upon speculative assumptions that go beyond scientific evidence as such. Therefore, many strictly psychological behaviorists of the more rigorous sort (such as Clark Hull and B. F. Skinner) might very well reject such conjectural generalizations—and quite properly, from their own point of view—as "nonscientific," because such assertions cannot be verified solely on the basis of observable/measurable phenomena under controlled conditions. In other words, *psychological behaviorism* in the Skinnerian tradition (which is discussed at some length at a later point) is closely related to *philosophical behaviorism* in many respects, but it tends to be more rigorously experimental in a purely scientific (operational) sense and to refrain from making any sort of extended interpretations about the conditions that might assumedly underlie observable patterns of behavior. This is one of the reasons why attaching a philosophical label to someone like Skinner is a hazardous undertaking (see Chapter VII).

Second, the statement that all belief is a *product of* behavior is clearly a different statement than the statement that all belief is *verified through* behavior. The former statement is the essence of philosophical behaviorism. The latter is central to pragmatism (and, by extension, to experimentalism as well) but it is not *necessarily* behavioristic. A pragmatist in the tradition of William James would, for example, accept the principle that all belief is verified by behavior but he would also accept the long-range phenomenological (subjective) consequences of believing in certain metaphysical assumptions—such as the existence of a personal God or traditional 'free will'—as constituting effective 'proofs' as well. This is an acceptable tradition within pragmatism, but it is not sanctioned by the behaviorists. The 'proofs' of a person like William James are essentially phenomenological vindications—that is, "the proof of the principle is in the *living*"—and do not reside in directly measurable behavioral consequences observed under controlled scientific conditions.

Third, philosophical behaviorism often rejects the traditional notion that one cannot obtain *oughtness* (prescriptions or moral admonitions) from *isness* (descriptions or empirical observations). The position that many behaviorists take—which is discussed in the pages concerned with the various approaches to self-actualization at the beginning of Chapter III—is that man is naturally an active 'structure-function' system who finds his fullest satisfaction (happiness) in expressing his dynamic and ongoing potentialities for action to the fullest possible extent. In this sense, the behaviorist frequently takes the position that isness is inherently dynamic, and, since it is grounded in certain objective conditions regarding the nature of the organism and the nature of the world in which it lives, it implies a certain kind of oughtness. This follows because the highest value is to become what one potentially is; that is, to *exist* in such a way as to realize the dynamic imperatives implicit within one's naturally active *essence*, to live in such a way as to realize fully one's implicit nature. For many behaviorists, then, man is not static. He is a vital and ongoing energy-system with a set of motivating tendencies that are "built in at the factory." The question is not *how* one can initiate appropriate kinds of values in order to impel the organism into action. The organism is designed to act, and it is already acting when it emerges into the world, endowed with what the existentialists term "a passion to be." The basic problem, then, is to understand *why* people act as they do, as well as what sort of needs and desires are appropriate for a certain kind of organism that is constrained to act under a limited set of definable conditions. Indeed, from the point of view of many behaviorists, values emerge naturally out of human behavior in a manner outlined in Figures 2–7 and 2–8. Viewed somewhat differently, and phrased in the distinctive language of cybernetics, the knowledge process might be diagrammed as in Figure 2–9.

FIGURE 2–7
THE EMERGENCE OF VALUES

Physical tension-systems (inherent action-tendencies—actually, internal physical behavior—preparatory to certain types of external behavior) give rise to

$\downarrow$

observable behavior (actual interaction with the external environment) which actively resolves

$\downarrow$

physical tensions through the appropriate types of consummatory behavior, which is experienced physiologically as pleasure, which gives rise to

$\downarrow$

modifications within the physical tension-system on a psychological (electrochemical) basis known as "learning," which allows

$\downarrow$

preconscious needs to become identified with the sorts of environmental goals (objects and events) that have led to success and survival (and which have therefore been confirmed by pleasure).

$\downarrow$

By means of symbolism, these goals are generalized into abstract principles termed *values*.

$\downarrow$

These values, through the exercise of reason and in light of further information, imply additional goals that also function effectively and are therefore confirmed indirectly by reason and directly by emotional feedback.

FIGURE 2–8
THE ETIOLOGY OF KNOWLEDGE

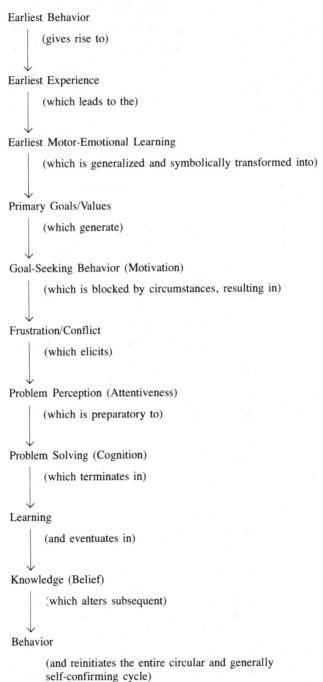

Earliest Behavior

    (gives rise to)

Earliest Experience

    (which leads to the)

Earliest Motor-Emotional Learning

    (which is generalized and symbolically transformed into)

Primary Goals/Values

    (which generate)

Goal-Seeking Behavior (Motivation)

    (which is blocked by circumstances, resulting in)

Frustration/Conflict

    (which elicits)

Problem Perception (Attentiveness)

    (which is preparatory to)

Problem Solving (Cognition)

    (which terminates in)

Learning

    (and eventuates in)

Knowledge (Belief)

    (which alters subsequent)

Behavior

    (and reinitiates the entire circular and generally
self-confirming cycle)

FIGURE 2–9
THE KNOWLEDGE PROCESS: A CYBERNETICS MODEL

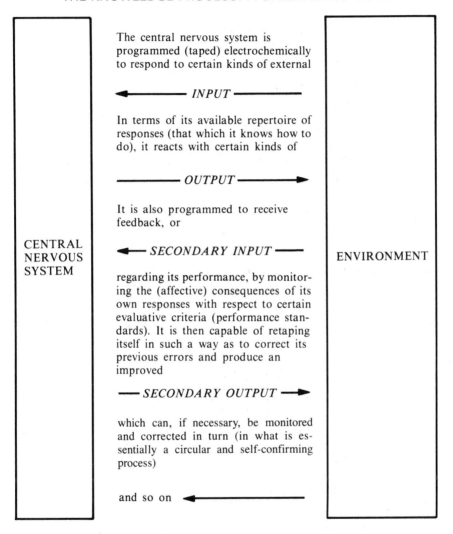

The central nervous system is programmed (taped) electrochemically to respond to certain kinds of external

◀——————— *INPUT* ———————

In terms of its available repertoire of responses (that which it knows how to do), it reacts with certain kinds of

——————— *OUTPUT* ———————▶

It is also programmed to receive feedback, or

◀—— *SECONDARY INPUT* ——

regarding its performance, by monitoring the (affective) consequences of its own responses with respect to certain evaluative criteria (performance standards). It is then capable of retaping itself in such a way as to correct its previous errors and produce an improved

—— *SECONDARY OUTPUT* ——▶

which can, if necessary, be monitored and corrected in turn (in what is essentially a circular and self-confirming process)

and so on ◀———————————

CENTRAL NERVOUS SYSTEM

ENVIRONMENT

For the philosophical behaviorist, then, values occur before the factual world (or, at least, the "factual world" as this is conventionally defined) is understood, and, if anything, it is *oughtness* (in terms of how the world is conatively and volitionally encountered) which precedes and determines *isness* (viewed as how the world is understood). Developmentally, then, we do not think before we act. We act and choose long before we think. Our beliefs are, in a basic sense, the products of our value commitments in the world. Again, this line of reasoning is perhaps best understood diagrammatically, as in Figure 2–10.

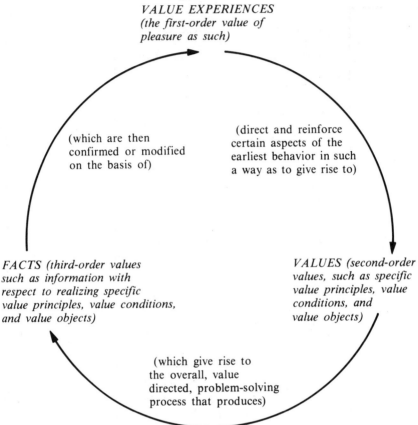

FIGURE 2–10
THE HEDONIC BASIS OF LEARNING

VALUE EXPERIENCES
(the first-order value of
pleasure as such)

(direct and reinforce
certain aspects of the
earliest behavior in such
a way as to give rise to)

(which are then
confirmed or modified
on the basis of)

FACTS (third-order values
such as information with
respect to realizing specific
value principles, value conditions,
and value objects)

VALUES (second-order
values, such as specific
value principles, value
conditions, and
value objects)

(which give rise to
the overall, value
directed, problem-solving
process that produces)

Correlation and Causation in Belief and Behavior

9. There is a significant difference between the educational practices that are logically implied by a particular philosophical position, on the one hand, and the educational practices that are merely psychologically related to (or correlated with) a particular philosophical position, on the other.

The philosophical followers of Saint Thomas Aquinas, for example, subscribe to the notion that the foremost goal of formal education is to train the student to comprehend the great religious truths that are required in order to secure the salvation of his immortal soul. This policy is a logical extension of the basic Thomistic worldview. On the other hand, most Thomists also subscribe to relatively formalized and didactic procedures in the classroom. As compared to the educational followers of existentialism and experimentalism, they are far less likely to use free inquiry techniques, activity methods, and similar practices. Here, however, we are dealing not so much with a practice that is a logical outgrowth of basic philosophical convictions as with one which is merely correlated (or associated) with the sort of personality structure that is predisposed toward the Thomistic approach in the first place.

Certain of the basic philosophical systems are logically incompatible with certain of the so-called educational philosophies. A traditional *theistic realist* such as a disciple of Saint Thomas Aquinas cannot, for example, logically subscribe to a pedagogical stance like *educational liberationism* which holds that the primary objective of education is to encourage humanistic social reforms by maximizing personal freedom within education and by advocating the extension of more humanitarian conditions within society at large.

In a similar sense, a philosophical experimentalist like John Dewey would be guilty of severe self-contradiction if he were to endorse the highly traditional *educational intellectualism* advanced by an individual like Robert Maynard Hutchins or Mortimer Adler. In addition, while it is very difficult to draw any convincing inferences about the ultimate philosophical assumptions underlying specifically educational philosophies, there are, as already noted, many indirect and essentially ''psychological'' relationships between those espousing certain philosophical positions and those advocating particular educational approaches. These relationships in themselves make it likely that persons advocating certain philosophical positions will be significantly more predisposed toward certain educational practices than toward others.

Traditional realists, for example, tend to be educational traditionalists, because they characteristically emphasize the formal mastery of subject matter content over the value of open-ended ''experimental'' inquiry. This is not to say that a traditional realist of, say, the Aristotelian variety is philosophically constrained to do so, however. *Theoretically,* he could focus almost entirely on problem-solving procedures or even veer in the direction of educational anarchism. *Factually,* however, this is not the case. There appears to be a rather convincing psychological relationship between subscribing to philosophical realism of the traditional sort and being predisposed toward a rather high degree of educational formalism.

In a similar sense, most experimentalists tend to be either educational liberals or educational liberationists. They are virtually always committed to the fullest expression of political freedom, usually centering around some form of representational democracy. This commitment, however, appears to be only indirectly related to experimentalism *as a philosophy.* It is quite possible to be a philosophical experimentalist—as the existence of B. F. Skinner testifies—and still have profound doubts about the wisdom of political democracy (see Chapter VII). Again, the correlation seems to be primarily rooted in a sort of prephilosophical agreement at the level of basic character structure which predates, and probably predisposes the individual toward, a particular type of philosophical commitment in the first place.

This sort of psychological relationship—whether exemplified by the Thomist's tendency toward academic formalism, by the experimentalist's tendency toward ''learning by doing,'' or by any of a number of other possible relationships—is perhaps most fully understood on the basis of the empirical behaviorist's worldview, which can be outlined as shown in Figure 2–11.

FIGURE 2–11
THE BEHAVIORAL BASES OF PERSONAL PHILOSOPHY:
THE EMPIRICAL BEHAVIORIST VIEW

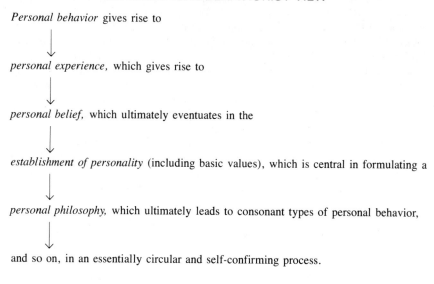

Personal behavior gives rise to

personal experience, which gives rise to

personal belief, which ultimately eventuates in the

establishment of personality (including basic values), which is central in formulating a

personal philosophy, which ultimately leads to consonant types of personal behavior,

and so on, in an essentially circular and self-confirming process.

Or, this can be diagrammed somewhat differently as shown in Figure 2–12.

FIGURE 2–12
BELIEF AND BEHAVIOR
(EMPIRICAL BEHAVIORISM)

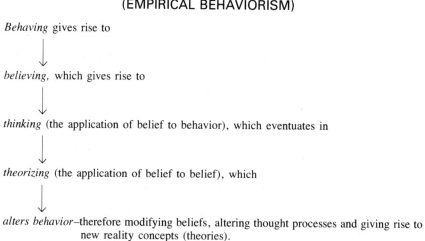

Behaving gives rise to

believing, which gives rise to

thinking (the application of belief to behavior), which eventuates in

theorizing (the application of belief to belief), which

alters behavior–therefore modifying beliefs, altering thought processes and giving rise to new reality concepts (theories).

What all of this suggests about the relationship between theory and practice can be summarized in three basic points.

The Psychological Foundations of the Philosophical. *Philosophical* similarities between individuals are generally based upon *psychological* similarities which, in turn, grow out of corresponding experiences caused by undergoing (and therefore learning from) the same and similar sorts of behavior during the earliest years of life. Similar personalities seek the same and similar sorts of experience, which ultimately gives rise to the same and similar types of belief. This commonality in belief ultimately generates a commonality in behavior, which confirms existing belief, and so on. [33]

The relationship between formal (philosophical) and informal (psychological) relationships is perhaps best explained from the point of view of the empirical behaviorist. The empirical behaviorist (whose philosophical stance is discussed at some length in Chapter VII) subscribes to a philosophical position that is based upon certain presuppositions about the empirical (and, specifically, behavioral) bases of all belief. In diagram form, the empirical behaviorist's point of view about the relationship between behavior and belief is presented in Figure 2–13.

FIGURE 2–13
KNOWING AND THE KNOWN: THE EMPIRICAL
BEHAVIORIST APPROACH

Implicit (behavioral) meaning, (organized behavior in the earliest phases of life) gives rise to

$\downarrow$

explicit (symbolic) meaning, (beliefs represented as knowledge in terms of images and symbols), which results in

$\downarrow$

behavior mediated by belief (practice directed by explicit knowledge). This eventuates in

$\downarrow$

belief mediated by belief (the internal criticism of knowledge on the basis of other knowledge: the verification of knowledge on the basis of accepted knowledge criteria; the reconstruction and correction of knowledge by means of accepted principles of knowing). This makes possible the

$\downarrow$

reconstruction and correction of behavior (by means of verified knowledge), including the

$\downarrow$

correction of explicit belief systems and the

$\downarrow$

improvement of behavior (by means of verified belief) which leads to the

$\downarrow$

continued verification of beliefs, and so on.

The essential circularity of the entire process is captured in Figure 2–14.

FIGURE 2–14
THE CIRCULARITY OF KNOWLEDGE

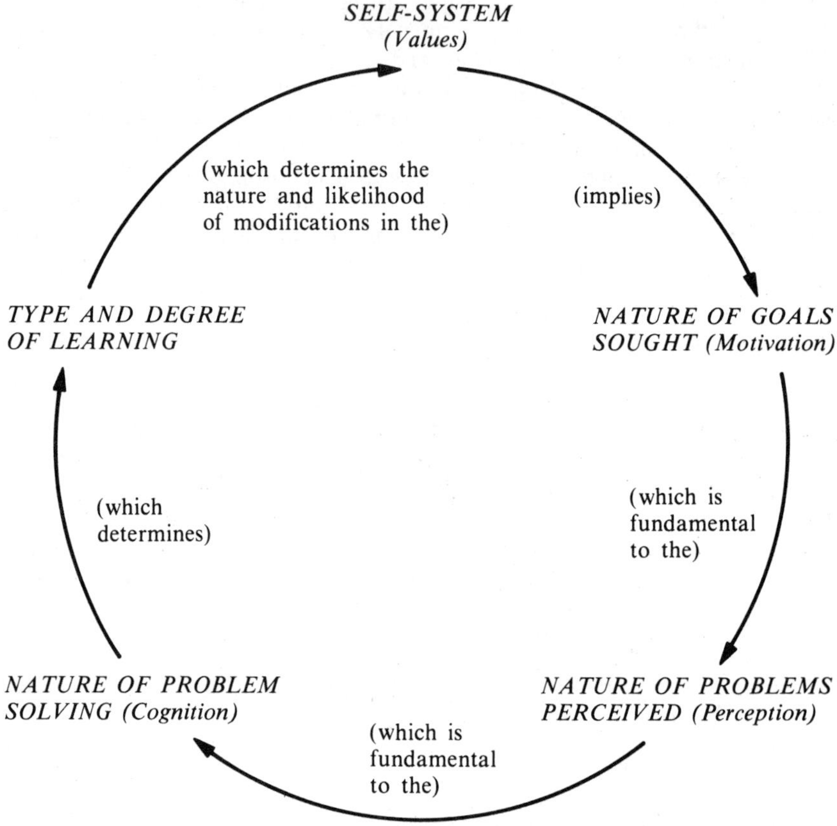

SELF-SYSTEM
(Values)

(which determines the
nature and likelihood
of modifications in the)

(implies)

TYPE AND DEGREE
OF LEARNING

NATURE OF GOALS
SOUGHT (Motivation)

(which
determines)

(which is
fundamental
to the)

NATURE OF PROBLEM
SOLVING (Cognition)

NATURE OF PROBLEMS
PERCEIVED (Perception)

(which is
fundamental
to the)

In short, common belief is rooted in common behavior. Common belief also *generates* common behavior, but only on an after-the-fact basis. Belief itself is rooted in the primary personality structure (basic to the establishment of the personal value system), which is determined during the essentially prerational years of infancy and early childhood.

Behavior as the Ground of Belief. *Behavior* (as previously indicated) is a broader concept than *belief,* and far broader than *philosophical belief. Belief* is merely a conscious distillation of the meaning inherent within overall behavior. Since common beliefs are grounded in common experience on the basis of common behavior, it is understandable that correspondences in behavior between individuals sharing the same or similar belief systems will be even broader and more encompassing than their agreements in the area of mere theory. In other words, since the *philosophical* evolves out of the *psychological,* the consensus between representatives of a particular educational philosophy with respect to virtually any significant educational question will tend to be much broader than would be suggested by merely examining the behavior logically necessitated by their common agreement in the area of theory. This consensus is fundamentally at the level of character structure and not in the realm of after-the-fact rationalization.

The Singularity and Circularity of Belief. Two factors virtually preclude any *total* philosophical agreement between individuals. These are, first, the fact that no person's behavior or experience can ever really be the same as any other's; and, second, that, once formulated, any system of beliefs generates behavior only in the light of particular (and largely uncontrollable) circumstances that, again, are never really identical for any two people. On the other hand, and despite these qualifications, personal experience does tend to be *generally* similar for almost everyone. Even basic differences in belief tend to fall into relatively predictable patterns because of the constancies and continuities that recur within overall human behavior as an unavoidable requirement for surviving and succeeding within a particular kind of world.

Thus, while behavior is subjective in one sense, "subjectivity" itself is "relative" to learned experience. Learned experience, however, is controlled by the objective conditions, the nature of the physical organism itself as well as the nature of the material world in which it operates. These conditions are never directly encountered, however, because we respond directly only to our responses (experience) and merely indirectly to the underlying conditions which elicit such responses. The underlying conditions are therefore simply "given" and are not either *subjective* or *relative* in any of the usual senses of these terms. In rough outline, then, we are confronted with the situation presented in Figures 2–15 and 2–16.

FIGURE 2–15
THE STRUCTURE OF EXPERIENCE

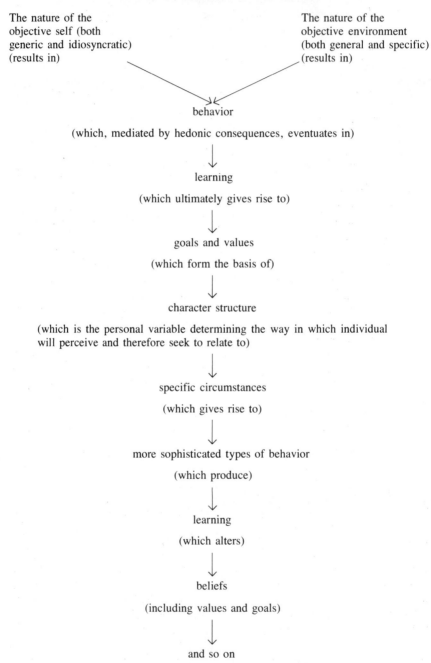

The nature of the objective self (both generic and idiosyncratic) (results in)

The nature of the objective environment (both general and specific) (results in)

behavior

(which, mediated by hedonic consequences, eventuates in)

learning

(which ultimately gives rise to)

goals and values

(which form the basis of)

character structure

(which is the personal variable determining the way in which individual will perceive and therefore seek to relate to)

specific circumstances

(which gives rise to)

more sophisticated types of behavior

(which produce)

learning

(which alters)

beliefs

(including values and goals)

and so on

(in what is fundamentally a self-confirming cycle)

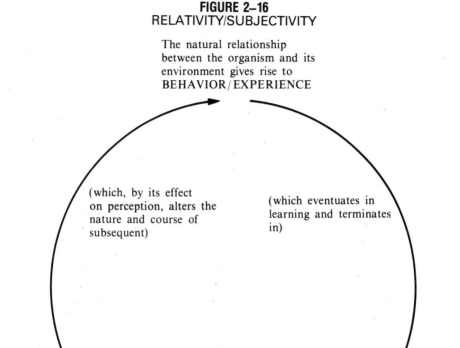

FIGURE 2–16
RELATIVITY/SUBJECTIVITY

The natural relationship
between the organism and its
environment gives rise to
BEHAVIOR/EXPERIENCE

(which, by its effect
on perception, alters the
nature and course of
subsequent)

(which eventuates in
learning and terminates
in)

THE SELF
(Subjectivity)

KNOWLEDGE

(an important aspect
of which comprises)

Values and Value-Priorities

10. In forecasting educational behavior, knowing a person's philosophy (including his basic values) is important, but knowing the specific priority ranking of the values contained within his philosophy tends to be even more important. In general, four questions are of central significance:

a) What are the person's basic values? (What is his overall value commitment?)

b) How intensely is he committed to these values? (How profound is this commitment?)

c) What, in general, is the priority ranking of these values, and how do they relate one to another? (What does he care for most, and what is the resulting *value-gestalt?*)

d) How does the individual perceive these values as relating to the situation at hand? (What is the situational relevance of this personal commitment?)

In Conclusion. These ten points are necessary considerations for a full understanding of philosophical discussions about education and related matters. Hopefully, they provide a basis for the more extended treatment of the various educational ideologies in the subsequent chapters. At the very least, they serve to explicate some of the more basic assumptions and/or concerns that pervade much of the material to come.

NOTES

1. John Dewey, *Democracy and Education* (New York: Macmillan Co., 1916), pp. 45–46.

2. Ibid., p. 60.

3. John Dewey, "Progressive Education: The Ideal and the Reality," in Ronald Gross, ed., *The Teacher and the Taught* (New York: Dell Publishing Co., 1963), p. x.

4. See Thomas Katen, *Doing Philosophy* (New York: Prentice-Hall, 1973).

5. Richard S. Peters, *Ethics and Education* (Chicago: Scott, Foresman & Company, 1966); Israel Scheffler, *Conditions of Knowledge* (Chicago: Scott, Foresman & Co, 1965); Jonas Soltis, *An Introduction to the Analysis of Educational Concepts* (Reading, Mass.: Addison-Wesley Co, 1968).

6. There are actually two basic formal systems approaches to the philosophy of education: (1) those emphasizing contemporary philosophies and systems of philosophy which are looked upon as being particularly significant for education (this is clearly the emphasis in such a book as Van Cleve Morris and Young Pai's *Philosophy and the American School*); and (2) those which are primarily concerned with the *history* of educational philosophy (either in general, as in Robert Ulich's *History of Educational Thought,* or with reference to particular problems and issues in education, as in John Brubacher's *History of Educational Problems*). Most of the existing textbooks in the area of educational philosophy use an eclectic approach, but virtually all tend to emphasize one of these two basic approaches.

7. J. Donald Butler, *Four Philosophies and Their Practice in Education and Religion,* rev. ed. (New York: Harper & Brothers, 1951). In the most recent revision of Butler's book (Second Edition, 1963) he has a brief consideration of two additional philosophical points of view, existentialism and linguistic analysis, but he continues to focus on the four traditional philosophies of naturalism, idealism, realism and pragmatism.

8. Butler, *Four Philosophies and Their Practice in Education and Religion,* 2d ed., pp. 261–62.

9. See Chapter VII.

10. This approach is not frequently encountered in the literature of educational philosophy, although the specifically educational aspects of the established philosophical systems are very often translated into equivalent educational theories (usually employing some variation of Brameld's categories of *essentialism, perennialism, progressivism* and *reconstructionism,* which are discussed further on). On the other hand, much of the discussion about such educational theories as perennialism, essentialism, progressivism and reconstructionism tends to be based upon the assumption that these can be regarded as if they were self-contained educational philosophies more or less independent of their antecedents in more profound philosophical differences.

11. Theodore B. Brameld, *Philosophies of Education in Cultural Perspective* (New York: Dryden, 1955); see also Theodore B. Brameld, *Toward a Reconstructed Philosophy of Education* (New York: Dryden, 1956).

12. Brameld, *Toward a Reconstructed Philosophy of Education,* pp. 4–19.

13. Ibid., p. 11.

14. Ibid., p. 8.

15. Ibid.

16. Ibid., p. 5.

17. Ibid.

18. Ibid., p. 4.

19. Ibid., p. 18.

20. This confusion relating to the so-called educational philosophies is compounded in some of the better-known textbooks on philosophy of education where terms ordinarily associated with systems of philosophy are used to represent additional educational philosophies, ordinarily supplementing, or partially qualifying, Brameld's four original positions. Van Cleve Morris, in his book *Philosophy and the American School: An Introduction to the Philosophy of Education* (Boston: Houghton Mifflin Co., 1961) adds existentialism as a fifth educational philosophy, augmenting Brameld's original list. In a similar sense, George F. Kneller (*An Introduction to the Philosophy of Education,* New York: John Wiley & Sons, 1964) replaces Brameld's term *progressivism* with the philosophical term *experimentalism,* and he, like Morris, adds existentialism as a fifth educational philosophy. There is certainly nothing indefensible with any of this, but it does make matters even more confusing by adding still a third category, systems of philosophy as they apply to education, to the two (political and pedagogical) already employed.

21. Robert B. McLaren, *A Study in Philosophical Curriculum Dissonance,* Dissertation for the degree of Doctor of Philosophy, School of Education, University of Southern California, 1972, p. 64.

22. Abraham Kaplan, *New World of Philosophy* (New York: Random House, 1961), p. 4.

23. This is not to suggest that there is any absolute distinction between *fact* and *meaning.* As Goethe states, "Everything factual is, in a sense, theory. The blue of the sky exhibits the basic laws of chromatics. There is no sense in looking for something behind the phenomena: they *are* theory."

24. Susanne K. Langer, *Philosophy in a New Key: A Study in the Symbolism of Reason, Rite and Art* (New York: New American Library, 1959), p. 246.

25. See Karl Popper and John Eccles, *The Self and Its Brain* (Heidelberg: Springer-Verlag, 1977) and Neils Bohr, *Atomic Physics and Human Knowledge* (New York: Science Editions, 1961).

26. Daniel Bell, ed., *The End of Ideology* (New York: Free Press, 1960); Seymour Lipset, *Political Man* (Garden City, New York: Doubleday and Company, 1960). Chaim I. Waxman, ed., *The End of Ideology Debate* (New York: Funk & Wagnalls, 1968).

27. Alasdair MacIntyre, *Against the Self Images of the Age* (New York: Schocken Books, 1971), pp. 8–9.

28. L. T. Sargent, *Contemporary Political Ideologies,* rev. ed. (Homewood, Illinois: Dorsey Press, 1972), pp. 1–2.

29. See the discussion of "Synergism" on pp. 78–83.

30. See the discussion of "Synergism" on pp. 78–83.

31. Carl Rogers, *Freedom to Learn* (Columbus, Ohio: Charles E. Merrill Co., 1969), pp. 286–87.

32. See pp. 29–36.

33. See the discussion on Synergism and other circular processes in reasoning on pp. 78–79.

BIBLIOGRAPHY

The following is a selected bibliography of books and selections from books which exemplify the various approaches to educational philosophy. The list is in no sense definitive. It is merely illustrative of some of the better representations of the three basic approaches to educational philosophy that were discussed in this section: educational philosophizing, the systems of philosophy as applied to education approach, and the educational philosophies approach.

Philosophical Systems and Education

CONTEMPORARY SYSTEMS

BRUBACHER, JOHN S. *Modern Philosophies of Education*. 4th ed. New York: McGraw-Hill, 1968.

BUTLER, J. DONALD. *Four Philosophies and Their Practice in Education and Religion*. New York: Harper & Brothers, 1951.

KNELLER, GEORGE F. *An Introduction to the Philosophy of Education*. New York: John Wiley & Sons, 1964.

MORRIS, VAN CLEVE, and PAI, YOUNG. *Philosophy and the American School: An Introduction to the Philosophy of Education*. 2d ed. Boston: Houghton Mifflin Co., 1961.

NATIONAL SOCIETY FOR THE STUDY OF EDUCATION, *Modern Philosophies and Education*. (The Fifty-fourth Yearbook of the NSSE, Part I), Edited by Nelson B. Henry. Chicago: University of Chicago Press, 1955.

NATIONAL SOCIETY FOR THE STUDY OF EDUCATION, *Philosophies of Education*. (The Forty-first Yearbook of the NSSE, Part I), Edited by Nelson B. Henry. Chicago: University of Chicago Press, 1942.

HISTORICAL SYSTEMS

BRUBACHER, JOHN S. *A History of the Problems of Education:* New York: McGraw-Hill, 1947.

BRUMBAUGH, ROBERT S., and LAWRENCE, NATHANIEL M. *Philosophers on Education: Six Essays on the Foundation of Western Thought*. Boston: Houghton Mifflin Co., 1963.

FRANKENA, WILLIAM A. *Three Historical Philosophers of Education: Aristotle, Kant and Dewey*. Chicago: Scott, Foresman & Co., 1965.

NASH, PAUL; KAZAMIAS, ANDREAS M.; and PERKINSON, HENRY J., eds. *The Educated Man: Studies in the History of Educational Thought*. New York: John Wiley & Sons, 1967.

ULICH, ROBERT. *History of Educational Thought*. 2d ed. Cambridge, Mass.: Harvard University Press, 1954.

ULICH, ROBERT, ed. *Three Thousand Years of Educational Wisdom*. 2d ed. Cambridge, Mass.: Harvard University Press, 1954.

THE EDUCATIONAL PHILOSOPHIES

BRAMELD, THEODORE B. *Patterns of Educational Philosophy: Divergencies and Convergencies in Culturological Perspective*. New York: Holt, Rinehart and Winston, 1971.

BRUBACHER, JOHN S. *Modern Philosophies of Education*. 4th ed. New York: McGraw-Hill, 1968.

MORRIS, VAN CLEVE. *Philosophy and the American School: An Introduction to the Philosophy of American Education*. Boston: Houghton Mifflin Company, 1961. See Part V.

KNELLER, GEORGE F. *An Introduction to the Philosophy of Education*. New York: John Wiley and Sons, 1964. See Chapter IV.

OZMON, HOWARD. *Dialogue in the Philosophy of Education*. Columbus, Ohio: Charles E. Merrill Publishing Co., 1972.

EDUCATIONAL PHILOSOPHIZING
(PHILOSOPHICAL ANALYSIS)

ARCHAMBAULT, REGINALD D., ed. *Philosophical Analysis and Education.* New York: Humanities Press, 1965.

PETERS, RICHARD S. *Authority, Responsibility and Education.* New York: Eriksson-Taplinger Co., 1960.

PETERS, RICHARD S. *Ethics and Education.* Chicago: Scott, Foresman & Co., 1966.

RYLE, GILBERT. "Knowing How and Knowing That," in Scheffler, Israel, ed. *Philosophy and Education: Modern Readings.* Boston: Allyn & Bacon, 1966.

SCHEFFLER, ISRAEL. *Conditions of Knowledge.* Chicago: Scott, Foresman & Company, 1965.

SCHEFFLER, ISRAEL, ed. *Philosophy and Education: Modern Readings.* Boston: Allyn & Bacon, 1966.

SCHEFFLER, ISRAEL, "Toward an Analytic Philosophy of Education." *Harvard Education Review* 24 (Fall 1954).

SMITH, D.O., and ENNIS, ROBERT H. *Language and Concepts in Education.* Chicago: Rand McNally, 1961.

SOLTIS, JONAS. *An Introduction to the Analysis of Educational Concepts.* Reading, Mass.: Addison-Wesley Co., 1968.

SOLTIS, JONAS F. "Philosophy of Education: Fourth Dimension." *Teachers' College Record* 67 (April 1966).

SOLTIS, JONAS F. *Seeing, Knowing and Believing.* Reading, Mass.: Addison-Wesley Co., 1966.

Chapter III

The Educational Ideologies: An Overview

There are significant differences between moral philosophers with respect to what constitutes the nature of the 'self': whether it is purely natural or, in some sense, supernatural; whether and to what extent it is socially determined; whether it is essentially individual and self-contained or merely one aspect of a larger social or cosmic 'self;' and so on. On the other hand, despite substantial differences, virtually all contemporary moral theorists seem to concur that man has a relatively stable nature, which is capable of being characterized in terms of certain fundamental potentialities for acting and being. In addition, they concur that, at least on some significant level, the individual's highest fulfillment resides—either directly or indirectly—in the sort of personal happiness that is a by-product of the realization of these potentialities. That is, it resides in his capacity to *become* that which he incipiently *is*.

VALUE AS SELF-ACTUALIZATION

Stripped to its essentials, the self-actualization argument—and virtually all moral philosophers today seem to subscribe to some variation of it—holds that (1) moral prescriptions apply only to those things that are humanly possible; (2) all possibilities refer to certain identifiable human potentialities for acting or being; and (3) the good life therefore can ultimately be defined (although at a very high level of generalization) in terms of human potentialities that exist in order to be perfected or realized.

On the other hand, and as previously mentioned, philosophers differ significantly in how they view these human potentialities. Most define them normatively, so that they encompass only *positive* capacities, such as the capacity to be rational, to be moral, to attain enlightenment, and so on. In such cases, the opposite or contrary potentialities are generally viewed as either the absence of the realized potentiality (for example, nonrationality, nonmorality, and such) or as the perverse misrepresentation of the potentiality (for example, fully realized immorality, a fully developed capacity for self-delusion, and so on) elicited by either ignorance or evil. Ironically, even those philosophers, such as the existentialists, who ostensibly reject the notion of a stable human nature, defining man as an 'absolute freedom'—that is, as being characterized by the capacity for total self-definition—invariably continue to discuss the boundaries of such freedom and to prescribe the "best" way to express it. Commonly, this is through exercising one's capacity for 'authenticity' (generally viewed as that mode of behavior which allows the individual to express most fully his *highest* potentiality, which is his capacity for autonomous self-determination).

Direct and Indirect Self-Actualization

The most central differences that occur with respect to the self-actualization point of view relate to certain central questions. One of these is the question of whether self-actualization (which is also frequently referred to as *self-realization* or *self-perfection*) is a direct and immediate good, being, in a sense, a different way of talking about personal happiness, or whether it is an indirect and merely mediate good. In the latter case self-actualization may be viewed as merely a means, simply allowing the individual to attain a higher level of existence (and therefore a different kind and/or degree of potentiality for experience) in some *other* dimension of being. In such an instance, the person may, for example, ascend to a spiritual "life-after-death" where *true* happiness is ultimately possible, but only on substantially different terms than those available in the temporal world. Even those philosophers and theologians who are less than totally optimistic about man's capacity for self-perfection in the natural world ordinarily hold that the highest *natural* good is to seek the perfection of one's (constructive) potentialities wherever possible in the course of temporal affairs, however.

Indeed, even where faith is looked upon as necessarily conferred by an inexplicable 'gift' of divine grace (as in Calvinism) the *potentiality* for faith nevertheless tends to be viewed as one aspect of man's intrinsic nature. Most theologians in this tradition would agree that, in the absence of faith, one should live as constructively as possible, fulfilling one's highest potentialities in order to warrant the gift of grace should it be forthcoming. In a similar sense, in traditional Hindu theology, where the different social castes are viewed as possessing decidedly different potentialities for being, and therefore for attaining spiritual liberation, the highest good is to realize fully one's special destiny as this is reflected in one's present capacities vis-á-vis existing conditions. Only by following this course of action can one aspire to substantially broader possibilities in some future life.

In the final analysis, few moral philosophers who subscribe to the self-actualization thesis vary significantly from the basic Aristotelian position which holds that (1) man is basically active, rational and social; and (2) a man who actively reasons about the sort of behavior that makes good sense in a world in which all men are quite obviously (that is, rationally) linked by a chain of mutual interdependence, will also be moral. Here, the term *moral* means quite capable of seeing the justification of subscribing to the kind of social behavior that benefits the group as a whole and therefore his own personal well-being, which is ultimately dependent upon his membership in the group.

Where moral philosophers do tend to differ is principally with respect to whether man's natural reason is sufficient to provide for the full realization of his potential or whether, and to what extent, some sort of external direction— or, in some cases, supernatural guidance—is also necessary in order to provide for the fullest realization of human happiness. The secular anarchist, for example, has generally been predisposed to believe that man is capable of exercising his intrinsic rationality in conjunction with his inherent sociability in such a way as to give rise to a sort of uncoerced moral order in which people are naturally predisposed toward cooperative and constructive social action. The social conservative, on the other hand, has generally had grave reservations about the sufficiency of unbridled reason, and, in a similar sense, the dominant traditions in both Christian and Judaic theology have always held that reason is necessary but not sufficient, that faith is also required in order to attain true self-perfection.

Not all moral philosophers, of course, would necessarily hold that man is naturally predisposed to be morally good. Some are inclined toward the position that man is essentially neutral in his moral makeup, equally inclined toward morally good *or* morally bad behavior. The basic objection to this point of view holds that, if one is willing to accept the basic notions that (1) the individual is naturally active; (2) he is naturally predisposed to seek pleasure and/or happiness; and (3) he is only capable of realizing such ends through behavior that is physically possible on the basis of a particular kind of psychobiological capacity operating in a certain kind of material environment; then the individual cannot be viewed as neutral, because he must necessarily do only some finite combination of what he is capable of doing under the kind of given physical circumstances. This makes only certain kinds of action possible, and only a limited number of these are capable of generating effective (and therefore pleasurable or happiness producing) responses.

Phrased somewhat differently, it is often argued that an organism can actively seek to do only what it *can* do, and that it becomes what it *is* by retaining and repeating the effective (and therefore pleasurable) aspects of what it has previously done. (This is because of an innate hedonic mechanism that relates certain kinds of behavior to certain kinds of emotional responses in what contemporary psychology ordinarily terms *reinforcement*.) From this point of view, human beings are therefore predisposed toward specific kinds of behavior—including specific kinds of social behavior—since men can only survive in some kind of social setting and become truly "human" through the medium of culture. Culture is, in turn, necessary because it acts to generate and sustain the best possible correlation between what man *is* (in terms of his objective potentialities) and what the world *provides* (in terms of its objective possibilities). In this sense, oughtness is ultimately rooted in isness, and the traditional dichotomy between fact and value becomes far less clear-cut than has previously been thought. See Figure 3–1.

Most experimentalists tend to reject the traditional distinction between facts and values, seeing a relationship between the two that might be summarized as in Figure 3–2.

For many experimentalists, then, a "scientific morality" is a distinct possibility, and such a morality might be summarized as in Figure 3–3.

Another alternative to the value-as-self-actualization point of view is the position that holds that the good life cannot ultimately be defined as self-actualization, not merely because man is neutral, but also because he also has an active proclivity for immoral or self-destructive behavior. This point of view, which sometimes takes the extreme position that man is objectively predisposed toward evil or is essentially depraved, is frequently associated with Saint Au-

FIGURE 3–1
THE RELATIONSHIP BETWEEN PERSONAL VALUES AND INTERPERSONAL VALUES (MORALITY)

Human behavior (which is invariably mediated by others)

↓

gives rise to pleasureful experience

↓

which produces learning.

↓

Therefore, the learning process itself ordinarily gives rise to a generalized psychological association between people and pleasure, in which people as such become secondary reinforcers (associated value objects). This marks the beginning of *altruism,* the subjective love of others as others.

↓

As reason matures, a person begins to recognize explicitly that certain conditions are objectively required for pleasure itself, and that these include a dependency upon others (society) and upon the interpersonal apparatus (culture) that sustains such interdependency.

↓

This is ultimately generalized into a code of conduct (moral code) pertaining to optimum relations with respect to other people and to culture in general.

↓

This expedites effective behavior, giving rise to pleasure and reinforcing the idea that pleasure occurs by and through other people, in what amounts to a sort of objective verification of subjective love.

FIGURE 3–2
SCIENTIFIC OBJECTIVITY

Scientific reasoning leads to

↓

objective knowledge which gives rise to

↓

more intelligent people in an increasingly intelligent world, which is precisely the condition necessary to guarantee

↓

even more advanced scientific reasoning, and therefore, continually increasing

↓

practical intelligence on the popular level.

gustine, in the theological tradition; and with Thomas Hobbes—or, more recently, with some of the sociobiologists and ethologists—in the secular realm.

FIGURE 3–3
SCIENTIFIC MORALITY

The scientific analysis of the nature of man and the natural world

identifies certain objective human requirements and the various possibilities for satisfying these requirements.

This, in turn, implies the optimum relationship that can, and should, exist between human needs and existing need-satisfaction, which constitute values.

This includes the demonstrable interdependency of mankind as well as the need for a culture oriented to the satisfaction of these values.

This implies the necessity for supportive types of personal behavior between individuals (a moral code),

which in turn, contributes to the cultural institutions that encourage the maximum realization of objective human needs

and so on.

The major objection that can be raised with respect to the innate depravity argument, in its more rigid and traditional *theological* phrasing, is that it assumes the possibility of *volitional evil,* generally positing that a person who comprehends the nature of the good is capable nevertheless of choosing what he understands to be bad. The primary difficulty here stems from the way in which the terms *good* and *bad* are used. If the *good act* is defined as that which, other things being equal, yields the most productive consequences with respect to what a person already considers to be of overriding value (that is, with respect to his understanding of what constitutes the *good life*), it would be impossible for him to perform *volitionally* a *bad act.* Here, a bad act is defined as one that would yield less than the most productive consequences with respect to what he considered to be of overriding value. This, they posit, would be impossible—*if he really understood* (and therefore yielded true intellectual assent to) *the nature of the good act.* Indeed, to do so would, of necessity, be either to deny the almost universally accepted axioms that (1) a person necessarily *seeks* to do what he *wants* to do, and (2) what a person *wants* is necessarily what he considers to *be* the good act. (This is not to argue that many people would not prefer to be faced with circumstances that would provide a substantially different kind of choice altogether, thereby generating a fundamentally different notion of what constitutes the good act. The point is, however, that the good act is always circumstantial. The good act is often a choice of comparative evils in the sense that the best option would not necessarily have been chosen at all if the problem confronted were different or if the individual confronting the problem had been capable of understanding it differently.)

On a somewhat different level, the very notion of saying that one can choose to do what one does not consider to be best (in the long run or everything considered) is virtually the same as saying that one can choose *not* to do what one *chooses* to do. In the final analysis, however, what one considers to be best *necessarily* takes priority over, and therefore logically determines, the nature of any conscious moral decision. As Socrates argued over 2500 years ago, no man who knows (and therefore really believes) a particular course of action to be good can act contrary to this belief *if his action is directed by conscious awareness* (and is therefore psychologically caused by his belief about what is good and desirable). To do so, would be both psychologically untenable (according to the conventional wisdom of contemporary scientific psychology) and a logical contradiction as well.

Volitional evil is therefore inevitably a contradiction in terms, and all ostensibly bad acts are really good acts (from the point of view of the person doing the acting). They are only bad from the point of view of some *other* person, who views the actions from a different point of view concerning good behavior or (on occasion) by the person himself if he subsequently reevaluates (and therefore makes a different choice at a later time) with respect to the moral status of his own previous behavior.

In short, even if there is such a thing as *categorically* (or objectively) good behavior, I may construe your act as bad—and it may be "bad" from my point of view—and even, conceivably, in an absolute sense. But you nevertheless cannot have performed this act *subjectively* with a conscious awareness that it was bad. Logically and psychologically, you had to consider it the best possible act or you would have been constrained, both logically and psychologically, to have done otherwise.

(The fact that the act was personally pleasurable but socially reprehensible—as might occur if you chose to embezzle money in order to gamble [perhaps throwing an entire firm into bankruptcy, with all the resultant consequences for the various other individuals involved]—is really quite irrelevant. If you were to consider the negative consequences for the other people involved to be the most significant consideration, you would not have embezzled the money in the first place, because you could not have construed embezzlement to be the *best* thing to do under the circumstances. This is not to say that you were not capable of understanding that others considered your act to be reprehensible. Such an insight may have generated a great deal of anxiety. Indeed, other things being equal, you yourself may consider embezzlement to be reprehensible. This too may give you pause. The fact that you nevertheless chose to embezzle indicates, however, if nothing else, that others' views of your behavior, and perhaps even your own reservations about it, did not take priority over your desire to gamble if and when you weighed the pros and cons of the situation. In other words, even your personal moral reservations about your own choice were not sufficient to cause you to do otherwise. They merely made you ambivalent. What you chose to do was inevitably what you considered to be the best course of action in terms of how you understood the particular situation at that time. Even if what you did was patently immoral from the point of view of others or society at large, you could not yourself have viewed it as less than the most moral act possible under the circumstances [in terms of your own understanding of what constituted right and wrong] or you would *necessarily* have done otherwise—you could not choose to do what you did not choose to do.)

The other basic point of view with respect to volitional immorality is essentially *naturalistic* rather than theological. It holds that, while man is not "consciously immoral" (in the sense discussed above), he is inherently predisposed toward immoral (antisocial) forms of behavior, such as aggressiveness or territoriality, which are quasi-instinctual in nature. This point of view does not contradict the self-actualization approach, but it does modify it in the sense that it takes a decidedly less than optimistic view of man's nature and of his potentialities for action. Thus, from the sociobiological point of view, man is frequently looked upon as having a "mixed" potential, with predispositions toward both constructive and destructive behavior. On the other hand, the sociobiological position generally assumes that man's "negative" tendencies toward aggressiveness, territoriality, competition (or whatever) are malleable predispositions of a very general sort that both can and should be subordinated to his more advanced (and generally stronger) potentialities for rational and cooperative behavior. (It should be noted that such antisocial or immoral tendencies as aggressiveness, while looked upon as inherent, are not ordinarily considered *volitional,* because they are unconscious and prerational aspects of man's species-behavior. They are *objectively* immoral in how they function with respect to human behavior in general, but they are not *subjectively* [intentionally] immoral in the sense of being based on conscious choice and intent.) They are, in this sense, 'prerational' (conative) expressions of man's intrinsic nature, and not acquired attitudes.[1]

THE VARYING CONCEPTS OF SELF

A second basic question around which moral philosophers who advocate self-actualization tend to divide concerns the ontological boundaries of the self. Here there tend to be four basic points of view (although, as is common in such matters, these differences are primarily theoretical, and it is not uncommon to find theorists who have quite hybrid concepts of what constitutes the self). These might be termed the *individualistic,* the *sociological,* the *corporate* and the *theistic* concepts.

1. The *individualistic* approach (which is perhaps most frequently associated with the names of such psychological theorists as Abraham Maslow and Carl Rogers) views the self as a relatively discrete psychological unit and looks upon self-actualization in what is substantially traditional Aristotelian terms. Thus, the individual is viewed as possessing an inherent human nature, characterized by certain potentialities (both generic and idiosyncratic) that continuously unfold and interact in response to changing conditions, giving rise to a constant dialectic of being and becoming. Political liberals, as well as some of the more

romantic anarchists, have generally leaned toward this view of self-actualization, which tends to look upon selfhood as essentially distinguishable from more basic sociopolitical considerations. (This is not to suggest that they would deny the relationship between personality and culture, but they frequently tend to disregard it, or at least to deemphasize it radically, treating the self *as if* it could be viewed as a relatively self-contained agent.)

2. The more *sociological* orientation stresses what might be termed *social self-actualization*. Here the self is viewed less as a separate psychological unit than as a part-function of the total field of cultural forces from which it emerges. From this point of view, the nature and degree of self-actualization is limited and defined by the nature and degree to which some particular concept of self is propagated within a particular society at a particular point in history. Thus, for the Marxist, as for many socialists of a non-Marxist persuasion, there can be no meaningful moral commitment to self-actualization in the psychological (or individualistic) sense unless the individual is allowed to operate within a society which is committed to the kind of goals and processes that are necessary for such a personal ideal to be a viable project in the first place. For most left-wing radicals (and particularly for those who are later described as "educational liberationists"), there can be no self-actualization in the absence of social justice, and there can be no social justice without radical reforms in the direction of fuller civil liberties and greater economic equity. From this point of view, then, *individualism* is ordinarily viewed as subordinate to more radical and logically prior socialistic reforms. The personal self is separate from, but radically contingent upon, the larger culture, which defines and determines its ultimate nature and activities.

3. Still another concept of self-actualization holds to the notion, reflected in the writings of such theorists as Hegel and Durkheim, that selfhood is basically a suprapersonal phenomenon located in the historical consciousness of entire cultures or nations. From this point of view, self-actualization is invariably a corollary of participating in some *corporate* or collective identity far broader than individual personality. For the fascist, for example, one finds oneself in losing oneself within the larger and superordinate Self of the state. The individual is invariably looked upon as a part-function of the group. The true self is the organic collective, viewed as the whole which is greater than the sum of its parts.

4. Finally, there is the *theistic* concept of self-actualization which, while accepting the basic reality of the psychological and sociological selves, sees the self as *primarily* a spiritual entity which discovers its fullest realization in a voluntary subordination to the ends of a personal God. From this point of view, the ultimate realization of the self lies in reconciliation with the far greater Self whose mysterious purposes transcend any final location or definition whatsoever. For such individuals—and most of the Western theological traditions in both Christianity and Judaism tend in this direction—true perfection resides only in the whole, and there is no whole except that which is revealed through a total subordination to the purposes of God. To view anything less than this as self-actualization is a form of self-limiting idolatry—the loss of the true self, which stems from mistaking a part of reality (psychological, sociological or intellectual) for the one true and total reality which exists beyond all finite limitations whatsoever.

SELF-ACTUALIZATION AND MORAL PHILOSOPHY

Extending beyond these foregoing considerations, but basically oriented to the overriding idea of self-actualization as the *summum bonum,* a whole host of different moral theories have sprung up to explain *how* it is possible to live the good, or self-actualized, life. In general, there would appear to be six fundamental points of view about how to live the good life that predominate in contemporary Western culture:

1. those which hold that the highest good grows out of adherence to intuitive and/or revealed standards of belief and behavior;
2. those which hold that the highest good grows out of philosophical and/or religious enlightenment based on speculative reason and metaphysical wisdom;
3. those which hold that the highest good grows out of adherence to established (conventional) standards of belief and behavior;
4. those which hold that the highest good grows out of practical intelligence (that is, effective problem solving);
5. those which hold that the highest good grows out of the development of new and more humanistic social institutions; and
6. those which hold that the highest good grows out of the elimination of institutional restraints, as a way of advancing the fullest realization of personal freedom.

It is interesting to note that all of the six basic moral philosophies that underlie the various educational ideologies view value as a particular sort of behavior related to a particular conception of knowing and the known. Thus two of the positions—fundamentalism (both in its secular and religious expressions) and theological intellectualism—see the highest truth as subordinate to nonrational modes of knowing. One—secular intellectualism—views reason as the preeminent mode of knowing but sees the ultimate verification of knowledge as residing in some mystical or quasi-mystical illumination that occurs through a special alchemy brought about when man (as an intelligent being) encounters the inherent intelligibility of the surrounding universe. The Conservative tends to equate value and knowledge, holding that the good life is essentially a matter of recognizing the intrinsic value of the status quo.

The Liberal ideologies all tend to equate the good life with behavior adapted to empirical and naturalistic assumptions about knowing and the known. Thus liberalism equates morality with functional intelligence; the good man is capable of effective thinking (problem solving) with respect to practical problems in the real world. Morality makes eminently good sense as a means of guaranteeing the greatest good for all, so intelligent people are moral. The liberationist agrees with the liberal's contention about the basic identity between intelligence and morality, but sees all intelligence (and therefore morality) as grounded in social conditioning and requiring a certain kind of social order as a preliminary requirement for both effective thinking and effective living. The anarchist, too, would concur that man's inherent morality resides in his intrinsic rationality but would be primarily concerned with the abolition of irrational (and therefore immoral) political constraints that distort and deny man's natural tendencies toward uncoerced rational cooperation.

All of the Conservative ideologies—fundamentalism, intellectualism and conservatism—share the common assumption that the ultimate value is self-realization and that self-realization is properly attained only indirectly, by identifying and adhering to natural and/or divine law. In addition, all three of the Conservative positions can be subdivided into two basic orientations, one *secular* and one *theistic*. The *secular* point of view, in all three positions, maintains that reality is restricted to natural experience and that, while there are metaphysical principles (that is, extremely abstract and pervasive propositions, like the laws of logic or the formal propositions of mathematics) that apply to *all* natural experience and which therefore defy ordinary explanation in common sense terms, even these are merely a different dimension of natural experience. The *theistic*, (or conventional religious) point of view (in Western culture), on the other hand, holds that reality is essentially dual, possessing both natural and supernatural dimensions, and that man, correspondingly, must realize both the natural and supernatural aspects of his nature in obedience to the universal laws that exist on both of these levels.

All of the Liberal persuasions—liberalism, liberationism and anarchism—share the Conservatives' overriding belief that the highest value is some form of self-realization. For the Liberals, however, the self to be realized is quite different than that envisioned by the Conservative. Thus, where the Conservative tends to view self-realization as an end to be approached only indirectly through an overriding dedication to some absolute reality—God, natural law, tradition, or whatever—that transcends ordinary personal experience, the Liberal ordinarily sees *man* as primary, the source of all knowledge whatsoever.

Phrased somewhat differently, if Conservatism tends to be an *indirect* humanism, seeing self-realization as a by-product of adhering to the dictates of a suprapersonal reality that exists above and beyond man's own experience, Liberalism tends to be a *direct* humanism, which views all reality as rooted in and deriving from personal or collective human experience. For the Liberal, then, all knowledge is rooted in human experience, and there are no absolutes that are not ultimately relative to being known, to emerging out of some sort of human involvement in the world. Thus, if the basic differences among the Conservative positions relate to different ways in which absolute knowledge can and should be known—God or reason; revelation or faith; intuition or authoritative tradition—the basic differences between the Liberals have to do with the relationship between the individual and his society.

The Liberal ideologies, like the Conservative ones, encompass both secular and religious positions. In the final analysis, however, the differences between the secular and religious proponents of the Liberal points of view are far less significant than these same differences as they exist within the Conservative orientations for reasons that are discussed at length in Chapter VII.

THE POLITICAL PHILOSOPHIES

Corresponding to these basic differences in the area of moral philosophy, and in large part growing out of these differing moral assessments, there are six basic political philosophies. These are the three basic political expressions of the Conservative point of view—*reactionary conservatism* (anti-intellectual authoritarianism), *philosophical conservatism* (intellectual authoritarianism), and mainstream *social conservatism* (authoritarian conventionalism); and the three basic political expressions of the Liberal point of view—*political liberalism, political liberationism,* and *political anarchism.*

It is difficult to discuss the various political philosophies out of cultural context, because all of the various expressions of both the Liberal and Conservative ideologies are relative to particular cultural traditions and social situations. Thus religious Conservatism in the Soviet Union today tends to confront significantly different problems and therefore to express itself differently from religious Conservatism in the United States. In a similar sense a politically reactionary stance in certain severely underdeveloped parts of the "Third World" may invoke a return to tribalism rather than a revival of fascism or a return to old-fashioned Bible-centered religion.

In a corresponding way, there are no special social organizations—no particular economic or religious institutions, for example—that are peculiarly "democratic," and, while the various Liberal ideologies all tend to advocate maximizing "democracy," the various expressions of ideological Liberalism frequently have significantly different notions of "democracy" in mind. In a similar sense, the indirect, representative democracy ("republicanism") favored by the social Conservative is far more "democratic" from the Conservative point of view than the more direct, participatory democracy envisioned by the more radical ideologies. For some, democracy means majority (or plurality) rule, where over 50 percent of those voting determine the proper course of action. For others it is a matter of proportional representation, where each special interest group collaborates in decision making. For some, democracy is a matter of direct mandate by the people; for others such a mandate is only acceptable if it has been qualified by some prior consensus, frequently embodied within a written constitution, which spells out the permissible limits of change.

For these and other reasons, the ideologies discussed here are intended to represent the basic spectrum of ideological differences that have primary importance in the United States at the present time. Examples from other countries, while they may occur, are used basically to clarify or extend the major ideological options that are most significant in our own society.

THE EDUCATIONAL IDEOLOGIES

From the six basic systems of social ethics, refracted through their corresponding political philosophies, emerge the six basic *educational ideologies*—the three Conservative ideologies (educational fundamentalism, educational intellectualism, educational conservatism) and the three Liberal ideologies (educational liberalism, educational liberationism, and educational anarchism)—and these educational ideologies consist primarily of the applications and implications of these underlying moral and political positions for the conduct of schooling.

The relationship between the various moral and political philosophies and the educational ideologies is presented graphically in Figure 3–4, while a more specific representation of the Conservative and Liberal educational ideologies is contained in Figures 3–5 and 3–6, which are presented at a later point.

Some Qualifications on the System of Classification

While a vast number of qualifications could easily be appended to a model of the sort presented here (Figure 3–4), three warrant special consideration.

1. Certain terminological problems invariably occur in this kind of enterprise. Three of these are especially confusing. First, and as indicated earlier, the terms *liberalism* and *conservatism* tend to be somewhat ambiguous, because they refer both to overall philosophical and political orientations (as they often do in everyday language) and also to specific educational orientations and ideologies *within these more basic orientations*. The ideology of educational conservatism is, for example, one of three educational positions that are generally characterized as being socially and politically conservative in nature. In a similar sense, the ideology of educational liberalism is merely one of three educational positions that are generally viewed as socially and politically liberal. This confusion is regrettable, but no other terms seemed more appropriate or less confusing, and every effort was made to avoid coining new and unfamiliar terms if at all possible. The choice was essentially one of comparative evils. As a weak compromise, and as mentioned before, the terms *conservative* and *liberal* have generally been capitalized whenever they refer to the generic philosophical and political orientations, and they have not been capitalized when they refer to the more particular educational expressions of these two overall points of view. Whenever reference is made to a conservative or liberal political orientation every effort has been made to specify that political philosophies are being dealt with and not the more particular educational ideology that is described by the same term. Whenever the term *conservatism* or *liberalism* is used without qualification or contextual grounding, it refers to the specific educational ideologies of educational conservatism and educational liberalism. Although these are specific traditions within more basic philosophical and political Conservatism and Liberalism, as well as representing educational positions that are normally considered to be Conservative or Liberal positions within political theory, they are much more delimited concepts than philosophical or political Conservatism or Liberalism as such.

Second, since this theoretical model is based largely on underlying political differences, every attempt has been made to use educational labels that accurately represent the political origins of the positions described. Unfortunately this has not been possible in two cases. After some consideration, the term *educational intellectualism* was settled upon as the pedagogical counterpart for philosophical and theological Conservatism, because no more satisfactory term became evident. This is unfortunate, because the term *intellectualism* has a

FIGURE 3–4
THE PHILOSOPHICAL BASES OF THE EDUCATIONAL IDEOLOGIES

PERSONAL HAPPINESS
(Self-Realization)

(can be attained by following
a moral philosophy based upon)

MORAL PHILOSOPHY

Adherence to Intuitive and/or Revealed Standards of Belief and Behavior	*Philosophical and/or Religious Enlightenment Based on Speculative Reason and Metaphysical Wisdom*	*Adherence to Established Standards of Belief and Behavior*
Teleological Totalitarians	Plato	Saint Augustine
Fascism (Italy)	Aristotle	Mainstream Reformation-
Naziism (Germany)	St. Thomas Aquinas	Based Protestant
American Fundamentalistic	Moses Maimonides	Traditions
Nationalism	St. Ignatius Loyola	Thomas Hobbes
John Birch Society	René Descartes	Thomas Harrington
Christian Crusade	Ralph Waldo Emerson	John Adams
Moral Majority		James Madison
Christian Voice		John C. Calhoun
"Common Sense" Populisim		Niccolo Machiavelli
George Wallace		Herbert Spencer
Max Rafferty		Georg W. F. Hegel
Christian Fundamentalism		Émile Durkheim
and Related Traditions		Winston Churchill
		Charles de Gaulle
		Milton Friedman
		Ayn Rand

(which expresses itself on
the political level as)

POLITICAL PHILOSOPHY

Reactionary Conservatism (Anti-intellectual Authoritarianism)	*Philosophical Conservatism (Intellectual Absolutism)*	*Social Conservatism*
Nationalistic or Religious Authoritarianism	Intellectual and/or Moral Meritocracy	Democratic Capitalism (Indirect Constitutional Democracy, Stressing Rule by Law, Due Process, and Property Rights Within a Relatively Uncontrolled Economy)

(which, in turn, applies to
education in the form of)

EDUCATIONAL IDEOLOGY

Educational Fundamentalism	*Educational Intellectualism*	*Educational Conservatism*

Practical Intelligence (Effective Problem Solving)	*Development of New and More Humanistic Social Institutions*	*Elimination of Institutional Restraints to Augment Personal Freedom*
John Dewey William H. Kilpatrick Boyd Bode Sidney Hook John Childs George Geiger	Jeremy Bentham Robert Owen Henri Saint Simon William Morris Karl Marx Nicholai Lenin John M. Keynes Eugene Debs Mao Zedong (Mao Tse-Tung) Herbert Marcuse Erich Fromm	William Godwin Peter Kropotkin Pierre Proudhon Henry David Thoreau Leo Tolstoi

Liberalism	*Liberationism*	*Anarchism*
Social Democracy (Representative Democracy in a Mixed Economy)	Democratic Socialism (Representative Democracy in a State-Controlled Economy)	Deinstitutionalized Free Cooperation (Direct Participational Democracy in a Post-Socialistic Era)

Educational Liberalism	*Educational Liberationism*	*Educational Anarchism*

history, as well as a host of connotations, that tend to be distracting and somewhat misleading. On the other hand, all of the other terms considered—*rationalism, absolutism, authoritarianism,* and others—were deemed even more defective in one way or another, and no new term seemed quite appropriate. In a similar sense, *educational fundamentalism* leaves a great deal to be desired, but other terms that were considered—*restorationism, revivalism, populism*—were even more inexact or inappropriate.

2. There are significant differences between the secular and religious expressions of the basic social ethics positions represented in the educational ideologies model. On the other hand, and as will be covered at greater length in the later chapters, religious and secular approaches within the same ideological tradition tend to converge in their recommendations for social action. And, in most cases, it is possible to disregard abstract explanatory principles pertaining to more profound metaphysical matters if these make no practical difference in applied ethics, political philosophy and educational theory.

In the case of the Liberal ideologies, and as previously indicated, there are clearly both religious and secular traditions in all three of the basic positions of liberalism, liberationism and anarchism, but these differences tend to occur almost entirely at the level of underlying philosophical explanation. Both the religious and secular expressions of each of the Liberal ideologies tend to favor essentially the same educational principles and practices, although for somewhat different reasons. Phrased somewhat differently, while there is a very real difference between the religious and secular traditions within all of the educational ideologies, these differences generally have more effect upon ideological rhetoric than upon the substance of actual recommendations at the practical level. Accordingly, in outlining the basic tenets of the various ideologies every attempt has been made to use nonreligious terminology when conveying ideas common to both the secular and religious traditions within a particular ideological position. Terms with religious associations, such as *God, spirit,* and *soul,* have been avoided in virtually all cases where religious subgroups within the various ideological positions were not explicitly being considered.

3. In almost all instances the range of ideological responses to the different educational topics discussed represent *continua* and not *dichotomies.* In other words, with certain exceptions, the educational ideologies differ primarily in *degree* and not in *kind.* In most instances, and with the possible exception of educational anarchism, they represent different perceptions of the same or similar problems (such as the objectives of the school or the nature of the curriculum), or they place different priorities and/or degrees of emphasis on somewhat similar ideas or approaches.

THE CONSERVATIVE EDUCATIONAL IDEOLOGIES

The Conservative educational ideologies consist of three basic traditions—educational fundamentalism, educational intellectualism and educational conservatism. They range from the religious expression of educational fundamentalism, at the most conservative or authoritarian end of the spectrum, to the secular variety of educational conservatism, at the least conservative end. The entire range of Conservative educational ideologies is presented in Figure 3–5.

Educational Fundamentalism.   Fundamentalism encompasses all of those types of political Conservatism that are basically anti-intellectual in the sense that they seek to minimize philosophical and/or intellectual considerations, and tend to ground their contentions upon a relatively uncritical acceptance of either revealed Truth or established social consensus (usually justified as "common sense"). In its political expression, the reactionary Conservative advocates a return to the real or imagined virtues of the past. There are two basic variations of such a point of view when applied to education: *religious educational fundamentalism,* as exemplified in certain of the more fundamentalist Christian churches that are profoundly committed to a rather rigid and literalistic view of reality as revealed through scriptural authority, and *secular educational fundamentalism,* which characteristically espouses an equally inflexible commitment to the consensual "common sense" worldview of the average man. In contemporary education, religious fundamentalism is perhaps best observed in the educational ideas of certain of the Bible-centered Christian groups, such as the Amish, which feature a strict adherence to the word of God as presented in the scriptures. The secular fundamentalist point of view within education is perhaps best exemplified by the "populistic" educational fundamentalism of such a well-known figure as Max Rafferty, the educational journalist and one-time Superintendent of Public Instruction for the state of California, with his strong emphasis on nationalism and patriotism.

Educational Intellectualism.   Intellectualism emerges out of those expressions of political Conservatism that are based upon closed and fundamentally authoritarian philosophical or theological systems of thought. In general, philosophical Conservatism seeks to change existing political (including educational) practices in order to make them conform more perfectly to some established and essentially unvarying intellectual or spiritual ideal. It is, for example, intellectual conservatism that is reflected in the writings of Plato and Aristotle, and that is central to the position of Saint Thomas Aquinas (which, in turn, continues to provide the philosophical basis for the dominant Roman Catholic point of view). In contemporary education, philosophical Conservatism expresses itself primarily as *educational intellectualism,* of which there are two basic variations: *philosophical intellectualism,* which is essentially secular and which can be observed in such contemporary educational theorists as Robert Maynard Hutchins and Mortimer Adler, and *theological intellectualism,* which is a religious orientation perhaps best reflected in the writings of such contemporary Roman Catholic educational philosophers as William McGucken and John Donahue.

Educational Conservatism.   Conservatism is fundamentally that position which espouses adherence to time-tested cultural institutions and processes, coupled with a deep respect for law and order, as a basis for any sort of constructive social change. Accordingly, on a political level, the Conservative tends to be well-represented by the writings of such men as Edmund Burke, James Madison and the authors of *The Federalist Papers.* In education, he views the central goal of the school as being the preservation and transmission of established social patterns and traditions. Within education, there are two basic expressions of the social Conservative point of view: *religious educational conservatism,* which stresses the centrality of spiritual training as a basis

FIGURE 3–5
THE CONSERVATIVE EDUCATIONAL IDEOLOGIES

MOST CONSERVATIVE

REACTIONARY CONSERVATISM
(Anti-intellectual Authoritarianism)

INTELLECTUAL CONSERVATISM
(Philosophical and/or Theological Absolutism)

Educational Fundamentalism

Educational Intellectualism

RELIGIOUS FUNDAMENTALISM	SECULAR FUNDAMENTALISM	THEOLOGICAL INTELLECTUALISM
Christian Fundamentalism and Related Traditions	Teleological Totalitarianism (Hegelian Totalitarianism)	St. Thomas Aquinas
Southern Baptist	Fascism	St. Ignatius Loyola (and the Jesuits)
Church of Christ	Benito Mussolini	Moses Maimonides
Many Independent Evangelical Churches	Giovanni Gentile	John Henry Newman
Many Independent Pentecostal Churches	Naziism	Dominant Tradition in Contemporary Roman Catholicism
Many Independent Religious Traditions	Adolf Hitler	Dominant Tradition in Contemporary Judaism
Latter-Day Saints	Ernst Huber	Dominant Tradition in Reformation-based Protestant Theology
Seventh-Day Adventists	More Extreme Forms of "Civil Religion" in the Prophetic Nation-as-Transcendent Tradition	Dominant Tradition in Most "Natural" Religions (such as Unitarianism, Universalism)
Jehovah's Witnesses	Religious Nationalism	
More Extreme Forms of "Civil Religion"* in the Prophetic Nation-Under-God Orientation	Robert Welch (John Birch Society)	
Evangelical Commitment to a Nondenominational Judeo-Christian Religious Orientation	Dan Smoot (Facts Forum)	
"Protestant Civic Piety"	Clarence Manion (Manion Forum)	
Edgar Bundy (Church League of America)	"Common Sense" Populism	
Billy James Hargis (Christian Crusade)	Max Rafferty	
Carl McIntire (*The Christian Beacon*)	George Wallace	
The Moral Majority	European Reactionary "Restorationism"	
Christian Voice	Joseph de Maistre	
	Louis de Bonald	
	François de Châteaubriand	

---

*The whole topic of "Civil Religion" is taken up at some length in Chapter IV.

———————————————————————————————— **LEAST CONSERVATIVE**

SOCIAL CONSERVATISM
(Social and/or Religious Traditionalism)

Educational Conservatism

PHILOSOPHICAL INTELLECTUALISM

Plato
Aristotle
René Descartes
Matthew Arnold
Dominant Tradition in
 Western "Liberal Arts"
 Orientation
 Robert Hutchins
 Mortimer Adler
 Jacques Barzun
 The Great Books Program
 St. John's College,
 Annapolis
 Major "Establishment"
 Prep Schools (Andover,
 Choate, etc.)
French Ideal of "culture
 generale" (as in the *lycée*)
German Mainstream
 Academic Tradition (as
 in the classical
 Gymnasium)
British "Great Public
 Schools" (Eton,
 Harrow, etc.)

RELIGIOUS CONSERVATISM

Mainstream Reformation-
 based Protestant
 Traditions
 Protestant Episco-
 palianism
 Lutheranism
 Presbyterianism
 Reformed Calvinism
Nondenominational Evangel-
 ical Christian Movements
 Billy Graham
 Campus Crusade
 for Christ
 Intervarsity Christian
 Fellowship
 Teen Challenge
Theological Augustinians
 St. Augustine of Hippo
 Reinhold Niebuhr
Theological Antirationalism
 and/or Intuitionism
 Tertullian
 John Duns Scotus
 Søren Kierkegaard
Most "Ethic Religions"
 Hungarian Reformed
 Church
 Norwegian Evangelical
 Lutherans
 Armenian Church of
 North America
Most Forms of "Civil
 Religion" in the Priestly
 Nation-as-Transcendent
 Tradition
 Qualified Religious
 Nationalism
Most Forms of "Civil
 Religion" in the Priestly
 Nation-Under-God
 Tradition
 Qualified Forms of
 "Protestant Civic Piety"

SECULAR CONSERVATISM

Establishment Conservatives
 (Tory Democracy)
 Edmund Burke
 Russell Kirk
 William Buckley
Laissez Faire Conservatives
 Adam Smith
 Thomas Malthus
 David Ricardo
 Milton Friedman
 Ayn Rand
Secular Augustinians and
 Related Traditions
 Political Realism
 (Hans Morgenthau)
 Hedonic Naturalism
 (Thomas Hobbes)
 Political "Conflict of
 Interest" Theories
 Thomas Harrington
 John Adams
 James Madison
 John C. Calhoun
Machiavelli and the Neo-
 Machiavellians
Social Darwinists
 (Spencerian
 Conservatives)
 Herbert Spencer
 William Graham Sumner
 Lester Ward
Teleological Nationalists
 (Hegelian Conservatives)
 Georg W. F. Hegel
 Auguste Comte
 Émile Durkheim
Various German Romantic
 Idealists (Fichte, Schelling)
Friedrich Nietzsche
Various Critics of Liberal
 Approaches to Education
 Council for Basic
 Education
 Hyman Rickover
 James Koerner
 Arthur Bestor

for proper moral character, and *secular educational conservatism,* which is concerned with the necessity of preserving and transmitting existing beliefs and practices as a way of ensuring both social survival and personal effectiveness. At the present time, religious conservatism is probably best represented by the educational orientation of the more evangelical and scripturally oriented traditions, which are decidedly less liberal theologically than the various mainstream Protestant denominations, such as the Southern Baptist Convention and the Lutheran Church (Missouri Synod)—see Chapter IV—while secular conservatism tends to be best exemplified by many of the more articulate critics of educational progressivism and permissivism, such as James Koerner and Hyman Rickover.

THE LIBERAL EDUCATIONAL IDEOLOGIES

The Liberal educational ideologies, like the Conservative, consists of three basic traditions—educational liberalism, educational liberationism, and educational anarchism. They range from the least liberal expression of educational liberalism (method liberalism) to the exceedingly radical proposals of the utopian anarchist at the other end of the continuum. The entire range of Liberal educational ideologies is presented in Figure 3–6.

Educational Liberalism.   For the educational liberal, the long-range goal of education is to preserve and improve the existing social order by teaching each child how to deal effectively with his own emerging life problems. Educational liberalism ranges in intensity, however, from the relatively mild *method liberalism* of a theorist like Maria Montessori, through the *directive* (or structured) *liberalism,* which is perhaps most characteristic of John Dewey's philosophy, to the virtually *nondirective,* or laissez faire, *liberalism* of the perspective of A. S. Neill or Carl Rogers.

Educational Liberationism.   Liberationism is the point of view that maintains we should seek the immediate large-scale reform of the established political order as a way of furthering individual liberties and promoting the maximum realization of personal potential. Educational liberationism covers a wide spectrum of views, ranging from the relatively conservative *reform liberationism* of the civil rights protests during the mid-sixties to the urgent and passionate commitment of the (frequently Marxist) *revolutionary liberationism*, with its call for the active collaboration of the educational system in the immediate overthrow of the existing political order.

For the educational liberationist, the school should be *objective* (rational-scientific) but not *neutral.* It has an ideological function: it exists not only to teach children how to think effectively (rationally and scientifically) but also to help them recognize the superior wisdom inherent within the most convincing intellectual solutions that are currently available with respect to significant human problems. Phrased somewhat differently, educational liberationism is founded on an open system of truth, but it encompasses a particular commitment to whatever course of action is supported by the informed and objective consensus of the intellectual community at any particular time. It is ultimately a problem- or procedure-centered orientation, but it also encompasses a strong secondary commitment to the best *answers* produced by trained intelligence. It maintains that the school is morally obligated to identify and promote constructive social programs and not merely to train the mind, that it should seek to advance the most convincing course of action that is supported by an objective analysis of the available facts.

Educational Anarchism. The educational anarchist, like the educational liberal and the educational liberationist, generally adheres to an open system of experimental enquiry (subscribing to the verification of knowledge through scientific reasoning [see pages 103–108]) or to assumptions held to be compatible with such a system of enquiry. In contrast to all of the other educational ideologies, however, the educational anarchist holds that we should emphasize the need for minimizing and/or eliminating institutional restraints on personal behavior, that we should, insofar as possible, *deinstitutionalize society.* Accordingly, he maintains that the best approach to education is one that attempts to precipitate immediate large-scale humanistic reforms within society by eliminating the existing system of schools altogether.

Probably best represented in education through the writings of Ivan Illich and Paul Goodman, the educational anarchist point of view covers a variety of positions, extending from the *tactical anarchist,* who would dissolve the schools as a way of freeing wealth and resources for the correction of more pressing social needs, all the way to the *utopian anarchist,* who envisions a society permanently liberated from virtually all institutional restraints.

Some Qualifications on the Ideologies Taxonomy

The classification scheme presented in Figures 3–4, 3–5 and 3–6 is intended to be suggestive rather than definitive, and several qualifications are necessary.

Virtually all of the individuals or movements indicated are twentieth-century phenomena. In certain cases historical personages or developments are cited, because they are exceedingly important in the emergence of a particular educational ideology. The practical empiricism of John Locke is, for example, a central theme in the development of educational liberalism, and there is very little that occurs in the nondirective expression of educational liberalism that was not previously anticipated in the writings of Jean Jacques Rousseau. Unfortunately, history does not stand still for taxonomic classifications, so individuals who were, in their own time, distinctively "liberal" in their approach to education (like Herbert Spencer) tend to sound very "conservative" when viewed in the context of some of the more radical educational ideas that currently exist.

Several individuals have been cited as representatives of more than one tradition within an ideological orientation (as is the case with Ivan Illich, who does perhaps the best job of formulating *all* of the various expressions of educational anarchism); but, except in the case of John Dewey, who was, for all practical purposes, the founder of both contemporary progressive education (in the sense of structured liberalism) and educational reconstructionism (in the sense of radical educational liberationism), no individual has been cited as a formative thinker or basic influence in two separate educational ideologies.

FIGURE 3–6
THE LIBERAL EDUCATIONAL IDEOLOGIES

LEAST LIBERAL ─── **(cont. below)**

LIBERALISM
(Change within the Established Social Order)

Educational Liberalism

METHOD	DIRECTIVE- (STRUCTURED)	NON-DIRECTIVE
J. Herbart	John Locke	*J. J. Rousseau (*Émile*)
*M. Montessori	Benjamin Franklin	A. S. Neill
J. B. Conant	H. Pestalozzi	Carl Rogers
E. L. Thorndike (and the	*F. Froebel	George Leonard
Standardized Testing	Francis W. Parker	
Movement)	John Dewey	
J. Bruner's "structure of	W. H. Kilpatrick	
knowledge" approach as	John Childs	
applied to curriculum	Susan Isaacs (Great Britain)	
reform (the "new math,"	Celestin Fréinet (France)	
PSSC, etc.)	Community Colleges (U.S.)	
"Scientific Management" in	British "Open University"	
Education (PPBS)	British "Open Classroom"	
Competency-Based	Learning Laboratories	
Curricula	Confluent Education	
Programmed Instruction	"University Without Walls" approach	
(including PSI—The	(G. I. Brown)	
Keller Plan)	Jean Piaget	
Teaching Machines	Lawrence Kohlberg	
	Values Clarification	
	(Louis Raths, Sidney	
	Simon, etc.)	
	William Glasser	
	Carl Orff (*Orffschulwerk*)	
	Rudolf Steiner	
	(Waldorf Schools)	

LIBERATIONISM
(Rapid and Large-Scale Changes in the Basic Nature of the Established Social Order)

Educational Liberationism (cont. below)

REFORM	RADICAL
Ethnic and/or Racial	John Dewey
Reform Movements	George Counts
(particularly during the early	Harold Rugg
60s) and movements toward	Theodore Brameld
eliminating discrimination	B. F. Skinner (*Walden Two*)
based on age, sex or sexual	Wilhelm Reich
preference	Anton Makarenko (USSR)
Black Student Unions	Jonathan Kozol
United Mexican-American	Charles Dederich (Synanon)
Students	Black Panthers (Radical
*Southern Christian	Faction)
Leadership Conference	Stokely Carmichael
Brown Berets	*Christian Marxism
Black Panthers (Moderate	Israeli Kibbutz (of the
Faction)	secular-socialist variety)
Students' Nonviolent	Post-Revolutionary
Coordinating Committee	Marxism–Leninism (as in
Women's Rights	Communist Cuba,
Movements (various)	Communist China, etc.)
Gay Student Unions	Secular Yiddish Progressive
Gray Panthers	Schools (c. 1910–1940)

(cont. from above) ———————————————— **MOST LIBERAL**

LIBERALISM cont.
(Rapid and Large-Scale Changes in the Basic Nature of the Established Social Order)

ANARCHISM
(Liberation of Mankind from Institutional Restraints)

Educational Liberationism (cont. from above)

Educational Anarchism

REVOLUTIONARY
Prerevolutionary Marxism-Leninism (to create "revolutionary consciousness")
Paulo Freire
Revolutionary SDS (late 60s)
Weather Underground
Third World Liberation Front
Regis Debray
Maoist "Red Guard Movement" (China in early 70s)

TACTICAL
I. Illich
E. Reimer
P. Goodman
J. Holt

RADICAL
I. Illich
E. Reimer
P. Goodman
J. Holt
*M. Gandhi

UTOPIAN
I. Illich
E. Reimer
P. Goodman
J. Holt
*M. Gandhi
*L. Tolstoi
Marx's Vision of a Utopian "Classless Society"

Some of the movements and practices employed as examples must necessarily be qualified by where and when they occurred. The ethnic and racial movements during the early and mid-sixties, for example, were essentially reform orientations, but they tended to become radicalized through their confrontation with the system, and many gave rise to offshoots which were essentially radical or even revolutionary.

Every attempt has been made to use examples only from Western culture and to avoid references to other parts of the world. Where clarity made it necessary to refer to individuals or movements from non-Western cultures (as in the case of the Maoist "Red Guard movement" in Communist China during the early seventies or in references to Mohandas Gandhi), every attempt has been made to make reference to well-known and relatively recent phenomena and not to become involved with comparatively obscure non-Western philosophical points of view or educational practices.

In virtually all instances, an attempt has been made to indicate (by a single asterisk to the left of the name or movement) an individual or movement that best represents a more or less religious approach to the various points of view within the liberal educational ideologies. This was not always possible. In the case of tactical anarchism, for example, none of the individuals cited appear to justify their position on the basis of assumptions that could reasonably be viewed as religious in a conventional sense of the term. The fact that Ivan Illich is a Roman Catholic priest has very little bearing on this. Whatever Illich's particular religious convictions may be, they are not readily identifiable in his writings on schooling, and it seems exceedingly unwise to assume that his educational philosophy is *necessarily* an outgrowth of his religious convictions.[2] Gandhi was clearly religious (the last word he said, as he was dying was "Ram," one of the incarnations of the god Vishnu), but he was scarcely representative of any of the conventional Hindu sects.

In a similar sense, no attempt was made to specify a religious expression of revolutionary educational liberationism, because no particularly good examples were apparent. Conceivably, of course, a Christian Marxist could also be a Leninist, and advocate violent revolution as a regrettable means toward a necessary Christian end. Some people assume that, since Paulo Freire is both a Christian and Marxist (presently serving as a consultant with the World Council of Churches in Geneva) that he is also a Christian revolutionary liberationist. This may be, but, again, since Freire does not explicitly justify his revolutionary stance on the basis of specifically Christian principles, it seems unwarranted to assume that his revolutionary liberationism is *necessarily* related to his religious convictions. Whether Rousseau was religious or simply had a penchant for "religiosity" is difficult to say. He is extremely ambiguous and inconsistent in his religious pronouncements but, on the other hand, he is clearly concerned with spiritual questions, and his educational ideas clearly reflect what are ordinarily viewed as religious concerns. In a similar sense, Froebel was something of a mystic, a rather nebulous Christian idealist, whose ideas about education were permeated by his beliefs about God and spiritual matters. He was not an orthodox Christian but he was clearly concerned with a spiritual dimension. Maria Montessori was a deeply religious woman, in the Roman

Catholic tradition, and she has a great deal to say about the spiritual aspects of education in her writings. On the other hand, it is entirely possible to accept Montessori's educational point of view without agreeing with her religious convictions, and one may subscribe to her basic philosophy without sharing her religious beliefs.

All of these qualifications simply indicate, as previously noted, that the religious and secular varieties of the Liberal educational ideologies are exceedingly difficult to isolate when it comes to specifically educational questions. The differences arise primarily at a far more profound (and abstract) level, involving philosophical disputes about *why* an individual has taken a particular position in the area of social ethics in the first place. Once a person has adopted a particular moral and political stance, however, the reasons for his doing so (whether religious or secular) become of decidedly secondary importance when viewed from the necessarily more delimited perspective of purely "educational" philosophy. In other words, however central a person's intellectual rationale for advocating a particular approach to education may be *to the individual himself* (in terms of what philosopher Abraham Kaplan calls the "act meaning" of his behavior)[3], for the external observer it is quite possible to talk about what the individual proposes purely descriptively (in terms of what Kaplan calls the "action meaning" of his behavior). One can compare and contrast it to other approaches to education on the basis of purely intramural considerations relating to educational questions such as the instructional objectives advocated or the nature of the curriculum prescribed. Such considerations are essentially "educational" matters that are capable of being discussed independent of the more profound (and necessarily prepedagogical) philosophical considerations that may have been centrally important in determining how and why the individual developed a particular educational philosophy in the first place. To use a rough analogy, one person may be a vegetarian because he subscribes to the sanctity of life, another because he wants to lose weight; nevertheless, vegetarianism can be defined and discussed as a concept with a specifiable meaning without the necessity of becoming involved in the complex and varying motives of particular vegetarians.

In a similar sense, it does not discount the significance of underlying philosophical or religious assumptions to say that educational philosophies, as *educational* philosophies, have an internal logic that can be analyzed and discussed relatively independent of the underlying motives or belief systems that may have led to their formulation. Again, the various individual movements and practices used to exemplify the various ideologies (as well as the subvarieties within these ideologies) are selective. Many other examples could have been used, and some of those employed are exceedingly contentious in the absence of extensive qualification. The examples are used primarily to illustrate the complexity and variety of ideas involved in the various ideological orientations and to provide the reader with a far more explicit idea of the sorts of individuals and practices that might legitimately be subsumed under the various conceptual divisions.

A basic problem confronting any conceptual scheme such as this is that of determining precisely which of the various ideological orientations are most or least *liberal* or *conservative* in the conventional senses of these terms. Perhaps the most difficult problem here occurs in relationship to *conservatism* and *intellectualism* as they relate to overall social and political considerations.

Obviously, there are types of political and educational conservatism that are more "conservative," rigid, and authoritarian than types of intellectualism, and vice versa. I have opted to view educational conservatism as a more Liberal orientation than educational intellectualism—other things being equal—for several reasons. First, in our culture, at this time, educational conservatives tend to be predominantly conflict theorists (that is, individuals who hold that progress grows primarily out of the competitive interaction between individuals and groups). Most seem to be generally disposed—although this is ordinarily an informal and somewhat eclectic commitment—to some form of social Darwinism, ordinarily allied to a predisposition for laissez faire economics. Virtually all tend to stress the total and organic nature of society, holding that the social necessarily takes both logical and psychological precedence over the individual. For the Conservatives, although value is almost invariably viewed as being experienced personally, or psychologically, the personal is always viewed as being channeled and therefore controlled by a variety of overriding social considerations. In other words, reality is invariably a personal experience, but personality is ultimately rooted in social membership. In contemporary American culture—which is characteristically predisposed toward democracy, science, psychology, technology and industry—the Conservative orientation is ordinarily cautionary. Somewhat pessimistic about the potentialities of the average man, Conservatism acts largely to temper inordinate enthusiasm for rapid changes in any of these areas (and therefore is frequently viewed as favoring predemocratic, prescientific, prepsychological, pretechnological and preindustrial practices that are actually far more characteristic of the reactionary point of view).

Second, *intellectualism,* as defined here, refers not merely to a belief in reason as the overriding means to effective behavior (which, with some qualifications, is perhaps a better definition of *liberalism,* with its roots in pragmatism/experimentalism). It also encompasses the idea that there is some kind of identifiable absolute Truth that has been substantially identified in the past and that can be transmitted through perfected reason to yield philosophical and/or religious enlightenment in the present. In other words, intellectualism, as the term is used here, refers to the point of view that holds that reasoning (linear, logical, subject-predicate thinking) can produce wisdom (in the sense of absolute Truth that is knowable and that is already known by those who have attained intellectual enlightenment). This is an active, cognitive approach, but it is also a closed ideological system that utilizes an absolute means (the process of reason) to yield an absolute end (substantive Truth). In short, the intellectualist demands not only conformity in what one learns and does but also in how one thinks.

The educational conservative may also frequently tend in this direction, but, on the whole, both his means (which are far less exclusively cognitive) and his ends (which are characteristically broader than philosophical or religious enlightenment) are more ambiguous and are fundamentally susceptible to "evolving" cultural definition. This is not to say that a rigid and authoritarian culture may not impose an educational conservatism more exacting in its demands for conformity than most forms of intellectualism, but this does generally appear to be the case.

Finally, intellectualism, in its very optimism, its belief that the child is naturally predisposed toward wisdom and virtue, is more inclined to impose heavy and rigorous intellectual demands on the child than conservatism. Intellectualism stresses the abstract and requires a high degree of intellectual discipline. It tends to be far more exacting and demanding in its educational prescriptions than conservatism, which is much more concerned with the less profound demands of a relatively simple moral and academic conformity. The conservative is, in the final analysis, more of a utilitarian rather than an (epistemological) idealist. For the conservative, truth is good because it is eminently useful for society and for the individual as a member of society. For the more "high-minded" intellectualist, Truth is ultimately good because it is Truth— that is, an intrinsic (virtually aesthetic) requirement for man's very being *as a man*. Far less oriented to the distant (classical) past than to the immediate past and the present, the conservative characteristically also tends to be less of an elitist than the intellectual. For the conservative, truth is not a matter of personal enlightenment so much as a collective achievement of a particular society over an extended period of time, a shared accomplishment of a particular culture that has confronted a succession of real problems and survived to establish itself as a viable historical creation.

In modern America, educational conservatism may be less optimistic about man's potentialities for immediate and self-initiated types of social reform than the various liberal positions, but it is clearly far less conservative than religious intellectualism (which demands the most arduous processes of rational discipline combined with dogmatic theological goals) and, in most cases, it is probably also less conservative than secular intellectualism as well. (The latter, however ostensibly liberal it may be in its social objectives, generally calls for much more of a "hard pedagogy," featuring rigorous academic training based upon absolute intellectual criteria and processes, than the far more practical and utilitarian programs espoused by most of the educational conservatives.) Phrased somewhat differently, at least when viewed in the context of contemporary American culture, the explicit intellectual authoritarianism of the intellectualist, founded upon theological or philosophical absolutes, appears to imply a much more rigid type of education than the "go slow" qualifications of the conservatives who, in the long run, appear to be much more concerned with curbing the excesses of the liberal's relatively unbridled devotion to social welfare than with formulating any sort of explicit counterideology.

The Ambiguous Transition from Fact to Value. The taxonomy developed here takes as its fundamental point of departure the *prescriptive* realm of moral theory and not the (essentially) *descriptive* realm of metaphysical and epistemological speculation. To be more specific, the ideologies are distinguished as Conservative or Liberal primarily on the basis of whether (as in the case of Conservatism) they prescribe obedience to some kind of overriding external or internal authority—revelation, mystical intuition, formal logic, or established social patterns of belief and behavior (or some combination of these)—which are viewed as taking precedence over individual experience. The Liberal positions prescribe individual experience and judgment—personal problem-solving ability, individual commitment to social liberation, or total and unrestrained self-determination—as taking precedence over all of the more traditional forms of authority and control.

In most cases, the way in which reality is described philosophically is closely correlated to the ethical course of action (and the related political and educational systems) prescribed. In some instances, however, there may *appear* to be some degree of conflict between the world *described* by particular philosophers and the moral course of action which they *advocate*. The philosophy of Karl Marx provides an example. On a *descriptive* (ontological) level, Marxism is very similar to the overall Conservative point of view. It is rigid, rationalistic, and, at least in the short run, authoritarian. It presents essentially a conflict theory of history that is, in large part, a special expression of social Darwinism. As in most Conservative positions, Marx holds that the social necessarily takes logical and psychological precedence over the individual, and that individual personality is invariably focused through and controlled by a variety of overriding social considerations. On the other hand, Marx differs markedly from the usual Conservative point of view in three basic respects.

1. While he holds to the logical and psychological primacy of society over the individual descriptively, Marx calls for the reconstruction of society for the ultimate purpose of correcting this situation. He advocates the sort of world in which the individual will ultimately become the fundamental political unit of society—thereby breaking the traditional dualism between the *individual* and the *group*. In short, with the "withering away" of the political state which Marx envisions, only society will remain, but such an emergent society will consist of an aggregate of self-determining individuals in a pure utopian vision of anarchy.

2. While Marx describes history as a social Darwinist "survival of the fittest" dominated by the conflict between different social classes, he envisions a future in which all social conflict will ultimately disappear in a "classless society" at the "end of history."

3. While Marx stresses the organic nature of society and the social origins of the self, he does not equate *society* with *state*. He predicts (and prescribes) a world in which political states will wither away to be replaced by the free and spontaneous cooperation between sane and self-directing individuals in the absence of conventional political constraints. Contrary to being pessimistic and cautionary about the potential of man, Marx is unabashedly optimistic and activistic, enthusiastically advocating large-scale and immediate action on behalf of a utopian tomorrow.

For these reasons, Marxism, which superficially bears many of the earmarks of the Hegelian conservatism from which it emerged, does not take a Conservative moral stance, and is therefore decidedly Liberal as an overall social orientation.

A potential source of confusion grows out of the tendency to classify systems of philosophy, such as pragmatism or classical realism, as "Liberal" or "Conservative." This may be defensible, but the terms are used here with reference to overriding moral philosophies, along with their associated political and educational theories, regardless of the underlying philosophical assumptions relating to knowing and the known upon which these positions are based. Thus, as is discussed at a later point, there are both religious and secular proponents of Liberal educational ideologies such as liberalism, liberationism, and anarchism. To confound matters, there is no necessary reason why a secular pragmatist might not embrace a Conservative social philosophy like fascism (which would express itself in a school setting as a variation of educational fundamentalism).

The point is that there is no inevitable and logical relationship—although there are generally correlations that are probably best explained psychologically or sociologically—between Liberal metaphysical and/or epistemological positions, such as the process-oriented, experience-based philosophies of pragmatism and (most) existentialism, and Liberal moral/social (including educational) philosophies. Liberal ontologies may eventuate—as they do (argumentatively) in the case of theistic existentialism—in rather conventional and conservative moral/social stances. In a similar sense, Conservative ontologies—such as Thomism—may ultimately subscribe to Liberal (or even quite radical) moral/social philosophies such as (again, argumentatively) the Christian Marxism of a person like Paulo Freire. This is assuming that it is possible to reach some sort of consensus on what constitutes a Liberal or Conservative ontology in the first place. But is *determinism* more Liberal than traditional notions of *free will*? Is *agnosticism* or *atheism* more Liberal than *theism*? Are procedural absolutes—like the "scientific process" (however defined)—more Liberal than substantive absolutes (as might be exemplified in a clearly defined concept of the supernatural nature and destiny of man)? Such questions are quite obviously very difficult. For present purposes, it is perhaps sufficient not to confuse ontologically (metaphysically and/or epistemologically) liberal positions—if such exist—with morally and socially liberal positions. *Liberal* and *Conservative* philosophies, as the terms are used here, have reference solely to moral and political positions, and do not purport to describe differences in underlying reality-orientations.

Perhaps the most contentious categories in the educational ideologies classification scheme apply to the most conservative representatives in all of the three Liberal positions. It can be argued quite convincingly that such orientations as method liberalism, reform liberationism and tactical anarchism are not legitimate representatives of the positions that they purportedly espouse. Thus, the method liberals may, as in the case of advocates of competency-based curricula, appear to be liberal because they propose a significantly new way of organizing the teaching-learning process, but the methodology that they propose may (at least on occasion) actually serve to strengthen conservatism in education because it reorganizes the old educational objectives and content in new and more efficient ways that actually tend to perpetuate the status quo. This point of view is discussed at some length in Chapter VIII. In a similar sense, it can be argued that the reform liberationist does not "liberate" at all but merely reinforces the existing system by correcting some of its more blatant abuses, abuses that, if allowed to run their course, might eventuate in a demand for truly radical changes within the overall system. In a similar sense, it is frequently held that the tactical anarchist is not a true anarchist in that he advocates not a utopian postpolitical society of freely determining individuals, but merely the temporary utilization of anarchism as a *means* (through deschooling) of correcting present political abuses and thereby dramatizing the ultimate need for a new kind of political and educational system.

The inclusion of tactical and revolutionary anarchists under the general category of educational anarchism is probably a venial sin to any but the comparatively small number of fervent utopian anarchists. In a similar sense, subsuming the reform liberationist under educational liberationism is not likely to discomfit many except those who feel (with Marx) that social reconstruction can occur *only* through violent revolution and that violent revolution requires the intensification of existing social ills rather than their remedy. They view reform as a socially regressive and antiprogressive attempt to tamper with the internal dialectic of history by muting the class conflict that is required for true "historical progress" to occur.

FROM PHILOSOPHY TO IDEOLOGY

One of the most vexing problems in talking about the relationship that exists between education and the underlying philosophical points of view is that of tracing a relatively clear-cut pattern of relationship between fundamental differences in the areas of ethics and political philosophy, on the one hand, and the educational ideologies, on the other.

Generally speaking, there are three patterns of relationship that occur between basic positions in social ethics and educational theory.

1. There are *logical relationships,* that occur where there are relatively explicit and necessary relationships implied between moral and political positions or between such positions (generally viewed in combination, as *social ethics*) and educational ideology. There is, for example, a fairly obvious logical relationship between philosophical or theological rationalism in the moral realm and a political commitment to some form of meritocracy, just as there is a relationship between political meritocracy and the use of the schools to develop an intellectual or moral elite.

2. *Psychological relationships* exist where, as noted earlier, there may be no *logical* necessity between a particular social philosophy and a particular educational stance but where there is a rather obvious correlation between the two that appears to be more associated with the psychodynamics governing the choice of both (possibly determined by something else altogether) than with any natural relationship inherent between the two.

3. *Social relationships* are visible associations that exist between moral and political positions within a specific culture at a particular time in history. Certain of the conservative positions (such as secular fundamentalism and certain varieties of secular conservatism) are particularly prone to define themselves in terms of "cultural traditions" or "prevailing patterns of belief and behavior," both of which are notoriously difficult to define with any exactitude and which are clearly very highly conditioned by the particular makeup of a particular culture at some specific point in time. Such points of view can only be discussed intelligently within the framework of well-defined cultural and historical boundaries. Thus, the specific program advocated by many of the social conservatives, both with respect to politics and education, tends to differ widely

between different cultures and between different eras occurring within the same culture. An American political conservative in 1783 would be a substantially different individual than an American political conservative in 1876 or 1978.

In the pages that follow, every attempt has been made to rely primarily upon *logical relationships,* the rational implications of basic philosophical assumptions with respect to the nature and conditions of education. Where it has been necessary to resort to descriptive relationships of a less formal nature (as in tracing psychological or social relationships associated with certain of the ideological points of view), every attempt has been made to make this transition quite evident. An exception to this rule occurs in the rather extended outline that compares and contrasts the various ideological positions in the latter part of the book (see Part Four). Here no attempt has been made to separate the formal (prescriptive) implications from the informal (descriptive) generalizations, which are essentially empirical generalizations rather than logical implications.

On the other hand, strictly speaking, there is no logical reason why a fundamentalist cannot have an absolute (revealed or intuitive) certitude that encompasses a moral and political commitment to an ''open-ended'' and relativistic political system like democracy, which emphasizes social justice and civil rights. In point of fact, however, such a relationship—while possible—is so improbable and rare as to be almost nonexistent.

As mentioned earlier, there appears to be some ulterior psychological logic—most probably explicable only on the basis of underlying psychodynamics—that virtually precludes such combinations of belief. Absolute and authoritative approaches to knowing and the known—that is, approaches featuring such avenues as revelation, faith or mystical intuition—seldom advocate flexible and process-oriented political philosophies and therefore seldom propose flexible and process-oriented approaches to education. Logically, however, they *could* do so. There is no *logical* reason why God's revelation should not expound the overriding value of democracy as a means of knowing truth, or why nonintellective intuition should not yield an indisputable conviction that the scientific method is superior to all other ways of understanding the world. However, these relationships seldom occur. *Rationalism*—viewed generally, as all philosophical orientations that hold that trained intelligence provides the best means to live one's life—tends toward open and liberal systems of government and toward similar and supportive types of education. Philosophical orientations that are essentially *nonrational* hold that the most significant truths are accessible only through nonrational means, such as revelation, faith or mystical intuition, or hold that active reason is far less trustworthy than conventional social patterns of belief and behavior. Such orientations almost invariably opt for relatively authoritarian political systems and correspondingly ''hard pedagogies.''

Educational conservatism holds that reason is good but that it necessarily remains subordinate to the previously reasoned (or potentially reasonable) patterns of social belief and behavior that have emerged out of previously unreasoned (but, assumedly, reasonable) cultural adaptations to emerging circumstances throughout a particular society's history.

The three Liberal ideologies—liberalism, liberationism and anarchism—all hold that the highest good is to live in such a way as to allow the fullest expression of trained intelligence (that is, critical thinking, viewed as the practical application of scientific problem-solving processes to the resolution of personal and social problems). They differ primarily in how they view the conditions necessary for such critical thinking to occur.

The liberal emphasizes individual critical thinking as the origin and basis for all enlightened social change. He is dubious about social ideologies that have not emerged out of inquiry founded on the basis of scientific objectivity. In a sense, the liberal gives the personal (the individual) priority over the social (including the political). The liberationist feels that individual critical thinking is impossible in the absence of a political system that encourages and sustains the social and intellectual conditions that are prerequisites for a fully developed popular intelligence. The anarchist feels that virtually all political and educational *systems* are necessarily alienating and oppressive forces that stand between the individual's natural predisposition toward self-actualization and his equally natural tendency to become culturally (but not socially) inducted into all types of critical thinking required by the demands for intelligent and cooperative social living.

In a sense, all of the Liberal ideologies see individual self-actualization as the ultimate goal, but they see this as emerging out of objective intelligence. Ethically, the liberal sees trained intelligence as both the ethical *end* and the ethical *means*. For the liberationist, it is the end, but it requires a prior commitment to essentially political means. For the anarchist, objective intelligence (good sense) is one of the means, but it is subordinated to the more immediate imperative of dissolving the existing political/educational system. Indeed, the existing system is viewed as essentially gratuitous, and, in a more immediate sense, even counterproductive, because it (1) exaggerates the value of the problem-solving process as both a means and end of education (even creating iatrogenic problems that are actually side-effects of a pathologically overcontrolled society); and (2) reduces "sensibility"—man's inherently cooperative and altruistic nature—by replacing man's natural sense of moral obligation with spurious obligations to impersonal bureaucratic organizations.

SYNERGISM AND OTHER CIRCULAR PROCESSES

One of the things that makes it particularly difficult to deal effectively with the relationship between theory and practice, the philosophical and psychological, the social and personal, or virtually any of the other dichotomies that traditionally arise in the attempt to discuss vexing questions of social policy is that, while conceptual distinctions can be clearly stated, the matters to which the ideas refer are seldom discrete and generally tend to serve as merely different aspects of a total and interrelated process. Such ostensibly different elements as the theoretical and the practical are inextricably interwoven together in a complex web of interaction. Thus, philosophers tend to talk *as if* theory caused practice, and many psychologists (or at least those of the strict behaviorist persuasion) are inclined to hold that practice causes theory. In a sense, of course, both are right. Sometimes theory causes practice—some behavior does stem from intellectual speculation—and, at other times, the contrary is true. The well-worn example of the blind men and the elephant is apt.

In a sense, of course, this may be precisely the issue that separates the various academic disciplines. Ultimately it is always necessary to talk about *something* rather than *everything,* because totality is inexpressible in conventional language and logic. Each discipline must therefore necessarily suspend belief in the organic and reciprocal interrelationship between all things, and must concentrate on one small set of phenomena that it ordinarily treats—by omission of other matters if not by direct declaration—as of supreme importance. Philosophers talk as if virtually all people were intellectually motivated, because they are singularly interested in those types of behavior that *are.* In a similar sense, musicians focus on what Suzanne Langer has called the "connotational semantic" of music, not as a way of denying the importance of the visual arts or literature, but because, in the academic division of labor, this is their distinctive concern. Mathematicians deal largely with quantitative relationships, not because the world can be expressed solely in these terms, but because this is the function of mathematicians *as* mathematicians.

These truisms merit repetition when it comes to philosophical explanations of why people act as they do. If pressed, most philosophers would grant that philosophical considerations are not all-informing. Much more than philosophy is involved in determining what and how a person will act with respect to a particular situation. On the other hand, philosophy is the place where the philosopher "holds on to the elephant," and it provides his singular contribution to the total enterprise of why people behave as they do.

Most philosophers—although certain metaphysical absolutists and certain of the antiphilosophical schools (as in certain forms of educational fundamentalism) would disagree—would concur with the proposition that it is a mistake to assume that there is a simple, causal relationship that runs in one direction from theory to practice. They would generally concur with the conventional wisdom in the contemporary social and behavioral sciences that holds that behavior occurs in feedback loops: actions eliciting reactions, which alter subsequent actions, which affect the nature and course of succeeding reactions, and so on. In short, there are no simple and linear one-way causal explanations. Explanations of reality are almost invariably complex, interaffecting—and frequently circular.

Whether logical explanations that end up as circular arguments are flawed as logical explanations—being, for all practical purposes, tautologies (in which the conclusion is implicit in the initial assumption)—or whether reality is best described in this manner, because reality *is* essentially circular and is best expressed as a series of interlocking and self-repeating circuits, in which certain types of action invariably give rise to reactions that create the conditions that cause or reinforce the initial actions (and so on), is a legitimate matter for philosophical debate. On the other hand, it is clear that a great many philosophical positions—and many that are discussed in this book—do end up presenting something approximating the kind of circular processes that are generally referred to as "synergism cycles."[4]

Synergism

Synergism is the process whereby certain kinds of behavior elicit the sort of conditions that, in turn, generate the subsequent kinds of behaviors and resulting conditions that ultimately lead to a repetition of the entire process (in what is essentially a self-sustaining cycle of cause-and-effect). So, for example, if only relatively affluent societies can afford the leisure to invest in liberal education (including theoretical science), and theoretical science is a precondition for applied science and technology, which, in turn, becomes the basis for industrial development—which ultimately provides the economic substructure required for sustained or enhanced affluence (and so on)—we are, in effect, faced with a synergism cycle. Affluence provides the basis for popular education, which provides the basis for enhanced affluence, and so on and on, in a positive and self-reinforcing spiral of progressively better conditions.

Positive synergism exists whenever this process (viewed as implicitly or explicitly purposive or goal-oriented) functions in such a way as to create the ongoing conditions that predispose toward the success of subsequent phases of the process—which, in turn, create the conditions necessary to generate successful behavior (in terms of the purpose or goal of the entire course of action) in subsequent phases of the process, and so on. Thus, from the point of view of the experimentalist, happiness is typically viewed as the actualization of distinctive personal potentialities for constructive behavior. These potentialities are released primarily through effective behavior (or, more specifically, through effective problem solving). Effective problem solving, in turn, requires an "experimental" (that is, scientific) approach to thinking, featuring open and critical inquiry directed to the solution of all significant human problems. Such an experimentalist approach to thinking is only possible in a social democracy (that is, in a democratic political system founded upon an equitable, "socialistic" distribution of wealth and power). To be more specific, then, for John Dewey, who was certainly one of the more central figures in founding the philosophy of experimentalism, we get the sort of positive synergism cycle represented in Figure 3–7.

In a somewhat more limited sense, Dewey also envisions a positive synergism cycle between experimental thinking, on the one hand, and constructive social and educational change, on the other. This is represented in Figure 3–8.

Negative synergism, which is the contrary of positive synergism, is well exemplified by the Marxist (or neo-Marxist) critique of American society that can be found in the writings of Herbert Marcuse. Thus, according to Marcuse, contemporary American culture can be viewed as essentially constituting a negative synergism cycle of the sort presented in Figure 3–9.

Synergism is, then, essentially a circular and self-confirming process—a sort of experiental or behavioral analogue of the well-known "self-fulfilling prophecy." The *self-fulfilling prophecy* is a special sort of synergism cycle that occurs when belief creates the sort of behavior that serves to verify the belief that generated the behavior in the first place. Thus, the teacher who believes that a particular student has limited abilities—as was the case in the well-known Rosenthal and Jacobson study, *Pygmalion in the Classroom*[5]—may very well act toward the student in such a way as to create precisely those

FIGURE 3–7
DEWEY ON THE RELATIONSHIP
BETWEEN SCHOOL AND SOCIETY

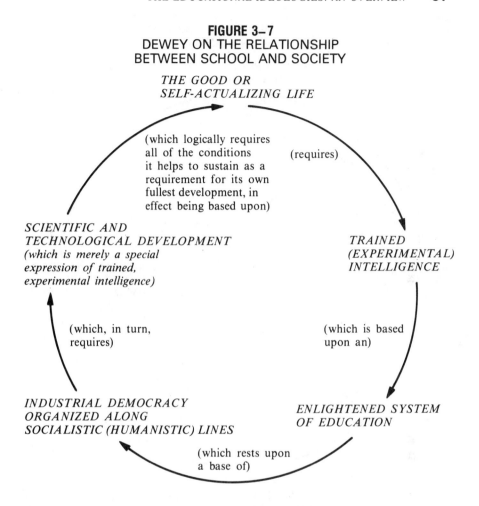

THE GOOD OR
SELF-ACTUALIZING LIFE

(which logically requires
all of the conditions   (requires)
it helps to sustain as a
requirement for its own
fullest development, in
effect being based upon)

SCIENTIFIC AND
TECHNOLOGICAL DEVELOPMENT
(which is merely a special   *TRAINED*
expression of trained,   *(EXPERIMENTAL)*
experimental intelligence)   *INTELLIGENCE*

(which, in turn,   (which is based
requires)   upon an)

INDUSTRIAL DEMOCRACY
ORGANIZED ALONG   *ENLIGHTENED SYSTEM*
SOCIALISTIC (HUMANISTIC) LINES   *OF EDUCATION*

(which rests upon
a base of)

conditions that cause him to respond *as if* he had limited ability, therefore con-
fiming the initial hypothesis.

Synergism also differs from the closely related concept of *heurism.* Generally speaking, heurism is a more restricted and specialized idea than synergism.
In heurism, the individual pursues a line of inquiry that generates new and
more productive lines of inquiry. The scientific process of inquiry is, for example, frequently viewed as essentially heuristic because scientific knowledge is
ordinarily looked upon as *cumulative.* The entire body of scientifically verified
knowledge becomes, in effect, a fund of justified (and therefore potentially
justifiable) beliefs that are capable of providing a reservoir of potential ideas
and information both for identifying and for solving future problems. It is also
generally looked upon as *self-correcting* in the sense that, however attractive an

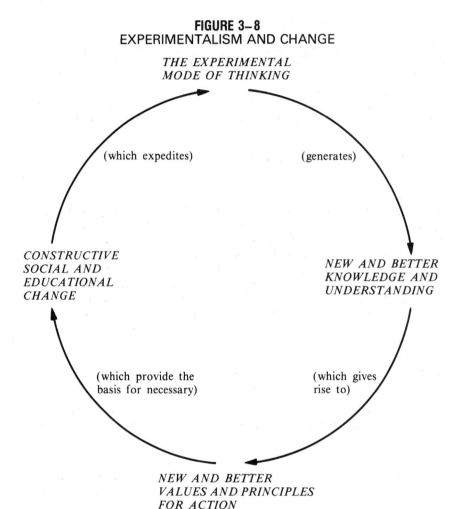

FIGURE 3–8
EXPERIMENTALISM AND CHANGE

*THE EXPERIMENTAL
MODE OF THINKING*

(which expedites)   (generates)

*CONSTRUCTIVE
SOCIAL AND
EDUCATIONAL
CHANGE*

*NEW AND BETTER
KNOWLEDGE AND
UNDERSTANDING*

(which provide the   (which gives
basis for necessary)   rise to)

*NEW AND BETTER
VALUES AND PRINCIPLES
FOR ACTION*

idea may be, it is automatically rejected if it does not "test out" when subsequently subjected to appropriate scientific procedures for the verification of knowledge.

Heurism can be viewed as a special sort of positive synergism, but it differs from the overall concept of synergism in three basic respects. First, heurism is invariably a positive phenomenon. Second, it relates primarily to cognitive processes—to inquiry or to lines of reasoning. Third, synergism, unlike heurism, tends to be a more specifically determinative process—less openended than heurism. It characteristically creates not only the possibility for a certain type of behavior—as through revealing new insights or relationships between ideas—but also the conditions that predispose a person toward a *specific* sort of behavior. In other words, heuristic ideas, which open up productive

FIGURE 3–9
CONTEMPORARY AMERICAN SOCIETY (AFTER MARCUSE)

The Establishment (an economic elite of vested interests)

↓

directly and indirecty controls the reward-structure of our society

↓

thereby controlling the conditions of intellectual development that are based upon re-ward (reinforcement)—that is, information, communications, advertising, education, political parties, etc.

↓

In this way, it systematically brainwashes and economically implicates the general popula-tion.

↓

This results in a sort of engineered consent in a pseudo-democracy in which the people are pacified by affluence and propaganda and therefore come to subscribe voluntarily, and even enthusiastically, to their own continued repression.

↓

This lends additional power to the vested interests who gradually fall victim to their own pervasive environmental controls and become "brainwashed" by their own system.

↓

This allows the system (the industrial-technological-economic apparatus) to function as a sort of impersonal "establishment."

lines of inquiry, are not ordinarily sufficiently compelling, in and of them-selves, to generate a more rigidly structured positive synergism cycle, even at the intellectual level. A rigid personality may be able to pursue a heuristic line of reasoning but fail to follow up on the heuristic insights revealed by his own inquiries. In the case of synergism, the system has a compelling dynamism that, other things being equal, tends to compel a certain sequence of behavior either because it dictates a certain mode of psychological responsiveness or because the entire process tends to take precedence over otherwise extenuating psychological factors.

PHILOSOPHY AND CULTURE

A philosophy necessarily interacts with, both influencing and being influenced by, all of the other elements within a culture—political, economic, educational and such. Thus, philosophy is always ideological, in a conventional sense of the term, and it invariably serves at least partially as a rationalization for exist-ing cultural assumptions as well as being a potential rationale for changing such assumptions. In short, philosophy is merely one of the interdependent and reciprocally interaffecting aspects that make up the totality of a particular culture at a particular time in history. It cannot be viewed, in and of itself, as determining social change in any literal, linear or simplistic way.

The whole question of circular processes, synergism cycles, the sociology of knowledge, and such is highly controversial in philosophy, and it is important to bear in mind that the circular process approach is merely one way to explain the relationship between theory and practice, thought and behavior. Important reservations pertaining to the entire topic are discussed on pages 99–108.

In most cases—although this too is ultimately a philosophical generalization that requires some qualification—there is an inevitable circularity about the relationship between a society's philosophical beliefs and its cultural assumptions. Particular societies tend to generate particular philosophical points of view, that, in turn, tend to reinforce or to sustain the dominant beliefs of the underlying social organization, and so on. Indeed, it is often argued that all philosophies are basically a posteriori rationalizations for socially conditioned belief systems that have generally emerged out of the essentially prerational or nonrational "lived" experience of a certain people over an extended period of time. In other words, from this point of view, the exalted prescriptions of traditional philosophies have typically been little more than idealized descriptions of the tacit values inherent within the host culture.

This is not to say that philosophy is unimportant. Most people may practice practice, but intellectuals are disproportionately important precisely because they practice theory. In short, they think before they act, and, if truly effective, they are sufficiently aware of how their various beliefs cohere and relate in an overall (or "philosophical") sense to be able to avoid much of the uncertainty, ambiguity, inconsistency and self-contradiction that characterizes the behavior of most people. In addition, most philosophies at least attempt to provide the individual with an encompassing set of general ideas which provide the basis for examining prevailing cultural assumptions from a frame of reference outside of the system itself. Archimedes' famous comment "Give me a place to stand, and I will lift the whole world" might be appropriately extended to the function of philosophy in the realm of cognition. Philosophy attempts to provide an intellectual stance, a way of viewing reality, outside of the conventional wisdom of any particular society. In so doing, it provides an external frame of reference, a sense of detachment, that allows prevailing social beliefs to be analyzed and examined on the basis of some more extended point of view than that provided merely by popular consensus or personal opinion. As discussed at a later point, one of the virtues of philosophy, viewed as a synthesizing discipline, is that it at least attempts to reassemble the pieces of reality presented by the other, less encompassing disciplines into something approximating a more complete picture of the whole.

For Karl Marx (and for virtually all contemporary social and behavioral scientists, who generally subscribe to his formative "sociology of knowledge" point of view regarding the cultural origins of belief systems) the *personal* necessarily and inevitably emerges out of the *social*. Or—to be more specific, the line of reasoning generally subscribed to is illustrated in Figure 3–10.

Viewed graphically as a circular process, the entire interaction might be represented as in Figure 3–11. Or, reduced even further, it can be represented schematically as in Figure 3–12.

FIGURE 3–10
SOCIOLOGY OF KNOWLEDGE (AFTER MARX)

Material conditions   (including the economic and political) interact to give rise to

↓

behavior,   which creates

↓

personal experience,   which, viewed collectively, gives rise to

↓

social experience,   which generates

↓

ideology,   which modifies and creates

↓

material conditions   (including the economic and political), which alter

↓

behavior,   which changes

↓

personal experience,   which causes changes within

↓

social experience,   which gives rise to revisions in

↓

ideology   (and so on in what is essentially a circular and self-confirming cycle).

It is important to bear in mind that these figures—and, indeed, virtually all of the diagrams that attempt to represent circularity and, particularly, synergism—are essentially misleading because they are two-dimensional. What actually occurs is a spiral progression in which, other things being equal, conditions either become progressively better (in the case of positive synergism) or progressively worse (as in negative synergism). In other words, synergism and circularity in philosophy seldom refer to a causal sequence in which there is a sterile and mechanical repetition. Thus, Marx's sociology of knowledge point of view, as represented in Figure 3–10, does not deny novelty or imply the constant recapitulation of the past. Indeed, it guarantees novelty and change. Physical and social conditions generate personal behavior, which creates personal experience, which provides the basis for organized social existence—which, in turn, generates ideology, which (ultimately) works to modify physical and social conditions (and so on and on). On the other hand, physical and social conditions are encompassing and infinitely complex. They defy total and effective understanding or control. Therefore personal behavior is never totally explicable or predictable *in fact*—only in principle. In a similar sense, ideology may dictate whether and to what extent overriding physical and social conditions will be sustained, but ideology is ultimately an effect of the interaction between such conditions, and, while it becomes a significant determinant (once it has emerged), it can still only affect conditions that are not themselves ideological in any primary sense, and even those conditions are altered by many other factors than the ideological.

FIGURE 3–11
SOCIOLOGY OF KNOWLEDGE

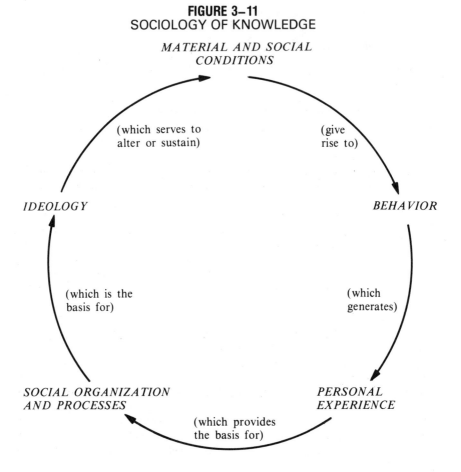

*MATERIAL AND SOCIAL
CONDITIONS*

(which serves to
alter or sustain)

(give
rise to)

IDEOLOGY

BEHAVIOR

(which is the
basis for)

(which
generates)

*SOCIAL ORGANIZATION
AND PROCESSES*

*PERSONAL
EXPERIENCE*

(which provides
the basis for)

In other words, what is circular and repetitive is the formal mode of relation-ship between the conceptual elements which comprise the cycle (spiral). The content, the actual nature of the circumstances that constitute the cycle as it really occurs at any particular point in time, is extremely variable. As in Marx and Hegel, the *meaning* of history varies but the process by which history *expresses* its meaning is constant. The ascending (or descending) corkscrew of synergism describes the constant pattern of formal relationships (at a very high level of abstraction) *within which* all the more concrete objects and events oc-cur. The way in which the circular process manifests itself—particular institu-tions, personal beliefs, and such—is constantly changing, but the process itself is objective and (for all practical purposes) immutable. Even slow change in the circular process ultimately leads to significant differences in how the particular elements of the cycle are expressed in the real world of objects and events. In the long run these differences, which are initially small differences in *degree,* may become so obvious that they begin to function as differences in *kind.* Indeed, in some instances, as in Marxism, drastic and revolutionary change is ultimately seen as a requirement of the entire process. What makes Marx so

FIGURE 3–12
SOCIOLOGY OF KNOWLEDGE

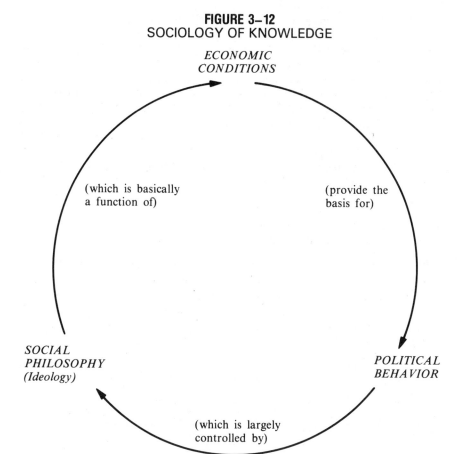

*ECONOMIC
CONDITIONS*

(which is basically
a function of)

(provide the
basis for)

*SOCIAL
PHILOSOPHY
(Ideology)*

*POLITICAL
BEHAVIOR*

(which is largely
controlled by)

difficult to deal with is, in part, the fact that he *describes* a dialectical "conflict" theory which terminates in—and actually *prescribes*—a state of social equilibrium in which the kind of class conflict that Marx has hitherto seen as the motivating force behind all human history, disappears, and "history" comes to an end. Unfortunately, this leads to at least two questions to which Marx did not address himself:

1. If conflict (and particularly class conflict) has been the motivating force in all recorded history, precisely what sort of conflict (if any) will succeed "class conflict" as the fundamental dynamic that directs the evolution of a purely "classless society"? and

2. If "conflict" is viewed as ultimately disappearing altogether, how is it possible to explain motivation and behavior in the utopian world that is to come, since it was the synergistic relationship of forces in conflict that led to the effective elimination of conflict itself? In short, how will a world, born out of conflict, endure without conflict? Does it make sense to *prescribe* equilibrium as the goal of a philosophical system that *describes* reality entirely in terms of conflict?

In the situation represented in Figure 3–12, it is important to note that economics, politics and ideology are an interpenetrating unity; to change one is to change all. On the other hand, it is very difficult to alter politics or ideology without first modifying the economic substructure. The economic is closer to the biological, and hence the material, foundations of reality. It therefore has developmental priority in the reciprocal sequence of interaction. Historically, the economic precedes the political, which precedes the philosophical, even if the three dimensions function in a contemporary sense as interrelated and complimentary forces.

Applied to contemporary American capitalism, the neo-Marxist of today (such as Marcuse) tends to see the sort of functional interaction represented in the line of reasoning as shown in Figure 3–13.

FIGURE 3–13
MARCUSE'S NEO-MARXISM

A technological economy activated by the competitive pursuit of wealth and power

↓

requires profit derived from the sale of goods and services.

↓

In general, maximum profit requires maximum production and maximum consumption.

↓

In a growing economy, profit (wealth) must be reinvested in the economy in order to grow (that is, to appreciate in value relative to wealth in general). In other words, the most productive wealth is capital (wealth invested in further production).

↓

Capital requires more production and therefore more consumption in order to grow (and reap profits).

↓

Since natural (biological) needs are finite and exhaustible, capitalism requires the artificial manipulation of needs beyond the natural level (by means of advertising, propaganda and so on) in order to insure the sort of consumption demands required to guarantee profitable production and the overall growth of the economy.

↓

This results in a secondary or psychological type of materialism in which people are systematically addicted to gratuitous physical needs in order to guarantee increased production.

↓

This leads to greater profit, enhanced production, improved production techniques (increased efficiency, automation, etc.), improved selling procedures, and so on.

↓

This results in enhanced consumption, which leads to a rise in expectancy with respect to future consumption needs, which blocks psychological access to leisure, keeps individuals enslaved to the system, and generates increased consumption.

↓

This, therefore, increases production, advertising, consumption expectancy, and so on and on, in what is essentially a circular and self-confirming cycle.

For Marx, true progress was looked upon as inexorably related to a circular and self-confirming process of positive synergy, which was a central aspect of his overall philosophy of dialectical materialism. Thus, from the Marxist point of view, personal value (happiness realized by means of self-actualization) ultimately required a humanistic society (social self-actualization, the synergistic interrelationship of all forces in a totally constructive and progressive system) which, in turn, contributed to ultimate social unification (the Marxist "end of history" where all natural forces are synergistically unified in one positive and ongoing social process that is capable of operating automatically and without the intervention of traditional political constraints). For Marx, then, the line of reasoning in Figure 3–14 would hold true:

FIGURE 3–14
MARX'S THEORY OF SOCIAL SELF-ACTUALIZATION

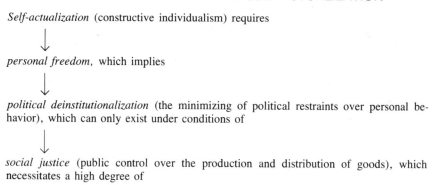

Self-actualization (constructive individualism) requires

$\downarrow$

personal freedom, which implies

$\downarrow$

political deinstitutionalization (the minimizing of political restraints over personal behavior), which can only exist under conditions of

$\downarrow$

social justice (public control over the production and distribution of goods), which necessitates a high degree of

$\downarrow$

material prosperity (the availability of adequate wealth for all), and an enlightened moral philosophy (Marxism), which emerges naturally out of the dialectical process of progressive material evolution throughout history.

Figure 3–15 views the same process in essentially reverse order:

FIGURE 3–15
THE POLITICS OF SELF-ACTUALIZATION (AFTER MARX)

The natural evolution of material conditions (*dialectical materialism)* leads inexorably to

$\downarrow$

improved social conditions and the *development of objective reason,* which implies the necessity for

$\downarrow$

revolutionary Communism, which terminates in

$\downarrow$

the *abolition of traditional politics* (the "classless society" and the "withering away of the state"), which generates

$\downarrow$

the highest expression of *self-actualization.*

Viewed as a synergism cycle, we have the situation presented in Figure 3–16.

FIGURE 3–16
THE MARXIST HIERARCHY OF VALUES (PRESCRIPTIVE)

SELF-ACTUALIZATION

(which both explains and implements)

(requires)

DIALECTICAL MATERIALISM

SOCIAL SELF-ACTUALIZATION

(which can only flourish on the basis of)

(which necessitates)

SCIENCE, TECHNOLOGY AND INDUSTRY

SOCIALISM

(which implies)

The essential circularity of social and intellectual forces is in no sense restricted to Marxism. Indeed, it is a pervasive theme in many contemporary non-Marxist philosophies that subscribe to empirical and relativistic assumptions about the nature of reality. John Dewey's experimentalism is, for example, and as indicated earlier, deeply circular in its conception of how the schools should ideally relate to society.

THE RELATIONSHIP BETWEEN CIRCULAR PROCESSES

What complicates the whole question of synergism — and indeed the entire problem of how the various physical, psychological, social and philosophical influences come together to act as reciprocally interpenetrating systems — is the fact that, generally, one synergism cycle tends to be related to still others, usually at different levels of abstraction, leading to an extremely complicated *metasystem* consisting of interrelated synergism cycles, each dealing with particular aspects of total reality.

Cosmic Synergism and Evolution.   Thus, to begin at the most abstract (and traditionally "philosophical" level), the well-known Jesuit paleontologist-philosopher Pierre Teilhard de Chardin is celebrated for his vision of cosmic evolution in which the entire universe is moving toward spiritual self-perfection.[6] While Teilhard's point of view is highly abstruse and extremely subtle, it is perhaps defensible to reduce it to a basic line of reasoning which might be outlined as in Figure 3–17.

FIGURE 3–17
TEILHARD'S CONCEPT OF EVOLUTION

Structure-function evolves into

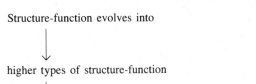

higher types of structure-function

resulting in man, that aspect of structure-function who is capable of comprehending and acting in terms of abstract (universal) structure-function that actually constitutes the regulative principles inherent within nature per se.

This gives man the unique capacity to alter structure-function (nature) itself in certain significant respects in order to expedite his own part-function (human nature).

These changes modify the overall field of forces (nature) and, in so doing, indirectly modify human nature itself.

Man increasingly humanizes (personalizes) the world by altering natural conditions to suit his own nature. He uses intelligence to shape a more intelligible universe. A more reasonable universe, in turn, improves functional reason. This leads to greater control over, and changes within, the natural world. In a sense, then, reason and the reasoned environment created by reason are synergistic: intelligence leads to a more intelligible world, which expedites intelligence, which promotes a more intelligible (rational) world, and so on and on.

Man therefore alters evolution (the world) through reason in order to expedite human purposes. He learns from a reasoned environment to be more reasonable and ultimately to reason about his own purposes. By changing the world, he changes himself and vice versa.[7]

A more succinct paraphrase is found in Figure 3–18.

FIGURE 3–18
TEILHARD'S CONCEPT OF EVOLUTION

The evolution of the *physical* environment (the possible) gives rise to
↓
the *biological* organism (the imperative), which is basic to
↓
the development of the *normative* (the desirable), which is basic in determining
↓
the *intellectual* (the comprehensible), which leads to
↓
modifications in the *physical* environment, and so on in a spiral progression.

A graphic presentation of this concept is found in Figure 3–19.

FIGURE 3–19
TEILHARD'S CONCEPT OF EVOLUTION

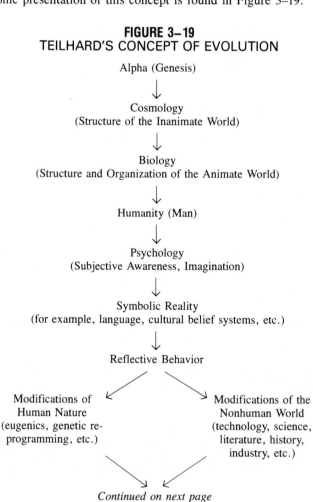

Alpha (Genesis)
↓
Cosmology
(Structure of the Inanimate World)
↓
Biology
(Structure and Organization of the Animate World)
↓
Humanity (Man)
↓
Psychology
(Subjective Awareness, Imagination)
↓
Symbolic Reality
(for example, language, cultural belief systems, etc.)
↓
Reflective Behavior

Modifications of
Human Nature
(eugenics, genetic re-
programming, etc.)

Modifications of the
Nonhuman World
(technology, science,
literature, history,
industry, etc.)

Continued on next page

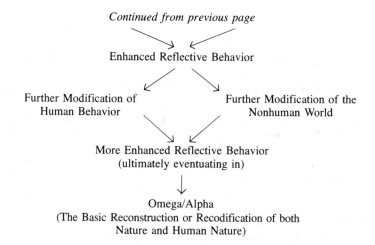

Continued from previous page

Enhanced Reflective Behavior

Further Modification of
Human Behavior

Further Modification of the
Nonhuman World

More Enhanced Reflective Behavior
(ultimately eventuating in)

Omega/Alpha
(The Basic Reconstruction or Recodification of both
Nature and Human Nature)

But Teilhard's theory is merely one special (''spiritualized'') version of the better known ''evolutionary behaviorist'' point of view which may be generally summarized as in Figure 3–20.

FIGURE 3–20
THE EVOLUTIONARY BEHAVIORIST VIEW OF EVOLUTION

The total field of forces (*reality*) shapes

↓

behavior, which is selectively reinforced by means of pleasure and pain in terms of its value for the survival and success of the species, which in the long run leads to

↓

modifications in the species-organism (*human nature*), which in turn expresses itself as a proclivity toward certain types of

↓

behavior that are compatible with the natural needs and potentialities of the organism, which leads to

↓

certain types of *learning,* which eventuates in

↓

certain types of *knowledge,* which may or may not be

↓

adaptive and therefore reinforced, but which thereby leads to subsequent modifications in

↓

behavior and therefore, in the long run, to evolutionary modifications in the

↓

biological structure of the species-organism

↓

and so on in a spiral progression.

Viewed more graphically as a circular process, the more conventional view of human evolution might be represented as in Figure 3–21.

FIGURE 3–21
THE EVOLUTIONARY CYCLE

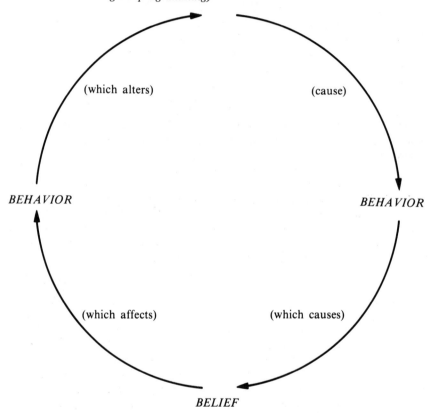

PHYSICAL CONDITIONS (including environmental circumstances as well as both genetic and acquired biological programming)

(which alters)   (cause)

BEHAVIOR   *BEHAVIOR*

(which affects)   (which causes)

BELIEF

At the very highest level of generalization, then, both the evolutionary behaviorists and the more metaphysical or spiritual traditions associated with an evolutionary theorist such as Teilhard might be graphically summarized as in Figure 3–22.

FIGURE 3–22
COSMIC SYNERGISM

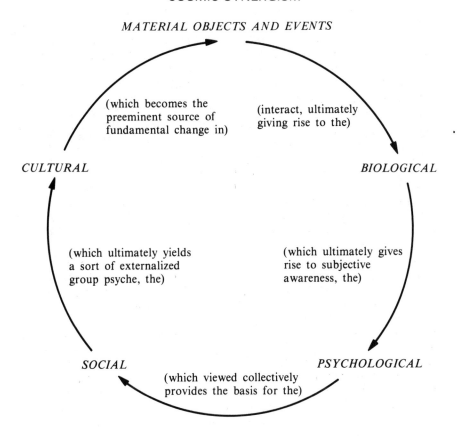

Cultural Synergism. If, on the other hand, one chooses to focus, not on the cosmos, but on culture (in the tradition of Marx and the Marxists, among others) one tends to get a similar sort of synergism cycle, but on a far less generalized scale. This might be represented as in Figure 3–23.

FIGURE 3–23
CULTURAL SYNERGISM

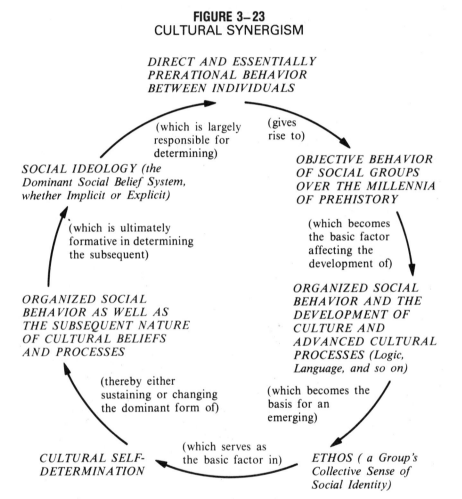

DIRECT AND ESSENTIALLY
PRERATIONAL BEHAVIOR
BETWEEN INDIVIDUALS

(which is largely
responsible for
determining)

(gives
rise to)

SOCIAL IDEOLOGY (the
Dominant Social Belief System,
whether Implicit or Explicit)

OBJECTIVE BEHAVIOR
OF SOCIAL GROUPS
OVER THE MILLENNIA
OF PREHISTORY

(which is ultimately
formative in determining
the subsequent)

(which becomes
the basic factor
affecting the
development of)

ORGANIZED SOCIAL
BEHAVIOR AS WELL AS
THE SUBSEQUENT NATURE
OF CULTURAL BELIEFS
AND PROCESSES

ORGANIZED SOCIAL
BEHAVIOR AND THE
DEVELOPMENT OF
CULTURE AND
ADVANCED CULTURAL
PROCESSES (Logic,
Language, and so on)

(thereby either
sustaining or changing
the dominant form of)

(which becomes the
basis for an
emerging)

CULTURAL SELF-
DETERMINATION

(which serves as
the basic factor in)

ETHOS (a Group's
Collective Sense of
Social Identity)

The cultural synergism diagram is necessarily an oversimplification. A cultural ethos is seldom a simple and monolithic matter in any but the crudest sort of primitive society. Most contemporary cultures are exceedingly complex, and encompass a host of component subcultures with distinctively different ideological orientations. Even totalitarian cultures have a difficult time suppressing pluralistic ideological considerations, and most cultures probably evolve largely through the conflict between opposing points of view that are constantly influential within the context of the dominant worldview.

Political and Economic Synergism.   By progressing one step further, and reducing the frame of reference, from culture in general to more specific political and educational matters, a somewhat different synergism cycle tends to emerge. This is diagrammed in Figure 3–24.

FIGURE 3–24
POLITICAL/EDUCATIONAL SYNERGISM

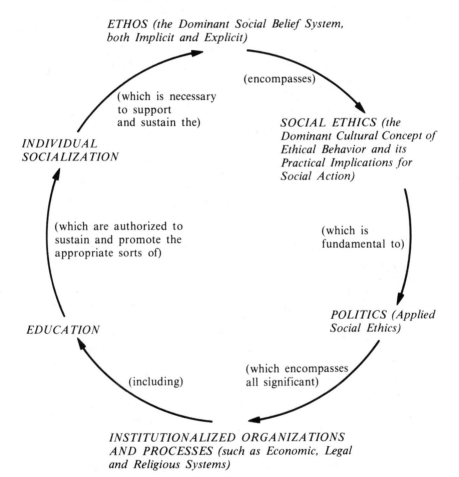

ETHOS *(the Dominant Social Belief System, both Implicit and Explicit)*

(encompasses)

(which is necessary to support and sustain the)

INDIVIDUAL SOCIALIZATION

SOCIAL ETHICS *(the Dominant Cultural Concept of Ethical Behavior and its Practical Implications for Social Action)*

(which are authorized to sustain and promote the appropriate sorts of)

(which is fundamental to)

EDUCATION

POLITICS *(Applied Social Ethics)*

(including)

(which encompasses all significant)

INSTITUTIONALIZED ORGANIZATIONS AND PROCESSES *(such as Economic, Legal and Religious Systems)*

The political/economic synergism cycle is, similarly, oversimplistic. The political almost invariably controls the educational (except where these are equated, and the school is used as the basic structure of the state—as in Plato's ideal republic). On the other hand, this is not a simple and one-directional type of relationship that precludes the use of the school as an agency for social change. There is no reason why a culture should not organize itself politically in such a manner as to utilize the schools as basic instruments for political reconstruction (as in Fascist Italy or in Communist China during the forties and fifties). In a truly democratic culture, committed to open and experimental inquiry, the schools would, ostensibly, become laboratories for furthering the fullest and most open-ended sort of continuous self-criticism and social change.

Psychological Synergism. Finally, by reducing the scope from the cosmic, the cultural and the political to the purely personal, what emerges is a psychological (developmental) synergism cycle which frequently resembles that presented in Figure 3–25.

FIGURE 3–25
PSYCHOLOGICAL (DEVELOPMENTAL) SYNERGISM

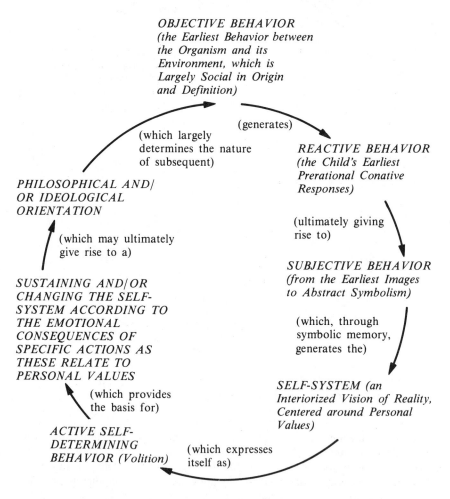

*OBJECTIVE BEHAVIOR
(the Earliest Behavior between
the Organism and its
Environment, which is
Largely Social in Origin
and Definition)*

(generates)

(which largely
determines the nature
of subsequent)

*REACTIVE BEHAVIOR
(the Child's Earliest
Prerational Conative
Responses)*

*PHILOSOPHICAL AND/
OR IDEOLOGICAL
ORIENTATION*

(which may ultimately
give rise to a)

(ultimately giving
rise to)

*SUBJECTIVE BEHAVIOR
(from the Earliest Images
to Abstract Symbolism)*

*SUSTAINING AND/OR
CHANGING THE SELF-
SYSTEM ACCORDING TO
THE EMOTIONAL
CONSEQUENCES OF
SPECIFIC ACTIONS AS
THESE RELATE TO
PERSONAL VALUES*

(which, through
symbolic memory,
generates the)

(which provides
the basis for)

*SELF-SYSTEM (an
Interiorized Vision of Reality,
Centered around Personal
Values)*

*ACTIVE SELF-
DETERMINING
BEHAVIOR (Volition)*

(which expresses
itself as)

Levels of Synergism

What compounds all of this circularity is ultimately, however, the fact that all four of these synergism cycles are also interrelated, and frequently even mesh to form still more encompassing double, triple, and quadruple cycles—and perhaps even an holistic gestalt which encompasses virtually everything. In short—and in a manner somewhat reminiscent of Teilhard's general synthesis—we appear (at least on the conceptual level) to have at least four completely distinct cycles that interact reciprocally with each other and that can even be viewed as forming an upwards spiral progression rather than merely a series of simple concentric circles as shown in Figure 3–26.

FIGURE 3–26
OVERLAPPING SYNERGISM CYCLES

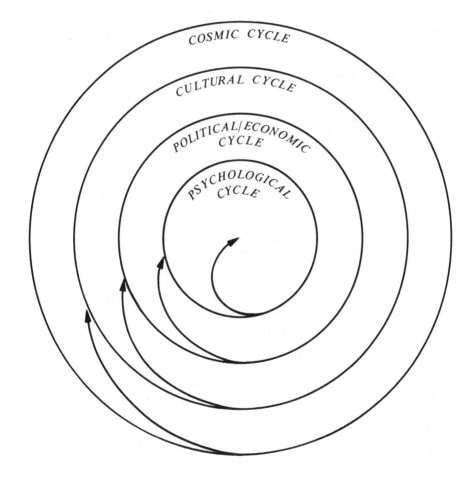

Some Qualifications Regarding Synergism

Certain qualifications should necessarily be appended to the preceding discussion on synergism.

1. It is important to recognize that the entire concept of synergism (as a philosophical explanation) is part and parcel of a particular philosophical point of view, and is not necessarily congenial to proponents of certain philosophical positions. In ideological terms, certain of the intellectualists (such as the classical realists and Thomists) and fundamentalists (such as the anti-intellectual "common sense" intuitionists) subscribe to absolute types of intuitive and/or revealed knowledge that are *not* viewed as being subordinate to overriding social or psychological experience. Many, perhaps most, empirical philosophers—and particularly those who are essentially naturalistic and/or behavioristic in orientation—*would,* on the other hand, be inclined to subscribe to synergistic lines of reasoning. Since most contemporary social and behavioral scientists tend to be predisposed toward a scientific worldview (which is implicitly empirical, behavioral and pragmatic in its underlying assumptions), most theorists in these areas are inclined toward synergistic explanations and tend to look upon those who hold more absolutistic and linear beliefs about the nature and origins of personal knowledge as being substantially prescientific and prepsychological. In a sense, this may be true, but it does not militate against the fact that *most* people's fundamental belief systems *are* probably absolutist and rather simplistically linear in nature and must therefore necessarily be confronted and understood as such. The notion that philosophy exists solely to explore ideas that are supported by evidence gathered through scientific and scientifically inclined disciplines, which are themselves rooted in particular philosophical assumptions about the nature of reality, is a somewhat naïve position. Most of the world is still committed to nonscientific points of view, and we disregard such worldviews only at great hazard. Religion may not be scientific in the usual sense of the term, but we ignore the practical significance of religious convictions only by excluding the majority of the world's peoples from consideration.

2. The different synergism cycles represent essentially different levels of abstraction. They are, however, merely conceptually distinct. They actually constitute an interpenetrating whole, in which all of the various levels (and the various elements within the levels) are constantly interacting. Thus the *cosmic* synergism cycle, at the highest level of abstraction, naturally encompasses and affects the social, but the social, once it evolves out of the material/biological, also exerts profound effects on the cosmic in a variety of different ways. In a similar sense, certain individuals—such as Newton, Einstein, Darwin or Freud—can substantially change the cultural ethos, and, in the long run, alter the political/educational and material/biological dimensions of reality very substantially. (See Figure 3–27.)

3. The cosmic synergism cycle, which is rooted in the interaction of physical (including biological) objects and events, has logical and developmental priority over the others, because it *encompasses* all of the others (which are essentially subsets or special expressions of the physical/biological). The cosmic

FIGURE 3–27
THE RELATIVE SELF

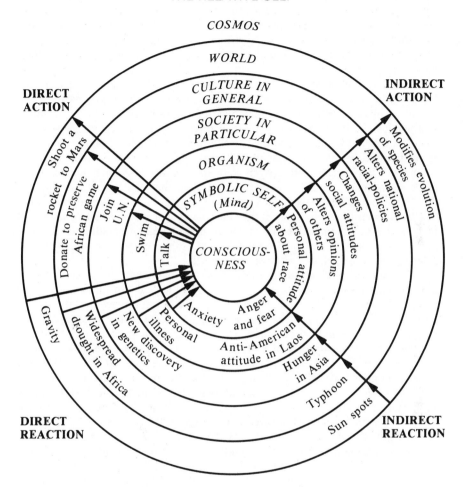

cycle provides the developmental origins for the other cycles, which are ulti-mately outgrowths of the evolution of more basic forces at the material and biological levels.

4. All of the various synergism cycles are based upon assumptions of causal determinism, but such determinism is not rigid and highly predictable because it works in a very complex manner with a virtually infinite number of different variables acting in combination. It does not necessarily deny the possibility of 'free will,' although it would reject the notion that the will itself is free from some kind of ultimate circumstantial determination emerging out of its own psy-

chological origins. In a similar sense, this determinism would not necessarily deny that certain cultures are more "open" and flexible than others, but it would tend to see such "openness" as a determined and determining commitment to certain social processes, such as science, reason or democracy. These processes encourage variety and variability rather than others, such as superstition, habit or totalitarianism, which tend to be more self-confirming in an essentially "closed" direction.

5. The various ideologies differ in large degree in their focus with respect to the different levels of abstraction represented by the various synergism cycles as well as in the attention they direct toward the various elements that constitute such cycles. A traditional secular intellectualist of the liberal arts persuasion, such as Robert Maynard Hutchins or Mortimer Adler, for example, tends to emphasize the cosmic, or metaphysical level. He tends to move rather directly from the metaphysical to the psychological, viewing the social (including the political and educational) as essentially no more than the logical extension of the demonstrable relationships that exist between the knower (the rational mind) and the known (metaphysical Truth). The pragmatist, on the other hand—and most of the educational Liberals are rooted in the pragmatic tradition—tends to move from the psychological to the logical, from the personal/social to the abstract, from the behavioral to the theoretical.

6. The extent to which the average individual or society directs its behavior through conscious and intentional intellectual/ideological considerations is open to debate. Since the central concern here is with the influence that theory has on practice, these diagrams are intended to indicate the sort of relationship that exists between theoretical considerations and practical behavior *where such a relationship exists*. In point of fact, however, and as already discussed, most personal and/or social behavior is probably best explained psychologically rather than philosophically or ideologically (see Chapter II). On the other hand, much *significant* personal and social behavior *is* ideological and can be adequately understood only if ideological considerations are taken into proper account. This discussion is directed at these types of behavior.

7. Despite the attention directed to synergism and circularity in the preceding pages, the circularity (or potential circularity) of the relationships between various of the philosophical positions and underlying social and psychological forces is not emphasized in the remainder of this book. This strategy is intentional and is employed for the sake of clarity and simplicity. Linear-causal lines of reasoning are more easily followed than those that focus on circular and mutually interaffecting elements. Holistic problems seldom lend themselves to holistic resolution. Thinking is—as the General Semanticists have long maintained—necessarily a linear, part-to-whole, subject-predicate process where one must make somewhat artificial distinctions between inseparable aspects of a total or continuous set of relationships. This is a difficulty inherent in using language and, indeed, in conventional logic itself. Separate academic disciplines exist largely by virtue of the fact that it is necessary to divide the world into bite-size pieces in order to analyze its complexity. One of the virtues of philosophy, viewed as a synthetic discipline, is that it at least attempts to reassemble the pieces in something approximating a more complete picture of the whole.

Science and the Scientific Method

Since the terms *science*, *scientific process*, *scientific method*, and such recur with striking frequency throughout this discussion — and, indeed, throughout the book — it is perhaps wise to dwell briefly on how these terms are used. Three qualifications are perhaps central.

1. Science and the philosophical bases of science are very difficult to identify and define because contemporary science is in a rather obvious state of perturbation caused, in large part, by disturbing discoveries made by science itself. Many of these developments seem to be fomenting a basic revolution in the way in which science views the nature of the scientific process itself. These discoveries include such matters as: quantum theory, the general and special theories of relativity, Werner Heisenberg's principle of uncertainty, developments in molecular biology and genetics, recent discoveries in physiological psychology (particularly relating to the electrical stimulation of the brain) and behavioral psychology (especially reinforcement theory), recent speculations about the holographic transmission of electrical patterns in the brain, such intriguing phenomena as "black holes" in space, antimatter, peculiar and partially inexplicable subatomic particles, to name but a few. We may be, as Thomas S. Kuhn points out in his well-known book *The Structure of Scientific Revolutions*, [8] on the verge of a radical "paradigm-shift." This involves a basic redefinition of the nature and conduct of science generated by inconsistencies and incongruities between the world discovered by new scientific techniques and the traditional assumptions about the world that are still largely implicit within the way science has traditionally been conceived. The sort of changes that may occur in the philosophical assumptions that underlie the scientific endeavor are obviously beyond the scope of this book, but, at the very least, it seems clear that very sophisticated and complicated assumptions about the metaphysical and epistemological bases of reality are currently evolving.

Since the publication of Kuhn's book, it has become popular to talk about the "scientific paradigm" and/or "scientific paradigms." Essentially, a *scientific paradigm* is a model containing the fundamental substantive and procedural assumptions on which research activities peculiar to science or a particular type of science are based. This is a rough definition of a very difficult concept. As Kuhn points out, one sympathetic reader prepared a partial analytic index of his book and concluded that the term *paradigm* had been used in at least twenty-two different ways. [9] At one point, Kuhn defines a paradigm as "what the members of a scientific community share, *and*, conversely, a scientific community consists of men who share a paradigm." [10]

With respect to scientific paradigms, there appears to be two basic points of view: They hold either that (1) there are a variety of different paradigms that are appropriate for different sorts of scientific activity; or (2) there is only one scientific paradigm, that which represents the most exacting statement of the conditions required for defensible scientific activity and which is best represented in those fields (particularly the physical sciences) that provide the most supportive conditions for the application of this model of research and verification.

Obviously, either or both of these positions may be true, but, for present purposes, the latter concept is used, and the term *science* is applied with reference to those activities most representative of "hard scientists" who deal with physical (and, preferably, inorganic) objects and events. "Soft scientists," like psychologists, sociologists, and anthropologists, can only hope to approximate the exactitude and rigor of work in such areas.

For present purposes, then, this book will use the rather conventional definition of science, which is still generally applicable beyond the more exotic frontiers of such areas as particle physics, astronomy and molecular biology, and which continues to command allegiance in virtually all of the less developed social and behavioral sciences. Thus, when the term *science* is used here, reference is made to the scientific *process,* and to scientific *knowledge.* Scientific process is conventionally understood here in terms of controlled variables, public verification, intersubjectivity, quantifiability, observability, and so on.[11] Scientific knowledge refers here to that body of information and ideas that has been confirmed *through* the scientific process or that, at the very least, appears to be highly *probable* on the basis of those things that have been verified, and are usually therefore verifiable in the future, through such scientific experimentation.

To be more specific — and all of these comments are amplified in Chapter VII — the assumption is made here that science (as conventionally conceived) is:

a. *empirical* (based upon sense-perceptual experience);
b. *behavioristic* (based upon the assumption that sense-perceptual experience is a function of psychobiological behavior);
c. *pragmatic* (based upon the assumption that the truth of an idea is determined by its consequences when applied to the solution of a real problem);
d. *materialistic* (based on the assumption that all behavior is elicited by the interaction between physical objects and/or events); and
e. *experimental* (based on the assumption that the best test is one in which one experiences/observes the consequences of discrete (separate and separable) objects or events under the rigorously controlled conditions conventionally described as constituting the "scientific method."

This is, as noted, a conventional definition of the terms *science* and *scientific process.* It discounts the notion that there are a multiplicity of *different* models of the scientific method that all possess equal (or at least partial) validity under certain circumstances. It also disregards legitimate questions about whether and to what extent the assumptive bases of science are changing. These are very important topics but they are not highly salient to the present discussion, which is essentially focused on social philosophy.

2. The terms *relativism* and *relativity* are the cause of great confusion in both science and philosophy. Again, and in general, relativism and relativity have reference to two points of view in philosophy. One position holds that all knowledge is relative in the sense of being fundamentally *indeterminate,* and

the other position holds that all knowledge is relative in the sense of being *relational* and therefore capable of being determined and defined only within some specified context.

The difficulty with the first position is that, as Bertrand Russell once pointed out, it does not make good sense. If *all* knowledge is relative, there can be no trustworthy knowledge at all, because there are no propositions that are ultimately specified as categorical cases that can be used as a basis for grounding subsequent communication. The statement "All knowledge is relative" therefore becomes the functional equivalent of the statement "All knowledge is subjective." But, if all truth is subjective, no "philosophical" knowledge of the conventional sort — which necessarily purports to be abstract and universal — is possible.

The second position — "All knowledge is relational" — presents a somewhat different situation. Here what is being stated is essentially reducible to two points: (1) that any truth-proposition is inevitably related to a broad field of other interrelated truth-propositions and cannot be *totally* defined and understood in isolation; and (2) that undergirding all particular truth-propositions are highly abstract truth-propositions (or *meta-assumptions*). These meta-assumptions, although themselves relational (in the final analysis), nevertheless provide an absolute basis (for all practical purposes) when it comes to establishing a basis for ongoing communication. Thus, as Aristotle stated, the terms by which we *express* differences or commonalities — terms such as *length, size, duration, intensity, movement* — are *not* relational, because they are the assumptive concepts by which we communicate about (and perhaps experience) all relationships. All communication is based on metaphor, which implies a recognition of basic similarities and differences.

For present purposes, the terms *relativism* and *relativity* will have reference to the latter sense of "relational but grounded in absolute concepts of relationship" and not to the earlier sense of "indeterminate." As such, the term *relational* implies an overriding unity and holism; the idea that the world is ultimately a dynamic Gestalt. Certainly, it is central to the concept of "synergism" which was discussed earlier.

3. With respect to the vexing question of cause-and-effect there appear to be two basic points of view in both science and philosophy. The first point of view is the traditional point of view of the cause-and-effect determinists who hold that all events are caused by the prior interaction between immediately preceding objects and events, which were themselves the products of the relationship between prior objects/events, and so on and on, ad infinitum. All such determinism implies *pre*determinism in the sense that anyone who is *hypothetically* possessed of *perfect* knowledge of the world as it exists at the present (in all of its complexity) would be able to predict the future without error and to reconstruct the past by logical implication on the basis of existing information.

The second point of view — frequently associated in philosophy with David Hume and in science with Werner Heisenberg — holds that, while reality is generally characterized by constant conjunctions (or correlations) between phenomena, there is no reason to assume that these conjunctions necessarily rest upon necessary causation in which the first element in the series gives rise to the next, which engenders the next, and so on, in a continuous sequence of inevitable determinism.

With respect to causality, perhaps the most central controversy at the present time exists in the area of physical science, and centers on Werner Heisenberg's well-known principle of uncertainty.

In his very provocative book *The Tao of Physics,*[12] physicist Fritjof Capra paraphrases Heisenberg's well-known principle of uncertainty in the following words:

> The crucial feature of atomic physics is that the human observer is not only necessary to observe the properties of an object, but is necessary even to define these properties. In atomic physics, we cannot talk about the properties of an object as such. They are only meaningful in the context of the object's interaction with the observer. In the words of Heisenberg, "What we observe is not nature itself, but nature exposed to our method of questioning."[Werner Heisenberg, *Physics and Philosophy*, p. 58.] The observer decides how he is going to set up the measurement, and this arrangement will determine, to some extent, the properties of the observed object. If the experimental arrangement is modified, the properties of the observed object will change in turn.
>
> This can be illustrated with the simple case of a subatomic particle. When observing such a particle, one may choose to measure — among other quantities — the particle's position and its momentum (a quantity defined as the particle's mass times its velocity)....Heisenberg's uncertainty principle...says that these two quantities can never be measured simultaneously with precision. We can either obtain a precise knowledge about the particle's position and remain completely ignorant about its momentum (and less about its velocity), or vice versa; or we can have a rough and imprecise knowledge about both quantities. The important point now is that this limitation has nothing to do with the imperfection of our measuring techniques. It is the principle limitation which is inherent in the atomic reality. If we decide to measure the particle's position precisely, the particle simply *does not have* a well-defined momentum, and if we decide to measure the momentum, it does not have a well defined position....John Wheeler sees this involvement of the observer as the most important feature of the quantum theory, and he has therefore suggested replacing the word "observer" by the word "participator." In Wheeler's own words..."the measurement changes the state of the electron. The universe will never afterwards be the same. To describe what has happened, one has to cross out that old word 'observer' and put in its place the new word 'participator.' In some strange sense the universe is a participatory universe." (Internal quote from J. I. A. Wheeler in J. Mehra, ed., *The Physicist's Conception of Nature*, p. 244.)[13]

Thus, according to Heisenberg, the difficulty in any of the natural sciences — and most particularly in physics — is that the acts of observation and measurement, being physical acts that insert new quanta of energy into the observational sequence, necessarily interfere with and alter that which is being observed. "Natural science," says Heisenberg, "does not simply describe and explain nature; it is part of the interplay between nature and ourselves."[14] Hence, in measuring extremely small particles of energy, the instruments and movements used in the process of measurement affect (and distort) the object/event being measured. One cannot, in effect, separate the observer and the observed, so pure *objective* data (emerging out of what is sometimes referred to in philosophy as the "doctrine of immaculate perception") becomes impossible when it comes to the matter of making subtle observations relating to extremely microscopic phenomena.

This, on occasion, gives rise to some rather strange anomalies. In quantum theory, for example, subatomic units of matter are very abstract entities that have a dual aspect. Again, and as Capra states:

Depending on how we look at them [these subatomic units] appear sometimes as particles, sometimes as waves; and this dual nature is also exhibited by light which can take the form of electromagnetic waves or particles.
This property of matter and of light is very strange. It seems impossible to accept that something can be, at the same time, a particle — i.e., an entity confined to a very small volume — and a wave, which is spread out over a large region of space. This contradiction gives rise to most of the *koan*-like paradoxes which finally led to the formulation of quantum theory. The whole development started when Max Planck discovered that the energy of heat radiation is not emitted continuously, but appears in the form of "energy packets." Einstein called these energy packets "quanta" and recognized them as a fundamental aspect of nature. He was bold enough to postulate that light and every other form of electromagnetic radiation can appear only as electromagnetic waves, but also in the form of these quanta. The light quanta, which gave quantum theory its name, have since been accepted as bona fide particles and are now called photons. They are particles of a special kind, however, massless and always traveling with the speed of light.
The apparent contradiction between the particle and the wave picture was solved in a completely unexpected way which called in question the very foundation of the mechanistic world view — the concept of the reality of matter. At the subatomic level, matter does not exist with certainty at definite places, but rather shows "tendencies to exist," and atomic events do not occur with certainty at definite times and in definite ways, but rather show "tendencies to occur." In the formalism of quantum theory, these tendencies are expressed as probabilities and are associated with mathematical quantities which take the form of waves. This is why particles can be waves at the same time. They are not "real" three-dimensional waves like sound or water waves. They are "probability waves," abstract mathematical quantities with all the characteristic properties of waves which are related to the probabilities of finding the particles at particular points in space and at particular times. All the laws of atomic physics are expressed in terms of these probabilities. We can never predict an atomic event with certainty; we can only say how likely it is to happen. Quantum theory has thus demolished the classical concept of solid objects and of strictly deterministic laws of nature. At the subatomic level, the solid material objects of classical physics dissolves into wave-like patterns of probabilities, and these patterns, ultimately, do not represent probabilities of things, but rather probabilities of interconnections.... As we penetrate into matter, nature does not show us any isolated "basic building blocks," but rather appears as a complicated web of relations between the various parts of the whole. These relations always include the observer in an essential way. The human observer constitutes the final length in the chain of observational processes, and the properties of any atomic object can only be understood in terms of the object's interaction with the observer. This

means that the classical ideal of an objective description of nature is no longer valid. The Cartesian partition between the I and the world, between the observer and the observed, cannot be made when dealing with atomic matter. In atomic physics, we can never speak about nature without, at the same time, speaking about ourselves.[15]

These anomalies, however, give rise to a basic question: If there appear to be exceptions to the universal law of cause-and-effect in some instances of the behavior of exceedingly small particles (or quanta) of matter — as there do — does this behavior indicate that (1) cause and effect is *not* an absolute principle that applies to all phenomena in the known world (since it is not predictably verifiable at certain subatomic levels); *or* (2) cause-and-effect *is* an absolute (metaphysical) principle of all known phenomena, but that in some instances in the area of particle physics, cause-and-effect is rendered indeterminate (but only *ostensibly* nonexistent) because man has not perfected (or is not, in principle, capable of perfecting) the instruments necessary to isolate and describe how it operates? Einstein opted for the latter hypothesis, which might be termed *indeterminable determinism* — that is, that all objects/events are absolutely determined but that we are (at least temporarily) *epistemologically* incapable of identifying and defining the determinants beyond a certain level of operations.[16] Heisenberg, on the other hand, opted for the former hypothesis of *metaphysical nondeterminism* — that is, cause-and-effect, although presenting a true description of reality at the macroscopic level, does not apply to certain types of subatomic particles at extremely microscopic ranges of behavior.

Unfortunately, there is no "scientific" solution to this problem, because the problem transcends the existing limits of science and even calls into question the conventional cause-and-effect assumptions upon which "normal science" is usually considered to be based. In this book, Einstein's assumption of *epistemological (indeterminable) determinism* is preferred over Heisenberg's more radical notion of *metaphysical nondeterminism* when it comes to explaining phenomena at the subatomic level.

In summary, then, "science," for present purposes, is defined as (1) essentially *one paradigm* (with certain accepted variations and approximations) rather than as a multiplicity of different paradigms; (2) *relativistic* in the sense that it subscribes to a grounded "relationalism" in its attempt to formulate ultimate laws or principles; and (3) assuming a *constant cause-and-effect determinism* that operates at the metaphysical level (despite epistemological difficulties and ambiguities that occasionally occur when it comes to describing how this cause-and-effect network operates at an extremely microscopic level).

The Remaining Chapters

In the following pages, the educational ideologies associated with the more basic systems of social ethics are identified and defined. The educational ideologies are considered in a sequence that would range on a political spectrum from the most Conservative (educational fundamentalism) to the most Liberal (educational anarchism). For purposes of clarity, the same format has been used in each of the six sections that deal with the six major ideologies. Each begins with a brief definition of the particular educational position in quite general terms. This is followed by an outline summary of the basic point of view as it addresses itself to the following eight questions:

1. What is the fundamental goal of education from the point of view of the ideology in question?
2. What are the specific objectives of the school as a social institution?
3. What are some of the more central features of the ideology that apply to virtually all aspects of teaching and learning?
4. What is the general nature of the child as learner?*
5. How and by whom should education be controlled?
6. What should be the general nature of the curriculum? †
7. What instructional methods and evaluation procedures should be employed?
8. How should classroom control be maintained?

In all instances, the outline summaries, which conclude the discussions of the various educational ideologies, are intended to be indicative rather than definitive.

NOTES

1. See Chapter II, pp. 28–31.
2. See Chapter X.
3. Abraham Kaplan, *The Conduct of Inquiry: Methodology for the Behavioral Sciences* (San Francisco: Chandler Publishing Company, 1964), p. 139.
4. Anthropologist Ruth Benedict is generally conceded to be the originator of the concept of synergism in the social sciences. The following books are a particularly useful introduction to her thought: Ruth Benedict, *An Anthropologist at Work: Writings of Ruth Benedict*, Margaret Mead, comp. (Boston: Houghton Mifflin, 1959); Ruth Benedict, *Patterns of Culture* (New York: New American Library, 1951); and Ruth Benedict, *Race and Racism* (London: G. Routledge and Sons, 1942).
5. Robert Rosenthal and Lenore Jacobson, *Pygmalion in the Classroom* (New York: Harper, Row & Winston, 1968).
6. The comments on the thoughts of Pierre Teilhard de Chardin are based primarily on his book *The Phenomenon of Man* (Introduced by Julian Huxley. Translated by Bernard Wall. New York: Harper, 1959). Teilhard, in his concept of evolution, includes the idea that man passes through a state of spiritual perfection (*Christogenesis*) on his way to Point Omega. I have left this aspect of Teilhard's theory out of the discussion, because it is based upon a particular religious point of view and because the general nature of Teilhard's philosophy can be understood without an explicit discussion of this phase. Those interested in the philosophy of Teilhard de Chardin should particularly see the following books: Pierre Teilhard de Chardin, *Christianity and Evolution*, René Hague, trans. (New York: Harcourt, Brace Jovanovich, 1971); Pierre Teilhard de Chardin, *The Future of Man*, Norman Denny, trans. (New York: Harper and Row, 1964); and J.M. Wildiers, *An Introduction to Teilhard de Chardin*, Hubert Hoskins, trans. (New York: Harper & Row, 1968).

---

*The question of who should be educated and to what degree is considered as an aspect of this topic.

†The question of what special subject matter should be taught is considered as an aspect of this topic (although it is treated as a separate topic in the taxonomy presented in Part Four).

7. Again, the discussion here is based primarily on Teilhard de Chardin's book *The Phenomenon of Man* (Introduction by Julian Huxley), Bernard Wall, trans. (New York: Harper, 1959). The Christogenesis phase of Teilhard's thought is also left out of this summarization.

8. Thomas S. Kuhn, *The Structure of Scientific Revolutions* (Chicago: University of Chicago Press, 1962).

9. Kuhn, *Scientific Revolutions,* 2d ed., Enlarged, 1970, p. 181.

10. Ibid., p. 176

11. Kaplan, *The Conduct of Inquiry,* pp. 126–40.

12. Fritjof Capra, *The Tao of Physics* (Berkeley: Shambhala Publications, 1975).

14. Ibid, pp. 140–41.

14. Heisenberg, *Physics and Philosophy,* p. 81, quoted in Capra, *The Tao of Physics,* p. 140.

15. Capra, *The Tao of Physics,* pp. 67–69.

16. Ibid.

BIBLIOGRAPHY

Political Ideologies

CHRISTENSON, REO M. et al. *Ideologies and Modern Politics.* New York: Dodd, Mead & Company, 1971.

CONNOLLY, WILLIAM E. *Political Science and Ideology.* New York: Atherton Press, 1957.

COX, RICHARD H., ed. *Ideology, Politics, and Political Theory.* Belmont, California: Wadsworth Publishing Co., 1969.

DOLBEARE, KENNETH N., and DOLBEARE, PATRICIA. *American Ideologies: The Competing Beliefs of the 1970's.* Chicago: Markham Publishing Co., 1971.

GOULD, JAMES A., and TRUITT, WILLIS H., eds. *Political Ideologies.* New York: Macmillan Publishing Co., 1973.

SARGENT, LYMAN TOWER. *Contemporary Political Ideologies: A Comparative Analysis.* rev. ed., Homewood, Illinois: Dorsey Press, 1972.

Philosophical Conservatism

THEOLOGICAL CONSERVATISM

AQUINAS, SAINT THOMAS. *Basic Writings of Saint Thomas Aquinas.* Edited by Anton C. Pegis. New York: Random House, 1945.

MAIMONIDES, MOSES. *The Guide for the Perplexed.* Translated by M. Friedlander. New York: Pardes Publishing House, 1946.

PHILOSOPHICAL CONSERVATISM

ARISTOTLE. *The Basic Writings of Aristotle.* Edited by Richard McKeon. New York: Random House, 1941.

DEMOS, RAPHAEL. *The Philosophy of Plato.* New York: Octagon Books, 1966.

PLATO. *The Republic.* Translated by Bernard Bosanquet. Cambridge: Cambridge University Press, 1908.

Reactionary Conservatism

NATIONALISM

JANOWSKY, OSCAR. *Nationalities and National Minorities.* New York: Columbia University Press, 1945.

KOHN, HANS. *The Age of Nationalism: The First Year of Global History.* New York: Harper & Brothers, 1962.

THE RADICAL RIGHT IN AMERICA

BELL, DANIEL. *The Radical Right.* New York: Doubleday & Co., 1963.

BOUSCAREN, ANTHONY. *Guide to Anti-Communist Action.* Chicago: Henry Regnery Co., 1958.

JOHN BIRCH SOCIETY. *The Blue Book of the John Birch Society.* Belmont, Massachusetts: Birch Society, 1961.

MANION, CLARENCE E. *The Key to Peace.* Chicago: The Heritage Foundation, 1951.

FASCISM

GREGOR, JAMES A. *The Ideology of Fascism: The Rationale of Totalitarianism.* New York: Free Press, 1969.

MUSSOLINI, BENITO. *Fascism: Doctrine and Institutions.* New York: Howard Fertig, 1968.

NOLTE, E. *Three Faces of Fascism.* New York: The New American Library, 1969.

NAZIISM

HITLER, ADOLF. *Mein Kampf.* Translated by Ralph Mannheim. Boston: Houghton & Mifflin Co., 1943.

NEUMANN, FRANZ. *Behemoth: The Structure and Practice of National Socialism.* 2d ed. New York: Octagon Books, 1963.

VIERECK, PETER. *Metapolitics: The Roots of the Nazi Mind.* New York: G.P. Putnam's Sons, 1961.

RELIGIOUS FUNDAMENTALISM

ELLWOOD, ROBERT S., JR. *One Way: The Jesus Movement and Its Meaning.* Englewood Cliffs, New Jersey: Prentice-Hall, 1973.

SCHWARTZ, GARY. *Sect Ideologies and Social Status.* Chicago and London: University of Chicago Press, 1970.

SYNAN, VINSON. *The Holiness-Pentecostal Movement.* Grand Rapids, Michigan: W. B. Eerdman's Publishing Co., 1971.

Social Conservatism

SOCIAL CONSERVATISM (RELIGIOUS CONSERVATISM)

CARNELL, J. E. *The Case for Orthodox Theology.* Philadelphia: Westminster Press, 1959.

STEVICK, D. B. *Beyond Fundamentalism.* Richmond, Virginia: John Knox Press, 1964.

SOCIAL CONSERVATISM (SECULAR CONSERVATISM)

BERLE, ADOLF A., JR. *The Twentieth Century Capitalist Revolution.* New York: Harcourt, Brace & Co., 1954.

CHASE, HAROLD W., and DOLAN, PAUL. *The Case for Democratic Capitalism.* New York: Thomas Y. Crowell, 1964.

ROSSITER, CLINTON. *Conservatism in America: The Thankless Persuasion.* 2d. ed., rev. New York: Alfred A. Knopf, 1962.

Political Liberalism

SCHAPIRO, J. SALWYN. *Liberalism: Its Meaning and History.* Princeton, New Jersey: D. Van Nostrand Co., 1958.

VIORST, MILTON. *Liberalism; A Guide to Its Past, Present and Future in American Politics.* New York: Avon Books, 1963.

VOLKOMER, WALTER E., ed. *The Liberal Tradition In American Thought.* New York: Capricorn Books, 1969.

Liberationism

AVINERI, SHLOMO. *The Social and Political Thought of Karl Marx.* Cambridge: Cambridge University Press, 1968.

BETTS, ROBERT. *Ideology of Blackness.* Boston: D. C. Heath & Co., 1969.

Brown v. *The Board of Education.* United States Supreme Court Decision of May 17, 1954.

HARRINGTON, MICHAEL. *Socialism.* New York: Saturday Review Press, 1972.

HAYDEN, TOM. *Rebellion and Repression.* New York: Meridian Books, 1969.

JACOBS, PAUL and LANDAU, SAUL. *The New Radicals: A Report With Documents.* New York: Vintage Books, 1966.

KING, MARTIN LUTHER, JR. *Why We Can't Wait.* New York: Harper & Row, Publishers, 1963.

LEIDEN, CARL, and SCHMIDT, KARL M. *The Politics of Violence.* Englewood Cliffs, New Jersey: Prentice-Hall, 1968.

NORTH, ROBERT C. *Chinese Communism.* New York: McGraw Hill Book Co., 1970.

NYERERE, JULIUS K. *Freedom and Socialism: A Selection from Writings and Speeches 1965 – 1970.* Dar es Salaam: Oxford University Press, 1968.

PETROVIC, G. *Marx in the Mid-Twentieth Century.* Garden City, New York: Doubleday & Co., 1967.

Anarchism

APTER, DAVID E., and JAMES JOLL. *Anarchism Today.* New York: Doubleday & Co., 1972.

HOFFMAN, ROBERT. *Anarchism.* New York: Atherton Press, 1970.

JOLL, JAMES. *Anarchists.* London: Eyre and Spottiswoode, 1964.

WOODCOCK, GEORGE. *Anarchism: A History of Libertarian Ideas and Movements.* Cleveland, Ohio: World Publishing Co., 1962.

PART TWO

THE CONSERVATIVE EDUCATIONAL IDEOLOGIES

Chapter IV

Educational Fundamentalism

THE BASIC PRINCIPLES OF
EDUCATIONAL FUNDAMENTALISM

The ethical position which holds that the good life stems from adhering to intuitive and/or revealed standards of belief and behavior generally subscribes to a line of reasoning that can be summarized in a sequence of five basic points:*

1. There are authoritative answers to all of life's really significant problems.

2. These answers are basically founded on external authority: either in prior religious revelation, supported by faith; or in the common sense, intuitive "folk wisdom" of the average man.

3. These answers are not only authoritative; they are simple and straightforward. They are unambiguous and directly comprehensible to the ordinary person, requiring neither special interpretation nor the intervention of certified experts. They are precisely what they *are*, and they are the *literal* truth.

Philosophical speculation (and most of the humanistic intellectualism with which this has been associated) is not only unnecessary but profoundly dangerous. The intellectual's characteristic posture holds that Truth is problematic. The result of this skepticism is widespread confusion and moral decay. The intellectual tends to misrepresent the basic simplicity of life, subverting self-evident truth by gratuitous reasoning that merely confounds the intuitive and/or revealed certainties, which provide the only effective basis for organized social existence. At basis, however, the truly significant questions concerning the nature and conduct of life are relatively uncomplicated, and the idea that they are

---

*The terms *intuition, revelation, common sense,* and *faith* are used in the following pages without any strict definition, because the terms tend to be inexact and somewhat ambiguous in the writings of the political, religious and educational fundamentalists themselves. In general, however, *intuitive* knowledge is what is known directly and spontaneously, requiring no supportive evidence or proof. *Common sense* knowledge is that which is known precognitively by the average man as a result of "lived" experience (in contrast to theory). Not all *intuitive* knowledge need be represented in *common sense,* and common sense, while generally intuitive, is ordinarily viewed as potentially demonstrable by evidence as well as personal experience. *Revelation* is undeniable knowledge communicated directly by God. *Faith,* in the religious sense of the term, is essentially belief in the authoritative nature of someone else's prior revelation (as well as the necessary consequences of such belief). These ideas are explored more fully in the chapter on educational intellectualism.

obscure is merely moral camouflage to protect those who seek to manipulate others or who attempt to avoid responsibility for their own evasions.

4. The answers provided by intuition/faith are sufficient for anyone who desires to live the good life.

5. To live the good life, however, it is not merely necessary to return to the certainties of folk wisdom or simple and straightforward religion. It is also necessary to purify contemporary society be eliminating the extraneous and distracting elements that keep people from focusing clearly on the basic requirements of life as it could and should be. It is therefore also necessary to restore the older and better ways as a means of reinstituting the kind of world that is more congruent with the demands of traditional belief and behavior. (Indeed, in some cases, a literal adherence to traditional ways of thinking and acting is only possible if the past — or some vision of what the past is thought to have been — can be restored in the present. Traditional precepts are generally difficult to reconcile with contemporary practices.)

The reactionary conservative is perhaps most often a sort of political evangelist who has a fervent conviction that "a small body of true believers can lead a return to the pristine fundamentals that once set this nation on a true course."[1] As Abcarian and Stanage note in their article "Alienation and the Radical Right," for the reactionary conservative

> the nation must be purified and redeemed. It is urgently necessary to expose the hydra-headed conspiracy that infects government, churches, educational institutions, and the mass media of communication. Purification is an urgent patriotic duty. . . . The U.S. is presumed to have attained a Golden or Heroic age, usually, but not invariably, located somewhere in the century preceding "that man" FDR. . . . Domestically, the golden age is sometimes equated with the *status quo*, though more frequently located in the past. Internationally, the golden age is typically regarded as lost by the early twentieth century, owing to seduction into degrading and humiliating foreign entanglements. Despite the obstacles, the golden age can and must be restored by achieving victory over the domestic forces that block the return to authenticity by preaching and practicing compromise, coexistence and cooperation with national enemies.[2]

Fundamentalism holds, then, to an absolutistic and closed system of belief. For the fundamentalist, truth can be known directly on a nonrational (or even, on occasion, antirational)* basis, and it is not conditional upon what is ordinarily viewed as "personal experience." Fundamentalists differ in their value commitments. Some favor a relatively closed-self orientation (like the

---

*The distinction between *nonrational* and *antirational* (or *irrational*), like many other important distinctions in philosophy, is based upon the difference between an *opposite* and a *contrary* in formal logic. Strictly speaking — although the rule is frequently violated — the *opposite* of something is its absence. The *contrary* of something is its antonym. Thus, the opposite of the term *rational* is nonrational; the contrary is irrational. The opposite of the term *white* is nonwhite; its contrary is black. In a similar sense, the opposite of moral is amoral; the contrary is immoral. Not all terms have both opposites and contraries, but most do, and the failure to distinguish between the two is frequently the cause of great confusion in intellectual discourse.

ethnocentric supernationalist) but most favor some expression of a more conventional altruistic ethic, although the boundaries of the larger social-self tend to vary according to the specific fundamentalist orientation being considered.

In most cases where the fundamentalist's value system encompasses a relatively conventional notion of a universalized altruism — as in Christian fundamentalism — there tends to be an implicit conflict between "closed-truth" epistemological ideas (concerning knowing and the known) and "open-self" axiological ideals (concerning the nature and conditions of value). That is, even where value is seen as universalistic — as for example where everyone is viewed as potentially capable of spiritual redemption through religious conversion and proper conduct — only a minority are ordinarily viewed as possessing "true knowledge," and the majority tend to be looked upon as warranting condemnation or as requiring authoritative guidance by those already possessing enlightenment. In the latter case — which is perhaps characteristic of most fundamentalists — authoritative truth (generally encompassing authoritative knowledge of what is good for one and all) ordinarily implies a corresponding commitment to authoritarian political ideals (viewed as a required means of ensuring the *objective* good of everyone). Such political ideals are either imposed upon those who already subscribe to the ideological persuasion or are adopted as a general program for the moral rectification of all. Since fundamentalism is based upon a recognition of authoritative truth — truth that is not, in the first instance, contingent on either reason or evidence — it generally advocates authoritarian approaches to education as well, and such eductional authoritarianism tends to complement and support the more basic authoritarian tendencies that characterize the fundamentalist political and moral stance.

REACTIONARY POLITICAL CONSERVATISM

Reactionary conservatism is an awkward term, but it is perhaps the best available to encompass all of those types of social conservatism which are basically anti-intellectual in the sense that they seek to minimize philosophical (or intellectual) arguments and tend to ground their contentions upon a relatively uncritical acceptance of either revealed Truth or established social consensus (frequently viewed as "common sense"). In his political expression, and as indicated, the reactionary conservative generally advocates a return to the real or imagined virtues of the past.

As in all of the conservative political orientations, there are two basic traditions within the overall point of view represented by the political reactionary, one essentially secular, the other basically religious.

SECULAR REACTIONARY CONSERVATISM

There are basically two "pure-type" traditions within secular reactionary conservatism. (1) One view might be termed *nonphilosophical* (or even *anti-intellectual*) *reactionary conservatism* (most generally associated with the sort of "restorationist" right-wing spokesmen who occur within virtually every modern nation). An individual like Robert Welch, founder of the John Birch Society, might serve as a cardinal example in our own society at the present time. (2) The other could be labelled *philosophical reactionary conservatism* (and is largely associated with the ideas of G.W.F. Hegel and Émile Durkheim, although these philosophers are not themselves representatives of *reactionary conservatism* in the usual sense of the term). Needless to say, this is a purely conceptual distinction, which is only approximated in the real world, and there are a vast number of combinations and permutations of these fundamental types. Indeed, some of the most interesting examples of secular reactionary conservatism occur primarily as hybrid phenomena, such as National Socialism (which, among other things, presents an intellectual, or quasi-intellectual, rationale for a return to intuitive thinking directed by a mystical *Volksgeist*)[3]

The secular reactionary of the more or less anti-intellectual variety is difficult to exemplify, but he is probably best represented in the United States today by the ethnocentric, nativistic, "Know-Nothing" orientation of the chauvinistic superpatriot, with his sentimental and simplified version of American beliefs and attitudes. Such an individual, who might be termed a *"common sense" populist,* constitutes an essentially nonintellectual, or even anti-intellectual, point of view that envisions a return to the intuitive "folk wisdom" of the "common man." Fundamentally opposed to the complex, the exotic, and the foreign, the common sense populist seeks some clear and simple consensus that is assumed to exist on a more or less intuitive and self-evident basis in the depths of the popular mind. Frequently associated with the "civil religion" orientation (discussed below), it often presents itself as a quintessential "Americanism" with a strong ethnocentric bias against virtually any sort of novel or unfamiliar ideas.

It if difficult to cite specific examples of common sense populism for several basic reasons.

First, the common sense populist is a political reactionary, and his ideas therefore tend, as the term *reactionary* suggests, to be a *reaction against* social change more than a coherent attempt to formulate a systematic theoretical alternative to such change. As a result, fundamentalism characteristically expresses itself as a polemical response to specific cultural conditions that are viewed as posing significant threats to accepted traditions. Since such threats inevitably occur in a specific historical context, the issues-oriented pronouncements of the reactionary conservative tend to become quickly dated and often have only transient significance as substantive positions.

Even in those instances where reactionary conservatives have employed intellectual approaches (as, for example, with the French reactionary Maurice Barrès and the German reactionary Alfred Rosenberg in the late nineteenth and early twentieth centuries) they tend to enjoy relatively brief tenure on the intellectual scene. In our own country such once-prominent American reactionaries of this sort, such as Father Charles Coughlin or Westbrook Pegler, tend to be recognized only by members of the older generation.

Second, such a reactionary conservative, as previously indicated, tends to be anti-intellectual. As a consequence, he characteristically rejects intellectual and scholarly approaches in favor of declarations that are largely either hortatory or polemical in nature. In the United States at the present time it is particularly difficult to find intellectual spokesmen within the common sense populist tradition who have made serious attempts to formulate systematic theoretical rationales for their positions.

Third, the ideas of such anti-intellectual reactionary conservatives tend to be intimately related to their own particular social situations as these exist at some particular point in history and are seldom expressed in the more abstract and theoretical terms more characteristic of the other ideological orientations. In most cases, and as already suggested, the anti-intellectual reactionary is a "social restorationist" who seeks a return to the real and/or imagined virtues of the historical past as this pertains to his own particular culture. Since cultural histories obviously differ according to time and place, the actual content of this kind of social restorationism is highly contingent upon where, when, and by whom it is advocated. Thus, in eighteenth century France, social restorationism was characteristically an aristocratic point of view envisioning the return of the monarchy, which was well represented in the writings of such individuals as Joseph de Maistre, François de Châteaubriand and Joseph de Bonald. In contemporary Austria, it still frequently takes the form of agitation for the return of the Hapsburgs. In our own relatively young country, it more typically expresses itself as either a nostalgic yearning for a return to the frontier (with the corresponding pioneer virtues, such as thrift, competition and hard work, associated with the old West during the late 1800s) or as an attempt to reinstitute the simpler (and ostensibly better) ways of small-town midwestern America around the turn of the century.

Fourth, and finally, there often tends to be a significant relationship between religious and secular fundamentalism. Since religion and other aspects of culture are closely interwoven, there are very few religious reactionaries who might not also be used as examples of political reaction and vice versa. The Christian Anti-Communism Crusade as it existed during the fifties and early sixties, as well as such prominent contemporaries as Robert Welch with his John Birch Society, the right-wing Reverend Carl McIntire, and the more recently established Christian Voice and Moral Majority movements, testify to the close affinity between the religious and political expressions of the "reactionary right" in our own country. Even among the ostensibly "secular" reactionaries there is frequently a quasi-religious devotion to the State which has occasionally led to its being characterized as a sort of nondenominational and largely secularized "civil religion."

Fundamentalism and Civil Religion

"Every functioning society," states Robin Williams in his *American Society: A Sociological Interpretation,* "has, to an important degree, a common religion. The possession of a common set of ideas . . . rituals, and symbols tends to play an overarching sense of unity even in a society otherwise riddled with conflict."[4] The term *civil religion,* as it is ordinarily used, refers precisely to such a unitive common religion. Originally coined by Rousseau in *The Social Contract* in 1762, the term was revived by sociologist Robert Bellah in his well-known article entitled "Civil Religion," which first appeared in the late sixties.[5] According to Bellah, "There actually exists alongside of and rather clearly differentiated from the churches an elaborate and well-institutionalized civil religion in America,"[6] which can generally be characterized in three ways.

First, it is a *general* religion — which is sometimes labeled "the American way of life," the common faith, the fourth major faith or American Shinto — in contrast to the far more particular religions usually identified with specific churches, synagogues, revivals, missions, and such.

Second, it has its own set of sacred symbols (like the Declaration of Independence or the flag), rituals (like the Pledge of Allegiance), shrines (like the Tomb of the Unknown Soldier or the Alamo), beliefs (like the "official" version of American history), individuals (like George Washington and Abraham Lincoln), and events (like Memorial Day or the Fourth of July). In general, these exist quite apart from the various denominations of formal religion. In addition, and as Bellah states, "The public-school system serves as a particularly important context for the cultic celebration of [these] civil rituals."[7]

Third, and finally, this civil religion generally functions as a "religiofication" of the nation, providing "a transcendent goal for the political process."[8]

Actually, the whole notion of civil religion is highly controversial, and, as Russell Richey and Donald Jones indicate in the Introduction to their book *American Civil Religion,* there are at least five basic concepts of civil religion which are closely connected and often overlapping.[9]

1. Civil religion as *folk religion* tends to be concerned with "the common religion of Americans descriptively as emerging out of the life of the folk."[10] In this approach to civil religion, and as Will Herberg states, ". . . national life is apotheosized, national values are religionized, national heroes are divinized, national history is experienced as a *Heilsgeschichte,* as a redemptive history."[11]

It is important to distinguish between this concept of *folk religion,* which is essentially a homogeneous and unitive phenomenon, and what might, from want of a better term, be called *ethnic religion.* Ethnic religion tends to be socially conservative, but it typically combines allegiance to a *particular* religious tradition with a commitment to the social traditions of a special subculture or ethnic group that exists within the confines of the overall culture. The ethnic religious orientation, then, becomes essentially the fusion of religion with ethnicity (both commonly rooted in a separate language) in which the religious tradition is used to maintain both cultural and religious *separateness* from the majority society in the face of strong pressures for assimilation and change. The ethnic religion orientation may be viewed as politically or religiously reactionary with respect to the dominant traditions of the majority culture, but this is not always the case. Its primary function is to protect the identity of a particular subculture from assimilation into the mainstream society.

2. Civil religion as *religious nationalism* is essentially the religion of patriotism, where the nation becomes the object of worship (as in the so-called German Christianity under the Third Reich).[12]

3. Civil religion as *Protestant civic piety* represents the fusion of Protestantism and nationalism in which, to quote Will Herberg, there is a compound of

"the two great religious movements that molded America — the Puritan way, secularized; and the Revivalist way, secularized."[13]

4. Civil religion as the *transcendent universal religion of the nation* is primarily what theologian Sidney Mead looks upon as the essentially cosmopolitan and prophetic "religion of the Republic."[14] As Mead notes, ". . . under religious freedom, because no denomination could plausibly claim to be or to function as 'the church' in the new nation, 'the nation came more and more so to function.'"[15]

5. Civil religion as *democratic faith* seems to occur where there is a commitment to "humane values and ideals of equality, freedom, and justice without necessary dependence on a transcendent deity or a spiritualized nation,"[16] as in the case of John Dewey's "common faith."

Martin Marty on Bellah.   Theologian Martin Marty, in a particularly trenchant analysis of Bellah's concept of civil religion, distinguishes between four basic types of civil religion, which emerge out of two fundamental distinctions that were not explicit in Bellah's original theory. One distinction is that between *priestly* and *prophetic* religious styles. The *priestly* civil religion is essentially "celebrative, affirmative, culture-building."[17] The *prophetic,* on the other hand, tends to be dialectical and judgmental. The two are, as Marty suggests, similar to Joseph Pulitzer's definition of the complete journalist: "one comforts the afflicted; the other afflicts the comfortable."[18]

Traditions within civil religion also differ in kind, however. Here Marty notes a second fundamental distinction between the type of civil religion (1) that sees the nation "under God," assuming "there is a transcendent objective reference of a kind which has traditionally been associated with deity,"[19] and (2) in which the nation displaces God; the nation itself assuming self-transcendence.[20] For Marty, then, by using the logical combination of these basic differences, there are four basic expressions of civil religion: (1) the priestly nation-under-God approach (exemplified by Eisenhower); (2) the prophetic nation-under God approach (exemplified by Lincoln); (3) the priestly nation-as-transcendent orientation (exemplified by Nixon); and (4) the prophetic nation-as-transcendent orientation (exemplified by a theologian like Sidney Mead).[21] The four basic traditions are presented schematically in Figure 4–1.

However valid these distinctions may be, all expressions of civil religion are not necessarily expressions of either political or educational fundamentalism. Indeed, the traditions that Richey and Jones term *transcendent universal religion of the nation* and *democratic faith* are far more likely to be allied with other political orientations (perhaps most frequently with social conservatism or even, on occasion, liberalism than with the radical right). Within the *nation-as transcendent* orientation, however, those types of civil religion that Richey and Jones term *folk religion, religious nationalism* and *Protestant civic piety* (either in combination or in relatively "pure-type") *do* frequently express themselves as fundamentalist points of view with respect to society in general and education in particular. And, in Marty's typology, the prophetic nation-as-transcendent mode of civil religion would seem to lend itself particularly well to political and educational fundamentalism.

FIGURE 4–1
CIVIL RELIGION

Nation-Under-God

Nationalistic Religion
  Edgar Bundy
  Billy James Hargis
  Carl McIntire
  Verne P. Kaub
  Moral Majority (Jerry Falwell)
  Christian Voice

Protestant Civic Piety
  Many Nondenominational
  Evangelical Christian
  Movements
    Campus Crusade for Christ
    Teen Challenge
    Intervarsity Christian Fellowship

Prophetic Mode ————————————————————————————— Priestly Mode

Religious Nationalism
  Robert Welch
  Dan Smoot
  Clarence Manion

Teleological Totalitarianism
  Fascism
  Naziism

Teleological Nationalists
  G.W.F. Hegel
  Emile Durkheim

Nation-as-Transcendent

SECULAR FUNDAMENTALISM IN AMERICA

In our own country the contemporary "radical-right" or "right-wing extremism" rose to prominence during the 1960s, largely in response to the development of the John Birch Society. Abcarian and Stanage indicate that the radical right encompasses any

> political grouping or ideological coalition occupying the political terrain between (but not including) Midwestern Republicanism and American Fascism, populated by organizations such as: The American Coalition of Patriotic Societies; The American Security Council; Americans for Constitutional Action; America's Future, Inc.; The Cardinal Mindszenty Foundation; The Christian Anti-Communist Crusade; The Christian Crusade; the Circuit Riders; The Christian Nationalist Crusade; The Church League of America; The Conservative Society of America; The Conservative Union; The Council of Christian Churches; Defenders of the American Constitution; Facts Forum, Inc.; For America; Freedom and Action; Human Events, Inc.; The John Birch Society; Liberty Lobby; Life

Lines, Inc.; The Manion Forum; The Minutemen; The National Education Program; National Indignation Convention; Veritas Foundation; We, The People!; Young Americans for Freedom, to name but a representative and prominent few.[22]

The ideology of the radical right, as Gould and Truitt identify it in their book *Political Ideologies*

consists of a strong belief in individualism along with a strong revulsion toward any form of collectivism; a belief in a Republican as opposed to a Democratic form of government; a fundamentalist interpretation of the Bible; a belief that world events and American politics as they presently exist are wholly conspiratorial, hence the consequent need to purify American society; the need to restore the United States to the golden age of its founding fathers; a belief that there are always solutions to both national and domestic problems; and a strong ultra-patriotism and belief in "direct action" in order to break the net of conspiracy and establish the "right" system. The radical right is different from the moderate right in that the latter includes most of the large corporation world, which has come to accept changes in American society during the past three decades, including trade unions, medical care, and other social reforms which the radical right sees as threats to the American system.[23]

The right-wing position in American politics today is well expressed by Ezra Taft Benson, who was the Secretary of Agriculture in Eisenhower's cabinet from 1953 to 1961. As he states:

What are these fundamental principles which have allowed the United States to progress so rapidly and yet remain free?

First, a written Constitution clearly defining the limits of government so that government will not become more powerful than the people.

Second, an economic system which is characterized by: Free enterprise — the right to venture, the right to choose; Private property — the right to own, develop and enjoy, and a Market economy — the right to exchange and to profit.

Third, building an open society where each individual enjoys the greatest opportunity to improve himself, to travel, to become educated, to invent, to compete, to build, to speak, to worship, and to pursue happiness in whatever way the individual finds most satisfying and worthwhile.

Fourth, assigning government the role of referee rather than competitor — giving it enough power to provide peace, order, and security but not enough power to rob people of their liberty or take away their property without due process of law.

*   *   *

My own political and economic creed is a simple one. I commend it to you:

I am for freedom and against slavery.

I am for social progress and against socialism.

I am for a dynamic economy and against waste.

I am for the private competitive market and against unnecessary government intervention.

I am for private ownership and against governmental ownership and control of the means of production and distribution.

I am for national security and against appeasement and capitulation to an obvious enemy.[24]

Philosophical Reactionary Conservatism

The *philosophical* tradition in reactionary conservatism has been primarily influenced by the antirationalist movement as it has developed since the latter part of the eighteenth century. It has probably been most significantly influenced by two figures who, ironically, were not themselves reactionary conservatives: the German philosopher G.W.F. Hegel and the French sociologist Émile Durkheim.

G.W.F. Hegel. Georg Wilhelm Friedrich Hegel (1770–1831) developed a "relationalistic" metaphysics, which views reality as a total and unified whole in process of teleological self-perfection. There is, as Hegel sees it, a *Weltgeist* (a sort of absolute cosmic-mind) which includes everything as an aspect of itself. This Weltgeist is both immanent within and, at the same time, transcendent over everything which is. It encompasses everything that is, including both *objective mind* (including the physical and social world) and the *subjective mind* of personal consciousness. The Weltgeist operates in and through universal reason, which expresses itself as history. History, in turn, evolves through a conflict (dialectic) between universal ideas, which are embodied in particular conditions and which occur in response to changes in such conditions.

The *subjective mind* of the individual is capable of comprehending both *objective mind* (that is, the physical and social worlds that represent the present status of the absolute mind) and the *absolute mind* itself, that is, the *ideal* logical contraries and/or opposites implied by the *real* conditions that presently exist. The conflict experienced between that which actually *is* and that which can or should *be* generates the conscious desire to change. The change that occurs as a result of this conflict between the real and the ideal alters both objective conditions and consequent subjective experience as well (as both of these are directed and controlled by the *total* process that is absolute mind).

For Hegel, then, "the truth is the whole."[25] The Weltgeist is the whole that is greater than the sum of its parts. The divine Idea (of a total reconciliation of all dialectical differences) is actualized through the process of evolution. Subjective mind (individual consciousness) and objective mind (the world of everyday objects and events) interact to produce absolute mind (Weltgeist).

Reason, acting in and through history, *is* universal will (Weltgeist). Since reason acts through conflict, conflict ensures progress. In the absence of a supra-State (such as Kant's idea of a world federation of states), war is the ultimate arbiter of what is right. World history is ultimately the only court of justice.

The objective mind of society is ideally reflected within the State. The State acts like a magnified person to implement universal reason, and "this Reason, in its most concrete form is God. God governs the world."[26] Therefore "whatever is, is right."[27] The predominant nation represents the dominant phase of universal reason — the highest Idea — and "...we must worship the State as the manifestation of the divine on earth."[28]

Émile Durkheim.   The French philosopher and sociologist Émile Durkheim was greatly influenced by Hegelian idealism (particularly as this was reflected in the earlier writings of Auguste Comte), and Durkheim's philosophy is perhaps best viewed as a type of sociological Hegelianism in the naturalistic tradition.

For Durkheim, as for Comte, "sociology is not a corollary of psychology,"[29] because "psychological" phenomena are always the result rather than the cause of social interactions. For Durkheim, the human mind is a reflection of the social world and its characteristics, and, as Sorokin notes, ". . . it is as wrong to try to explain social phenomena through the psychological as it is wrong to explain the cause through its effect."[30]

In addition, Durkheim posits the existence of a "collective consciousness"[31] that differs quite specifically from individual consciousness. Thus, for Durkheim, there has been an evolution from *mechanical society* (which was essentially an aggregate of individuals) to an organic society, characterized by a collective consciousness consisting of social structures and processes that determine individual awareness. Once the organic level has been reached — through "social condensation" and increased social cohesiveness — the "collective consciousness" assumes an independent status as a separate and controlling "group mind." The collective consciousness is, however

> ...something more than a mere epiphenomenon of its morphological basis. . . . In order that the [collective consciousness] may appear, a synthesis *sui generis* of particular consciousness is required. Now this synthesis has the effect of disengaging a whole world of sentiments, ideas and images which, once born, obey laws all their own. They attract each other, repel each other, unite, divide themselves, and multiply, though these combinations are not commended and necessitated by the condition of the underlying reality. The life thus brought into being even enjoys so great an independence that it sometimes indulges in manifestations with no purpose or utility of any sort, for the mere pleasure of affirming itself.... this is often precisely the case with ritual activity and mythological thought.[32]

For Durkheim, then, the collective consciousness, once established, is no longer the product of collective individual behaviors. Rather, it is individual behaviors that largely "reincarnate"[33] group consciousness. In a similar sense, material behavior (such as economic activity) is also epiphenomenal, representing primarily the predispositions of the collective consciousness, and not merely the demands of external conditions.

Once established, the collective consciousness includes both "conscious awareness" (including ways of thinking) and "conscience" — subjectively experienced moral ideas and ideals.[34] The collective representations of the group mind include certain basic structures that represent universal principles of collective psychological processes.[35]

As Durkheim sees it, then, the collective consciousness functions autonomously of individual consciousness, and it has the power to act upon and to modify itself, obeying its own laws. Collective consciousness leads to the idealization of group belief and behavior. It crystallizes a tacit way of life into explicit and communicable ideas.

Each culture has a collective consciousness—a national spirit—which exists more or less independent of historical changes and which constitutes its highest identity and supreme value. The value of an act or idea is ultimately determined by whether it contributes to "social solidarity" as determined in terms of these archetypal "collective representations."

The collective consciousness gives rise to virtually all significant social institutions. Religion arises when a people become aware of the power and significance of their own collective consciousness, and religion is the most concentrated expression of group mind, indirectly giving rise to most other social institutions as well. Accordingly, God is merely the externalized idea, or apotheosis, of the collective consciousness.[36]

In summary, Durkheim's theory of collective consciousness can be outlined as in Figure 4–2.

FIGURE 4–2
DURKHEIM'S CONCEPT OF SOCIAL REALITY

Each society (as a *mechanical* collection of individual consciousnesses)

$\downarrow$

evolves, by mean of *social condensation,* toward an

$\downarrow$

organic society (based upon contributions of behavior to the *social solidarity* of the group),

$\downarrow$

giving rise to *collective consciousness* (which centers around "elementary structures" within the group mind and which is unique to each people as a people).

$\downarrow$

Continued on next page

Continued from previous page

This collective consciousness becomes autonomous of individual consciousness (in effect, obeying its own laws), and tends to express itself in two basic ways:

The collective consciousness is apotheosized as God and gives rise to religion

The collective consciousness "reincarnates" its archetypal collective representations directly within individual consciousness so that

which is the most concentrated expression of the collective consciousness, giving rise (indirectly) to most significant social institutions

individual experiences are channelled and shaped by the collective consciousness to produce collective ideas, which serve to harmonize individual and social behavior (leading to enhanced communication and greater social solidarity)*

which channel and control behavior (even giving rise to "nonpractical" types of behavior caused by the expressive needs of the collective consciousness as such — for example, rituals, myths, etc.) —

all of which becomes self-sustaining, self-perfecting, more intense, more complex, etc. — in a synergistic cycle of reciprocal confirmation.

---

*Not all behavior is collective consciousness; some is ordinary empirical experience elicited by practical behavior, but even this occurs within the parameters established by the overriding collective consciousness.

Quasi-Mystical Nationalism

In the tradition of reactionary political conservatism, the philosophies of Hegel and Durkheim are perhaps best represented in a position that might be termed *quasi-mystical nationalism*. The quasi-mystical nationalists are perhaps most visible in the philosophies of fascism and naziism, both of which seek the voluntary subordination of individual reason to the superordinate will of the entire people, as this is expressed through the instrumentality of a totalitarian state.

Fascism and National Socialism

The social theories of fascism and national socialism were so significantly influenced by the philosophy of Hegel that both have occasionally been characterized as extreme expressions of the "Hegelian Right," or even as "Hegelian Totalitarianism." Certainly, Italian fascism owes a special debt to the neo-Hegelian philosophers Benedetto Croce (1866–1952) and Giovanni Gentile (1874–1944), the latter even serving for several years as Minister of Education under Mussolini. In a similar sense, both seem indebted, however indirectly, to many of Durkheim's ideas as well.

On the other hand, both fascism and national socialism are indebted to a variety of other philosophical sources as well. There is, for example, a strong dose of social Darwinism (see Chapter VI) in both positions, and both Mussolini and Hitler were clearly inspired by various social theories that glorify war as a means toward national and/or racial purification. The national socialists were also influenced by a variety of racist and selectionist theories–perhaps most significantly by those associated with such names as Arthur de Gobineau, Houston Stewart Chamberlain, Victor de Lapouge and Otto Ammon.

Clearly, all reactionary conservatism is not fascistic, but fascism (and naziism) nevertheless represent perhaps the most developed *intellectual* expression of what are probably the four most basic characteristics of all radical right-wing ideological movements: irrationalism (or nonrationalism), nationalism (with its corresponding patriotic attitudes), social Darwinism, and a predisposition toward totalitarian government.

Irrationalism. As previously indicated, the reactionary conservative has a strong penchant for avoiding intellectual approaches to knowing. For the reactionary, truth is beyond proof. The State is often viewed as a spiritual unit infused with its own collective consciousness. This is clearly indicated in Italian fascist ideology where the State is viewed as the physical embodiment of the spirit of the nation.[37] "The State is absolute," states Mussolini, "individuals and groups relative."[38] Accordingly, for Mussolini, and as Sargent states, it stands to reason that ". . . the state is the carrier of the culture and spirit of the people or nation; that it is the past, present, and future; that it represents the 'immanent conscience of the nation'; and that it educates the citizens in all the virtues."[39] Thus, as Mario Palmieri indicates:

[Fascism] presupposes ... that the nation state is gifted with an organic life of its own, which far transcends in meaning the life of the individual, and whose development, growth and progress, follow laws which man cannot ignore or modify, but only discover and obey.[40]

Nationalism.   Hans Kohn, who is perhaps the best known scholar on nationalism, defines it as

> . . . a state of mind, permeating the large majority of a people and claiming to permeate all of its members; it recognizes the nation-state as the ideal form of political organization and the nationality as the source of all creative cultural energy and of economic well-being. The supreme loyalty of man is therefore due to his nationality, as his own life is supposedly rooted in and made possible by its welfare.[41]

In line with Kohn's comments, the nationalist is, by definition, patriotic in the sense that Leonard Doob defines this term in his book *Patriotism and Nationalism: Their Psychological Foundations.* "Patriotism," states Doob, is ". . . the more or less conscious conviction of a person that his own welfare and that of the significant groups to which he belongs are dependent upon the preservation or expansion (or both) of the power and culture of his society."[42]

Both of these attitudes are characteristic of the reactionary conservative, and they reach perhaps their supreme expression in the formulated philosophy of fascism. Fascism, states A. James Gregor in his book *The Ideology of Fascism: The Rationale of Totalitarianism,* was "the first revolutionary mass movement regime which aspired to commit the totality of human and natural resources of an historic community to national development."[43] As "a 'calling forth' of the tight-knit, racially and culturally homogeneous preindustrial community, relying on such concepts as common traditions, nationalistic feelings, and racial solidarity," fascism signifies, as Gould and Truitt indicate

> . . . the very reverse of liberal ideological values: constitutional and representative government gives way to dictatorship, minority rights give way to persecution of minorities, the party system gives way to one-party domination, freedom of speech gives way to oppressive censorship, religious toleration is suspended, and throughout this broad transformation capitalist control of the means of production is retained.[44]

According to fascist doctrine, the State or Nation is central, a mystical entity replete with an historical mission. As Mussolini sets forth in his essay "The Doctrine of Fascism," the State is truly *organic,* and it is the duty of the individual to raise himself to the national consciousness and to lose his own identity in it. In this way, the individual exists only in and through the nation-state: "Social groups as fractions of the species receive thereby a life and scope which transcends the scope and life of the individuals identifying themselves with the history and finalities of uninterrupted series of generations."[45]

National socialism differs from fascism primarily in emphasis rather than in kind. Both see man as merely one part of the larger unit of the State or Nation, and both look upon individual identity as far deeper than conscious reason, being rooted in such things as political identification, soil, race or blood. For the Fascist, the organic unity of the State is based upon national and ethnic considerations; the State is primarily the geographical entity inhabited by people who share a common history and culture. For naziism, however, geographical and historical considerations are secondary to race. The *nation* is viewed as primarily a racial stock of peoples sharing the same underlying human nature.

In this sense, naziism functions as a sort of racial fascism. Thus, as Gould and Truitt state:

> Mussolini maintained that the state created the nation; Hitler argued that the state was an instrument of the nation or the people. Racism played a greater role in Naziism than in Italian Fascism, and this emphasis by the Nazis was partly responsible for the unmatched persecution of the Jews and other minorities.[46]

This difference in regard to the fundamental political unit can be clearly seen in the writings of Mussolini and Hitler. For Mussolini the state is fundamentally a geographical and historical entity:

> Fascism is a religious conception in which man is seen in his immanent relationship with a superior law and with an objective will that transcends the particular individual and raises him to conscious membership in a spiritual society. Whoever has seen in the religious politics of the Fascist regime nothing but mere opportunism has not understood that Fascism besides being a system of government is also, and above all, a system of thought.[47]

> The man of fascism is an individual who is nation and fatherland, which is a moral law, binding together individuals and the generations into a tradition and a mission, suppressing the instinct for a life enclosed within a brief round of pleasure in order to restore within duty a higher life, free from the limits of time and space: a life in which the individual, through the denial of himself, through the sacrifice of his own private interests, through death itself, realizes that completely spiritual existence in which his value as a man lies.[48]

In naziism, on the other hand, the emphasis is on the race as the basis of both nation and state. As Hitler states in *Mein Kampf:*

> The state is a means to an end. Its end lies in the preservation and advancement of a community of physically and psychically homogeneous creatures. This preservation itself comprises first of all existence as a race and thereby permits the free development of all the forces dormant in this race. Of them a part will always primarily serve the preservation of physical life, and only the remaining part the promotion of a further spiritual development. Actually the one always creates the precondition for the other.[49]

Since the fascist State is an organic unit, it stands to reason that, while private property should remain, it should be coordinated and directed by the State. Indeed all property, and the relationships between all owners, managers and workers should come under the unified control of the State.[50] This doctrine of the organic State is clearly reflected in fascist educational theory. Giovanni Gentile, a philosopher who became Minister of Education under Mussolini, was heavily influenced by pragmatism but he nevertheless maintained that individual liberty could only be realized through the State. The same theme of the organic or corporate State recurs in national socialism with Hitler's concept of the *folkish* state. ''The highest purpose of a *folkish* state,'' states Hitler in *Mein Kampf*

. . . is concern for the preservation of those original racial elements which bestow culture and create the beauty and dignity of a higher mankind. We, as Aryans, can conceive of the state only as the living organism of a nationality which not only assures the preservation of this nationality, but by the development of its spiritual and ideal abilities leads to the highest freedom.[51]

Accordingly, in Germany, too, widespread educational reforms were instituted. "The State," directed Hitler, "must undertake a thorough reconstruction of our national system of education. . . . The curricula of all educational establishments must be brought into line with the necessities of practical life. With the first dawn of intelligence, the schools must aim at teaching the pupil to know what the State stands for (instruction and citizenship)."[52]

The kinds of reforms that Hitler referred to are well illustrated in the sorts of directives that were issued to all German schools. The *Times* of London describes one of these as follows:

Teachers are directed to instruct their pupils in "the nature, causes, and effects of all racial and hereditary problems," to bring home to them the importance of race and heredity for the life and destiny of the German people, and to awaken in them a sense of their responsibility toward "the community of the nation" (their ancestors, the present generation, and posterity), pride in their membership of the German race as a foremost vehicle of hereditary Nordic values, and the will consciously to cooperate in the racial purification of the German stock. Racial instruction is to begin with the youngest pupils (six years of age) in accordance with the desire of the Fuhrer "that no boy or girl should leave school without complete knowledge of the necessity and meaning of blood purity."[53]

Social Darwinism. Both fascism and its racial variation of naziism adhere to the belief that history must be viewed primarily in terms of conflict between nations and between peoples. The survival of the fittest is true not only within the species but also between nations and races. It is simply in the nature of things that inferior races should be either dominated or, in the case of naziism, eliminated. A dominant people, supported by God, is destined to come forward. "Only force rules," states Hitler. "Force is the first law."[54]

It is evident that the stronger has the right before God and the world to enforce his will. History shows that the right as such does not mean a thing, unless it is backed up by great power. If one does not have the power to enforce his right, that right alone will profit him absolutely nothing. The stronger have always been victorious. The whole of nature is a continuous struggle between strength and weakness, an eternal victory of the strong over the weak. All nature would be full of decay if it were otherwise. The states which do not wish to recognize this law will decay.[55]

---

*The use of the term *social Darwinism,* which is frequently equated with the thought of Herbert Spencer, is not meant to suggest that Spencer himself was a social or political reactionary. As is discussed in the chapter on Educational Conservatism, Spencer was essentially a social conservative but one who saw the evolution of society as ultimately terminating in a fundamentally conflict-free society where the "survival of the fittest" would have been banished by the triumph of human reason.

The first fundamental of any rational *Weltanschauung* is the fact that on earth and in the universe force alone is decisive. Whatever goal man has reached is due to his originality plus his brutality. Whatever man possesses today in the field of culture is the culture of the Aryan race. The Aryan has stamped his character on the whole world. The basis for all development is the creative urge of the individual, not the vote of majorities. The genius of the individual is decisive, not the spirit of the masses. All life is bound up in three theses: Struggle is the father of all things, virtue lies in blood, leadership is primary and decisive.[56]

The value of man is determined in the first place by his inner racial virtue; second, by the ability of the race to bring forth men who in turn become leaders in the struggle for advancement; third, this entire process takes place in the form of eternal struggle. As a consequence struggle is the father of all things in this world.[57]

The borderline between man and the animal is established by man himself. The position which man enjoys today is his own accomplishment. We see before us the Aryan race which is manifestly the bearer of all cultures, the true representative of all humanity. All inventions in the field of transportation must be credited to the members of a particular race. Our entire industrial science is without exception the work of the Nordics. All great composers from Beethoven to Richard Wagner are Aryans, even though they were born in Italy or France. Do not say that art is international. The tango, the shimmy, and the jazzband are international but they are not art. Man knows everything that is of any importance to the principle of struggle and the one race which carries itself forward successfully. Take away the Nordic Germans and nothing remains but the dance of apes. . . . Because we recognize the fact that our people can endure only through struggle, we National Socialists are fighters.[58]

Totalitarianism.   Reactionary conservatism tends to favor a centralized system of government characterized by absolute state control over virtually all significant forms of individual behavior. For the radical right, and as Abcarian and Stanage state: "In a 'true republic,' the will of the masses will be represented, but only through the consciences of representatives whose task it is to evaluate and interpret the intent of such will. Only . . . government for the people by a qualified elite can save us from the ravages of immoral mob rule...."[59] In fascism, for example, the individual finds his highest individual self-expression in dedicating himself to the highest interests of the State. Ironically, the highest individual freedom is to be found in the destiny of the race or nation and requires the voluntary subordination of the self to the political dictates of the State, which embodies the collective will of the people. Since the State is ultimately a "spiritual" unit, it justifiably commands the loyalty of all citizens. Accordingly, those who control the State, at all levels, are really expressing the best interests of the nation and of each individual citizen, and they should, accordingly, command both the respect and obedience of all. Thus, in Nazi Germany, and as national socialist theoretician Rudolf Huber states, the Fuhrer represents the collective will of the people. He is almost infallible, because, as long as he correctly interprets the nation he represents, "his will is not the subjective, individual will of a single man, but the collective national will...."[60] Accordingly, the leadership (Fuhrer) principle states "that each subordinate holds absolute obedience to his immediate superior, with everyone ultimately subordinate to the absolute leader, the *Fuhrer.*"[61]

> The Fuhrer Reich of the [German] people is founded on the recognition that the true world of the people cannot be disclosed through parliamentary votes and publicized plebiscites but that the will of the people in its pure and uncorrupted form can only be expressed through the Fuhrer. Thus a distinction must be drawn between the supposed will of the people in a parliamentary democracy, which merely reflects the conflict of the various social interests, and the true will of the people in the Fuhrer-state, in which the collective will of the real political unit is manifested. . . .
>
> The Fuhrer is the bearer of the people's will; he is independent of all groups, associations, and interests, but he is bound by laws which are inherent in the nature of his people. In this twofold condition: independence of all factional interests but unconditional dependence of the people, is reflected the true nature of the Fuhrer principle.

*　　*　　*

> The Fuhrer principle rests upon unlimited authority but not upon mere outward force. It has often been said, but it must constantly be repeated, that the Fuhrer principle has nothing in common with arbitrary bureaucracy and represents no system of brutal force, but that it can only be maintained by mutual loyalty which must find its expression in a free relation.[62]

RELIGIOUS REACTIONARY CONSERVATISM

The religious reactionary is perhaps most often represented by various of the Bible-centered, fundamentalist Protestant denominations that take a literalistic view of the Scriptures. It is also the position that is most congenial to such significant offshoots from the basic Christian tradition as the Latter-Day Saints (Mormons), Seventh-Day Adventists, and the Jehovah's Witnesses. For such groups, truth is primarily founded upon revelation and faith, centering in a literalistic interpretation of accepted Scriptures. Accordingly, they advocate a return to biblical truth, black-and-white moral categories and the sort of simple Christian living that is generally looked upon as more characteristic of an earlier era. They are typically other-worldly in their overall orientation, and vehemently oppose any sort of theological speculation that would suggest that essential truth has not already been satisfactorily determined.

The Varieties of Christian Belief: Some Terminological Distinctions

Christianity and the Varieties of Protestantism. The terms *Christianity* and *Protestantism* are scarcely synonymous, but their usage in various contexts is frequently very confusing. Many independent Christian churches of the evangelical and/or pentecostal persuasions do not consider themselves to be *Protestant* in the sense that they necessarily trace their origins back to theological distinctions that emerged during the Reformation. In a similar sense, many organized denominations that have emerged during approximately the last century (such as the Church of Christ, the Church of God, and the Church of Christ, Scientist) also tend to view themselves as constituting essentially *Christian* movements and not merely variations of established *Protestant* traditions. Most of the more distinctive Christian sects, or special traditions, that have emerged in the last two centuries (Latter-Day Saints, Jehovah's Witnesses, Seventh-Day Adventists, and Christian Scientists) also tend to represent themselves more properly as special expressions of the Christian tradition (albeit stemming largely from the Protestant orientations) than of Protestantism viewed as a distinctive scriptural or experiential orientation.

In a similar sense, the term *Protestantism* covers a wide range of different points of view. As Williams states in his book *What Americans Believe and How They Worship:*

> Trying to describe Protestantism is like trying to describe the United States; one can say almost anything about it—and almost anything one says can be shown to be false in some particular. Protestants range in belief all the way from the supernaturalism of the right-wing Lutherans to the agnosticism of the left-wing Unitarians. Protestants range in worship forms all the way from the complexity of the high-church Episcopalians to the simplicity of the silent-meetings Quakers. Protestants range in emotionalism all the way from the restraint of the Congregationalists to the exuberance of the Pentecostals.
>
> Probably there are close to three hundred non-Roman denominations in the United States. However, many of these groups are by no means representative of the main line of Protestant thought and tradition. Some are churches which are Roman Catholic in all important respects except acceptance of the authority of the Pope; for example, the Polish National Catholic which has a quarter of a million members, and the Old Roman Catholic which has eighty thousand. Then there are such nontraditional groups as the Spiritualists, the Bahaists, Jehovah's Witnesses, and the followers of Father Divine.[63]

Classical Protestantism finds its historical locus in the Protestant Reformation. As Robert McAfee Brown indicates, there is no "party line" in the classical Protestant tradition, but, generally speaking,

> ...a "classical protestant" is one who aligns himself with the point of view that what happened at the Reformation was fundamentally right— that is, that the essentials of the faith were rediscovered and made normative once again in the life of the church. This does not mean that he flails himself until he has had an "experience" identical with the anguish of Martin Luther, or that he checks every statement he makes against Calvin's *Institutes*. It *does* mean that through Luther or Calvin he may find himself once more inescapably confronted by the gospel and thereby quickened, renewed, and made whole once again. The classical protestant thus has tremendous respect for heritage and tradition, not as ends in themselves, but as indications that there is an on-goingness about God's activity in the world, and that men may understand that on-goingness more fully as they are related to the ways in which other men have understood it

in the past. Protestants today are not committed to the Reformers' formulas and statements as final truth, but they do find that those things to which the Reformers' formulas and statements point coincide with something which they have found true for themselves.[64]

The classical protestant takes his stand somewhere close...to the Bible. He can no longer . . . go to proof texts, or assume the verbal inerrancy and historical accuracy of every single statement in the record. He must thus, in a sense, not point to the Bible, as such, as his authority, but rather to that to which the Bible itself points, namely, the "mighty acts of God" which are transmitted to each age through the Bible.[65]

Fundamentalism errs in assuming that God gives *information* about himself. The classical protestant counters by asserting that God gives *himself,* and that this is precisely what the Bible is trying to tell us. The point of the Bible is not that we may believe in the Bible, but that we may believe in the God to whom the Bible witnesses.

Perhaps an analogy can clarify this important distinction. Imagine that you are standing in front of a brick wall. You can see beyond it only if there is a window in it. But do you look *at* the window? If you do, you may see the details of the sash very clearly, perhaps a few thumbprints on the panes themselves, but as long as you look just *at* the window, the scene beyond will be blurred and fuzzy. No, you must look *through* the window, at what is going on outside. If you focus on the activity beyond, an occasional thumbprint on the pane isn't going to blur your vision too drastically. So with the Bible. To look *at* it, at the statements, is to fail to perceive God's activity with clarity. But to look *through* it is to make use of it as a "window" by means of which we can see God at work, and make our active response to what he is doing.[66]

If one subscribes to the basic distinction offered by Philip Schaff, it is possible to distinguish between two different traditions in American Protestantism, the English and the German. As Schaff puts it:

In Protestantism we may again distinguish the English and the German groups of confessions. To the English belong the Congregationalists, the Presbyterians, the Episcopalians, the Quakers, the Methodists, and the Baptists; the last two having also German branches. The Reformed Dutch are, it is true, of Low Dutch origin, but they have become in language entirely English, and are closely related to the Presbyterians. The Huguenots, who emigrated after the revocation of the Edict of Nantes, have clearly all fallen in with the Presbyterian and Episcopal churches, and the French language is rarely used in public service in the United States, excepting for the numerous Roman Catholic Frenchmen in some of the southern states, especially Louisiana. The German group embraces the Lutheran, Reformed, and United Churches, and the Moravian Brethren.

All these may be reckoned to orthodox and evangelical Protestantism, since they adhere in their symbols to the fundamental doctrines of the Scriptures and the Reformation, and manifest a corresponding Christian life. The Baptists and Quakers stand on the extreme limit of orthodox Protestantism, and accordingly come nearest to being sects in the strict sense; though the Baptists are very numerous. The Episcopalians, on the other hand, form the extreme right wing of Protestantism and are the nearest akin to Catholicism, especially in the high-church or Puseyite section. The German churches, we may say, generally hold middle ground between the Episcopal and the Presbyterian.[67]

Liberal Protestantism tends to be more adapted to modern thought, which is dominated by science. More than any other major Christian persuasion, the liberal Protestants tend to emphasize the right of individuals to decide what is true in religion for themselves. Correspondingly, "the belief in freedom from theological domination by creeds, councils, bishops, and pastors amounts to about the most basic religious conviction . . . [so] theological divergence among Liberals is, accordingly, great."[68] As Edwin Aubrey states, "The liberal starts with the proposition that experience precedes theological formulas. In other words, religious experience is more fundamental than theology. Therefore, in order to understand the theology we must go to the experience behind it."[69] (The three basic traditions that constitute the more "liberal" Christian [and generally Protestant] traditions, ranging from classical Protestantism to the ultraliberal "natural religions" are presented in Figure 4–3.)

FIGURE 4–3
CHRISTIAN (PROTESTANT) LIBERALISM

Critical Biblicism

Scripture construed by expert scholarship (the classical Protestant tradition) Mainstream Reformation-based Protestantism (Reformed Calvinism, Episcopalianism, Presbyterianism, Lutheranism, etc.)	Scripture interpreted and supplemented by direct personal inspiration from God Quakers Pentecostals	Scripture interpreted and supplemented by personal reason Unitarianism/Universalism Ethical Culture Society

Evangelicalism and Fundamentalism. The difference between Christian *evangelicalism* and Christian *fundamentalism* (both of which tend to be largely special expressions of Christian Protestantism—although not invariably so) is also somewhat vague and contentious. As a general rule, *evangelicalism* is the more encompassing orientation, and all fundamentalists are evangelical (even though the contrary is not true). At basis, as Richard Pierard states,

The evangelical is identified by his emphasis upon the inspiration and authority of the Scriptures and the need for individual spiritual regeneration (salvation) through faith in Jesus Christ and the action of the Holy Spirit....[T]here is a continuum of doctrinal solidarity on these basics reaching from fundamentalism to many who would prefer to identify themselves as "evangelicals" or "confessionalists." The confessing evangelical differs from the fundamentalist particularly in that he is seriously trying to place conservative Christianity in the mainstream of contemporary life and make the orthodox position a live option for modern man.[70]

The confusion here is even further compounded by two additional distinctions that are frequently made in religious scholarship between *evangelicalism* and *neo-evangelicalism*, on the one hand, and between *orthodoxy* (defined essentially as adherence to one of the classical Protestant theologies) and *neo-orthodoxy*, on the other. In essence, *neo-evangelicalism* (or *new evangelism*) is a post World War II movement—named by a Boston minister, Harold Ockenza, and largely popularized by Billy Graham and editor Carl F. H. Henry of *Christianity Today*—which seeks to retain the religious fervor of evangelical fundamentalism while, at the same time, rejecting its " 'wowser' worship, its cultural isolationism, its sectarian separatism, its monastic ethics, its theological hair-splitting.''[71] In addition, and as Martin Marty indicates, "while both [Evangelicals and Fundamentalists] are normally seen to be conservative (though many Evangelicals and Fundamentalists through the years have voted for the New Deal and for progressive legislation, as citizens and not as representatives of their churches), Evangelicals are closer to the political mainstream, while almost all radical rightists and those dismissed by others as demagogues come out of Fundamentalism.''[72]

Neo-orthodoxy, on the other hand, began as an attack on Christian liberalism. Rejecting liberalism's characteristic optimism and faith in reason, neo-orthodoxy holds that man, while made in the image of God, is nevertheless flawed by innate depravity and is therefore subjected to a tragic fate. As Eston states: "The basic truths of Christianity are a part of the divine revelation and we either accept them or we don't. The Christian faith . . . is not something that is arguable.''[73]

> Neo-orthodox thinkers accept the results of the modern study of the Bible. They hold that while reason has no power to communicate God's revelation, it has power to deal with nature. The Bible is a natural product; therefore, reason is applicable to biblical problems just as it is applicable to all problems which are of the natural order. Some of the most radical of the biblical scholars are neo-orthodox in their theological point of view, even to the point of rejecting a large part of the biblical account of the life of Jesus as literal historical truth.

*　　*　　*

> However, the neo-orthodox theologian makes one fertile suggestion concerning our understanding of the miraculous events of the Bible. He says many of the narratives of miraculous events are myths, that is, stories whose actual details never happened but whose central teachings are true to the basic principles of existence. For example, the first chapters of Genesis do not describe the actual creation of the universe; nor was there ever a first man by the name of Adam who was lured by his wife to eat an apple and thereby corrupt the human race. But the first chapters of Genesis are true in the sense that there was a creation, that God was the creator, that man is rebellious against the order that God has established, and that man is estranged from God because of his sins. Many of the greatest truths of the Bible are thus mythologically stated, according to neo-orthodox belief.
>
> Basically Neo-orthodoxy is a reassertion of the judgment of God. It is a reaction against the comfortable theology which stresses God's love at the expense of His majesty.[74]

While its doctrines go well back into history, *fundamentalism* is largely a product of the twentieth century. As Marty states:

> By the middle of the nineteenth century, although no one would have been called Fundamentalist, most Protestants called themselves Evangelical, which then could have been equated with "Mainline Protestant." Robert Baird, in *Religion in America,* simply divided his map into "Evangelical" and "Nonevangelical" spheres, relegating only a few minuscule Protestant churches like Unitarianism and Universalism to the latter camp."[75]

Contemporary fundamentalism, as Clabaugh notes

> ...can be traced to a series of twelve pamphlets, *The Fundamentals: A Testimony to the Truth,* which appeared in the years 1910 to 1912. These pamphlets were a reaction to the spread of modernism. They dealt with subjects like the virgin birth of Christ, his physical resurrection, the literal infallibility of the Bible, and the substitutionary blood atonement.
>
> A group of conservative Protestant leaders adopted the term "Fundamental" from this series of pamphlets and set about to combat the spread of modernism. To this end the World Christian Fundamentals Association was founded in 1918. Although the original movement was primarily Baptist in origin, it soon spread to other denominations.
>
> The Fundamentalists stood four square against any other interpretation of the Bible than it was directly inspired by God and literally infallible. They bitterly resisted any use of modern historical research and criticism. They maintained that the Bible contained no myths and that it could only be interpreted as a series of statements of fact. They also opposed religious involvement in the achievement of social justice and declared the social gospel movement to be an apostasy. . . .
>
> The movement's most marked characteristic was its predilection for opposing virtually every aspect of modern life. This negativism was not confined to theological matters. It became the last ditch position of rural and small-town Protestant America. It was here that the encroachments of cosmopolitan sophistication and its attendant rationalism were to be resisted to the end.
>
> Fundamentalism may have reached its apogee, in terms of its national influence, during the evolution controversy of the 1920's. Nevertheless, it is currently attracting many new members. In fact, shorn of some of its dogmatism and self-righteousness by the abrasive effects of the twentieth century, the Fundamentalist movement contains some of the fastest growing church groups in the country.[76]

In a social sense, then, fundamentalism appears to have emerged as a "defense of the agrarian culture of the nineteenth century against the developing urban culture."[77] From a theological point of view, however, and, as Williams notes,

> ...Fundamentalism is an effort to assert traditional dogma, reaffirming the ancient and medieval view of the relation of God to nature. The Catholic view of God and of nature is accepted, except that most fundamentalists deny that miracles have happened since Biblical times. God's purpose in performing the miracles, they say, was simply to make clear to

mankind that the Bible is His special revelation and is to be taken literally. This purpose having been accomplished, there is no reason for God to interfere further with the course of nature. But Fundamentalists have no doubt about the Biblical miracles. The sun stood still, the ax floated, the water turned to wine, actually and literally, just as narrated in the Bible. Fundamentalists are just as sure these things happened as they are of the things that occur in their own living rooms, and surer than they are of what they read in the newspapers.

The five minimum basic doctrines of Fundamentalism are:

1. The inerrancy and infallibility of the Bible.
2. The virgin birth and the complete deity of Christ Jesus.
3. The resurrection of the same body of Jesus which was three days buried.
4. The substitutionary atonement of Jesus for the sins of the world.
5. The second coming of Jesus in bodily form.[78]

EVANGELICAL FUNDAMENTALISM

Perhaps the most visible representatives of religiously grounded educational fundamentalism are those associated with the Christian evangelical-fundamentalist tradition. This tradition, unlike the basic denominational or-thodoxies of the larger and less militant "establishment" Protestant churches, is less a matter of adhering to a particular church doctrine than it is a more general approach to Christianity. Thus, while it is clearly fundamentalist in its extreme biblicism, it is far more than this. As Robert S. Ellwood phrases it in his book *One Way: The Jesus Movement and Its Meaning:*

> In America evangelicalism [a term that Ellwood uses essentially in ref-erence to the more specific orientation of evangelical-fundamentalism] is a particular manner of interpreting Christianity. We might almost say it is a particular Christian mood or style, though it also implies a certain doctrin-al and psychoexperiential content. It is not a denomination, though it has spawned many and represents a party or school in many others.
>
> But characteristically the evangelical movement is not involved with denominationalism. Its most potent institutions, whether the old-time revi-val or the coffeehouse of the present [1973] Jesus movement, have few denominational ties and have drawn persons to its most central experience from all churches or from none. Evangelicalism's most effective continu-ing organizations, from the old National Holiness Alliance to the modern Campus Crusade for Christ, have been organized independently of de-nominations and are cross-denominational in support. Many major evangelical churches and Bible Schools are independent.[79]

The basic tenet of evangelicalism is that a person must have a defi-nite, deeply experienced, personal relationship with Jesus Christ. He must believe that, though no longer visible to physical eyes, Jesus is living today as much as ever; that you can know him and talk with him; that he is, moreover, all-powerful; and that you can trust him to answer all your problems in this world and the next, particularly problems of sorrow, emp-tiness and the anxiety caused by guilt.

The evangelical believes, with other orthodox Christians, that in his death on the cross Jesus paid a price demanded by God for all the sins of the world. He stresses this atonement by personally affirming—as the keystone of the personal relationship—that the paid price specifically applies to his own sins.

Typically, though not always, evangelicals emphasize that the establishment of the personal relationship with Christ and the acceptance of forgiveness of sins should be attained in a single powerful experience. Whether it is coming forward during an invitational hymn at a church service or revival meeting, or in deep prayer alone, somewhere a person will have his hour with God when he will sense the deep power of the holy Spirit stir within him and will see the cross before his mystic eyes, and will know that the past is past and all his scarlet sins are made white as snow. The experience is commonly called "being saved" or "becoming a Christian." The literature is full of accounts of them. The evocation of this experience in "sinners"—those who have not had it—is the main purpose of revivals and evangelical preaching. Personal expressions of "accepting Christ" are often quasi-ritualized by such tokens as raising the hand or coming forward. And they also include ecstatic phenomena such as shouting, trance, and uncontrollable tears.

The evangelical does not forget the Christian's life after the initial experience. With the experience or, according to some, in subsequent experiences, comes the power of the Holy Spirit, the Third Person (with God the Father, and Jesus Christ the Son) of the triune Christian God. He gives joy and inward guidance ("I've got those Holy Ghost grins") to the believer who has accepted Christ's salvation. For some (the pentecostalists) his presence is made known by "speaking in tongues." Many evangelicals (those in the "holiness" tradition) affirm that after receiving the Holy Spirit, it is possible for the Christian to live, with his help, entirely free from further sin.

Evangelicals have always stressed experience more than forms of church government or sacraments. They do insist on certain points of doctrine: the Trinity, Christ both God and man, the Virgin Birth, the atonement for sin. While not overly preoccupied with philosophical theology, they will attack strongly those they feel to be "watering down" such central doctrines as these. Almost always they affirm vehemently the full verbal inspiration and infallibility of the Scriptures. While it may have greater or less psychological importance to individual evangelicals, they generally look toward the imminent Second Coming of Christ to judge the world. In this world, which is passing away, they expect frequent signs and wonders of the other world and its power: answer to prayer, guidance, conversion, healing.

Spiritual rebirth, infallible Scripture, signs and miracles, explicit doctrine, and awareness of the approaching End, combine to build around the evangelical a magic circle invisibly cutting him off from those for whom these things have no meaning. Here he lives as in an alternative world. There is no criticism; all persons have made their own world to a large extent, and all religion is grounded in man's hunger for "otherness," for a transition or rebirth to another kind of world, a hunger as biting as hunger for food and sex.[80]

One of the things that makes the evangelical-fundamentalist Christian deeply conservative—and occasionally socially regressive—in his fundamental approach to living is the fact that he frequently needs to create the kind of social environment that is compatible with the kind of moral and spiritual perfection to which he aspires. Because of his literalistic interpretation of Scripture, he finds himself faced with the necessity of reconstructing society along rural-agrarian lines as a way of guaranteeing the kinds of conditions that are congruent with his Bible-centered worldview. In a sense, and as Ellwood states, such an evangelical has an "inner reality anchored outside of present time,"[81] and this creates a sense of invulnerability in this world, but it also creates a sense of disquietude about this world. "The evangelical must make himself a man of another time while living in this."[82] "The more you talk about the other, Biblical-time world, and the more others are brought into it, the more its reality in the present day is reinforced."[83]

> Within the evangelical's magic circle, time moves in a different way. It flows by like a great river too deep and turgid to differentiate; the circle, like a refracting lens, resolves its secret motions into splendid clarity. He sees mighty rocks on the river's bed and the creatures that dwell there; in one place the currents are seen to run with tremendous speed, in another the river stops and appears not to flow at all; in still others it eddies into strange side diversions.
>
> The infallibility of Scripture sets the whole narrative of the Bible, for the evangelical, in a special time capsule. It happened in the course of history, but it has not been borne away on the splashing waves of the river. Instead the Bible and its time stands like a lighthouse in the midst of history. Bible time is special; it stands in equal relation to all other points in time. The evangelical is always contemporaneous with it, particularly with the time of Christ. He always wants to collapse into nothing all time between himself and the New Testament. He strives to negate all customs and attitudes which have evolved in the life of the church between then and now. He wants to walk into the time capsule which is the New Testament world, with its miracles, its expectation of an immediate end, and above all the mighty tangible presence of Jesus Christ. He wants to be the thirteenth disciple and to write in his life the twenty-ninth chapter of the book of Acts. He yearns to merge the magic circle of his own "otherness" world, his alternative reality, with the New Testament capsule.[84]

American evangelical fundamentalism has always functioned in part as a protest against the sophisticated and learned elite of the institutional establishments. Far more concerned with preaching and singing than with the analysis of scriptural texts, such evangelicals generally reject bookishness and avoid close-reasoned disputes over doctrinal niceties in favor of "a Spirit-inspired eclecticism."[85] The history of evangelical fundamentalism in America has been intimately connected with the history of religious revivals, and such revival meetings, ending in personal decisions for Christ, are ordinarily conducted by preachers independent of ordinary churches, by men of the people, who do "not descend with priestly blessings, or smelling of the library."[86] Theirs is, on the whole, a popular culture religion, making an "appeal for decision rather than intellectual comprehension."[87]

All of the great religions of the world have a majority tradition. Such a tradition, states Ellwood, "is cool, official, and deeply learned."[88]

> Within all these traditions, however, are counter movements emphasizing intensity of personal experience more than tradition, scholarship, dignity, or sanction by the elite. Usually appealing most to the outcasts and

dissatisfied, these movements say, "We can give *you* directly and intensely what is only hinted at in the official temples. We have a 'short path,' a special plan or technique which can give you right away what would take years and years in the temple.

*   *   *

Evangelicalism makes a similar odd appeal, couched in Christian phraseology, offering a comparable sudden individual transformation through the "short path" of "accepting Christ" and the power of the Holy Spirit, not in a nominal but in a deeply felt way induced by various means . . . principally by intense preaching, hymns, and the use of confrontational psychology.[89]

The primary call of evangelical fundamentalism is for "the resolution of inner complexity."[90] Seeking the "old-time religion," such a person has a "sense of nostalgia for an earlier time when life was presumably simpler and more integrated, with less disparity between religious, personal, and social values."[91]

The man attracted to a short path is a man of complexity, a person in some ways more complicated, more torn apart by inner conflicts, than the ordinary person of his society. The process of resolving the complexity is not one of simple decomplexification. It is rather one of rearrangement of psychic constituents into a balanced pattern, like a mandala. For the evangelical this means the production of something like a dumbbell-shaped map of the psyche. Everything is grouped around two poles, with a channel of access between them. The two poles are the "world" and the alternative New Testament Reality, and the latter is sovereign, the "sovereignty of Christ."[92]

In the "confrontational psychology of evangelicalism," continues Ellwood, "the alternative reality is a whole world, requiring inner consistency, one is either in it or not. . . . Belief either takes you to the other side, or you are nowhere."[93] " . . . evangelical rhetoric, whether in sermons, or in one-to-one encounters, seeks to focus issues down to stark, black and white dimensions. . . . Spiritual issues are reduced to one: acceptance or rejection of the 'claims of Christ.' "[94]

Accordingly, in its attitude toward American society Ellwood summarizes the evangelical tradition (in its more fundamentalistic expressions) as follows:

1. The evangelicals feel nostalgic for an earlier America of the pioneers in which the faith of their spiritual fore-bears is idealized; this leads to a conservative affirmation of traditional American symbols and institutions.
2. There is also a reformism which usually centers around a few symbolic issues, such as opposition to the liquor trade or to foreign or Roman Catholic influences. These issues essentially set evangelical life styles and moral values against strongly contrasting ones. Thus in the nineteenth century evangelicals lent support to the temperance and abolition of slavery causes and to the founding of colleges in the West where their value systems were taught.

3. Evangelicals in any given period will be opposed to a current educational, urban, and cultural "Establishment" from which they feel alienated: people who drink, do not believe the Bible literally, and are changing the country in directions contrary to evangelical values.

4. The individual experience emphasis leads to confrontational as well as withdrawal attitudes toward the "outside." Rhetoric stresses the drawing of lines between sides; forays such as urban missions and revivals are sent into the "other camp." The combined sense of reformism and alienation, incidentally, has led to a difficult ambivalence toward education, especially higher education. Awareness that a word-centered faith ought to give priority to study is balanced by the fact that evangelicals have very often deprecated intellectualism and education, insofar as they conflict with the conversion experience and the gifts of the Spirit as the criteria of salvation or as the main qualification for preaching. Education which raises difficulties for the concept of full verbal inspiration of Scripture has been held especially dangerous.

5. This confrontational attitude necessitates an almost unavoidable mentality of an isolated, alienated, almost oppressed minority among the adherents of evangelicalism, even while they also feel they are the "real" Americans and that in some paradoxical sense the great "silent majority" of Americans are like them. In a way this is true; while serious evangelicals are a minority, probably most Protestant Americans have somewhere guilty feelings that if they were serious about religion, they would be like the evangelicals.

6. The activism and the sense of isolation from the "outside" reinforce each other in evangelical mentality. With a vigor like that of small town lodges and chambers of commerce, evangelical institutions work hard to promote rallies, Sunday schools, tours, programs, and revivals. Sporting and military terms, and often heroes of these fields, are part of the vocabulary. Yet evangelicalism rarely lacks the feel of a belligerent but beleaguered army surrounded by its foes. It must be that this mentality is somehow necessary to the self-identity evangelicalism gives to its adherents. They are happiest as a minority assured that a revival is going on which may vindicate them in the near future. They love statistics indicating growth and often post them conspicuously in churches. This is activism induced by deferred reward thinking, in contrast to those more mystical religions stressing enjoying the present moment with God.[95]

The Pentecostals

Within the American evangelical tradition exists the comparatively recent tradition of pentecostalism. Beginning about the turn of the century among the most dispossessed members of American society, the poor whites and blacks of both the rural and urban South, pentecostalism is perhaps America's most significant contribution to Christianity. It is currently the most rapidly expanding of the generally recognized types of Christianity in the so-called Third World, numbering over thirty-five million adherents across the globe.

Pentecostalism is based in John Wesley's doctrine of Christian perfectionism as a result of the conversion experience. According to the pentecostal interpretation of this "holiness" doctrine, it is possible to live a sinless life after "becoming a Christian'' and receiving the Holy Spirit. By receiving a ''second blessing,'' after the baptism of the Holy Spirit, the true believer is allowed to continue living a sinless life. ''It was,'' as Ellwood indicates,

> but a short step to believe that a community informed with this blessing should possess all the marks of the New Testament church and its spiritual signs and powers as well—healing, the power to pick up serpents, and above all the ability to speak in new tongues (glossolalia) as did the apostles on the day of Pentecost, when witnesses at first thought them full of new wine.[96]

Pentecostalism is not restricted to particular churches such as the Assemblies of God or the Pentecostal Assemblies. In recent years it has occurred with increasing frequency in some of the more staid Protestant denominations such as the Episcopalian and the Presbyterian. In the late sixties, the ''tongues'' movement became active in the Roman Catholic Church, and there is presently a rather active Catholic pentecostal movement that holds annual conferences. Most pentecostalists believe fervently in the power of prayer, and they frequently pray with great intensity for quite specific outcomes. Pentecostalist groups, whether within or without particular established church groups, tend to be deeply involved with healing, and they frequently employ such approaches as direct prayer and the laying on of hands in this pursuit.

The Apocalyptics

Some fundamentalist Christian groups also tend to be apocalyptic, holding that the end of the world, with the return of Christ and the beginning of the millenium (the one-thousand-year kingdom of God on earth) is imminent. Apocalypticism is only one of the ways in which Christian evangelism incorporates the temporal world into the essentially supernatural dimensions of its alternative worldview. In most instances, the Coming, the Final Judgment and the Kingdom of God are viewed as occurring at the end of a series of progressively deepening catastrophies, such as wars and plagues. Such apocalyptic visions are usually substantiated by means of biblical sources, usually calling upon the books of Daniel, Ezekiel and Revelation as well as certain parts of the Gospel of Mark.

Such apocalyptic fervor is not a new thing. There was a floodtide of apocalyptic hysteria before the year 1000, with many Christians believing that Christ would reappear in that year. Today many look upon the year 2000 as a probable date for the end of history. In all events, Christianity, like the other fundamental Western religious orientations of Judaism and Islam, have always rejected the Eastern religions' view that history is essentially ''circular,'' encompassed within an eternal process of divine play, featuring an unending round of cycles and reincarnations, and has opted instead for the idea that time is essentially linear, ''a straight line marked by irreversible periods and unrepeatable events starting with the creation of the world by God and ending with his final judgment.''[97]

> [The apocalyptic] style involves reading contemporary historical events in the light of expectations based on Scripture and vision concerning specific events believed to be indicators of the coming End. Today this pattern

is certainly connected to the rise of "historicism." Ours has been an age of a radical rediscovery of history—the definitive discovery that events move in an irreversible sequence and can be interpreted as having a meaning which points toward the future. That is, events can be signs. The Marxist, the evolutionist, the Biblical apocalypticist all have their meaning-giving pattern to lay over the puzzle of historical events.[98]

In some cases, of course, the temporal world as it presently exists is looked upon as intolerable, subverting religious needs to the extent that the individual or group must retreat from it altogether as a way of salvaging its spiritual integrity. In such cases, which most often occur within apocalyptic religious groups, the group most frequently tends to form a community apart from the general society. Such Christian communities tend to be of two basic sorts: (1) those which presume a reasonably long future and which are therefore oriented toward social stability and economic survival within the present society, such as the Hutterian Brethren (the Hutterites), or the Bruderhof communities within the Protestant tradition, or the monastic movement within the Roman Catholic and Orthodox traditions; or (2) those which (like the Qumran community in ancient Palestine) assume a relatively imminent apocalypse and which are therefore oriented toward immediate spiritual self-perfection without regard for the development of new and sustaining social and economic institutions. (Here would occur such contemporary "Jesus movement" communes as The Children of God.)[99]

RIGHT-WING CHRISTIAN FUNDAMENTALISM

The fundamentalist Christian (and generally Protestant) radical right—what Clabaugh terms "the Fundradists"[100]—is only one expression of the basic fundamentalist tradition in this country, and the contention that America is God's country is probably viewed with deep misgiving by most fundamentalists.[101] In a similar sense, any attempt to equate the fundamentalist Christian radical right with the remainder of the Radical Right is also extremely hazardous. As Clabaugh states:

> While it is easy *in principle* to establish the distinction between Fundradists and the remainder of the Radical Right, it is not as easy *in practice*. This is because Fundradists organizations are arranged on a continuum which ranges from the Radical Right with no *overt* Fundamental Protestant beliefs or attitudes to Fundamental Protestant with the suggestion of Radical Right propensities. As a consequence of this distribution along a continuum, any attempt to clearly distinguish Fundradists from the rest of the Radical Right, or from groups bordering on the Radical Right, is subject to some very basic limitations.
>
> The problematic nature of the situation is further compounded by the fact that the continuum is multidimensional. Not only must the overt display of beliefs and attitudes be dealt with, but the matter of covert factors as well. For example, we may be confronted with a Radical Rightist organization which never overtly endorses any Fundamental Protestant

theology. Yet, this organization might well be a secular offshoot of this very same theology. In other words, they could be "fundamentalist" in everything but their overt expression of opinion about theological matters.[102]

However this may be, the hybrid blend of nationalism and religion introduces a fervent chauvinistic religious nationalism—what Jorstad calls "the politics of doomsday"[103]—as the distinguishing characteristic of one type of "civil religion" that is probably best exemplified by such individuals as Dr. Carl McIntire (leader of the American and International Councils of Christian Churches and the Twentieth Century Reformation), Dr. Billy James Hargis (leader of Christian Crusade and member of the International Council of Christian Churches), Mr. Edgar C. Bundy (leader of the Church League of America and member of the American and International Councils of Christian Churches), and Mr. Verne P. Kaub (leader of the American Council of Christian Laymen, which merged with the American Council of Christian Churches following Mr. Kaub's death in 1964).[104] As Jorstad indicates, throughout recent American history, but probably most actively during the decade of the sixties,

a tiny but vehement band of Protestants denounced every change as being for the worse, and not only "worse" but in fact disastrous for the cause of Christianity in the world. Instead of relevance their leaders call for a "Twentieth Century Reformation," a "Christian Crusade," a total sweeping out of every element in American church life which deviated from their understanding of pure New Testament Christianity. American church people stood not on the threshhold of a creative new age, but on the brink of total destruction. The myriad of changes was absolute proof that this nation and the world now faced the Last Days. Satan had cleverly disguised his soldiers as clergymen who had convinced most Americans that they were simply trying to make Christianity meaningful in society. What this really meant was that Satan had laid his plans for the Battle of Armageddon. Soon, at any moment now, he would come out of hiding and challenge God for control of this planet. Unless America repented at once, it would face the horrors of doomsday.

These leaders were "the fundamentalists of the far right," or "ultrafundamentalists." Their bill of particulars was very long and precise. The changes in church-state relations, the ecumenical movements, and the increasing social outreach of the churches were nothing more than the Devil fornicating with the whore of Babylon (Rev. 17). An insidious conspiracy was at work uniting Washington, Rome, Moscow, and Geneva (the World Council of Churches) into the kingdom of Lucifer. Every social reform from civil rights to fluoridation, from the income tax to social security, was the creation of the Communists who took orders from Satan.[105]

Overview of Christian Fundamentalism. In general, Christian fundamentalism can be viewed as a continuum that ranges from (1) the extreme fundamentalism of the Pentecostal groups (such as the Assembly of God and Foursquare Gospel), stressing direct communication with the Holy Spirit; through (2) the less extreme but nevertheless rigid and Bible-centered fundamentalism represented by many of the independent evangelical churches who are members of the Interdenominational Fundamentalist Churches of America; to (3) the more institutionalized fundamentalism of certain of the established Protestant denominations like the Southern Baptists and Lutherans (who frequently term themselves "neo-evangelical" to distinguish themselves from the more vehemently anti-intellectual evangelism true of the independent churches).

Still another way of viewing the differences between Christian (and generally Protestant) fundamentalist groups—one which makes the locus of authority its essential point of departure—is presented in Figure 4–4. In a broader sense, if the ultimate source of authority is employed as the basic means of distinguishing between *all* Christian groups, the sort of classification presented in Figure 4–5 emerges.

Overview of Reactionary Conservatism

Reactionary Conservatism is not a monolithic point of view, and, in general, the reactionary Conservatives tend to differ most significantly with respect to two basic considerations: (1) religion, and (2) the intellectual basis (or lack thereof) for claims about revealed and/or intuitive truth. At basis, then, there are four fundamental types of reactionary conservatism: (1) those religious reactionary Conservatives who ground their beliefs upon a more or less literal interpretation of accepted scriptures or authoritative teachings (as in most evangelical fundamentalist churches); (2) those religious reactionary Conservatives who ground their beliefs upon a more or less literal interpretation of accepted scriptures or authoritative teachings but place primary emphasis upon some personal conversion or rebirth experience (such as the pentecostal fundamentalists); (3) those secular reactionary Conservatives who emphasize intellectual, direct intuition or "common sense" as a matter of philosophical principle (as in naziism or fascism); and (4) those secular reactionary totalitarians who emphasize either nonintellectual, direct intuition or "common sense" without recourse to any sort of theoretical rationale whatsoever (as in some expressions of the prophetic nation-as-transcendent brand of "civil religion"). These various subvarieties of reactionary conservatism are diagrammed in Figure 4–6.

FUNDAMENTALISM IN EDUCATION: A SUMMARY

For the educational fundamentalist, contemporary society is faced with imminent moral collapse, and the highest imperative is consequently to reform conventional standards of belief and behavior by returning to the morally superior virtues characteristic of an earlier day and age. Accordingly, the goal of the school is to restore the older and better ways in order to reconstruct the existing social order.

As in all of the educational ideologies, there are two basic types of educational fundamentalist, the *secular* educational fundamentalist and the *religious* educational fundamentalist. The secular fundamentalist has no explicit religious

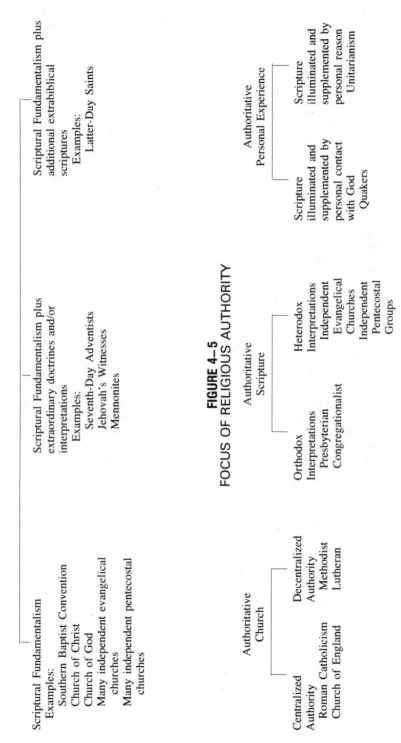

FIGURE 4–4
CHRISTIAN (PROTESTANT) FUNDAMENTALISM

Scriptural Fundamentalism
Examples:
Southern Baptist Convention
Church of Christ
Church of God
Many independent evangelical
churches
Many independent pentecostal
churches

Scriptural Fundamentalism plus
extraordinary doctrines and/or
interpretations
Examples:
Seventh-Day Adventists
Jehovah's Witnesses
Mennonites

Scriptural Fundamentalism plus
additional extrabiblical
scriptures
Examples:
Latter-Day Saints

FIGURE 4–5
FOCUS OF RELIGIOUS AUTHORITY

Authoritative
Church

Centralized
Authority
Roman Catholicism
Church of England

Decentralized
Authority
Methodist
Lutheran

Authoritative
Scripture

Orthodox
Interpretations
Presbyterian
Congregationalist

Heterodox
Interpretations
Independent
Evangelical
Churches
Independent
Pentecostal
Groups

Authoritative
Personal Experience

Scripture
illuminated and
supplemented by
personal contact
with God
Quakers

Scripture
illuminated and
supplemented by
personal reason
Unitarianism

FIGURE 4–6
REACTIONARY CONSERVATISM
SECULAR

More Extreme Types of Civil Religion in the Prophetic Nation-as-Transcendent Tradition
  Religious Nationalism
    Robert Welch (John Birch Society)
    Dan Smoot (Facts Forum)
    Clarence Manion (Manion Forum)
  "Common Sense" Populism
    Max Rafferty
    George Wallace
  European Reactionary Restorationism
    Joseph de Maistre
    Louis de Bonald
    François de Châteaubriand
	Teleological Totalitarianism (Hegelian Totalitarianism)
	  Fascism
	    Benito Mussolini
	    Giovanni Gentile
	  Naziism
	    Adolf Hitler
	    Ernst Huber

NONPHILOSOPHICAL AND/OR NONTHEOLOGICAL (NONDENOMINATIONAL) ANTI-INTELLECTUALISM*	PHILOSOPHICAL AND/OR THEOLOGICAL (DENOMINATIONAL) ANTI-INTELLECTUALISM

More Extreme Types of Civil Religion in the Prophetic Nation-Under-God Tradition
  Evangelical commitment to a nondenominational Judeo-Christian religious orientation
    Protestant "civic piety"
      Edgar Bundy (Church League of America)
      Billy James Hargis (Christian Crusade)
      Father Charles Coughlin (late 30s)
      Carl McIntire *(The Christian Beacon)*
      Jerry Falwell (Moral Majority)
    Christian Voice Movement
	Christian Fundamentalism and Related Traditions
	  Southern Baptists
	  Church of Christ
	  Many independent evangelical churches
	  Many independent pentecostal churches
	  Many independent religious traditions
	    Latter-Day Saints
	    Seventh-Day Adventists
	    Jehovah's Witnesses

RELIGIOUS

---

*This category includes both *anti-intellectual* orientations, which view any sort of intellectual speculation as counterproductive, and *nonintellectual* orientations, which place their primary emphasis on revelation, faith, mystical intuition, or some combination thereof, rather than on conventional intellectual approaches.

convictions, and, while he may occasionally employ religious or quasi-religious terminology, he tends to ground his position in more or less intuitive or "common sense" assumptions rather than on revelation or faith. The religious fundamentalist maintains that the ultimate purpose of education—that is, to revive and reaffirm the older and better ways, to reestablish traditional standards of belief and behavior—is always decidedly secondary to the overriding universal goal of working for the salvation of the immortal soul, and that such salvation is primarily a matter of recognizing and obeying the will of God as this has been revealed through accepted scriptures.

Temporarily disregarding the differences between the secular and religious points of view within the tradition of educational fundamentalism, the basic ideology of the educational fundamentalist can be summarized as follows:

The Overall Goal of Education.   The central purpose of education is to revive and reaffirm the older and better ways, to reestablish traditional standards of belief and behavior.*

The Objectives of the School.   The school exists for two basic reasons: (1) to help reconstruct society by encouraging a return to its original purposes, and, in so far as this is consistent with the foregoing objective, (2) to transmit the information and skills necessary to succeed within the existing social order.

General Characteristics.   Educational fundamentalism can be characterized in the following ways:

It maintains that knowledge is primarily a tool for reconstructing society in pursuit of some earlier pattern of moral excellence.

It emphasizes man as moral agent, stressing adherence to a clear and comprehensive moral code and emphasizing the value of patriotism, narrowly defined.

It is tacitly anti-intellectual, opposing the critical examination of preferred patterns of belief and behavior.

It views education primarily as a process of moral regeneration.

It focuses on the original purposes of existing social traditions and institutions, emphasizing a return to the past as a corrective reorientation to the current overemphasis on the present and future.

It emphasizes the reintroduction of time-tested earlier ways, the need to return to the real or imagined virtues of a prior era.

It is based on a closed social and/or religious system characteristic of an earlier era, advocating a return to the ostensibly superior conditions that once prevailed.

---

* Fundamentalist orientations differ in their concepts of what constitutes the "idealized past." Some locate it in the "shallow past" (for example, the American frontier in the late nineteenth century or a romanticized version of small-town America around the turn of the century) while others tend to locate the ideal past further back in history (for example, in an idealized vision of the Holy Land in biblical times). In other words, the "golden age" varies from one fundamentalist point of view to another, so qualifications about "the older and better ways," "traditional standards of belief and behavior," "a return to original purposes," and such, must necessarily remain somewhat ambiguous, because the meaning of such phrases necessarily differs between the various expressions of the fundamentalist point of view, and is radically dependent upon considerations of time and place.

It is grounded on implicit and/or unexamined assumptions about the nature of reality that are generally based on either "common sense," intuitive certitude or religious faith.

It holds that the ultimate intellectual authority resides in a community of true believers, that truth is determined through a consensus of the morally enlightened.

The Child as Learner.   The child is predisposed toward error and evil in the absence of firm guidance and sound instruction.

Individual similarities are more important than individual differences, and these similarities are properly determinative in establishing appropriate educational programs.

Children are morally equal in a world of objectively unequal opportunities; they should have equal opportunities to strive for the limited number of rewards available, but success should be conditioned upon personal merit in a world characterized by vigorous competition for moral and material success.

The child is essentially self-determining; he has personal free will in the traditional sense.

Administration and Control.   Educational authority should be invested in trained academic managers who are not necessarily either intellectuals or professional educators.

Teacher authority should be based on the superior moral stature of the teacher.

The Nature of the Curriculum.   The school should emphasize proper moral character, training the child to be a good person in terms of traditional standards of moral conduct.

The school should focus on the renewal of prior cultural patterns; it should help the child to rediscover the values inherent within basic cultural traditions.

Emphasis should be placed on moral regeneration, on rebuilding society along the lines of traditional approaches to belief and behavior.

The course of study should be heavily prescribed.

Emphasis should be placed on *ideological conformity* (moral indoctrination) over the *academic* (learning how to learn, and mastering the sort of technical knowledge and skills that are only indirectly related to more central human problems) and the *practical* (the immediately useful), minimizing the *intellectual* (that is, the ideational, dealing with broad interpretive theory).*

The school should stress moral training and the sort of academic and practical skills required to help the child become an effective member of an appropriately regenerated social order: the basic learning skills, character training, physical education (including health instruction), American history, American literature, religious instruction, and so on.

---

* These same definitions will be utilized in corresponding discussions of the other educational ideologies. In discussing curricular content the *academic* will always have reference to learning how to learn, and mastering the sort of technical knowledge and skills that are only indirectly related to more central human problems; the *intellectual* will refer essentially to the ideational, dealing with broad interpretive theory; and the *practical* will refer to the immediately useful.

Instructional Methods and Evaluation. Emphasis should be placed upon traditional classroom procedures, such as lecture, recitation, supervised study, and highly structured group discussion.

Drill is the best way of establishing proper habits at the lower levels, but it should evolve toward more student initiative and more self-directed approaches at advanced levels; a significant amount of memorization and drill is necessary.

Teacher-determined and teacher-directed learnings are best, because the student is not sufficiently enlightened to direct his own process of intellectual development.

The teacher should be viewed as a model of moral and academic excellence.

Tests that measure skills and information are preferable to those that emphasize analytic ability and abstract speculation.

Interpersonal competition for grades between students is both necessary and desirable in order to foster excellence.

Emphasis should be placed on the cognitive (particularly the informational) with a heavy secondary emphasis on the affective and the interpersonal.

Emphasis should be placed upon the restoration of traditional (national and/or ethnic) educational principles and practices.

Personal counseling and psychotherapy are functions of the family and/or the church, not the school.

Classroom Control. Students should be good citizens in conformity with the ideal of a morally regenerated society.

Teachers should generally be nonpermissive in procedures for maintaining classroom control, and students should be expected to conform to duly constituted authority.

Moral education (character training) is the basic and overriding purpose of schooling.

NOTES

1. Gilbert Abcarian and Sherman M. Stanage, "Alienation and the Radical Right," *The Journal of Politics,* 27, November 1965, pp. 776–96.
2. Abcarian and Stanage, "Radical Right," pp. 184–85.
3. See the discussion of national socialism later in this chapter.
4. Robin Williams, *American Society: A Sociological Interpretation* (New York: Alfred A. Knopf, 1952), p. 312.
5. Robert N. Bellah, "Civil Religion in America," *Daedalus,* Journal of the American Academy of Arts and Sciences; Boston, Massachusetts; Winter 1967; Reprinted in Russell E. Richey and Donald G. Jones, eds., *American Civil Religion* (New York: Harper & Row, 1974), pp. 21–44.
6. Bellah, "Civil Religion," p. 21.
7. Ibid., p. 33.
8. Robert N. Bellah, *Beyond Belief* (New York, 1970), p. 172; quoted in Herbert Richardson, "Civil Religion in Theological Perspective," in Richey and Jones, *American Civil Religion,* p. 161.
9. Richey and Jones, *American Civil Religion,* pp. 15–17.
10. Ibid., p. 15.

11. Will Herberg, "America's Civil Religion: What Is It and Whence It Comes," in Richey and Jones, *American Civil Religion*, p. 78.

12. Richey and Jones, *American Civil Religion*, p. 16.

13. Will Herberg, quoted in Richey and Jones, *American Civil Religion*, p. 17.

14. Sidney E. Mead, "The 'Nation With the Soul of a Church,' " in Richey and Jones, *American Civil Religion*, p. 64.

15. Ibid., p. 66.

16. Richey and Jones, *American Civil Religion*, p. 17.

17. Martin E. Marty, "Two Kinds of Civil Religion," in Richey and Jones, *American Civil Religion*, p. 145.

18. Ibid.

19. Ibid., p. 144.

20. Ibid., p. 144.

21. Ibid., pp. 145–54.

22. Abcarian and Stanage, "Radical Right," p. 180. In specific contrast to Abcarian and Stanage's delimitations, the term *reactionary conservatism* is used here to provide the fullest theoretical expression of the reactionary conservative point of view as it exists in Western society at the present time. Fascism and naziism did not originate as American movements, it is true, but there are clearly American expressions of such movements, and it is very difficult to talk about the meaning of many of the existing movements within the radical right without making reference to perhaps the most coherent and persuasive statements of extreme right-wing political philosophy in the writings of such individuals as Mussolini, Gentile, Rosenberg, and Hitler. It is quite true that many of the radical right movements are fascistic purely on a tacit level, unwittingly and unintentionally. On the other hand, it is quite possible to advocate what is, for all practical purposes, the equivalent of fascist principles and practices without being explicitly aware that one is doing so.

23. James A. Gould and Willis H. Truitt, eds., *Political Ideologies* (New York: Macmillan Co., Inc., 1973), p. 169.

24. Ezra Taft Benson, from the *Congressional Record*, March 7, 1962, p. 3263.

25. G.W.F. Hegel, quoted in William S. Sahakian, *History of Philosophy from the Earliest Times to the Present* (New York: Barnes & Noble Books, 1968), p. 189.

26. Ibid., p. 199.

27. Ibid.

28. G.W.F. Hegel, *The Philosophy of Right*, trans. J. Loewenberg, quoted in *Hegel Selections* (New York: Charles Scribner's Sons, 1929), p. 282.

29. Émile Durkheim, *Sociological Method*. 1895. pp. 125-28; quoted in Pitirim Sorokin, *Contemporary Sociological Theories*, (New York: Harper & Brothers, Publishers, 1928), p. 465.

30. Sorokin, *Contemporary Sociological Theories*, p. 442.

31. Durkheim, *Sociological Method*, 1895, pp. 125–28; quoted in Sorokin, *Contemporary Sociological Theories*, p. 464.

32. Émile Durkheim, *The Elementary Forms of the Religious Life*. Translated by J. W. Swain (London: Allen & Unwin, 1912), pp. 423–24; quoted in Marvin Harris, *The Rise of Anthropological Theory* (New York: Thomas Y. Crowell, 1968), pp. 479–480.

33. Harris, *Anthropological Theory*, p. 473.

34. Ibid., p. 473.

35. Ibid., p. 479

36. Ibid., p. 478.

37. L. T. Sargent, *Contemporary Political Ideologies: A Comparative Analysis*, rev. ed. (Homewood, Illinois: Dorsey Press, 1972), p. 112.

38. Benito Mussolini, "The Doctrine of Fascism," in Mussolini, *Fascism: Doctrine and Institutions* (New York: Howard Fertig, 1968), p. 27.

39. Sargent, *Contemporary Political Ideologies,* pp. 111–12; quoting Mussolini, *The Doctrine of Fascism,* p. 27.

40. Mario Palmieri, *The Philosophy of Fascism* (1936); quoted in Gould and Truitt, *Political Ideologies,* p. 111.

41. Hans Kohn, *The Idea of Nationalism, A Study of Its Origins and Background* (New York: Collier Books, 1944), p. 16.

42. Leonard W. Doob, *Patriotism and Nationalism: Their Psychological Foundations* (New Haven, Connecticut: Yale University Press, 1964), p. 6.

43. A. James Gregor, *The Ideology of Fascism: The Rationale of Totalitarianism* (New York: Free Press, 1969), p. xii.

44. Gould and Truitt, *Political Ideologies,* p. 2.

45. Adolf Hitler, *The Speeches of Adolf Hitler, April 1922–August 1939,* Norman H. Baynes, ed. (London: Oxford University Press, 1942), vol. 1, p. 188; Speech of September, 1930.

46. Gould and Truitt, *Political Ideologies,* p. 102.

47. Benito Mussolini, *The Doctrine of Fascism* (1932); from Michael Oakeshott, *Social and Political Doctrines of Contemporary Europe* (London: Cambridge University Press, 1950), pp. 164–68.

48. Ibid.

49. Adolf Hitler, *Mein Kampf.* Translated by Ralph Mannheim. (Boston: Houghton Mifflin Co, 1943), p. 393.

50. Ernst Rudolf Huber, *Verfassungsrecht des Grossdeutschen Reiches* (Hamburg, 1939), p. 195; *Readings on Fascism and National Socialism* (Denver, Colorado: Alan Swallow, Publisher, n.d.), p. 75.

51. Ibid., p. 394. Emphasis in the original.

52. Adolf Hitler, *Mein Kampf,* from Michael Oakeshott, *Doctrines of Europe,* p. 192.

53. Quoted in the *Times* (London), 29 January 1935, p. 12; reprinted in George L. Mosse, *Nazi Culture: Intellectual, Cultural and Social Life in the Third Reich* (New York: Grosset & Dunlap, 1966), pp. 282–84.

54. Adolf Hitler, quoted in *Hitler's Words, The Speeches of Adolf Hitler from 1923–1943.* Edited by G. Prange (Washington, D.C.: Public Affairs Press); quoted in Gould and Truitt, *Political Ideologies,* p. 116.

55. Ibid.

56. Ibid., p. 118.

57. Ibid.

58. Ibid., p. 117.

59. Abcarian and Stanage, "Radical Right," p. 183.

60. Huber, *Verfassungsrecht,* p. 125.

61. Ibid., p. 115.

62. Ibid., p. 125.

63. J. Paul Williams, *What Americans Believe and How They Worship*, rev. ed. (New York: Harper & Row, Publishers, 1962), p. 94. Copyright © 1952, 1962 by Harper & Row, Publishers, Inc. Reprinted by permission of the publisher.

64. Robert McAfee Brown, "Classical Protestantism," in F. Ernest Johnson, *Patterns of Faith in America Today*, in Williams, *What Americans Believe*, p. 21. Copyright © 1957 by The Institute for Religious and Social Studies. Reprinted by permission of Harper & Row, Publishers, Inc.

65. Brown, "Classical Protestantism," p. 25.

66. Brown, "Classical Protestantism," p. 28.

67. Philip Schaff, *America: A Sketch of Its Political, Social, and Religious Character* (Cambridge, Massachusetts: The Belknap Press of Harvard University Press, 1961), pp. 105–6.

68. Williams, *What Americans Believe,* p. 110.

69. Edwin Aubrey, quoted in F. Ernest Johnson, *Patterns of Faith in America Today* (New York: Collier Books, 1962), p. 61.

70. Richard V. Pierard, *The Unequal Yoke: Evangelical Christianity and Political Conservatism* (New York: J. B. Lippincott Co., 1970), p. 21.

71. Harold Ockenza, quoted in Martin E. Marty, *A Nation of Behavers* (Chicago: University of Chicago Press, 1976), p. 98.

72. Martin E. Marty, *A Nation of Behavers,* p. 94.

73. W. Burnet Eston, Jr., *The Faith of a Protestant* (New York: Macmillan, 1946), p. 20.

74. Williams, *What Americans Believe,* pp. 119–20.

75. Marty, *A Nation of Behavers*, p. 85. Reprinted by permission of The University of Chicago Press. © 1976 by University of Chicago.

76. Gary K. Clabaugh, *Thunder on the Right: The Protestant Fundamentalists* (Chicago: Nelson-Hall Publishers, Chicago, 1974), pp. 122–23.

77. Winthrop S. Hudson, quoted in Williams, *What Americans Believe,* p. 105.

78. Williams, *What Americans Believe,* p. 105.

79. Robert S. Ellwood, Jr., *One Way: The Jesus Movement and Its Meaning* (Englewood Cliffs, New Jersey: Prentice-Hall, 1973), p. 25.

80. Ibid., pp. 30–32.

81. Ibid., p. 34.

82. Ibid., p. 33.

83. Ibid.

84. Ibid., pp. 30–32.

85. Ibid., p. 48.

86. Ibid., p. 38.

87. Ibid.

88. Ibid., pp. 27–28.

89. Ibid.

90. Ibid., p. 35.

91. Ibid., pp. 18–20.

92. Ibid., p. 34.

93. Ibid., p. 33.

94. Ibid.

95. Ibid., pp. 36–37.

96. Ibid., p. 45.

97. Ibid., p. 87

98. Ibid., p. 88.

99. Ibid., pp. 97–105.

100. Clabaugh, *Thunder on the Right,* p. 119.

101. Ibid., p. 139.

102. Ibid., pp. 119–20.

103. Erling Jorstad, *The Politics of Doomsday: Fundamentalists of the Far Right* (New York: Abingdon Press, 1970), p. 17.

104. For a full discussion of the Right-Wing Christian Fundamentalism of these four individuals, see Erling Jorstad's book *The Politics of Doomsday: Fundamentalists of the Far Right* (New York: Abingdon Press, 1970).

105. Jorstad, *The Politics of Doomsday,* pp. 12–13.

BIBLIOGRAPHY

Educational Fundamentalism

RELIGIOUS FUNDAMENTALISM

BYRNE, HERBERT W. *A Christian Approach to Education,* Grand Rapids: Zondervan Publishing House, 1961.

CLABAUGH, GARY K. *Thunder on the Right: The Protestant Fundamentalists.* Chicago: Nelson-Hall Publishers, 1974.

EAVEY, C. B. "Aims and Objectives of Christian Education," in Hakes, J. Edward, ed. *An Introduction to Evangelical Christian Education.* Chicago: Moody Press, 1971, pp. 57–70.

GAEBELEIN, FRANK E. "Toward a Philosophy of Christian Education," in Hakes, *An Introduction to Evangelical Christian Education,* pp. 37–56.

GANGEL, KENNETH O. "Toward a Biblical Philosophy of Church Education," in Gangel, Kenneth O. *Leadership for Church Education.* Chicago: Moody Press, 1971.

HARGIS, BILLY JAMES. *Communist America: Must it Be?* Tulsa, Oklahoma: Christian Crusade, 1960.

JORSTAD, ERLING. *The Politics of Doomsday: Fundamentalists of the Far Right.* New York: Abingdon Press, 1970.

PIERARD, RICHARD V. *The Unequal Yoke: Evangelical Christianity and Political Conservatism.* New York: J. B. Lippincott Co., 1970.

SECULAR FUNDAMENTALISM

HOFSTADTER, RICHARD. "The Pseudo-Conservative Revolt," in Bell, Daniel, ed. *The Radical Right.* Garden City, New York: Doubleday-Anchor, 1964, pp. 75–96.

How "Progressive" is Your School? America's Future, Inc., n.p., n.d.

JOHN BIRCH SOCIETY. *The Blue Book of the John Birch Society.* Belmont, Massachusetts: Robert Welch, 1961.

KAUB, V. B. *Communist-Socialist Propaganda in American Schools.* Madison, Wisconsin: American Council of Christian Laymen, 1960.

OAKES, C. P., ed. *Education and Freedom in a World of Conflict.* Chicago: Regnery, 1963.

O'NEILL, WILLIAM F. *Readin, Ritin and Rafferty: A Study of Educational Fundamentalism.* Berkeley, Calfornia: Glendessary Press, 1969.

OVERSTREET, HARRY, and OVERSTREET, BONARO. *The Strange Tactics of Extremism.* New York: W. W. Norton & Co., 1964.

ROOT, E. MERRILL. *Collectivism on the Campus.* New York: Devin-Adair Co., 1956.

RAFFERTY, MAX. *Classroom Countdown: Education at the Crossroads.* New York: Hawthorn Books, 1970.

RAFFERTY, MAX. *Max Rafferty on Education.* New York: Devin-Adair Co., 1968.

RAFFERTY, MAX. *Suffer, Little Children.* New York: Devin-Adair Co., 1962.

RAFFERTY, MAX. *What They are Doing to Your Children.* New York: New American Library, 1965.

Chapter V

Educational Intellectualism

PHILOSOPHICAL ASSUMPTIONS OF EDUCATIONAL FUNDAMENTALISM

Educational intellectualism, like all of the other ideologies, is based upon certain overriding considerations in the areas of moral and political philosophy. As the moral philosophy that identifies the highest good with philosophical and/or religious enlightenment based upon perfection of reason, intellectualism is generally founded upon three philosophical assumptions.

1. The world is inherently meaningful. There are certain fundamental truths—natural or divine laws—that are absolute and unchanging, and these truths precede and determine personal experience.

2. Men are not born with an *explicit* knowledge of these truths, so a conscious awareness of them must be acquired through learned experience in the natural world.

3. In all but the most exceptional cases — such as religious revelation or mystical intuition — these truths are apprehensible through the exercise of reason.

Rationalism.   Phrased somewhat differently, the rationalist tradition associated with intellectualism (and particularly secular intellectualism) subscribes to the notion that the individual is rationally disposed to recognize certain basic truths when they occur. This takes place either through "reminiscence" in the Platonic sense (that is, because they are inherent within the mind to begin with and therefore are, in a sense, "matched up" and remembered when such ideas are evoked by some actual experience in the natural world); or because, in the less esoteric and mystical Aristotelian tradition, they tend to invoke a sense of almost aesthetic closure (experienced as a sort of intuitive certitude) because of the inherent "match" between the individual's potentiality for knowing (the individual's distinctive intelligence) and the infinitely rational nature of that which is known (the ultimate structure of the intelligible world).

This "verification by reason" argument of the intellectualist warrants special comment, because, at least from an empirical point of view, it appears to be in error on two counts. First, reason (in the strict sense of formal logic) does not address itself to the nature of *truth-assumptions* but, rather, to the relationships (inferences) that are possible on the basis of given truth-assumptions. Logically, the empirical generalizations (truth-assumptions) that derive from pure reasoning must have been implicit within the assumptions employed as logical propositions at the beginning of the reasoning process. Not even the laws of logic themselves can be established logically, because they constitute primary truth-assumptions that are necessary before logical reasoning can commence. Second, truth-assumptions cannot be established through some process of purely "empirical" logic such as scientific verification procedures, because such empirical procedures themselves exist merely to *test* truth-assumptions and not as a *source* of such assumptions in any primary sense. In an even more basic way, then, even such empirical procedures represent assumptive-truths (primary assumptions) that cannot be tested in and of themselves without falling into a process of unavoidably circular reasoning.

Absolute Truth.   For the intellectualist, Truth is not man-made, and it is no private matter. On the contrary, there are certain truths and values that exist independent of being known. These qualities do not "exist" (from the Greek *exstasis*, "to stand out") so much as they "subsist," or undergird, all personal experience. They do not "adhere" to Being so much as they "inhere" within Being, and constitute the very essence of the world as we know it. These essential qualities of Being (which may be defined in a variety of different ways, ranging from the abstract concept of beauty or the formal principles of mathematics to the basic laws of physics) are 'absolute' in the sense that they have no context, but, rather, constitute the very ground of Being.

First Principles.   Behind the flux of transitory existence, then, there lies an intransitive (or, at the very least, imperceptibly evolving) core of meaning, an irreducible set of metaphysical first principles, that are not *derivative* in the sense of growing out of experience but *fundamental* in the sense that they *cause* us to experience the world in the way in which we do. Implicit within Being there are certain 'essential' and abstract properties that exist independent of the "accidental" aspects of life and which constitute the very center of universal meaning.

There is, then, such a thing as absolute knowledge (Truth), and this knowledge transcends mere personal experience. As philosopher Mortimer Adler notes "...philosophy does not exist unless it is absolute and universal knowledge — *absolute* in the sense that it is not relative to the contingent circumstances of time and place; *universal* in the sense that it is concerned with essentials and abstracts from every sort of merely accidental variation."[1]

As pertains to such overriding and absolute truths, man is epistemologically infallible and therefore incapable of reasonable doubt. Indeed, these absolute truths not only exist, they exist on an intuitive (but undemonstrable) basis. They are absolute and indubitable precisely because they are not relative to being known or to being proven in terms of other things that have already been experienced. They are, in this sense, "true," not on the basis of *evidence* (personal experience) but *self-evidently,* in and of themselves. Such ideas cannot be proven in the usual sense, because to be true *by proof* is to be relative to *being proven.* Indeed, to know *prior to proof,* as a condition for all *subsequent* proof, is an unavoidable requirement for any sort of ultimate philosophical "objectivity" (as this term is ordinarily used in traditional philosophy).

These intrinsic truths — cause-and-effect, free will, or the existence of God are frequently cited examples—defy either verification or refutation, then, because they are first principles (primary assumptions), which precede all particular experience whatsoever and provide the necessary basis for any sort of intelligent behavior. They are exempt from the verdict of experience, because they serve as the necessary *conditions* for experience itself. They cannot be "known" in the usual sense at all, because they are a priori and intuitive. Their existence is perceived directly and requires no external verification whatsoever. They are *true* by definition, tautologically; they *are* because they *are*. Taken together, such ideas comprise the *essence of Being*. They serve as the internal dynamic, the reason and regulating force, behind everything that *is*. They provide the eternal possibilities — what philosopher George Santayana calls "the realm of essences" — which are expressed in the world of appearance.

At basis, then, the underlying nature of the *physical* is the metaphysical. The *raison d'être* of existence is essence. The most "real" knowledge is ultimately, abstract, for the abstract designates a persisting set of relations that transcends all temporary embodiment in the material. Ultimately, all material objects and events are merely superficial expressions of underlying forms or ideas. "Qualities are *exemplified* by particular items in the world, i.e., by instances. The instances co-exist with other instances. Thus, an instance of gold will be instances of qualities of yellowness, malleability, and so on, co-existing in the same area of space at a given time."[2] Ultimately, however, every actual object *is* no more than a particular expression of certain general attributes or qualities. In the final analysis, we can only know the cup through its whiteness, its fragility, its roundness, its smoothness, and so on. We can only know the chair through its solidity, its roughness, its brownness, its angularity.

The metaphysical philosophies in which the intellectualist tradition is rooted are ultimately nonempirical in the sense that they reject the idea that all knowledge is ultimately personal knowledge, that all knowing is necessarily "evident" and grounded in sense-perceptual encounters with particular objects and events. If essence (Truth) precedes and determines existence (personal experience), it necessarily stands to reason that essence must be knowable in some significant sense prior to any personal act of knowing. Such absolute and objective knowledge may occur as either *immanent knowledge* or *transcendent knowledge*.

Immanent knowledge is, quite simply, knowledge (meaning) that exists prior to any sort of purely personal experience whatsoever and is therefore independent of any personal act of *knowing*. Such knowledge (the "inherent knowledge" of man's inalienable free will might serve as an example) is simply implicit within human nature as such. It is man's nature to know these things; they are intuitive in the sense that they defy any sort of reasonble doubt.*

---

*The term *immanent* is frequently associated with the related terms *instinctual* and *innate*. They are closely related but not necessarily synonymous. To be very simplistic, the terms *innate* and *instinctual* generally refer to behavior rather than to knowledge, or, at the least, to a predisposition toward the sort of behavior that tends to elicit certain types of knowledge. Thus, innate or instinctual behavior is inborn, and, other things equal, such behavior *indirectly* generates a certain kind of knowing. In most instances, innate or instinctual behavior is determined biologically, often emerging developmentally, and its psychological (including cognitive) components—if they exist at all—emerge out of such intrinsic behavior patterns.

Generally speaking, immanent knowledge differs from innate or instinctual behavior in three basic senses. (1) Immanent knowledge is "cognitive" in a primary sense; it is not contingent upon

Transcendent knowledge exists in a metaphysical realm beyond the individual's awareness but is capable of being communicated directly to him without any sort of personal (empirical) mediation whatsoever. In such cases — revelation, mystical intuition, and so forth — the truths are communicated quite involuntarily by some higher power who speaks *through* the individual. Such truths are beyond doubt, because they signify a direct contact with the realm of essence that is in no way adulterated by the usual sort of subjective processes. There are three basic ways in which transcendent knowledge occurs: through revelation, through mystical intuition, and through reason.

The Paths of Transcendent Knowledge

In *revelation*, truth is revealed directly through a recognized spiritual source, usually God. Such knowledge is infallible, because it is not subject to the usual processes of knowing. In revelation, the knower is generally characterized as passive. God talks through one, one is enlightened. When God spoke to Moses, Moses received a revelation. Most revelation is known indirectly by means of faith. *Faith* (in the usual sense of the word) is the act of believing in someone else's revelation. Faith necessarily goes beyond reason and natural evidence, and is ultimately grounded in mystical intuition. *Mystical intuition,* as it applies to notions of transcendent truth, is actually a sort of crypto-revelation. One knows directly and immediately, and one knows beyond all doubt, but what is known is in no sense evidential (in the respect that it reflects merely a sudden explicit awareness of the meaning inherent within purely personal experience). As in revelation, one is seized by a nonempirical certitude, but, unlike revelation, this knowledge cannot be traced to an identifiable supernatural source.

Reason, viewed as an approach to transcendent, or metaphysical, knowledge — which is essentially a "rationalist" approach to reason and therefore significantly different than the view of "reason-as-applied-logic" which is more characteristic of the empirical point of view in philosophy — holds that the best way to discover the meaning inherent within existence is through reflection and logical analysis. In this process, the individual distinguishes those things that are metaphysically certain (self-evident) from those that are merely probable (evident) and develops a full and coherent system of general beliefs by logicial inference on this basis. While such reason is not always capable of directly verifying ultimate truths, since many are ultimately based upon revelation, faith or intuition, it is capable of verifying them indirectly by proving that they are the most coherent and convincing explanations possible. In this way "rational

---

experienced structure-function or biological development sequences. (2) It is (at least in contrast to more instinctual behavior) capable of being suppressed or denied. It can be replaced with volitional error and does not necessarily take priority over acquired knowledge. (3) Immanent knowledge is not necessarily biological but may itself be an invariable concomitant of the unavoidable relationship between self and world (mind and matter), which provides the ultimate basis for even the physiological. In other words, immanent knowledge may be an ontological, and not merely a biological, phenomenon—an experienced quality of the total field of forces that comprise reality in general.

thinking'' is the best means of attaining speculative wisdom, which is the ultimate source of philosophical or religious enlightenment.

The metaphysical philosopher's contention that truth is directly apprehensible
by means of reason is very controversial for a number of reasons, but, in general, his fundamental line of reasoning would seem to be captured in three basic
ideas.

1. Man, being rational, finds the most "rational" answers unavoidably con-
    vincing.
2. The most "rational" answers are those that are most logical and coherent
    in terms of those things—for instance, free will, the existence of a per-
    sonal God, and such—that are already *known* to be true on a self-evident
    basis.
3. Therefore, Truth is directly accessible to reason, because (a) certain things
    are self-evidently true *to begin with* and represent either immanent or
    transcendent knowledge, and (b) rational inferences based upon these self-
    evident beliefs lead inexorably to certain overall conclusions that simply
    defy any sort of reasonable doubt.

Intellectualism, like fundamentalism, tends to wed authoritarian means to
authoritarian ends. In most cases, the intellectualist concept of reality, like that
of the fundamentalist, is relatively definitive, offering a general prescription for
a certain way of thinking and acting. Virtually all intellectualists propound a
universalistic "open self" ethic, and almost all tend to prescribe the training of
the intellect as the preeminent (natural) means for leading the individual toward
philosophical or religious enlightenment. The overall goal is the enlightened
(and therefore self-realized) person, and it is these enlightened individuals who
should control the state, thereby guiding the educational process, which will
ultimately determine the enlightenment of others. The exact nature of the political system required is largely determined by how potentially capable of enlightenment the average person is considered to be. Since most intellectualists
view reason as the preeminent characteristic of natural man, most tend to be
relatively optimistic about the average person's capacity for attaining enlightenment through proper training and education.

The classical Aristotelian position holds that man is rational in nature, is
predisposed to exercise this rationality in living, and is preinclined to recognize
the truth by means of reason—in other words, an intelligent being is inherently
harmonized with an intelligible world and therefore possesses a sort of "aesthetic" recognition of the truth when he finally arrives at it. This is perhaps the
most commonly encountered point of view among contemporary intellectualists
of both the secular (generally Aristotelian) and religious (generally Thomistic)
varieties, both of whom tend in their political orientation to be democratic
rather than aristocratic. Generally speaking, they posit the desirability of a
meritocracy, but the elitism inherent in such a meritocratic vision is ameliorated
by the fact that they tend to see virtually all men as potentially meritorious and
therefore capable of participating in the political system. A few intellectualists
would adhere to the less optimistic—and far more aristocratic—Platonic position,[3] which holds that only a few men are destined for enlightenment and that

these few should govern, selected to rule through an educational system designed to separate the potentially enlightenable from those destined for less exalted ends.

In either case, however, the intellectualist's ideas about education tend to flow logically from his overall moral and political philosophy. The schools should exist primarily to bring everyone to the peak of their potentialities. Those who attain the ideal moral and intellectual stature should properly assume control over the state, and the schools, as one of the central agencies within the state, should guarantee the appropriate education for everyone. (The secular intellectualists are perhaps more rigorous in their intellectual orientation than the religious intellectualists, because the religious intellectualists tend to place less reliance in reason as such, looking upon it as basically the means of arriving at a coherent presentation of an eminently reasonable point of view which, however, can ultimately only be known fully through an act of faith).*

SECULAR AND THEISTIC INTELLECTUALISM

Within the intellectualist tradition, which posits the ultimate value of philosophical or religious enlightenment, there are two basic points of view, one theistic and one secular.

The *theistic* orientation consists of all of those positions that assume the existence of a personal God who can be characterized in four ways: (1) He is an active force in the determination of contemporary events. (2) He has personality; that is, he is person-like, thinking and feeling in a manner very much like human beings. (3) He can be communicated with. (4) He can, on occasion, be induced to intercede in human affairs.†

The *secular* point of view, on the other hand, is represented by all of those philosophies that hold either that (1) there is no personal God (atheism); or (2) there is no way to determine the existence or nonexistence of a personal God (agnosticism). Agnosticism, because it denies the possibility of knowing God regardless of his existence, *functions* as a secular tradition, because it denies the practical usefulness of any sort of theological speculation. Atheism is implicitly a metaphysical point of view, because it is based on the conviction that it is possible to possess certain knowledge that a personal God does *not* exist.

---

*Another philosophy that is strongly intellectualist in its approach to education is that of the well-known novelist-philosopher Ayn Rand. Rand's philosophy of "objectivism," which is perhaps the best known expression of right-wing "libertarianism," advocates a rigorous intellectualism in education (as well as the elimination of free, universal, and compulsory public education as it presently exists). Since she advocates what might be described as a sort of "right-wing anarchism," a more complete description of her ideas is reserved for Chapter VII.

†It should be emphasized here that only theistic and secular intellectualism as they exist in Western culture are being discussed here. Eastern societies do not necessarily subscribe to these distinctions. Judaism, like Thomistic Catholicism, tends to be an intellectualistic position in all of its three basic expressions (orthodox, conservative and reform). Judaism is, however, a very complicated religious and philosophical tradition unto itself, and it is treated in a special appendix entitled "Judaism and Jewish Education" at the back of the book.

With respect to theism, the term *religious* is frequently confusing, because it is often used to encompass three "religious" orientations that are fundamentally nontheistic. These are *pantheism, deism,* and *panentheism. Pantheism* is the position that holds that God is to be found in everything, that God is immanent within all Being. It is essentially an identifying of God with nature and therefore constitutes a denial of God *as a personality. Deism* is the point of view that accepts God only as an historical agent, a force that originally created the universe but is no longer actively involved in its operations. *Panentheism* is the less well-known position that holds that God is nothing less than the active interrelating of all of the determinative principles (truths, ideas) that shape and control the universe. Phrased somewhat differently, the panentheist holds that God is, in effect, a sort of transcendent and impersonal "idea-gestalt" or "cosmic consciousness."

At basis, all three of these points of view, while they may superficially appear to be religious, are not religious in the traditional sense, because they are nontheistic and serve implicity to deny the *personal relevance* of God as an active and identifiable force in contemporary affairs. In short, whatever word homage they may pay to the idea of "God," all of these orientations actually *function* as secular points of view, because they deny the *personality* of God, his concern for the individual, or his possible intercession in human affairs.

Theism, on the other hand, and as philosopher Alan Watts so acutely notes, is fundamentally a "political cosmology" that "presupposes a fractured way of experiencing the world."[4]

> God is not, as in Hindu cosmology, the underlying identity of the differences, but one of the differences — albeit the ruling difference. Man is related to God as to another distinct person, as subject to king or as son to father. The individual is, from the beginning and out of nothing, created separate and must bring himself to be brought to conformity with the divine will.[5]

In general, the secular and theistic traditions within the intellectualist point of view take very similar positions; the overall intellectualist orientation is summarized graphically in Figure 5–1.

FIGURE 5–1
INTELLECTUALISM

Self-realization

↓

is based upon proper conduct

↓

guided by true knowledge

↓

founded upon the apprehension of natural and/or divine laws

↓

guided by faith and reason.

The Secular View

The secular tradition differs from the theistic primarily in how it defines ultimate Truth. For the *secular* rationalist, Truth is ultimately *metaphysical* in the sense that it is highly abstract and consists of meaning that transcends any particular objects or events in the natural world. It is not, however, necessarily *supernatural* in the sense of existing in a realm apart from the physical world as such. Phrased somewhat differently, Truth is frequently viewed as the meaning of the whole—the qualities of the gestalt, or total system—which is not found in any particular aspect or aspects of the whole. Such meaning, which describes what modern physics might term "characterisitics of the total field," transcends any particular representation and can only therefore be known intuitively, in a way that resists satisfactory verbal (part-to-whole) definition.

For the secular rationalist, such intuitions transcend reason, strictly speaking, but they are also the global insights that ideally provide the consummation for all speculative reason. Indeed, it is reason that leads the mind, step by step, to the point of visionary transformation where reason itself is able to integrate all the painstaking knowledge that was previously acquired into certain global insights that constitute a suprarational sense of certitude that goes beyond the boundaries of natural reason altogether. Thus, in the philosophy of Aristotle, which is perhaps the best representation of the secular rationalist position, we are presented with a line of reasoning that can be roughly summarized as follows:

1. All men are rational.

2. A rational man naturally seeks Truth through the application of reason, and finds the most rational answers inherently convincing beyond all reasonable doubt.

3. Intellectual consensus about the nature of Truth is implicit within reason itself. Man is rational (predisposed toward the discovery of ultimate meaning through the application of reason), and he exists in an inherently rational (meaningful) world. When man's reason encounters the Reason inherent within Being, the inevitable result is Truth. Understanding is the relationship between an intelligent knower and an intelligible world. In knowing, man transcends the sensible limits of the body. He relates to a wider context, to the intelligibility of the universe itself. Therefore truth is the inevitable convergence of subjective (personal) reason and objective (universal) reason.

4. Therefore the best preparation for wisdom (Truth) is to cooperate with man's rational nature by training the mind, by developing his natural capacity to reason effectively. (See Figure 5–2.)

The Religious View

The *religious* attitude differs from the secular tradition primarily in that it views reason as merely one step in the enlightenment process. Where the secular rationalist sees reason as necessary *and* sufficient, culminating in rationally directed intuitive leaps that defy doubt, the religious rationalist sees reason as necessary but not sufficient, requiring both faith and revelation as additional bases for true knowing. Indeed, from the religious rationalist's point of view, faith ideally *precedes* reason, and it is reason that justifies faith by generating an intuitive certitude in the inevitability of revealed Truth. From the point of

FIGURE 5–2
SECULAR RATIONALISM

Self-realization

↓

is based upon proper conduct

↓

guided by true knowledge

↓

which is founded upon the apprehension of natural laws

↓

by means of reason.

view of the religious rationalist, faith without reason is wrong, because man is a rational animal, and this rationality, fully developed, inevitably terminates in true faith. Indeed, true faith is ultimately the most reasonable answer to the most important of life's problems.

The Thomistic Philosophy.   The religious rationalist's position is perhaps best represented in the philosophy of Saint Thomas Aquinas, and can be summarized roughly as follows:

1. Reality (Truth) is both natural and supernatural.

2. *Natural Truth* (metaphysical knowledge with respect to the ultimate nature of the temporal world) is apprehensible by means of reason. Man is naturally rational; he seeks the Truth by employing reason and finds the most reasonable answers inherently convincing.

3. Reason is a *necessary* but not a *sufficient* condition for apprehending Truth. *Supernatural Truth* — that is, knowledge concerning the ultimate nature of the external world, including such things as a knowledge of the existence of God, a belief in the divinity of Christ, and so on — transcends ordinary experience and does not lend itself to purely natural determination by means of reason and evidence.

4. In order to grasp Truth, it is necessary to supplement reason with faith in the perfect knowledge that derives (directly or indirectly) from divine revelation or from the authority of the Church (which serves as God's agent on earth). There is no inherent conflict between reason and faith, and whatever differences appear to exist are merely ostensible differences growing out of the imperfect state of contemporary knowledge and man's natural intellectual fallibility. Ultimately, when reason is perfect and evidence is complete, reason will confirm the teachings of faith, and the two will be found to be not merely compatible but mutually supporting.

5. Supernatural knowledge is *nonrational*, but it is not *irrational*. Ideally, the teachings of faith should be presented through reason, as a logical inference from the known. When this is done, the supernatural pronouncements of faith become convincing beyond all doubt, because (a) they are the logical outgrowth of man's innate powers of rational inference and (b) they reflect a vision of reality that is so overwhelmingly meaningful as to be rationally irresistible. (See Figure 5–3.)

FIGURE 5–3
THEISTIC RATIONALISM

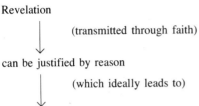

Revelation

    (transmitted through faith)

can be justified by reason

    (which ideally leads to)

a natural (if suprarational) intuitive confirmation of essentially supernatural truths (which were initially transmitted on a prerational basis by revelation and/or faith).

Some Roman Catholic Traditions. It should be added here, particularly in view of the foregoing discussion of differences within some of the non-Catholic (and generally Protestant) fundamentalist groups and also in view of subsequent discussions of other non-Catholic Christian orientations, that not all Roman Catholicism is based upon the Thomistic philosophy discussed here. Thomism is the official philosophy of the Roman Catholic Church, but Roman Catholicism, like all large and complex religions, encompasses a variety of different points of view that deviate in significant degree from official policy. Thus, to be completely fair to the variations of belief that exist wihtin Roman Catholicism, it is perhaps wise to view this religion as a continuum of beliefs, as represented in Figure 5–4, ranging from the relatively simple sort of "folk religion" that might be found in a place like Haiti to the theological "anarchism" exemplified by such individuals as St. John of the Cross.

VALUES

The distinction between theistic and secular points of view within the overall orientation of intellectualism is particularly significant in the area of values. Here proponents of the intellectualist tradition tend to break down into two major groups on the basis of religious orientation.

The position of the secular intellectualist can be essentially summarized in two points:

1. The question of value is basically a question of effective behavior within the natural world, of being able to live in harmony with that which *is*, of being able to adapt oneself to the imperatives of temporal reality.
2. In general, the best guide to effective behavior is a profound insight into the nature of such reality — that is, a true knowledge of that which is objectively good and true.

The position of the theistic intellectualist is more complicated, because he accepts a *double-truth* theory, which assumes that truth (and value) is both *natural* and *supernatural*. The practical result of this is to break the world up

FIGURE 5–4

MAJOR TRADITIONS WITHIN CONTEMPORARY ROMAN CATHOLICISM

Conservatism						Liberalism
Folk Religion	Ethnic Religion (Ethnodoxy)	Augustinian Conservatism	Thomistic Intellectualism	Theological Liberalism	Theological Liberalism	Mysticism
Religious convictions emerging out of beliefs and practices indigenous to a particular people and, in large part, unmediated by Church authority The nature and degree of folk religion present is highly dependent upon the particular cultural context	Orthodox beliefs adapted to the needs and requirements of a specific ethnic group that has retained its separate identity within a larger and otherwise dominant culture	Conservative orthodoxy that emphasizes intuition and faith over reason	Mainstream orthodoxy that places a greater emphasis on reason than on intuition or naive faith	Orthodoxy made less restrictive by an emphasis on the critical examination of traditional beliefs and practices (generally viewed as a continuing form of spiritual renewal)	An emphasis on the social interpretation of the scriptures and church authority, frequently bordering on so-called *liberation theology* in which the role of the church is seen as encompassing an active commitment to the political and economic reconstruction of society in order to expedite the fullest realization of man's natural and supernatural potentialities	The religious counterpart of political anarchism; the belief that personal revelation and/or mystical intuition takes precedence over established church authority and accepted theological doctrine (at least with respect to significant aspects of religious practices)

into not only two but three basic spheres: (1) the self (the natural subject with supernatural attributes — the supernatural aspect frequently being referred to as the "soul"); (2) the world (the natural object); and (3) God (the supernatural determinative reality that transcends and, in some sense, determines both subject and object). What this means with respect to values can, again, be summarized roughly in two points:

1. There are *natural values* that represent the principles of action governing effective behavior in the ordinary, temporal world. Such values — the laws of logic, the principles ensuring civic order, and so on — are not separate from supernatural values in any absolute sense, since the temporal world is also founded upon eternal principles, which are ultimately grounded in the divine (supernatural). On the other hand, such natural laws represent a lower order of moral reality than that expressed in explicitly *supernatural values* such as the Ten Commandments or the Golden Rule, which emanate directly from the divine by means of revelation and which are not fundamentally reliant upn natural evidence or reason.

2. In the moral realm, supernatural values take precedence over natural values, and the violation of divine injunctions is a graver transgression than trespasses against natural laws. There is, then, a natural hierarchy of values that can be outlined as follows:

I. SUPERNATURAL VALUES
   A. *Ultimate Supernatural Values* (for example, salvation, immortality, a reconciliation with God, and such)
   B. *Immediate Supernatural Values* (obedience to God's will as *directly* revealed within the natural world — for example, the Ten Commandments, obedience to church authority as a temporal expression of Divine Will, and so on)

II. NATURAL VALUES (obedience to God's will as *indirectly revealed* in the moral principles that inhere within the natural world—for example, standards for good citizenship, rational behavior and such)

POLITICAL AND EDUCATIONAL INTELLECTUALISM

At the level of political philosophy, the moral stance of the intellectualist generally translates into what might be termed *philosophical conservatism*. Philosophical conservatism includes all of those expressions of political conservatism that are based upon authoritarian (absolute) philosophical or theological systems of thought and which maintain that "right reason" inexorably leads to true conclusions. In general, philosophical conservatism seeks to change existing political (including educational) practices in order to make them conform more perfectly to some established and essentially unvarying intellectual or spiritual ideal. It is, for example, intellectual conservatism that is reflected in the writings of both Plato and Aristotle and which is central to the position of Saint Thomas Aquinas (who, in turn, provides the philosophical basis for the dominant point of view within the Roman Catholic Church).

Educational intellectualism, as indicated, is closely related to the traditional (metaphysical) approaches to philosophy, and most of the conventional representatives of the traditional philosophies tend to speak in intellectualist terms when they address themselves to the problems of education. In general, then, educational intellectualism holds that there are certain absolute and enduring truths that transcend any particular time and space; that such truths are eternal and universal; that they have always existed; and that they apply to mankind in general and are not the unique possession of any particular individual or group. Such truths can be discovered either by reason or — in the case of the theological tradition within educational intellectualism — by reason supplemented by revelation or faith.

Accordingly, educational intellectualism tends to be past-oriented and to emphasize stability — the continuity of the great, enduring ideas — over change. In general, the eternal truths are best represented in the abiding masterworks of the world's greatest minds as these are conveyed through the cultural heritage of mankind. The overall goal of education is to identify, preserve and transmit essential Truth (that is, the central principles that govern the underlying meaning and significance of life). More specifically, the immediate role of the school as a particular social institution is to teach the students how to think (that is, how to reason) and to transmit the best thought (the enduring wisdom) of the past.

In contemporary education, philosophical conservatism expresses itself primarily as *educational intellectualism*, which encompasses two basic variations: *philosophical intellectualism* and *theological intellectualism*. Philosophical intellectualism is probably best represented in America today by such individuals as Robert Maynard Hutchins and Mortimer Adler, who are both primarily concerned with metaphysical wisdom in the traditional Aristotelian sense and who both tend to place great emphasis on traditional "liberal arts" education in the spirit of the "Great Books."

Theological rationalism is a religious orientation that is perhaps best reflected in the writings of such contemporary Roman Catholic educational philosophers as Jacques Maritain, William McGucken, John Donohue and James Ryan. As indicated earlier, the theological intellectualist distinguishes between natural truths and supernatural truths (and therefore between two different ways of knowing and learning); he believes that the supernatural takes precedence over the natural, and he holds that educational practices should be established upon an intellectual basis that integrates the deepest and most profound insights of both philosophy and religion. From the point of view of the theological intellectualist, the ultimate purpose of education is always secondary to the ultimate purpose of life itself, which is to bring the individual into a perfect union with God.

Probably the best known and most influential type of theological intellectualism is the Thomist point of view growing out of the writings of Saint Thomas Aquinas, which has traditionally dominated the Roman Catholic approach to education since the Middle Ages. There are, however, two other varieties of theological intellectualism that are less well known but also important. These are (1) the Jewish intellectualist tradition, which is perhaps best represented in the writings of Moses Maimonides and which is still fundamental in virtually all persuasions within organized Judaism; and (2) the essentially nondenominational (or interdenominational) Christian intellectualism that extends from the earliest beginnings of the Christian faith through contemporary theologians such as Paul Tillich and Reinhold Niebuhr.

Empirical Philosophies and Education. The more contemporary *empirical* philosophies—positions such as behaviorism and experimentalism—are most frequently associated with the more liberal educational ideologies. On the other hand, this is a *correlation* rather than a *causal relationship*, and it is possible in principle—however improbable in fact—for a person who subscribes to one of the "process," or empirical philosophies, such as experimentalism, to subscribe to a relatively traditional educational position (such as educational intellectualism) that may appear to be logically incompatible with his more basic philosophical assumptions. (See Chapter 2.)

An experimentalist might, for example, evolve through the following line of reasoning toward the ideology of educational conservatism:

1. The goal of life is effective behavior.
2. Effective behavior is based upon effective thinking.
3. All effective thinking is effective problem solving.
4. The most effective problem solving is that which is guided by the experimental (scientific) mode of inquiry or which is probable on the basis of information that has emerged from such a process of verification.
5. Many of the more significant moral and political problems that exist today, however, are demonstrably too complex to be solved "experimentally" by the average man.
6. Therefore, the best course of action for people in general is to reduce such problems to simpler dimensions that are more comprehensible to the average person and that are capable of being resolved on the basis of traditional *code morality* as this prevails within the established social system.

In a similar manner, it would be *possible* (if generally improbable) for a philosophical experimentalist to veer in the direction of *educational intellectualism* of a theological sort by pursuing something approximating the following line of reasoning:

1. The goal of life is effective behavior.
2. Effective behavior is based upon effective thinking.
3. All effective thinking is effective problem solving.
4. The most effective problem solving is that which is guided by the experimental (scientific) mode of inquiry or which is probable on the basis of information that has emerged from such a process of verification.
5. Science, as well as information growing out of scientific inquiry and that which is compatible with established scientific beliefs, supports the idea that man has an ontological need for some kind of supernatural "overbelief," including the need for some transcendent sense of commitment to a personal God.
6. The most effective way of satisfying this need for "philosophical closure" is by means of established religion.
7. Therefore a religious system of belief is warranted on the basis of a fully conceived scientific worldview, and the best educational system is one that accepts the most convincing religious expression of man's overriding need to relate to a personal God and organizes its activities around the sort of intellectual and moral requirements implied by such a belief.

Again, this is not to say that such positions are either prevalent or probable. Merely that they are logically possible and that they do not necessarily violate more basic experimentalist assumptions about the nature of reality.

Natural and Supernatural Metaphysics

At basis the various expressions of intellectualism tend to divide on two main questions: (1) the question of religion (that is, whether there is a personal God and what this implies for human conduct); and (2) the nature of metaphysical reality (more specifically, whether absolute truth is *transcendent*, and therefore exists in some realm superordinate to personal and/or natural experience), or *immanent* (that is, universally inherent within all personal and/or natural experience). In terms of these two basic distinctions, there are four basic subvarieties of intellectualism, which are represented diagrammatically in Figure 5–5 and somewhat simplified in Figure 5–6.

FIGURE 5–5
PHILOSOPHICAL CONSERVATISM

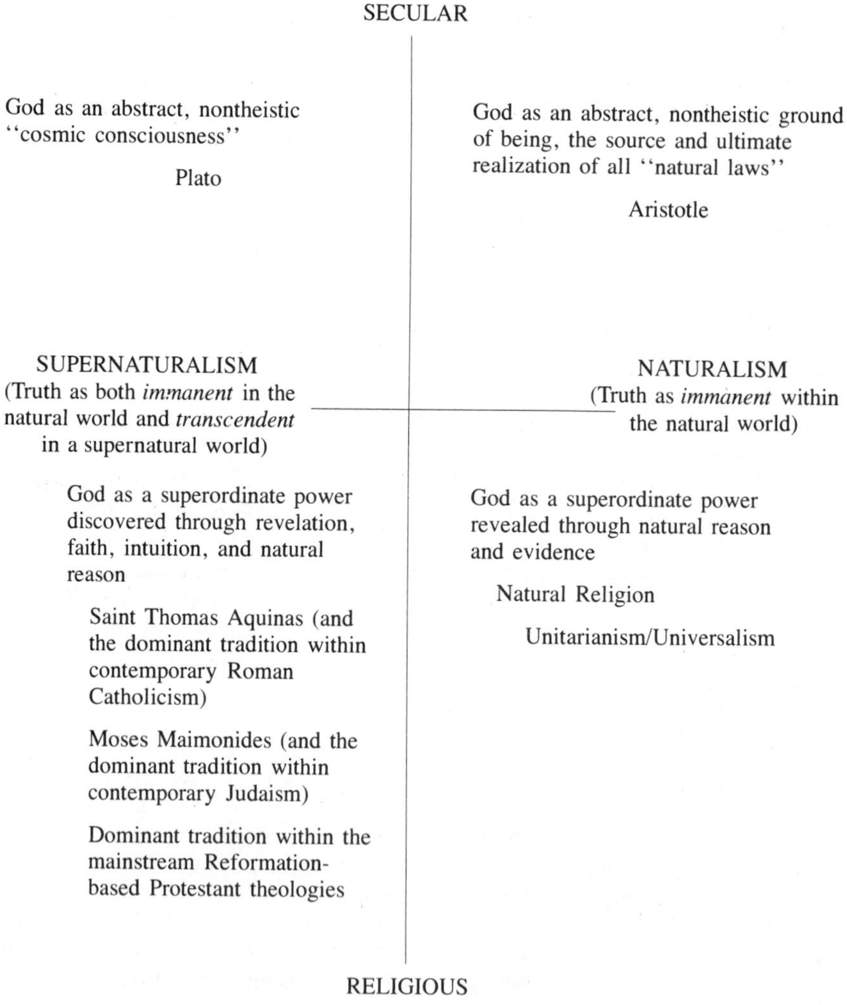

SECULAR

God as an abstract, nontheistic "cosmic consciousness"

Plato

God as an abstract, nontheistic ground of being, the source and ultimate realization of all "natural laws"

Aristotle

SUPERNATURALISM
(Truth as both *immanent* in the natural world and *transcendent* in a supernatural world)

NATURALISM
(Truth as *immanent* within the natural world)

God as a superordinate power discovered through revelation, faith, intuition, and natural reason

Saint Thomas Aquinas (and the dominant tradition within contemporary Roman Catholicism)

Moses Maimonides (and the dominant tradition within contemporary Judaism)

Dominant tradition within the mainstream Reformation-based Protestant theologies

God as a superordinate power revealed through natural reason and evidence

Natural Religion

Unitarianism/Universalism

RELIGIOUS

FIGURE 5–6
PHILOSOPHICAL CONSERVATISM (SIMPLIFIED)

SECULAR

Plato	Aristotle
SUPERNATURALISM (Transcendent Truth)	NATURALISM (Immanent Truth)
Saint Thomas Aquinas	Natural Religion Unitarianism/Universalism

RELIGIOUS

INTELLECTUALISM IN EDUCATION: A SUMMARY

Temporarily disregarding the differences between the secular and religious points of view within the tradition of intellectualism, the basic ideology of the educational intellectualist can be summarized as follows:

The Overall Goal of Education.   The central purpose of education is to identify, preserve, and transmit Truth (that is, knowledge about the underlying meaning and significance of life).

The Objectives of the School.   The school exists for two basic reasons: (1) to teach students how to reason (how to think clearly and coherently), and (2) to transmit the enduring wisdom of the past.

General Characteristics.   Educational intellectualism can be characterized in the following ways:

It maintains that knowledge is an end-in-itself, that knowing is not simply a means of improving the effectiveness of practical behavior.

It emphasizes man *as man*, that is, that man has a universal nature which transcends specific circumstances.

It stresses the values of traditional intellectualism, that is, the cultivation of reason and the transmission of speculative (philosophical) wisdom.

It views education as an orientation to life in general, not as a matter of situational adaptation.

It focuses on the intellectual history of man as this is identified with the dominant Western intellectual tradition (classicism).

It emphasizes philosophical stability over the need for change, stressing intellectual stability and continuity, the so-called perennial truths that transcend time and place.

It is based on a closed ideological system of philosophical absolutes.

It is grounded on self-evident truths that are inherent within reason and/or reality itself.

It holds that the ultimate intellectual authority resides within the intellect itself, that truth is apprehensible by means of pure reason.

The Child as Learner.   The child is predisposed toward wisdom and virtue, because he is by nature both rational and social.

Individual similarities are more important than individual differences, and these similarities are properly determinative in establishing appropriate educational programs.

Children are morally equal in a world of objectively unequal opportunties; they should have equal opportunity to strive for intellectual excellence although the capacity to attain such excellence is not equally distributed throughout the population.

The child is essentially self-determining; he has personal free will in the traditional sense.

Administration and Control.   Educational authority should be invested in a highly educated intellectual elite.

Teacher authority should be based on the teacher's superior wisdom.

The Nature of the Curriculum.   The school should emphasize intellectual discipline, training the child to be capable of clear and coherent reasoning.

The school should focus on reason and speculative wisdom.

Emphasis should be placed on abstract ideas and theory.

The course of study should be almost totally prescribed.

Emphasis should be placed on the *intellectual* (that is, the ideational, dealing with broad interpretive theory) over the *practical* (the immediately useful) and the *academic* (learning how to learn, and mastering the sort of technical knowledge and skills that are only indirectly related to actual human problems).

The school should stress philosophy and/or theology, literature (particularly the established literary and intellectual classics of the Western world), and broad-scale interpretive history in the tradition of Edward Gibbon, Oswald Spengler and Arnold Toynbee.

Instructional Methods and Evaluation.   Emphasis should be placed upon traditional classroom procedures, such as lecture, recitation, Socratic (teacher-directed) questioning, and highly structured group discussion.

Drill is the best way of establishing proper habits at the lower levels, but it should evolve toward more open and intellectual approaches, featuring formal (deductive) reasoning during the later phases of learning.

Teacher-determined and teacher-directed learnings are best, but the teacher should always attempt to cooperate with the child's naturally rational nature rather than seeking blind obedience through indoctrination procedures.

The teacher should be viewed as a model of intellectual excellence and an arbiter of Truth.

Tests that measure intellectual acuity (as in essay-type examinations) are preferable to those that emphasize factual content (as in objective-type examinations).

Since intellectual aptitude is unequally distributed and intellectual excellence is difficult to attain, some degree of interpersonal competition is virtually implicit in any good academic situation, and the competitive pursuit of intellectual excellence can be utilized to advance legitimate intellectual goals.

Emphasis should be placed on the cognitive over the affective and the interpersonal.

Emphasis should be placed upon adhering to the classical educational principles and practices identified and defined by the great thinkers of the Western intellectual tradition.

Personal counseling and psychotherapy are not proper concerns of the school, and should be handled by other social agencies better suited to provide guidance and therapy.

Classroom Control. Students should be good citizens in terms of certain absolute moral standards, and they should be held morally accountable for their own behavior.

Teachers should generally be nonpermissive in procedures for maintaining classroom control but authority should always be justified and/or justifiable by reason.

Moral education (character training) is a necessary and unavoidable aspect of schooling, but the school should focus its attentions on explaining and clarifying the intellectual basis of fundamental moral principles.

NOTES

1. Mortimer J. Adler, "In Defense of the Philosophy of Education, " in The National Society for the Study of Education Yearbook (Forty-first Yearbook, Part 1; Nelson B. Henry, ed.), *Philosophies of Education* (Chicago, Illinois: National Society for the Study of Education, 1942), pp. 221–22.

2. John Hospers, *An Introduction to Philosophical Analysis* (Englewood Cliffs, New Jersey: Prentice-Hall, 1963), p. 209.

3. The case can be made that Aristotle was far more of an aristocrat than Plato. Aristotle, unlike Plato, held quite explicitly to the notion that women were inherently inferior to men and that certain peoples were essentially subhuman and therefore "natural slaves." On the other hand, Aristotle was essentially inductive and scientific in orientation, and these beliefs probably reflect the state of knowledge in that essentially prescientific era rather than deep-set philosophical convictions. Certainly, contemporary Aristotelians, like Robert Maynard Hutchins and Mortimer Adler, subscribe to a meritocratic democracy in which the average person (regardless of sex or race) is regarded as potentially capable of intellectual enlightenment.

   At basis, both Plato and Aristotle subscribe to the notion that individuals are inherently unequal in abilities, both prescribe education as the best way of realizing the maximum development of these abilities (however inequitably distributed), and both advocate extending equal educational opportunity to all so that natural inequalities will sort out on the basis of achievement during the course of the schooling process. They differ primarily in their concept of "man." Aristotle views "man" as essentially a masculine category (relegating women to a subordinate status) and assigning certain peoples to an essentially subhuman role as "natural slaves." With these qualifications, however, he views all "men" as potentially capable of enlightened action. Plato is not recorded as having made any invidious distinctions between the sexes or the various races, but he clearly believed that only a small proportion of "men" (defined generically to encompass both sexes) were capable of true intellectual enlightenment and that only this minority should (as per his "myth of metals" in *The Republic*) be allowed to govern. If it is to be assumed that Aristotle's statements were based on insufficient or erroneous evidence while Plato's were based upon philosophical principle (grounded in the more basic fabric of his overall philosophy), Aristotle is, at least in principle, more democratic and equalitarian than Plato both in his political theory and in his corresponding educational ideas.

4. Alan W. Watts, *Nature, Man and Woman* (New York; New American Library — Mentor, 1960), p. 56

5. Ibid.

BIBLIOGRAPHY

Educational Intellectualism

THEOLOGICAL INTELLECTUALISM

Roman Catholicism (Thomism)

AQUINAS, SAINT THOMAS. *Basic Writings of St. Thomas Aquinas.* Edited by Anton C. Pegis. New York: Random House, 1945.

AQUINAS, SAINT THOMAS. *The Teacher —The Mind.* Chicago: Henry Regnery Co., 1953.

DONOHUE, JOHN W. *Saint Thomas Aquinas and Education.* New York: Random House, 1968.

FITZPATRICK, EDWARD A., ed. *Saint Ignatius and the Ratio Studiorum.* Translated by A. R. Ball. New York: McGraw-Hill & Co., 1933.

HENLE, ROBERT J. "A Roman Catholic View of Education," in *Philosophies of Education,* edited by Philip H. Phenix. New York: John Wiley & Sons, 1961.

LEE, JAMES MICHAEL, ed. *Catholic Education in the Western World.* Evanston, Illinois: University of Notre Dame Press, 1967.

KOLESNIK, W. H., and POWER, E. J., eds. *Catholic Education: A Book of Readings.* New York: McGraw-Hill, 1965.

McGUCKEN, WILLIAM, S.J. *The Catholic Way in Education.* Milwaukee, Wisconsin: Bruce Publishing Co., 1934.

McGUCKEN, WILLIAM, S.J. "The Philosophy of Catholic Education," in National Society for the Study of Education. *Philosophies of Education.* (The Forty-first Yearbook of the NSSE, Part I). Edited by Nelson B. Henry, Chicago: University of Chicago Press, 1942.

MARITAIN, JACQUES. *Education at the Crossroads.* New Haven, Conn.: Yale University Press, 1943.

MARITAIN, JACQUES. "Thomist Views on Education," in National Society for the Study of Education. *Modern Philosophies and Education.* (The Fifty-fourth Yearbook of the NSSE, Part I). Edited by Nelson B. Henry. Chicago: University of Chicago Press, 1955, pp. 57–90.

PIUS XI, "Encyclical on the Christian Education of Youth," in *Five Great Encyclicals.* New York: Paulist Press, 1939.

REDDEN, J. D., AND RYAN, F. A. *A Catholic View of Education.* Rev. ed. Milwaukee, Wisconsin: Bruce Publishing Co., 1956.

RYAN, JAMES H. *A Catechism of Catholic Education.* Washington, D.C.: National Catholic Welfare Conference, 1922.

Traditional Judaism

COHEN, A. *The Teachings of Maimonides.* New York: KTAV Publishing House, 1968.

MAIMONIDES, MOSES. *The Guide for the Perplexed.* Translated from the Arabic by M. Friedlander. New York: Pardes Publishing House, 1946.

Nondenominational and/or Interdenominational Christianity

BUTLER, J. DONALD. *Idealism in Education.* New York: Harper & Row, 1966.

FULLER, EDMUND, ed. *The Christian Idea of Education.* New Haven, Conn.: Yale University Press, 1957.

FULLER, EDMUND, ed. *Schools and Scholarship: The Christian Idea of Education, Part Two.* New Haven, Conn.: Yale University Press, 1962.

GREENE, THEODORE, M., "A Liberal Christian Idealist Philosophy of Education," in NSSE, *Modern Philosophies and Education,* pp. 91 – 136.

GREENE, THEODORE M. *Liberal Education Reconsidered.* Cambridge, Mass.: Harvard University Press, 1953.

HORNE, HERMAN H. *Idealism in Education.* New York: Macmillan Co., 1910.

HORNE, HERMAN H., "An Idealistic Philosophy of Education," in NSSE, *Philosophies of Education,* pp. 139–96.

SECULAR INTELLECTUALISM

ADLER, MORTIMER J. and PETER WOLFF. *A General Introduction to the Great Books and to a Liberal Education.* Chicago: Encyclopedia Brittanica, 1959.

ADLER, MORTIMER J. *Great Ideas from the Great Books.* New York: Washington Square Press, 1961.

ADLER, MORTIMER J. *How to Read a Book: The Art of Getting a Liberal Education.* New York: Simon & Schuster, 1940.

ADLER, MORTIMER J., "In Defense of the Philosophy of Education," in NSSE, *Philosophies of Education,* pp. 197 – 250.

ADLER, MORTIMER J., and MAYER, MILTON. *The Revolution in Education.* Chicago: University of Chicago Press, 1958.

ARISTOTLE. *Aristotle on Education.* Edited and translated by John Burnet. Cambridge: Cambridge University Press, 1967.

ARISTOTLE. *The Basic Writings of Aristotle.* Edited by Richard McKeon. New York: Random House, 1941.

BARZUN, JACQUES. *The House of Intellect.* New York: Harper, 1959.

BROUDY, HARRY S., "A Classical Realist View of Education," in *Philosophies of Education,* edited by Philip H. Phenix. pp. 17 – 24.

BRUMBAUGH, R. S., and LAWRENCE, N. M., JR. "Aristotle's Philosophy of Edu-Realization," in Brumbaugh and Lawrence, *Philosophers on Education.* Boston: Houghton Mifflin Co., 1963.

BRUMBAUGH, R. S., and LAWRENCE, N. M., JR. "Aristotle's Philosophy of Education," *Educational Theory 9,* no. 1 (Jan. 1959), pp. 1–15.

CHAMBLISS, J. J. "The Guardian: Plato," in *The Educated Man: Studies in the History of Educational Thought.* Edited by Paul Nash, Andreas M. Kazamias, and Henry J. Perkinson. New York; John Wiley & Sons, 1967, pp. 29 – 54.

DEMOS, RAPHAEL. *The Philosophy of Plato.* New York: Octagon Books, 1966.

HARWOOD, A. C. *The Rediscovery of Man in Childhood: A Study in the Educational Work of Rudolph Steiner.* New York: Hodder & Stoughton, 1970.

HIGHET, GILBERT. *Man's Unconscious Mind*. New York: Columbia University Press, 1960.

HUTCHINS, ROBERT M. *The Conflict in Education in a Democratic Society*. New York: Harper, 1953.

HUTCHINS, ROBERT M. *Freedom, Education and the Fund: Essays and Addresses, 1946–1956*. New York: Meridian Books, 1956.

HUTCHINS, ROBERT M. *Great Books, The Foundations of a Liberal Education*. New York: Simon & Schuster Co., 1954.

HUTCHINS, ROBERT M. *The Higher Learning in America*. New Haven, Conn.: Yale University Press, 1936.

KIRK, RUSSELL. *Academic Freedom*. Chicago: Henry Regnery Co., 1955.

PLATO, *The Education of the Young in the Republic of Plato*. Translated by Bernard Bosanquet. Cambridge: Cambridge University Press, 1908.

ST. JOHN'S COLLEGE. *The St. John's Program: A Report*. Annapolis, Md.: St. John's College Press, 1955.

STEINER, RUDOLF (and other writers). *Education as an Art*, edited by Paul M. Allen. Blauvelt, New York: Rudolf Steiner Publications, 1970.

WHITEHEAD, ALFRED N. *The Aims of Education*. New York: Macmillan Co., 1929.

VAN DOREN, MARK. *Liberal Education*. Boston: Beacon Press, 1965.

Chapter VI

Educational Conservatism

POLITICAL CONSERVATISM

The political philosophy of social conservatism is essentially that position which espouses adherence to time-tested cultural institutions and processes, coupled with a deep respect for law and order, as a basis for any sort of constructive social change. The mainstream social conservative does not, unlike the reactionary conservative, distrust reason; but, in contrast to the philosophical conservative, he does not exalt it either. Rather he advocates a proper relationship between reasoned change and reasonable conformity, with his enthusiasm for either depending largely on his assessment of existing conditions.

The Conservative tends to distrust pure theory, free-floating intellectual speculation. Skeptical of both the moral fervor of the reactionary conservative on the one hand and the intellectual passion of the philosophical conservative on the other, the social conservative is dubious about utopian visions and romanticized notions of man's potential for self-improvement. He favors ideas that are grounded in concrete situations and that are clearly relevant to the practical problems of everyday living. While he favors trained intelligence and democratic procedures, he hesitates to relinquish the best of the past except for the most urgent reasons. "The stimulus to conservatism," states the Conservative thinker Samuel P. Huntington, "comes not from the outworn creeds of third-rate thinkers but from the successful performance of first-rate institutions." [1]

Typically committed to a stance that might be described as *democratic capitalism*, the American Conservative today tends to be staunchly committed to the capitalistic economic system of individualistic free enterprise, and he typically views this system as characterized by (1) either private ownership of property (or, at the least, private ownership of *most* property); (2) little or no limitation on the accumulation of property; and (3) the absence of governmental intervention in the economy (or, at the least, restricted governmental regulation of the economy and a radically restricted welfare system). [2]

The Conservative, states Gould and Truitt,

> . . . agrees with the liberal that constitutional and representative government is good, [but] he will argue that it is only good to the extent that it stays out of the affairs of individuals' private lives. Governments, he says, have no right to legislate matters of social equality, housing, education,

and so forth. With great stress on individual self-determination, the conservative believes that social injustice and inequality will best be overcome by means of personal initiative and hard work. Even the lowliest of individuals on the social scale, it is maintained, are capable of improving themselves within the institutions of capitalism and economic free enterprise.[3]

In a similar sense, F.J.C. Hearnshaw, in his book *Conservatism in England* sees Conservative philosophy as it exists in the modern world as reducible to twelve basic principles:

. . . (1) reverence for the past, (2) the organic conception of society, (3) communal unity, (4) constitutional continuity, (5) opposition to revolution, (6) cautious or evolutionary reform, (7) the religious basis of the state, (8) the divine source of legitimate authority, (9) the priority of duties to rights, (10) the prime importance of individual and communal character, (11) loyalty, (12) common sense, realism, and practicality. [4]

THE SUBVARIETIES OF CONSERVATISM

What further complicates any discussion of social conservatism as an overall political philosophy is that there are at least two basic varieties of social conservatism; one the secular variety, the other fundamentally religious in orientation. Within the secular orientation alone, there are at least four basic approaches to social conservatism. These might be termed (1) the Establishment Conservatives (the Tories); (2) the Laissez Faire Conservatives (or Free Marketeers); (3) the Social Darwinists (or Spencerian Conservatives); and (4) the Teleological Nationalists (or Hegelian Conservatives).

The Establishment Conservatives (The Tory Conservatives)

In contemporary parlance, the term *Tory* generally means an old-fashioned conservative. From the late 1600s to the early nineteenth century (when it broke up over the question of free trade) the Tories were, along with the Whigs, one of the two chief political parties of Great Britain. Unlike the Whigs, the Tories emphasized the supremacy of the King over Parliament, and generally expounded the interests of the precapitalist landed gentry rather than those of the more enterprising commercial and industrial classes. Probably the most prominent spokesman for establishment conservatism was Edmund Burke (1729–1797), a British statesman who, ironically, was not a Tory but a Whig, yet who nevertheless articulated perhaps the most persuasive presentation of the profoundly conservative point of view that is often referred to as "Tory Democracy."

Conservative philosophy is frequently said to have begun with the publication of Edmund Burke's *Reflections on the Revolution in France* in 1790, although there was already a good deal of conservative political theory before that. Burke is, however, still considered by many to have been both the originator and the most articulate spokesman for the conservative point of view, and Gould and Truitt in their book, *Political Ideologies*, characterize Burkean Conservatism as follows:

> First, it definitely argues that radical social change is wrong, especially radical change that is instigated by force. Second, the conservatives believe that it is the main function of government to maintain peace and order. It should do little else. Third, conservatives view human nature as complex, unpredictable, and often immoral. Regarding this last point, they contend that such immoral characteristics as cruelty and greed are inevitably present in human existence. Consequently, political and social institutions cannot be perfected. We must accept their necessary inadequacies. Related to this is the belief of conservatives that institutions as well as people can only become adequate for society through historical development. Individuals learn how to govern others by practice and example. Hence those best suited to rule come from the members of a long-established ruling class. Such aristocrats, it is argued, have had the tradition, have had the education, and have had the experience of living with successful rulers. It is the same with institutions. Only those institutions that have survived the many decades and centuries—such as the state, the church, the family—are those society should want. Those institutions that have long existed must be workable, successful institutions. Finally, these conservatives are usually quite religious. They usually believe in God and God's role in history. Not all conservatives agree with each of these tenets. Many reject Burke's autocratic element. Others support change, that is, those changes which will preserve the fundamental elements of their society. . . . there is no single ideology of conservatism.
>
> Yet . . . note how many of the following scenes appear: the need of a ruling aristocracy, the uncertainty of progress, the primary role of private property, the necessity of social classes and orders, the natural inequality of men in their mental abilities, the imperfect and sinful nature of men, the existence of God and the need for organized religion, the limitations of human reason, and the inadequacy of majority rule and its potentiality for tyranny. [5]

In general, the conservative orientation of the so-called Tories subscribes to a somewhat pessimistic view of human nature. They reject the idea that individual reason should reign supreme; they hold, instead, that the collective wisdom of the group, as this is embodied in established institutions and processes, represents the highest expression of human intelligence at any particular time.

For the Tory Conservative, history itself provides a sort of informal and pragmatic verification for the viability of established ways of behaving and believing. In general, the very complexity of real problems rules against the reliability of pure reason. Habit is generally more trustworthy than precept, and one should make a presumption in favor of the established order precisely because of its longevity, if for no other reason.

Certain individuals and institutions have come to dominate because they have been patently more effective than others in meeting certain continuing human needs. The collective historical experience of the group, which is contained within existing traditions, is far less fallible than individual reason, and should properly take precedence over it. The corporate society in historical frame of reference is continuous and evolves gradually out of its own formative traditions.

Intelligent action is basically practical and contextual, rooted in the specific realities of particular situations. Radical prescriptions for wholesale change tend to violate the integrity and continuity of the total process, as this exists in all of its historical richness and particularity. Accordingly, it is important to guard against excessive zeal for large-scale reforms based upon purely abstract conceptions of reality. Intelligent change is basically a matter of compromise in which conflict is minimized to the point where it consists primarily of adaptations within the established frame of reference.

Law and order are not legitimately opposed to individual freedom. Rather, individual freedom requires some preestablished order for its fullest expression, and, in a similar sense, all law and order represent the exercise of free choice by those who have lived in previous generations. Contrary to restricting personal liberty, then, current laws and the existing distribution of goods merely represent the decisions of previous peoples who found themselves confronted with the necessity of making intelligent choices in response to many of the same problems that exist today. To reject existing laws, with the existing distribution of property, is to reject the cumulative wisdom of the past as this is embodied in present patterns of behavior.

The Laissez Faire Conservatives (The Free Marketeers)

It has been said that there was no conservative social philosophy before Burke, because, before Burke, *all* social philosophy was conservative. A variation of the same observation can be applied to the Laissez Faire Conservatives: there was no "free market" philosophy before the middle of the eighteenth century, because before "the busting, scurrying, free-for-all of the eighteenth century"[6] there was nothing that really approximated a free market. Indeed, and as economist Robert Heilbroner indicates, land, labor and capital — the basic elements of production in a "market system" of economics — did not exist until about the eighteenth century, and "the profit motive was conspicuous by its absence over most of recorded history."[7] "As long as the problem of survival was handled by tradition or command, the economic problem never gave rise to that special field of study called economics."[8] (The school of economics known as Physiocracy, propounded by François Quesnay in France during the reign of Louis XV, agreed with the later laissez faire economists that real wealth was not contained in gold and silver but, rather, sprang from production and flowed through the nation, from person to person, replenishing society like the circulation of blood. It also held, however, that only agricultural classes produced true "wealth" and that the manufacturing and commercial classes merely manipulated it in an essentially sterile way. Thus, while they advocated a policy of laissez faire, which influenced such thinkers as Adam Smith, their basic position ran counter to the rising tide of industrialism and therefore failed to take hold.)

For all practical purposes, laissez faire economics and the laissez faire social philosophy associated with this economic doctrine grew out of the writing of one man, Adam Smith, who was a professor of moral philosophy at the University of Edinburgh. Smith published his epochal *Inquiry Into the Nature and Causes of the Wealth of Nations* in 1776. In this work — which was a massive attack on the then-dominant mercantile system — Smith for the first time formulated the laws of the open and uncontrolled market. The good, as Smith saw it, emerged as a by-product of selfishness. People naturally seek to maximize profits and minimize losses. "It is best to abolish slavery, because to do so will probably be cheaper in the end."[9] "Individual self-interest will result in competition, and competition will result in the provision of necessary goods. Competition gives rise to the socially beneficial consequence of the conflicting self-interests of all the members of society. The unexpected result of competition is social harmony."[10]

There are, then, according to Smith, imperative natural laws that govern the market mechanism, and these laws work inexorably if they are not tampered with. Left alone, such natural forces guarantee the positive evolution of society, propelling the market system ever upward, in an ascending spiral of greater productivity that ultimately advances the best interests of all. Smith does not oppose all government, but he does condemn any meddling of the government with the market system. The least government is decidedly the best government.

What frequently goes unremarked is the fact that Adam Smith was generally hostile to the motives of the business men of his day. In an earlier book (*The Theory of Moral Sentiments,* published in 1759) Smith propounds the notion that man is a creature of self-interest, but that a person always has the ability to empathize and identify with a third person, in this way forming a sympathetic notion of the moral merits of a case quite apart from personal considerations. [11] Even with respect to government, the great enemy to Smith's system is not so much government per se as *monopoly*, and, as Heilbroner indicates,

[t]he fact that Smith had written of "the mean rapacity, the monopolizing spirit of the merchants and manufacturers" and that he had said that they "neither are nor ought to be, the rulers of mankind" . . . was ignored in favor of the great point which Smith drew from his inquiry: *let the market alone.*"[12]

. . . Smith is not necessarily opposed to *all* government action which has as its end the promotion of the general welfare. He warns, for example, of the stultifying effect of mass production, which robs men of their creative natural powers, and prophesies a decline in the manly virtues of the laborer, "unless the government takes some pains to prevent it." Similarly he is in favor of public education to raise the citizenry above the level of mere uncomprehending cogs in a vast machine.[13]

Smith's views were basic in influencing the ideas of the other major figures in the late eighteenth and early nineteenth century laissez faire economics like Thomas Malthus and David Ricardo. Both Malthus and Ricardo, unlike the fundamentally optimistic Smith, present essentially tragic visions of life. Malthus, whose major contributions were concerned with the issue of population, went so far as to urge the abolition of poor relief and even opposed providing low cost housing for the working classes on the grounds that all such charities were ultimately destined to produce cruel results. Ricardo, who was perhaps the first effective champion of industrialism and free trade, went on to develop the theory that capitalism inevitably generates a bitter contest for supremacy between different economic interests and classes who are constantly maneuvering for gain. As Ricardo saw it, the basic contest was between the capitalists and the landlords, whose interests were intrinsically opposed. Indeed for Ricardo, "the interest of the landlords is always opposed to the interests of every other class in the community.[14]

> The landlord benefited from the powers of the soil, and his income—his rent—was not held in line by either competition or by the power of population. In fact, he gained at everyone else's expense. . . . the growing population caused more and more land to be put into use, the cost of grain would rise—not on the good fields previously in use, but on the newly added second-rate fields. Hence, the rents of the well-situated landlord would rise. And not only rents, but wages would rise, too. For as grain became more expensive to produce, the laborer would have to be paid more, just to enable him to buy his dry crust and to stay alive. . . . The worker was forever condemned to the margin. . . . the capitalist, who worked and saved and invested, found that all his trouble was for nothing: his wage costs were higher, his profits smaller, and his landed opponent far richer than he. And the landlord, who did nothing but collect his rents, sat back and watched them increase.[15]

Today the ideas of the "classical economists," such as Smith, Malthus, and Ricardo, continue to be influential in both the economic and philosophical spheres. Economically, they are perhaps best represented in the ideas of such present-day economists as Ludwig von Mises and, perhaps more significantly, Milton Friedman (who was one of the first voices to call for the formal disestablishment of public education by providing for a "voucher system" approach to the financing of schools). Philosophically, the laissez faire position is perhaps best represented today by the ideas of the right-wing libertarians who are frequently indebted to the philosophical "objectivism" of philosopher Ayn Rand.[16] On the national political scene, the Libertarian party — which seems to draw across a wide range of different conservative orientations, although its leadership seems to be primarily inspired by the ideas and ideals of laissez faire economics and philosophy — has been particularly visible during the last decade.

In general, the laissez faire conservative favors individual liberty within a free economic system. He tends to be optimistic about human nature, viewing man as naturally active, rational, competitive, acquisitive and value-maximizing (within the constraints imposed by the objective and impersonal mechanisms of the free market). Thus, capitalist society is naturally good, and, accordingly, capitalist man is the expression of a basically benign social reality. Individual reason can be trusted so long as it is directed by self-interest, and self-interest is always *enlightened* self-interest when viewed in the long run.

For the laissez faire conservative, human intelligence is preeminently practical and conditioned by the nature of existing circumstances. Institutions are good only insofar as they harmonize with the contemporary demands of the open market system. Only the automatic mechanism of the open market should take precedence over and limit the exercise of individual reason, and, within an open economic system, individual errors in judgment are fundamentally self-correcting over time.

The laissez faire conservative advocates the elimination of traditional restraints on trade and competition. He favors a radical decentralization of political power, opposing all central controls over economic enterprise that would tend to tamper with natural market forces.

He stresses property rights and personal liberty over the need for law and order, because he tends to view law and order as by-products of natural forces governing social behavior and not as artificial creations of external government. He stresses only the bare minimum of governmental restraints over personal behavior, and only insofar as these are required to guarantee the fullest realization of an open economic and political system. He prefers to limit controls to those areas where they would be difficult to provide by voluntary groupings of like-minded individuals (as in providing for courts of justice or protecting the national security from foreign aggression).

The laissez faire conservative is basically committed to a "conflict" model of social relationships. Cooperation exists, but primarily as but one way of fostering the competitive pursuit of individual excellence.

The Social Darwinists (Spencerian Conservatives)

The social Darwinist point of view emerges through, and is usually most closely identified with, the writings of the great British social philosopher Herbert Spencer (1820–1903). It was Spencer, above all, who adapted the ideas of Darwinian and post-Darwinian biology to the study of society, fusing Auguste Comte's views concerning the nature of society as a superorganism with Darwin's concepts of natural selection, variation, adaptation, and struggle for existence. Thus Spencer, and not Darwin, popularized the term *evolution,* and it was also Spencer who introduced the phrase "survival of the fittest."

For Spencer, society is a living unity with a supraindividual reality. It originates spontaneously, and evolves according to its own natural laws. "Society," states Spencer, "is an organism,"[17] and it evolves in a manner analogous to the way the physical organism of the species itself evolves. Society is also the highest form of organism, and for Spencer, as for his German contemporary Lilienfeld, there is a logical progression from the cell to the tissue (as a complex of cells), to the organs (as a complex of tissues), to the person (as a complex of organs), and to society itself (as a complex of persons).[18]

Spencer, like most of the evolutionary naturalists who have succeeded him, from Albert Keller, Lester Ward and William Graham Sumner down to such contemporaries as Leslie White and Julian Stewart, is a meliorist who sees industrial society evolving toward more rational, cooperative, and altruistic modes of action. Indeed, there is much in Spencer's vision of the goals implicit within the process of social evolution that is reminiscent of Marx's quasi-anarchist views of a classless society at the "end of history." As Marvin Harris states, "Spencerism combines Malthusian pessimism about the immediate with Helvetian optimism about the distant future."[19] There is also, Harris continues, "a curious similarity between Spencer's ultimate industrial phase and the nebulous stateless and classless utopia which Marx had promised would follow the proletarian victory."[20]

The social Darwinist is pessimistic about the individual human being in the short run, then, but he is optimistic about the future of man in general when the species is viewed in evolutionary perspective. Accordingly, he tends to view the present in terms very similar to those employed by the laissez faire conservative, seeing man as involved in a competitive struggle for survival and success in a world characterized by continuing conflict. For most social Darwinists however — and as for Spencer himself — this conflict is seen as ultimately eventuating in the natural selection of individuals and institutions which will have gone beyond the necessity for the old conflict paradigm altogether, having perfected new processes based on a heightened capacity for rational cooperation. For the social Darwinist, then, man, *as he presently exists,* is not good, but natural selection on both the individual and social levels provides him with the mechanism for realizing his potential *to be good.* Through social evolution, in other words, cooperation is emerging out of conflict; reason out of passion.

In an immediate sense however, the social Darwinist opposes social changes that block the natural processes of competition and struggle required for real evolutionary progress to occur. To demand premature cooperation from a humanity not socially or psychologically prepared for such sophisticated forms of behavior is useless and frequently even dangerous (because it contradicts the very nature of man and society as these presently exist).

Competition, conflict, and struggle—however dispensable they may prove to be in the distant future—are necessary means to the kind of humanity that may *ultimately* prove itself capable of acting on entirely different (and even altruistic) motives. In short, the superordinate goals of evolution itself require a willingness to allow the oftentimes cruel processes of natural selection to occur without interference. The nation that protects its people or institutions from the natural consequences of their own errors or inadequacies courts disaster, because it fails to learn (and therefore improve) from its own experience. That nation which sustains or rewards weakness will never grow strong enough to afford the luxury of being gentle. Social dissonance, however harsh it may seem, is a necessary step toward creating self-perfection in the universal order of things. The good society exists only *in potentia;* its birth requires unavoidable pain and struggle. An emergent society grows only out of the crucible of conflict. That society which demands exalted standards of personal and social morality before the conditions have emerged which make such perfection possible, merely freezes itself into a weak and futile posture, eventually blocking access to its own long-range possibilities for growth and advancement.

Individual intelligence is very real, but it exists primarily as a function of a more encompassing natural evolution (including the evolution of social structures and processes). It is the entire process of natural evolution that creates the kinds of social and individual consciousness that make the expression of certain kinds of ideas and actions possible. The value of keeping the process of natural selection open and emergent is greater than any particular values, whether personal or social, that exist within the process itself. In the final analysis, only the forces of evolution will reveal the true nature of the good person and the good society, and these are only vaguely foreshadowed in the world as it presently exists.

Specific questions dealing with such matters as the permissible limits of political authority and the particular nature and rate of changes in institutional structure (such as those governing property rights or inheritance) are always ultimately determinable only on the basis of after-the-fact evolutionary decisions. They can never be determined by contemporary ideology, because they are finally decided on the basis of their contribution to the survival and success of the species itself. Even occasional social mutations — such as those generated by revolutions or wars—may eventually prove to be successful adaptations to the demands for social change, and only the requirements of the species as a whole, over extended periods of time, can serve to assess the viability of particular social changes. Ultimately, then, the only sort of change that is categorically wrong is that which blocks the process of social struggle that is necessary for any sort of natural selection to take place.

For the social Darwinist, then, conflict is the central mechanism for contemporary society, and only through the relatively unbridled exercise of competitive struggle over extended periods of time will effective modes of rational cooperation become possible.

The Teleological Nationalists (Hegelian Conservatives)

The teleological nationalists need to be distinguished from the far more extreme teleological totalitarians represented by such groups as the fascists and the nazis on the extreme "Hegelian right." The teleological nationalists are essentially conservatives rather than reactionaries, and they probably represent the mainstream of thought within the Hegelian tradition. [21]

The teleological nationalists are not optimistic regarding the nature of individual human beings, but they do tend to be optimistic about the nature of the collective (whether defined as *nation, state* or *race*) to which the individual belongs. Thus, as the teleological nationalist sees it, the individual basically discovers his nature and identity as a person in and through his participation in some collective. The individual realizes himself, but only indirectly, through the group. It is ultimately the group that realizes itself, through the teleological unfolding of its inner soul or spirit, and not the individuals that comprise it. Accordingly, the individual realizes his personal destiny by voluntarily subordinating himself to the higher Self of the nation or race. The highest good always resides in the whole, and the *Volksgeist* always takes precedence over the lesser imperatives of the individual psyche.

The teleological nationalist views society, then, as an organic unity possessing its own singular sort of collective consciousness.[22] Past, present and future coexist wihtin the institutions of the state, and these institutions are the essence of the transcendent group mind. Accordingly, it is important to protect the integrity of the national soul both from the excesses of individual reason and from radical social changes that might violate the nature and integrity of the collective ego.

For the teleological nationalist, individual reason is always legitimately subordinate to the collective wisdom of the nation. The highest reason is beyond effective expression, because it exists only within the totality of dynamic social experience, and this experience defies individual analysis. At basis, the *Volksgeist* can only be *experienced*. It can be approached by means of myth and poetry, but it can never be fully *explained* in the usual sort of explicit and prosaic terms. In its fullest expression it can only be known intuitively and ambiguously — a whole that is inevitably greater than the sum of its parts.

The nature and rate of cultural change is necessarily an expression of the unique *Volksgeist* of a particular people. Only those changes that are organically related to the total needs of the entire group are truly good. In a similar sense, the extent to which governmental centralization or decentralization is desirable is ultimately contingent upon the unique needs of a particular people. Only the dynamic requirements of the people as a whole can determine what constitutes the appropriate limits of individual liberty, property rights, and so on.

Ultimately, then, the teleological nationalist offers an hybrid "conflict and cooperation" model of society. Both conflict and competition may be good, providing that they serve to advance the shared purpose of the entire nation (which can only be known intuitively, by a mystical identification with the transcendent *Volksgeist* of the entire group).

An overview of the four basic traditions in secular conservatism is given in Figure 6–1.

Some Additional Considerations.   Conservatism, as an overall philosophy, is difficult to translate into a specific political or educational theory — or, at least, in any categorical sense — because (1) conservatism, and as already discussed, actually represents a compilation of somewhat different points of view that tend to assume much the same political and educational stance but which frequently do so for substantially different reasons; and because (2) the particular content of any specific conservative political philosophy depends on the nature of the particular culture (or subculture) being discussed as well as upon its particular stage of historical development.

Thus, a social conservative in the Russia of the 1820s or even 1880s held clearly different views than a social conservative in the Soviet Union of the 1920s. In a similar sense, a social conservative in the United States in 1774 endorsed a substantially different position than the social conservative of 1870 whose views, in turn, are clearly distinguishable from those of the contemporary who might be described by the same label. In other words, who is or is not "conservative" is a highly relative matter. A conservative in one culture at one time may not be viewed as conservative in another culture or era or even in the same culture during consecutive generations.

A second qualification to bear in mind about conservatism is that the conservative tends to be skeptical about the efficiency of unbridled reason as a way of arriving at appropriate answers to social questions. Conservatism relies largely on a sort of tacit intuitionism in which primary reliance is placed not on intellectual discipline or even upon effective individual or group problem-solving procedures (as in the Liberal ideologies) but on established (conventional) standards of belief and behavior.

The difficulty with applying this sort of standard is precisely what the United States Supreme Court has encountered in attempting to limit pornography to "contemporary community standards relating the the description or representation of sexual matters." [23] That is, beyond the level of rhetoric, precisely what are these "contemporary standards"? Who is to define them? What constitutes

FIGURE 6–1
THE SECULAR CONSERVATIVES: THE FOUR BASIC TRADITIONS

ESTABLISHMENT CONSERVATIVES (Tory Conservatives)	LAISSEZ FAIRE CONSERVATIVES (Free Marketeers)	SOCIAL DARWINISTS (Spencerian Conservatives)	TELEOLOGICAL NATIONALISTS (Hegelian Conservatives)
Pessimistic regarding human nature; no exorbitant confidence in individual reason; the status quo as naturally good	Generally optimistic concerning individual human nature within the context of the objective natural laws controlling the free market; man is naturally active, rational, competitive, acquisitive, and value-maximizing within a fundamentally self-regulating economic system	Pessimistic about human nature in the short run but optimistic about human nature in the long run; man as evolving through conflict toward cooperation	Optimistic regarding the collective but pessimistic regarding the individual acting independent of the group; the collective is naturally good and the individual is good only when voluntarily subordinating himself to the higher interests of the group
Collective wisdom, embodied in establisted institutions and processes, takes precedence over individual reason; a closed society representing the funded wisdom of the group over a long period of time; the natural selection of the superior individuals and institutions through social evolution	Individual reason, seeking to maximize self-interest, indirectly contributes to the enlightened self-interest of all; individual self-interest in an open society	Opposed to any sort of social changes that would block the superordinate goals of the evolutionary process itself	Collective consciousness as superior to and superordinate over individual reason

FIGURE 6–1 (cont.)

ESTABLISHMENT CONSERVATIVES (Tory Conservatives)	LAISSEZ FAIRE CONSERVATIVES (Free Marketeers)	SOCIAL DARWINISTS (Spencerian Conservatives)	TELEOLOGICAL NATIONALISTS (Hegelian Conservatives)
Intelligence as essentially practical and contextual; skeptical of abstract and ideological prescriptions for change	Intelligence as practical and contextual within the constraints imposed by the automatic mechanisms of the free market; a naturally benign and self-correcting economy	Individual intelligence as contained within and limited by teleological evolutionary forces which transcend particular individuals and institutions	Individual intelligence as contained within and subordinate to the collective consciousness (which can be apprehended only intuitively)
Stress on the continuity and gradual evolution of established institutions	Favors radical liberty from traditional constraints on trade and competition; favors only institutions compatible with a free and open economy	Nature and rate of social changes as a function of long-range evolutionary necessity	Nature and rate of social changes as a function of the collective consciousness

Emphasis on established cultural traditions as the basic criterion for determining desirable political processes and institutions

Favors radical decentralization; opposed to any sort of central controls that violate free market mechanisms

Nature and degree of political controls as a function of evolutionary necessity

Nature and degree of political controls as a function of collective consciousness

Tends to view property and law as extensions of individual personality

Property rights are fundamental, but legal restraints should be minimized to those which maintain free competition in an open market

Civil liberties and property rights as a function of evolutionary necessity

Civil liberties and property rights as a function of collective consciousness

Tends toward a compromise model of social change, stressing minimal conflict within the context of established social institutions

Favors a conflict model of reality; cooperation only as by-product of free competition

A conflict model postulating the possibility of evolution toward a new type of society governed by rational cooperation

Nature and relationship of conflict and cooperation determined by overriding collective consciousness a "culture" or "community"? What is meant by a "standard" of belief or behavior? When, and according to whom, is a standard "contemporary"? Are "contemporary standards" those which are supported by a "silent majority" (a sort of "tacit" consensus) or are they traditional standards that have met the test of time and have endured through custom and usage? What amount of time must transpire before a belief or type of behavior becomes a "contemporary standard"? And so on.

There are, quite obviously, no simple answers to these questions, but it is precisely such questions that frequently make conservatism an ambiguous position, even when the term has been severely restricted to describing a particular position in a particular society at one specific point in history. In the United States at the present time, for example, the establishment conservatives (who are largely in the tradition of Edmund Burke), as well as related traditions, such as adherents of the various political "conflict of interest" theories (as John Adams, John Madison and John C. Calhoun were in their day) tend to view conventional belief and behavior as being rooted in the collective experience of the past, viewed as a sort of "funded wisdom" that inheres within the corporate structure of organized society.

For the laissez faire conservatives, on the other hand, conventional wisdom is equated primarily with the automatic and unconscious mechanism of the open market — less a set of established answers than a sure and certain economic basis for effective social organization. For the teleological nationalists, such as Hegel and Durkheim, on the other hand, cultures are looked upon as functioning largely by means of a distinctive collective consciousness which complements, but nevertheless takes priority over, the more delimited consciousness of individuals within such cultures. (Accordingly, different cultures have significantly different historical destinies, and societies, like individuals, are in a constant competitive struggle for survival and dominance.)

All of the conservative points of view, however, see the individual as legitimately subordinate to the requirements of the larger social system, which (whether viewed structurally, as a funded set of ironclad economic laws, or, more functionally, as the manifestation of large-scale evolutionary or historical forces) is looked upon as being a more authoritative and trustworthy source of guidance than the far more limited and potentially fallible processes of individual reason.

Virtually all of the conservative orientations in the United States at the present time accept some form of constitutional respresentative democracy as the most desirable form of government. In addition, virtually all feel that democracy operates best under a relatively open form of capitalistic economic enterprise, combining a high degree of economic freedom with intelligent political restraints (such as separation of powers or adherence to due process of law) over the excesses of unbridled majoritarianism.

The conservatives would perhaps differ most markedly in their historical orientation with respect to what constitutes desirable contemporary social organization. Thus, the establishment conservatives (or Tories) and the teleological nationalists tend to place a higher premium on the past than do the laissez faire conservatives or the social Darwinists. The first two groups feel very strongly that culture is a continuous organic process in which past and present coexist through the medium of a kind of collective intelligence, viewing the *traditional* as a defining characteristic of the *conventional*. The laissez faire conservatives tend to be more exclusively concerned with the economic substructure than with the overall cultural content, and the social Darwinists tend to be more concerned with a culture's practical efficiency with respect to its dominant purposes than with the nature and content of the purposes themselves.

In line with these considerations, conservatives generally tend to advocate the kind of education that will promote the preservation of established (convetional) social beliefs and behavior and that, in most cases, also serve to restore once dominant ideas and institutions which have been allowed to wither through neglect in a world committed to a misplaced sense of destructive "individualism."

RELIGIOUS CONSERVATISM

Edmund Burke, like most major figures in philosophy, actually bridges several philosophical positions. He assumes, for example, the existence of a rational God who has implanted a rational order in human history. As Burke sees it, anything that runs contrary to the divine plan is not permitted to continue in existence and is not therefore part of the status quo.[24] He also holds that there are certain laws of nature that are known on a self-evident basis. As Bluhm notes:

> There is, for example, "the natural taste and relish of equity and justice." There is the religious instinct, for "man is by his constitution a religious animal; [and] athesim is against, not only our reason, but our instincts." There are the ties of blood relationship, "the ties of nature, which are the laws of God." These ties of nature are "the first bond of society." "The love that God has implanted in the hearts of parents toward their children," Burke says, "is the first germ of the second conjunction which is ordered to subsist between them and the rest of mankind." And there is "a hatred of the unjust and cruel" which "a kind Providence has placed in our breasts . . . in order that we may preserve ourselves from cruelty and injustice." These are a few of the moral instincts which Burke saw in human nature.[25]

Although some Tory conservatives would agree with Burke's position with respect to divine Providence and natural laws, Tory democracy, as it exists today, seldom stresses this kind of philosophical or religious reasoning, and representatives of the other three basically "secular" traditions within social conservatism are also generally reluctant to ground their ideas on explicity theistic assumptions.

On the other hand, there is a significant tradition of religious conservatism that exists apart from the essentially secular orientations. In contrast to his secular counterpart, the religious conservative is willing to accept both faith and reason, but he veers away from excesses in both. He recognizes the necessity for adapting the historical message of his faith to contemporary circumstances, and he accepts the need for theological interpretation that does not violate the basic spirit of his creed, but he remains basically content to view his religion as a sacred contract that ultimately resists rational explanation.

The Augustinian Tradition. The philosophical and theological tradition associated with Saint Augustine of Hippo (354–430) has been a particularly important source of inspiration for conservatives of all persuasions. Saint Augustine, unlike Saint Thomas Aquinas, was primarily influenced by the Platonic and neo-Platonic traditions in philosophy rather than by Aristotle (whose writings were only rediscovered and translated into Western languages in the tenth and eleventh centuries). For Augustine, God is the one eternal Being, absolutely real and absolutely good. He is the source of all other things. Man in and of himself is innately depraved, "bound by original sin"[26] which is inherited from the transgressions of Adam. But God is merciful. Although his Will is inscrutable, all of his decisions are just, and he elects to save certain individuals by a free gift of divine grace which no one can resist. Through this gift of grace the sinner is changed and brought to a sanctified state. For others, grace never arrives. Such individuals are predestined to damnation. (For Saint Thomas Aquinas, on the other hand, grace is potentially available to all, and the individual has free will to opt for or against God's freely offered gift of salvation. Aquinas, in contrast to Augustine, holds that "Grace does not do away with the natural order, but rather perfects it."[27] According to Bluhm, "Burke, whose antecedents are Thomistic rather than Augustinian tended to view the Christian-Aristocratic culture of pre-1789 Europe, which had been slowly developed over the ages, as a close approximation of an ideal order.")[28]

During the Reformation, John Calvin adopted Augustine's concepts of divine election and predestination. "By predestination," wrote Calvin, "we mean the eternal decree of God, by which he determined with himself whatever he wished to happen with regard to every man. All are not created on equal terms, but some are preordained to eternal life, others to eternal damnation."[29] For Calvin, the believer is not saved by his works but by God's election. He is, however, elected into a state of righteousness that abounds in good works, and, as philosopher Noss notes, "his righteousness is the only assurance he has of his election."[30]

Still another area where the Augustian tradition in Christianity differs from the Thomistic is in regard to the relative merits of faith and reason. For Aquinas, reason is a necessary but not a sufficient basis for faith. Reason does, however, lead the individual in the direction of true faith, predisposes him toward such faith once revealed, and indirectly acts to bolster and support the teachings of the Church. Augustine, on the other hand, tends to be much more skeptical about the ultimate efficacy of reason as a path toward religious enlightenment, placing his primary reliance on faith: "I believe in order to know." While he does not forsake reason — "faith seeks the support of the intelligence"[31] — Augustine places his primary confidence in the formative act of faith. Indeed, throughout the history of Christian theology, ranging from the pre-Nicene writings of the anti-rationalist Tertullian (165 – 220) through the Platonic scholasticism of individuals like Anselm of Canterbury (1033 – 1109) and on through such post-Thomist Aristotelian scholastics as John Duns Scotus (1265 – 1308), William of Occam (1285 – 1349) and Nicholas of Cusa (1401 – 1464) the preeminence of intuition and faith over reason and evidence is a recurring theme.

There is much in Tory conservatism that is reminiscent of Saint Augustine's insistence on the innate depravity of human nature since the Fall. Thus, as for

Augustine, the individual tends to be viewed as partially reasonable but as primarily controlled by his passions and appetites. Until the end of history, when God comes to establish the City of God, all men must continue to exist in the necessarily imperfect Earthly City, where God's will is expressed only indirectly through the wills of particular men and where, in Augustine's words, "Order is good, disorder is evil. Therefore, any kind of order is better than chaos."[32]

Today the Augustinian tradition, combining a basically pessimistic concept of human nature with a fundamental distrust of reason continues to exert a strong influence in both the Roman Catholic and Protestant traditions. In a viewpoint sometimes described as "secular Augustinianism," it is occasionally ascribed to certain contemporary social theorists, such as political "realist" Hans Morgenthau, who tend to be less than sanguine about the prospect for realizing human perfection through political action in the temporal world. Thus, as Morgenthau writes in his book *Scientific Man and Power Politics* (1946):

> [Political realism] believes that the world, imperfect as it is from the rational point of view, is the result of forces which are inherent in human nature. To improve the world one must work with those forces, and not against them. This being inherently a world of opposing interests and of conflict among them, moral principles can never be fully realized, but are best approximated through the ever temporary balancing of interests and the ever precarious settlement of conflicts. [Political realism], then, sees in a system of checks and balances a universal principle for all pluralist societies. It appeals to historic precedent rather than abstract principles, and aims at achievement of the lesser evil rather than the absolute good.[33]

Throughout the history of political philosophy, a variety of individuals—ranging from Machiavelli (and such latter-day "Machiavellians" as Vilfredo Pareto, Gaetano Mosca and Robert Michels) through the rationalized self-interest theory of Thomas Hobbes and the "interest"-based conflict model of Thomas Harrington (reflected in the writings of John Adams, James Madison and John C. Calhoun, among others)—also seem to be tinged with Augustinian pessimism and who also seem to represent essentially conservative points of view in political thought.

RELIGIOUS CONSERVATISM IN CONTEMPORARY AMERICA

While most conservatives tend to favor religion and the institutionalized church, the more explicitly religious tradition within American social conservatism is located largely in the more religiously conservative, established Protestant churches (such as the Presbyterian, Reformed, Episcopal, and Methodist, which are based upon the major Reformation theologies). What distinguishes the more religiously orthodox, or mainline, Protestant churches as a group from the more religiously heterodox (fundamentalist) churches, such as the Southern Baptist or the various independent evangelical and pentecostal groups, is difficult to specify, but in general there appear to be ten basic differences between the more traditional denominations and the more "enthusiastic" groups.

1. The mainline religiously orthodox churches tend to be more explicitly concerned with doctrinal differences. They tend to have relatively clear-cut ideas about what constitutes theological legitimacy, often tracing these ideas to standard Reformation doctrines rooted in church history.

2. The more traditional and established churches ordinarily have more stable and systematic systems of church governance and administration. Many, such as the Episcopalians, Congregationalists, and Presbyterians, take their names from the characteristic attitudes that they assume with respect to preferred patterns of church organization (see Chapter IV).

3. Their church organizations tend to be better integrated into the basic structure of the surrounding secular society. They are law-abiding and are generally willing to conform to the established patterns of civil government. They do not view their beliefs as "alternative realities" that are opposed to the common sense, everyday world.

4. They tend to place a greater stress on formalized and standardized religious forms, such as traditional rites, rituals, sacraments, and services.

5. They tend to reject, or to be deeply skeptical of, *contemporary* supernaturalism. They view reality as essentially natural and this-worldly, looking upon religion as an integrated aspect of everyday living. They tend to regard religion as a practical way of living in the world as it is; they view virtue primarily as a matter of scrupulous behavior within the everyday world, which accumulates as a warrant for salvation in the world to come. They generally view Jesus as the supreme example of moral perfection rather than as a living spirit to be encountered in the present. They tend to be uncomfortable with the entire notion of the Holy Ghost and are generally skeptical of present-day miracles and religious prophesies.

6. They believe in mediated grace. They accept the moral equality of men, as well as the priesthood of all believers, but they believe that the proper interpretation of scripture often calls for special training and education. Scripture is fundamental in all of the Protestant denominations, but personal interpretations are not viewed as being particularly authoritative in the more traditional groups, and special clergy are looked upon as extremely useful in elucidating the true meaning of the Bible.

7. Individual subjective belief is necessary but not sufficient to guarantee truth. True faith resides in the scripture as mediated and construed by the Church. Salvation is less a matter of personal conversion (spiritual rebirth by accepting Christ as Saviour) than of becoming a fully functioning member of a corporate Christian community of true believers who are able to aid each other in the continuing process of spiritual rebirth. Grace is perfected through appropriate participation in a fellowship of believers. Religion in the mainline Protestant churches is more a social than a psychological phenomenon. Religious ecstasy is primarily an end to be sought in the next world, and not a means of ensuring salvation in the present. Perfect holiness — the ability to live without sin — is not ordinarily possible in this life.

8. Man lives primarily in historical time, not in biblical time. The scriptures must necessarily be interpreted in such a way as to guarantee their applicability to present situations. We cannot restore the world of the Bible, so we must adapt the Bible to the realities of the world as it presently is.

9. The end of the world is not immediately at hand. The spiritual realm will continue to coexist in an uneasy alliance with the requirements of a profane existence.

10. There is no "cheap grace." Man is free to change, to turn away from sin, but the act of conversion is not sufficient to guarantee salvation, for true salvation is the product of a lifetime of virtuous living. Conversion per se does not negate sin, and it does not elevate the individual to the possibility of a sinless life in the present. It is God's judgment of a person's total behavior weighed over a lifetime that determines whether or not he shall be "saved." Only those who survive and succeed in the rigorous competition for moral excellence that goes on unceasingly throughout life will ultimately merit salvation. In effect, then, salvation depends on hard work and the accumulation of merit over an extended period of time. It does not occur in the present, but is the delayed reward growing out of a lifetime of virtuous living.

This last point is a particularly interesting one, because what the conservative churches advocate is essentially the "capitalist ethic" of hard work (in the cause of the Lord), saving (the acquisition of merit in order to earn salvation) and the survival of the fittest (in the arena of spiritual competition). Ironically, what the conservative churches seem to object to most vehemently in the more evangelical (and particularly pentecostal) persuasions is the position that holds that (1) one can be saved without effort (merely by accepting responsibility for one's sins and choosing to live in Christ); (2) salvation can be earned without cost (without accumulating worldly virtue over time); and (3) it can be bestowed upon the "unworthy" (that is, those who have clearly lost the worldly competition for moral status).

Phrased somewhat differently, the conservative churches, like the politically conservative groups, emphasize freedom — that is, the individual's freedom to choose, with its corollary responsibility for assuming the consequences for his own actions. The fundamentalist churches — which are frequently more rigid in their biblical literalism on the personal level — tend to be political radicals in the kingdom of Heaven, emphasizing equality and holding that all men have the same potential for salvation at any given time quite regardless of their prior moral stature. All are free to accept Christ and therefore to be saved at any moment regardless of who they are or what they have previously accomplished.[34]

RELIGIOUS AND SOCIAL CONSERVATISM: SOME FINAL COMMENTS

The question of precisely what individuals or groups exemplify the religious *fundamentalist* as opposed to the religious *intellectualist* or the religious *conservative* orientation is difficult to answer. The position taken here — which is certainly open to debate—concurs with the position presented by Dean Kelley in his book *Why Conservative Churches are Growing*, published in 1967, in which he presents what he terms "the Exclusivist-Ecumenical Gradient" with respect to certain major Christian traditions in contemporary America.[35] According to Kelley, existing religious groups range from the most exclusivist and antiecumenical (least related to "mainline religions" discussed by Will Herberg in his epochal book *Protestant-Catholic-Jew* [1955]), to those typical of the mainstream American religious traditions. Thus, as Kelley sees it, the least mainstream, most exclusivist and antiecumenical, were (listed in order of comparative separatism and rigidity) as follows:

Black Muslims
  Jehovah's Witnesses
    Evangelicals and Pentecostals
      Orthodox Jews
        Churches of Christ
          Latter-Day Saints (Mormons)
            Seventh-Day Adventists
              Church of God
                Church of Christ, Scientist[36]

Next in line, come the large and more mainstream churches that provide a good degree of social integration with the larger culture while nevertheless retaining a significant degree of separateness from the dominant religious consensus. Again, in degree of separateness and rigidity when contrasted to the mainline religious traditions, these are listed as follows:

Southern Baptist Convention
  Lutheran Church — Missouri Synod
    American Lutheran Church
      Roman Catholic Church
        Conservative Jews
          Russian Orthodox
            Greek Orthodox[37]

Finally, there are the churches that typically represent the mainstream American religious tradition. In descending order with respect to exclusiveness and antiecumenicism, these are as follows:

Southern Presbyterian Church
  Reformed Church in America
    Episcopal Church
      American Baptist Convention
        United Presbyterian Church
          United Methodist Church
            United Church of Christ
              Reform Jews
                Ethical Culture Society
                  Unitarian-Universalists[38]

In exemplifying religious expressions of the moral/political/educational ideology of fundamentalism, Kelley's lists of exclusivist/antiecumenical churches (except for the Orthodox Jews and the Church of Christ, Scientist) serve well. The two exceptions, while they seem to meet Kelley's criterion of exclusivism and antiecumenicism, are not socially *fundamentalist* in the sense that the term is used here. Orthodox Judaism (like Thomistic Catholicism) is intellectualistic (although in a rather narrow sense) in its overall orientation — as discussed in Appendix 1 (Judaism and Jewish Education).

Christian Science has no clearly identifiable social ideology, but it is quite apparently not fundamentalist, and the vast bulk of Christian Scientists appear to be very much in the sociopolitical mainstream, probably being best represented as tending toward one of the two dominant cultural ideologies of either Conservatism or Liberalism. Christian Science is perhaps the only example of Christian Liberalism (critical biblicism) that combines the teaching of the Bible with extraordinary doctrines and/or intrepretations. In general, the Christian Scientists tend to favor the conventional separation of church and state, preferring to advance their religious convictions through their own special programs.

Evangelical fundamentalists are virtually always educational fundamentalists as well. If the term "evangelical" is used only with reference to fundamentalists (or even in the somewhat broader sense, with reference to all of those who emphasize the authority of the Scriptures and the need for individual salvation through faith in Jesus Christ[39] and who, at the same time, are substantially committed to proselytizing for these views within society at large), "evangelicals" are also probably best represented as educational fundamentalists. On the other hand, the term "evangelicalism" is sometimes used to describe any group that accepts the basic authority of the scriptures (the Evangel) whether or not they subscribe to the needs for individual salvation through faith in Jesus Christ. The term is also frequently applied to groups that do not actively proselyte for converts within the larger society. Indeed, many of the churches listed in Kelley's second and third categories (as either quasi-mainstream or mainstream religious traditions in America) would tend to view themselves as integral parts of the "evangelical" tradition in this broader sense.

In a similar manner, while there is probably a correlation between being pentecostal (see Chapter IV) and being socially Conservative and educationally fundamentalist, it is hazardous to be very dogmatic about this. Most Pentecostals are evangelical (in the strict sense of the term), and most are also fundamentalists. But this is not invariably the case, and it is entirely possible to be a Roman Catholic, Quaker, or Episcopal pentecostal.

It is difficult to generalize about the educational preferences of the various Christian fundamentalist groups. Some, like the Seventh-Day Adventists, maintain an extensive system of parochial schools to advance their own point of view. Some favor compulsory religious instruction and/or prayer (usually with a denominational flavor) within the public schools. Virtually all seem to reject the idea that schooling should be truly secular, and almost all of these groups at least advocate supplementing public school instruction with special church schools after regular public school hours or with camps that meet during public school vacations; released-time religious instruction offered by the various churches themselves; Sunday schools; and so on. Most of these groups also tend to favor such quasi-educational activities as evangelical campaigns, revivals, religious proselytizing, missionary activities, missionary schools, contributions to nondenominational Christian activities (such as the Y.M.C.A., the Salvation Army), and so on.

Ideological intellectualism, as previously indicated, is best represented within a religious context by Roman Catholicism in its dominant Thomistic expression as well as by all three of the major orientations (Orthodox, Conservative, and Reform) within contemporary Judaism. It is also represented on occasion by spokesmen from some of the liberal Protestant traditions and by others representing such "humanistic religions" as Unitarianism/Universalism or quasi-religious movements like Ethical Culture.

Ideological Conservatism within a religious frame of reference is probably best characterized by all of the groups that Kelley lists as quasi-mainstream except for the Conservative Jews (who are basically intellectualists, as discussed in Appendix 1), the dominant Thomistic tradition within Roman Catholicism (which is almost universally conceded to be perhaps the most prevalent type of religious intellectualism), and the "natural humanistic" traditions represented by such movements as Unitarianism/Universalism and the Ethical Culture Society. Most nonfundamentalist evangelicals (except those in the intermediate and mainstream churches listed by Kelley who prefer to view themselves as "evangelical" in the very broad sense that they subscribe to the authority of the Scriptures or "Evangel") as well as most nonfundamentalist pentecostals are generally better represented as ideological conservatives than as ideological fundamentalists. As Marty notes, the nonfundamentalist evangelicals (such as the vast bulk of Baptists who belong to churches in the American Baptist Convention or Presbyterians, whether Southern Presbyterians or members of the United Presbyterian Church)

> . . . seem to . . . offer much of what Dean Kelley observed churches needed in order to grow. They display much but not too much commitment, discipline, missionary zeal, absolutism, conformity, and fanaticism. . . . Their success, in a sense, lies in their ability to offer prospective converts and members the best of both worlds. On the one hand, they provide meaning, belonging, and identity apparently *over against* other Americans while on the other hand they are taught to *fit in with other Americans,* to be the real and true citizens. The [nonfundamentalist] Evangelicals address near majorities and then give them a sense of clear minority status. The continuing denominationalism of the member groups serves well here. Each one has something to which it adheres in particular, a way of baptizing or communing or observing the church calendar. All these are decided on the basis of variant readings of the Scriptures, which they all believe to be inerrant and clear. Yet they are also increasingly ecumenical and worldly, and can offer their clienteles the assets that go with such commitments. Their formula provides both identity and exposure; it is hard to match as a combination for tens of millions of Americans on this part of the religious map.[40]

It is difficult to generalize about the educational proclivities of the more theologically liberal Protestant and quasi-Protestant traditions ranging from nonfundamentalist evangelical groups through the humanistic religions like Unitarianism. In general, the "natural" religions like Unitarianism and Universalism, as well as the Quakers, who represent a substantially different point of view, tend to favor the separation of Church and State. Many Pentecostals and many in the mainstream Reformation-based Protestant churches also tend to favor such a separation. On the other hand, some Pentecostals favor parochial schools or compulsory religious instruction and/or prayer in the public schools. The Lutherans maintain a very extensive system of parochial schools, and the Protestant Episcopalians run a number of schools as well. Within Protestant liberalism, most groups tend to favor Sunday Schools, special supplementary types of religious instruction outside of the public schools, special church camps or schools during public school vacation periods, and missionary schools.

The greatest difficulty with using church membership as a sign of ideological orientation is, of course, that many church members—perhaps even most—are only nominally religious, and their identification with a particular religious group may not be representative of their fundamental convictions. Thus, as Schaff comments with respect to Protestantism, "The nominal Protestants, many of them not even baptized, correspond to the numberless nominal Christians in European state churches, who, though they have been baptized and have professed their Catholic or Lutheran or Reformed faith, care no more about the church, than if they were heathens or Mohammedans."[41]

Summary of Differences

In general, the moral and social philosophies that are essentially conservative in nature subdivide along two basic questions: (1) the question of religion, and (2) the question of teleology (that is, whether or not there is some sort of emergent design inherent within history). Accordingly, if the secular/religious division is used as one dividing line and the teleological/nonteleological question is used as the other, the basic traditions within social Conservatism can be graphically represented as in Figure 6–2.

CONSERVATISM IN EDUCATION: A SUMMARY

The educational conservative views the central goal of education as being the preservation and transmission of established social patterns and traditions. Characteristically present-oriented, the educational conservative has a deep respect for the past, but he is primarily concerned with the usefulness and applicability of learning within the present social context. He seeks to promote the fullest development of the contemporary society by ensuring the sort of slow and organic change that is compatible with preestablished legal and institutional requirements. In a similar sense, and while he retains a deep concern for both character training and intellectual discipline, the secular conservative is primarily devoted to the sort of schooling designed to ensure a deep respect and appreciation for existing social institutions and practices. In contrast to the intellectualist's stress on the study of philosophy and humanities, the conservative tends to focus his attentions on the more practical (and more recent) disciplines, such as history and the biological and physical sciences, which are viewed as more directly relevant to the immediate problems of contemporary living.

As was the case with the other two "conservative" educational ideologies of educational fundamentalism and educational intellectualism, there are two basic traditions within educational conservatism that correspond to different attitudes with respect to religion.

FIGURE 6–2
SOCIAL CONSERVATISM

SECULAR

Social Darwinists
(Spencerian Conservatives)
  Herbert Spencer
  William Graham Sumner
  Lester Ward
Teleological Nationalists
(Hegelian Conservatives)
  Georg W. F. Hegel
  Auguste Comte
  Émile Durkheim
Various German Romantic Idealists
  (Fichte, Schelling, etc.)
Friedrich Nietzsche
Henri Bergson's "Intuitionism"

Establishment Conservatives
(Tory Democracy)
  Edmund Burke
  Russell Kirk
Laissez Faire Conservatives
(The Free Marketeers)
  Adam Smith   Milton Friedman
  Thomas Malthus   Ayn Rand
  David Ricardo
Secular Augustinians and Related Traditions
  Political Realism (Hans Morgenthau)
  Hedonic Naturalism (Thomas Hobbes)
  Political "Conflict of Interest" Theories
    Thomas Harrington
    John Adams
    James Madison
    John C. Calhoun
Machiavelli and the Neo-Machiavellians

TELEOLOGICAL	NONTELEOLOGICAL
(Historical Predeterminism)	(History as Open and Problematic)

Most Forms of "Civil Religion" in the
Priestly Nation-as-Transcendent Tradition*

Mainstream Reformation-based
Protestant Traditions
  Protestant Episcopalianism
  Lutheranism
  Presbyterianism
  Reformed Calvinism
Nondenominational Evangelical
Christianity
  Billy Graham
  Campus Crusade for Christ
  Teen Challenge
Intervarsity Christian Fellowship
Theological Augustinians
  Saint Augustine of Hippo
  Reinhold Niebuhr
Theological Antirationalism and/or
Intuitionism
  Tertullian   Søren Kierkegaard
  John Duns Scotus
Most "Ethnic Religions"
  Hungarian Reformed Church
  Norwegian Evangelical Lutherans
  Armenian Church of North America
Most Forms of "Civil Religion" in the
Priestly Nation-Under-God Tradition
  "Protestant Civic Piety"

*The "civil religion" approaches used here (following Martin Marty's classification scheme) are very difficult to categorize in terms of the various social ethics approaches. This is true for three basic reasons. First, they are somewhat ambiguous to begin with. Second, some (like civil religion in the prophetic nation-as-transcendent tradition) tend to be very close to other positions discussed (such as teleological nationalism or teleological totalitarianism). Finally, the proponents of these positions tend to differ in the intensity of their commitment, the more extreme advocates of the prophetic nation-under-God tradition, for example, tending to be reactionary, while the more muted proponents of such a position might very well be merely conservative.

RELIGIOUS

Secular Educational Conservatism. The secular conservative is perhaps best represented by such prominent educational theorists and critics as Arthur Bestor and Hyman Rickover. They do not necessarily reject the spiritual aspects of education, but they tend to be much more utilitarian and practical in their approach to schooling than those with more decided religious inclinations. Their primary concern is with the schools' role in preserving and transmitting established social institutions and processes, and they seek to propagate the sort of information and skills that are necessary in order to ensure the individual's success within the secular society that presently exists.

Religious Educational Conservatism. The religious conservative is less rigid and moralistic than the religious fundamentalist. He is also less concerned with justifying and comprehending the intellectual bases of religion than is the theologically inclined intellectualist. He is primarily concerned with transmitting the established beliefs and practices—the time-tested moral and religious orthodoxies—of his own particular church or denomination. He is perhaps best represented by certain of the more establishment-oriented members of the mainstream Protestant denominations (such as the Lutherans, Presbyterians or Methodists) and various members of the Roman Catholic Church who are inclined toward a more liberal theology than that offered by the mainstream Thomistic tradition.

The religious conservative agrees with the secular conservative in virtually every instance but he also believes that spiritual training is a basic aspect of our established social traditions and that some form of religious instruction is therefore a proper and significant aspect of the child's basic education.

Temporarily disregarding the differences between the secular and religious points of view within the tradition of social conservatism, the basic ideology of the educational conservative can be summarized as follows:

CONSERVATISM IN EDUCATION:
A SUMMARY

The Overall Goal of Education. The central purpose of education is to preserve and transmit conventional patterns of social behavior.

The Objectives of the School. The school exists for two basic reasons: (1) to encourage an understanding of, and an appreciation for, time-tested cultural institutions, traditions and processes, including a deep respect for law and order; and (2) to transmit the information and skills necessary to succeed within the existing social order.

General Characteristics. Educational conservatism can be characterized in the following ways:

It maintains that the basic value of knowledge resides in its social utility, that knowledge is a means of realizing established social values.

It emphasizes man as citizen; man in his role as a member of an established state.

It stresses reasoned conformity; placing reliance on the best answers of the past as the most trustworthy guide to present action.

It views education as socialization to the established system.

It focuses on existing social traditions and institutions, emphasizing the present situation (viewed in a relatively shallow and ethnocentric historical perspective).

It emphasizes cultural stability over the need for reform, accepting only changes that are basically compatible with the established social order.

It is based on a closed cultural system (ethnocentrism), stressing dominant social traditions and emphasizing gradual change within a generally stable social situation.

It is grounded on time-tested convictions and on the belief that established ideas and practices are more reliable than those which arise from relatively uncontrolled speculation.

It holds that the ultimate intellectual authority is the dominant culture with its established system of beliefs and behavior.

The Child as Learner.   The child requires firm guidance and sound instruction before he becomes effectively socialized as a responsible citizen.

Individual similarities are more important than individual differences, and these similarities are properly determinative in establishing appropriate educational programs.

Children are morally equal in a world of objectively unequal opportunities; they should have equal opportunity to strive for the limited number of rewards available, but success should be conditioned upon personal merit.

The child is essentially self-determining; he has personal free will in the traditional sense.

Administration and Control.   Educational authority should be invested in mature and responsible professional educators who have a deep respect for due process and who are sufficiently prudent to avoid intemperate changes in response to popular demand.

Teacher authority should be based on ascribed social role and status.

The Nature of the Curriculum.   The school should emphasize political socialization, training the child to be a good citizen.

The school should focus on cultural conditioning; helping the child to acquire conventional cultural values.

Emphasis should be placed on basic skills, practical knowledge and character training.

The course of study should be heavily prescribed.

Emphasis should be placed on the *academic* over the *practical* and the *intellectual*.

The school should stress basic training in the fundamental learning skills (the three R's), an overview of the basic natural sciences, physical education (including health instruction), and a relatively academic approach to the more conventional social sciences (American history, American political institutions, world history, and so on).

Instructional Methods And Evaluation.   There should be a practical compromise between traditional and progressive classroom procedures; the teacher should use whatever methods are most effective in expediting learning, but should be inclined toward modifying traditional procedures by such means as demonstrations, field trips, laboratory work, and such, rather than tending toward radical departures from established practices (such as free schools, non-directive teaching, or individualized instruction).

Drill is the best way of establishing proper habits at the lower levels, but it should evolve toward more open and intellectual approaches (such as lecture and directed discussion) during the later phases of learning; a significant amount of memorization and drill is necessary.

Teacher-determined and teacher-directed learnings are best, but the student should be allowed to participate in the less crucial aspects of educational planning.

The teacher should be viewed as an expert disseminator of specific knowledge and skills.

Tests that measure skills and information are preferable to those that emphasize analytic ability and abstract speculation.

Interpersonal competition for grades between students is both necessary and desirable in order to foster excellence.

Emphasis should be placed on the cognitive with a heavy secondary emphasis on the affective and the interpersonal.

Emphasis should be placed upon the preservation of conventional educational principles and practices.

Personal counseling and psychotherapy should be restricted to children with severe emotional problems that affect their capacity to learn in a normal school situation.

Classroom Control.   Students should be good citizens in terms of the dominant cultural view of good citizenship and proper behavior.

Teachers should generally be nonpermissive in procedures for maintaining classroom control, but teacher authority should be supplemented by reason.

Moral education (character training) is one of the necessary aspects of schooling.

NOTES

1. Samuel P. Huntington, "Conservatism as an Ideology," *American Political Science Review,* 1958, p. 472.

2. Sargent, *Contemporary Political Ideologies,* p. 84.

3. Gould and Truitt, *Political Ideologies*, pp. 2–3.

4. F. J. Hearnshaw, *Conservatism in England* (New York: Howard Fertig, 1968), p. 22.

5. Gould and Truitt, *Political Ideologies,* pp. 133–34.

6. Robert L. Heilbroner, *The Worldly Philosophers* (New York: Simon & Schuster, 1953), p. 20.

7. Ibid., p. 15.

8. Ibid., p. 11.

9. Ibid., p. 62.

10. Ibid., p. 47.

11. Ibid., p. 39.

12. Ibid., p. 60.

13. Ibid., p. 61.

14. David Ricardo, quoted in Heilbroner, *The Worldly Philosophers,* p. 74.

15. Heilbroner, *The Worldly Philosophers,* pp. 87–90.

16. See Chapter VII.

17. Herbert Spencer, *The Inductions of Sociology,* pp. 447–62; quoted in Pitirim Sorokin, *Contemporary Sociological Theories* (New York: Harper & Brothers, 1928), p. 202.

18. P. Lilienfeld, *Zur Vertidigung,* pp. 9–12 and *passim*; quoted in Sorokin, *Contemporary Sociological Theories*, p. 203.

19. Marvin Harris, *The Rise of Anthropological Theory* (New York: Thomas Y. Crowell Co., 1968), p. 133.

20. Ibid., p. 468.

21. See the discussion of Hegel in Chapter IV.

22. See the earlier discussion of Durkheim in this chapter.

23. In the majority decision rendered by the United States Supreme Court in *Roth v. United States* (1956), the Court defined "obscenity" on the basis of "whether to the average person, applying contemporary community standards, the dominant theme of the material taken as a whole appeals to a prurient interest." In a subsequent case, *Memoirs v. Massachusetts* (1966), the same theme was restated in the following words: " . . . the material is patently offensive because it affronts contemporary community standards relating to the description or representation of sexual matters . . ." (Roy C. Rist, comp., *The Pornography Controversy: Changing Moral Standards in American Life.* [New Brunswick, New Jersey: Transaction Books, 1974], p. 100).

24. Edmund Burke, quoted in Francis Canavan, *The Political Reason of Edmund Burke* (Durham, North Carolina: Duke University Press, 1960), p. 55.

25. William T. Bluhm, *Theories of the Political System,* 2d ed. (Englewood Cliffs, New Jersey: Prentice-Hall, 1971), p. 430.

26. Saint Augustine, in *A Select Library of Nicene and Post-Nicene Fathers,* first series, 14 vols.; vol. 5, *Marriage and Concupiscence,* 1.27 (New York: Christian Literature Co., 1886–1890), p. 275.

27. Saint Thomas Aquinas, quoted in Bluhm, *Theories of the Political System,* p. 209.

28. Bluhm, *Theories of the Political System*, p. 194.

29. John Calvin, *Institutes of the Christian Religion,* trans. Henry Beveridge, 3 vols. (Edinburgh: Calvin Tract Society, 1845), vol. 2, p. 534.

30. John Calvin, quoted in John B. Noss, *Man's Religions,* rev. ed. (New York: Macmillan Co., 1956), p. 646.

31. John Calvin, quoted in Noss, *Man's Religions,* p. 629.

32. Saint Augustine, quoted by Bluhm, *Theories of the Political System,* p. 184.

33. Hans J. Morgenthau, "Another Great Debate: The National Interests of the United States," *American Political Science Review 46* (1952), p. 962.

34. Even Calvinism in its original stress on predestination and divine election did not do away with a concern for moral competition, a sort of theological version of social Darwinism. Quite the contrary, what Calvin originally maintained might be summarized as follows:
    1. Man is innately depraved as a consequence of Adam's fall.
    2. God, in His divine wisdom, has elected to receive certain individuals into his favor. He bestows upon these the gift of divine grace, just as He withholds it from others.
    3. Certain individuals are predestined by divine election to be saved, others to be damned. "By predestination," wrote Calvin, "we mean the eternal decree of God, by which he determined with himself whatever he wished to happen with regard to every man. All are not created on equal terms, but some are preordained to eternal life, others to eternal damnation." (Noss, *Man's Religions,* p. 646).
    4. Despite these considerations, no one can ever be *certain* of whether or not he has been elected for salvation by God. The Church invisible is constituted of all the elect of God in heaven and on earth; the Church visible is the company of professing believers on earth which is organized in accordance with God's word in the Scripture. As philosopher John Noss phrases it, "In the Church visible the believer is not saved by his works, since it is God's election alone that saves him; if he is saved unto a righteousness abounding in good works; in fact, *his righteousness is the only assurance he has of his election.*" (Ibid.)

Phrased somewhat differently, even in orthodox Calvinism it is necessary to rely on the outward (visible and worldly) signs of inward and invisible grace as a sort of secular verification of spiritual exaltation. These outward signs of incipient salvation are to be found in a good and virtuous life—characterized by all of the Protestant-capitalistic virtues. Hence good works signify salvation, and, other things being equal, the man who lives a Christian life is generally assumed to be the one who is predestined for eternal life in Christ. (Ibid., pp. 646–47).

In contrast to Reformation Calvinism, the mainline Protestant denominations today tend to be *Arminian.* That is, they hold that God has elected all men to salvation through the atonement of Christ, which saved all men from complicity in Adam's original sin, but all men must reaffirm their right to salvation through proper faith and right action in the course of their own individual lives on earth. (Ibid., p. 654).

35. Dean M. Kelley, *Why Conservative Churches are Growing: A Study in the Sociology of Religion* (New York: Harper and Row, 1972), pp. 88–90.

36. Ibid.

37. Ibid.

38. Ibid.

39. Richard V. Pierard, *The Unequal Yoke: Evangelical Christianity and Political Conservatism* (New York: J. B. Lippincott Co., 1970), p. 21.

40. Martin E. Marty, *A Nation of Behavers* (Chicago: University of Chicago Press, 1976), p. 105.

41. Philip Schaff, *America: A Sketch of Its Political, Social, and Religious Character* (Cambridge, Massachusetts: The Belknap Press of Harvard University Press, 1961), p. 105.

BIBLIOGRAPHY

Educational Conservatism

RELIGIOUS CONSERVATISM

BEN-HORIN, MEIR, "Jewish Education," in Park, Joe, *Readings in the Philosophy of Education,* 2d ed. New York: Macmillan, 1963. pp. 472–83.

BEGGS, DAVID W., and McQUIGG, R. BRUCE, eds. *America's Schools and Churches.* Wilmington, Illinois: Indiana University Press, 1965.

BLANSHARD, PAUL. *Religion and the Schools: The Great Controversy.* Boston: Beacon Press, 1963.

BOLES, DONALD E. *The Bible, Religion, and the Public Schools.* New York: Collier Books, 1963.

BOROWITZ, EUGENE B., "A Jewish View of Education," in Phenix, Philip, H., ed., *Philosophies of Education.* New York: John Wiley & Sons, 1961, pp. 86–93.

CUNINGGIM, MERRIMON, "A Protestant View of Education," in Phenix, ed., *Philosophies of Education,* pp. 67–73.

DIERENFIELD, RICHARD B. *Religion in American Public Schools.* Washington, D.C.: Public Affairs Press, 1962.

HUEGLI, ALBERT C., ed. *Church and State Under God.* St. Louis: Concordia, 1964.

JAHSMANN, ALLAN HART, "What's Lutheran in Education?" in Park, *Readings in the Philosophy of Education,* pp. 453–69.

LOWRY, HOWARD. *The Mind's Adventure.* Philadelphia: Westminster Press, 1950.

PANOCH, JAMES and BARR, DAVID. *Religion Goes to School.* New York: Harper & Row, 1968.

RELIGIOUS EDUCATION ASSOCIATION. *Religion in Public Schools: A Symposium.* New York: Religious Education Association, 1964.

SIZER, THEODORE R., ed. *Religion and Public Education*. New York: Houghton Mifflin, 1967.

STOOPS, JOHN A. *Religious Values in Education*. Danville, Illinois: Interstate Publishers, 1967.

SECULAR CONSERVATISM.

BESTOR, ARTHUR E. "Education for Intellectual Discipline," in Phenix, ed., *Philosophies of Education*, pp. 35–44.

BESTOR, ARTHUR E. *The Restoration of Learning*. New York: Knopf, 1955.

BREED, FREDERICK S. *Education and the New Realism*. New York: Macmillan Co., 1939.

BREED, FREDERICK S., "Education and the Realistic Outlook," in National Society for the Study of Education. *Philosophies of Education* (The Forty-first Yearbook of the NSSE, Part I). Edited by Nelson B. Henry. Chicago: University of Chicago Press, 1942.

CONANT, JAMES B. *The American High School Today*. New York: McGraw-Hill, 1959.

CONANT, JAMES B. *Education and Liberty*. Cambridge, Mass.: Harvard University Press, 1953.

CONANT, JAMES B. *Slums and Suburbs: A Commentary on Schools in Metropolitan Areas*. New York: McGraw-Hill, 1961.

COUNCIL FOR BASIC EDUCATION. *The Case for Basic Education: A Program of Aims for the Public Schools*. Boston: Atlantic-Little, Brown, 1959.

KOERNER, JAMES D. *The Miseducation of American Teachers*. Boston, Mass.: Houghton Mifflin Co., 1963.

RICKOVER, HYMAN G. *Education and Freedom*. New York: E. P. Dutton Co., 1959.

PART THREE

THE LIBERAL EDUCATIONAL IDEOLOGIES

Chapter VII

The Liberal Ideologies: An Overview

THE PHILOSOPHICAL ASSUMPTIONS OF SOCIAL LIBERALISM

Generally speaking, the Liberal ideologies—*liberalism, liberationism* and *anarchism*—tend to be rooted in a series of theoretical assumptions that can be summarized in the following line of reasoning:*

All knowledge is the product of personal experience (*Empiricism*).

Personal experience is the product of the behavior (interaction) between the organism and its physical and social environment (*Philosophical Behaviorism*).†

All behavior grows out of the interaction between physical objects and/or events (*Materialism*).

All personal experience is based in biological processes, growing out of the sense-perceptual encounter between the physical organism and the material world (*Qualified, or Biological, Empiricism*).

An idea is "true" if (and to the extent that) it leads to effective consequences when applied to the solution of a real (practical) problem *(Pragmatism)*.

All thinking is problem solving. We think because we are motivated to act in pursuit of a goal that is not immediately capable of realization. The need to attain this goal constitutes a "problem," and all thinking is the attempt to solve the problem and therefore to

---

*It can well be argued that only the secular Liberal ideologies subscribe to this line of reasoning. This seems unlikely for the reasons covered at some length on pp. 237–244 where the differences between the secular and religious expressions of the Liberal ideologies are discussed.

† The term *behaviorism* is ambiguous in both psychology and philosophy. *Philosophical behaviorism,* as indicated, is a broader position than psychological behaviorism in at least three respects: (1) It is explicitly empirical, holding that behavior is knowable only *indirectly* on the basis of personal experience (which is only secondarily explicable as an expression of *personal behavior*); (2) It tends to view behavior very broadly, as applying to the responses of all animate beings interrelating to the totality of the objects and events that make up their environment; and (3) It is speculative in the sense that it is willing to make extended inferences about the existence of apparently prebehavioral conditions that defy effective scientific verification but that are viewed as fundamental requirements for any sort of personal experience and/or behavior to occur.

realize the goal *(Instrumentalism)*. (When we solve a problem through the application of an idea, we pragmatically verify the truth of the idea with respect to that problem.)

The best way to think is to perfect the natural (instrumental) process of problem solving by imposing certain controls on inquiry that will give rise to more objective (that is, trustworthy and effective) knowledge. Knowledge should be verified by applying ideas to the solution of practical problems that exist within the real world. To do this, one should seek to be as scientific as possible in how one thinks and in what one subsequently believes. A common-sense adaptation of scientific problem-solving procedures is the best way to think and therefore the best way to live, since effective thinking is the best guide to effective living *(Philosophical Experimentalism)*.*

The best way to understand human experience is to study its basis in human behavior, and the best way to conduct such a study is through the application of experimental (and especially more exacting scientific) procedures. This gives rise to scientific psychology *(Psychological, or Scientific, Behaviorism)*.

All personal knowledge is relative to the nature and content of the personal experience by which it has been confirmed *(Psychological Relativism)*.

All knowledge is acquired psychologically, as it emerges through and is affected by the psychobiological processes of knowing (as this, in turn, relates to whatever experience has already been interiorized symbolically through the prior acquisition of knowledge). After the earliest, purely physical, encounters with the world, a person does not respond to the world *as such,* he responds to his own psychological *responses* to the world *(Subjectivism)*.

Since all personal knowledge is (1) relative to personal (sense-perceptual) experience; (2) since the earliest personal experience becomes "subjectified" (interiorized and organized through memory and symbolism), giving rise to basic subjectivity (selfhood); and (3) since subsequent experience is increasingly organized (and made meaningful) on the basis of the existing subjective self-system, virtually all knowledge—after the earliest purely sensory encounters—emerges developmentally out of psychological transactions between the existing psychic structure (self-system) and the surrounding physical

---

*The relationship between instrumentalism and experimentalism (and particularly *scientific experimentalism*) is difficult to arrange in any sort of logical sequence. Strictly speaking, instrumentalism (the theory that all thinking is a means of solving personal problems) is verified (or is generally accepted to be verifiable) on the basis of scientific behavior applied to psychology, and is therefore an outgrowth of scientific (psychological) behaviorism. On the other hand, since scientific behaviorism (in psychology and otherwise) is based upon the assumption that effective inquiry (thought) is the product of a particular type of problem solving, experimentalism is based upon the assumption of instrumentalism. The whole problem is reminiscent of the chicken and the egg. In all likelihood instrumentalism (as an assumption) precedes experimentalism, but experimentalism, once accepted as a theory incorporating instrumentalism as one of its assumptions, then offers a sort of (circular) quasi-verification for one of its own assumptions. In short, the two theories can only be separated on an artificial, conceptual basis. Strictly speaking, they are different aspects of one overall point of view.

Not all experimentalists are scientists, and, conversely, not all scientists are experimentalists. In other words, experimentalism is a philosophical position that advocates a common-sense adaptation of scientific problem-solving procedures as the best way to think and therefore the best way to live. Clearly, one can be an experimentalist and not be a scientist in the more rigorous sense of the term. In a similar sense, most scientists function in a relatively compartmentalized fashion and do not extend their scientific orientation over as a central method of acting and thinking in everyday life.

and social world. This makes the process of psychological development of primary importance in determining how and to what extent the individual will subsequently come to comprehend the world in which he lives. In short, the individual does not respond to the world, *he responds to his responses to the world;* his responses are basically mediated by his personality, and his personality is primarily contingent upon the development of personal identity during the earliest years of life (*Psychological Developmentalism*).

With respect to personal values, the highest good is the experience of pleasure. Men are not naturally ''good'' in the sense of being intrinsically ethical in their interpersonal relations, but they are naturally predisposed toward happiness—the maximum realization of pleasure (both qualitatively and quantitatively) over the longest period of time— and happiness is logically predicated on supportive social and psychological conditions. Man is inherently active—he seeks to be what he is, to exist in such a way as to realize his essential nature as a person—and rational—that is, capable of understanding the nature of the world in which he lives, including his own nature as one aspect of that world. In a fundamental sense, the highest good is to be self-actualizing, that is, to be totally alive in terms of one's potentialities for being the sort of creature one is. ''Pleasure'' is the expression of natural human potentialities as these relate to natural possibilities with respect to specific situations. More specifically, it is the maximum correlation between inclination and opportunity (ability) when measured against some existing state of frustration or discomfiture. The interaction between human potentialities and factual possibilities in the light of perceived problems gives rise to hedonic behavior, that is, behavior directed by pleasure and pain (*Psychological Hedonism*).

Man learns by the emotional consequences of his behavior. Other things being equal, he learns only those things which entail emotional consequences, and he retains that knowledge which is confirmed by pleasurable effects (*Reinforcement Theory*).

All personal experience is largely relative to (and reliant upon) existing social conditions (the nature of childrearing patterns, family organization, dominant political, economic and religious institutions, and so on). Human personality is essentially a sociovocal creation, and man's highest capacity is his ability to construct an indirect, or symbolic, universe (*Cultural Relativism*).

Experimental thinking necessarily implies an experimental society, which in turn implies the existence of a number of ''open'' social institutions and processes, which are prerequisites for any sort of objective inquiry (*Social Democracy*).

In summary, then, man naturally seeks pleasure and happiness. These require effective behavior. Effective behavior, in turn, requires effective thinking by means of trained intelligence founded upon science and reason. These, in turn, require a supportive culture. A supportive culture necessitates humanistic moral values (freedom of speech, freedom of religion, freedom of association, and such). All of these, in turn, generate (and are also largely based upon) the fullest realistic expression of self-potential. This gives rise to pleasure and happiness (and so on) in what is essentially a *positive synergism* cycle, as discussed in Chapter III. This line of reasoning is well exemplified in the philosophy of John Dewey as illustrated in Figure 3–11.

Viewed diagrammatically, using only the key terms of the various positions described, the above line of reasoning is outlined in Figure 7–1.

FIGURE 7-1
THE PHILOSOPHICAL BASES OF SOCIAL LIBERALISM:
A LADDER OF ABSTRACTION

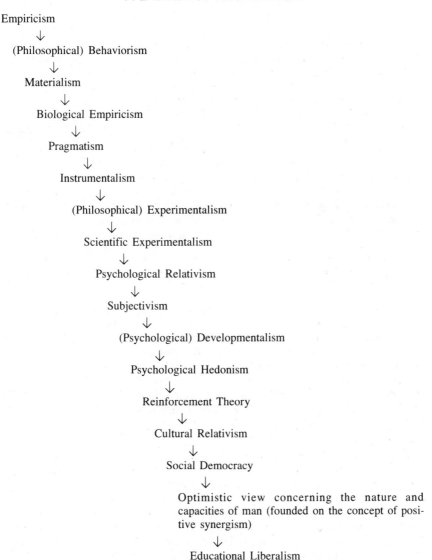

Empiricism
↓
(Philosophical) Behaviorism
↓
Materialism
↓
Biological Empiricism
↓
Pragmatism
↓
Instrumentalism
↓
(Philosophical) Experimentalism
↓
Scientific Experimentalism
↓
Psychological Relativism
↓
Subjectivism
↓
(Psychological) Developmentalism
↓
Psychological Hedonism
↓
Reinforcement Theory
↓
Cultural Relativism
↓
Social Democracy
↓
Optimistic view concerning the nature and capacities of man (founded on the concept of positive synergism)
↓
Educational Liberalism

EDUCATIONAL COROLLARIES

As might be expected, certain educational principles tend to flow logically out of these basic philosophical positions. These might be summarized as follows (and as presented in outline form in Figure 7–2).

1. All learning is relative to the nature and content of personal experience. Personal experience gives rise to personal knowledge, and all personal knowledge is therefore a product of personal experience/behavior with respect to some particular set of objective conditions. (This is the educational corollary of psychological relativism).

2. Once subjectivity (a sense of conscious intentionality, which progressively evolves toward a full-blown self-system, or personality) emerges through the processes of personal development, all significant learning tends to be subjective, in the sense that it is largely governed by volitional, and therefore selective, attention. (This is the educational corollary of subjectivism).

3. All learning is ultimately rooted in active sense-perceptual involvement. (This is the educational corollary of the various philosophical principles relating to empiricism, behaviorism, materialism, and biological empiricism).

4. All learning is primarily a process of testing ideas in practical problem-solving situations. (This is the educational corollary of pragmatism and instrumentalism).

5. The best way to learn—and, by implication, the best way to live, since effective learning is the key to effective living—is to exercise critical inquiry governed by the experimental precepts that characterize scientific thinking. (This is the educational corollary of both philosophical and scientific experimentalism).

6. The earliest psychological experience—the experience that the learner undergoes during childrearing, including the earliest emotional and cognitive training—is inordinately important because it takes both logical and psychological priority over all subsequent experience. It provides the formative basis for the subsequent establishment of the self-system (which gives rise to subjectivity) as well as for all of the more involved personality processes that emerge at a later date. (This is the educational corollary of the psychological developmental point of view).

7. Learning is controlled by the emotional consequences of personal behavior—the principle of reinforcement. Other things being equal, the individual learns only those actions that yield hedonic consequences (pleasure or pain), whether physical or psychological. Affectively (hedonically) neutral actions are not learned (for all practical purposes), and negatively reinforced behavior is ordinarily abandoned in favor of other types of behavior that elicit (or give promise of eliciting) more positive types of reinforcement.

The pleasure principle governs all human experience. In learning, other things being equal, the pleasure experience determines what shall be learned, and the experimental mode of inquiry provides the best modality for effective learning and therefore for maximizing pleasurable experience over the longest period of time. (This is the educational corollary of psychological hedonism).

8. Since man is a social creature who relies upon other people for survival in infancy and for the cultural conditions that guarantee successful behavior both in the competition between species and in the competition between individuals and societies within the species itself, personal learning always occurs within the context of social experience, and the nature and content of social experience takes logical and psychological priority over purely personal experience. Therefore all personal experience is contingent upon some preexisting and predomi-

nant social definition of reality. (This is the educational corollary of cultural relativism).

9. Experimental inquiry, as well as the sort of schooling implied by such a value orientation, can exist only under the sort of social conditions that make possible true scientific inquiry, particularly the application of scientific methods of inquiry to personal and social problems, and not merely to value-neutral areas in the physical sciences. In short, an open and critical process of personal inquiry, adopted as a collective goal for society as a whole, implies a supportive sort of cultural organization that is capable of providing the social, economic, and political prerequisites for the effective realization of experimental thinking. Any significant exercise of open and critical personal inquiry requires an open (democratic) society founded upon a relatively equalized distribution of economic power and featuring clearly specified political rights in such central areas as freedom of speech, freedom of association, and such. (This is the educational corollary of the ''social democracy'' ideal).

10. On the basis of the conditions specified above, the average child can become both personally effective and socially responsible. Trained practical intelligence, viewed as an overriding social goal, can provide the necessary basis for a positive synergism cycle of the sort described earlier, and therefore justifies an optimistic attitude with respect to man's capacity for intelligent self-regulation.

FIGURE 7–2
EDUCATIONAL LIBERALISM: BASIC PROPOSITIONS

All learning is personal knowledge via personal experience.

All learning (after the earliest era in psychological development during infancy) is subjective and selective.

All learning is rooted in activity, based upon sense-perceptual involvement.

All learning is based upon a process of active trial-and-error problem solving.

The best learning is governed by critical inquiry directed by experimental precepts characteristic of the scientific method, and the best knowledge is that which corresponds most highly (or is most probable) in terms of previously validated scientific evidence.

The earliest experience is the most influential on subsequent development and therefore the most important.

Learning is directed and controlled by the emotional consequences of behavior.

The nature and content of social experience directs and controls the nature and content of personal experience and therefore personal knowledge.

Critical inquiry of a significant sort can only occur in an open and democratic society committed to the popular expression of individual thought and feeling.

Given optimum conditions, the average child is capable of becoming both personally effective and socially responsible.

LIBERALISM AND POLITICAL PHILOSOPHY

Liberalism as it relates to politics is reducible to three basic points of view: *political liberalism, political liberationism* and *political anarchism.*

Political Liberalism

This rather diffuse concept generally advocates gradual, small-scale reforms within the framework of the existing political system in order to further individual freedom and to maximize the fullest realization of human potential. In contrast to the social conservative, the political liberal has a good deal of faith in human nature. He tends to favor reasonable change, and is willing to use the government as an instrument for improving the human condition.

Just as social conservatism is largely rooted in the ideas of Edmund Burke, many of the key ideas of liberalism in Great Britain and the United States have grown out of the theories of John Locke and, later, of Jeremy Bentham, James Mill and John Stuart Mill. Virtually all contemporary American liberals advocate private ownership of the means of production and limited constitutional government. Similarly, and as Gould and Truitt point out, liberals are inclined to advocate doctrines such as political representation, a party system of loyal opposition, majority rule qualified by minority rights, and equality of opportunity (as opposed to socialist equality of access to all goods and services within society).[1] They tend to stress specific personal and social liberties, such as the right to vote, freedom of speech, freedom of the press, freedom from arbitrary treatment by the political-legal system, freedom of religion, freedom of movement, and freedom of assembly. Most, however, are clearly opposed to the conservative tenets of laissez faire capitalism as viewed by its earliest proponents—Adam Smith, David Ricardo, and Thomas Malthus. They tend to advocate a "mixed economy," holding, with liberal economist John Maynard Keynes that it is necessary to ". . . clear from the ground the metaphysical or general principles upon which from time to time, *laissez-faire* has been founded."[2] They would also agree with Keynes in his contention that

> it is *not* true that individuals possess a prescriptive "natural liberty" in their economic activities. There is *no* "compact" conferring perpetual rights on those who Have or on those who Acquire. The world is *not* so governed from above that private and social interests always coincide. It is *not* so managed here below that in practice they coincide. It is *not* a correct deduction from the Principle of Economics that enlightened self-interest always operates in the public interest. Nor is it true that self-interest generally *is* enlightened; more often individuals acting separately to promote their own ends are too ignorant or too weak to attain even these. Experience does *not* show that individuals, when they make up a social unit, are always less clear-sighted than when they act separately.[3]

Political Liberationism

This point of view maintains that we should seek the immediate, large-scale reform of the established social order as a way of augmenting individual liberties and promoting the maximum realization of personal potential. Generally advocating a position that might be termed "democratic socialism," the contemporary American liberationist ordinarily favors a limit on the accumulation of private property (including public ownership of all major industries, utilities and transportation) and extensive government regulation of the economy. Largely inspired by the final, utopian vision of Marxist ideology and the teachings of Marxism-Leninism, liberationists frequently envision the ultimate abolition of all conventional political parties and their replacement by strictly social-managerial institutions.

Liberationism is a somewhat awkward term, and some liberationists prefer to refer to themselves as "libertarians." Unfortunately, *libertarianism* is a confusing term, because two radically different "libertarian" movements currently exist in this country. The left-wing libertarians represented by the "student liberation" movement of the late sixties, for example, is a significantly different thing than the "right-wing libertarianism" that can be observed in the "objectivist" followers of novelist-philosopher Ayn Rand, with her fervent commitment to laissez faire capitalism and the abolition of traditional altruistic ethics. Despite obvious similarities, the latter is probably closer to anarchism[4] than to left-wing libertarianism for two reasons. First, left-wing libertarianism is humanistic in the traditional sense. Its ultimate goal is the fullest liberation of the individual within society, viewing man as an interdependent social being. It is founded upon the traditional ethics of altruism. Second, left-wing libertarianism aims at establishing new social institutions which are capable of initiating, supporting and sustaining the sort of society which guarantees the utilitarian ideal of the maximum realization of happiness for all. The right-wing "libertarianism" associated with the objectivist philosophy of Ayn Rand, on the other hand, characteristically denies the necessary interdependence of men, viewing each individual as an autonomous moral unit, and seeking to liberate the individual, insofar as possible, from the traditional institutional restraints of organized society, actively advocating the abolition of everything but the most minimal institutional restraints upon personal freedom. In educational terms, the right-wing libertarian would not necessarily eliminate schools, but he would eliminate both *public* schools and *compulsory* school attendance as violations of basic human rights. (These matters are considered at greater length later in this chapter.) Because of the radically different "libertarian" orientations, I have chosen to refer to what is sometimes viewed as "left-wing libertarianism" as "liberationism," reserving the "libertarian" label for the right-wing groups represented by the Libertarian Party in contemporary American politics, the followers of Ayn Rand, and various others who share the same or similar persuasions.

Most political liberationists would concur with Marx's *materialist* point of view, agreeing that

in the social production of their means of existence men enter into definite, necessary relations which are independent of their will, productive relationships which correspond to a definite state of development of their material productive forces. The aggregate of these productive relationships constitutes the economic structure of society, the real basis on which a juridical and political superstructure arises, and to which definite forms of social consciousness correspond. The mode of production of the material means of existence conditions the whole process of social, political, and intellectual life. It is not the consciousness of men that determine their existence, but, on the contrary, it is their social condition that determines their consciousness. At a certain stage of their development the material productive forces of society come into contradiction with the existing productive relationships within which they had moved before. From forms of development of the productive forces these relationships are transformed into their fetters. Then an epoch of social revolution opens. With the change in the economic foundation the whole vast superstructure is more or less rapidly transformed.[5]

Despite extensive criticism, Marxist socialism has shown a remarkable ability to flourish under changing conditions. The New Left movement exemplified by the Students for a Democratic Society during the late sixties was, for example, deeply affected by the early Marxist essays that were largely preoccupied with the theme of alienation. On the other hand, and as Gould and Truitt indicate

... there has been an infusion of such Freudian concepts as repression and sublimation in the works of new-Marxists like Herbert Marcuse, Erich Fromm, and Norman Brown. The general result has been that the political ideology of traditional Marxism was expanded by the New Left so that the focus goes far beyond an examination of the conditions of the working classes to encompass a general critique of the total culture.[6]

Even the statements of the initially "reformist" liberationists of the oppressed minorities who demanded equity within the existing system during the early and mid-sixties have tended to take on an increasingly Marxist ring over the years. This tone—which has become somewhat muted of late—is reflected in the words of onetime Black Panther Eldridge Cleaver (now a "reborn" Christian), who, writing from the perspective of 1967, states

... the ideology of the Black Panther Party is the historical experience of Black people and the wisdom gained by Black people in their four hundred year long struggle against the system of racist oppression and economic exploitation in Babylon, interpreted through the prism of Marxist-Leninist analysis by our Minister of Defense, Huey P. Newton. ... Essentially, what Huey did was to provide the ideology and the methodology for organizing the Black Urban lumpenproletariat. Armed with this ideological perspective method, Huey transformed the Black lumpenproletariat from the forgotten people at the bottom of society into the vanguard of the proletariat.[7]

Much of the educational criticism of the New Left is directed against the public schools, viewed as political agents of the existing totalitarian state. Thus, for the liberationist, most formal education appears to be motivated by the urge to avoid confronting the real issues of political power and social control. "A great deal of contemporary research," states Richard Lichtman, appears to be similarly motivated. If it is not immediately useful to established power it tends to withdraw and place between itself and the anxieties and responsibilities of the world what Bullough calls "aesthetic distance" and what W. H. Auden referred to as "lecturing on Navigation while the ship is going down."[8]

Writing in *The New Left Reader* in 1969, liberationist Carl Oglesby observes that

... the composition of the work force has been significantly altered by the massive assimilation of industry and technology. Students and workers are from now on one and the same. "There are no student problems," begins *The Appeal From The Sorbonne*. The factory of the post-industrial state is the multiversity. Students are the new working class.

   . . . [Another] position . . . has not yet been argued in a sustained way, although it is perhaps suggested in some of the writings by André Gorz, Louis Althusser, and Martin Nicolaus. Diverging from the conclusions but not the methods of Marx, this view would share with the new-working-class theory the notion that students can no longer be understood as if the modern university retained all the key features of the medieval university. Students constitute the beginnings of a new historical class, produced by a workers' revolution which (within the West) is not still to come but which has already taken place. Such a view implies several departures from classical Marxism. First, it denies that bourgeois society in anything like the original model still exists: bourgeois society was above all a scarcity society, a fact which determined its chief legal, political, and economic features. What we have now, inadequately termed post-scarcity and post-industrial, is, in fact, merely the fulfilled industrial society. Second, it denies that bourgeois society (or any other) is the last of the contradictory social systems. On the contrary, there is more reason to believe that each historically successful revolution will produce a new class with a new conception of need and possibility, new objectives which will motivate new historical practices. Third, it denies that the mission of the proletariat was to make the socialist revolution. The objective evidence indicates, rather, that its mission was to industrialize society—a mission which brought it into sharp conflict with the bourgeoisie. Fourth, it denies that current world politics can be understood as a class of rival socio-ethical systems. Capitalism and socialism, as defined by their practice, are different means, corresponding to different material and political situations, for pursuing the common and general aim of industrialization. Fifth, far from hero-worshiping the proletariat, the new class (unnamed and no doubt at this point unnameable) repudiates in part and in part carries forward the proletarian culture in much the same way that the proletariat both absorbed and transcended bourgeois culture. That an embryonic new class will seek alliance with the proletariat in its struggle with the bourgeoisie—this has made the same kind of meaning as the fact that the embryonic proletariat made alliance with the bourgeoisie in the latter's struggle against Versailles.[9]

The basic problems of contemporary society, states Ernest Mandel, are in large part the outgrowth of a third industrial revolution in which increasing numbers of people are being channeled into service functions and recognized tasks in a variety of large-scale bureaucratic institutions. As Mandel states:

> The third industrial revolution can be seen at one and the same time as a process of *expulsion* of human labor from traditional industry, and of tremendous *influx* of industrial labor into all other fields of economic and social activity. Whereas more and more people are replaced by machines and industry, activity like agriculture, office administration, public administration and even education become industrialized—that is, more and more mechanized, streamlined and organized in industrial forms.
>
> This leads to very important social consequences. These may be summed up by saying that, in the framework of the third industrial revolution, manual labor is expelled from production while intellectual labor is reintroduced into the productive process on a gigantic scale. It thereby becomes to an ever-increasing degree alienated labor—standardized, mechanized, and subjected to rigid rules and regimentation, in exactly the same way that manual labor was in the first and second industrial revolutions. This fact is very closely linked with one of the most spectacular recent developments in American Society: the massive student revolt, or, more correctly, the growing radicalization of students. To give an indication of the scope of this transformation in American society, it is enough to consider that the United States, which at the beginning of this century was still essentially a country exporting agricultural products, today contains fewer farmers than students. There are today [1969] in the United States 6,000,000 students, and the number of farmers together with their employees and family-help has sunk below 5,500,000. We are confronted with a colossal transformation which upsets traditional relations between social groups, expelling human labor radically from certain fields of activity, but reintroducing it on a larger scale and at a higher level of qualification and skill in other fields.[10]

Political Anarchism

This point of view advocates the abolition of virtually all institutional restraints over human freedom as a way of providing the fullest expression of fully liberated human potentialities. This position as it presently exists in this country continues to reflect many of the ideas of the classical anarchists like William Godwin, Pierre Proudhon, and Peter Kropotkin, but it tends to deliberately downplay the violence-prone teachings of such individuals as Georges Sorel and Mikhail Bakunin in favor of the less violently oriented theory of Kropotkin and others.

The neoanarchists of today's radical youth culture generally espouse communitarian values with emphasis on individual moral commitment. Like the classical anarchists, they tend to "have a shared consensus in anarchism as a 'way of life' rather than as a 'view of the future.' "[11] "Very few of the new anarchists," states Max Lerner

> either wish to or believe they can destroy the state completely. What they hope to achieve by violence is either a fundamental modification of

the state or (and this is more true of the commune dwellers) the *de facto* right of counter-culture communities to control their own affairs at a local level.[12]

"What characterizes contemporary anarchism, as contrasted with earlier forms," notes Irving Horowitz

is the highly personal nature of the revolt against authority. There might very well be a sense in which the anarchism of intellectuals is a very special variant of anarchism. It possesses three distinguishing qualities: (1) emphasis on individual responses, on the 'politics of truth'; (2) rejection of professionalism and departmental academicism; and (3) belief in the sanctity of the 'private life.' In the intellectual's powerful sense of the distinction between public and private, which D. H. Lawrence in particular has pointed out, and the image of the private fighting intellectual there is perhaps an anomic kind of anarchism, if one may speak of *anomie* in this connection.[13]

Contrary to general opinion, political anarchism is ordinarily not opposed to order—a position best characterized as *nihilism*—but, rather, seeks to eliminate coercive controls over others. As Pierre Proudhon (the first person to call himself an "anarchist") states, *anarchism* is

... the name given to a principle or theory of life and conduct under which society is conceived without government—harmony in such a society being obtained, not by submission to law or by obedience to any authority, but by free agreements concluded between the various groups, territorial and professional, freely constituted for the sake of production and consumption, as also for the satisfaction of the infinite variety of needs and aspirations of a civilized being.[14]

There are a confusing variety of different "anarchisms," but there would appear to be three basic types: (1) communist anarchism (which stresses that government, law and capitalism are root evils—Kropotkin, Alexander Berkman, Herbert Read); (2) anarcho-syndicalism (which emphasizes the reorganization of industries on the basis of independent worker communes); and (3) individualist anarchism (which emphasizes immediate personal self-expression rather than social reconstruction). The remarks made here apply generally to all of the various subexpressions of political anarchism, but anarchists are notoriously difficult to generalize about, and there tend to be exceptions to virtually any generalizations which may be made in this area.

The central theme in anarchism is not economic relations but coercion. Economic reforms are not enough. The point is to eliminate the need for virtually any political decisions; to administer *things* and not *people*. The key terms are self-expression, cooperation, community (*Gemeinschaft* as opposed to *Gesellschaft*), and voluntary association. A basic summary of the secular anarchist point of view as it generally exists in America today is presented in Figure 7–3.

FIGURE 7–3
SECULAR ANARCHISM

Man is a natural organism who is predisposed to seek personal happiness.

Personal happiness is realized through productive reason (effective practical problem solving).

Since man is basically social, depending upon other people and a supportive social environment both for physical survival during the earliest years and for intellectual development during subsequent phases of this development

productive reason emerges in a social context of shared experience and patterned relationships.

Therefore society itself is a value, because it provides the basis for individual survival and intellectual development; it is therefore an implied necessity (or value) required as a condition for true "individual" identity to emerge.

Therefore other people and organized social behavior are experienced as natural values from the very beginning of an individual's personal experience, and man is basically social, naturally altruistic.

Therefore there is no basic conflict between the individual and society; personality is a social construct; individualism only exists in a society carefully designed to support and encourage it.

Therefore society (the natural interrelationship of mutually supporting individuals) does not violate individual self-expression, it provides the basis for it; self-centered atomistic individualism, which denies the significance of man's social nature, is unnatural and therefore irrational.

But conventional social institutions that purport to support individual self-actualization actually subvert it by forcing man to fulfill the dictates of abstract and impersonal institutions, which ultimately cause men to lose their capacity for effectively regulating their own experiences; they become the servomechanisms of an external state.

Therefore the state and its institutional apparatus of nonvoluntary coerced participation in required types of behavior should be eliminated insofar as possible—a step which ordinarily requires the positive resocialization of man through the expedient of a temporary socialistic state which demands conformity to a new social ethic that seeks the benefit of all rather than the domination of a few.

The eventual elimination of conventional social and political institutions (when the transitional socialist state is abolished) will release man to act on the basis of his naturally rational and cooperative nature, allowing him to respond critically and creatively to whatever problems emerge at the time they occur

which will generate a whole new and positive synergistic relationship between the individual and society,

eliminating the necessity for any sort of monolithic philosophical and political system of beliefs or behavior (since social consensus will be implicit within enlightened reason—rational men facing reasonable problems arrive at the same and similar answers)

resulting in a state of rational and productive cooperation with other men

in which *being* is no longer equated with *doing* or *having* (and in which man is properly viewed as an *end* and not as an alienated *means* to production and/or consumption),

the entire process being regulated by the free and unhampered exercise of individual and collective reason in response to emerging problems, a truly self-renewing and self-transcending society, characterized both by mutual aid and maximum individualism.

Right-Wing and Left-Wing Anarchism. In the area of anarchism there is, as indicated previously, legitimate conflict between the main body of anarchist sentiment, which is essentially an extending—and ultimately a transcending—of radical liberationism, and the less well known position of what might be termed "right-wing anarchism" represented by the "libertarian" philosophies of such individuals as Ayn Rand, Nathaniel Branden, and John Hospers. The distinction between these two positions is difficult to clarify, because both left-wing and right-wing anarchists tend to reject self-perpetuating political institutions, which are viewed as violating the integrity of individual personality. On the other hand, most of the right-wing "anarchists" tend to reject the *anarchist* label altogether, and they seem to have a good case, because the traditional left-wing anarchist (for whom the term *anarchist* is generally reserved) tends to be relativistic in his approach to knowing, altruistic (and utilitarian) in his moral philosophy, and socialistic in his short-range political orientation. He envisions a postcollectivist society of freely cooperating individuals coming together on the basis of rational necessity in order to form temporary, *ad hoc* alliances for the solution of common problems. However, he generally views such a system as emerging out of socialism, which he tends to regard as providing a temporary and transitional resocialization of human consciousness to the new and positive kind of social ethic required as one condition for realizing anarchist freedom. For left-wing anarchists, socialism is not necessarily a self-perpetuating system but is capable of self-destructing at the proper time, abdicating in favor of a new individualistic era.

The right-wing anarchist, on the other hand, tends to be absolutistic in his approach to knowing, "egotistic" in his moral philosophy, and capitalistic in his politics. (See Figure 7–4.) In the case of Ayn Rand's "objectivism," for example (which is perhaps the best known of the right-wing "anarchist" points of view), certain basic truths—such as the proposition that *good* consequences can never be caused by *bad* (irrational and/or unproductive) behavior, as through monopolistic restraints over free trade—are simply self-evident.

In a similar sense, for Rand, the altruist's contention that man can legitimately experience value by identifying with the happiness of others is a fallacy, for man is an isolated moral agent who finds his highest value in and through his own personal experience on the basis of productive labor, guided solely by reason. Accordingly, the kind of society that Rand's "objectivist" philosophy envisions is a laissez faire capitalism in which the rational-productive capacity of the individual is freed from gratuitous, and essentially destructive, social restraints. The State would, in effect, be eliminated, except for the basic minimum of unavoidable services—perhaps a small army, a small police force and a small judiciary—which would be very difficult to provide solely through private enterprise.[15]

In the final analysis, traditional "left-wing" anarchism and the right-wing "anarchism" of Ayn Rand seem to differ in four basic respects:

1. For the traditional anarchist, human experience is ultimately social in both its nature and its origins. For Rand experience is purely personal.
2. For the traditional anarchist, praxis (rational action) is ultimately social in both its nature and its origins. For Rand, praxis is purely personal.

FIGURE 7–4
SECULAR RIGHT-WING ANARCHISM
(AYN RAND'S OBJECTIVIST PHILOSOPHY)[16]

Man is a natural organism who is spontaneously predisposed to seek personal happiness.

↓

Personal happiness is realized through individual productive reason; rational action (praxis).

↓

Other people are values only insofar as they contribute to individual happiness; man is not basically social (ethical egotism).

↓

Therefore social controls that force individuals to serve the needs of other people violate the basic value of reason/happiness; in a similar sense, conventional morality and the sort of society that is based upon such morality is essentially founded upon a destructive lie. Man is only indirectly moral, through the exercise of his individual reason. A personal commitment to a more or less unqualified love of others is intrinsically unreasonable. It is not natural for man to seek his natural happiness through the happiness of other people.

↓

The conventional ethics of altruism cause man to misrepresent himself, both to himself and to others.

↓

This gives rise to a basic irrationality that generates a sort of circular frustration: delusion breeds unhappiness, which strengthens delusion as a means of coping with unhappiness, and so on.

↓

The way out of this dilemma is to develop a new social ethic based upon unrestrained individualism, an ethic founded upon a new system of philosophy that correctly emphasizes the importance of reason and objective belief. The new society created by such a philosophy would be, in effect, a laissez faire capitalism.

↓

In such a capitalistic society productive reason would automatically generate the acquisition of wealth, for, since man is a material being, he finds the highest expression of his nature in the production and consumption of material goods and services.

↓

On purely philosophical grounds, the wealth that is created by productive reason can never be abused by the establishment of monopolies or unworthy inheritance. The law of cause-and-effect and the law of identity in formal logic have their corollaries in ethics: wealth that does not grow out of the good (productive reason) can never yield good consequences (happiness); and bad action (action governed by irrational belief) can never yield good results (wealth).

↓

In the final analysis, reality itself is governed by certain natural laws that govern both the operation of individual intelligence and the relationship of individual intelligences in the marketplace. These natural laws transcend and control individual reason, and they should never be tampered with in a vain attempt to fight against the ironclad strictures of objective reality.

3. For the traditional anarchist, the value experience is ultimately social (interpersonal) in both its nature and its origins. For Rand, all value experiences are personal.

4. For the traditional anarchist, true individualism emerges through stages, and, in the latter stages before the abolition of the state can occur, an imposition of positive social controls by means of a socialist state is necessary in order to correct the abusive nature of existing capitalist conditions. In this sense, the road to traditional anarchism goes through socialism, because personal freedom, fully conceived, requires the positive reconditioning of personal consciousness during a transitional era of positive political controls. For Rand, true individualism emerges out of a return to laissez faire capitalism and is incompatible with socialistic attitudes and approaches.

Where the left-wing radical differs most significantly with Rand—and with most of the other right-wing ''libertarians''—is in her description of the utopian state. As the traditional anarchist sees it, what Rand proposes is not the elimination of the *State* but the elimination of the *public state* and its replacement by a whole host of private-enterprise organizations (such as multinational corporations), which would function collectively as a sort of updated industrial feudalism. Thus, for the left-wing anarchist, to free the individual from a set of bureaucratic, socialistic, public institutions only to turn him over to bureaucratic, capitalistic, private institutions, would be no gain at all, but a substantial loss.

Rand's contention is that capitalist institutions can never be totalitarian, because even continuing corporate or legal entities of the most powerful sort can only sustain their existence if they constantly reaffirm their value by continuing to be the most effective (rational-productive) means of guaranteeing human happiness. In this sense, they cannot be abused, because the misuse of wealth (which, as Rand sees it, is the good *end* of the good *means* of productive reason) would be illogical. It would violate the law of cause-and-effect as it applies to moral matters: that is, good (wealth) cannot be the source of bad (unwarranted suffering or deprivation). It cannot be used to create happiness that is unearned—as might occur, for example, if a person were to inherit a great deal of wealth that he (ostensibly) did not merit on the basis of his subsequent behavior. In a sense, a wealthy man who experiences satisfaction from his wealth *must* be good. By objectivist logic, if he did not *deserve* to be wealthy, even if by inheritance, his wealth would simply destroy him as an inevitable moral consequence of his own defective character.[17]

For the traditional anarchist, of course, this line of reasoning is not particularly compelling. He does not accept Rand's self-evident truths (such as the application of the principle of cause-and-effect in the moral sphere). He rejects the idea that unwarranted wealth is implicitly bad (in the sense that it is incapable of yielding happiness to its possessor). Indeed, even if unmerited and the cause of great personal misery to its possessor, such monopolized wealth is effectively denied to others who might conceivably warrant it. Perhaps most significantly, of course, the traditional anarchist would reject the objectivist contention that a society organized around private corporations in hot pursuit of wealth is ''free.'' For the anarchist, the state is *any* external organization of power that denies the individual the possibility of determining his own fate, and private totalitarianism is no adequate substitute for public tyranny.

For these reasons, the so-called right-wing anarchists are probably quite correct in rejecting the *anarchist* label (and the term will be used henceforth solely with reference to the left-wing tradition). Certainly, in its more explicit formulation, in the writings of Rand, Branden and Hospers, we seem to be dealing with a philosophical conservatism that advocates a political meritocracy—a position that requires the highest development of trained reason and that generally eventuates on the educational level in a type of secular intellectualism very close to that advocated by some of the contemporary neo-Aristotelians like Robert Maynard Hutchins and Mortimer Adler.

THE LIBERAL CONTINUUM

For the *educational liberal* the highest good is critical intelligence, defined in terms of effective problem solving on both the personal and social levels. Man is rational, and his reason alone is capable of establishing the necessary relationship between his own enlightened self-interest and the overall best interests of others. For the liberal, then, critical intelligence, ordinarily defined as experimental problem solving, is the *means-value* that takes precedence over any particular *ends-values*. Indeed, the governing assumption is that the specific values to be discovered in any actual situation will be defined within the situation itself by applying the more encompassing *meta-value* of critical intelligence.

The *educational liberationist* does not disagree with the liberal's commitment to experimental inquiry, but he does disagree with the *sufficiency* of critical intelligence as a guide to practical action in most *existing* situations. As the liberationist sees it, the individual understands the world only *indirectly* on the basis of his behavior within it, and this behavior is invariably determined by quite specific social constraints and conditions. Thus, problem solving is invariably subordinate to problem perceiving, and problem perceiving is always fundamentally determined by social experience. In this way, the creation of a society that allows and encourages critical intelligence is a logical prerequisite for the effective *exercise* of such critical intelligence. The "critical thinking" that the liberals champion can only be a viable *personal* goal in a society that is first dedicated to changing those social conditions that preclude the effective exercise of critical intelligence by *all*. The rational man requires a rational society, and the development of such a society requires the elimination of all of those social conditions—including all forms of economic, political and intellectual authoritarianism—that keep men from thinking and acting freely in response to constantly changing conditions.

For the *educational anarchist,* on the other hand, both the liberal and the liberationist are partly right and partly wrong. Like the liberal, the anarchist advocates individualism. Like the liberationist, he accepts the necessity for new standards of social justice. For the anarchist, however, true individualism can only occur after the new socialist state—which is generally viewed as one stage on the path to anarchism—has begun to self-destruct. Indeed, true "individualism" can only occur in a *postsocialist* era, which is only possible when man's consciousness has been liberated from the pervasive social delusions perpetuated by authoritarian systems, and he has become capable of acting independent of virtually all of the usual institutional restraints.

For the anarchist, man is naturally rational and naturally good (that is, well-disposed toward his fellows). It is the state that has traditionally denied him the right to *exercise* his natural proclivities toward rational self-determination in voluntary cooperation with others.* Free men require, not new social controls, but the radical elimination (or at least the radical minimization) of social controls *as such*. For the anarchist, liberalism correctly perceives the end—self-realization—but it sadly misconstrues the means, for these require the formation of a totally new and deinstitutionalized social order. In a similar sense, the liberationist properly perceives the *means*—political reconstruction of the existing social order—but he misconceives the inherently antihumanistic *consequences* of any society that forces men to regulate their lives indefinitely by even the most well intentioned system of external controls. The answer, says the anarchist, is to return man to himself, to free him of all of the unnecessary social bonds that deny him the right of *self*-determination. The goal lies beyond society as it has been traditionally conceived; it requires a free and rational system of voluntary cooperation between self-determining individuals. (See Figure 7–5.)

Politically, then, all three of the "liberal" social ethics assume similar but nevertheless significantly different forms. As indicated in Figure 7–5, the differences between the three Liberal positions tend to be more matters of *degree* or *priority* than of *kind*. For the educational liberal, the preferred course of social action entails the liberation of the individual *within the state*. The social is looked upon as a natural by-product of collective "individual" behavior, and the emphasis is on liberty (political freedom) rather than equality (economic freedom), on equity *within the system* rather than striving for a more equitable *system*. Thus, and although educational liberalism, like all of the more "liberal" ideologies, expresses itself differently in different cultures and at different times, the contemporary American liberal tends to be a social democrat, who is more concerned with expanding freedom and self-expression within the established capitalistic order than with supplanting capitalism with socialism. If socialistically inclined—as many educational liberals tend to be—he tends to

---

* How the anarchist *knows* that man is naturally active, rational, social, and (therefore) moral is a contentious point. Most anarchists seem to hold to this point of view on philosophical principle. Most would also, however, take the position that such a proposition is experimentally verifiable (in principle, if not in fact) through appropriate scientific observations. In the latter case, anarchists tend to fall into two general categories: (1) those who subscribe to the position that there is sufficient scientific evidence (usually anthropological) currently available to justify such a contention about the nature of man; and (2) those that would reject the notion that there is sufficient scientific evidence currently available to support the point of view but who would hold that such scientific evidence is *not* available precisely because the political organization of contemporary society has so perverted the nature of man as to make his behavior misleading as an indicator of his underlying potentialities for constructive behavior (and who generally also hold to the point of view that scientific evidence *will become* available only in an objective—that is, anarchist—society where man will be capable of being observed in a truly natural, and therefore moral, state).

FIGURE 7–5
THE LIBERAL CONTINUUM

Self-realization

↓

requires proper conduct

↓

guided by true knowledge

↓

which is founded upon effective thinking (critical problem solving)

↓

guided by experimental/pragmatic precepts about the verification of knowledge

↓

which is currently best represented within the intellectual consensus of the best experimental thinkers

↓

who concur that man is naturally a rational, social, and moral being

↓

whose personality is fundamentally derived from his social conditioning within a particular cultural setting

↓

which indicates that social reforms leading to the development of an open and experimental society necessarily precede any effective concern with individual critical thinking

↓

but which also indicates that man's natural abilities and inclinations toward critical thinking is blocked by the deadening conformity to established social institutions, which blocks any satisfactory expression of personal autonomy and self-expression just as it blocks the evolution of new and more effective types of thought and behavior.

↓

Therefore the highest immediate imperative is to free the individual from all prescribed institutional restraints that can possibly be eliminated so that he can determine his own destiny in voluntary concert with other free men who are equally unhampered by the tyranny of both social majorities and minorities.

Liberalism, Liberationism and Anarchism

Liberationism & Anarchism

Anarchism

view change within a rather expanded time-frame, advocating a gradualistic and nonviolent evolution of social forces directed by the slow growth of critical intelligence within society at large.

For the educational liberationist, too, the ultimate value of self-realization requires a commitment to the process of critical intelligence, but this commitment also implies a more specific commitment to the sort of society— democratic socialism—in which this goal is both possible and practical. In short, effective self-realization implies a corollary *social* self-realization, the development of a total society committed to the collective self-realization of *all* of its members. Phrased somewhat differently, the liberal states that, *if* critical intelligence is effectively exercised, *then* all particular problems can be resolved. The liberationist counters with the observation that, since critical intelligence *cannot* be effectively exercised under existing conditions, the best course of action is properly one that envisions establishing the kind of social order that is willing to accept critical intelligence as both necessary and desirable for all.

The left-wing anarchist, on the other hand, is willing to accept both the crucial value of critical intelligence and the necessity of social reform, but his fundamental concern is with personal liberty as the basic value that overrides all others. Thus, as the anarchist sees it, science and reason both lead us inexorably to the conclusion that man is demonstrably rational and social. Other things being equal, then, the individual is naturally predisposed to be good, and to cooperate voluntarily with others in behavior that advances the best interests of all. Unfortunately, however, other things seldom are *equal*. Man is *forced* everywhere to believe and behave, not according to the dictates of his own reason, but according to the requirements of generally unnecessary and frequently tyrannical social institutions that force him to think and act in violation of his own intrinsic needs. As the anarchist sees it, such institutions generally elicit irrelevant and anachronistic responses because they represent the answers of previous generations to problems that either no longer exist or that exist in significantly new forms. Thus they interfere with the individual's ability and inclination to think for himself. They frustrate and block his innate tendency toward critical thought and creative action, forcing him to be what he *is* rather than to *become* what he *might be*.

While there is no one individual or movement within the Liberal continuum that propounds all three of the basic Liberal ideologies—liberalism, liberationism, and anarchism—there is at least one major figure, the American philosopher John Dewey, who has served as perhaps the formative figure in at least two of these traditions: educational liberalism and educational liberationism. In a manifesto that was first published as a pamphlet in 1897, Dewey outlined both his "progressive" (directive liberal) and "reconstructionist" (radical liberationist) tenets in one succinct and eloquent statement of educational principles. Since there is no other single document that summarizes so well the essential spirit of mainstream Liberal thinking in education, it is perhaps justifiable to break the normal continuity of presentation at this point by allowing Dewey to speak for himself. The following is John Dewey's famous statement of educational beliefs entitled "My Pedagogic Creed."

MY PEDAGOGIC CREED*

ARTICLE I–What Education Is (1897)

I Believe that

—all education proceeds by the participation of the individual in the social consciousness of the race. This process begins unconsciously almost at birth, and is continually shaping the individual's powers, saturating his consciousness, forming his habits, training his ideas, and arousing his feelings and emotions. Through this unconscious education the individual gradually comes to share in the intellectual and moral resources which humanity has succeeded in getting together. He becomes an inheritor of the funded capital of civilization. The most formal and technical education in the world cannot safely depart from this general process. It can only organize it or differentiate it in some particular direction.

—the only true education comes through the stimulation of the child's powers by the demands of the social situations in which he finds himself. Through these demands he is stimulated to act as a member of a unity, to emerge from his original narrowness of action and feeling, and to conceive of himself from the standpoint of the welfare of the group to which he belongs. Through the responses which others make to his own activities he comes to know what these mean in social terms. The value which they have is reflected back into them. For instance, through the response which is made to the child's instinctive babblings the child comes to know what those babblings mean; they are transformed into articulate language, and thus the child is introduced into the consolidated wealth of ideas and emotions which are now summed up in language.

—this educational process has two sides—one psychological and one sociological—and that neither can be subordinated to the other, or neglected, without evil results following. Of these two sides, the psychological is the basis. The child's own instincts and powers furnish the material and give the starting-point for all education. Save as the efforts of the educator connect with some activity which the child is carrying on of his own initiative independent of the educator, education becomes reduced to a pressure from without. It may, indeed, give certain external results, but cannot truly be called educative. Without insight into the psychological structure and activities of the individual, the educative process will, therefore, be haphazard and arbitrary. If it chances to coincide with the child's activity it will get a leverage; if it does not, it will result in friction, or disintegration, or arrest of the child nature.

—knowledge of social conditions, of the present state of civilization, is necessary in order properly to interpret the child's powers. The child has his own instincts and tendencies, but we do not know what these mean until we can translate them into their social equivalents. We must be able to carry them back into a social past and see them as the inheritance of

---

* This was published originally as a pamphlet by E. L. Kellogg and Co., 1897.

previous race activities. We must also be able to project them into the future to see what their outcome and end will be. In the illustration just used, it is the ability to see in the child's babblings the promise and potency of a future social intercourse and conversation which enables one to deal in the proper way with that instinct.

—the psychological and social sides are organically related and that education cannot be regarded as a compromise between the two, or a superimposition of one upon the other. We are told that the psychological definition of education is barren and formal—that it gives us only the idea of a development of all the mental powers without giving us any idea of the use to which these powers are put. On the other hand, it is urged that the social definition of education, as getting adjusted to civilization, makes of it a forced and external process, and results in subordinating the freedom of the individual to a preconceived social and political status.

—each of these objections is true when urged against one side isolated from the other. In order to know what a power really is we must know what its end, use, or function is, and this we cannot know save as we conceive of the individual as active in social relationships. But, on the other hand, the only possible adjustment which we can give to the child under existing conditions is that which arises through putting him in complete possession of all his powers. With the advent of democracy and modern industrial conditions, it is impossible to foretell definitely just what civilization will be twenty years from now. Hence it is impossible to prepare the child for any precise set of conditions. To prepare him for the future life means to give him command of himself; it means so to train him that he will have the full and ready use of all his capacities; that his eye and ear and hand may be tools ready to command, that his judgment may be capable of grasping the conditions under which it has to work, and the executive forces be trained to act economically and efficiently. It is impossible to reach this sort of adjustment save as constant regard is had to the individual's own powers, tastes, and interests—that is, as education is continually converted into psychological terms.

In sum, I believe that the individual who is to be educated is a social individual, and that society is an organic union of individuals. If we eliminate the social factor from the child we are left only with an abstraction; if we eliminate the individual factor from society, we are left only with an inert and lifeless mass. Education, therefore, must begin with a psychological insight into the child's capacities, interests, and habits. It must be controlled at every point by reference to these same considerations. These powers, interests, and habits must be continually interpreted—we must know what they mean. They must be translated into terms of their social equivalents—into terms of what they are capable of in the way of social service.

ARTICLE II–What the School Is

I Believe that

—the school is primarily a social institution. Education being a social process, the school is simply that form of community life in which all those agencies are concentrated that will be most effective in bringing the child to share in the inherited resources of the race, and to use his own powers for social ends.

—education, therefore, is a process of living and not a preparation for future living.

—the school must represent present life—life as real and vital to the child as that which he carries on in the home, in the neighborhood, or on the playground.

—that education which does not occur through forms of life, forms that are worth living for their own sake, is always a poor substitute for the genuine reality, and tends to cramp and to deaden.

—the school, as an institution, should simplify existing social life; should reduce it, as it were, to an embryonic form. Existing life is so complex that the child cannot be brought into contact with it without either confusion or distraction; he is either overwhelmed by the multiplicity of activities which are going on, so that he loses his own power of orderly reaction, or he is so stimulated by these various activities that his powers are prematurely called into play and he becomes either unduly specialized or else disintegrated.

—as such simplified social life, the school life should grow gradually out of the home life; that it should take up and continue the activities with which the child is already familiar in the home.

—it should exhibit these activities to the child, and reproduce them in such ways that the child will gradually learn the meaning of them, and be capable of playing his own part in relation to them.

—this is a psychological necessity, because it is the only way of securing continuity in the child's growth, the only way of giving a background of past experience to the new ideas given in school.

—it is also a social necessity because the home is the form of social life in which the child has been nurtured and in connection with which he has had his moral training. It is the business of the school to deepen and extend his sense of the values bound up in his home life.

—much of present education fails because it neglects this fundamental principle of the school as a form of community life. It conceives the school as a place where certain information is to be given, where certain lessons are to be learned, or where certain habits are to be formed. The value of these is conceived as lying largely in the remote future; the child must do these things for the sake of something else he is to do; they are mere preparations. As a result they do not become a part of the life experience of the child and so are not truly educative.

—the moral education centers upon this conception of the school as a mode of social life, that the best and deepest moral training is precisely that which one gets through having to enter into proper relations with others in a unity of work and thought. The present educational systems, so far as they destroy or neglect this unity, render it difficult or impossible to get any genuine, regular moral training.

—the child should be stimulated and controlled in his work through the life of the community.

—under existing conditions far too much of the stimulus and control proceeds from the teacher, because of neglect of the idea of the school as a form of social life.

—the teacher's place and work in the school is to be interpreted from this same basis. The teacher is not in the school to impose certain ideas or to form certain habits in the child, but is there as a member of the community to select the influences which shall affect the child and to assist him in properly responding to these influences.

—the discipline of the school should proceed from the life of the school as a whole and not directly from the teacher.

—the teacher's business is simply to determine, on the basis of larger experience and riper wisdom, how the discipline of life shall come to the child.

—all questions of the grading of the child and his promotion should be determined by reference to the same standard. Examinations are of use only so far as they test the child's fitness for social life and reveal the place in which he can be of the most service and where he can receive the most help.

ARTICLE III–The Subject-Matter of Education

I Believe that

—the social life of the child is the basis of concentration, or correlation, in all his training or growth. The social life gives the unconscious unity and the background of all his efforts and of all his attainments.

—the subject-matter of the school curriculum should mark a gradual differentiation out of the primitive unconscious unity of social life.

—we violate the child's nature and render difficult the best ethical results by introducing the child too abruptly to a number of special studies, of reading, writing, geography, etc., out of relation to this social life.

—the true center of correlation on the school subjects is not science, nor literature, nor history, nor geography, but the child's own social activities.

—education cannot be unified in the study of science, or so-called nature study, because apart from human activity, nature itself is not a unity; nature in itself is a number of diverse objects in space and time, and to attempt to make it the center of work by itself is to introduce a principle of radiation rather than one of concentration.

—literature is the reflex expression and interpretation of social experience; that hence it must follow upon and not precede such experience. It, therefore, cannot be made the basis, although it may be made the summary of unification.

—once more that history is of educative value in so far as it presents phases of social life and growth. It must be controlled by reference to social life. When taken simply as history it is thrown into the distant past and becomes dead and inert. Taken as the record of man's social life and progress it becomes full of meaning. I believe, however, that it cannot be so taken excepting as the child is also introduced directly into social life.

—the primary basis of education is in the child's powers at work along the same general constructive lines as those which have brought civilization into being.

—the only way to make the child conscious of his social heritage is to enable him to perform those fundamental types of activity which make civilization what it is.

—in the so-called expressive or constructive activities as the center of correlation.

—this gives the standard for the place of cooking, sewing, manual training, etc., in the school.

—they are not special studies which are to be introduced over and above a lot of others in the way of relaxation or relief, or as additional accomplishments. I believe rather that they represent, as types, fundamental forms of social activity; and that it is possible and desirable that the child's introduction into the more formal subjects of the curriculum be through the medium of these activities.

—the study of science is educational in so far as it brings out the materials and processes which make social life what it is.

—one of the greatest difficulties in the present teaching of science is that the material is presented in purely objective form, or is treated as a new peculiar kind of experience which the child can add to that which he has already had. In reality, science is of value because it gives the ability to interpret and control the experience already had. It should be introduced, not as so much new subject-matter, but as showing the factors already involved in previous experience, and as furnishing tools by which that experience can be more easily and effectively regulated.

—at present we lose much of the value of literature and language studies because of our elimination of the social element. Language is almost always treated in the books of pedagogy simply as the expression of thought. It is true that language is a logical instrument, but it is fundamentally and primarily a social instrument. Language is the device for communication; it is the tool through which one individual comes to share the ideas and feelings of others. When treated simply as a way of getting individual information, or as a means of showing off what one has learned, it loses its social motive and end.

—there is, therefore, no succession of studies in the ideal school curriculum. If education is life, all life has, from the outset, a scientific aspect, an aspect of art and culture, and an aspect of communication. It cannot, therefore, be true that the proper studies for one grade are mere reading and writing, and that at a later grade, reading, or literature, or science, may be introduced. The progress is not in the succession of studies, but in the development of new attitudes towards, and new interests in, experience.

—education must be conceived as a continuing reconstruction of experience; that the process and the goal of education are one and the same thing.

—to set up any end outside of education, as furnishing its goal and standard, is to deprive the educational process of much of its meaning, and tends to make us rely upon false and external stimuli in dealing with the child.

ARTICLE IV—The Nature of Method

I Believe that

—the question of method is ultimately reducible to the question of the order of development of the child's powers and interests. The law for presenting and treating material is the law implicit within the child's own nature. Because this is so I believe the following statements are of supreme importance as determining the spirit in which education is carried on:

—the active side precedes the passive in the development of the child-nature; that expression comes before conscious impression; that the muscular development precedes the sensory; that movements come before conscious sensations; I believe that consciousness is essentially motor or impulsive; that conscious states tend to project themselves in action.

—the neglect of this principle is the cause of a large part of the waste of time and strength in school work. The child is thrown into a passive, receptive, or absorbing attitude. The conditions are such that he is not permitted to follow the law of his nature; the result is friction and waste.

—ideas (intellectual and rational processes) also result from action and devolve for the sake of the better control of action. What we term reason is primarily the law of orderly or effective action. To attempt to develop the reasoning powers, the powers of judgment, without reference to the selection and arrangement of means in action, is the fundamental fallacy in our present methods of dealing with this matter. As a result we present the child with arbitrary symbols. Symbols are a necessity in mental development, but they have their place as tools for economizing effort; presented by themselves they are a mass of meaningless and arbitrary ideas imposed from without.

—the image is the great instrument of instruction. What a child gets out of any subject presented to him is simply the images which he himself forms with regard to it.

—if nine-tenths of the energy at present directed towards making the child learn certain things were spent in seeing to it that the child was forming proper images, the work of instruction would be indefinitely facilitated.

—much of the time and attention now given to the preparation and presentation of lessons might be more wisely and profitably expended in training the child's power of imagery and in seeing to it that he was continually forming definite, vivid, and growing images of the various subjects with which he comes in contact in his experience.

—interests are the signs and symptoms of growing power. I believe that they represent dawning capacities. Accordingly the constant and careful observation of interests is of the utmost importance for the educator.

—these interests are to be observed as showing the state of development which the child has reached.

—they prophesy the stage upon which he is about to enter.

—only through the continual and sympathetic observation of childhood's interests can the adult enter into the child's life and see what it is ready for, and upon what material it could work most readily and fruitfully.

—these interests are neither to be humored nor repressed. To repress interest is to substitute the adult for the child, and so to weaken intellectual curiosity and alertness, to suppress initiative, and to deaden interest. To humor the interests is to substitute the transient for the permanent. The interest is always the sign of some power below; the important thing is to discover this power. To humor the interest is to fail to penetrate below the surface, and its sure result is to substitute caprice and whim for genuine interest.

—the emotions are the reflex of actions.

—to endeavor to stimulate or arouse the emotions apart from their corresponding activities is to introduce an unhealthy and morbid state of mind.

—if we can only secure right habits of action and thought, with reference to the good, the true, and the beautiful, the emotions will for the most part take care of themselves.

—next to deadness and dullness, formalism and routine, our education is threatened with no greater evil than sentimentalism.

—this sentimentalism is the necessary result of the attempt to divorce feeling from action.

ARTICLE V–The School and Social Progress

I Believe that

—education is the fundamental method of social progress and reform.

—all reforms which rest simply upon the enactment of law, or the threatening of certain penalties, or upon changes in mechanical or outward arrangements, are transitory and futile.

—education is a regulation of the process of coming to share in the social consciousness; and that the adjustment of individual activity on the basis of this social consciousness is the only sure method of social reconstruction.

—this conception has due regard for both the individualistic and socialistic ideals. It is duly individual because it recognizes the formation of a certain character as the only genuine basis of right living. It is socialistic because it recognizes that this right character is not to be formed by merely individual precept, example, or exhortation, but rather by the influence of a certain form of institutional or community life upon the individual, and that the social organism through the school, as its organ, may determine ethical results.

—in the ideal school we have the reconciliation of the individualistic and the institutional ideals.

—the community's duty to education is, therefore, its paramount moral duty. By law and punishment, by social agitation and discussion, society can regulate and form itself in a more or less haphazard and chance way. But through education society can formulate its own purposes, can organize its own means and resources, and thus shape itself with definiteness and economy in the direction in which it wishes to move.

—when society once recognizes the possibilities in this direction, and the obligations which these possibilities impose, it is impossible to conceive of the resources of time, attention, and money which will be put at the disposal of the educator.

—it is the business of every one interested in education to insist upon the school as the primary and most effective interest of social progress and reform in order that society may be awakened to realize what the school stands for, and aroused to the necessity of endowing the educator with sufficient equipment properly to perform his task.

—education thus conceived marks the most perfect and intimate union of science and art conceivable in human experience.

—the art of thus giving shape to human powers and adapting them to social service is the supreme art; one calling into its service the best of artists; that no insight, sympathy, tact, executive power, is too great for such service.

—with the growth of psychological service, giving added insight into individual structure and laws of growth; and with growth of social science, adding to our knowledge of the right organization of individuals, all scientific resources can be utilized for the purposes of education.

—when science and art thus join hands the most commanding motive for human action will be reached, the most genuine springs of human conduct aroused, and the best service that human nature is capable of guaranteed.

—the teacher is engaged, not simply in the training of individuals, but in the formation of the proper social life.

—every teacher should realize the dignity of his calling; that he is a social servant set apart for the maintenance of proper social order and the securing of the right social growth.

—in this way the teacher always is the prophet of the true God and the usherer in of the true kingdom of God.

THE LIBERAL RELIGIOUS TRADITIONS

The religious expressions of the Liberal ideologies tend to be less important than those within the Conservative ideologies for two basic reasons.

1. In the Liberal persuasions, the social ethic very seldom, if ever, differs significantly between religious and secular proponents of the same ideological position. Religious liberalism differs from secular liberalism primarily in that the religious liberals accept some categorical ethical principle (almost always either the love-ethic—"Do unto others"—or some variation thereof) as a divinely prescribed injunction based upon some sort of sacred revelation that is capable of serving as a supraempirical (supernatural) basis for moral behavior. They are often willing to subscribe to certain preferred rules for behavior associated with a particular religious tradition, providing that these rules appear (pragmatically and on quite empirical grounds of evidence) to provide the best means of maximizing the realization of this categorical (if unavoidably ambiguous) love-ethic in the light of some particular set of conditions. Phrased somewhat differently, the religious liberal accepts a supernatural ethical imperative grounded (generally historically) in some sort of revelation and founded upon personal faith, but, for all practical purposes, he functions in the same manner as the secular liberal when it comes to virtually all of his other basic beliefs. For all practical purposes, it is very hard to distinguish between the secular and the religious traditions within the various liberal ideologies, because virtually all of the secular liberals also subscribe to some variation of the love-ethic and also adhere to the same general rules for ethical conduct (including such values as truth-telling, refraining from theft, sexual fidelity, and such) although they would generally verify these on purely naturalistic and empirical bases.

What differences exist between religious and secular liberals tend to occur almost entirely in the area of theory, at a level of abstraction far beyond that required to deal with specific political and educational questions. The differences between the Christian socialist and the secular socialist, for example, are not readily apparent at the operational level of social action, but occur primarily at the explanatory level with respect to underlying philosophical preconceptions. In a similar sense, the religious liberal will *explain* the love-ethic—the "Do unto others" injunction—differently than the secular liberal, viewing it as a divine absolute emanating from a personal God. Indeed, for the religious liberal, altruistic love may be viewed as rooted in the brotherhood of man, but the brotherhood of man may be explained, in turn, by the fatherhood of God. In a similar sense, the religious liberal's view of the ultimate consequences of adhering to the love-ethic will ordinarily envision a more transcendent and enduring sort of happiness (frequently encompassing some concept of life-after-death) than that of the secular liberal. For the religious liberal, then, the love-ethic is both explained differently, and it also leads to somewhat different (or, at least, more extended) consequences than those envisioned by the secularist. For the secular liberal, on the other hand, the ethic remains essentially the same proposition, but it is explained on a purely naturalistic level (ordinarily on the basis of enlightened self-interest), and it is looked upon as leading to purely natural consequences (that is, as generating the highest degree of self-realization or happiness, both personally and socially, within the confines of the temporal world).

For all practical purposes, however, the fact remains that the ethical, political and educational programs espoused by both the secular and religious liberals are essentially the same on the *descriptive* level. They advocate the same sort of policies for significantly different reasons, but, since these differences in underlying belief exist on a level of abstraction far beyond that reflected in specific types of moral and political behavior, these differences can be effectively ignored for present purposes, and the two approaches to the various liberal ideologies within education can be treated, as they are here, as essentially one position.

2. While fundamentally dualistic—assuming the existence of both natural and supernatural experience—the religious liberals tend to downplay the supernatural in two respects.

a) They tend to hold that the supernatural is in most respects amenable to partial (if imperfect) verification on the basis of reason and natural evidence. "Altruistic love" is, for example, generally viewed as *both* a divine prescription *and* a rational imperative, which can be defended on either religious or secular grounds. They maintain that the supernatural love-ethic is essentially compatible with natural reason and experimental evidence.

b) They tend to view fewer ethical sanctions as emanating from the divine, and they generally define these less literally, at a higher level of generalization which requires a significant degree of personal interpretation as a basis for application. Phrased differently, they are more disposed to prescribe abstract principles than specific policies and practices. (They tend, for example, to be more inclined to believe that a person should treat other people as *ends* and not *means,* but less inclined to specify *how* this should be done in a categorical sense—as, for example, by specifying that one should *always* love one's mother or father, that one should *always* tell the truth, or whatever.) Accordingly, they are less inclined toward traditional "code morality" with its definitive prescription of particular do's and don'ts regardless of particular circumstances.

Religious Liberalism and Moral Choice

At the ethical level, most religious liberals tend to view values as existing on five basic levels.

1. God.   God himself is the highest value as well as the highest truth. He is the ground of Being who encompasses all less particular values as well as the process of valuation itself.

2. A Divinely Ordained Moral Principle.   The divinely ordained moral principle is almost invariably some form of the so-called love-ethic—that is, the injunction to love others and to treat others as objects of supreme concern: "Do unto others as you would have others do unto you.'' There may be other divine injunctions as well—such as ''truthfulness'' (the value of telling the truth)—but for most religious liberals the supreme divine injunction, and the only one that exists without additional qualification, is that which enjoins one to care deeply about the well-being of other people. (See also the discussion of Judaic ethics in Appendix 2.)

3. Divine Reward. One who adheres to the dictates of God earns some sort of reward that transcends the daily satisfactions that might otherwise accrue to a satisfactory natural existence. Such rewards may exist in a realm beyond ordinary experience (heaven, life-after-death, preferred modes of reincarnation, release from involvement in natural existence, realization of racial or ethnic destiny, absorption into the divine presence, etc.) or involve special types of personal experience (religious ecstasy, cosmic consciousness, and so on).

4. Reason. The value subordinate only to love for most theistic liberals is the value of critical intelligence. If the supreme end is *love,* the supreme means is *reason.* Indeed, reason provides the manner of determining which course *is* most loving and therefore most ethical. The supreme value of altruistic love can be confirmed by reason, but it is not subordinate to reason. Altruistic love is the categorical *end*; reason is merely the categorical *means.*

5. A Code of Moral Precepts. Virtually all religious liberals accept some code of moral precepts (policies, recommended practices, rules, and such) that is rooted in religious faith. Such precepts—and the bulk of the Judaic-Christian Ten Commandments would be examples of such—may be viewed as highly desirable or even divinely inspired, but for the religious liberal they are not taken as prescriptive absolutes that allow for no exceptions. Rather, they call for intelligent interpretation, a prudential analysis of the best way of acting in any given situation if one is to realize most effectively the supreme injunction of the love-ethic.

In general, then, religious liberals espouse ''situational'' (or ''contextual'') morality. And while the predetermined ''code morality'' of the conservative is not totally disregarded, it tends to be viewed primarily as a set of exceedingly valuable ''hypotheses'' (or *preferred maxims,* to use theologian Joseph Fletcher's term[18]) about the nature of proper behavior, not as an inexorable and binding code of conduct that admits no exceptions. For the religious liberal, for example, the moral dictate ''Thou shalt not commit adultery'' would probably be closely adhered to because of the probable consequences of acting otherwise (when these are measured against the standard of truly loving behavior). Phrased somewhat differently, in most cases, and other things being equal, the religious liberal would concur with the religious conservative that it is best not to covet other people's wives or husbands, and that the advisability of refraining from such behavior can be verified by the practical consequences of acting in a contrary fashion when such acts are measured against the absolute and overriding moral criterion of overriding concern for the well-being of others. On the other hand, even such a maxim as that proscribing adultery might well be suspended in certain extreme situations. The proverbial person shipwrecked on a desert island might, for example, reconsider such a maxim as this if the alternative were a lifetime of total continence.

For the religious liberal, then, the moral act is the intentionally "loving" act that is guided by useful and generally trustworthy religious maxims, and that is tested by the real or imagined consequences of acting on such maxims. The religious liberal, unlike his secular counterpart, takes certain things on faith. He has faith in the existence of a personal God or God-event—the divinity of Christ, the actuality of Buddha's enlightenment, the reality of Moses' communications with the Lord, or whatever. He has faith in the absolute morality of a divine ethic of a rather general and encompassing sort, usually the "love-ethic," or golden rule, which is shared by so many of the world's religions. He has faith in the reality of certain extraordinary rewards—whether natural or supernatural—that come to those who consistently follow this ethic. He has faith in the wisdom of guiding his behavior by certain divinely inspired principles of action—such as the moral precepts revealed in scripture—viewing these as preferred options in determining a practical course of action in the face of specific problems. (See Figure 7–6.)

FIGURE 7–6
RELIGIOUS LIBERALISM

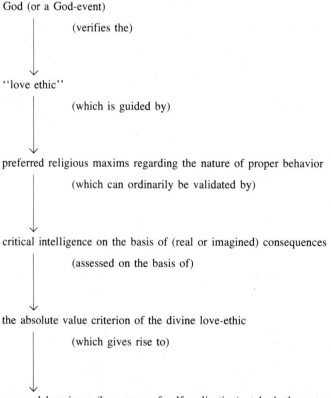

God (or a God-event)

    (verifies the)

"love ethic"

    (which is guided by)

preferred religious maxims regarding the nature of proper behavior

    (which can ordinarily be validated by)

critical intelligence on the basis of (real or imagined) consequences

    (assessed on the basis of)

the absolute value criterion of the divine love-ethic

    (which gives rise to)

personal happiness (by means of self-realization) at both the natural and supernatural levels of existence.

Religion and Social Action

There are, in essence, two ways in which a religious orientation can veer in a philosophically or politically "liberal" direction. The first and most important path toward religious liberalism occurs when a person views the "open society" as a logical correlate of the divine love-ethic as this applies to existing social conditions. Thus, for some Christians, the golden rule implies the necessity of working actively for the correction of certain social inequities. Both the Christian Marxism of the Brazilian educational philosopher Paulo Freire and the Christian anarchism of social critic Ivan Illich might well serve as examples of such a stance. A second basic path to religious liberalism—although this is significantly less common and more contentious than the first—occurs in those instances where the believer construes the teachings of the Scriptures and/or the Church itself as directly advocating the necessity for certain basic social reforms. Thus, for certain Christians, the words of Jesus are viewed as the basis for a "social gospel" whose practice would solve man's more pressing political and economic problems. For some, Jesus assumes the proportions of a prophet of social justice whose principles imply radical social reforms and even, in some cases, political revolution. Even where such an interpretation is plausible, however, it tends to be a less persuasive approach to religious liberalism than that based on a rational application of the love-ethic. For the Christian liberal, only the love-ethic (as measured by its practical and/or probable consequences with respect to ongoing behavior) can *ultimately* constitute a real criterion for ethical choice. Indeed, even socially radical admonitions based on interpretations of scripture can only be justified in the final analysis on the basis of enlightened reason inspired by divine love. In short, even "social gospel" interpretations of the scriptures are no more absolute as a basis for choice than the more explicit "moral maxims" that are also founded upon scriptural authority.

Religious Anarchism. Religious anarchism takes two basic forms that are closely related and that often occur together. These are (1) a religious *perfectionism,* in which the group attempts to practice or even proselyte for religious ideals that encompass anarchistic principles while choosing to remain as a part of the general culture; and (2) a religious *separatism,* in which the group retreats into an isolated and relatively self-contained community that exists apart from the general culture as a way of sustaining anarchistic or quasi-anarchistic communes.

Religious anarchism in the perfectionist tradition seeks spiritual perfection in and through the existing social order. Leo Tolstoy's Christian anarchism is, at least in part, an example of such a position. Tolstoy believed that, according to the teachings of Christ, all men are naturally and spontaneously "loving" in the true Christian sense of the word. Love resides in man's very nature. It is the "fundamental essence of the soul."[19] Only by substituting the laws of man for the law of God do men lose sight of their own implicitly loving natures, justifying violence, oppression, and inequality. If men were to follow their own divine natures, which exemplify the law of God, they would naturally care for and cooperate with each other. They would live in peace and harmony, having no use for government, man-made laws, courts, prisons, police, armies, or private property. For Tolstoy, the world as it exists is corrupt. Both State and

Church are evil, and man should return to the simple agricultural life, which is best suited to the requirements of human nature itself.[20]

 For Tolstoy, then, as for Emerson, "the one thing of value in the world is the active soul; this every man contains within him. The soul active sees absolute truth and utters truth and creates."[21] The creative individual soul, which is the source of all truth and value, must be reborn from the fetters imposed by traditional religion, property, and government, which have assumed domination over man's mind. God is within man, but His expression is blocked by social restraints. By freeing Christian conscience, individual man will be free to create a new Christian world that will require no coercive restraints over man's naturally loving inclinations. Accordingly, for Tolstoy, the individual must resist government itself—all laws and regulations—but in the only loving way possible, by nonviolent civil disobedience. Only by eliminating violence, including the institutionalized, tacit violence imposed by the institutionalized force of traditional social organizations such as the Church and the State, can man be truly liberated. Only by releasing the natural and spontaneous goodness of the individual can individual men be perfected; only by perfecting individual men can the kingdom of God on earth be achieved.

 In a similar sense, in India, Mohandas Gandhi preached much the same kind of benevolent anarchism, envisioning an entire Indian society based upon "self-sufficient, self-governing village republics."[22] Whether and to what extent Gandhi's philosophy of love, based upon massive campaigns of nonviolent civil disobedience, were inspired by "religious" principles in the usual sense of the word is difficult to say, but it is usually represented as being rooted in traditional Hindu (Vedic) principles, as was Thoreau's approach, which inspired many of Gandhi's ideas.

 The religious anarchist in the "separatist" tradition is perhaps best represented by some of the original Anabaptist groups that flourished in the sixteenth century. Some of these groups established separatist colonies that were relatively anarchistic, tending to focus on highly individualized religion in which the word of God was viewed as a "living spirit" that addressed itself directly in and through a priesthood of believers. A deeply sincere people, the Anabaptists held fervently to the principle of nonviolence, maintaining that the New Testament teaches that evil should be overcome with good. Accordingly, Anabaptists refused to join the armed forces of the state or, indeed, even to participate in the civil administration during peacetime, as a way of protesting against the relatively coercive policies of virtually all established governments.

 Even in the arena of religion itself, the Anabaptist tended to be anticlerical, holding that priests and ministers were prone to compromise with civil authority. They regarded regular church houses as implicitly idolatrous and met regularly in their own houses. While they were generally tolerant in matters where there was a reasonable difference of opinion about the meaning of Scripture, some Anabaptists practiced Christian communism modeled after the early Christian fellowship in Jerusalem.[23]

 The radical Christianity of the Anabaptists frequently evoked the hostility of the established civil government, and their insistence on separating from the established churches and the state earned them the name of "Separatists." Even in the Separatist tradition, as in several contemporary pietistic communities (such as those of the Amish[24] or the Bruderhof, which have chosen to separate themselves from the regular course of secular society), life within the religious community itself is scarcely "individualistic" in the usual sense of the term. The believers are constrained to act and to believe within a generally prescribed manner. Although they may be governed more by tradition than by explicit political force, there tends to be a strong pressure directing the individual toward conformity with the communal group itself. Of the separatist religious groups, probably the only one that practices anything approximating true anarchism is the Dukhobors (the Christians of the Universal Brotherhood), a Russian sect that emigrated to North America and that follows several of the principles of Leo Tolstoy, such as selective disobedience of governmental authorities in matters of conscience, passivism, rejection of official church structure, and agricultural living.[25]

The Quakers (The Society of Friends), initially an English nonconformist group, is in many respects a return to the truly radical Christianity of the earlier Anabaptists. The Quakers were founded in England as a revolt against religious formalism during the Puritan Revolution in the seventeenth century by the famous mystic George Fox. For Fox and his Quakers, as Noss comments in his book *Man's Religions,*

> [t]rue Christianity was ... not a matter of conforming to a set of doctrines or believing in Scripture without having "a concern" as a result of so doing; nor was it going to a "steeple-house" to listen to a sermon or prayers read by professional priests; it was being illuminated by an *inner light*. The Word of God is a living thing not confined to the Scriptures, though it is there; it comes directly into the consciousness of the believer whom God chooses for the purpose of speaking through him.
>
> Fox would hear nothing of a professional ministry; God speaks to whom He will when He will. Every man—or woman, for that matter—is potentially God's spokesman. Fellow men are to be treated as friends, with infinite reverence for the divine possibilities in any personality. War or any violence are therefore thoroughly wicked. Slavery is abhorrent. The requirement to take an oath should not be imposed upon a Christian, for he always speaks soberly and truthfully.
>
> At a religious meeting of Friends there were no sacraments (sacraments by their material symbolism are the occasion of leading the mind out of its subjective state of contemplation into the idolatry of fixation on an object) and no prepared discourses (God will stir up thought in someone present, at need). It was admitted that prayer is appropriate to begin with, but let it be followed by silent meditation, until the inner light illumines someone's understanding.[26]

The Quakers remain somewhat anarchistic in their mode of worship. They believe that God's spirit exists in every man, and they hold to no particular interpretation of the Bible. Advocating spontaneous worship on the basis of personal inspiration, which occurs when God speaks through any individual within the group, they reject clergy, defined rituals, sermons, and the usual sorts of organized services. They gather in relatively simple "meeting houses" rather than in conventional churches. They believe in honesty, sincerity, truthfulness and nonviolence; and they advocate treating all men as brothers in a spirit of universal love.

Obviously, the Quaker religion is an open and individualistic faith, and there is much in it that is implicitly opposed to almost any sort of state that is organized along fundamentally closed and authoritarian lines. Thus the Quakers have always been in the vanguard of movements for the abolition of slavery and for the rights of women. They have traditionally been opposed to force and violence, and many Quakers have refused to serve in the armed forces or to take politically imposed oaths. On the other hand, and regardless of the anarchistic tendencies implicit in the Quaker's passionate adherence to individual freedom, most Quakers tend to be quite selective in their civil disobedience. In historical terms, they are more in the tradition of the "nonconformists" than of the "separatists," and they have traditionally been willing to work for greater freedom within the normal constraints imposed by organized society, granting civil obedience to most of the requirements of government in return for freedom of conscience at the religious level.

Many of the contemporary separatist groups who subscribe to apocalyptic beliefs, like the contemporary Children of God or the Christian Foundation,[27] tend to appear anarchistic because they reject participation in normal secular affairs. However, these groups tend to be very authoritarian in the governing of internal affairs within the religious community itself, and even their reluctance to become involved in normal civil matters appears to stem primarily from their view that the temporal world faces imminent collapse in the final days before the Second Coming.

With respect to separatist religious communities, then, three important qualifications should be made. First, not all religious movements that advocate either separation from, or civil disobedience to, the existing secular order are "anarchistic" when it comes to matters of internal community organization and administration. Many are simply countercultures that are highly directive when it comes to structuring the lives of the members within the religious community itself.

Second, and as indicated, some apocalyptic groups tend to be anarchistic not out of active commitment to anarchistic social ideals, religious or otherwise, but because they view the secular order as in a state of terminal dissolution that merits no serious involvement.

Finally, not all religious anarchism—even where a particular movement may be seriously committed to an anarchistic life-style either within its religious practices or as a separate social system—necessarily subscribes to anarchism as a preferred method of organization for the larger secular society that exists outside of the religious community proper.

NOTES

1. Gould and Truitt, *Political Ideologies,* p. 2.

2. John Maynard Keynes, *Essays in Persuasion* (New York: W. W. Norton & Company, 1963).

3. Ibid.

4. See subsequent discussion of right-wing and left-wing anarchism in this chapter.

5. Karl Marx, "Preface," in *A Contribution to the Critique of Political Economy,* translated by N. I. Stone (Chicago: Charles H. Kerr & Co., 1913), pp. 11–12.

6. Gould and Truitt, *Political Ideologies,* pp. 3–4. The ideology of the so-called New Left is generally a revisionist Marxism. A full description of the New Left obviously exceeds the scope of this book, but Sargent in his book *Contemporary Political Ideologies,* has an interesting discussion of the New Left doctrine on pages 142–43.

7. Eldridge Cleaver, from a pamphlet published by the Ministry of Information, Black Panther Party, San Francisco, 1967; quoted in Gould and Truitt, *Political Ideologies,* p. 372.

8. Richard Lichtman, "The University: Mask for Privilege?" *The Center Magazine,* a publication of the Center for the Study of Democratic Institutions in Santa Barbara, California, January 1968; quoted in Gould and Truitt, *Political Ideologies,* p. 314.

9. Carl Oglesby, "The Idea of the New Left," from Carl Oglesby, ed., *The New Left Reader* (New York: Grove Press, 1969), pp. 19–20.

10. Ernest Mandel, "Where is America Going?" *New Left Review,* no. 54 (March–April 1969), pp. 5–6.

11. Irving Louis Horowitz, ed., *The Anarchists* (New York: Dell Publishing Co., 1964), p. 17.

12. Michael Lerner, "Anarchism and the American Counterculture," from David E. Apter and James Joll, *Anarchism Today* (Garden City, New York: Doubleday, 1971), p. 127.

13. Horowitz, ed., *The Anarchists,* p. 20.

14. Peter Kropotkin, "Anarchism," *Encyclopaedia Britannica,* Eleventh Edition (Cambridge, England: Cambridge University Press, 1910), vol. I, p. 914.

15. While Rand champions Aristotle, as the founder of all respectable philosophy, her views are actually at significant variance from the conventional wisdom of virtually all of the other intellectualists, both secular (such as Robert Maynard Hutchins) and religious (such as the dominant Thomism of the Roman Catholic Church) which are (at least purportedly) founded on Aristotelian notions. It can be argued either that Rand has a rather strange concept of what Aristotle actually said—she does regard Aristotle's law of identity in logic as an empirical principle, encompassing a particular interpretation of reality, and not, as is generally the case, as a stricture about the use of language in rational discourse—or that she has every right to offer a substantially different notion of what constitutes the "real" Aristotelian point of view.

  Rand is overtly atheistic and ostensibly a proponent of secular intellectualism in education. A close examination of her position reveals that she holds substantive convictions about the nature of reality (positing, among other things, a severe psychological hedonism, which views "selfishness"—in a relatively conventional and common sense use of this term—as being the highest moral good, and rejecting conventional altruism as a pernicious lie). Since Rand's description of reality is exceedingly close to Adam Smith's laissez faire capitalism stripped of its auxiliary assumptions about man's inherently altruistic nature, she actually describes a world that corresponds much more closely to that of either laissez faire or social Darwinist conservatism than to that of the usual intellectualist. She is, in a sense, a strange sort of hybrid—a sort of intellectualistic social Darwinist who subscribes to an ethical system that is very close to unadulterated laissez faire capitalism.

  A particularly good discussion of "right-wing libertarianism," which roughly corresponds to what is termed "right-wing anarchism" here, is to be found in the book *Libertarianism: A Political Philosophy Whose Time Has Come* by John Hospers (Santa Barbara, California: Reason Press, 1971). This book contains an excellent discussion on pages 417–64 of how, and to what extent, the elimination of government is possible.

16. William F. O'Neill, *With Charity Toward None: An Analysis of Ayn Rand's Philosophy* (Totowa, New Jersey: Littlefield, Adams & Co., 1972).

17. O'Neill, *With Charity Toward None,* pp. 60–61.

18. Joseph Fletcher, *Situation Ethics: The New Morality* (Philadelphia: The Westminster Press, 1966). *Situation* (or "contextual") *ethics* is a controversial and involved school of thought, and many individuals other than Joseph Fletcher—such individuals as Paul Lehmann, Paul Ramsey, George Doherty, and Rudolf Bultmann—have participated in the "movement." Fletcher's point of view, however, is best known outside of theological circles, and he presents perhaps the most convincing case for a radically nonlegalistic love-ethic. A brief but excellent discussion of the differences between the major spokesmen for situation ethics is to be found in the book *All to the Good: A Guide to Christian Ethics* by Robert B. McLaren and Homer D. McLaren (New York: The World Publishing Co., 1969, pp. 45–50).

19. Derry Novak, "The Place of Anarchism in the History of Political Thought," *The Review of Politics,* July 1958; quoted in Robert Hoffman, ed., *Anarchism* (New York: Atherton Press, 1970), p. 27.

20. Ibid.

21. Tolstoy, quoted in Emma Goldman, *Anarchism and Other Essays* (New York: Mother Earth Publishing Association, 1911), p. 58.

22. Gandhi, quoted in *Jayaprakash Narayan, A Plea for Reconstruction of Indian Polity* (London: Wardha, 1959), p. 63.

23. Noss, *Man's Religions,* p. 653.

24. The Anabaptist tradition is perhaps best represented today by the Mennonites (of whom the Amish are a subgroup). This group bases its faith on the New Testament, particularly the Sermon on the Mount. The ministers are loyal to civil government, but they will not bear arms or take oaths. They live and dress quite simply, and each congregation elects its own minister.

25. Derry Novak, "The Place of Anarchism," p. 27.

26. Noss, *Man's Religions,* pp. 559–60.

27. The Children of God and the Christian Foundation are two of the best known fundamentalist groups that are associated with the contemporary "Jesus movement." Both seem to make a particularly powerful appeal to adolescents, and they have attracted a good deal of attention because of the extremely visible religious communities they have established. These groups, among others, are discussed at length in Robert S. Ellwood's previously cited book *One Way: The Jesus Movement and Its Meaning* (Englewood Cliffs, New Jersey: Prentice-Hall, 1973). Both of these groups are controversial, and both—like many of the more extreme expressions of the "Jesus movement"—appear to be undergoing significant changes at the present time.

Chapter VIII

Educational Liberalism

For the educational liberal, the long-range goal of education is to preserve and improve the existing social order by teaching each child how to deal effectively with his own emerging life problems. In a more specific sense, he holds that the school as a particular educational institution should attempt to: (1) provide students with the information and skills necessary to learn effectively for themselves; and (2) teach students how to solve practical problems through the application of individual and group problem-solving processes based upon rational-scientific procedures for testing and proving ideas.

SCHOOL AND SOCIETY

Where the liberal ideologies differ is primarily in how they confront the relationship between the school and society—i.e., what particular interpretation they give to the concepts of cultural relativism and "social democracy," which were discussed in the previous chapter.

When it comes to the relationship between school and society, the educational liberal takes what is essentially a psychological (or personalistic) approach, in which the individual takes precedence over the demands of society. He takes this position for two basic reasons.

First, while the liberal agrees that the psychological is ultimately conditioned by the social, he holds that the psychological remains the ultimate basis for verifying the truth or falsity of any knowledge-claims. The individual learns through the emotional consequences of acting upon his beliefs, and these consequences can never be *experienced* "collectively" regardless of their logical relationship to underlying social experience. Learning may occur within a social matrix, but learning, as such, is always personal and psychological in nature. Even in the midst of culture, the individual does not experience society directly and objectively; he responds to his responses—to his perceptions and interpretations—of culture, not to culture per se. Thus, the social affects the psychological, and vice versa, but the psychological (the subjective) remains fundamental, because it is the ultimate basis for all experience. Learning is personal therefore in a far more fundamental sense than it is group-centered, and the subjective necessarily takes priority over objective social conditions when it comes to educational matters.

Second, there are virtually no cultures that are truly "open" and "critical," and that would therefore serve as a valid model for the pursuit of trained practical intelligence viewed as a collective social goal. This being the case, the liberal finds it difficult to argue for the superiority of the state over the school, and, indeed, in most cultures, he tends to view the schools as more open, critical, and responsible than the political systems in which they exist. As the liberal sees it, the social and behavioral sciences are in a very ambiguous and imperfect state of development at the current time, and they frequently reflect dominant social beliefs—as in the "objective" laws of capitalist economics contrasted to the "objective" laws of socialist economics—rather than trustworthy scientific generalizations.

Schooling should therefore be governed by the requirements of experimental (scientific) intelligence as applied to the solution of personal problems rather than being involved in the attempt to advance particular dogmas concerning the nature and organization of "the good society." We simply lack sufficient information about human nature at present to prescribe what is or is not a truly "humanistic" or "humanizing" society. We should, instead, use the schools to advance individual critical inquiry in the hope that a collective commitment to open inquiry and objective knowledge will result in the kind of information that will ultimately prove sufficient to formulate enlightened ideas about what constitutes the most desirable sort of social organization. We should not use the schools to proselyte prematurely for some sort of predefined social system that cannot, as yet, derive any clear and adequate justification from existing experimental evidence.

In short, until scientific knowledge is more fully developed, we should hesitate about drawing "scientific conclusions" about what kind of social structure is necessary or sufficient for the general good, and place our reliance, instead, in the far more objective, and substantially more "culture-fair," scientific *process* as the most trustworthy goal for education.

For the liberal, then, the best education is that which exists to train the child to think critically and objectively, following the basic format of the scientific process, and to believe those things that are most plausible on the basis of existing scientific knowledge. The reconstruction of society should evolve out of the perfecting of practical intelligence at the individual level. Enlightened personal behavior, viewed collectively, yields enlightened collective behavior and, ultimately, gives rise to the sort of critical and objective culture that is presently conceivable only in broad outline.

THE AMBIGUITY OF EDUCATIONAL LIBERALISM

In our culture at this time educational liberalism is *essentially* an outgrowth of the empirical point of view, and, more specifically, of the philosophical position called "experimentalism," which adheres to the idea that the highest value—happiness, self-actualization, or however it may be stated—is fundamentally a by-product of "practical intelligence" (that is, the ability to solve personal problems effectively by being as scientific as possible both in how one thinks and in what one believes).

On the other hand, this overall generalization requires three rather significant qualifications.

Phenomenology and Behaviorism

1. When it comes to the ultimate nature of personal experience, empiricists tend to fall into two opposing camps, the phenomenologists (who are most frequently associated with the philosophy of existentialism), and the behaviorists (who are generally inclined toward experimentalism).

The *phenomenologist* is, in essence, the true empirical solipsist who holds that all a person can ever know is his own processes of awareness, his own "subjectivity." For the phenomenologist reality is ultimately personal knowledge, a consciousness of one's own thoughts and feelings. Ultimately, each of us is irremediably locked into his own stream of consciousness. We can only *know* our own knowing and the knowledge that evolves out of this knowing process. This personal knowledge is fundamental; it is all we know and determines all of our specific beliefs and convictions. Ultimately, it is both *self-evident,* in the sense that it *is* experience and therefore constitutes all evidence, and *self-determining,* because it is the primary datum that underlies and gives rise to all more particular conclusions.

Behavior is motivated by and directed through personal consciousness; action is relative to belief. Our very perceptions of the world are acts of personal choice that are mediated by subjective goals, intentions, and anticipations. Our very responsiveness to the external world is determined by internal (personal) requirements, such as needs, values, and so on. We only encounter the objective *subjectively.* At basis, personal experience is irreducible.

The *behaviorist* agrees with the radical empiricism of the phenomenologist as a starting point, but he rejects the position that personal experience viewed as subjectivity is an irreducible datum. As the behaviorist sees it, the meaning inherent within personal experience itself suggests that all experience is contingent upon circumstances that precede and determine the nature and course of experience itself.

Phrased somewhat differently, on the basis of experience itself, it is reasonable to assume that experience is ultimately neither self-evident nor self-determining; rather, it is an interaction phenomenon that is caused by the relationship between two entities, the physical organism and the physical environment. These entities are known only indirectly through behavior and, even less directly, through the resulting experience process.

At basis, then, experience is merely a type of *internal* behavior that occurs as a consequence of *external* behavior created by the interaction between defined entities that provide the objective conditions necessary for the existence of all purely "subjective" consciousness. In other words, while experience is all that we can know *directly,* it is not all that we can know *indirectly.*

We can also make rational inferences on the basis of personal experience that lead us to recognize the necessity for a world apart from the purely subjective. Ultimately reality resides not in the processes of personal response but in the conditions that create and mediate such processes in the first place. We can only know our own *subjectivity,* but this is ultimately rooted in the *objective* and represents merely a particular response to universal circumstances.

All consciousness is an expression of behavior, and all behavior is ultimately relative to the nature of those entities that behave. Personal experience is basically an awareness of personal behavior and of the meaning (pattern) that is inherent within such behavior. We only know our own subjective knowing, but our knowing is an awareness of our behavior which is, in turn, an objective relationship between given physical entities. Even our subjectivity is, then, ultimately objective and behavioral.

The *evidence* that underlies consciousness is the preconscious *behavioral ground* that is required for all experience whatsoever. All experience is caused by and mediated through physical behavior. Belief is relative to action and not vice versa. We encounter the subjective *objectively.* Personal *experience* is analytically reducible to *behavior.*

Experimentalism and Behaviorism

2. *Experimentalism,* like most general philosophical systems, is somewhat ambiguous. While the relationship of experimentalism to pragmatism, instrumentalism, behaviorism, and other philosophical positions was discussed at some length in the previous chapter, it is perhaps helpful to reestablish some basic terminology. *Experimentalism,* as was discussed, is essentially a marriage between *philosophical behaviorism*—the point of view that holds that personal experience is the product of the behavior (interaction) between the organism and its physical and social environment—and *pragmatism*—the position that holds that an idea is "true" if (and to the extent that) it leads to effective consequences when applied to the solution of real (practical) problems. It is, in essence, the philosophical position—perhaps best represented in the thought of John Dewey—that holds that a common-sense adaptation of scientific problem-solving procedures is the best way to think and therefore the best way to live, since effective thinking is the best guide to effective living.

On the other hand, not all philosophical behaviorists are pragmatists. Some—such as Karl Marx, certain of the classical anarchists (such as Kropotkin and Proudhon), and various of the leading figures in speculative psychology, such as Freud and Jung (at least with respect to the central tenets of their theories)—tend to be "soft" behaviorists who wed the overall worldview of behaviorism with the epistemological orientation of traditional rationalism, relying more on speculative reason than on observable consequences in order to establish their systems.[1]

In a similar sense, not all pragmatists are experimentalists. William James tends to be more phenomenological than behavioristic in his approach to pragmatic verification. For James—unlike Dewey and his school—certain significant ideas (such as the idea that a personal God exists or that man has "free will" in the conventional sense of the term) can only be tested experientially, through the "lived" (subjective or phenomenological) consequences of applying such ideas to the conduct of one's own life over an extended period of time. Such consequences are not objective, behavioral, quantifiable, or intersubjective, so they do not meet the requirements for verification prescribed by philosophical experimentalism or by science (which is a particularly rigorous expression of the experimentalist point of view).

Experimentalism and Ideology

3. What greatly complicates any attempt to establish a simple and straightforward relationship between philosophical experimentalism, on the one hand, and social and educational liberalism, on the other, is the fact that—contrary to popular opinion—not all experimentalists are *necessarily* liberals. To be more specific, while it is true that *most* experimentalists can, and should, be classified as educational liberals and that educational liberalism is *characteristically* an outgrowth of experimentalism, experimentalism actually tends to branch out in three basic directions, one (mainstream experimentalism) terminating in what is ordinarily viewed as "educational liberalism," and the other two (consisting of those experimentalists who end up advocating either radical socioeconomic programs or certain types of large-scale behavioral engineering approaches) culminating in what are essentially forms of "educational liberationism."

THE THREE BASIC EXPRESSIONS OF EXPERIMENTALIST THOUGHT

Mainstream Experimentalism

The mainstream of experimentalist thought, as indicated, takes the position that a commitment to open and critical inquiry necessarily implies a corresponding commitment to an open and critical society, the sort of society that allows and encourages such inquiry in the first place. They then proceed to define an "open society" as a democracy where the majority (or at least the concerned plurality) rule, where everyone has the right to be wrong, and where civil liberties are viewed as taking priority over any particular concept of social justice (and, in most cases, even over experimental inquiry itself). This point of view is perhaps the dominant theme in the philosophy of John Dewey, and represents the basic philosophical rationale for most educational liberalism.

Egalitarian Experimentalism

On the other hand, not all experimentalists necessarily subscribe to this line of reasoning. Some, as discussed earlier (see Chapter III and Figure 3–10) would reject conventional social and educational liberalism altogether on the grounds that the democratic process, while desirable in the long run, must necessarily be subordinated under existing circumstances to the more immediate goal of social justice, which provides the cultural base for any viable democratic process. For experimentalists in this tradition, then, critical thinking may *ultimately* imply a critical society, but the relationship is, at best, indirect.

In the final analysis, a truly critical society can only take root where there has been an effective reallocation of resources and power that provides the practical social and economic conditions required to make personal choice a truly meaningful option. For these individuals, then, critical thinking implies not so much a "democratic society" as a society founded upon the kind of economic and social conditions (giving rise to social justice), which is a logical prerequisite for the intelligent exercise of critical thinking and therefore ultimately for the development of a truly viable democratic society that is capable of functioning in fact and not merely in theory.

This tradition within experimentalism, which is perhaps well represented by the more liberationist (or reconstructionist) line of reasoning in John Dewey's philosophy, as well as by many social philosophers who (like Dewey) advocate the establishment of a socialist economy, tends to accord (developmental) priority to the *means* required to create and sustain a democratic process. Priority goes to social justice and science (the latter being viewed as the basis for technology and therefore for the wealth required as a logical precondition for the effective redistribution of goods and power)—rather than to the ultimate (but logically subsequent) *end* of the democratic process itself.

Technocratic Experimentalism

Still a smaller group of experimentalists—representing a sort of "technocratic" point of view—tends to see critical thinking as fundamentally dependent upon an objective (scientific) society in which the pursuit of scientific knowledge is a prerequisite for social justice and therefore, in the long run, for individual self-actualization.

The Controversial Ideas of B. F. Skinner. One of the things that makes most people very uncomfortable with the scientific meritocracy envisioned by B. F. Skinner in his book *Walden Two* is that Skinner takes precisely this point of view. For Skinner, truly effective critical thinking in the scientific mode requires a society committed primarily to the pursuit of scientific truth and governed by those who are capable of discovering and applying scientific principles to the regulation of human behavior. For Skinner, all people should have the right to be totally free within the constraints imposed by a rigorously conceived experimentalist society, but, within this society, the pursuit and application of scientific knowledge always takes precedence over social justice (which is necessarily defined by and imposed through a scientifically enlightened elite). Social justice is, in turn, the basis for personal self-actualization (viewed as the gratification of "objective," or scientifically determined, human needs). Contrary to mainstream experimentalist thinking, Skinner rejects popular democracy as a form of political organization, because he believes that significant social decisions should be made only by those who have been trained scientifically to make responsible and enlightened choices about complex scientific questions.[2]

Skinner, like a number of other educational theorists, can be used as an example of both educational liberalism and educational liberationism. When he is speaking strictly as a psychologist, as in many of his shorter writings dealing with behavioral modification techniques in the classroom and with teaching machines, Skinner frequently sounds very much like a "method liberal." On the other hand, when Skinner addresses himself more speculatively to questions of how education might ideally be redesigned, as in his utopian novel, *Walden Two,* he presents himself primarily as a "radical liberationist." In other words,

Skinner, like many others, has both a highly conjectural "if-then" philosophy coupled with a much more practical and conservative "however-hence" philosophy.[3]

Skinner is a highly controversial thinker, but he is also greatly misconstrued. What Skinner says in his more conjectural works in which he advocates a sort of social engineering is frequently at substantial variance from what he is interpreted as having said. His actual position, which is worth looking at more closely because it represents a point of view significantly different from that presented by both the mainstream experimentalists and the social liberationist extension of that position, can be characterized in the following seven points.

a) Skinner, *as a psychologist,* restricts himself to operational ·definitions regarding the laws of behavior. He does not become involved in philosophical speculation about the nature of man, moral philosophy, and such. It can be argued that he *should,* but the fact is that he does not.

Skinner is, above all, a "scientific behaviorist" working in psychology, but, since science is a special expression of philosophical experimentalism, and is based upon the observation and analysis of only certain kinds of quantifiable and replicable behavior (as opposed, say, to studying data presented directly through subjective personal experience, as in phenomenology), Skinner actually functions philosophically as an "experimental behaviorist."

On the other hand, he is relatively reluctant to make philosophical generalizations about the conditions that assumedly give rise to observable behavior. He views such generalizations as beyond scientific verification and tends to regard the conditions that assumedly underlie behavior itself as scientifically invisible (and thus also beyond scientific verification). He prefers to remain an agnostic about speculative psychological questions and to view himself as totally committed to scientific experimentalism as an open-ended and self-correcting process. In this sense, his intention is certainly to function as a pure *scientific* experimentalist, and his psychological "behaviorism" is more a description of the data to which he addresses himself than it is a reference to any set of hard and fast *philosophical* convictions about the ultimate nature of reality.*

b) Skinner, in his more speculative works, such as *Walden Two, Beyond Freedom and Dignity* and *About Behaviorism,* develops many of the philosophical implications of his work in behavioral psychology, and, in some of his work, he does extrapolate a position of *philosophical behaviorism* that is related to, but not the same as, his psychological point of view.

---

* Strict, or "hard," behaviorism in psychology holds to the position that only behavior is observable and that therefore no assertions about the conditions that ostensibly underlie behavior as such can be the object of legitimate psychological inquiry. For the "hard behaviorist," the object of psychology is to formulate laws about behavior, not to make inferences about the nature of reality above and beyond truly observable responses. For the less rigorous, or "soft," behaviorists, the behavior of the organism in specified circumstances remains the basic focus, but certain influences about "why" certain patterns of behavior occur—explanations rather than merely correlations—are also deemed admissible. B. F. Skinner, at least in his earlier, purely psychological, works is often cited as a "hard behaviorist." Such psychologists as Carl Rogers and Abraham Maslow—while often referred to in totally nonbehavioristic terms—are essentially "soft behaviorists" in the sense that they continue to view themselves as representing the scientific (and therefore implicitly behavioristic and materialistic) traditions despite whatever reservations they may hold about the sufficiency of narrow scientific behaviorism in the strict sense.

c) In his philosophical statements, Skinner does not deny "inner qualities or capacities." He simply explains these biologically and behavioristically rather than in the conventional "mentalistic" terms. He views man as essentially a biological organism that can be best explained on the basis of electrochemical activity at the molecular level but he leaves the explanation of how these activities occur to experts in the area of neurophysiology.

d) Skinner does not deny either *mind* (as a function of the central nervous system in situational context) or *agency* (volition or personal "will"). He does not deny *psychological* free will—that a person can choose what he wants to do—he merely denies *metaphysical* free will—the contrary notion that a person is free to choose what he does not *want* to choose. His quarrel is not with psychological freedom (freedom to choose) or political freedom (freedom to act, "liberty"). It is with metaphysical freedom—freedom to act in violation of the law of cause-and-effect (i.e., actions violating the established assumptions of physical, including psychological, determinism) or of the formal law of self-contradiction in logic (i.e., actions where the individual purportedly chooses to do what he does not consider to be "best" under the given circumstances).

e) Skinner does not deny the value or efficiency of the love-ethic (that is, the golden rule). On the contrary, he advocates the love-ethic and goes on to explain how it can be augmented and implemented.

For Skinner the best evidence emerging from the contemporary behavioral sciences indicates that man is a naturally social animal who requires systematic cooperation with others in order to survive and in order to be fully effective in the pursuit of his ends.

> One advantage of being a social animal is that one need not discover practices for oneself. The parent teaches the child as the craftsman teaches his apprentice because he gains a useful helper, but in the process the child and the apprentice acquire behavior they would very probably not have acquired under nonsocial contingencies.[4]

All *prescriptions*—all moral rules—are implicitly *descriptions,* statements that convey the probable reinforcing effects of acting upon given principles. "Love," for example, "is another name for use of positive reinforcement."[5] In general, it is a pleasurable experience to be loved, and a person seeks behavior that gives rise to this experience. In a similar sense, the old admonition "Love your enemies" has two great advantages: (1) it helps us avoid the negative emotions of hate and anger; and (2) it ultimately helps us to control the behavior of our enemies by controlling a very important aspect of their reinforcement.

There is, as Skinner sees it, such a thing as a scientific system of values, and such a system already exists as a basis for establishing constructive social relationships. The ultimate goals of Skinner's utopian community of Walden Two are the basic human values identified by contemporary scientific psychology: the more or less self-evident values of health, adequate nutrition and such; leisure; satisfying and constructive social contact; and the exercise of natural talents and abilities.[6] In accordance with these values, the members of Walden Two reject such things as interpersonal competition, the acquisition of unnecessary possessions, and the profit motive.

At basis, Skinner is an experimentalist, and, like all experimentalists, he holds that all values reside within nature, in the natural objects and events of the physical world. He also holds that to understand these natural values, it is necessary to study nature, and in so doing, to define the underlying character of both man himself and the world in which he lives. In a sense, then, the highest good for man is to recognize what is objectively true (real) and to bring his behavior into accord with objective reality.

Accordingly, the best way to determine what is factual is to use some rational-empirical method of proof that features the testing of truth-propositions in terms of their observable consequences. Like all experimentalists, Skinner maintains that the best way to verify (prove) an idea is to employ it as a conjectural solution to some practical (behavioral) problem—in effect, to use it as an hypothesis or prediction that should generate certain observable results—and then to see whether the idea does in fact "work" or "test out" in the sense of producing the results that were anticipated.

f) Skinner does not reject "individualism" but, on the contrary, advocates it.

True "individualism," as Skinner sees it, is not a matter of "free will." The "individualist's" beliefs are just as *determined* by his prior behavior as those of anyone else. What sets the individualist apart from the average person is that he recognizes the nature of his ultimate beliefs and that he is capable of examining these beliefs (including his value convictions) critically on the basis of their foreseeable (reinforcing) consequences, as determined by objective (scientific) evidence. Phrased somewhat differently, an "individualist" is a person who is capable of subjecting his own belief-system to critical scrutiny on the basis of an overriding commitment to the experimental verification of knowledge. (Such experimental verification is viewed as the most satisfactory model for structuring reinforcement contingencies at the personal level of operation.) Or, put in still another way, the "individualist" seeks happiness (maximum reinforcement) by modifying his own behavior in such a way as to make it approximate the behavior implied by the best evidence growing out of contemporary scientific research. In outline form, this might be expressed as in Figure 8–1.

FIGURE 8–1
REINFORCEMENT AND EXPERIMENTAL BEHAVIORISM

Maximum reinforcement (happiness)

↓

is a product of maximum behavioral effectiveness

↓

which requires the modification of belief in the direction of objectivity (rational-scientific conclusions)

↓

which calls for a critical examination of existing beliefs on the basis of scientific evidence viewed as the best available intellectual strategy

↓

which can ultimately be vindicated by the emotional consequences growing out of maximum reinforcement (personal happiness).

It is fruitless to talk about whether a society should or should not control personal character. All societies exist primarily to control behavior, and all behavioral controls serve to generate appropriate sorts of beliefs and attitudes. Whether a society is or is not going to control behavior, then, is not a legitimate question. *All* societies control behavior by definition. This is why they exist in the first place, and, since man is a social organism, we have no viable alternative to cultural conditioning.

The real choice, then, reduces itself to two basic options: (1) a society can choose to shape behavior both consciously and intentionally in some kind of serious attempt to exert public control over personal character; or (2) a society can choose not to institute any sort of conscious and intentional program of significant public control over individual personality, leaving such changes up to the discretion of private agencies and chance circumstances.

There is no inherent conflict between controlled behavior and "individualism." Since man is naturally a social animal, individual choice must always be tempered by some sort of prior commitment to the well-being of the group. Strictly speaking, the only way in which individualism will ever be a viable social goal is if we systematically and intentionally begin to design societies that require the kind of behavior which makes individualism possible as a realistic goal for everyone.

Phrased somewhat differently, any collective commitment to individualism implies the imposition of the kind of controls that are necessary in order to force people to *conform* to the ideal of *nonconformity*. Ironic though it may be, individualism—if it is to be more than an accidental offshoot of uncontrolled conditions, as it has been in the past—requires a serious social commitment to the kinds of belief and behavior that make such a personalistic orientation more than merely rhetorical.

g) Politics is ultimately applied moral philosophy. The purpose of the State is to use power in order to achieve some vision of what constitutes the collective good. The major failing of politics in the past has been not only the inefficiency of its means but, even more important, the inhumanity of its ends. It has been concerned primarily with compelling obedience by such means as coercion and propaganda in order to more fully realize economic and psychological exploitation. Such political methods have not only made people miserable throughout most of recorded history, they have also blocked the otherwise positive course of human progress by indoctrinating people to believe either that they were not miserable at all or that certain types of institutionalized misery, like war, hate, or systematic self-denial, were actually ends-to-be-sought. The net result has been that politics has been used almost continuously throughout history as both an instrument of oppression and as a way of keeping people unaware of the fact that they were being oppressed in the first place.

Today, however, values are capable of being determined scientifically, and a well developed technology for the engineering of human behavior exists. This means, among other things, that the traditional ends and means of politics are largely obsolete. A science of human government that places social control on an experimental basis quite apart from politics is now possible.

Scientific morality, however, is the outcome of a rigorous process of controlled intellectual investigation. It grows out of a careful consideration of the weighted conclusions of scientific specialists in a large number of different areas. The average man is relatively unreflective. He has neither the time, the training, nor the inclination to undertake a profound intellectual inquiry into the ultimate bases of his own beliefs and behavior, and he cannot, in this sense, be looked upon as "moral" in the traditional sense of possessing insight into the more profound meaning of his own actions.

At best, democracy is merely the lesser of many evils among the existing political systems. At worst, it is a travesty, a "pious fraud"[7] in which the government is neither *by* nor *for* the people; a despotism of the majority, characterized by ignorance, neglect, irresponsibility, and accident.[8] "In a democracy," notes Skinner's spokesman Frazier in *Walden Two*, "there is *no* check against despotism, because the principle of democracy is supposed to be itself a check. But it guarantees only that the *majority* will not be despotically ruled."[9]

The basic flaw in democracy stems from the fact that it is founded upon a scientifically invalid concept of man, for, before man determines the operation of the State, he is himself determined *by* the State.[10] To expect a laissez faire system of social control to produce the kind of people who are capable of enlightened political decision making and responsible action is pure fancy. The choices that govern a democracy can never be better than the citizenry that such a system has created through its basic institutions, such as the family and the school.

Properly viewed, democracy should be a way of investing power with public opinion, and not merely a procedure for polling it.[11] Ironically, however, the true goal of democracy—the fullest realization of each individual as an individual, within a supportive social setting—is more fully advanced (as in Walden Two) through nondemocratic means than it could ever be through the majoritarian procedures used within existing democratic states.

For better or for worse, popular skill in governing declines with the complexity of culture. Society today is far too sophisticated and sensitive to be run by a consensus of the uninformed and unskilled. The government of Skinner's utopia, Walden Two, is essentially a scientific technocracy run primarily by carefully selected generalists (the Planners) on the basis of the most enlightened conclusions growing out of research in the contemporary behavioral sciences. As such, it is a government *for* but not *by* the people. Its ends as well as its means emerge from the scientific study of human behavior.

In a sense, then, the state is regulated by an applied "science of government" which, like any other science, is properly controlled by experts, for, if special knowledge is required to govern, the average person is no longer capable of making responsible decisions about social policy. Indeed, and as Skinner's spokesman, Frazier, notes, the people

> ... become less and less skilled, relatively speaking, as the science of government advances . . . when we've once acquired a behavioral technology, we can't leave the control of behavior to the unskilled. Your answer is to deny that the technology exists—a very feeble answer, it seems to me. . . . The one thing the people know . . . and the one thing about which they should be heard is how they like the existing state of affairs, and perhaps how they would like some other state of affairs. What they conspicuously don't know is how to get what they want. That's a matter for specialists. . . . The actual practice in a democracy is to vote,

not for a given state of affairs, but for a man who claims to be able to achieve that state. I'm not a historian . . . but I suspect that that's always what is meant by the rule of the people—rule by a man chosen by the people.

"Isn't that a possible way out, though?" said Castle. "Suppose we need experts. Why not elect them?"

"For a very simple reason. The people are in no position to evaluate experts. And elected experts are never able to act as they think best. They can't experiment. The amateur doesn't appreciate the need for experimentation. He wants his expert to *know*. And he's utterly incapable of sustaining the period of doubt during which an experiment works itself out. The experts must either disguise their experiments and pretend to know the outcome in advance or stop experimenting altogether and struggle to maintain the status quo."[12]

In Walden Two the government operates pragmatically, by correcting its course of action in terms of the social consequences of its own policies. Its basic experimental feedback is the observable satisfaction—the personal happiness—of the people themselves. In a sense, then, even the government's errors tend to be self-correcting, because they generate popular discontent, which ultimately serves to elicit a change of policy (which, in turn, goes on to be judged on the basis of its own long-range contribution to overall satisfaction, and so on). The people judge and criticize the government on the basis of its practical effectiveness, measured on the basis of overall personal satisfaction (that is, on the basis of positive reinforcement produced by organized social arrangements). The government, in turn, directs, assesses and corrects its own behavior on the basis of this same criterion of popular satisfaction. In this way, the government of Walden Two effectively institutionalizes the method of effective (experimental) intelligence at the level of social action while, at the same time, striving for the realization of the overall common good.

Restated in outline form, this might be viewed as in Figure 8–2.

FIGURE 8–2
SCIENCE AND POLITICS (AFTER SKINNER)

Rule by experts on the basis of an objective science of government (scientific technocracy)

↓

results in more effective problem-solving behavior within society as a whole

↓

which terminates in greater positive reinforcement for all citizens

↓

which confirms and consolidates popular enthusiasm for scientific technocracy,

↓

eventuating in even more effective social action, hence more happiness, hence more popular enthusiasm and so on, in a self-perpetuating cycle of mutual self-confirmation; a synergistic spiral.

As a result of this process, then, the success of Skinner's Walden Two and the perfecting of a science of human behavior are positively interrelated and interdependent. It is Walden Two that provides the sort of objective, humanistic society that permits the sort of objective, humanistic behavior that makes the serious study of human behavior possible.

EXISTENTIALISM AND EDUCATIONAL LIBERALISM

The philosophy of existentialism is frequently viewed as leading to a type of educational liberalism. This is unfortunate, because, contrary to popular opinion, existentialists are difficult to place in any of the standard categories of the educational ideologies.

Existentialism and the Problem of Free Choice

All existentialists are in principle radical empiricists who subscribe to the overarching idea that *existence (personal experience) precedes and determines essence (truth, knowledge, or meaning)*.[13] The existentialist subscribes to the basic tenet of traditional realism, the principle of independence—that is, there is a world independent of the personal process of knowing.

Unlike the traditional (classical) realist of the Aristotelian sort, however, the existentialist does not accept the idea that this world which is independent of being known (i.e., which constitutes 'being' as opposed to 'existence,' or 'experienced Being') is both real *and* meaningful. For the existentialist, the world independent of being known (Being) is real but not meaningful. It is therefore fundamentally 'absurd,' that is, "meaningless" in any transcendent or overarching sense. Instead, it is the individual person who brings "meaning" into the world through the continuous process of cognitive *choice* (perceptual selection) that occurs in the course of normal goal-directed intentional behavior.

Such choice is free, because it is determined *personally.* The individual projects his intentions into the world and thereby throws himself into conflict with the circumstances that must be dealt with if such intentions are to be realized. Thus, the attempt to realize personal intentions generates conflict (problems) and elicits consciousness (a sequence of cognitive decisions generated by the attempt to solve personal problems in some particular situation).

All men are free *to choose*—to perceive—the world as it has relevance for their own particular set of values/goals/intentions. Indeed, man is not free *not to be free.* He cannot reject his goal-oriented intentionality, which generates his particular consciousness-making collision with the world of real objects and events outside of himself. He is not *metaphysically* free—that is, free to choose *not* to choose, or to choose some other *ground for choice* than the conditions under which he finds himself. He is also not *politically* free (he may or may not have such *freedom to act,* depending on the circumstances).

Perhaps most significantly—and implied by the above—he is not free to choose the *nature* of his own intentionality, the basic value orientation that elicits his particular intentional goals as these manifest themselves at any particular moment. The individual assimilates these quite uncritically during the earliest weeks and months of life, during the essentially *prerational* era before he has become fully "human" (and before he can therefore be characterized as "free" in any meaningful sense).

In short, the value set (which constitutes the individual's basic intentionality and the basis for all of his subsequent *choices*) cannot itself be "chosen," because it is the necessary, if fortuitous, foundation for all subsequent choices. In other words, *men* are free—but infants are not yet "men." The uncritically assimilated beliefs and values that take form during infancy are simply part of the absurd Being within which man subsequently comes to exercise his total freedom of choice.

The individual 'transcends' the world (and even himself) because he constantly goes *beyond* himself in a constant state of 'becoming' based upon the constantly changing consequences of a continuing interaction with varying life circumstances. In short, existentialism does not deny that the child is free only within the context of overriding social and psychological determinism. He merely disregards this overriding determinism by emphasizing the fact that the individual—once he reaches a certain stage of cognitive maturation and thereby becomes a "man"—has total *psychological freedom* to relate to (and therefore construe) his *external* circumstances any way he prefers.

In other words, a man is free to choose, and therefore experience, the world any way he likes, but he is not free *to choose what he likes to begin with* (in any basic sense), because this is inevitably determined by the prerational character structure (the basic intentionality) that was established through operant conditioning during the era of psychological development before he was capable of making any *conscious* choices whatsoever.

Existentialism takes the position that it is possible to make a free choice to *reject* the necessarily subjective (personal) nature of all meaning by "choosing" to believe otherwise—for example, by subscribing to a *nonempirical* system of beliefs grounded in metaphysical convictions arrived at through revelation, faith, or mystical intuition. Where this occurs, a person is, at basis, making an existential choice to *reject* existentialism as a belief system in favor of some nonexistential point of view.

A twofold problem occurs in such a situation. First, if the individual has chosen a metaphysical position through existential free choice, he can no longer call himself an "existentialist" except in an historical sense. Existentialism may describe how he *arrived at* his metaphysical system, but the metaphysical system so chosen is, by no stretch of the imagination, "existential" in the sense that it subscribes to the radical subjectivity of all Truth.

Second, if an individual makes an existential choice to adopt a metaphysical system, he can only justify describing himself as an "existentialist" in a *contemporary* sense in two ways.

One, he can hold that he has not subscribed to a metaphysical system but merely sequentially and continuously "chooses it without exception" over alternative systems of belief and over an indefinite period of time (which seems to be a semantic problem, since most people would describe "constant choice" as "subscribing to").

Two, he can state that he retains the existential conviction that all thought is radically subjective but, at the same time, construe his own subjective experiences in such a way as to arrive at a metaphysical definition of reality. This, again, seems to devolve into a semantic problem: Can one have *objective* (metaphysical) certitude about the interpretation of one's own avowedly *subjective* experience? Or, perhaps more basic: Can one who gives priority to the notion of radical subjectivity ever have *objective* knowledge of anything?

Existential Theology and Theological Existentialism. The relationship between existentialism and theism is a very difficult problem to discuss. On the other hand, a great deal has been written about "existentialist theology" and "theological existentialism," and the topic merits some comment.

In general, there are two ways in which certain of the existentialist philosophers have attempted to broaden their point of view to encompass the idea of a personal God. These are: (1) by means of phenomenological demonstration, and (2) by means of existential choice.

It is very difficult—and probably not possible—to reconcile existentialism and theism. Strictly speaking, theism is not possible on the basis of phenomenological demonstration, because any sort of metaphysical position violates the basic premise of phenomenology, which holds that all meaning is radically personal and subjective. One cannot, in short, begin with the assumption that all truth is subjective and then proceed to establish an objective set of transcendent truths rooted in the proven existence of a personal God.

(Although, it can be argued that phenomenological demonstration itself, in which the phenomenologist performs a phenomenological reduction of his own personal experience, rigorously pursuing the interior meaning of his own subjectivity, is based upon the paradoxical notion that there are objective dimensions to subjectivity. If one is willing to grant this premise, it would not be impossible to establish the existence of a personal God through phenomenological demonstration.)

Those existentialists who ground their theistic contentions in choice take the position that the existence of God cannot be *proven* but can only emerge out of *personal commitment*. There are actually two variations of this position, what might be termed *existentialist theology* and what might be termed *theological existentialism*. The existentialist theologian can be described as that person who maintains that he has made an existential choice of a nonexistential (metaphysical) position. The theological existentialist holds that it is possible to be a theist within the overriding context of existential doubt.

Phrased somewhat differently, where the existentialist theologian states "I know there is a personal God, but I arrived at this knowledge through an act of free choice in which I could just as easily have come to a different conclusion," the theological existentialist takes the much more guarded position that might be summarized as follows: "I know that all knowledge is beyond certitude, but I *believe* that a personal God exists."

It is very difficult to see that either one of these positions makes particularly good sense. The existentialist theologian uses existential free choice to opt for a position that is opposed to the basic assumptions of the empirical point of view, which lies at the basis of all existentialist beliefs. He is an "existentialist" only in the past tense. The theological existentialist retains his existentialism, but only at the price of reducing his theism to little more than personal speculation grounded in overriding skepticism. He is a theist only by inclination and not by fundamental conviction.

Existentialism and Education

All of this is not to say that philosophical existentialism may not, as is popularly conceived, eventuate in some sort of educational liberalism, but, in this regard, three qualifications need to be made.

1. *Existentialism* is an exceedingly ambiguous term, and it frequently covers a multitude of different points of view that have very little in common except the fact that the term *existentialism* is used to describe them. To compound difficulties, the term *existentialism* is frequently used quite differently in psychology (and particularly in psychotherapy) than it is in philosophy.

2. Existentialism as a philosophy does not prescribe freedom as the cure for either personal or social ills. Thus, for the existentialist, man has radical psychological freedom (that is, free perceptual choice) by definition, and there is no way that he can avoid exercising this total psychological freedom. The ultimate value for the existentialist is not therefore "freedom" but "authenticity"—which is a particular life-style that entails a highly controlled and well-defined sort of educational preparation.

The existentialist value schema envisions a very specific sort of individualism as constituting the desirable product of the educational process. Again, and despite assertions to the contrary, "freedom" is not the central value for the existentialist. From the existentialist point of view, all men are unavoidably and categorically free on a *descriptive* basis, so freedom as such cannot be *prescribed* as a good. Rather it is the way in which the individual confronts and uses his personal freedom that allows him to become "authentic," and it is authenticity that is the central value for the existentialist.

The authentic individual is "moral" in the sense that he assumes conscious responsibility for his own personal freedom. He is "good," as a subset of the "moral," if, and to the extent that, he commits himself to creating the sort of world in which others are also allowed to be authentic (and therefore moral). The authentic individual is, then, typically an intellectual who has a deep sense of social commitment to the creation of a more humanistic (authentic) world.

3. Existentialists are not opposed to experimental problem solving as a basic approach to education. The confusion arises primarily from the fact that the existentialist emphasizes *problem perception* (which is a necessary antecedent to problem solving) over problem solving itself.

In other words, where Dewey and most experimentalists emphasize that all personal experience (consciousness) is a concomitant of a continuing sequence of problem-solving behavior, the existentialist tends to emphasize the choice (or selection) of the problem itself rather than its resolution. The difference is, however, principally one of focus rather than of two essentially contradictory positions.

The existentialist position might (very roughly) be summarized as follows: Subjectivity acts intentionally (by seeking the realization of personal purposes or goals). Intentionality (in any particular set of circumstances) functions through choice, the perceptual identification of one meaning among the multiplicity of meanings that are hypothetically possible under the circumstances. The choice of a particular interpretation elicits a sequence of subchoices with respect to how to realize the intention in question under the particular conditions that prevail. The sequence of choices (directed by any overall intention) works instrumentally to resolve what are normally called "problems," thereby reducing conflict and, other things being equal, leading to the fulfillment of the intention. Throughout the process, the experienced consequences of choosing (and experiencing the feedback from acting on one's choices) alters the nature and strength of intentions, and therefore modifies the way in which the situation itself is perceived.

Generally speaking, the existentially "authentic" individual is that person who is passionately committed to the realization of a well-defined system of values (intentions) and who is cognitively equipped—by virtue of being well-informed and capable of sophisticated reasoning—to solve a maximum number of the problems entailed by such a commitment within a given period of time.

The experimentalist (at least rhetorically) seems to subscribe to an equilibrium theory in which the value experience is seen as the resolution of the particular problem at hand (the problem-solving process generating the sense of fulfillment experienced as pleasure and happiness).

The existentialist, on the other hand, appears to be basically preoccupied with a life-style in which the individual is encouraged to intensify conflict by emphasizing the conditions—existential lucidity (conscious affirmation of free choice), commitment to the active resolution of large and challenging problems, and intellectualism—which are viewed as being necessary to both *creating* and *resolving* problems. Indeed, "existential anxiety" at least connotes not the "neurotic anxiety" of having problems that cannot be solved but, rather, the more radical problem of "meaninglessness," of existing in the world without significant and urgent problems to deal with.

In short, the existentialist, like the experimentalist, is very much concerned with problems and problem solving, but the existentialist is more inclined to see problems as opportunities for becoming fully alive (that is, actively conscious) and not (as some experimentalists seem to suggest) as temporary difficulties to be overcome.

For the existentialist, effective problem solving has two facets: (1) it leads to pleasure through the resolution of experienced needs; and (2) it leads to the reformulation of new problems that, in turn, provide the opportunity for future need-gratifications.

On the other hand, since the existentialist stresses conflict (as a precondition for the pleasurable reduction of conflict) over conflict resolution (which tends to be the dominant theme in experimentalism), there is clearly far less of an emphasis on such themes as group consensus and compromise in existentialism than there is in experimentalism.

Whether these differences between the two philosophies are differences in kind or merely expressed differences in mood or emphasis is difficult to say, and goes significantly beyond the parameters of the present discussion. The differences do, however, exist, and they make the attempt to make generalizations that encompass both experimentalism and existentialism very hazardous.

The Philosophical Bases of Educational Liberalism: In Summary

At basis, then, three general observations can be made about the philosophical bases of educational liberalism.

1. Educational liberalism—in our culture and at this time—is primarily an expression of the dominant tradition in experimentalism associated with John Dewey. It holds that the best way to think is to perfect the natural (instrumental) process of problem solving by imposing certain controls on inquiry that will give rise to more objective (trustworthy and effective) knowledge. In other words, knowledge should be verified by applying ideas to the solution of practical problems that exist within the real world; to do this, one should seek to be as scientific as possible in how one thinks and in what one subsequently believes.

2. Not all experimentalists are educational liberals. Some (such as the social reconstructionists of the thirties) go beyond liberalism, advocating liberationism as the only effective means of instituting the social conditions required for a viable social democracy. Others, such as psychologist B. F. Skinner, reject the notion of democratic government altogether, preferring a truly "experimental society" dedicated to the fullest realization of personal potential but directed by a cadre of expert scientific planners and managers who are devoted to the fullest expression of the common good.

3. Contrary to popular opinion, existentialists are seldom educational liberals. Their emphasis on *intellectualism* (in both the informational and reasoning dimensions of the term) make them clearly sympathetic to much that the educational intellectualist advocates. On the other hand, their stress on commitment—and particularly social commitment in pursuit of the kind of world that envisions authenticity as a viable objective for all—makes them highly sympathetic to the educational liberationist point of view as well.

Some existentialists are probably best described as "directive liberals," but others are probably more appropriately categorized as educational intellectualists, educational liberationists or, on occasion, educational anarchists. Certainly secular existentialism in the tradition of Jean-Paul Sartre—which is probably the dominant expression of existentialism in our own culture at the present time—would probably be best characterized as a hybrid phenomenon when it comes to educational ideology, a sort of "intellectualist liberationism" when it comes to the question of education.

TYPES OF EDUCATIONAL LIBERALISM

In essence, there seem to be three central types of educational liberalism: (1) method liberalism (which is ostensibly nonideological because it focuses on new and improved means to expedite existing educational goals); (2) directive (or structured) liberalism, which is perhaps best represented by John Dewey and his followers, and which is closely associated with the central tradition of American pragmatism/experimentalism; and (3) nondirective (or laissez faire) liberalism, which is perhaps best represented today by the rather ambiguous "psychological" liberalism of such individuals as A. S. Neill and Carl Rogers.

Method Liberalism

Method liberals are those liberals who take the position that, while instructional methods (or means) should be updated to encompass new psychological insights into the nature of human learning, the goals (or ends) of education, including traditional content, are fundamentally sound and do not require significant modification.

Maria Montessori might serve as a good example of a method liberal, because she suggests a new way of teaching but is basically not critical of existing educational goals and content. The present movement directed toward the establishment of behavioral objectives in learning, "competency-based curricula," and such, also appears to be a type of method liberalism on the whole.

Some method liberals are concerned in a narrow sense with merely one type of learning (for example, the Suzuki method of teaching children to play the violin, the Delgado approach to the teaching of reading, the NSSC physics curriculum, and so on), but, for present purposes, only method liberals who are concerned with the *total* teaching-learning process are considered.

Some who have been called "method liberals" are frequently individuals who have no clear-cut philosophical orientation and who do not therefore comfortably fit into any of the normal "ideological" categories. Many consider themselves as essentially specialists or technicians who operate in a relatively "value-free" realm of curricular and methodological problem solving. As such, they do not view themselves as implicated in the *philosophical* arena at all. They would deny that their behavior is appropriately described as "ideological" in any meaningful sense.

Thus, for example, many would argue that a person like Edward Lee Thorndike (who is considered by many to be virtually the father of the standardized testing movement in education) is *liberal* in the sense that he was instrumental in bringing a whole new innovative dimension to educational diagnosis and evaluation. Others would tend to look upon him as fundamentally *conservative*, a major figure in the introduction of a deadening and dehumanizing new approach to educational "sorting and selecting."

Whether Thorndike was either is, of course, open to indefinite debate. Was he, in his role as a psychologist, acting *ideologically* at all? Is it possible to evaluate what he did ideologically—in terms of its "action-meanings"—quite apart from the meanings the acts may or may not have had for Thorndike himself (that is, the "act-meanings")?[14] Did Thorndike's work on standardized testing have a different ideological function—and therefore a different ideological *meaning*—in the America of the first part of the century than it does today?

It can well be argued that movements such as those advocating "behavioral objectives," "competency-based curricula," programmed instruction, teaching machines, and "scientific management" approaches are not truly "liberal" and are therefore misplaced in this taxonomy—probably being more representative of "educational conservatism." The point—which is discussed at length in such books as Raymond E. Callahans' *Education and the Cult of Efficiency,* Ralph A. Smith's *Regaining Educational Leadership: Critical Essays on PBTE/CBTE, Behavioral Objectives and Accountability,* and Don Martin, George Overholt and Wayne Urban's *Accountability in Education: A Critique*[15]—is well-taken, at least in part.

It has been argued and extensively documented that such movements have been characteristically more geared to "efficiency" ("doing things right," in the sense of helping educators do what they are already doing—but doing it better) rather than "effectiveness" ("doing the right things," in the sense of helping educators reexamine the value and relevancy of *what* they are doing in the first place).

It seems increasingly evident that this has in fact often been the case. Many of these new (and at least ostensibly) "liberal" approaches to teaching and organizing schools have had the latent function of freezing the curriculum by directing an inordinate attention to the wrong questions—questions of *means* rather than those of *ends*—or of investing exorbitant amounts of time and energy in a fruitless attempt to find scientific ways of expediting the achievement of essentially anachronistic, and even inhumane, curricular objectives.

This may very well be true, but, on the other hand, three things need to be noted.

First, the definition of "method liberal" is, as stated, "one who suggests a new way of teaching but who is not basically critical of existing educational goals and content." The movements identified above clearly meet this criterion.

Second, it is important to bear in mind that, as the distinguished educational historian R. Freeman Butts points out in his book *Public Education in the United States: From Revolution to Reform*,[16] even at the height of the "progressive era" during approximately the first two decades of the twentieth century, there was a clear divergence between two fundamentally different groups of educational progressives. Butts identifies these as "the *business-oriented progressives*, who were speaking more and more of 'social control' and 'social efficiency,' and those *welfare-oriented progressives* who were speaking more of 'social service.' "[17]

After World War I, reform progressivism in politics, economics, and education tended to lose much of its original vitality, and the term "progressive" was largely taken over by a new group of essentially middle-class "reformers" who concentrated primarily on individual development divorced from social reform. (When the Progressive Education Association was organized in 1919, its stated principles pertained almost wholly to individual development and said very little about social reform.) Butts suggests that, even during the twenties and thirties, there was a significant schism in the "progressive education" movement and that, during this period, it might be useful to distinguish between "child-centered progressive education" and "social reform progressive education."[18]

It is also important to bear in mind that an inordinate number of those involved in the contemporary movements for behavioral objectives, competency-based curricula, and such are either educational psychologists or educators strongly inclined toward the application of scientific psychology to classroom behavior. What makes this noteworthy is that educational psychology tended early on, as Butts notes, to ally itself to the "social efficiency" wing of progressivism, which sought to perfect a thorough and efficient system of public schools and not to the "welfare-oriented" reformers. As Butts indicates,

Educational psychology after John Dewey's and G. Stanley Hall's early psychological studies tended to reject the social reform elements that characterize the "new education" prior to 1905. . . . [It] broke away from its social reform impetus to be found in William James and John Dewey, and became profoundly conservative in its acceptance of the social order and its search for "norms" that describe *what was* rather than *what should be*.[19]

In other words, educational liberalism—whether viewed as a contemporary movement or as the "new education" or "progressive education" movements during the first half of the century—is (and was) clearly a collection of substantially different movements that were frequently going in somewhat different directions.

"Method liberalism" is necessarily an ambiguous position, and any attempt to define it normatively to encompass only benign, "humanistic," "child-centered" or "social reform" orientations does violence to a far broader and more useful concept of "method reform" in education.

Third, it is important to distinguish between the *nature* (or, more properly, the apparent nature) of an educational program, the *motives* of those advocating such a program, and the social (including educational) *consequences* of the program, once it has been put into effect.

In a very general sense, a program can be viewed as "liberal" if it meets one of three basic conditions:

1. It has "face validity" as being *liberal* in the sense that it is truly innovative and represents a perceived departure from conventional educational practices.

2. It is motivated by recognizably "liberal" ideological considerations; it does not seek to sustain existing beliefs and practices or to revive previous ones.

3. It leads to consequences that effectively contribute to the realization of liberal social objectives.

Ideally, of course, a *liberal* educational practice would be one that met all of these conditions. It would be liberal in appearance, intent, and effects. Unfortunately, reality does not fall into such neat categories, and many "liberal" programs satisfy only one or two of these criteria, and these only ambiguously and on occasion.

The motivations of those who propose changes is a significant factor when it comes to understanding educational innovations. Thus, the same educational practice may be advocated by two different individuals for two substantially different reasons.

Behavioral modification approaches, featuring programmed instruction, behavioral objectives and controlled reinforcement schedules, may, for example, be used for "liberal and humanistic" purposes (as, for example, by channeling the child's thinking in the direction of open inquiry and by reinforcing divergent thinking) or for "conservative and authoritarian" ends (as by engineering conformity to established beliefs and by reinforcing convergent thinking or unquestioned obedience to authority).

In a similar sense, the *consequences* of any given educational practice may not necessarily correspond to the intent of those who initiated the practice in the first place. The educational liberal who advocates personal problem solving as the ultimate goal of education may actually foster a conservative social system if the children within the system have been socialized in such a way as to perceive the world as a battleground for competing ego needs. If the child defines his problems in terms of the pathological value of "getting ahead at all costs," is effective problem solving a viable "liberal" goal?

Even if, as is frequently charged, the consequences of applying industrial sociology and behavioral psychology approaches to the problems of instruction are ultimately socially regressive, there is certainly little evidence to warrant the assumption that the social-efficiency liberals have set out with malice aforethought to create or sustain conservative social or educational principles. If they have sinned, their sins appear, on the contrary, to be more those of omission than of commission. The problem—if there is one—appears to be less a matter of conscious conspiracy than one of what Silberman calls "mindlessness"—an ignorance of larger philosophical considerations.[20]

Contemporary educational psychology has become so fragmented that most of its practitioners operate more as narrow specialists or technicians within the established system than as more global theorists who perceive their role as critics of the profession. If they create pedagogical Frankensteins, they do so with the best of intentions by addressing holistic problems on the basis of re-ductionistic psychological assumptions—which may appear to make very good sense in a purely psychological frame of reference. If they create systems that are inhumane or dehumanizing, it is because their own education has not led them to a concern with the larger questions at hand, questions that are generally viewed as beyond the boundaries of legitimate psychological debate.

Directive Liberalism [21]

Directive liberalism, which constitutes the mainstream of American educational liberalism, has already been discussed at length in the chapter devoted to an overview of the liberal educational ideologies, as well as in the earlier pages of this chapter. In brief summary, the *directive liberal* seeks basic reform in both the means and ends of the schools as they presently exist. He holds that compulsory instruction is necessary, and he favors maintaining certain basic educational requirements pertaining to attendance and prescribed course content. On the other hand, he takes the position that, within these limits, both traditional ends and means (including objectives, content, and methods) need radical revision from their traditional authoritarian orientation to the more appropriate objective of teaching every child to think effectively for himself.

Nondirective Liberalism

The *nondirective liberal* would agree that educational ends and means need to be radically redirected from their traditional authoritarian orientation to the proper educational objective of teaching each child to think effectively about his own problems. He would, however, reduce virtually all constraints within the conventional school situation by eliminating (at least to a very significant degree) such things as compulsory school attendance and compulsory instruction as well as most prescribed learning experiences.

In effect, and as is well exemplified in A. S. Neill's famous Summerhill, he would replace institutional authority with the students' freedom to choose both *whether* and *what* they want to learn, providing them with the freedom to select whatever educational experiences appear to be most relevant to their own personal needs. Phrased somewhat differently, from the point of view of the nondirective liberal, the student himself should, within very broad limits, determine *whether* or not he wants to learn any particular lesson as well as *when*, *where* and *to what extent* he desires to do so.

Naturally, even nondirective liberals demonstrate different degrees of nondirection, ranging from those who would eliminate prescribed content but retain both compulsory attendance and relatively traditional instruction in elective programs, down to those who would favor a virtually laissez faire approach, eliminating prescribed content, prescribed instruction, and prescribed attendance more or less altogether.

PROBLEMS ASSOCIATED WITH EDUCATIONAL LIBERALISM

The difficulty in providing examples of the various sorts of educational liberalism is compounded by the fact that very few theorists present "puretype" points of view. Most nondirective liberals, for example, can be construed as *directive* in some respects if their entire position is closely examined.

In a similar sense, what constitutes an educational *means* and what an educational *end* is difficult to determine with any degree of exactitude, so just what *degree* of "method liberalism" terminates in a significantly different *kind* of educational product, therefore becoming more "liberal" in the usual sense of the term, is a difficult question to answer.

Phrased somewhat differently, the subvarieties of educational liberalism refer primarily to differences in *degree* within a generally similar orientation and not to absolute differences in *kind*. An educational *liberal* is basically one who seeks to alter existing educational practices and policies without, at the same time, seeking to modify existing social institutions in any significant sense in the process. (Whether significant social changes necessarily *occur* as a result of such methodological reforms is a substantially different question.)

Nondirective liberalism is also a particularly difficult position to pin down because, at the present time, it seems to encompass at least two philosophical points of view.

On the one hand, it includes a number of experimentalists and individuals inclined toward experimentalism who believe that existing scientific evidence implies the superiority of nondirective liberalism as a general approach to education. Many of the followers of the well-known Swiss psychologist Jean Piaget seem to fall into this category.

Second, it includes a number of "soft experimentalists," like Carl Rogers and Abraham Maslow, who view themselves as fundamentally "scientific" in orientation but who are unwilling to accept the notion that conventional scientific procedures and assumptions are totally adequate to explain human behavior in its full complexity. Most of these individuals tend to fuse a basic commitment to experimentalism with a strong secondary commitment to the notion that some types of experience are only capable of being understood as the basis of phenomenological (subjective) experience directed by speculative reason and confirmed by the overall emotional consequences emerging out of long-term personal involvement in the world. (This brings it very close to the phenomenological pragmatism of someone like William James.)

Thus the humanistic psychology of such a person as Carl Rogers, to take but one well-known example of the soft experimentalist position, is probably best viewed as a hybrid development that seems to present a synthesis of at least the following four points of view:

1. traditional scientific or quasi-scientific experimentalism drawing upon both the hard data of scientific psychology as well as the soft data of clinical observations drawn from the practice of individual and group psychotherapy;

2. phenomenological assumptions about the ultimate subjectivity of the self, (which are sometimes very close to the ego-centered phenomenological assumptions of such existentialists as Sartre who see all individuals as inhabiting separate psychological universes, and, at other times, far more reminiscent of the suprapersonal phenomenology of Eastern philosophical positions like Zen Buddhism, which see "subjectivity" writ large as the holistic unity of an ultimate cosmic "Self" in which all separate personality—or ego—is a mere illusion to be overcome);

3. a sort of Jamesian "phenomenological pragmatism" that accepts long-range emotional confirmation of ideas that do not lend themselves to experimental verification of a conventional sort; and

4. a tendency to seek large and synthetic "philosophical" explanations based primarily on speculative reason but using all of the sources of information indicated above.

In other words, a nondirective liberal such as Carl Rogers is essentially a "soft experimentalist" in the sense that he is a psychotherapist who generalizes on the basis of his clinical observations and yet, at the same time, supplements his clinical understanding with wide-ranging speculation. With the latter, he attempts to synthesize the objective-experimentalist knowledge derived from conventional psychology with the subjective-phenomenological insights emerging out of the practice of therapy.

At basis, however, even a person like Carl Rogers is not representative of all nondirective liberals because, at basis, there are two types of "soft experimentalists" who feed into this tradition: (1) those—like Abraham Maslow—who are essentially scientific in a conventional sense, subscribing to the information provided by mainstream scientific psychology but, at the same time, expressing important reservations about the adequacy of existing scientific procedures and information as a basis for explaining the full range of human behavior; and (2) those—like Carl Rogers and a number of individuals associated with the Freudian and neo-Freudian psychoanalytic tradition—who are "scientific" in the less exacting sense that they derive their data primarily from relatively uncontrolled clinical observations conducted in a psychotherapeutic setting (but who also have important reservations about the adequacy of the conventional scientific process and scientific knowledge as a basis for explaining the full range and variety of human behavior).

LIBERALISM IN EDUCATION: A SUMMARY

As indicated, it is particularly difficult to generalize about educational liberalism as a total and encompassing position, both because the three major varieties of educational liberalism frequently present substantially different points of view and because there is legitimate dispute about the "liberal" nature of some of the more significant expressions of "method liberalism." In view of these considerations, the following summary, while, as usual, disregarding the differences between the secular and religious points of view within the tradition of educational liberalism, is primarily addressed to directive liberalism in the mainstream experimentalist tradition associated with John Dewey and his followers. With these qualifications, the basic ideology of the educational liberal can be summarized as follows:

The Overall Goal of Education. The central purpose of education is to promote effective personal behavior.

The Objectives of the School. The school exists for two basic reasons: (1) to provide students with the information and skills necessary to learn effectively for themselves; and (2) to teach students how to solve practical problems through the application of individual and group problem-solving procedures based upon rational-scientific methods.

General Characteristics. Educational liberalism can be characterized in the following ways:

It maintains that knowledge functions primarily as a tool to be used in practical problem solving, that knowledge is a means toward the end of more effective behavior in dealing with everyday situations.

It emphasizes the unique personality of each individual, the singularity of each person as a person.

It stresses effective thinking (practical intelligence), directing its primary attention to the ability of the individual to solve his own personal problems effectively.

It views education as the development of personal effectiveness.

It focuses on individual and group problem solving procedures, emphasizing the present situation and the immediate future as perceived in the light of the individual's existing needs and problems.

It emphasizes indirect cultural change brought about by developing each person's capacity for effective practical behavior in pursuit of his own personal goals; it stresses continuous small-scale changes within a generally stable situation.

It is based on an open system of experimental inquiry (the rational-scientific verification of knowledge) and/or assumptions that are compatible with such a system of inquiry.

It is grounded on rational-scientific verification procedures.

It holds that the ultimate intellectual authority resides in knowledge derived through experimental verification and/or democratic decision-making procedures.

The Child as Learner.   The child is generally predisposed to be good (that is, to seek effective and enlightened action) on the basis of the natural consequences of his own ongoing behavior.

Individual differences are more important than individual similarities, and these differences are properly determinative in establishing educational programs.

Children are morally equal and they should have equal opportunity to strive for basically equalized (equitably distributed) social rewards.

Selfhood (personality) grows out of social conditioning, and this social self becomes the basis for all subsequent "self"-determination; the child is "free" only within the context of overriding social and psychological determinism.

Administration and Control.   Educational authority should be invested in highly trained educators who are committed to the process of critical inquiry and who are capable of making required educational changes in the light of relevant new information.

Teacher authority should be based primarily on pedagogical skills.

The Nature of the Curriculum.   The school should emphasize personal effectiveness, training the child to adapt effectively to the requirements of his own situation as he perceives it.

The school should focus on practical problem solving.

Emphasis should be placed on practical problem-solving procedures.

The course of study should be both prescribed and elective, with approximately equal stress on both.

Emphasis should be placed on the *intellectual* and *practical* over the *academic*.

The school should stress open and critical exploration of contemporary problems and issues as these are perceived to be significant by the students themselves; primary emphasis should be directed toward activity-based and interdisciplinary group problem-solving approaches involving training in such areas as the three R's, practical logic, scientific method, the behavioral and social sciences, history and most of the natural sciences and humanities.

Instructional Methods and Evaluation.   The teacher should rely primarily upon individual and group problem-solving procedures applied to the solution of problems identified on the basis of the students' personal interests; emphasis should be placed on more open and experimental classroom procedures.

Drill has some value when it is required in order to master a skill that will ultimately be necessary in order to deal effectively with some significant personal problem, but learning tends to be a side-effect of meaningful activity, and drill should be minimized wherever possible.

Student-directed learning, along with collaborative educational planning between teachers and students, is better than teacher-determined and teacher-directed learning.

The teacher should be viewed as the organizer and expediter of learning activities and experiences.

Evaluations based upon classroom simulations of practical, life-like situations tend to be better than those derived from the usual paper and pencil examinations.

Interpersonal competition and traditional grading should be minimized and/or eliminated as fostering poor attitudes and discouraging self-motivation.

Emphasis should be placed on the affective (motivational), which forms the basis for the cognitive; the sense-perceptual and motor-emotional bases of learning are also very important.

Emphasis should be placed upon the modification of existing educational principles and practices.

Personal counseling and psychotherapy are a central aspect of normal schooling, because they serve to guarantee the emotional conditions necessary for effective learning to occur.

Classroom Control. Students should be held accountable for their own actions in an immediate sense, but it should be recognized that student accountability is ultimately untenable in terms of any traditional concept of "free will."

Teachers should be generally democratic and objective in determining standards for conduct, soliciting student advice and consent in establishing rules for classroom behavior.

Since the moral act is ultimately the most intelligent act that is available in any particular situation, moral education (character training) is necessarily a by-product of helping the child develop his capacity for effective problem solving.

NOTES

1. To compound matters even further, there are two distinctly different traditions in philosophical behaviorism itself, *psychological behaviorism* and *evolutionary behaviorism*. The psychological behaviorists hold that all personal meaning derives from personal experience via personal behavior as this is directed through the instrumentality of hedonic reinforcement. The evolutionary behaviorists hold that the human species (and all human culture) has evolved out of behavioral "shaping" on the basis of the practical consequences of emerging structure-function over the millenia of human existence.

   In our culture at this time, most behaviorists are pragmatic, and virtually all pragmatic behaviorists are experimentalists (more or less by definition). In turn, most experimentalists subscribe to some version of both psychological *and* evolutionary behaviorism. It is important to bear in mind, however, that not all behaviorists are pragmatists or experimentalists.

2. It should be noted in this regard, that Skinner advocates the subordination of all other values to the scientific process, and he views the scientific process as fundamentally self-correcting. Skinner does not advocate a society organized around a set of substantive and static "scientific answers."

   This is perhaps the major problem, however, with most other philosophies that purport to be "scientific." In the case of Marxism, for example, Marx proposes that all human behavior be subordinated to a "scientific philosophy" based upon a particular "scientific" (that is, dialectical materialist) interpretation of history, derived at one particular point in time. This, in a sense, exalts a particular set of *scientific conclusions* over and above the "scientific process" itself, thereby eliminating the open and self-correcting element that is central in the proposals of an individual like Skinner.

3. The same qualification might very well be attached to Jerome Bruner. Bruner is best known for his theoretical work on the "structure of knowledge" as a basis for redesigning various components of the existing educational curriculum. He is not, however, concerned *solely* with

improving the way in which we teach existing content, and in some of his writings it is clear that his reservations about the nature and conduct of contemporary education go far beyond methodological and organizational concerns.

For a thorough exposition of Skinner's theory, the best books are probably the following. B. F. Skinner, *About Behaviorism* (New York: Knopf, 1974). B. F. Skinner, *Beyond Freedom and Dignity* (New York: Alfred A. Knopf, 1971). B. F. Skinner, *Reflections on Behaviorism and Society* (Englewood Cliffs, New Jersey: Prentice-Hall, 1978). B. F. Skinner, *Walden Two* (New York: Macmillan, 1948). Also see Richard Isadore Evans, *B. F. Skinner: The Man and His Ideas* (New York: Dutton, 1968).

The application of Skinner's behaviorism to actual problems of teaching and learning in contemporary American society is examined in two books: B. F. Skinner, *The Analysis of Behavior: A Program for Self-Instruction* (New York: McGraw-Hill, 1961), and B. F. Skinner, *The Technology of Teaching* (New York: Appleton-Century-Crofts, 1968).

4. B. F. Skinner, *Beyond Freedom and Dignity*, in *Psychology Today*, vol. 5, no. 3, August 1971, p. 61.

5. B. F. Skinner, *Walden Two* (New York: Macmillan Co., 1948), p. 300.

6. Ibid., pp. 158–62.

7. Ibid., p. 265.

8. Ibid., p. 268.

9. Ibid.

10. Ibid., p. 273.

11. Ibid., p. 266.

12. Ibid., pp. 266–67.

13. For a more thorough exposition of the relationship between existentialism and education the following books are useful. Maxine Greene, ed, *The Teacher as Stranger* (New York: Random House, 1967). George F. Kneller, *Existentialism and Education* (New York: Philosophical Library, 1958). Van Cleve Morris, *Existentialism and Education* (New York: Harper & Row, 1966). Donald Vandenberg, *Being and Education: An Essay on Existential Phenomenology* (Englewood Cliffs, N.J.: Prentice-Hall, 1971).

14. Abraham Kaplan, *The Conduct of Inquiry: Methodology for Behavioral Science.* (San Francisco: Chandler Publishing Co., 1964), p. 139.

15. Raymond E. Callahan, *Education and the Cult of Efficiency.* (Chicago: University of Chicago Press, 1962); Ralph A. Smith, ed., *Regaining Educational Leadership: Critical Essays on PBTE/CBTE, Behavioral Objectives and Accountability.* (New York: John Wiley & Sons, 1975); and Don Martin, George Overholt, and Wayne Urban, *Accountability in American Education: A Critique.* (Princeton: Princeton Book Co., 1976; see particularly Chapter II, "The Theoretical Background: Basic Assumptions of Accountability").

16. R. Freeman Butts, *Public Education in the United States: From Revolution to Reform.* (New York: Holt, Rinehart & Winston, 1978).

17. Ibid., p. 175.

18. Ibid., pp. 207–8.

19. Ibid., pp. 204–6.

20. Charles E. Silberman, *The Crisis in the Classroom.* (New York: Random House, 1970), p. 472.

21. The term *directive liberal* is inexact and somewhat misleading. It is, however, probably preferable to *structured liberal*, which seems to imply that the method and nondirective liberals are not "structured" (which is not the case), and it is less awkward than the term *method and content liberal*, which would be a possible option.

It is perhaps sufficient to indicate that *directive* is not meant to imply "authoritarian." The directive liberal does not attempt to dictate what the course of the educational experience should be, but he does see the teaching-learning process as clearly subordinate to certain prescriptive requirements—such as the requirement that the child should learn the three R's or become conversant with the "scientific method"—which grow out of more overreaching philosophical considerations.

BIBLIOGRAPHY

Educational Liberalism

METHOD LIBERALISM

AMERICAN INSTITUTE OF BIOLOGICAL SCIENCES. *Biological Sciences Curriculum Study*. Washington, D.C.

ASHTON-WARNER, SYLVIA. *Teacher.* New York: Simon & Schuster, 1963.

BELLFLOWER UNIFIED SCHOOL DISTRICT. *Orff-Schulwerk: Design for Creativity*. Bellflower, California, 1968.

BROWN, GEORGE ISAAC. *Human Teaching for Human Learning: An Introduction to Confluent Education*. New York: Viking Press, 1971.

BRUNER, JEROME S. *The Process of Education*. New York: Vintage Books, 1960.

ENDORE, GUY S. *Synanon*. Garden City, New York: Doubleday, 1968.

GLASSER, WILLIAM. *Schools Without Failure,* New York: Harper & Row, 1968.

GORMAN, RICHARD M. *Discovering Piaget: A Guide for Teachers*. Columbus, Ohio: Merrill, 1972.

LILLARD, PAULA P. *Montessori: A Modern Approach*. New York: Schocken Books, 1972.

MCLUHAN, MARSHALL. *Understanding Media: The Extensions of Man*. New York: McGraw-Hill, 1964.

MONTESSORI, MARIA. *The Absorbent Mind*. Translated by Claude A. Claremont. New York: Holt, Rinehart & Winston, 1968.

PHYSICAL SCIENCE STUDY COMMITTEE. *Physical Science Study Committee Physics*.

PIAGET, JEAN. *Judgment and Reasoning in the Child*. Patterson, New Jersey: Littlefield, Adams & Co., 1959.

PIAGET, JEAN. *Science of Education and the Psychology of the Child*. Translated by Derek Coltman. New York: Orion Press, 1970.

RAMBUSCH, NANCY M. *Learning How to Learn: An American Approach to Montessori*. Baltimore: Helican Press, 1963.

RUSSELL, BERTRAND. *Education and the Modern World*. New York: W. W. Norton & Co., 1932.

SIDWELL, ROBERT T., "Cooling Down the Classroom: Some Educational Implications of the McLuhan Thesis," in Stoff, P. Sheldon, and Schwartzberg, Herbert, eds., *The Human Encounter,* 2d ed. New York: Harper & Row, 1973.

SKINNER, B. F., "The Science of Learning and the Art of Teaching," in Fullager, William A., Lewis, Hal G., and Cumbee, Carroll F. *Readings for Educational Psychology*. New York: Thomas Y. Crowell, 1956.

SKINNER, B. F., "Why We Need Teaching Machines," *Harvard Educational Review,* 31: 377–98, Fall, 1961.

STANDING, E. M. *The Montessori Revolution in Education*. New York: Schocken Books, 1966.

TRUMP, J. LLOYD, and DORSEY, BAYNHAM. *Focus on Change: Guide to Better Schools*. Chicago: Rand McNally & Co., 1961.

DIRECTIVE LIBERALISM (MAINSTREAM EXPERIMENTALISM)

BODE, BOYD H. *Progressive Education at the Crossroads*. New York: Lawson, 1938.

CHILDS, JOHN L. *American Pragmatism and Education.* New York: Henry Holt & Co., 1956.

DEWEY, JOHN. *The Child and the Curriculum.* Chicago: University of Chicago Press (Phoenix), 1962.

DEWEY, JOHN. *Democracy and Education.* New York: Macmillan Co., 1916.

DEWEY, JOHN. *Experience and Education.* New York: Collier Books, 1963.

DEWEY, JOHN. *Experience and Nature.* Chicago: Open Court Publishing Co., 1925.

DEWEY, JOHN, "My Pedagogic Creed," in Ulich, Robert. *Three Thousand Years of Educational Wisdom,* 2nd ed. Cambridge, Mass.: Harvard University Press, 1954, pp. 629–38.

DEWEY, JOHN. *The School and Society.* Chicago: University of Chicago Press (Phoenix), 1962.

GEIGER, GEORGE R., "An Experimentalist Approach to Education," in National Society for the Study of Education. *Modern Philosophies and Education.* (The Fifty-fourth Yearbook of the NSSE, Part I). Edited by Nelson B. Henry. Chicago: University of Chicago Press, 1955, pp. 137–74.

HULLFISH, H. GORDON, and SMITH, PHILIP G. *Reflective Thinking: The Method* Philip. *Philosophies of Education.* New York: John Wiley & Sons, 1961, pp. 9–16.

HULLFISH, H. GORDON, and SMITH, PHILIP G. *Reflective Thinking: The Method of Education.* New York: Dodd, Mead & Co., 1961.

JAMES, WILLIAM. *Talks to Teachers.* New York: Holt, Rinehart & Winston, 1899.

KILPATRICK, WILLIAM HEARD. *Philosophy of Education.* New York: Macmillan Co., 1951.

KILPATRICK, WILLIAM HEARD, "Philosophy of Education from the Experimentalist Outlook," in National Society for the Study of Education. *Philosophies of Education* (The Forty-first Yearbook of the NSSE, Part I). Edited by Nelson B. Henry. Chicago: University of Chicago Press, 1942, pp. 39–86.

MEAD, MARGARET. *Culture and Commitment.* Garden City, New York: Doubleday & Co., 1970.

PARKER, FRANCIS W. *Talks on Pedagogics.* New York: John Day Co., 1937.

RAUP, R. BRUCE; BENNE, KENNETH D.; AXTELLE, GEORGE E.; and SMITH, OTHANEL B. *The Improvement of Practical Intelligence.* New York: Harper, 1950.

ROUSSEAU, JEAN JACQUES, *Rousseau on Education.* Edited by Leslie H. Claydon. London: Collier-Macmillan, 1969.

TOLSTOI, LEO. *Tolstoi on Education.* Translated by Leo Wiener. Chicago: University of Chicago Press, 1967.

NON-DIRECTIVE LIBERALISM

HOLT, JOHN. *How Children Fail.* New York: Dell Publishing Co., 1964.

HOLT, JOHN. *How Children Learn.* New York: Pittman Publishing Corporation, 1969.

HOLT, JOHN. *Freedom and Beyond.* New York: Dell Publishing Co., 1973.

KOHL, HERBERT. *The Open Classroom: A Practical Guide to a New Way of Teaching.* New York: New York Review, 1970.

LEONARD, GEORGE B. *Education and Ecstasy.* New York: Delacorte Press, 1968.

NEILL, A. S. *Summerhill: A Radical Approach to Child Rearing.* New York: Hart Publishing Co., 1964.

NEILL, A. S. *Talking of Summerhill,* London: Gollancz, 1967.

ROGERS, CARL R. *Freedom to Learn.* Columbus, Ohio: Charles E. Merrill Publishing Co., 1969.

ROGERS, CARL R., "Personal Thoughts on Teaching and Learning," in Rogers, *Freedom to Learn,* pp. 151–56.

SHIEL, BARBARA J., "A Sixth-Grade Teacher 'Experiments' ", in Rogers, *Freedom to Learn,* pp. 11–28.

SILBERMAN, CHARLES E. *Crisis in the Classroom.* New York: Random House, 1970.

TENENBAUM, SAMUEL, "Carl R. Rogers and Non-Directive Teaching," from Rogers, Carl R. *On Being a Person.* New York: Houghton Mifflin, 1961.

Chapter IX

Educational Liberationism

As the educational liberationist sees it, the ultimate goal of education should be to implement the reconstruction of society along truly humanistic lines that emphasize the fullest development of each person's unique potentialities as a human being. This can only occur within the framework of a social system that is committed to the maximum expression of individual civil liberties compatible with a stable and equitable democratic process. More specifically, the school should provide students with the information and skills necessary to learn effectively for themselves; it should teach students how to solve practical problems through the application of individual and group problem-solving techniques based upon the rational-scientific verification of knowledge; and it should help students to recognize and respond to the need for whatever constructive social reforms appear required by the demands of the time.

THE SOCIAL FOUNDATIONS OF SELFHOOD

For the liberationist, unlike the liberal, the social necessarily takes precedence over the individual. Thus, as the liberationist sees it, two points are of supreme importance.

1. The distinction between the social and the psychological is essentially spurious. Personal experience is always experienced in and through some particular cultural framework. The learner is essentially and necessarily social, and he always operates by and through a "socialized psyche"—based on a particular set of cultural constraints that govern the nature of virtually all personal experience. Civilized man is essentially a social phenomenon, and it is culture that serves as the fundamental agency for indoctrinating him in how he will subsequently encounter and experience the world in which he lives. In this sense, the individual is always a particular expression of the social. Whether "individualism" will exist, and how such "individualism" will be expressed, is invariably determined by the nature and dynamics of some particular culture at some particular point in time.

2. In a similar sense, whether science will be utilized as a viable approach to thinking and learning—whether it will be applied to the solution of relatively ambiguous personal and social problems—is also ultimately determined by the overall orientation of the particular culture in question. To ask that cultural institutions and processes be determined through the popular application of scientific inquiry applied to critical questions of personal and social import, is to assume that the culture in question already has the ability and inclination to use

experimental inquiry as a basic instrument for arriving at appropriate social changes—which is very seldom the case. Closed and totalitarian cultures are very unlikely to undergo significant revision on the basis of open and democratic approaches to thinking and learning, precisely because they reject such approaches in the first place. An open educational system requires an open and experimental approach to learning. Such an approach, in turn, requires the sort of open political and economic institutions and processes that include such an educational system as one of its aspects from the very beginning.

For the liberationist, then, the school's central purpose is to create the political and economic conditions necessary to initiate and sustain the sort of society that makes a truly liberal and liberating education of an open and experimental sort possible. Without a "learning society," no objective learning is possible, and objective schools are logically precluded. Without a collective commitment to individual self-actualization as an overall *social* ideal, the attempt to promulgate "individualism" as an educational objective is merely a rhetorical device to distract attention from underlying social authoritarianism.

Three Types of Educational Liberationism

There are three basic types of educational liberationism. Their adherents might be termed the *reform liberationist,* the *radical liberationist,* and the *revolutionary liberationist.*

Reform Liberationism. This position maintains that we should correct basic social inequities both within the educational system itself (as through racial desegregation, school busing, compensatory instruction for the educationally disadvantaged, and so on) and also within the overall society (by publicizing social injustices, educating children about the necessity for certain types of social action, and such). In short, the school should actively proselyte for the fullest implementation of democratic principles within the existing system.

Reform liberationism is perhaps best represented at the present time by five "reformist" movements in contemporary American society: The Black (Afro-American) liberation movement, the women's liberation movement, the Hispanic-American liberation movement, the Native American (American Indian) liberation movement, and the gay (homosexual) liberation movement. Of these, perhaps the two that have attracted the greatest attention are the Blacks' and the women's movements.

Reform liberationism, in its purest expression as a demand for equity (equal rights and participation) within the existing system, is a relatively nonideological matter. In effect, it merely reaffirms dedication to the "American creed" and asks that our society live up to its rhetoric by providing disadvantaged minorities with fair and equitable treatment equivalent to that granted to the majority of others (in what tends to be viewed as a largely male-dominated, heterosexual, white and Western European culture).

Characteristically, however, most of the significant *reform* movements—such as the Black civil rights movement of the early sixties—have tended to become radicalized through their confrontation with the system, and, in most cases, *radical* and *revolutionary* forms of what were initially *reform* movements have made their appearance. In the case of the Black movement, for example, what was primarily a struggle for equal rights within the system during the early days of the civil rights confrontation under the leadership of a moderate like Martin Luther King, has gradually evolved (at least in a significant degree) into a far more radical call for either separatism (the Black Muslims) or for a radical redefinition of basic social institutions on Marxist or quasi-Marxist grounds (Angela Davis, Stokely Carmichael, and the more extreme members of the remaining Black Panthers). More recently, small groups of radicals, such as Weather Underground, the new World Liberation Front, and so on, have even engaged in direct revolutionary action against the prevailing system.

Radical Liberationism.   This position would use the schools to criticize and reconstruct the very foundations of our culture. As the radical liberationist sees it, we need to rethink and radically revise certain of the most fundamental institutions upon which our society is founded (for example, the traditional churches, capitalism, democracy, sex roles, the family, and so on).

The *radical liberationist* — a group that ranges all the way from John Dewey to such contemporary figures as the Brazilian educator Paulo Freire—are divided into two major points of view. What might be termed "prerevolutionary" liberationism advocates the sort of education necessary to create "revolutionary consciousness" as a way of eliciting a popular demand for restructuring the existing socioeconomic system. What is perhaps best regarded as "postrevolutionary" radical liberationism is primarily concerned with the sort of education that is required in order to construct and consolidate the new, reconstituted socialist state in the era after a political turn-around has been accomplished. If the traditional "reconstructionism" of John Dewey, George Counts, and Theodore Brameld has traditionally been a type of prerevolutionary radical liberationism that addressed itself to correcting some of the more significant defects within the capitalist system, there is also a significant body of literature, ranging all the way from the writings of the postrevolutionary Soviet and Chinese communist educators through the various works that have been done on such radical institutions as the secular Israeli *kibbutz,* which addresses itself primarily to how the school can "resocialize consciousness" within the framework of the new socialist order.

Revolutionary Liberationism.   This position holds that, since the schools are institutions that serve the larger interests of the general culture, and, since the culture itself is the major educational force in the life of the child, the schools themselves cannot realistically hope to reconstruct the society by any sort of *internal* criticism of existing practices. Rather, the only way the schools can effectively counter a dehumanizing social system is by eliminating all pretense of "educating" children who have already been rendered uneducable by more profound social forces, and by working instead for the active abolition of the existing system and for its replacement by a different kind of society founded upon truly humane and rational principles. Only a new society of this sort will ultimately provide the possibility for establishing "real" schools rather than the kind of pseudoeducational agencies for social repression that presently prevail.

Phrased somewhat differently, revolutionary liberationism holds that the school should become the basic agency for fomenting social revolution. This approach, which was perhaps best exemplified in the famous "Red Guard" era in Communist China during the late sixties where the students were, in effect, activated as a counterinsurgency force to combat reactionary threats to the leadership of Mao, can be observed in works as various as Lenin's *What Is to Be Done?*, the "Port Huron Statement" of the Students for a Democratic Society, and Paulo Freire's *Pedagogy of the Oppressed.*

LIBERATIONISM IN EDUCATION: A SUMMARY

Temporarily disregarding the differences between the secular and religious points of view within the tradition of educational liberationism, the basic ideology of the educational liberationist can be summarized as follows:

The Overall Goal of Education.   The central purpose of education is to encourage necessary social reforms by maximizing personal liberty within the school and by advocating more humanistic and humanizing conditions within society at large.

The Objectives of the School.   The school exists for three basic reasons: (1) to help students to recognize and to respond to the need for necessary social reforms; (2) to provide students with the information and skills necessary to learn effectively for themselves; and (3) to teach students how to solve practical problems through the application of individual and group problem-solving techniques based upon rational-scientific methods.

General Characteristics.   Educational libertarianism can be characterized in the following ways:

It maintains that knowledge is a necessary tool for bringing about required social reforms.

It emphasizes man as a product of culture, the social determinants of selfhood.

It stresses the objective (rational-scientific) analysis and evaluation of existing social policies and practices.*

It views education as the fullest realization of each person's unique potentialities as a distinctive human being.

It focuses on those social conditions which block the fullest realization of individual potentialities, emphasizing the future (that is, changes in the present system required to bring about a more humanistic and humanizing society).

---

*"Science"—and even "reason" in the traditional Aristotelian sense of the term—are obviously not "culture-free." Both are clearly the outgrowth of a particular way of thinking that has emerged out of the Western European experience. In this sense, "the rational-scientific analysis and evaluation of existing social policies and practices" is clearly not neutral. Science does not give equal time to evidence based upon revelation or mystical intuition, and reason does not ordinarily defer to the nonrational (as sometimes occurs in Zen) or the antirational (as is expressed in some religious orientations). On the other hand, "objectivity" is not "neutrality." Neutrality specifies no preference between knowledge-claims. "Objectivity" declares the clear-cut superiority of those knowledge-claims that meet the (necessarily philosophically slanted) criteria for representing *reality,* as opposed to error or illusion. As previously discussed, "science" is based upon certain philosophical presuppositions. It is empirical, behavioristic, experimental, and so on. To the extent that knowledge-claims meet these criteria, they are deemed "objective."

It emphasizes immediate large-scale changes within the existing society, stressing significant changes that would affect the basic nature and conduct of the established social system.

It is based on an open system of experimental inquiry (the rational-scientific verification of knowledge) and/or on assumptions compatible with such a system of inquiry.[1]

It is grounded on Marxist or neo-Marxist assumptions about the socioeconomic determination of all personal consciousness.

It holds that the ultimate intellectual authority resides in those who accurately perceive the pathological consequences of contemporary capitalism and its associated social attitudes.

The Child as Learner. The child is predisposed to be good (that is, to seek effective and enlightened action) when reared in a good (that is, rational and humanistic) society.

Individual differences are more important than individual similarities, and these differences are properly determinative in establishing educational programs.

Children are morally equal and they should have equal opportunities to strive for a far broader, more accessible and more equitably distributed range of intellectual and social rewards.

Selfhood (personality) grows out of social conditioning, and this social self becomes the basis for all subsequent "self"-determination; the child is free only within the context of overriding social and psychological determinism.

Administration and Control. Educational authority should be invested in an enlightened minority of responsible intellectuals who are fully aware of the objective need for constructive social changes and who are capable of implementing such changes through the schools.

Teacher authority should be primarily based on intellectual acuity and enlightened social consciousness.

The Nature of the Curriculum. The school should emphasize socioeconomic reforms.*

The school should focus on both self-understanding and social action.

Emphasis should be placed on intelligent action in pursuit of social justice.

The course of study should be elective within generally prescribed limits.

---

*Obviously, where society has been effectively liberated and reformed in such a way as to preclude the necessity for any further sort of socioeconomic reforms—as would ostensibly occur in Marx's vision of the "classless society" after the triumph of Communism—the school would no longer be obliged to emphasize "socioeconomic reforms." Most liberationists do not envision a state of euphoric social equilibrium, however, so hypothetical utopias (such as Marx's "classless society") are not ordinarily taken into consideration. Assumedly, however, successful liberationists would be constrained to adopt one of the other educational ideologies (with the possible exception of educational fundamentalism), if a successful liberation (and subsequent social reconstruction) were to occur. The particular educational orientation that would be adopted in such an eventuality would be primarily contingent upon the extent to which such an individual would view continued change (as opposed to institutional stability) as being necessary in order to guarantee the continued existence of the new social order.

Emphasis should be placed on the *practical application of the intellectual (praxis)* over the narrowly *practical* or *academic*.

The school should stress controversial social problems and issues, emphasizing the identification and analysis of underlying values and assumptions, and demonstrating a special concern for the application of relevant classroom learnings to socially significant after-school activities; the school should typically feature interdisciplinary problem-centered approaches that draw upon such subject matter areas as philosophy, psychology, contemporary literature, history, and the behavioral and social sciences.

Instructional Methods and Evaluation. There should be approximately equal emphasis on problem perceiving (the identification and analysis of appropriate problems) and problem solving (the resolution of such problems).

Drill may occasionally be required in order to master a skill that will ultimately be called for in order to deal effectively with some significant personal problem or social issue, but learning is generally a side effect of meaningful activity, and drill should be minimized and/or eliminated wherever possible.

Student-directed learning within the framework of a predetermined socially relevant curriculum is superior to teacher-determined and teacher-directed learning.

The teacher should be viewed as a model of intellectual commitment and social involvement.

Evaluations on the basis of students' unrehearsed behavior in response to significant social problems is preferable to that derived from the usual sort of in-class examinations.

Interpersonal competition and traditional grading should be minimized and/or eliminated wherever possible because they lead to poor social attitudes and diminished self-motivation.

Emphasis should be placed on the cognitive and affective as they relate to the interpersonal; the school should emphasize the social basis of all significant personal experience.

Emphasis should be placed upon the necessity for new social (including educational) institutions.

Personal counseling and psychotherapy, as they exist in our schools at the present time, generally function as covert forms of social control and conformity-training that serve to block children's awareness of the underlying social conditions that gives rise to individual psychological problems.

Classroom Control. Students should be held accountable for their own actions in an immediate sense, but it should be recognized that student accountability is ultimately untenable in terms of any traditional concept of "free will."

Teachers should be democratic and objective in determining standards of conduct, and such standards should be determined collaboratively with the students as a means of developing the child's sense of moral responsibility.

Since the moral act is the most intelligent act in any situation, the improvement of practical intelligence is the most effective type of moral education; on the other hand, intelligent action, as a prescribed social ideal, requires an intelligent (objective) society in which everyone is given the opportunity to make enlightened choices on the basis of equal educational opportunities.

NOTES

1. It can be argued that Marxist and neo-Marxist assumptions are incompatible with an "open system" of experimental inquiry. In this respect, two considerations merit comment.

    A. There are at least three basic Marxist (and neo-Marxist) philosophies of education that relate to the various stages of social development that occur in the course of attaining a classless utopia:

        1. the prerevolutionary point of view, which advocates the development of "revolutionary consciousness" as a precondition for effective social revolution;

        2. the immediate postrevolutionary point of view, which advocates the development of the "new Communist man" as a way of resocializing personal consciousness and making the population amenable to the development of new and constructive forms of interpersonal behavior during the transitional era in which the Communist Party controls the political apparatus of the state; and

        3. the utopian, long-range postrevolutionary point of view, which pertains to the sort of education appropriate to the totally resocialized society that theoretically emerges after the "withering away of the state" has taken place (during the era in which all significant class conflict has been overcome).

    B. Marxism rejects an open system of experimental inquiry *under the authoritarian and dehumanizing conditions that they deem to be characteristic of stages 1 and 2 above* (pre- and postrevolution). The rationale that they offer for this violation of civil rights rests on three assumptions:

        1. An open system of experimental inquiry is both possible and desirable in principle.

        2. Such a system of open inquiry cannot occur in a "closed" (non-Marxist) society.

        3. Subscribing to Marxist tenets is the only way to create the kind of world in which such an open (classless) society can eventually be brought about.

    In other words, assumedly, Marxists subscribe to the value of individualism (and the open and critical society required for real individualism to occur), but they reject the notion that individualism is a viable goal *under existing conditions*. For Marx, the means to true individualism is a coerced collectivism, but the end (true individualism) justifies such a means.

BIBLIOGRAPHY

Educational Liberationism

REFORM LIBERATIONISM

CARMICHAEL, STOKELY, and HAMILTON, CHARLES V. *Black Power: The Politics of Liberation in America*. New York: Random House, 1967.

CASTAÑERA, ALFREDO, and RAMIREZ, ALFREDO, et al. *Mexican Americans and Educational Change*. Riverside, California: University of California Press, 1971.

FRIEDAN, BETTY. *The Feminine Mystique*. New York: Norton, 1963.

FRIEDENBERG, EDGAR Z. "The Image of the Adolescent Minority," in Friedenberg, Edgar Z. *The Dignity of Youth and Other Atavisms*. Boston: Beacon Press, 1966.

GREER, GERMAINE. *The Female Eunuch*. New York: McGraw-Hill, 1971.

MAZON, MANUEL REYES, ed. *Adelante: An Emerging Design for Mexican-American Education*. Center for Communication Research: The University of Texas at Austin, 1972.

MILLETT, KATE. *Sexual Politics*. Garden City, New York: Doubleday, 1970.

RED BUTTERFLY PUBLICATIONS. "Gay Liberation," in *Radical Ideas and the Schools,* edited by Jack L. Nelson, Kenneth Carlson, and Thomas E. Linton. New York: Holt, Rinehart & Winston, 1972, pp. 163–66.

SILBERMAN, CHARLES E. "Education and Equality," in Silberman, Charles E. *Crisis in the Classroom.* New York: Random House, 1970, pp. 53–112.

SILBERMAN, CHARLES E. *Crisis in Black and White.* New York: Random House, 1954.

WRIGHT, NATHAN, JR., ed. *What Black Educators Are Saying.* New York: Hawthorne Books, 1970.

RADICAL LIBERATIONISM

Right-Wing Radical Liberationism

BRANDEN, NATHANIEL. *The Psychology of Self-Esteem.* Los Angeles: Nash Publishing Co., 1972.

HOSPERS, JOHN. *Libertarianism: A Political Philosophy for Tomorrow.* Los Angeles; Nash Publishing Co., 1971.

O'NEILL, WILLIAM F. *With Charity Toward None: An Analysis of Ayn Rand's Philosophy.* Totowa, New Jersey: Littlefield, Adams & Co., 1972.

RAND, AYN. *For the New Intellectual.* New York: Signet Books, 1961.

RAND, AYN. *The New Left: The Anti-Industrial Revolution.* New York: New American Library, Signet Books, 1971.

Left-Wing Radical Liberationism (Prerevolutionary)

BRAMELD, THEODORE B. *Patterns of Educational Philosophy: Divergence and Convergence in Culturological Perspective.* New York: Holt, Rinehart & Winston, 1971.

BRAMELD, THEODORE B. *Philosophies of Education in Cultural Perspective.* New York: Dryden, 1955.

BRAMELD, THEODORE B. "A Reconstructionist View of Education," in *Philosophies of Education,* edited by Philip H. Phenix. New York: John Wiley & Sons, 1961, pp. 103–12.

BRAMELD, THEODORE B. *Toward a Reconstructed Philosophy of Education.* New York: Dryden Press, 1956.

COHEN, ROBERT S. "On the Marxist Philosophy of Education," in National Society for the Study of Education. *Modern Philosophies and Education.* (The Fifty-fourth Yearbook of the NSSE, Part I). Edited by Nelson B. Henry. Chicago: University of Chicago Press, 1955, pp. 175–214.

COUNTS, GEORGE S. *Dare the Schools Build a New Social Order?* New York: Arno Press, 1969.

GUREK, GERALD L. *The Educational Theory of George S. Counts.* Columbus, Ohio: Ohio State University Press, 1971.

STANLEY, WILLIAM O. *Education and Social Integration.* New York: Bureau of Publications, Teachers College, Columbia University, 1953.

Left-Wing Radical Liberationism (Postrevolutionary)

BETTELHEIM, BRUNO. *The Children of the Dream.* New York: Macmillan Co., 1969.

BOWEN, JAMES. *Soviet Education: Anton Makarenko and the Years of Experiment.* Madison, Wis.: University of Wisconsin Press, 1962.

ELON, AMOS. *The Israelis: Founders and Sons.* London: Sphere Books, 1972.

FRASER, STEWART E., ed. *Chinese Communist Education: Selected Documents, Speeches and Articles, 1949–1960.* Nashville, Tenn.: George Peabody College for Teachers, 1964.

FRASER, STEWART E., ed. *Education and Communism in China: An Anthology of Commentary and Documents.* London: Pall Mall Press, 1971.

KING, EDMUND J., ed. *Communist Education.* Indianapolis, Indiana: Bobbs-Merrill, 1963.

MAKARENKO, ANTON S. *The Road to Life: An Epic of Education.* Translated by Ivy and Tatiana Litvinov. Moscow: Foreign Languages Publication House, 1951.

PINKEVITCH, ALBERT P. *The New Education in the Soviet Republic.* Edited by George S. Counts. New York: John Day, 1929.

SPIRO, MELFORD E. *Children of the Kibbutz.* Cambridge, Mass.: Harvard University Press, 1958.

SUCHODOLSKI, BOGDAN. "Poland—A Statement of Aims and Achievements," in Edmund J. King, ed. *Communist Education.* Indianapolis: Bobbs-Merrill Co., 1963. 1963.

REVOLUTIONARY LIBERATIONISM

FARBER, JERRY. *The Student as Nigger.* North Hollywood, California: Contact Books, 1969.

FREIRE, PAULO. *Pedagogy of the Oppressed.* Translated by Myra Bergman Ramos. New York: Herder & Herder, 1971.

FANON, FRANTZ. *The Wretched of the Earth.* Translated by Constance Farrington. New York: Grove Press, 1968.

LENIN, VLADIMIR. "What Is to Be Done?" in Christman, ed. *Essential Works of Lenin.*

MARCUSE, HERBERT. "Beyond Tolerance," in *A Critique of Pure Tolerance*, edited by Robert Paul Wolff, Moore Barrington, Jr., and Herbert Marcuse. Boston: Beacon Press, 1965.

MARCUSE, HERBERT. *One-Dimensional Man.* Boston: Beacon Press, 1966.

O'NEILL, WILLIAM F., and DEMOS, GEORGE D. *Education Under Duress: Behavior Modification Through Thought Reform.* Los Angeles: LDI Books, 1971.

ROSZAK, THEODORE, ed. *The Dissenting Academy.* New York: Vintage Books, 1968.

ROSZAK, THEODORE. "Youth and the Great Refusal," in *The Politics and Anti-Politics of the Young*, edited by Michael Brown. Los Angeles: Free Press, 1968, pp. 1–22.

SAVIO, MARIO. "An End to History," in *The New Radicals: A Report with Documents*, edited by Paul Jacobs and Saul Landau. New York: Vintage Books, 1966, pp. 230–33.

STUDENTS FOR A DEMOCRATIC SOCIETY. "The Port Huron Statement," in *The New Radicals*, edited by Jacobs and Landau, pp. 149–61.

Chapter X

Educational Anarchism

Anarchism is the point of view that advocates the abolition of virtually all institutional restraints over human freedom as a way of providing the fullest expression of liberated human potentialities. The anarchist would favor the psychological individualism of the liberal in principle, but he would be even more predisposed toward the social determinism of the liberationist when it comes to matters of immediate, practical action.

ANARCHISM AND THE LIBERAL TRADITION

Where the anarchist would differ from both of the other Liberal positions would be in two basic respects.

1. For the anarchist, the individual is *descriptively* subordinate to society (in a psychological, or developmental, sense) because he is determined essentially by his social membership. On the other hand, the individual is *prescriptively* superior to society (in a purely philosophical sense), and he becomes truly human and self-actualizing only when he transcends the imperatives of organized society altogether.

Phrased somewhat differently, for the anarchist, the fact that organized society currently holds primacy over individual self-expression is a factually correct, but nonetheless regrettable, situation because the individual is objectively capable of direct and uncoerced moral behavior that does not require externalized social controls.

As the anarchist sees it, then, man is naturally social—he naturally requires other people and is actively predisposed to cooperate with them in a rational and constructive manner, on a purely voluntary basis. The difficulty stems primarily from the fact that society has become inextricably identified with political institutions and processes that have systematically reduced the individual to a function of the group. Increasingly, then, the individual has become institutionalized. His personal autonomy has been taken from him, and he has been constrained—both directly, by force, and indirectly, by socialization—to obey externalized rules and to adhere to the ostensibly beneficent controls imposed by preestablished political agencies. These controls have actually functioned to make him less responsible (and more passive), less rational (and more reactive), and less social (and more obedient).

2. *Society* (and culture) is both necessary and good. The *state*, however, which serves to subordinate the individual to predetermined organizations and institutions that serve to perpetuate a given type of collective behavior over an indefinite period of time, should not be equated with *society*. The state is both dispensable and, generally, iatrogenic in its effects (that is, its authoritarian cures tend to create pathological ills in its citizens far more severe than the disorders they were designed to correct). In the attempt to socialize man, the state has actually dehumanized him by making him lose both the ability and inclination to think and act for himself. In a sense, then, the state is tacitly immoral, because it subordinates individual experience—which is, after all, the source and basis of all value—to an impersonal collective process that militates against most forms of (personal) moral decision altogether. Subjectivity is lost in the vast objective mechanism of the political organization.

Education versus Schooling

For the anarchist, then, *education*—viewed as an inevitable process of learning through one's natural social experience—should not be confused with *schooling*, which is merely one type of education and which constitutes a far more restricted concept. Schools, as they presently exist, are merely one arm of the authoritarian state. By reducing personal responsibility, they make children uneducable in any true sense; they help to subordinate true education to mere training.

The school, like the state itself, exists primarily to minister to needs of its own creation. We require a radical deinstitutionalization—including deschooling. In a decentralized, deinstitutionalized society people would be returned to themselves, to a radically simplified world of I-thou relationships based on significantly fewer needs, significantly greater vitality, enhanced rationality, and the sort of true morality that is based upon enlightened personal responsibility. In such a world, the political would be transmuted into the interpersonal; cooperation on a manageable scale would replace coerced conformity to the anonymous forces of government.

THE THREE BASIC TYPES OF EDUCATIONAL ANARCHISM

There are three basic types of educational anarchism. Their adherents might be termed the *tactical anarchist*, the *revolutionary anarchist*, and the *utopian anarchist*.

Tactical Anarchism

The *tactical anarchist* feels that society educates the individual far more effectively than the schools, as such. Accordingly, he feels that the real *educational* problems of our time are actually such ostensibly "social" problems as poverty, racism, and war—problems that also serve to keep the majority of children fixated at motivational levels below those required for effective education in the schools. Therefore, the most "educational" thing we can do is to eliminate the schools altogether. We can use the immense wealth we are presently expending on an inefficient and authoritarian system of formal education to correct the more pressing *social* injustices that ultimately preclude the possibility of real education for most children.

Revolutionary Anarchism

The *revolutionary anarchist* views the schools as tools of the dominant culture. As such, they are not only useless as vanguards of significant social reform, they actually function as the primary bulwark of the status quo. As the revolutionary anarchist sees it, the schools at present serve to program obedient producer-consumers who subsequently serve and support an oppressive system of social controls. The most effective way to further the necessary social revolution is to recognize our educational institutions themselves as the pathological agents that reproduce the "sick" system, and to rise up and eliminate the schools. Such a course of action would be the single most important step toward overthrowing the existing system and establishing a new and enlightened society in which, hopefully, new and truly meaningful schools would eventually emerge.

Utopian Anarchism

The *utopian anarchist* holds that, in our culture at this time, we live on the brink of a utopian postindustrial society characterized by affluence and leisure for all, the sort of society in which only a small number of trained workers will be necessary in order to maintain an almost entirely automated system of production. In line with this, our schools, which exist primarily to force people into socially useful vocational roles in the industrial apparatus, are no longer necessary. People are now free to learn for themselves voluntarily on the basis of their own spontaneous interests. If we simply leave people alone, a sufficient number will naturally choose to learn those things which society requires and which are not capable of being done better by machines, and those who choose to perform a given job on a voluntary basis are likely to be better and more productive than those who have been forced to perform against their natural inclinations. In short, under anarchism there will be ample numbers of people who will spontaneously seek to do a sufficient number of the socially required tasks to eliminate the necessity for continuing the usual sort of institutional coercion over human behavior. We have entered the postschool era.

THE DIFFICULTY OF MAKING DISTINCTIONS

The subvarieties of educational anarchism are difficult to exemplify for several reasons. First, the difference between *tactical, revolutionary,* and *utopian* anarchists is basically a conceptual distinction that is implied by, but not directly stated within, the writings of the educational anarchists.

Second, and related to this point, is the fact that, while the utopian anarchist may favor a deinstitutionalized society in theory, he is aware that this goal is very difficult to attain. Consequently, many of those who are favorably disposed toward a utopian position are willing to concede that, under present conditions, it is better that educational anarchism be employed as a strategy for bringing about required social change *within* the existing system or for developing a more equitable set of social institutions in the immediate future, than that it be applied as an all-or-none ideological proposition.

Phrased somewhat differently, even the utopian anarchist often subscribes to a hierarchy of anarchist options in which the highest good is a deinstitutionalized society but in which he is also willing to subscribe (at least temporarily) to the abolition of schools as a basis for either correcting existing social problems or for developing a more humanistic institutional state. Thus, ironically, the writings of Ivan Illich probably make the best case for *all* of the varieties of educational anarchism, because, while Illich appears to be a utopian anarchist, he is also deeply sympathetic with both the reform and revolutionary potentialities of the deschooling movement.

Finally, what separates the tactical, revolutionary, and utopian subvarieties of educational anarchism is basically the question of *intent.* For the tactical anarchist, the abolition of schools provides access to the wealth presently invested in the cumbersome and counterproductive school apparatus, and such wealth becomes capable of being released for the purpose of carrying out necessary social reforms within the existing system.

For the revolutionary anarchist, the elimination of the schools effectively destroys the keystone of the existing system and therefore foments the sort of social revolution necessary in order to initiate a new era of democratic socialism.

For the utopian anarchist, on the other hand, the abolition of schools is not only a means of effecting required social reforms, but also serves as one of the key reforms to be sought, because the ultimate goal is to create a noninstitutional, constantly self-transcending and self-renewing society in which necessary social arrangements are arrived at through free cooperation on the basis of mutual need. The utopian anarchist is not *opposed* to schooling. He is, however, vehemently opposed to the self-perpetuating institutions that force people to learn certain things in certain ways and at certain times. For the utopian, *education* cannot be equated with traditional *schooling,* let alone with *public schooling,* and the good society does not require compulsory patterns of teaching and learning.

If intent is central to identifying the various subvarieties of educational anarchism, however, such intent is frequently difficult to identify. What makes the underlying purposes of most educational anarchists particularly difficult to determine is that they are more acute in their negations than in their affirmations. Their diagnosis of what is wrong with the existing system of schools is often convincing, but their prescriptions for change frequently tend to be vague and unpersuasive. This often makes it difficult to determine whether one is dealing with a person who views the abolition of formal schooling as a means of correcting existing social inequities, as a way of overthrowing the existing social system in favor of a more humane socialism, or as a way of eliminating traditional political restraints altogether and setting up a totally new society based on "collective individualism."

ANARCHISM IN EDUCATION: A SUMMARY

Temporarily disregarding the differences between the secular and religious points of view within the tradition of educational anarchism, the basic ideology of the educational anarchist can be summarized as follows:

The Overall Goal of Education.   The central purpose of education is to bring about immediate large-scale humanistic reforms within society by eliminating compulsory schooling.

The Objectives of the School.   The present system of formal schooling should be abolished altogether and replaced with a pattern of voluntary and self-directed learnings; free and universal access to educational materials and opportunities should be provided, but no compulsory system of instruction should be imposed.

General Characteristics.   Educational anarchism can be characterized in the following ways:

It maintains that knowledge is a natural by-product of daily living.

It views individual personality as a value that transcends the requirements of any particular society.

It stresses free choice and self-determination in a sane and humanistic (person-oriented) social setting.

It views education as a natural function of everyday living in a rational and productive social environment.

It focuses on the development of an "educational society" that either eliminates or radically minimizes the necessity for formal schools as well as all other such institutional constraints on personal behavior. It emphasizes the posthistorical future in which people will be capable of functioning as self-regulating moral beings.

It emphasizes continuous change and self-renewal within a constantly emerging society, stressing the need for minimizing and/or eliminating institutional restraints on personal behavior (deinstitutionalization).

It is based on an open system of experimental inquiry (the rational-scientific verification of knowledge) and/or on assumptions compatible with such a system of inquiry.

It is grounded on anarchistic or quasi-anarchistic assumptions about the moral perfectability of man under optimum social conditions.

It holds that intellectual authority properly resides in those who have correctly diagnosed the basic conflict that exists between the requirements of the individual and the demands of the state.

The Child as Learner.   The child is predisposed to be good (that is, to seek effective and enlightened action) when he is reared in a good (that is, a rational and humanistic) society.

Individual differences militate against the wisdom of prescribing the same or similar educational experiences for all people.

Children are morally equal, and they should have equal opportunities to study whatever they choose in order to obtain whatever objectives they consider desirable.

Selfhood (personality) grows out of social conditioning, and this social self becomes the basis for all subsequent "self"-determination; the child is free only within the context of overriding social and psychological determinism. *Society* and the *state* are not synonymous: society is necessary for self-fulfillment, but the state blocks the fullest realization of society, as fully conceived.

Administration and Control. Educational authority should be returned to the people by allowing each person to control the nature and course of his own personal development.

No special authority should be delegated to the teacher as teacher.

The Nature of the Curriculum. The school should be eliminated in order to augment free personal choice.

Education is not the same as *schooling*; the only true learning is self-determined learning, and this can only occur effectively in a "deschooled" society.

Emphasis should be placed on allowing each individual to determine his own purposes for learning.

Within the requirements imposed by any system of social existence (which implies the necessity of certain collective experiences and therefore common learnings), all learning should be self-determined.

Emphasis should be placed on the *personally relevant* at the expense of traditional distinctions between the *academic,* the *intellectual,* and the *practical.*

Every person should be free to determine the nature and extent of his own learning.

Instructional Methods and Evaluation. The individual student should be the arbiter of whatever instructional methods are best suited to his own educational purposes and projects.

The value of drill and other such related considerations should be left to the discretion of the individual learner; those who desire directive or authoritarian approaches to learning should be free to opt for these on an individual basis.

Traditional teacher and student roles as institutional requirements imposed upon everyone should be eliminated.

The teacher is a dispensable (or, at the very most, an optional) aspect of the educational process.

The best evaluations are self-evaluations, which should be utilized almost exclusively for purposes of self-competition.

Man is naturally social and cooperative, and, accordingly, learning should emphasize cooperation and minimize interpersonal competition for rewards. Since the individual is naturally self-actualizing, he is intrinsically self-competitive and requires no artificial motivation for learning.

The traditional distinctions between the *cognitive, affective,* and *interpersonal* are artificial and unproductive ways of viewing an otherwise total and organic learning process.

Virtually all continuing and self-perpetuating social institutions (such as schools) should be eliminated altogether.

Educational counseling and psychotherapy, as these are conducted through the schools, are merely one part of the system of social restraints that actually *cause* many of the psychological problems they purportedly attempt to cure.

Classroom Control. Children should be fundamentally self-determining, and the very idea that *children* are synonymous with *students* is an implicit violation of this notion; the nature and content of school experiences (if any) should be determined by the individuals involved and not dictated by external agencies.

Only situational rules of conduct, cooperatively derived by all participants under given conditions, are acceptable; general rules imposed upon specific situations are not organically related to the requirements of the situations and therefore misrepresent the kind of controls that may actually be necessary.

Moral action is invariably the by-product of moral living in a moral society; schools as such play only an incidental role in determining moral conduct.

BIBLIOGRAPHY

Educational Anarchism

COHN-BENDIT, DANIEL, and COHN-BENDIT, GABRIEL. *Obsolete Communism: The Left-Wing Alternative.* Translated by Arnold Pomerans. New York: McGraw-Hill Book Co., 1968.

GOODMAN, PAUL. *Compulsory Mis-education.* New York: Vintage Books, 1966.

HOLT, JOHN. *Freedom and Beyond.* New York: E. P. Dutton, 1972.

ILLICH, IVAN, et al. *After Schooling, What?* Edited by Allen Gartner, Colin Greer, and Frank Riessman. New York: Harper & Row, 1973.

ILLICH, IVAN. *Deschooling Society.* New York: Harper & Row, 1971.

ILLICH, IVAN, "School: The Sacred Cow," in Illich, Ivan. *Celebration of Awareness: A Call for Institutional Revolution.* Garden City, New York: Doubleday, 1970, pp. 121–36.

ILLICH, IVAN. *The Tools of Conviviality.* New York: Herder & Herder, 1973.

REICH, CHARLES A. *The Greening of America.* New York: Random House, 1970.

REIMER, EVERETT. *School Is Dead: Alternatives in Education.* Garden City, New York: Doubleday, 1971.

PART FOUR

THE EDUCATIONAL IDEOLOGIES: AN OUTLINE SUMMARY

Chapter XI

Comparative Overview

The various educational ideologies, along with their theoretical bases in social ethics and political philosophy, have already been discussed in previous chapters, but because they have been considered individually and in sequence, an overview comparing and contrasting the various ideological positions serves as a useful summary. Accordingly, the following chart attempts to outline the ideological positions in such a way that their similarities and differences become more clearly apparent.

The ideologies are characterized with respect to the positions they take with regard to nine basic topics: (1) the overall goal of education; (2) the objectives of the school; (3) general characteristics; (4) the child as learner; (5) administration and control; (6) the nature of the curriculum; (7) subject matter;* (8) instructional methods and evaluation; and (9) classroom control.

Subject matter is treated here as a separate category for the sake of clarity, rather than as part of *the nature of the curriculum*, as was done in previous discussions of the ideologies.

Educational Fundamentalism	Educational Intellectualism	Educational Conservatism	Educational Liberalism	Educational Liberationism	Educational Anarchism
THE OVERALL GOAL OF EDUCATION					
Revive and reaffirm the older and better ways	Identify, preserve and transmit Truth	*Preserve and transmit established patterns of social behavior	Promote effective personal behavior	Encourage necessary social reforms by maximizing personal liberty within the school and by advocating more humanistic and humanizing conditions within society at large	Bring about immediate large-scale humanistic reforms within society by eliminating compulsory schooling
THE OBJECTIVES OF THE SCHOOL					
Reconstruct society by encouraging a return to its original purposes	Teach students how to reason	*Encourage an understanding of, and appreciation for, time-tested cultural institutions, traditions, and processes, including a deep respect for law and order	***Provide students with the information and skills necessary to learn effectively for themselves	Help students to recognize and respond to the need for necessary social reforms	Abolish the present system of formal education altogether and replace it with a pattern of voluntary and self-directed learnings; provide free and universal access to educational materials and opportunities but impose no compulsory system of instruction

*The asterisks at the immediate left of some of the headings indicate my personal assessment of the ideological stance taken by contemporary American public education. A single asterisk indicates a primary commitment. Double asterisks indicate a secondary characteristic, and, on those rare occasions when they occur, three asterisks indicate a third-level priority. In most instances, and as can be seen, I felt that the American public schools at the present time are somewhat ambivalent in their stand on the various issues discussed, so at least two levels of priority are generally indicated. In some cases (as in the instance of teacher-rights), even a third level of involvement seems to merit consideration. My overall feeling, as the system of notations indicates, is that American public education is predominantly conservative with a strong secondary commitment (perhaps largely rhetorical) in the direction of liberalism.

	Educational Fundamentalism	Educational Intellectualism	Educational Conservatism	Educational Liberalism	Educational Liberationism	Educational Anarchism
THE OBJECTIVES OF THE SCHOOL *(cont.)*						
	Transmit the information and skills necessary to succeed within the existing social order	Transmit the enduring wisdom of the past	**Transmit the information and skills necessary to succeed within the existing social order	Teach students how to solve practical problems through the application of individual and group problem-solving procedures based upon rational scientific methods	Provide students with the information and skills necessary to learn effectively for themselves† Teach students how to solve practical problems through the application of individual and group problem-solving techniques based upon rational scientific methods	

GENERAL CHARACTERISTICS

	Educational Fundamentalism	Educational Intellectualism	Educational Conservatism	Educational Liberalism	Educational Liberationism	Educational Anarchism
	Knowledge as a tool for reconstructing society in pursuit of some prior pattern of moral excellence	Knowledge as an end-in-itself; truth as an intrinsic value	*Knowledge for social utility; knowledge as a means of realizing existing social values	**Knowledge as a necessary tool to be used in practical problem-solving	Knowledge as a necessary tool for bringing about required social reforms	Knowledge as a natural by-product of daily living
	Man as a moral agent; code morality (including patriotism narrowly defined)	Man *as man* (that is, man's universal nature, which transcends specific circumstances)	*Man as citizen, who finds his highest fulfillment as an effective member of the established social order	**The individual as a unique personality, who finds his greatest satisfaction in self-expression in response to changing conditions	Man as a product of culture, who finds his highest fulfillment along the lines defined and controlled by the existing social system	Individual personality as a value that transcends the requirements of any particular society

Tacit anti-intellectualism; opposed to the critical examination of preferred patterns of belief and behavior	Traditional intellectualism (stressing reason and speculative wisdom)	*Reasoned conformity; reliance on the best answers of the past as the most trustworthy guide to present action	**Effective thinking (practical intelligence); the ability to solve personal problems effectively	The objective (rational-scientific) analysis and evaluation of existing social policies and practices	Free choice and self-determination in a sane and humanistic social setting
Education as moral regeneration	Education as an orientation to life in general	*Education as socialization to the established system	**Education as the development of personal effectiveness	Education as the fullest realization of each person's unique potentialities as a distinctive human being	Education as a natural function of everyday living in a rational and productive social environment
Focus on the original purposes of existing social traditions and institutions; emphasis on a return to the past as a corrective reorientation to the current overemphasis on the present and future; traditionalism.	Focus on the intellectual history of man (generally identified with the dominant Western intellectual tradition); classicism	*Focus on existing social traditions and institutions; emphasis on the present situation, viewed in relatively shallow historical perspective; conventionalism	**Focus on individual and group problem-solving procedures; emphasis on the present situation and the immediate future as perceived in the light of the individual's existing needs and problems	***Focus on social conditions that block the fullest realization of individual potentialities; emphasis on the future (that is, on changes in the present system required to bring about a more humanistic and humanizing society)	Focus on the development of an "educational society," that either eliminates or radically minimizes the necessity for formal schools and other such institutional constraints on personal behavior; emphasis on a posthistorical future in which people function as self-regulating moral beings

†On occasion the same characteristic is listed under two different educational ideologies. In this particular instance, this objective is sought by both the liberal and liberationist with only a difference in priority. In some cases, however (as in the seventh point under General Characteristics) exactly the same position may be taken by two or more of the various educational ideologies.

GENERAL CHARACTERISTICS (cont.)

Educational Fundamentalism	Educational Intellectualism	Educational Conservatism	Educational Liberalism	Educational Liberationism	Educational Anarchism
Reintroduction of time-tested earlier ways; a return to the real or imagined virtues of a prior era	Philosophical stability over the need for change	*Cultural stability over the need for change; accepts only changes that are basically compatible with the established social order	**Indirect cultural change by developing each person's capacity for effective practical behavior in pursuit of his own personal goals; stresses continuous small-scale changes within a generally stable situation	Immediate large-scale changes within the existing society; stresses significant changes that would affect the basic nature and conduct of the established social system	Continuous change and self-renewal within a constantly emerging society; stresses the need for minimizing and/or eliminating institutional restraints on personal behavior (deinstitution-alization)
Based on a closed social and/or religious system characteristic of an earlier era; advocates changing back to the ostensibly superior conditions that once prevailed	Based on a closed ideological system (philosophical absolutism)	*Based on a closed cultural system (ethnocentrism); stresses dominant social traditions; gradual change within a generally stable social situation	**Based on an open system of experimental inquiry (the rational-scientific verification of knowledge) and/or assumptions compatible with such a system of inquiry	Based on an open system of experimental inquiry (the rational-scientific verification of knowledge) and/or assumptions compatible with such a system of inquiry	Based on an open system of experimental inquiry (the rational-scientific verification of knowledge) and/or assumptions compatible with such a system of inquiry
Grounded on implicit and/or unexamined assumptions about the nature of reality	Grounded on self-evident truths that are inherent within reason itself	*Grounded on time-tested convictions, and the belief that established ideas and practices are more reliable than those that are purely theoretical	**Grounded on rational-scientific verification procedures	Grounded on Marxist or neo-Marxist assumptions about the socioeconomic determination of all personal consciousness	Grounded on anarchistic or quasi-anarchistic assumptions about the moral perfectability of man under optimum social conditions
Holds that ultimate intellectual authority should reside in those who have most fully realized their intellectual potentialities	Holds that decisions should be made on the basis of intellectual reflection	*Holds that ultimate intellectual authority is the dominant culture with its established system of beliefs and behavior	**Holds that ultimate intellectual authority resides in knowledge derived through experimental verification and/or democratic decision-making procedures	Holds that ultimate intellectual authority resides in those who accurately perceive the pathological consequences of contemporary capitalism	Holds that intellectual authority resides in those who have correctly diagnosed the basic conflict that exists between the requirements of the individual and the demands of the state

(With respect to multicultural education narrow cultural nationalism and/or a rigid subcultural ethnic or religious particularism (ethnocentrism); the norms of a particular religious, cultural, or political group should take precedence over all others	*Cultural assimilationism (generally oriented toward some overriding set of religious or philosophical absolutes rooted within the Western intellectual tradition)	*Social assimilationism; the dominant social institutions and processes should take precedence over all special religious, philosophical, or ethnic traditions	**Social and psychological pluralism; each individual should be free to pursue his own interests and confront his own problems as these emerge within changing social circumstances	(Immediate) ideological assimilationism directed toward an "objective" (and usually socialistic) social philosophy; envisioning an (ultimate) psychological and social pluralism (which is only possible within a fully realized humanistic society restructured along proper and constructive ideological lines)	Psychological pluralism (established within the parameters of a purely informal culture, divested of all coercive political and economic constraints)

THE CHILD AS LEARNER

The child as predisposed toward error and evil in the absence of firm guidance and sound instruction	The child as predisposed toward wisdom and virtue	*The child as requiring firm guidance and sound instruction before he becomes effectively socialized as a responsible citizen	**The child as generally predisposed to be good (that is, seek effective and enlightened action) on the basis of the natural consequences of his own ongoing behavior	The child as predisposed to be good (that is, to seek effective and enlightened action) when reared in a good (that is, rational and humanistic) society	The child as predisposed to be good (that is, to seek effective and enlightened action) when reared in a good (that is, rational and humanistic) society
Individual similarities as more important than individual differences, and properly determinative in establishing appropriate educational programs	Individual similarities as more important than individual differences, and properly determinative in establishing appropriate educational programs	*Individual similarities as more important than individual differences, and properly determinative in establishing appropriate educational programs	Individual differences as more important than individual similarities, and properly determinative in establishing appropriate educational programs	Individual differences as more important than individual similarities, and properly determinative in establishing appropriate educational programs	Individual differences militate against the wisdom of prescribing the same or similar educational experiences for all people

	Educational Fundamentalism	Educational Intellectualism	Educational Conservatism	Educational Liberalism	Educational Liberationism	Educational Anarchism

THE CHILD AS LEARNER (cont.)

Educational Fundamentalism	Educational Intellectualism	Educational Conservatism	Educational Liberalism	Educational Liberationism	Educational Anarchism
The individual as a part-function of a chosen people or an especially enlightened group; individualism as participation in the corporate identity of a special subgroup possessed of unique capabilities	The individual as a rationally self-determining agent predisposed to recognize some absolute vision of reality; individualism as the capacity for recognizing one's inalienable relationship to a rational universe	*The individual as a part-function of the dominant social-system; individualism as participation in the superordinate corporate identity of the established society	**The individual as a relatively autonomous psychological unit operating in response to constantly changing personal and social conditions; psychological individualism	Individualism as one expression of the individual's social membership in a particular society at a particular time; individualism as conditioned and controlled by overriding social forces; fully realized "individualism" as the psychological by-product of a social system *collectively* committed to the political realization of each person as a unique being; sociopsychological individualism	The individual (fully conceived) as the supreme expression of autonomous personal reason cooperating freely with others in a totally open culture uncontrolled by conventional political and economic institutional restraints; "romantic individualism"
The moral inequality of people with respect to their intrinsic value; the fundamental superiority of those who accept and adhere to revealed and/or intuitive standards of belief and behavior	The natural inequality of people with respect to basic abilities, but faith in the essentially equal capacity of virtually all people to reach philosophical and/or religious enlightenment through reason; equality of opportunity extended to all regardless of natural differences in ability in order to allow all individuals to realize	*Natural inequality of people reflected in the naturally unequal distribution of goods and power within society; the moral imperative to grant equality of opportunity to all within the context of the existing (and essentially unequal) distribution of goods and power; everyone should be allowed equal access to social oppor-	**The moral equality of all people with respect to their intrinsic value as persons, and faith in the fundamental equality of people when it comes to the exercise of practical intelligence in order to solve practical problems of a personal and social nature, combined with the very real, but politically and morally irrelevant, in-	The natural, but morally and politically irrelevant, inequality of people with respect to abilities, combined with the moral equality (the equal intrinsic value) of persons *as persons*, despite these real differences in ability; the capacity of virtually all people to behave intelligently and morally with respect to practical	The natural, but morally and politically irrelevant, inequality of people with respect to abilities, combined with the moral equality (the equal intrinsic value) of persons *as persons*; all people substantially unique with respect to the nature and degree of natural abilities, but virtually all have the capacity to behave intelli-

their differing potentialities for reaching wisdom and goodness	equality between people with respect to natural abilities	tunities as they are presently structured on the basis of the prior competition between individuals and groups, which provides the basis for the established social structure		problems of a personal and social nature; existing society functions in such a way as to foster the illusion of moral inequality (which, in turn, legitimizes the oppression of the many by the few)	gently and morally with respect to realistic personal and social problems; the existing political structure functions to create dependency and passivity on the part of most people, giving rise to the impression that people are morally unequal or that the average person is not capable of participating effectively in a society organized along the lines of moral and political equality

ADMINISTRATION AND CONTROL

Educational authority invested in trained academic managers who are not necessarily either intellectuals or professional educators	Educational authority invested in a highly educated intellectual elite	*Educational authority invested in mature and responsible professional educators who have a deep respect for due process and who are sufficiently prudent to avoid intemperate changes in response to popular demand	**Educational authority invested in highly trained educators who are committed to the process of critical inquiry and who are capable of making required educational changes in the light of relevant new information	Educational authority invested in an enlightened minority of responsible intellectuals who are fully aware of the objective need for constructive social changes and who are capable of implementing such changes through the schools	Educational authority returned to the people by allowing each person to control the nature and course of his own development
Teacher authority based on superior virtue	***Teacher authority based on superior wisdom	*Teacher authority based on ascribed social role and status	**Teacher authority based on pedagogical skills	Teacher authority based on intellectual acuity and social involvement	No special authority delegated to the teacher as teacher

Educational Fundamentalism	Educational Intellectualism	Educational Conservatism	Educational Liberalism	Educational Liberationism	Educational Anarchism

ADMINISTRATION AND CONTROL (cont.)

Educational Fundamentalism	Educational Intellectualism	Educational Conservatism	Educational Liberalism	Educational Liberationism	Educational Anarchism
Teacher rights (academic freedom, tenure, ability to determine professional obligations, and such) subordinate to the teacher's recognition of, and adherence to, revealed and/or intuitive standards of belief and behavior; teacher rights relative to teacher's responsibilities to uphold absolute standards	***Teacher rights as a corollary of superior enlightenment based on superior wisdom and virtue; teacher rights relative to teacher's responsibility to attain and exemplify true reason	*Teacher rights subordinate to and determined by dominant social standards of belief and behavior; teacher rights relative to teacher's responsibility to uphold the conventional social system	**Teacher rights determined situationally through the exercise of practical intelligence in relationship to significant social problems; intelligent compromise—teacher rights relative to teacher's responsibilities to exercise open and objective critical intelligence with respect to emerging social problems	Teacher rights determined and defined by the particular imperatives required in order to institute humanistic social change in a particular society at a particular time; teacher rights relative to teacher's responsibilities to advance constructive social reforms	Teacher rights essentially the same as student rights, that is, the *human rights* to exercise rational and uncoerced persuasion in the natural intercourse between people living in a free and open social system; teacher rights relative to teacher's responsibilities to refrain from arbitrary authority and to foster the autonomous intelligence of each student

THE NATURE OF THE CURRICULUM

Educational Fundamentalism	Educational Intellectualism	Educational Conservatism	Educational Liberalism	Educational Liberationism	Educational Anarchism
Emphasis on proper moral character	Emphasis on intellectual discipline	*Emphasis on political socialization (social control)	**Emphasis on personal effectiveness	Emphasis on socioeconomic reforms	Emphasis on free personal choice
Focus on renewal of prior cultural patterns	Focus on reason and speculative wisdom	*Focus on cultural conditioning; the acquisition of conventional cultural values	**Focus on practical problem solving	Focus on self-understanding and social action	Focus on self-determined learning
Emphasis on moral regeneration	Emphasis on abstract ideas and theory	*Emphasis on basic skills, practical knowledge and character training	**Emphasis on practical problem-solving procedures	Emphasis on intelligent action in pursuit of social justice	Emphasis on allowing each individual to determine his own focus for learning

Heavily prescribed course of study	Almost totally prescribed course of study	*Heavily prescribed course of study	**Approximately equal emphasis on prescription and election	Emphasis on election within generally prescribed limits	Almost total self-determination of learning
Emphasis on *ideological conformity* (moral indoctrination) over the *academic* and the *practical*; minimizes the *intellectual*‡	Emphasis on the *intellectual* over the *practical* and the *academic*	*Emphasis on the *academic* over the *practical* and the *intellectual*	**Emphasis on the *intellectual* and *practical* over the *academic*	Emphasis on the *practical application of the intellectual* over the narrowly *practical* or *academic*	Emphasis on the *personally relevant* at the expense of traditional distinctions between the *academic*, the *intellectual*, and the *practical*

SUBJECT MATTER

Stresses moral training and the sort of academic and practical skills required to be an effective member of an appropriately regenerated social order: the basic learning skills, character training, physical education (including health instruction), American history, American literature, religious instruction, and so on	Stresses philosophy and/or theology, literature (particularly the established literary and intellectual classics) and broad-scale interpretive history	*Stresses basic training in the fundamental learning skills (the three Rs), an overview of the basic sciences, physical education (including health instruction) and a relatively academic approach to the more traditional social sciences (American history, American political institutions, world history, and so on)	**Stresses open and critical exploration of contemporary problems and issues perceived to be significant by the students themselves; primary emphasis on activity-based and interdisciplinary group problem solving approaches involving training in such areas as the three Rs, practical logic, scientific method, the behavioral and social sciences, history, and most of the natural sciences and humanities	Stresses controversial social problems and issues; emphasizes the identification and analysis of underlying values and assumptions; special concern for the application of relevant classroom learnings to socially significant out-of-school activities; typically features interdisciplinary problem-centered approaches that draw upon such subject matter areas as philosophy, psychology, contemporary literature, history, and the behavioral and social sciences	Holds that every person should be free to determine the nature and extent of his own learning

‡As indicated earlier in this book, the term *academic* has reference to learning how to learn, and mastering the sort of technical knowledge and skills which are only indirectly related to the more central human problems. The term *intellectual* refers essentially to the ideational, dealing with broad interpretive theory. The term *practical* refers to the immediately useful.

Educational Fundamentalism	Educational Intellectualism	Educational Conservatism	Educational Liberalism	Educational Liberationism	Educational Anarchism
Inclined toward traditional classroom procedures, such as lecture, recitation, supervised study, and highly structured group discussion	Inclined toward traditional classroom procedures, such as lecture, recitation, Socratic (teacher-directed) questioning, and highly structured group discussion	*Inclined toward a practical compromise between traditional and progressive classroom procedures; generally willing to use whatever methods are most effective in expediting learning, but inclined toward modifying traditional procedures rather than toward radical departures from established practices	Inclined to rely primarily upon individual and group problem-solving procedures applied to the solution of problems identified on the basis of students' personal interests; tends to emphasize more open and experimental classroom procedures	Inclined toward approximately equal emphasis on problem perceiving (the identification of appropriate problems) and problem solving (the resolution of such problems)	Holds that the individual student should be the arbiter of whatever instructional methods are best suited to his own educational purposes and projects
Tends to favor drill as a way of establishing proper habits at the lower levels, but encouraging more student initiative and more self-directed approaches at advanced levels; generally tends to favor memorization and drill	Tends to favor drill during the earlier years, but evolving toward more open and intellectual approaches, featuring formal (deductive) reasoning, during the later phases of learning	*Tends to favor drill as a way of establishing proper habits at the lower levels, but evolving toward more open and intellectual approaches during the later phases of learning; generally tends to favor a significant amount of memorization and drill	**Tends to view learning as a side effect of meaningful activity and to discount the value of drill except when it is required in order to master a skill that will ultimately be necessary to deal effectively with some significant personal problem	Tends to view learning as a side effect of meaningful activity and to discount the value of drill except when it is required in order to master a skill that will ultimately be called for in order to deal effectively with some significant personal problem or social issue	Tends to leave questions relating to the value of drill and other such related matters up to the discretion of the individual learner

Favors the elimination or radical minimization of traditional teacher and student roles	Favors a high degree of student-directed learning within a framework of a predetermined socially relevant curriculum	Favors a high degree of student-directed learning with collaborative educational planning between teachers and students	*Favors teacher-determined and teacher-directed learning but advocates student participation in less central aspects of educational planning	Generally favors teacher-determined and teacher-directed learning	Generally favors teacher-determined and teacher-directed learning
Views the teacher as a dispensable aspect of the educational process	Views the teacher as a model of intellectual commitment and social involvement	**Views the teacher as the organizer and expediter of learning activities and experiences	*Views the teacher as an expert disseminator of specific knowledge and skills	Views the teacher as a model of intellectual excellence and an arbiter of Truth	Views the teacher as a model of moral and academic excellence
Tends to favor self-evaluation, self-competition and cooperative learning	Tends to favor evaluations on the basis of students' unrehearsed behavior in response to significant social problems; tends to be opposed to interpersonal competition and traditional grading	Tends to favor evaluations based upon classroom simulations of real-life situations; tends to minimize interpersonal competition and traditional grading	*Tends to favor tests that measure specific skills and information over those that emphasize analytic ability and abstract speculation; tends to emphasize interpersonal competition and traditional grading	Tends to favor general evaluations of intellectual acuity (as in essay-type examinations) over evaluations that stress merely factual content (as in objective-type examinations)	Tends to favor tests that measure specific skills and information over those that emphasize analytic ability and abstract speculation; emphasizes interpersonal competition and traditional grading
Sees traditional distinctions between the cognitive, affective and interpersonal as artificial and unproductive ways of viewing an otherwise total and organic learning process	Sees the cognitive and affective as an aspect of the interpersonal; emphasizes the social basis of all significant personal experience	**Sees the cognitive and affective as based upon the affective; emphasizes the sense-perceptual and motor-emotional bases of learning	*Stresses the cognitive but with a heavy secondary emphasis on the affective and the interpersonal; emphasizes identification and imitation	Stresses the cognitive over the affective and the interpersonal	Stresses character training; emphasizes the cognitive (particularly the informational) but with a heavy secondary emphasis on the affective and the interpersonal; emphasizes identification and imitation

Educational Fundamentalism	Educational Intellectualism	Educational Conservatism	Educational Liberalism	Educational Liberationism	Educational Anarchism
Emphasizes the restoration of traditional principles and practices rooted in our national heritage	Emphasizes the adherence to classical educational principles and practices identified and defined by the great thinkers of the Western intellectual tradition	*Emphasizes the preservation of conventional educational principles and practices	**Emphasizes the modification of existing educational principles and practices	Emphasizes the necessity for new social (including educational) institutions	Emphasizes the necessity for eliminating most social and educational institutions altogether
Tends to view personal counseling and psychotherapy as functions of the family and/or the church	Tends to view personal counseling and psychotherapy as something outside the province of the school that should be handled by other social agencies	*Tends to favor restricting personal counseling and psychotherapy to children with extreme emotional problems that affect their capacity to learn in a normal school situation	**Tends to view personal counseling and psychotherapy as a central aspect of normal schooling which serves to guarantee the emotional conditions necessary for effective learning	Tends to view personal counseling and psychotherapy conducted through the schools as a form of covert social control and conformity training which serves to block children's awareness of the underlying social conditions which give rise to individual psychological problems	Tends to view educational counseling and psychotherapy conducted through the schools as part of the system of social restraints that actually causes many of the psychological problems that they attempt to cure

CLASSROOM CONTROL

Educational Fundamentalism	Educational Intellectualism	Educational Conservatism	Educational Liberalism	Educational Liberationism	Educational Anarchism
Expects students to be good citizens in conformity with the ideal of a morally regenerated society	Maintains absolute moral standards and holds students morally accountable for their behavior	*Expects students to be good citizens in terms of the dominant cultural view of good citizenship and proper behavior	**Holds students accountable for their own actions in an immediate sense but recognizes that student accountability is ultimately untenable in terms of any traditional concept of "free will"	Holds students accountable for their own actions in an immediate sense but recognizes that student accountability is ultimately untenable in terms of any traditional concept of "free will"	Holds that the child should be fundamentally self-determining

Generally nonpermissive in procedures for maintaining classroom control; features conformity to duly constituted authority	Generally nonpermissive in procedures for maintaining classroom control; features authority justified by reason	*Generally nonpermissive in procedures for maintaining classroom control; features authority supplemented by reason	**Generally democratic and objective in determining standards of conduct; solicits student advice and consent in establishing rules of classroom behavior	Generally democratic and objective in determining standards of conduct; frequently seeks to have students determine own standards of conduct in collaboration with teacher as a means of developing a sense of moral responsibility	Generally favors only situational rules of conduct, cooperatively derived by all participants in a given learning situation
Assumes that moral education (character training) is the basic and overriding purpose of schooling	Assumes that moral education (character training) is a necessary and unavoidable aspect of schooling	*Assumes that moral education (character training) is one of the necessary aspects of schooling	Holds that the most moral act is ultimately the most intelligent act	Holds that the most moral act is the most intelligent act, but that intelligent action requires an intelligent (objective) society in which everyone is given the opportunity to make enlightened choices on the basis of equal educational opportunities	Holds that moral action is invariably the by-product of moral living in a moral society

Appendix I

Judaism and Jewish Education

If one is not to misrepresent the philosophical and religious approaches to education in this country it is necessary also to take note of the very rich Jewish tradition.

THE DISTINCTIVE CHARACTERISTICS OF JUDAISM

Judaism differs from mainstream Christianity, including both Protestantism and Roman Catholicism, in eight basic respects.

1. Judaism is a significantly more ancient tradition than Christianity. Dating back to approximately twelve or thirteen hundred years B.C. (or, in Jewish parlance, B.C.E., before the common era), with its origins in Abraham's decision to serve the Lord and his subsequent migration from Mesopotamia to the land of Canaan, Judaism has a long and eventful history. Moses and the Exodus from Egypt, Joshua's conquest of Canaan, the kingdoms of David and Solomon, the Assyrian conquest of Samaria (with the loss of the ten northern tribes of Israel), the Babylonian conquest of Israel (with the destruction of the First Temple and the fifty-year exile of the Jews to Babylonia), and the return to Jerusalem, including the construction of the Second Temple, are all events that predate the life of Christ.

By the time Jerusalem was destroyed by the Romans in 70 A.D. (or C.E., common era)—and long before Christianity was a significant world power—the political life of ancient Israel had come to a close, and the Jews had begun the great dispersion throughout the Near and Middle East, North Africa, Europe, and Russia that was to remain their destiny for almost two thousand years.

2. From the time of the diaspora—the dispersion of the Jews, dating roughly from the destruction of the Second Temple by the Romans until the establishment of the modern state of Israel in 1948—the Jewish people have had no national territorial identity. Most of the Christian religions, on the other hand, have possessed some sort of geographical focus, even where this has transcended national boundaries—for example, northern Europe for the Lutherans, western Europe for the Roman Catholics, Greece and related territories for the Greek Orthodox, and so on. Since the emancipation of the Jews—which began in the latter part of the eighteenth century and was virtually completed in western Europe by 1870—the Jews have lost the ethnic religious autonomy that was

ordinarily vested in the scattered Jewish communities by the secular authorities of the various nations in which they were situated. In the United States, the Jews were emancipated at the federal level (although not in some of the colonies) from the very start, but, beginning with the formal enfranchisement of the Jews in France in 1791, the traditional Jewish community has become increasingly subordinate to the new "hyphenated Jew" (the German-Jew, the Polish-Jew, etc.).

3. The Jewish cultures, in common with most non-Western societies, did not tend to distinguish between *religion* and *culture,* and many specifically Jewish "problems" appear to derive from this fact.[1]

Throughout the history of the dispersion, the Jews have lived primarily in relatively isolated, self-governing communities that were endowed with a high degree of ethnic and religious autonomy. These communities—probably most frequently recalled by the Eastern European *shtetl* of the years prior to the Holocaust—were the primary force influencing traditional Jewish life. All other Jewish institutions—synagogues, cemeteries, orphanages, slaughter houses, bakeries, ritual baths, and such—were secondary to the overall Jewish community.

4. Judaism, in its evolution, unlike Christianity, tended to move almost directly from the Middle Ages to the Enlightenment—largely skipping the Renaissance and (until Herzl) the nationalist era. As Louis Ginzberg has written: "Judaism passed from the fifteenth century into the nineteenth, and this could not take place without a formidable shock. That it withstood the shock is the best proof of the power and energy inherent in Judaism."[2]

Modern Judaism really begins in the late eighteenth and early nineteenth centuries. Before this time Jewish culture was a unified whole, which was well characterized as "corporate, collective and segregated."[3] Even the great massacres of 1648–1649 generated no significant political or religious response from the Jews. It was only with the rise of the Enlightenment in Western Europe (perhaps best reflected in the writings of such Jewish *illuminati* as Moses Mendelssohn and Napthali Wessely) and the impact of the pietistic hasidism of Eastern Europe that the old unity was effectively shattered and the new forms of Jewish thought began to emerge. It was, in turn, the legal emancipation of the Jews (which was itself largely a product of Renaissance individualism and Enlightenment rational humanitarianism) that destroyed the basic reason for the traditional Jewish communities, leading both to the threat and the promise of cultural assimilation into the mainstream culture of the various non-Jewish nation-states.

5. Modern Jewish traditions primarily reflect differences in the Jewish community with respect to contemporary Jewish identity as this has emerged from the Jewish response to emancipation and the consequent possibility of assimilation into the dominant cultures of the host-nations. Emancipation, as indicated, destroyed the *raison d'etre* for the traditional Jewish community as it had existed for almost two thousand years. As such, it served to cast doubt upon the very basis of traditional Jewish identity. In a sense, all of the current movements that exist within Jewish life—reform, conservative, neo-orthodox, and many others that are less well known—are attempts at "reverification,"[4] ways

of redefining "Jewishness" in response to the ever-present threat of cultural absorption.

6. The Jews have traditionally viewed themselves as a "holy people" who have a sacred covenant with God. The Jew is born, the Christian must be *reborn* through individual conversion and faith.[5]

The special mission of Israel is to live as a sacred, or clerical, people; to proclaim the sacred duty of man as being service to God. The law (Torah)[6] is a special mission, an ethical imperative that isolates, protects, and enhances the visibility of the Jewish people.[7] Many of the great scholars of Judaism would agree with the great Jewish philosopher of the middle ages, Judah Halevi, that the Jews possess a special religious faculty and are therefore destined to serve as the spiritual organ of humanity in general.[8] In this sense, the Jews are, as Franz Rosensweig indicates, like seed—transformed by history and yet also transforming history to a final point of universal salvation for all.[9] The redemption of Israel, then, precedes and determines the redemption of *all* men. The "mission of Israel" is the "redemption of mankind."[10] The messianic monotheism of traditional Judaism has universal validity. It is not just for Jews.

7. As compared with mainstream Christianity, Judaism tends to be a relatively nontheological and nondoctrinal religion. Indeed, and as orthodox Jewish philosopher Eliezer Berkovits notes in his book *Major Themes in Modern Philosophies of Judaism,* abstract and universalistic interpretations of Judaism tend to lose their Jewish particularism. More a matter of revealed *law* than of revealed *religion* (in the traditional sense of "doctrines and beliefs"), Jewish theology is primarily a matter of exegesis (Jewish scholarly interpretation of Torah) and not of "philosophy" in the usual sense of the term. "Christianity is centered on the question of faith; Judaism centers on proper action and observances (based on nonspeculative faith in the Torah). Jewish faith is manifest in lawful doing."[11]

8. Judaism, at least in comparison to much of Christianity, is characteristically this-worldly and life-affirming. God is manifest in the world and in others. The central question in Judaism is not *what* but *how;* it is the existential question of how to apply the supernatural law to specific natural conditions.[12]

JUDAISM IN AMERICA

American Judaism differs from traditional (pre-emancipation) Judaism in five basic respects.

1. Jews were emancipated in the United States (except in certain of the colonies) from the very beginning of our national existence. (The first legal emancipation, or enfranchisement, of the Jews in Europe occurred in France in 1791). There is therefore no history of organized and systematic national oppression of Jews in the United States.

2. There were, as the result of this, no pre-emancipation Jewish communities of the traditional sort in the United States. There were only voluntary synagogues—the earliest in New York City and Philadelphia—that were essentially autonomous from the very beginning (probably in the spirit of the prevailing

Congregationalism), and which began to function as the center for Jewish community activities. In a similar sense, there were virtually no Jewish men of learning and no trained body of religious leaders in the United States, and the tendency was, from the beginning, to rely heavily on enlightened opinions of eminent Jewish scholars in Western Europe.

3. For Jews, America was generally experienced as a double "exile": (1) a continued exile from the promised land of Israel, and (2) an exile from the traditional European Jewish community.[13]

4. In the United States two substantially different Jewish traditions have emerged at different points in time. The earliest Jewish emigrants were Sephardic (largely Spanish and Portuguese), and later Ashkenazic (basically from Germany, Holland, and England). During the nineteenth century, many of these emigrants—perhaps most significantly the group in Charleston, which was the largest Jewish community in the United States in 1820—were influenced by the reform Judaism that was emerging in Germany.

The second major wave of Jewish emigration in the country began around the end of the nineteenth century. As Joseph Blau states in his book *Modern Varieties of Judaism:*

> In the 1870's and 1880's . . . there began a massive migration of Jews from Eastern Europe that continued until World War I and brought to American shores a Jewish population that dwarfed the older and slowly growing Western European group. The new arrivals brought with them a type of Orthodox Jewish piety that previous Jewish settlers in America had never known, not even in their Western European homelands before migration. The newcomers brought with them their own communal traditions, their own men of learning—in some cases, men of broad learning. They brought their own semi-sacred language, Yiddish, not merely as an ancestral tradition, to be preserved out of reverence, but as a touchstone of Jewishness. The prevalence of Yiddish served, temporarily, as a barrier to Americanization, although it became, later, one of the most potent forces for Americanization. The use of Yiddish in daily communication, the publication of newspapers and magazines in Yiddish, the carrying on of instruction in the schools and preaching in the synagogues in Yiddish insulated this group of emigrants from the currents of American life for a far longer period than had been true of any previous group of Jewish arrivals.[14]

5. American Judaism has, in many respects, become the most fragmented and diversified expression of Judaism in the world today. Again, as Blau indicates:

> All the modern varieties of Judaism reveal, to a greater or lesser degree, the influence of emancipation and of the full entry of the Jews into the secular life of their communities. This influence is shown at its clearest in American Judaism, because the United States of America had few, if any, residues of a pre-emancipation outlook to overcome. Consequently American Judaism has been productive of the greatest number of interpretations of what it means to be a Jew under modern conditions and of the widest variety in these interpretations.[15]

WHO IS A JEW?

A central problem in contemporary Judaism is precisely that of determining who is or is not a "Jew." Definitions range widely. According to traditional Jewish law, defined by rabbis for almost a thousand years and codified in the Talmud, a Jew is a person who was born of a Jewish mother or who has been converted to Judaism. In a more specific sense, the great Jewish philosopher-theologian Moses Maimonides, who synthesized a neo-Platonic version of Aristotle's philosophy with the Torah around 1150 A.D. (in much the same way as Saint Thomas Aquinas had reconciled the teachings of Aristotle with Christianity), held that there are thirteen articles of faith to which every Jew must necessarily subscribe. These, to quote Jacob Neusner's paraphrase, are as follows:

1. The existence of God;
2. his unity;
3. his incorporality;
4. his eternity;
5. the obligation to worship him alone;
6. prophecy;
7. Moses is the greatest of the prophets;
8. the Torah is of divine origin;
9. the Torah is eternally valid;
10. God knows the deeds of man;
11. he punishes the evil and rewards the good;
12. he will send a Messiah; and
13. he will resurrect the dead.[16]

On the other hand, for Hillel, the great Jewish sage who lived at the time of Christ, the essence of "Jewishness" could be reduced to far simpler terms. His definition (which is so brief that he is reputed to have offered to state it while standing on one foot) was "What is hateful to yourself do not do to your fellow-man. That is the whole Torah. All the rest is commentary. Now go and study."[17]

THE DEVELOPMENT OF CONTEMPORARY JUDAISM

Modern Judaism really begins in the late eighteenth and early nineteenth centuries in Europe. Perhaps the two most formative influences in generating change in traditional Judaism were (1) the pietistic movement termed *Hasidism*, which emerged around 1750 and which was largely localized in Eastern Europe; and (2) the rationalistic humanism of the Enlightenment *(Haskalah)* in Western Europe, which emerged at about the same time and which initially had the largest effect on the Jewish population in Germany (as covered in the subsequent discussion of Reform Judaism).

Hasidism was essentially a mystical pietistic movement within traditional (orthodox) Judaism as it existed in Eastern Europe in the mid-eighteenth century. It stressed the devout heart over the ingenious mind, and, in this sense, ran counter to the prevailing emphasis on Jewish scholarship and rabbinic learning as the pinnacle of Jewish virtue. Hasidism's period of pure, mystical fervor, emphasizing religious charisma, was relatively short-lived, and, even so, it tended to be largely a regional phenomenon. Hasidism rapidly evolved into a bastion of ultraconservatism within orthodox Judaism, emphasizing a sort of devout literalism, with respect for scripture coupled with a scrupulous adherence to a strict interpretation of religious laws—in many respects, a sort of Judaic equivalent to Christian fundamentalism. On the other hand, the hasidic revolt against rabbinic intellectualism gave rise to a counter movement within orthodoxy, the *Mitnaggedim* (literally, "the Opponents") who supported the more traditional claims of religious intellectualism. Contemporary expressions of orthodox Judaism seem to have arrived at a reasonable compromise between devout piety and traditional learning. The distinctions between the hasidic orthodox and the dominant tradition of mainstream orthodox (or, perhaps more properly, "neo-orthodox") Judaism is still significant to many Jews, but it is increasingly difficult to use either philosophical or mystical distinctions within the Jewish traditions as ways of distinguishing between different points of view. Elements of mystical pietism, as it existed during the efflorescence of Hasidism in Eastern Europe during the latter part of the 18th century, can still be found in Judaism, particularly within the Orthodox movement, and, in a similar sense, interest in the esoteric mysticism of the Kabbalah is still prevalent in and around the Jewish tradition. There do not, however, appear to be any particularly visible forms of Jewish mysticism that are important at the present time.

As regards Jewish philosophy, there are both religious and secular expressions of Jewish philosophy, and there is great controversy, even within Judaism, as to whether a major philosopher like Martin Buber is essentially theological or philosophical (that is, secular) in his basic orientation. Certainly, there is a vast gulf between such theologically inclined philosophers as Hermann Cohen and Franz Rosenzweig and such essentially secular theorists as Mordecai Kaplan and Horace Kallen. In short, any attempt to distinguish a distinctively "mystical" or "philosophical" approach to Judaism/Jewishness is precluded by the fact that both mysticism and philosophy are represented in some manner and to some extent in virtually all of the different Jewish traditions.

THE CENTRAL TRADITIONS WITHIN CONTEMPORARY JUDAISM

Within mainstream American Judaism there are at present three central traditions: *Reform, Orthodox,* and *Conservative.*

Reform Judaism

Interestingly enough, of the three basic traditions in contemporary Judaism, the Reform movement, the most liberal of the three, was the first to emerge as a distinct tradition within overall Judaism. It probably received its initial impetus during the period of the Enlightenment (*Haskalah*) in Europe through the work of the "Jewish Socrates," Moses Mendelssohn (1729–1826). Mendelssohn was quite traditional when it came to matters of ritual and ceremonial law, but he was very liberal in many of his interpretations of orthodox Judaism. In his book *Jerusalem* (1783), he attempted to bridge the gulf between traditional Judaism and the secular rationalism of the Enlightenment. The book appears to make two central points: (1) Freedom of thought is essential, and requires a separation between church and state; and (2) Judaism is revealed *law* but it is not a revealed *religion* (that is, only Judaism's ceremonial laws are unique, and these govern behavior, not belief; all of its doctrines and beliefs are universal and should therefore be open to reason).[18] Several of Mendelssohn's disciples subsequently sought to liberalize traditional synagogue services as well as the established Jewish approaches to education. The first successful reform synagogue—featuring the first Jewish prayerbook in German, as well as Westernized rituals and a sermon—was established in Hamburg in 1818.

The man who is generally acknowledged to be the greatest figure in the establishment of Reform Judaism was Abraham Geiger (1810–1874). Geiger was very much influenced by the German philosopher Friedrich Schleiermacher, who held that inwardness was the essence of religion. Geiger took the position that all religion was essentially an "aspiration to perfection,"[19] and, in the words of Joseph Blau,

> . . . if religion is, as Geiger puts it, the attitude generated by man's simultaneous consciousness of his "eminence and lowness, the aspiration to perfection, coupled with the conviction that we can not reach the highest plane," then theology and ritual, belief and ceremonial, are at best secondary and derivative from personal attitudes and have no compelling force.[20]

It was Geiger who provided the basic theoretical rationale for reform Judaism. He was especially concerned with moving beyond Jewish ethnicity, toward a point of view more in tune with the era of emancipation. For Geiger, Judaism had gone beyond its "peculiar nationality."[21]

> The implication of this assertion for Reform Judaism is that it can, without loss, eliminate the surviving particularistic expressions in its liturgical and doctrinal formulations. Most significantly Reform liturgy can cut out any reference to the "Chosen People" doctrine. In Geiger's interpretation there is nothing left that can conflict with total political allegiance to any modern nation. Even before Geiger, Reform ritual had excised this doctrine from its liturgy and also had edited out all references in the traditional prayers to a return to Zion. The doctrine of a personal Messiah, so centrally important in earlier Judaism, was transformed, though with less care and consistency, into a doctrine of a Messianic Age, in order to avoid any hint of Jewish particularism. From its inception Reform Judaism involved a reforming of traditional doctrine to accord with the needs of an era of emancipation; Geiger gave this tendency its theoretical justification.[22]

For Geiger, *change* is central to the Jewish tradition. He seemed to be in basic agreement with his contemporary, Samuel Holdheim who stated: "The Talmud speaks with the ideology of its own time, and for that time it was right. I speak for the higher ideology of my time, and for this age I am right."[23]

In America, too, a number of Jewish leaders were concerned with central questions about orthodox Jewish beliefs and practices—liturgical practices, traditional laws of marriage and divorce, dietary laws, sabbath observances, "outmoded" practices (such as circumcision), the doctrine of a personal Messiah, the resurrection of the body after death, and others. These leaders sought to simplify, clarify, and, generally, make Judaism more rational, relevant, and inspiring.

In addresses and articles Reform leader after Reform leader presented the approach to Judaism in the spirit of the most optimistic voices of the nineteenth century. [Max] Lilienthal, in 1854, took up the theme of the "transient and the permanent," which Theodore Parker had raised in the Christian context a decade before. Lilienthal asked, "when religious ceremonies have to yield to the necessities of life and when they have to be kept at any price, subjugating life and its exigencies . . . . what in our law is God's command and what is the transient work of mortal man?" [David] Einhorn urged that "the divine law has a perishable body and an imperishable spirit. The body is intended to be the servant of the spirit, and must disappear as soon as bereft of the latter." The Decalogue, he insisted, is the spirit; all the rest of the ordinances "are only *signs* of the covenant."[24]

In the United States perhaps the most central reconsideration of the three central themes of Judaism (God, Torah, and Israel) were summarized in the epochal "Pittsburgh Platform" (at the Pittsburgh Conference of the Union of American Hebrew Congregations in 1885), which was written by Rabbi Kaufmann Kohler. In a radical and decisive break with Jewish tradition that has been characterized as the coming of age of Reform Judaism "as a completely self-conscious movement,"[25] Kohler reduced the spirit of the Reform movement to ten basic principles that Joseph Blau summarizes in the eight following points in his book *Modern Varieties of Judaism:*

1. The sanctity and sincerity of other religions was acknowledged at the same time as Judaism was described as presenting "the highest conception of the god-idea as taught in our holy Scriptures and developed and spiritualized by the Jewish teachers in accordance with the moral and philosophical progress of their respective ages."

2. The Bible was "the record of the consecration of the Jewish people to its mission as priest of the one God." The concept of literal inspiration was not mentioned; by implication it was abandoned and the value of the Bible was founded on its use as "the most potent instrument of religious and moral instruction." In the discussion [of the Pittsburgh Platform] Kohler's motion to amend this section by including the words "divine Revelations" was defeated, because of the ambiguities and the interpretation of the idea of revelation. With the quiet abandonment of the doctrine of literal inspiration, it was possible for the platform to deny any antagonism between Judaism and the scientific discoveries of the nineteenth century. Darwinism was the issue at the time the platform was composed.

3. Only the moral law in the Bible was to be regarded as binding; of the other parts of the Mosaic legislation the group accepted "only such ceremonies as elevate and sanctify our lives, but reject all such as are not adapted to the views and habits of modern civilization."

4. Dietary laws and regulations concerning priestly purity and dress were explicitly rejected.

5. The traditional Messianic concept was transformed into a universal hope for "the establishment of the Kingdom of Truth, Justice and Peace among all men." This change was combined with the rejection of the idea of Jewish nationhood; the Jews were designated "a religious community."

6. Judaism was declared "a progressive religion, ever striving to be in accord with the postulates of reason." Interfaith cooperation with Christianity and Islam were welcomed.

7. By retaining the doctrine of the immortality of the soul, the Reform rabbis cast out the belief in bodily resurrection and the doctrine of punishment in the life after death.

8. The participants, very much in tune with their time, introduced a plank calling for social justice. "In full accordance with the spirit of Mosaic legislation . . . we deem it our duty to participate in the great task of modern times, to solve on the basis of justice and righteousness the problems presented by the contrasts and evils of the present organization of society."[26]

Orthodox Judaism

For all practical purposes, from roughly the time of the destruction of the Second Temple in 70 A.D. until the end of the eighteenth century, Orthodox Judaism was the *only* Judaism. In the centuries before Jewish emancipation—and Eastern Europe was emancipated after the First World War, *if* then—it was the self-governing, separated, and isolated communities of orthodox Jews who were barred from the secular schools, who kept the Jewish heritage and the Hebrew language alive. Even the conflict between the pietistic Hasidism and the proponents of the more traditional Judaic scholarship (in Eastern Europe during the latter part of the eighteenth century) were essentially differences in degree and not in kind, and they ultimately led to a basic rapprochement within the context of orthodox Judaism.[27]

Before the Enlightenment era, orthodox Judaism was characterized by a severe traditionalism.

In the belatedly medieval situation of Poland such a statement as the following, from the rabbis of Lissa, may have retained relevance as a guide to life for the Jews: "All commandments and prohibitions contained in the books of Moses, and that, too, in the form that they were received by Talmudical interpretation, are of divine origin, binding for all time upon the Jews, and not one of these commandments or prohibitions, be its character what it may, can ever be abolished or modified by any human authority.''[28]

Since virtually all Judaism was "orthodox" prior to the beginning of the nineteenth century, the term "orthodoxy"—which is really a type of "neo-orthodoxy" or "neo-traditionalism"—is itself of comparatively recent origin and was first directed as an epithet at traditional Judaism by advocates of Reform Judaism during the first decade of the nineteenth century in Germany.

Samson Hirsch, who was the rabbi at Oldenburg (near Hamburg) and later at Frankfurt during the early part of the nineteenth century, was the first major spokesman for the newly recognized "orthodox" position in its earliest confrontation with the emerging forces of reform. In common with most other orthodox spokesmen, Hirsch stressed the power of gradual change available in the prevailing rabbinic tradition rather than insisting upon a rigid fixity of belief and practice.[29]

The basic contribution of Samson Hirsch was to formulate a rationale for orthodox Judaism that was essentially compatible with the intellectual climate of the nineteenth century. For Hirsch, orthodox Judaism was not inconsistent with reason, but it did *transcend* reason. Contrary to the ideas of the reformers, the role of Judaism was not to interpret the Torah through "the spirit of the age" but rather to interpret the spirit of the age through the eternal and immutable principles of the Torah. As Blau states, "True reform would be to reform ourselves in accordance with the eternal principles of Judaism. The Reform party seeks to ally religion to progress; Neo-Orthodoxy seeks to ally progress to religion.''[30] For orthodoxy, Torah is central over ethnicity or peoplehood, and, as Hirsch saw it, the central purpose revealed by the Torah is mutual service, "continual reciprocal activity. . . . None has power, or means, for itself; it receives in order to give; gives in order to receive.''[31]

The Jew must give priority to being a Jew, because the Jews are spiritually isolated from other peoples. The Jew is the divine bridge, the eternal "other" who bears witness. His "Jewishness" is his special mode of being human and thereby advancing the spiritual destiny of all peoples. As Blau states:

> To proclaim that the sacred duty of man is service to God is the special mission of Israel. Israel's responsibility has been to proclaim this message both through its history and through the daily life of its people, who are commanded to make the fulfillment of the will of God their only aim. In order to carry out its mission Israel must remain ethically and spiritually separate from the other peoples of the world. The people of Israel are forbidden to live as the other peoples of the world, because Israel may not idolize wealth and pleasure while announcing the great truth that there is one God who is the creator, the law giver, and the father of all beings. The complex of laws, precepts, and commandments in the Torah was given to Israel alone in order to enforce its isolation from the rest of mankind. Hirsch agreed with Mendelssohn that the Torah does not contain those general truths of religion that are addressed to all mankind. It assumes these and enunciates only those special laws laid down for Israel alone. The emphasis of the Torah falls upon observance of the law in every detail rather than upon belief in any particular doctrines. For observance of the

law is the essence of Judaism, within the overarching purpose of God. God's intent in these laws was to train the Jews for their mission and destiny.

Hirsch, in this way, took his stand firmly with those disciples of Mendelssohn who denied that Judaism is a creedal faith. Most emphatically he asserted that "Judaism enjoins 613 duties, but knows no dogmas." In the same context, he rebuked the barren intellectualism of those Jews of his time who dedicated themselves to "abstract and abstruse speculation," and he argued that the purpose of all thought is to discover our "life-duties." [As Hirsch writes:]

> True speculation does not consist, as many would-be thinkers suppose, in closing the eye and the ear to the world round about us and in constructing out of our own inner Ego a world to suit ourselves; true speculation takes nature, man, and history as facts, as the true basis of knowledge, and seeks in them instruction and wisdom; to these Judaism adds the Torah, as genuine a reality as heaven or earth. But it regards no speculation which does not lead to active, productive life as its ultimate goal; it points out the limits of our understanding and warns us against baseless reasoning, transcending the legitimate bounds of our intellectual capacity, however brilliantly put together and glitteringly logical it may appear to be.[32]

"Judaism," states Hirsch,

> is not a religion, the synagogue is not a church, and the Rabbi is not a priest. Judaism is not a mere adjunct to life: it comprises all of life. To be a Jew is not a mere part, it is the sum total of our task in life. To be a Jew in synagogue and kitchen, in the field and the warehouse, in the office and the pulpit, as father and mother, as servant and master, as man and as citizen, with one's feelings and one's thoughts, in word and in deed, in enjoyment and privation, with the needle and the graving-tool, with the pen and the chisel—that is what it means to be a Jew. An entire life supported by the Divine idea and lived and brought to fulfillment according to the Divine will.[33]

Conservative Judaism

Both Conservative Judaism and Neo-Orthodoxy grew out of a reaction to Reform Judaism but the Conservative movement in Judaism emerged more slowly and attained a substantial definition somewhat later than either of the other two orientations. Filling the rather significant gap that existed between the moderate Reform and liberal Orthodox positions, the emerging Conservative movement was influenced by several protoconservative trends that existed in Europe during the early part of the nineteenth century. Perhaps the most significant of these was the so-called historical school, a centrist group that viewed Judaism as a slowly evolving tradition, but that did not look upon all aspects of the tradition as being either divinely inspired or of equal value. Tending to downplay the traditional authority of rabbinical interpretations of scripture, the historical school placed its basic confidence in the Jewish people themselves—the so-called totality of Israel *(K'lal Yisrael)*—and viewed the historical continuity of the Jewish people as the central and formative principle of Judaism. The historicists did not reject novelty but they felt strongly that it should always be consonant with the overriding spirit of the Jewish people as revealed through the study of Jewish history. Accordingly, the historicist placed great stock on the permanent value of the literary and cultural achievements of the Jewish spirit, as this was expressed at different times and places in Jewish history.

> Unlike the Reformers, they were unwilling to cut away the bulk of this slowly evolved tradition in one radical excision. Unlike the Orthodox, they did not regard every jot and tittle of the tradition as of equal (and divine) authority. Their position was, rather, that the tradition contained the responses of the Jewish spirit to the conditions of Jewish life in other times and places, and that any novelty of response in their own age had to be in consonance with the spirit revealed in the tradition as well as with contemporary needs. They were not opposed to change as such, but they insisted that the guiding principles of change had to be discovered within the experience of the Jewish people rather than outside it.[34]

> The reinstitution of the Jewish community, in some form, became a major objective of [the historicist's] work. All Jews, regardless of their "party" affiliations, shared in the millenial Jewish tradition, had a common concern for the fate of Jewry in the present age, and bore a responsibility for the transmission and preservation of Judaism in the future. Historical continuity itself is the factor transcending contemporary divergences and, therefore, the constitutive principle of the Jewish community.[35]

In time the historical school evolved toward the Conservative point of view, placing increasingly greater emphasis on traditional practices and observances, such as the observance of the sabbath, dietary laws, Jewish education, political Zionism, and the importance of the Hebrew language.

Conservative Judaism, as it presently exists, was first explicitly formulated by the chief rabbi of Dresden, Zechariah Frankel (1801–1875) during the 1840s. Frankel sought to establish his approach "by scientific research based on positive-historical foundations,"[36] and, while Frankel was never entirely clear about what he meant by "positive-historical" (he seemed to have been using "positive" in the sense that Comte employed it, as a synonym for "scientific," but his concept of the "people" frequently seemed to be redolent of Durkheim's quasi-mystical concept of "collective consciousness"),[37] Frankel's "positive-historical Judaism" became, as Louis Ginzberg has remarked, "the shibboleth of the party founded by him."[38] In all events, and as Joseph Blau notes, Frankel attempted to separate "the religious question of whether this particular tradition still expressed a living reality in the Jewish soul from the scholarly question of its origin."[39]

> [Frankel's] studies of the history of Jewish law tried to discover what needs of the spirit of the Jewish people were given overt form through the

law. Behind this effort to understand lay the conviction that Judaism is the religious expression of the spirit of the Jewish people—its "total popular will."[40]

The basic objective of the Conservative movement was to mediate between the extremes of Reform and Orthodoxy, to establish a reunified Jewish community that transcended the divisive influence of particular doctrines and ideologies. The term "Conservative," remarked Cyrus Adler, one of the leaders in defining the initial direction of the Conservative movement, "is a general term which nearly everybody uses but which is, I believe, technically applied to those congregations which have departed somewhat in practice from the Orthodox, but not to any great extent in theory."[41] To this, states Blau, should be added the comment of still another of the basic authors of Conservative Judaism in America, Solomon Schechter (1850–1915) who held that the American-born second generation of Jews "accept all the ancient ideas, but they want modern methods, and this, on the whole, may be the definition of Conservative Judaism."[42]

It is, however, a mistake to view Conservative Judaism in America from the standpoint of only its leading intellectual proponents. "It is," states Blau, "the laity to whom we must turn to find out what Conservative Judaism really means, because much of the impulse to the development of a Conservative organization came from the laity and because (apart from the [Jewish Theological Seminary of America] and its offshoot, the Rabbinical Assembly) Conservative Judaism has been dominated by the ideas and the motivations of its lay members."[43]

What, then, is the meaning of Conservative Judaism to its laity? In the first place, it is an identification that can be maintained in consonance with other identifications. The members of Conservative congregations basically identify with middle-class American values, one of which is membership in a religious organization. The Orthodox synagogue retains behavior patterns which, in America, are identified as lower-class, though they may not have been so in the time and place of their origin. The Reform synagogues, permitting middle-class identification, provide a less satisfactory sense of Jewish identification, especially for those whose family background and upbringing was within Eastern European Orthodoxy. The Conservative Jewish identification is, if the distinction may be allowed, more ethnic than religious. It emphasizes a feeling of "Jewishness" rather than a practice of Judaism. Certain customs tend to be stressed as evidence of "Jewishness" while others, equally grounded in tradition, are disregarded. A special aura of sanctity attaches to food customs and dietary laws, probably because of their association with childhood. In the homes of many members of Conservative congregations, some of the dietary laws are observed, while others are disregarded; many who maintain fairly strict observance in their homes make no pretense of conforming to the dietary laws when they eat in restaurants or in the homes of others. There is a high percentage of holiday observance and far less Sabbath observance. Hebrew schooling, to some degree, for children is felt to be virtually obligatory, but the participation of the parents in Jewish cultural activities is far less common.[44]

FIGURE A1–1
THE THREE TRADITIONS WITHIN JUDAISM

ORTHODOX	CONSERVATIVE	REFORM
Judaicity as the ultimate source of Jewishness	Jewishness as the ultimate source of Judaicity	Attempt to move toward a contemporary redefinition of Jewishness and Judaism, as well as to redefine the relationship between the two
Judaism as a total and encompassing way of life	General adherence to traditional beliefs but some variations from traditional observances and rituals; generally more traditional in belief than in practices	Adaptation of traditional beliefs and practices in accordance with the "spirit of the age"
Judaism as a composite of belief and practice		
Scriptural exegesis over theology and speculative philosophy	Novelty and innovations acceptable if consonant with the dominant spirit of the Jewish people as a continuous and collective entity	The belief that "change" is a central characteristic of the Jewish tradition, that novelties and innovations are fully within the spirit of Judaism; Judaism as a constantly evolving religion—"continuous revelation"
Torah as interpreting the "spirit of the age" and not the contrary; progress as allied to religion and not vice versa		
General adherence to Maimonide's traditional thirteen Jewish articles of belief, including the belief that God punishes evil, that he will send a personal Messiah, and that he will resurrect the dead	Judaism defined as the religious expression of the Jewish people, the Jewish *Volksgeist* determined by the "totality of Israel" (the continuity of the Jewish people throughout history and across various cultures); religion as a function of cultural ethos (ethnic identity)	Replacement of Jewish religious nationalism (Jewishness as a corporate identity of a chosen people with a specific historic mission) with the concept of a Jewish religious community of individual believers characterized by shared personal concerns
Authoritative belief in a code of Jewish laws compiled by Joseph Karo in 1565 (*Shulḥan Arukh*); a generally static and antihistorical orientation	The Jews as a special people with a corporate identity and a divine mission—religious nationalism	Religion as a personal and individualistic experience rather than as a corporate enterprise
		Rejection of traditional belief in literal revelation; selective acceptance of biblical revelation
		General rejection of certain traditional beliefs, such as physical resurrection and the coming of a personal Messiah

Adherence to Judaic law as the highest ethical imperative

Adherence to the authority of the rabbinate (including traditional methods of rabbinical interpretation of scripture)

Redemption of mankind to be attained through the redemption of the Jewish people

The Jews as a distinctively "holy people" bound to a sacred covenant with God (religious nationalism)

Stress on Torah over God and Israel (as relates to the three traditional themes of Judaism: God, Torah, and Israel)

Stresses specifically Jewish scholarship and learning over general (secular) intellectual training

---

Strong emphasis on the authority of the laity in interpreting scripture; reduced reliance on traditional rabbinical authority

Emphasis on the permanent value of the literary and cultural monuments of the Jewish spirit, as expressed differently at different times and places

Stresses Israel (*K'lal Yisrael*) over Torah and God (in the three classic themes of Judaism)

Seeks approximate parity between specifically Jewish scholarship and learning, and secular intellectual training

---

Stresses the universal mission of Jewish people to redeem mankind over the restoration of Israel as a specific nation-state

Emphasizes general beliefs and conduct over traditional laws, rituals, and observances

Holds that beliefs and practices should be open to reason and critical scrutiny

Emphasizes universal applicability of Judaic principles over the more traditional "chosen people" doctrine

More predisposed to theological and philosophical speculation than either Orthodoxy or Conservatism

Stresses interfaith cooperation based on religious and ethical commonalities

Tends to favor the hope for a messianic age of Justice—where all nations will be united under one God in a common pursuit of truth, justice and peace—rather than the coming of a personal Messiah to restore the Jewish people

Stresses God over Torah and Israel (in the three traditional themes of Judaism)

Favors separation of church and state

Emphasizes general (secular) intellectualism over specifically Jewish scholarship and learning

RECONSTRUCTIONISM AND THE EMERGENCE OF "ETHNIC JEWISHNESS"

A special Jewish movement that is, in many respects, more closely related to Conservative Judaism than to either Orthodox or Reform, and yet which is perhaps most appropriately viewed as providing one of the most central theoretical rationales for what might be termed secular "ethnic Jewishness," is the "reconstructionist" approach formulated by Mordecai Kaplan (1881–   ).

Kaplan, who was deeply influenced by the philosophy of John Dewey and who also appears to have been profoundly affected by the social philosophy of Émile Durkheim, tends to regard all religion, including Judaism, as the apotheosis of culture, the highest expression and most spiritualized manifestation of the "collective consciousness" of a particular people. For Kaplan, then, communal life is the source of worship and not, as is frequently thought, the other way around. In the spirit of Dewey, he sees believing as primarily a by-product of acting, rather than the contrary.

For Kaplan, who is ultimately a scientific naturalist, there is no personal God in the traditional sense, and Torah is not divinely revealed or supernatural. Rather, Judaism is the "advancing civilization of the Jewish people."[45] As Blau states:

> Kaplan follows the French sociologists in seeing religion as primarily an affair of the group, rather than of individuals. A central reality of the Jewish tradition is neither God nor the Torah, but Israel, the Jewish people. The individuality of the individual Jew is a product of the group life of the Jewish people. There is an organic connection of the individual and the group.[46]

Reconstructionism requires ... that we recognize the qualities of the times in which we live and reinterpret Judaism so that it can serve as a guide to living in the world.

*   *   *

... [Kaplan] says that an "objective and adequate rationale for Judaism of our day . . . has to *select* from the Judaism of the past those beliefs and practices which, either in their original or in a reinterpreted form, are compatible with what we now recognize to be authentic." What we now recognize as authentic must cohere with our other knowledge; it must not be a special compartment which we open only on those occasions conventionally called "religious" and keep tightly closed all the rest of the time.[47]

For Kaplan the highest value is individual self-actualization. *God* expresses "the highest ideals for which men strive and, at the same time, points to the objective fact that the world is so constituted as to make for the realization of those ideals."[48] *Faith* in the sovereignty of God is viewed as "faith that in mankind there is manifest a power which, in full harmony with the nature of the physical universe, operates for the regeneration of human society."[49] There is no personal and omnipotent God, then, and the cosmic process is finite and in a state of continuous self-perfection. Man is part of this process, however, and, through his "enthusiasm for living,"[50] he can help to shape the universe itself in his own progressively rational image.

The Jewish people in America have been secularized, and they live in a secular society. It is therefore in the highest interests of Jewish religion to stress Jewish secular culture. Indeed, Judaism is primarily an ethical enterprise in which a special people has sought to perfect itself through a rational-democratic way of life founded upon an inspired tradition. The hope for the future of Judaism lies in the democratic reconstruction of the Jewish community itself.

> Every organized Jewish community will have a general membership, a democratically representative governing council that shall determine its policies, an administrative committee and executive officers to supervise the execution of these policies, various functional bureaus to direct the day-to-day activities of the community under the control of the council, and organizations for specific Jewish purposes such as already exist.[51]

Horace Kallen and Isaac Berkson

A somewhat different tradition of ethnic Jewishness is represented in the writings of individuals like Horace Kallen and Isaac Berkson. Largely inspired, like Kaplan, by the philosophy of John Dewey, both Kallen and Berkson hold to the notion that cultural diversity is intrinsic to a fully realized democratic way of life, and that Jewish ethnicity is a legitimate form of cultural identification within the larger context of American society.

Kallen, a Harvard-educated American Jew, argues that a culturally pluralistic society is a natural state for human beings with differing needs, and that the development of cultural differences should be encouraged. He conceives of an American nation consisting of a voluntary "Federation of Nationalities" united into a single state. "The American way," states Kallen,

> is the way of orchestration. As in an orchestra, the different instruments, each with its own characteristic timbre and theme, contribute distinct and recognizable parts to the composition, so in the life and culture of a nation, the different regional, ethnic, occupational, religious, and other communities compound the different activities to make up the national spirit.[52]

Like Kallen, Berkson, who served as supervisor of schools and extension activities for the Bureau of Jewish Education, disagrees with the traditional American "melting pot" ideal. Unlike Kallen, however, Berkson emphasizes individual self-determination over ethnic self-determination as such. While he, like Kallen, seeks to preserve ethnic communities,

> his primary concern was with reducing, if not eliminating, the forces in the large society that would pressure a minority to either dissolve or perpetuate itself. This means that if an ethnic community decides to eliminate itself, or if an individual member of the ethnic community decides to leave the group and join the dominant group, such a decision should be accepted as proper and legitimate....[53]

With respect to Judaism, both Kallen and Berkson represent a less fervent and mystical approach to ethnic Jewishness than that presented by Kaplan. Both are less concerned with Jewish cultural autonomy than with the more encompassing question of cultural pluralism in general, and both would be in substantial agreement with the statement put forth by the National Coalition for Cultural Pluralism in 1971, which held that "cultural pluralism" is

> a state of equal co-existence in a mutually supportive relationship within the boundaries or framework of one nation of people of diverse cultures with significantly different patterns of belief, behavior, color, and in many cases with different languages. To achieve cultural pluralism there must be unity with diversity. Each person must be aware of and secure in his own identity, and be willing to extend to others the same respect and rights that he expects and enjoys himself.[54]

Viewed as a whole, encompassing both Kaplan's "reconstructionism" and the secular-nationalist orientation of individuals like Kallen and Berkson, the contemporary ethnic Jewish orientation can be characterized in five ways:

1. It stresses "Jewishness," as an ethnic identification with a distinctive cultural orientation, over Judaic religious beliefs and practices.
2. It seeks a contemporary non-Judaic definition of "Jewishness."
3. It tends to view Jewish communal life as a source of Judaic religion and not vice versa; it sees Judaism as merely one aspect of the evolving culture of the Jewish people.
4. It tends to be secular and naturalistic, rejecting the supernatural assumptions of traditional religion.
5. It seeks to reestablish the traditional Jewish sense of ethnic identity and community as a way of restoring the historical, moral, and political vision of the Jewish people.

THE ETHICS OF JUDAISM

Whether or not there is a special ethical tradition that is distinctively "Jewish"— a question that frequently recurs in discussions of Judaism and Jewishness—is open to debate, but it merits some discussion. Jews, and especially secular Jews, constitute a disproportionate number of those involved in various movements working for social justice on behalf of the oppressed throughout the world, and it is often Jews who constitute the most visible and aggressive leaders of these movements.

In essence, there appear to be two basic moral traditions in Judaism. There is still inherent in much Judaic thought a sort of intellectual authoritarianism that seems to stem back to the period from about 1000 B.C. (with David's establishment of the Kingdom) until the destruction of the Second Temple by the Romans in 70 A.D. During this era, religious authority was centered in the Temple and controlled by a hereditary caste of priests, and secular power was invested either in traditional monarchical or theocratic arrangements.

The period beginning with the dispersion, during which there was no Temple and no hereditary priesthood, and the Jews were without political power (except within their own self-governing communities), was essentially a period of intellectual and political liberalism within Judaism (or, at least, as compared to the period before the Babylonian conquest). During the dispersion, the Jews lived primarily in self-governing communities; their synagogues were similarly autonomous and directed by teachers (rabbis) rather than priests, and even God took on a much less imperial presence than before, being viewed far more as a merciful source of solace, a redeemer, than as an avenger.

Obviously, elements of both of these traditions coexist in contemporary Judaism, but the emphasis has clearly shifted in the rational-democratic direction that was laid down during the diaspora rather than that which is much more characteristic of "Old Testament" authoritarianism.

When it comes to the question of ethics, it is important to note that the Judaic tradition has characteristically been more concerned with the question of *justice* than with the more characteristic Christian theme of *love*. Indeed, it is interesting to contrast the Christian love-ethic—"Do unto others as you would have others do unto you"—with the Judaic "justice-ethic." Needless to say, there are a vast number of interpretations of what constitutes "justice" within the Jewish tradition, and the entire topic is extremely complicated and controversial.

For practical purposes, however, the Judaic concept of justice, with its corresponding notion of the just man, is perhaps best summarized in Hillel's famous definition of Judaism, which was quoted earlier: "What is hateful to yourself do not to your fellow-man. That is the whole Torah. All the rest is commentary. Now go and study."

The essence of Hillel's definition is contained in the first sentence. While the Christian ethic is phrased positively (or prescriptively)—as an imperative to change others in one's own vision of what constitutes the "good," the Hillel concept is essentially phrased negatively (or proscriptively) as a call for judicious non-action: one should refrain from doing that which he would find antithetical to his own best interests if he were to find himself in the same situation as the other.

The difference between the two ethical traditions is not insignificant. The difficulty with the Christian love-ethic—as many commentators have noted—is that it potentially gives a person license to coerce another *for the benefit of the other* if one views the other as being basically ignorant or in error. Thus, if I have found consolation in Christ, I may construe my Christian duty to lead you toward the same realization—whether you like it or not—because I am morally enjoined to provide you with the same opportunity to find eternal life in Christ, which has been the supreme joy in my own life; I am morally constrained to do good *to you* and *for you*. The problem with "doing unto others" is that, as the old saying has it, "tastes vary." What you would do unto others, others may not choose to have done to them, and vice versa.

The Judaic justice-ethic, on the other hand—at least in Hillel's liberal construction—basically enjoins a person not to act in the best interests of the other (as the Christian might perceive these interests to exist) but, rather, *not* to act in such a way *as he would not like to be acted upon* (regardless of his particular notion of what constitutes *good* and *positive* action).

At basis, then, the Judaic justice-ethic differs from the Christian love-ethic in four basic respects:

1. The justice-ethic is phrased as an ethic that enjoins nonaction—refraining from evil, rather than action (the active pursuit of good behavior intended directly to benefit others). It is always an *indirect* pursuit of the good.

2. As such, it is both more specific and, at the same time, less directive than the Christian admonition. Consensus about what constitutes bad or negative behavior—behavior leading to death, distress, or deprivation—is probably far broader than that pertaining directly to good or positive behavior. There are far fewer arguments about categorical *disvalues* than about categorical *values*—probably because disvalues are more directly related to basic and intractable biological realities and are therefore less susceptible to personal or cultural distortion than are values framed in a more positive sense.

3. The justice-ethic can be construed as a positive ethic, but only with some difficulty and only by altering the basic nature and direction of Hillel's fundamental admonition. In other words, it is entirely possible to follow a line of reasoning such as the following:

I believe that a personal God revealed absolute truth to Abraham and to Moses.

My entire life and my happiness is founded upon my Judaic convictions, which are, in turn, based upon these beliefs.

Therefore, if I were unenlightened or misinformed, I would find it hateful for anyone possessing such knowledge to withhold it from me or to fail to convince me of its transcendent truthfulness.

Accordingly, I am enjoined to convince one and all of the ultimate truth of the Judaic point of view, to convert the unfortunate unbelievers to the Truth.

The difficulty with this line of reasoning is twofold. First, it misrepresents the actual situation. It transmutes the unenlightened other into an enlightened other, by saying, in effect, that, if I knew what I presently know, I would want the other to convert me so that I could be a good Jew and therefore not be subjected to the anguish growing out of ignorance or error. In point of fact, however, what Hillel's admonition suggests is that I should not do unto others what I would not have them do unto me *if I were the other*—that is, if I were unenlightened or living in error.

In other words, for Hillel, coerced conversion is intrinsically hateful to the unconverted regardless of its intent and regardless of its (conceivably) positive consequences in the long run. What Hillel advocates is refraining from behavior that would be perceived by the other, as he assumedly experiences himself, as hateful or negative. He does not countenance loving ''violations'' of the other's integrity in behalf of still another person's perception of what constitutes the other's best interests. He asks a person always to perceive the situation on the basis of a hypothetical identification with the other *as he actually is,* empathizing with the other *as other* and acting accordingly.

In addition, Hillel clearly emphasizes the negative: Do *not* do the hateful. If he had meant ''Do unto others as you would have others do unto you,'' because unless you do so, your action could ultimately lead to hateful consequences, he would in all likelihood have expressed himself quite differently.

4. Hillel's concept, by logical implication, places its central emphasis on the autonomy of the individual. It says, in effect: Avoid evil (which is more or less self-evident and universally recognized), but do not force your concept of the good on others. What one *should do* is not directly prescribed.

Finally, the last sentence in Hillel's famous definition, "Now go and study," is of central importance. To discover what one should do, one must study, one must apply reason to the central questions of conduct, using the best reasoning from the past ("commentary") as one's guide. In a sense, then, the concept of "justice" viewed as an essentially negative concept of noninterference—when taken in conjunction with the positive admonition to study—gives rise to the ideal of autonomous reason: the highest good is to allow each person to choose for himself while exercising informed reason as the paramount means for making appropriate kinds of choices. When applied to society in general, this tends to translate into rational-democratic self-determination.

The fundamental Jewish tendency toward *social justice,* defined in the negative phraseology of Hillel, probably predisposes more toward political liberalism than political radicalism, because of its emphasis on allowing the other person full rational authority to determine his own course of action within very broad limits. On the other hand, the negative ethic can also be construed as possessing positive (or directive) implications and frequently has been. Thus, to refrain from coming to the aid of the suffering is to cause distress, which is clearly not countenanced in Hillel's concept of justice.

Phrased somewhat differently, Hillel's concept of justice, while focused on nonaction, actually implies two types of ethical response. First, one should not do that which is hateful—"sins of commission." Second, one should not do that which causes or sustains a hateful or distressing action that is already under way by failing to do anything whatsoever—"sins of omission." In other words, Hillel abjures prescribing how the other should live, but he strongly admonishes against doing that which would (by commission) cause distress or (by omission) sustain distress that already exists. The latter case is capable of serving as a potent rationale for social activism in the cause of social justice.

Ethical Judaism and Ethical Jewishness

It is sometimes held that there is a position that might be termed "ethical Judaism," which is closely related to still another orientation that constitutes a sort of "ethical Jewishness." Whether there actually is a special ethical tradition that is distinctively "Judaic" as apart from the Judaic religion as such is open to debate. Many people would take the position that "ethical Judaism" is the position which holds that the essence of Judaism/Jewishness is the unique moral vision of a "just society" characterized by the establishment of the Kingdom of Truth, Justice and Peace among men.

The exact nature and varieties of this tradition are open to much dispute, but two basic types of Judaic/Jewish ethics are often identified: (1) *supernaturalistic ethical Judaism* ("ethical Judaism"), which holds that the Decalogue is authoritative in the sense of being divinely inspired—that is, the Ten Commandments are the essential spirit of Judaism, and all other Jewish laws, rituals and observances are only "signs of the covenant," and (2) *naturalistic ethical Judaism* ("ethical Jewishness"), which holds that the Jews are not a chosen people, but that they have been inspired throughout history with a singular sense of moral mission and ethical idealism that is perhaps best embodied in the Decalogue, but which is perhaps even better summed up in Hillel's famous definition, which already has been stated.

Supernaturalistic ethical Judaism is a moral fundamentalism based upon an absolute code of ethics which, for all practical purposes, is not substantially different than the corresponding sort of supernaturalistic ethical Christianity. The naturalistic orientation, based upon Hillel's "negative" ethic—which enjoins nonaction (refraining from evil) more than action (the active pursuit of good behavior intended to benefit others directly, as in the Christian "golden rule")—seems to lead toward more of a "situation ethics" than toward the strictures of a conventional "code morality."

ZIONISM

Zionism, the belief that the Jews are destined to be restored to their homeland in Palestine, has a long history in Judaism. It first emerged during the Babylonian captivity of the Jewish people (586–538 BCE) and was closely associated with the belief in the imminent coming of the "anointed one" of God, the Jewish messiah prophesied in the scriptures who would lead the Jewish people to salvation, restoring the kingdom of the Jews in Israel at the end of time. The Zionist movement received a new impetus after the destruction of the Second Temple in 70 AD when the Jews began the great dispersion—viewed by most as an "exile"—from Israel and when they began to evolve from a political to a religious community.[55]

The prayer for the Messiah, and for the return to Jerusalem, became a permanent feature of traditional Jewish life. As Blau notes:

> Preachers in the synagogues invariably concluded their addresses with a formula invoking the miraculous redeemer: the most sacred service of the year, on the Day of Atonement, ended with the words "Next year in Jerusalem". . . . prayers for restoration were incorporated into every Jewish service. Religion and nationality were so welded together that it became impossible to separate the spiritual elements from the political. For all its universality, Judaism developed as a religious nationalism.[56]

Zionism is scarcely a simple movement, however, and it is important to bear in mind that there are at least three basic concepts that are, in some sense, "Zionist":

1. political Zionism—which may be either religious or secular in nature—which seeks the restoration (or, as of the present, "continuation") of a politically independent Jewish Israel, generally through secular means;

2. supernatural Zionism, which holds to the more traditional belief in a miraculous return to the homeland and the restoration of political sovereignty under the leadership of the prophesied Messiah, and

3. what might be termed "spiritual Zionism," which envisions not a reinstituted Jewish state but the advent of a messianic age in which the entire world will become spontaneously perfected as a new and universal Zion through the enlightened moral and religious consciousness of a perfected Judaism.

Political Zionism

There are actually two forms of political Zionism: that which is religiously inspired and that which is essentially secular in nature. Even with respect to *religious* political Zionism, there appear to be two basic traditions: (1) that which functions as a sort of religious nationalism, seeing the establishment of a Jewish state as the fulfillment of scriptural prophecy; and (2) that which views the Jews as basically a religious community rather than as a political entity but which sees the establishment of a Jewish state as a necessary means to the realization of Judaism's "spiritual" mission to the rest of the world.

There is, however, no significant Jewish equivalent to Christianity's yearning for a "heavenly Zion," a promised land in a supernatural realm rather than in an earthly sphere. Restoration as a spiritual ideal—something to be experienced in another dimension of being (generally after death)—is not a central tradition in Judaism. Even Jews who posit the coming of a personal Messiah, the apocalyptic restoration of the Israeli nation, and the physical resurrection of all dead Jews to enjoy the millennial kingdom of God in association with the living, envision such a restoration as occurring in the physical land of Israel and not in a purely spiritual dimension.

Political Zionism of the secular sort is perhaps the dominant tradition in Zionism, and today the term "Zionism" is probably best reserved for those who advocate the restoration—or perhaps, more properly, the continued existence—of a politically independent Jewish state.

While there has been a long history of proto-Zionism in much the same tradition since the beginning of the nineteenth century (particularly through the activities of such men as Yehudah Alkalai, Zvi Kalischer and Moses Hess), this tradition of Zionism is essentially the creation of Theodore Herzl (1860–1904). Herzl, a Westernized and secular "assimilated Jew" who covered the famous Dreyfus Trial in Paris for a Vienna paper, really gave birth to modern Zionism in his book *The Jewish State,* which was published in 1896. For Herzl, "Jewishness" was primarily an expression of anti-Semitic persecution. As Blau notes, "Herzl did not see the common link of the Jewish people as religion or language, land or 'blood.' It is, he insisted, affliction that establishes the cohesiveness of the Jewish people."[57]

His attempts to establish a Jewish state were really a secular nationalist approach to Zionism, a quite unsentimental attempt to develop a modern state (not necessarily in Palestine—both Uganda and Argentina were also considered) with the power to defend the Jews against continuous oppression by others. As Blau notes:

The resurgence, in the nineteenth century and after, of persecutions, pogroms, blood accusations, and "blood and soil" theories of nationalism destroyed the very conditions that have made Jewish acceptance of emancipation so easy. Thus Zionism begins in confrontation with modern irrationalism, a different aspect of the modern world from that faced by Reform and Neo-Orthodoxy.[58]

The forces facing Herzlian Zionism were further strengthened by the Balfour Declaration of 1917 in which Great Britain went officially on record as favoring "the establishment in Palestine of a national home for the Jewish people"[59] and by Hitler's persecution of the Jews, terminating in the Holocaust.

Supernatural Zionism

Supernatural Zionism is perhaps most apparent today in the Orthodox tradition, but even Orthodox Judaism contains serious differences of opinion with respect to the issue of Zionism. The differences lie primarily between the dominant *Mizrachi* group, who accept a religiously inspired political Zionism in place of the traditional "miraculous" restoration, and the *Agudat Israel* group, who continue to advocate traditional Messianic Zionism. This division continues, but the Agudat Israel movement has very little support at present in the United States. In the state of Israel itself secular Jews such as those in the Labor Zionist movement, are able to work in close cooperation with Orthodox members of the Mizrachi movement to advance common political goals. Interestingly enough, in contemporary Israel an entente between secular and religious Zionists exists. While only fifteen percent or less of the population in Israel is actively religious, the Orthodox wing of Judaism operates almost as an established church. Israel does not maintain freedom of religion for its Jewish citizens. There is no provision for civil marriage ceremonies, and the Orthodox groups have forced the government to adopt extremely rigorous Sabbath observances and dietary laws.

Spiritual Zionism

Spiritual Zionism, which is closely related to what is sometimes termed "ethical Judaism" or "ethical Jewishness," is the position which holds that, while the Jews will not be returned geographically to their traditional homeland through the leadership of a personal Messiah, the world in general will ultimately become enlightened through the religious consciousness of the Jews, ushering in a "messianic age," a utopian era in which the kingdom of God will exist on earth not through the reign of a personal Messiah but rather through the messianic spirit of a triumphant Judaism.[60]

For such individuals, as Samuel Holdheim has stated, "The negative understanding of dispersion gave way to a positive understanding, according to which dispersion was a necessary step in the fulfillment of Israel's mission."[61] "The mission of Israel is to spread the pure ethical teachings of Judaism among the nations of the world without, at the same time, destroying the individual characters of the nations—or of Judaism."[62]

It is the destiny of Judaism to pour the light of its thoughts, the fire of its sentiments, the fervor of its feelings upon all souls and hearts on earth.

Then all of these peoples and nations, each according to its soil and historic characteristics, will, by accepting our teachings, kindle their own lights, which will then shine independently and warm their souls. Judaism should be the seedbed of the nations filled with blessing and promise, but not a fully grown matured tree with roots and trunk, crowned with branches and twigs, with blossoms and fruit—a tree which is merely to be transplanted into a foreign soil .... Judaism wants to purify the languages of the nations, but leave to each people its own tongue. It wishes for one heart and one soul, but not for one sound and one tone.[63]

Contemporary Zionism

In America today the various Jewish groups take somewhat varying stances with respect to the dominant tradition of political Zionism (or Jewish nationalism).

Although Reform, Conservative, and Orthodox groups went through similar stages in the acceptance of the Zionist cause, they passed through these stages at different rates of speed. Zionists were, at first, a small party within each group. The great bulk of each group was either indifferent or opposed to Jewish nationalism. Within the Conservative Movement the shift to a Zionist majority came most rapidly and with least disruption. For a time some difficulty was felt about the problem of dual allegiance, to America and to Zion, but the Zionist emphasis, within the Conservative Movement, tended to be more cultural than political, so it was relatively easy to show that the true forms of nationalism were not in conflict. Once this resolution had been achieved, Conservative Jews had little trouble accepting Zionism, especially since the Conservative orientation was so largely directed toward the Jewish community. In both the Reform and the Orthodox groups the difficulty was a more complicated one and far less easy to resolve.[64]

In the formulation of Reform Judaism in the late nineteenth century, the universal mission of Israel was seen as implicitly antithetical to political Zionism. Thus, in the Pittsburgh Platform of the American Reform movement, in 1885, the following statement occurs:

We recognize, in the modern era of universal culture of heart and intellect, the approaching of the realization of Israel's great Messianic hope for the establishment of the kingdom of truth, justice, and peace among all men. We consider ourselves no longer a nation, but a religious community, and therefore expect neither a return to Palestine, nor a sacrificial worship under the sons of Aaron, nor the restoration of any of the laws concerning the Jewish state.[65]

By 1937, however, the Reform lay organization, the Union of American Hebrew Congregations, came out in favor of "the obligation of all Jewry to aid [in building Palestine] as a Jewish homeland by endeavoring to make it not only a haven or refuge for the oppressed but also a center of Jewish culture and spiritual life."[66] In 1943 the Central Conference of American Rabbis finally passed a resolution asserting the compatibility of Zionism and Reform Judaism. Today each Reform congregation is free to determine its own stand on the question, but virtually all support the continued existence of the Israeli nation.

Prior to World War II, nationalistic Zionism was perhaps the most controversial issue within the American Jewish community. Zionism is still controversial but, since the state of Israel was established in 1948, virtually all religious Jews have rallied to the support of the reestablished Jewish nation despite whatever misgivings they might have had about the advisability of establishing such a state in the first place. There are, as mentioned, still some members of the Orthodox faction who oppose what they view as the politicalization—and, hence, secularization—of Judaism through the establishment of a modern nation-state, but these are a small minority at present (largely members of the Agudat group—many of whom live, ironically, in Israel) and, for all practical purposes, nationalistic Zionism has become tacitly accepted in all significant expressions of the Judaic/Jewish community. It is no longer the highly controversial matter that it was during the first part of the century.

Even proponents of religiously inspired political Zionism, such as the majority of the Orthodox and Conservative groups, support secular Zionism as one (if admittedly imperfect) step in the direction of establishing the prophesied Kingdom of Justice under the leadership of the coming Messiah. Among secular Jews, the ethnically oriented are generally predisposed to support the state of Israel. Even the nonethnic "secular internationalists" (sometimes called the "Jewish radicals") are supportive, if somewhat ambivalent, on the issue. They tend, on the whole, to see the state of Israel as a necessary evil, a protection against the irrational persecution of the Jews by other peoples in a world that is still (regrettably) dominated by pathological nationalism. At basis, then, "Jewish internationalists" tend to be supportive of Israel and are seldom willing to appear to be "anti-semitic semites" by coming out in active opposition to the continued existence of a Jewish homeland.

In short, the Zionist/anti-Zionist conflict has not entirely disappeared within the contemporary American Jewish community, but it has ceased to be a central issue, because virtually all self-identified Jews now tend to accept the Israeli state as a *fait accompli* and therefore tend to view it as an unavoidable aspect of contemporary Jewishness.[67]

JEWISH EDUCATION

Despite the differences that exist between the different orientations within contemporary Judaism, the Judaic religion is essentially one basic theme with variations. Accordingly, and as Neusner states: ". . . the entire structure of Jewish learning has got to be seen as essentially one and unified, interrelated and interdependent."[68] Always encouraging the dual purposes of knowledge and action—assuming that "the will to do presupposes a knowledge of what to do, obtainable only through proper instruction,"[69] Jewish education has, in the words of educational historians Frederick Eby and Charles Arrowood, ". . . outlasted every other system whatsoever [and is therefore] . . . the most successful educational experiment ever staged in the history of education."[70]

With respect to the overall nature of Jewish education probably most religious Jews would be in fundamental agreement with Rabbi Joseph Lookstein of (Orthodox) Yeshiva University. According to Lookstein, as Judah Pilch and Meir Ben-Horin state in their book *Judaism and the Jewish School,*

. . . Jewish education is characterized by five qualities: (1) Universality — Jewish education was open to all, to the rich and poor alike, to priest and layman. It did not necessarily limit itself to educating a special caste; (2) Maximalism—study was a lifelong process. It began in early childhood and it continued all through life; (3) Religious Motivation—Jewish education was more than a cultural enterprise. To engage in Jewish education was a precept of law, a commandment of the Torah; (4) Reverence for Learning—the scholar was the aristocrat of Jewish society. The teacher performed the most sacred function of Jewish life. The student received every possible encouragement; (5) Education is Jewish living—Jewish learning was more than absorption in an ancient culture. It was designed to encourage intelligent religious practice, to cultivate national loyalty and to emphasize ethical conduct.[71]

Historical Context

Judaism has always embraced the idea that education is the responsibility of the entire Jewish community. As Jewish historian Salo Baron notes:

Ever since the days of the Talmud, the legal maxim prevailed that a school was even more "sacred" than a synagogue and that, hence, a house of prayer could be converted into a house of learning but not the other way around. Asher ben Yehiel, one of the greatest medieval rabbis, whose decisions often became binding legal precedents, ruled that, if someone established a foundation for such religious purposes as a synagogue or cemetery, the community might at any time alter the terms of the foundation and use its funds for educational purposes, even against the will of the donor. But, if on the other hand, the foundation had been established for the sake of Jewish education, it must never be diverted to any other more strictly religious uses. In short, in the hierarchy of values, in the hierarchy of the 613 commandments of Judaism (the *taryag mitswot*) education was considered on a par with all the other commandments put together.[72]

*   *   *

Centuries later, a great rabbi, Ezekiel Landau of Prague, voiced a widely accepted explanation that the existence of a communal "school for children" was the main cause for Jewish survival through the ages of severe persecutions. What is more, unbiased observers will recognize in retrospect the essential validity of this claim.[73]

In a similar sense, and as historian Julius Maller writes:

The survival of Jews and Judaism is in a large measure due to the continuous emphasis, throughout Jewish history, upon the transmission of ideas and practices from old to young and from one generation to another. The educative process, an integral part of all varieties of religion and culture, was at the very core of Judaism and the Jewish way of living since biblical times.
    The quest for an understanding of the meaning of life and the sustained effort to pass that meaning on from generation to generation has eternally motivated Jewish endeavor. This searching for knowledge, which in its

practical aspect we call education, served as a central factor in Jewish life. The chief preoccupation of the Jewish sages of all time was learning and teaching—Torah and Talmud.

During the First and Second Commonwealth, for approximately a thousand years of Jewish self-government—with one brief interruption, the Babylonian Exile—the process of developing the way of the good life and teaching it to the people was the major responsibility of the nation's judges, priests, and prophets. After the conquest of Palestine by the Roman legions and the first dispersal of the Jews, *The Book* became the portable homeland. The loss of territorial unity strengthened the urge to preserve spiritual continuity. Community of ideas took the place of physical community; indeed, the Jews became known as "the People of the Book." The transmission of a complete system of ideas became the bulwark against disintegration, and education moved to the head of the Jewish table of values.[74]

During the middle ages, Jewish communities were scattered widely across Europe and no fixed pattern of Jewish education prevailed. On the other hand, as a general rule

> . . . the training of children started in the home, continued in an elementary school, and from there the pupil was sent to a religious academy or college, over which a famous scholar presided. Practical training began with active participation in holiday services and ceremonies.[75]

Historians point out that intellectually the Jews suffered no medieval relapse into ignorance, that they were more educated than those among whom they lived, and that even the ordinary Jew knew the Scriptures better than the churchmen of that time. The Jews contributed in large measure to the rebirth of civilization and Europe, disseminating Greek culture as interpreted by the Arabs. Jews were prominent in the Spanish cultural revival in the early renascence in Provence and in Sicily under Frederick II.[76]

The migrations of Jews from western to eastern Europe occurred in the centuries following the Middle Ages. In Russia and Poland, and in neighboring countries, where the vast majority of Jews settled, education continued to be the consuming interest of the Jewish communities.

The educational institutions that grew up in east European countries were similar to those in other countries from which the Jews came. At the beginning of the sixteenth century there was a huge wave of immigration from Bohemia into Poland, and the Jews who came from Bohemia and Germany brought with them their language, which developed into Yiddish, as well as their culture and communal organizations.

*   *   *

The educational institutions consisted of the *heder* and the *Yeshiva*. The curriculum of the *heder* included the Bible with its Hebrew commentaries, Hebrew prayers and other Hebrew books. The *Yeshiva* developed the lay scholar and the learned rabbi; it emphasized a knowledge of the sources of Jewish literature. To the extent that the Pentateuch, Mishna, and especially

Talmud and the Codes were the means of regulating the life of the Jewish people, their study had functional value, preparing its students for life in the Jewish community.[77]

Throughout the history of Jewish education certain basic ideas about education have been continually stressed and survive to the present. Among these basic ideas, notes historian Maller, are the following:

1. An abiding faith in the efficacy of education, that human character is modifiable and improvable.
2. Learning and doing must be integrated; knowledge of ethics must be expressed in proper conduct.
3. Education is a continual process, to be carried on literally from the cradle to the grave.
4. Environment is an important factor in the educative process.
5. Education, to be most effective, must start with the very young.
6. Individual differences among pupils must be recognized; tests reveal differences in knowledge and convictions.
7. The process of education must be gradual from the known to the unknown, from the simple to the complex, and from the immediate to the remote.
8. Responsibility for education rests with the parents and the community.
9. Training for work is regarded as both essential and honorable.
10. The teaching of history illustrates the continuity and meaning of Jewish experiences.

Jewish teaching emphasized above all else that study is essential and worth while and must be brought to the people for guidance in everyday affairs. The emphasis was definitely on the pragmatic aspects of education. The Greek concepts of contemplation or dialogue as forms of diversion and enjoyment were uncommon in Jewish lore.[78]

Contemporary American Jewish Education

In America today there tend to be three basic types of Jewish schools that offer instruction below the college or university levels. "Intensive Jewish schools" (such as the *yeshivot* of the Orthodox and the Solomon Schechter Day Schools of the Conservatives) offer Jewish education as a substitute for the secular public schools. Most day schools are Orthodox in ideological orientation and mainly enroll students at the elementary level. The Conservative movement also supports some day schools. Its system of Solomon Schechter Day Schools has sought to attract children from less religious homes who would not attend an ideologically Orthodox school. The Reform movement sponsors some day schools, but has traditionally favored part-time Jewish schooling.[79] These intensive Jewish schools, according to Neusner, "provide for the Jewish elite [and] are the means of education for the most committed Jews.... [creating] an informed laity, Jews who read Jewish books and keep

Jewish laws...."[80] Approximately 80 percent of all day school students attend Orthodox-sponsored day schools (in 1967) and about 80 percent of these were enrolled in the elementary level (including kindergarten) programs.[81]

"Supplemental Jewish schools"—generally supplementing public school institutions with part-time programs—are usually offered by synagogues or Jewish community centers anywhere from one to five afternoons a week. These schools—often called "synagogue schools," although they are not necessarily associated with particular synagogues—generally have programs at the primary, secondary, and adult levels. Voluntary in character, such schools generally offer elementary and somewhat superficial religious instruction to the masses, but, as Neusner notes, such schools are perhaps the most important and influential of the Jewish schools because the vast majority of American Jews who get any Jewish education, however limited, get it in the synagogue schools (and their community-sponsored counterparts).[82]

Finally, there are "informal Jewish educational programs" that include youth movements of all sorts—programs of various kinds in Jewish community centers, extracurricular activities in synagogue schools, Jewish camps (such as the Conservative movement's Ramah Camps), and so on.

The different kinds of Jewish schools have tended to attract substantially different populations of Jewish students.

> "Intensive Jewish schools" (day schools and *Yeshivot*) have generally attracted first generation men and women from all kinds of home backgrounds. *Chedarim* generally enrolled only first generation men, again from all kinds of home backgrounds. Supplemental schools have attracted second, third and fourth generation men and women, especially those raised in "more Jewish" home environments. Three-day to five-day supplemental schools have been most attractive to Jewish men, regardless of their family background or generation. One-day and two-day supplemental schools have been most popular among later generation Jews, especially women. In general, sex and generation are the principal factors affecting the type of school individuals have attended.[83]

THE PHILOSOPHICAL BASES OF JEWISH EDUCATION

It is difficult to generalize about Jewish educational philosophy, because not a great deal of systematic study has been directed to this area, and, as Ben-Horin states, "no book-length systematic treatment of Jewish education has been completed to date."[84] On the other hand, most of the contemporary interpretations of Judaism have corresponding points of view that relate to education, and there are also several Jewish educational philosophies that are far more concerned with "Jewishness," in a secular or quasi-secular sense, than with "Judaicity" as such. In general, there would appear to be four basic approaches to contemporary Jewish education in America: (1) Orthodox, (2) Conservative, (3) Reform, and (4) Ethnic.

Orthodoxy and Education. Orthodoxy, as previously discussed, is a Judaic orientation that encompasses a number of different points of view. Regardless of differences, however, Orthodox Jews advocate what Ben-Horin terms "revelation-centered re-construction."[85]

> Only *divine knowledge* can elevate secular learning "to a higher spiritual status." The Torah is not a mere constitution or code. It is the law of God, "represents divine authority and contains the highest wisdom and loftiest truths." It is "sufficient for our time and should control and guide the entire life and destiny of our people." The problem is how to bring back to "our theocracy, our sacred mode of living," those of our people who have become alienated from it. "It is our duty to reconstruct our lives so that they are in agreement with the eternal traditions."
>
> The Torah ideals such as the fatherhood of God, brotherhood of man, and sanctity of our lives can become meaningful only when integrated with a Judaism "practiced in accordance with the basic principles of the *Shulhan Aruch*." Our lives must be reconstructed, not our traditions.[86]

Accordingly, for the Orthodox the supreme purpose of education is to study, master, and live by Torah-Talmud.

Conservatism and Education. Conservatism, as discussed earlier, places its chief emphasis on the Jewish people as a continuing corporate entity. In the words of Solomon Schechter, one of the formative influences in defining the Conservative movement

> Since . . . the interpretation of Scripture or the Secondary Meaning is mainly a product of changing historical influences . . . some *living body* . . . is best able to determine the nature of the Secondary Meaning. This living body, however, is not represented by any section of the nation, or any corporate priesthood, or rabbihood, but by the collective conscience of Catholic Israel as embodied in the Universal Synagogue. . . . This Synagogue . . . must also retain its authority as the sole true guide for the present and the future.[87]

In terms of educational philosophy, as well as in the realm of religious convictions, the Conservative movement is difficult to pin down. It seems to range all the way from what Pilch and Ben-Horin characterize as "the Hebraic-Essentialist" position at the "conservative" end of the continuum, to a position roughly equivalent to that taken by the less progressive members of the Reform movement, at the other. The Hebraic-Essentialist position holds that "the schools' chief function is the transmission of Judaism's literary Hebraic essentials." This implies "that main consideration is given to subject matter, especially Hebrew language and literature. . . [requiring] the inculcation of a predetermined body of subject matter and complex of attitudes. [T]he 'essentials' [are] stated in terms of materials to be taught rather than capacities to be released and refined."[88]

Reform and Education. Reform education, like Conservative educators, encompasses a wide range of ideas and attitudes. Thus, according to Pilch and Ben-Horin, Reform education

> . . . in common with other revelationists . . . [maintain] that the crucial fact in the life of the Jewish people is God's covenant with Israel. In some

way and for His own good reasons, He has chosen our forefathers and us, their spiritual heirs, so to order our lives as to reflect that original cove- nant, whether entered into, once and for all, at Sinai, or whether con- cluded at earlier or subsequent occasions, rare or frequent. All essential and characteristic Jewish values derived from this decisive experience of the covenant through which God linked Israel's destiny to His being. This includes values and ways of modern Jews which may be quite different from those formulated in ancient and medieval rabbinic writings.

The supreme purpose of Jewish education is the transmission to the young of the feeling for and the understanding of Judaism's chief loyalty—the loyalty to the covenant with God.[89]

According to Emanuel Gamoran, who has been called the chief architect of Reform Jewish education in America, the goal of Jewish education in America should be "the continuous and progressive socialization of the child into the Jewish group in harmony with the conditions of the new environment."[90] Such socialization, states Ben-Horin, denotes

1. preservation of the group,
2. adjustment to modernism—science and democracy,
3. adjustment to America—democratic government, social relations, eco- nomic system,[and]
4. functionalism—attention to present practice and belief.[91]

According to Gamoran,

. . . the core of our Jewish education in the future should consist of:

a. The great intrinsic values—especially those which Rabbi Max Kadushin has referred to as "value concepts"—Israel, Torah, God, Jus- tice, and the like.
b. The Hebrew language.
c. Jewish customs and traditions which are of cultural esthetic value.
d. Jewish literature, music, and art.
e. Jewish history interpreted as creative living on the part of the Jewish people.
f. Our relation to Israel.
g. Our relation to America and to mankind.

Our traditional level of learning should be encouraged and fostered but it should be made relevant, as it will be if we relate it to our own life and to the problems of our day.[92]

On the more "progressive" end of the Reform spectrum, is what Pilch and Ben-Horin term the "Communal-Hebraic-Progressive Viewpoint."[93]

The writers in this group may disagree on the place of religion in the curriculum, the interpretation of the Zionist idea, the role of the synagogue, and the stress on Hebrew. But they agree that the Jewish people constitute a world-wide community, that the State of Israel is both a fulfillment of an age-old dream and a most important factor in the en- hancement of Jewish life in the diaspora, that Hebrew is central in any scheme of Jewish education and that the Jewish community is greater than the sum of its component constituents (synagogues, civic groups, et cetera). They also hold in common the belief in progressive education, i.e., the truth that children and youth learn what they live as they themselves accept it to live by and that the school, therefore, is a place where living goes on and where each learner is helped to grow up to effective living within the social group. For the Jewish school this calls not only for opportunities of Jewish experience (holiday celebrations, club activities, Keren Ami, junior congregations and the like). It also calls for a democratic school atmosphere, for democratic teacher-pupil-home relationships and continuity of Jewish education beyond the elementary level.[94]

Ethnic Jewishness and Education. The ethnic Jewish approach to education encompasses three basic traditions:

1. the Jewish "reconstructionism" of Mordecai Kaplan,
2. the nationalist-secular orientation of such individuals as Horace Kallen and Isaac Berkson, and
3. the Yiddish-Progressive movement (as it existed during roughly the first half of this century).

The quasi-naturalistic *Jewish "reconstructionism"* of Kaplan, as previously discussed, holds that the highest good for anyone is self-realization as a person, but that, for the Jew, self-realization as a person is necessarily attained through the instrumentality of one's very involvement within the evolving "religious civilization" of the Jewish people. This civilization, "under science and democracy, . . . is entering a new stage of existence which requires fundamental reconstructions in community organization, in world-wide status, in theological affirmations."[95]

The supreme purpose of Jewish education according to [Kaplan and his followers] is to transform learners into competent and devoted pioneers and participants in the reconstruction of Jewish civilization, to the end that the Jewish people may once again experience a new birth of religio-cultural creativity.[96]

The principal aim to be kept in mind in the Jewish education of the American-Jewish child, from the standpoint of his maximum self-fulfillment as an American and as a Jew, is . . . to render the Jewish heritage relevant to his moral and spiritual needs, and to qualify him, when he matures, to establish the kind of Jewish communal environment that will provide opportunities for the satisfaction of those needs.[97]

Thus, for Kaplan, and as Pilch and Ben-Horin indicate,

. . . American Jews should live in two civilizations, the American and the Jewish, each supplementing the other. Dr. Kaplan stresses the need for Jewish education which makes for at-homeness in the three components of Judaism: the Jewish people as a transnational community of faith and fate; Jewish culture, comprising the products of Jewish creativity throughout the ages; and Jewish religion, understood as Israel's millennial faith in God, the Power that makes for salvation.[98]

The *naturalist-secular* orientation (generally associated with Kallen and Berkson) was perhaps most strongly influenced by the educational philosophy of John Dewey and by the educational methodology of Dewey's colleague William Heard Kilpatrick. This movement would generally like to see American Jews retain their identification as a distinctive subculture but would also emphasize the dynamics of social change. They look upon American Jews as a central part of a constantly evolving American community. Closely akin to what Pilch and Ben-Horin call the "Cultural-Progressive" outlook in Jewish education,"[99] the naturalist-secular representatives of the ethnic point of view hold that "transmission of the cultural heritage need not be the sole concern of the schools; its program should rather aim to develop in learners a desire to want to live creatively as Jews in the modern world."[100]

The *Yiddish-Progressive* movement in education, which first emerged in Eastern Europe, was largely focused in New York City around the Yiddish schools (particulary the Workmen's Circle Schools and the Sholem Aleichem Schools) organized through the Jewish Education Committee of New York around the time of the First World War. Among the central figures associated with this movement (and frequently working with the Workmen's Circle Teacher Institute, the Jewish People's University, and the Congress of Jewish Culture) were such well-known "Yiddishists" as Shmuel Niger, Yudel Mark, and Mark Bass. The movement still exists, but it is markedly less important today than it was during the period between the two world wars. Greatly weakened by the establishment of Hebrew as the official language of the new Jewish state in 1948, it continues to exert some influence on Jewish education.

During the height of its influence, in the period between the wars, the Yiddish-Progressive movement in American education could be characterized in six ways.

1. It generally advocated the establishment of secular Yiddish schools to advance the cause of secular American Jewishness. As S. Niger stated,

> Our problem is how to arouse the desire among American Jewry (and before that, among Jewish leaders), to live a cultural and creative life as Americans and as Jews. The influence of other Jewish centers can be effectively utilized here only if our own resources are first developed. The center of our deliberations and efforts must be American Jewry which is an integral part of our country, America, and at the same time an integral part of the Jewish people which is still a worldwide people. It would be a grievous error to make Israel (or, more accurately, to let it remain) the focal point or goal of our social and pedagogic thought. . . .[101]

American Jewishness, remarks Mark Yudel, is "a synthesis of separation from the world in otherness and confrontation with the world, even when it is hostile, in order to take from it all that is worth taking and in order, ultimately, to establish it so that life may become worthwhile."[102]

2. It strongly favored the kind of education that would be compatible with, and supportive of, the democratic and pluralistic nature of American society.

3. It was far more concerned with offering the kind of education suitable for Jews in the era of the dispersion than with advocating Zionist nationalism. It was, if anything, an anti-Zionist orientation that viewed Jewishness as an international culture and not as a national identity.

4. It was primarily an ethnic—or folk—orientation rather than an approach to Judaic religion in the conventional sense. It took a positive attitude toward lasting traditional values but tended to be unorthodox and anti-traditional with respect to conventional Judaic beliefs and practices. The Yiddish-Progressives advocated a selective traditionalism that, in Yudel's words, wished "to take only that which adds beauty, uplift, color and [did] not conflict with our freedom-loving spirit."[103]

As Ben-Horin notes, the central objective of the Yiddish School was

> [in Yudel's words] "to accustom the pupil to Jewish ways of behavior, to take him into the circle of Jewish thinking and caring, to awaken an innermost interest for Jewish customs, develop the feeling of linkage with Jewish destiny and, on later levels, to render it intellectually meaningful and strong." The subjects are Yiddish language and literature, *Tanakh* [Torah], Jewish history, Jewish holidays, the Land of Israel—all in the spirit of a this-worldly, that is democratic-relativistic, orientation.[104]

5. The movement was strongly influenced by socialist ideas, and particularly by those of Karl Marx. (It is interesting to speculate on the extent to which "Jewish socialism"—and particularly that of the Marxist variety—may not represent a secular translation of quite traditional Jewish ways of thinking. Certainly, for some secular Marxists, the intellectuals—someone has described "intellectualism" as an "ecumenical Jewishness"—have become the new Israel, the "chosen people." Out of this people have come certain prophets and messiahs [Marx, Lenin, Mao] who, through the scrupulous exegesis of previous scholarship and, perhaps more importantly, of history itself, have generated a compelling vision of reality, and have inspired scripture [such as *Das Kapital*] that both describes and prescribes, and which includes a central prophecy—the promise of a messianic age of justice [the classless society], which will come after a political apocalypse [the revolution]. During this coming age of justice, the people will become fully humanized—that is, intellectual—thereby becoming truly enlightened and capable of total rational autonomy, obviating the necessity for traditional authoritarian political restraints altogether.)

On the other hand, the Yiddish-Progressives tended to reject socialist-anarchist cosmopolitanism, just as they rejected bourgeois cosmopolitanism, viewing it as incompatible with the centrality of Jewish ethnic identity. As time went by, the movement became less concerned with the "Jewish worker's child"[105] and more concerned with the Jewish child as such, less "progressive" in the radical socialist sense and more ethnically Jewish.

6. As the name indicates, the movement placed a central emphasis on Yiddish language and literature over the Hebraist orientation of the more conventional Jewish schools. Deeply concerned with the culture of the Eastern European Jewry, who constituted the ethnic background for the numerical majority of American Jews, they felt that

> only in Yiddish, the language of a thousand years of Jewish life, can one understand the humaneness of the ordinary Jew, his faith, his character, the wisdom of the Jewish child, the love of the Jewish mother, the revolution which raised a generation to seek a full Jewish and human emancipation.[106]

Yiddish and Hebrew

The conflict between the Yiddishists and the Hebraists in Jewish education is not entirely resolved by any means, but the adoption of Hebrew as the official language of Israel has given the Hebraists a definite edge over those who advocate the centrality of Yiddish in Jewish education. Today most Jewish educators in America would probably agree with Samuel Dinin's bilingual orientation. "I believe," states Dinin,

> that Hebrew is an indispensable element in any kind of Jewish education. It is the language of our sacred writings, it is the language of modern-day Israel; it is the language of our national renaissance; it is the only common avenue of communication for people scattered over the entire world. Jewish education must enable Jews to make use of the Hebrew language and literature. I realize that Yiddish is the mother-tongue of millions of Jews, that it has created and is still creating a rich literature and a rich culture. I believe that Jews should be taught to use and enjoy the Yiddish language and literature wherever and whenever they can acquire both languages. If, however, it comes to a choice, I believe in the priority of Hebrew and Hebrew literature.[107]

There are, on the other hand, many Jewish educators who are not at all comfortable with the extreme emphasis placed on any kind of "foreign language" training—and particularly the extreme emphasis placed on Hebrew—as a prerequisite for effective Jewish education. As Jewish scholar Jacob Neusner comments:

> Why is it taken for granted that mastery of the Hebrew language is the single most important educational achievement? That criterion represents an expression of an ideology no less than does the stress in the traditional *Yeshivot* on the study of Talmud and related literature. I am not a Hebraist, I am a Judaist; to me, knowing Hebrew is a means, not an end. True, it is an indispensable means, but that is all. The Hebraist may suppose it is harder to learn Hebrew well than to learn anything else well, and that may be so. But I can make a case for the difficulty of studying Talmud, for one thing, or the theology of Hermann Cohen and Franz Rosenzweig, and I think these are far more important for the building of American Judaism than is reading a poem by Tchernichovsky or a short story by Hazaz, both more important and more Jewish. In my view the single most formidable obstacle in the development of the Hebrew colleges as centers of Jewish learning is the narrowness of their commitment to Hebraism, to the near exclusion of many other legitimate and productive modes of Jewish creativity.[108]

Jewish Education: Some Final Considerations

In terms of the ideological taxonomy employed here, virtually all of the more significant expressions of Judaism and Jewishness in education can be characterized as types of educational "intellectualism," advocating the attainment of religious and/or philosophical enlightenment through the perfection of reason. On the other hand, virtually all of the educational expressions of Judaism/Jewishness tend to combine this overriding commitment to intellectualism with other concerns as well. For religious Jews, study is holy—the central ritual of the faith. After the destruction of the Temple, the study of Torah replaced ritual sacrifice as the central divine service, and, with the elimination of the priestly class, the Jews became "a kingdom of priests and a holy nation."[109] In Judaism study is ritual piety. The learned Rabbi (teacher) *is* Torah, a living Torah.[110]

The Orthodox Jew clearly combines educational intellectualism with elements of educational fundamentalism and educational conservatism, but he is clearly more traditional in his approach than the Conservative Jew. In a similar sense, the Conservative Jew tends to be an educational conservative within the context of his dominant intellectualism, but he is clearly less traditional than the Orthodox and more conservative than the Reform. Both the Orthodox and Conservative are, in a sense, "conservative" (in the usual sense of that term) within a religious and cultural tradition that is profoundly committed to intellectual and scholarly ideals that are themselves normally viewed as "liberal."

What makes the Reform Jew appear to be more of an educational intellectualist than the Orthodox or Conservative is the fact that he defines "intellectualism" more in the secular *liberal arts* tradition than in the time-honored terms of Jewish scholarship and learning. Within Reform Judaism, the ambivalence between ethnic and/or religious conservatism on the one hand and critical inquiry on the other still exists, but the ideal of autonomous reason seems to have taken precedence over the demands for conformity in belief and behavior.

If the three traditions of Orthodox, Conservative, and Reform Judaism are all primarily expressions of religious intellectualism in education, the ethnic Jewish orientation in all of its various expressions tends to combine a secular form of educational intellectualism with either educational liberalism or educational liberationism. The reconstructionism of Kaplan is more ethnic and less "universalistic" than the nationalistic-secularism of an individual like Berkson, and the Marxist radicalism that characterized the Yiddish-Progressive movement in the first part of the century was clearly a far more radical and liberationist expression of the Jewish commitment to the establishment of a "just society" than any of the other expressions of ethnic Jewishness. An attempt to represent the extremely complex range and variety of contemporary Judaism/Jewishness is provided in Figure A1–2, which covers three pages.

IN SUMMARY

At basis, Judaism can be summarized as follows:

1. It is a tradition based on the unique vision of God—viewing God as one and transcendent. Strictly speaking, God is beyond human understanding. God reveals himself only indirectly through his laws and through his covenant with the Jewish people. In a sense, then, Judaism is a nontheological orientation which defines itself through adherence to divine law and not through subscription to abstract beliefs. God is revealed in Torah, and it is difficult to reconcile either philosophical systems (such as those derived by Cohen, Rosenzweig, Buber or Heschel) or mystical speculation (as in the Kabbalah) with the central tenets of Judaism.

2. Judaism is based on an exalted moral idealism. The Jews are a "chosen people" with a holy vision. Mankind will be redeemed in and through the redemption of Israel.

3. The Jews share a corporate and continuous identity. A Jew is an individual, but he is, first and foremost, a representative of a special people whose individual identity can only be expressed properly within the context of his overriding Jewishness.

4. Judaism is future-oriented. The scripture prophesies that the Jews will be redeemed through supernatural intervention (either by a personal messiah or through the inception of a messianic age of justice) and be restored to the grace of God through the restoration of Zion—whether viewed as a political restoration to the Jewish homeland in Palestine or as a supernatural resanctification of the Jewish people in the eyes of God.

5. Judaism is not an evangelical religion. It will accept converts, but it does so only reluctantly and after careful scrutiny. A religion based on law and the observance of law is probably less predisposed to attract outsiders than one predicated on abstract beliefs that can be more fully understood by those standing outside of the system itself.

6. While it is very difficult to generalize about Jewish values, the core of the Jewish ethic appears to be *justice* — often phrased negatively, after Hillel, as "refraining from evil"—rather than *love,* viewed conventionally as the imperative to "do good" (as is the dominant tradition in Christianity).

7. Judaism places the highest value on learning and scholarship. Since the destruction of the Temple and elimination of the hereditary priesthood, study has become the holy duty of all Jews, replacing ritual sacrifice. For most Jews, study guarantees a sort of "progressive revelation." The enlightened interpretation of the Scripture becomes an extension of Scripture itself, because it explicates and clarifies the meaning of Torah. Thus, since meanings are implicit within the Torah itself, the "whole Torah" is more than Torah; it is also Talmud and the contemporary extensions of the Talmudic tradition.

8. Since the destruction of the Second Commonwealth—since the diaspora—Judaism has been a singularly democratic religion. Judaism has no priests, only rabbis (teachers). The synagogue, like the self-contained Jewish communities in Europe during the dispersion, are characteristically self-governing institutions. Study, reason, and disputation, rather than political coercion, have been the conventional Jewish approaches to the solution of social problems.

9. Whatever differences may occur between Jews, Judaism today is basically one theme with variations. Orthodox, Conservative, and Reform orientations may differ, but they differ primarily in emphasis and degree rather than in kind. The basic themes of Judaism—God, Torah, and Israel—remain the same throughout.

10. American Judaism today seems to have successfully traversed the long road from segregation and persecution to social assimilation. The central problem of contemporary American Judaism is far less a matter of assimilation, then—which has become much more a reality than a promise—than a matter of redefining the very nature of Jewish identity. Who is a Jew, and what does it mean to be a Jew at this particular juncture in history?

FIGURE A1–2
JUDAISM AND JEWISH EDUCATION:
BASIC CONTEMPORARY APPROACHES

TRADITIONAL/CONSERVATIVE————————————————————————

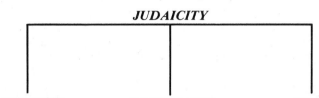

JUDAICITY

ORTHODOX*	*CONSERVATIVE*	*REFORM*
Judacity as the ultimate source of Jewishness	Jewishness as the ultimate source of Judaicity	Attempt to move toward a contemporary redefinition of Jewishness and Judaism, as well as to redefine the relationship between the two
Scriptural exegesis over theology and speculative philosophy	Strong emphasis on the authority of the laity in interpreting scripture; reduced reliance on traditional rabbinical authority	Religion as a personal and individualistic experience rather than as a corporate enterprise
Adherence to the authority of the rabbinate (including traditional methods of rabbinical interpretation of scripture)	Emphasis on the permanent value of the literary and cultural monuments of the Jewish spirit, as expressed differently at different times and places	Holds that beliefs and practices should be open to reason and critical scrutiny
Stress on specifically Jewish scholarship and learning over general (secular) intellectual training	Seeks approximate parity between specifically Jewish scholarship and learning, and secular intellectual training	More predisposed to theological and philosophical speculation than either Orthodoxy or Conservatism
Stresses intensive Jewish day schools (*yeshivoth*) which are closely related to the traditional Jewish schools (*chederim*) in Europe and which function primarily at the elementary level	Supplemental (part-time) Jewish schools	Emphasizes general (secular) intellectualism over specifically Jewish scholarship and learning
Central emphasis on Torah-Talmud training and Hebrew language study	Some intensive day school programs (e.g., the Solomon Schechter Day Schools)	Supports the separation of church and state, including the established tradition of secular public schools
Study as holy, a scared responsibility	Various informal programs Jewish community centers	Stress on supplementary extended-day religious instruction
Yeshiva University	Camping movements (e.g., Ramah camps)	Various informal Jewish education programs
	Club activities and youth associations	Community centers
	Jewish Theological Seminary	Camping movements
	University of Judaism	Club activities and youth associations (e.g., Young Mens Hebrew Association)
		Hebrew Union College

————————————————

*This position includes the ultraorthodoxy of contemporary Hasidism.

FIGURE A1–2 (cont.)

───────────── **TRADITIONAL/CONSERVATIVE** continued ─────────────

JEWISHNESS

ETHNIC

MORDECAI KAPLAN'S
"RECONSTRUCTIONISM"
AND
"JEWISH AMERICANISM"

Reconstructionism:

The Jewish people as the major
instrument in bringing about a
secular vision of the "just
society"
Supports the separation of
church and state, including
the established tradition of
secular public schools
The Jewish community
center movement
Stress on supplementary
extended-day religious
instruction
Various informal Jewish
education programs
Community centers
Camping movements
Club activities and youth
associations

Jewish-Americanism:

Jewish secular-nationalism as a
vital component of ethnic
pluralism in American
democracy
"Jewishness" as a vital
attachment to residual
ethnicity
Supports the separation of
church and state, including
the established tradition of
secular public schools
Various informal Jewish
education programs
Community centers
Camping movements
Club activities and youth
associations (e.g., Young
Men's Hebrew
Association)
Isaac Berkson
Horace Kallen

SECULAR ZIONISM

Political autonomy as a means
of ensuring the survival and
fullest self-expression of the
Jewish people
Nationalism as a political
cure for "Jewishness" viewed
as a manifestation of
persecution
The successful assimilation
of the Jews through the
effective use of counter-
vailing political power
Supports the separation of
church and state, including
the established tradition of
secular public schools
Various informal Jewish
education programs
Community centers
Camping movements
Club activities and youth
associations (e.g., Young
Men's Hebrew
Association)
The secular Israeli
kibbutzim
Theodore Herzl

YIDDISH
SECULAR-SOCIALISM

Jewish socialism integrated with
Jewish-Yiddish ethnicity
Generally secular and inter-
nationalistic in orientation
Characteristically opposed to
political Zionism (Jewish
nationalism)
Supports the separation of
church and state, including
the established tradition of
secular public schools
Stress on special schools
integrating Yiddish-Jewish
culture with socialist
political training
The Workman's Circle
schools and the Sholem
Aleichem schools in New
York City during the first
half of this century
Various informal Jewish
education programs
Community centers
Camping movements
Club activities and youth
associations (e.g., Young
Men's Hebrew
Association)

LIBERAL/SECULAR

ETHICAL

SUPERNATURALISTIC ETHICAL JUDAISM

Holds that only the Decalogue (the Ten Commandments) is authoritative in the sense of being revealed by God; the Commandments are the essential spirit of Judaism, and all other laws, rituals and observances are secondary and potentially dispensable

A religious commitment to a divinely revealed code-morality

Only the moral law as revealed in the Decalogue is truly binding

  Stress on supplementary extended-day religious instruction

  Various informal Jewish education programs

    Community centers

    Camping movements

    Club activities and youth associations (e.g., Young Men's Hebrew Association)

NATURALISTIC ETHICAL JUDAISM

The Jews, not as a "chosen people" but as a people who have been inspired throughout history with a singular sense of moral mission, an ethical idealism which is reflected in the Ten Commandments, but which is perhaps even better summed up as a supreme committment to a particular version of "justice" perhaps best expressed in Hillel's words: "What is hateful to yourself do not to your fellow-man. That is the whole Torah. All the rest is commentary. Now go and study." This moral vision of the "just man" has been the implicit core and central contribution of the Jewish people. It indirectly implies a sort of "situation ethics" based upon the application of individual and collective (democratic) reason as the predominant means of realizing the ultimate goal of universal justice.

  Privatistic situation ethics based on an overriding commitment to the goal of "justice" in channeling interpersonal behavior

    Supports the separation of church and state, including the established tradition of secular public schools

      Felix Adler and the Ethical Culture Society (in New York City)

SOCIALISTIC ETHICAL JUDAISM ("JEWISH SOCIALISM")

Accepts the goal of the "just man" in the "just society," but rejects the notion that effective ethical action can be privatistic and personal; maintains that "justice", which is based upon trained intelligence and democratic processes, necessarily imples a corollary commitment to a full and equitable distribution of power among all people in order to provide the most effective social basis for the fullest functioning of the intellectual democracy necessary to realize fully the ultimate goal of universal justice

  The "just man" can only exist in and through some vision of the "just society"

  Collectivistic ethics— commitment to "justice" as a means of reconstructing society and therefore reordering the underlying nature and content of inter-personal relationships

  The political universalization of the Jewish "justice-ethic"

    Education as an agency for social reform and reconstruction

NOTES

1. Jacob Neusner, *The Way of Torah: An Introduction to Judaism,* 2d ed., (Encino, California: Dickenson Publishing Co., 1974), p. 65.

2. Louis Ginzberg, *Students, Scholars, and Saints,* (Philadelphia: Jewish Publication Society, 1928), p. x.

3. Neusner, *The Way of Torah,* p. 68.

4. Joseph L. Blau, *Modern Varieties of Judaism,* (New York: Columbia University Press, 1964), pp. 26–27. Used by permission of the publisher.

5. Eliezer Berkovits, *Major Themes in Modern Philosophies of Judaism,* (New York: KTAV Publishing House, 1974), p. 45.

6. *Torah* literally means "revelation" in Hebrew. Strictly speaking, the Torah consists of the Five Books of Moses in the Old Testament, which constitute the basic Scriptures of Judaism.

7. Blau, *Modern Varieties of Judaism,* p. 76.

8. Neusner, *The Way of Torah,* p. 56.

9. Ibid., p. 46.

10. Samson R. Hirsch, quoted in Neusner, *The Way of Torah,* p. 78.

11. Berkovits, *Modern Philosophies of Judaism,* p. 27.

12. Ibid., p. 146.

13. Blau, *Modern Varieties of Judaism,* p. 13.

14. Ibid., p. 86.

15. Ibid., pp. 152–53.

16. Neusner, *The Way of Torah,* p. 53. The thirteen articles of faith are separated typographically here, although they constitute one unitary paragraph in Neusner's book.

17. Ibid., p. 95.

18. Blau, *Modern Varieties of Judaism,* p. 2.

19. Abraham Geiger, quoted in Blau, *Modern Varieties of Judaism,* p. 37.

20. Blau, *Modern Varieties of Judaism,* p. 38.

21. Abraham Geiger, quoted in Blau, *Modern Varieties of Judaism*, p. 38.

22. Blau, *Modern Varieties of Judaism,* pp. 38–39.

23. Samuel Holdheim, quoted in Blau, *Modern Varieties of Judaism,* p. 37.

24. Blau, *Modern Varieties of Judaism,* p. 53.

25. Ibid., p. 58.

26. Ibid., pp. 57–58. All of the internal quotations are from Kaufmann Kohler (writing in the so-called "Pittsburgh Platform"). The eight basic points are separated typographically here, although they constitute one unitary paragraph in Blau's book.

27. There are groups within contemporary Judaism that are even more traditional than mainstream Hasidism. These groups—advocating such things as the revival of ritual sacrifices, the rebuilding of the Temple in Jerusalem, the reinstitution of the hereditary priesthood and the priestly caste, and an extremely rigid definition of Torah (frequently to exclude the Talmud altogether)—are small and do not merit extended consideration within the scope of the present work, but they do exemplify the fact that Orthodoxy, like the other basic Judaic orientations, is much more diverse than a necessarily simplistic overview such as this would tend to suggest.

28. Blau, *Modern Varieties of Judaism*, p. 63, quoting Philipson, *The Reform Movement in Judaism* (New York: Macmillan, 1907), p. 82.

29. Hirsch differed from the strict traditionalists of his time in two basic respects: (1) he opposed Reform Judaism but he favored secular education as a desirable adjunct to religious training; and (2) he was willing, if need be, to break the traditional unity of the Jewish community by leading orthodox groups in secession from reform-dominated communities.

30. Blau, *Modern Varieties of Judaism,* p. 78.

31. Samson Hirsch, quoted in Blau, *Modern Varieties of Judaism,* p. 75.

32. Blau, *Modern Varieties of Judaism,* pp. 76–77. Hirsch's emphasis on behavior over belief in particular doctrines is not, however, the only point of view in orthodox Judaism. During the controversial exchanges that took place in Germany during the early years of the nineteenth century between Rabbi Geiger, representing the Reform point of view, and Rabbi Titkin, representing traditional Orthodoxy, an ally of Titkin, Solomon Eger, Chief Rabbi of Posen, took a far more absolutistic point of view than that subsequently adopted by Hirsch. He stated that ''only he can be considered a conforming Jew who believes that the divine law-book, the Torah, together with all the interpretations and explanations found in the Talmud, was given by God himself to Moses on Mt. Sinai.'' (Ibid., p. 63.)

This point of view is, of course, far more demanding in its definition of true Jewishness than that offered by Hirsch, because it takes the position that *belief* rather than *practice* is the basis of Judaism. It also holds to the loose interpretation of Torah, which holds that ''whole Torah'' encompasses the Talmud as well as the Torah defined narrowly as the first five books of Moses.

Modern orthodox Judaism is generally predisposed toward defining Judaism in terms of behavior and observances, in the tradition of Hirsch, rather than in terms of particular creeds and doctrines.

33. Samson Hirsch, quoted in Blau, *Modern Varieties of Judaism,* p. 79.

34. Blau, *Modern Varieties of Judaism,* p. 96.

35. Ibid., p. 98.

36. Zechariah Frankel, quoted in Blau, *Modern Varieties of Judaism,* p. 92.

37. See Chapter VI.

38. Louis Ginzberg, quoted in Blau, *Modern Varieties of Judaism,* p. 92.

39. Blau, *Modern Varieties of Judaism,* p. 94.

40. Ibid., p. 93.

41. Cyrus Adler, quoted in Blau, *Modern Varieties of Judaism,* p. 112.

42. Solomon Schechter, quoted in Blau, *Modern Varieties of Judaism,* p. 112.

43. Blau, *Modern Varieties of Judaism,* p. 113.

44. Ibid., pp. 113–14.

45. Mordecai Kaplan, quoted in Blau, *Modern Varieties of Judaism,* p. 171.

46. Blau, *Modern Varieties of Judaism,* p. 171.

47. Ibid., p. 168.

48. Mordecai Kaplan, quoted in Berkovits, *Modern Philosophies of Judaism,* p. 153.

49. Ibid., p. 154.

50. Berkovits, *Modern Philosophies of Judaism,* p. 158.

51. Mordecai Kaplan, quoted in Blau, *Modern Varieties of Judaism,* p. 173.

52. Horace N. Kallen, *The Education of Free Men,* (New York: Farrar, Straus, 1949), p. 117.

53. Van Cleve Morris and Young Pai, *Philosophy and the American School: An Introduction to the Philosophy of Education,* 2d ed., (Boston: Houghton Mifflin Co., 1976), p. 436.

54. National Coalition for Cultural Pluralism, quoted in William R. Hazard and Madelon D. Stent, ''Cultural Pluralism and Schooling: Some Preliminary Observations,'' in Madelon D. Stent *et al.,* eds. *Cultural Pluralism in Education: A Mandate for Change,* (New York: Appleton-Century-Crofts, 1973), p. 14.

55. The term *dispersion* is sometimes used synonymously with the term *exile* in Judaism. The two terms are not, however, the same. As Arthur A. Cohen notes in his book *The Natural and the Supernatural Jew: An Historical and Theological Introduction* (New York: Pantheon, 1962), ''dispersion'' is a fact of history while ''exile'' is an interpretation of this fact on the basis of religious conviction. (Arthur A. Cohen, quoted in Blau, *Modern Varieties of Judaism,* p. 157.) ''The Exile is a cosmic, not an historical, event in Jewish tradition. . . . The historical catastrophe is elevated to a metahistorical reality.'' (Ibid., p. 158.)

With the founding of the modern state of Israel, dispersion, as a necessary fact, has come to an end. For Cohen, however, as for the well-known orthodox theologian and philosopher Eliezer Berkovits, "exile" is not over, because "the exile is a universal principle and signifies man's alienation from God." (Blau, *Modern Varieties of Judaism*, p. 158.) Indeed, for Berkovits, and as Blau indicates, "emancipation was altogether a mistake, a curse, not a blessing, because it led the Jews to renounce their special status as eternal strangers and to secularize their lives." (Blau, *Modern Varieties of Judaism*, p. 159.) For Berkovits, emancipation has led to secularization. The political Israel violates the spiritual mission of the Jewish people. The political power of the Jews has created guilt in a sacred people. [As Blau states:]

...the very fact that this modern Israeli is creating a secular state leads Berkovits to criticize him for being only doubtfully a Jew. Zionism is not acceptable to Berkovits, then, because "The new Jewish reality in Palestine is, for the time being, overwhelmingly of a nature that cannot be reconciled with the aims and intentions of historic Judaism."

*   *   *

"Let us be grateful to the [Exile]," states Berkovits. "It has freed us from the guilt of national existence in a world in which national existence meant guilt." (Blau, quoting Berkovits, *Modern Varieties of Judaism*, p. 159.)

56. Blau, *Modern Varieties of Judaism*,, p. 120.

57. Ibid., p. 143.

58. Ibid., p. 129.

59. Blau, quoting from the Balfour Declaration, *Modern Varieties of Judaism*, p. 146.

60. Blau, *Modern Varieties of Judaism*, p. 125.

61. Ibid., p. 125.

62. Ibid., p. 126.

63. Samuel Holdheim, quoted in Blau, *Modern Varieties of Judaism*, pp. 125–26.

64. Blau, *Modern Varieties of Judaism*, pp. 147–48.

65. Kaufmann Kohler, quoted in Blau, *Modern Varieties of Judaism*, p. 127.

66. Blau, *Modern Varieties of Judaism*, p. 149.

67. Blau, *Modern Varieties of Judaism*, p. 150. Beneath the ostensible unanimity, however, many Jews—both religious and secular—still have very real trepidations about the existence of Israel as a secular nation-state. In an article entitled "The Tangibles of Jewish Education" Simon Greenberg expresses a preference for Mordecai Kaplan's concept of "the peoplehood of Israel" over that of the Jews as a political nation. As he states:

the first and most dramatic tangible of Jewish peoplehood I believe to be Erets Yisrael, rather than Medinat Yisrael, the State of Israel. With all of my concern for the welfare of the State of Israel, I have no doubts in my mind that the peoplehood of Israel is bound up with Erets Yisrael, the land of Israel, as a physical reality rather than with Medinat Yisrael, the State of Israel, as a political reality. Indeed, whatever spiritual significance Medinat Yisrael has for Jews living beyond the reach of its political sovereignty, it derives from the fact that it is located in Erets Yisrael. If it were located in Uganda or Biro Bidjan, it would have no unique spiritual claim upon us at all, except perhaps as a place of refuge for the persecuted. It was because of its association with Erets Yisrael that the Zionist movement captured the hearts of the Jews of the world. A Jewish state in Uganda was rejected not by the Zionists of the free West, but by the persecuted Jews of Eastern Europe.

Moreover, Jewish education in the United States cannot and should not weave bonds of allegiance between the Jewish child and the State of Israel as a political entity. But it must and properly may weave bonds of affection between the American Jewish child and the Land of Israel, as the concrete geographic locale where the Jewish people achieved its most glorious spiritual triumphs. (Judah Pilch and Meir Ben-Horin, eds., *Judaism and the Jewish School: Selected Essays on the Direction and Purpose of Jewish Education*. [New York: Bloch Publishing Company for the American Association for Jewish Education, 1966, p. 253.])

68. Jacob Neusner, "Seven Settings for Jewish Learning," *Synagogue School,* Vol. 33, No. 1–2 (Winter, 1973–1974), p. 2.

69. William W. Brickman, "Education for Eternal Existence: The Philosophy of Jewish Education," in Judah Pilch and Meir Ben-Horin (eds.), *Judaism and the Jewish School,* p. 207.

70. Frederick Eby and Charles F. Arrowood, *The History and Philosophy of Education: Ancient and Medieval.* (Englewood Cliffs, New Jersey: Prentice-Hall, 1956), p. 157.

71. Pilch and Ben-Horin, *Judaism and the Jewish School,* p. 214.

72. Salow Baron, "The Jewish Community and Jewish Education," in Pilch and Ben-Horin, *Judaism and the Jewish School,* p. 5.

73. Ibid.

74. Julius B. Maller, "The Role of Education in Jewish History," in Louis Finkelstein (ed.), *The Jews: Their History, Culture and Religion,* 3rd ed. volume 2, Philadelphia: The Jewish Publication Society of America, 1960, p. 1234.

75. Ibid.

76. Ibid.

77. Ibid., p. 1250.

78. Ibid., p. 1235. The ten ideas are separated typographically here, although they constitute one paragraph in the original.

79. Geoffrey E. Bock, "Does Jewish Schooling Matter?" Colloquium Papers, published by The American-Jewish Committee, January 1977, p. 11., n.p.

80. Neusner, "Seven Settings for Jewish Learning," p. 8.

81. Bock, "Does Jewish Schooling Matter?" p. 17.

82. Neusner, "Seven Settings for Jewish Learning," p. 7.

83. Bock, "Does Jewish Schooling Matter?", pp. 3–4.

84. Meir Ben-Horin, "Major Writings in American Jewish Education 1929–1959," *Jewish Education,* Vol. 30, No. 2, Winter, 1960, p. 13.

85. Ibid.

86. Ibid.

87. Solomon Schechter, quoted in Pilch and Ben-Horin, *Judaism and the Jewish School,* p. 227.

88. Pilch and Ben-Horin, *Judaism and the Jewish School,* p. 124.

89. Ibid., p. 265.

90. Ben-Horin, "American Jewish Education," p. 265.

91. Emanuel Gamoran, quoted in Ben-Horin, "American Jewish Education," p. 6. Although all one paragraph in the original, these four points have been separated typographically here.

92. Emanuel Gamoran, quoted in Pilch and Ben-Horin, *Judaism and the Jewish School,* p. 85.

93. Pilch and Ben-Horin, *Judaism and the Jewish School,* p. 72.

94. Ibid., p. 32.

95. Ibid., p. 306.

96. Ibid.

97. Mordecai Kaplan, quoted in Ben-Horin, "American Jewish Education," pp. 14–15.

98. Pilch and Ben-Horin, *Judaism and the Jewish School,* pp. 328–29.

99. Ibid., p. 144.

100. Ibid.

101. Shmuel Niger, "Theses on Jewish Education," in Pilch and Ben-Horin, *Judaism and the Jewish School,* p. 196.

102. Mark Yudel, in Ben-Horin, "American Jewish Education," p. 14.

103. Ibid.

104. Ben-Horin, "American Jewish Education," p. 14.

105. Ibid., p. 12.

106. Hyman Bass, "Some Problems of Jewish Education," in Pilch and Ben-Horin, *Judaism and the Jewish School,* p. 191.

107. Samuel Dinin, "My Educational Credo," in Pilch and Ben-Horin, *Judaism and the Jewish School,* p. 321.

108. Neusner, "Seven Settings for Jewish Learning," p. 13.

109. Blau, *Modern Varieties of Judaism,* p. 119.

110. Neusner, *The Way of Torah,* p. 44.

BIBLIOGRAPHY

Judaism and Jewish Education

JUDAISM AND THE JEWISH TRADITION

BECK, LEO. *The Essence of Judaism.* New York: Schocken, 1948.

BERKOVITS, ELIEZEP. *Major Themes in Modern Philosophies of Judaism.* New York: KTAV Publishing House, 1974.

BLAU, JOSEPH L. *Modern Varieties of Judaism.* New York: Columbia University Press, 1966.

COHEN, ARTHUR A. *The Natural and Supernatural Jew: An Historical and Theological Introduction.* New York: McGraw Hill, 1962.

DEUTSCHER, ISAAC. *The Non-Jewish Jew and Other Essays.* New York: Oxford, 1968.

ELON, AMOS. *The Israelis: Founders and Sons.* New York: Holt, Rinehart, and Winston, 1971.

FINKELSTEIN, LOUIS, ed. *The Jews: Their History, Culture, and Religion,* 3rd ed. Philadelphia: Jewish Publication Society, 1960.

GLAZER, NATHAN. *American Judaism.* Chicago: University of Chicago, 1957.

HERBERG, WILL. *Judaism and Modern Man.* Philadelphia: Jewish Publication Society, 1951.

HERTZBERG, ARTHUR. *The Zionist Idea.* New York: Herzl Press, 1959.

HESCHEL, ABRAHAM J. *God in Search of Man: A Philosophy of Judaism.* Philadelphia: Jewish Publication Society, 1956.

MAHLER, RAPHAEL. *A History of Modern Jewry.* New York: Schocken Books, 1971.

MEYER, MICHAEL A. *The Origins of the Modern Jew.* Detroit: Wayne State University Press, 1967.

NEUSNER, JACOB. *The Way of Torah: An Introduction to Judaism,* 2nd ed. Encino, Calfornia: Dickenson Publishing Company, 1974.

ROSENBERG, STUART E. *The Search for Jewish Identity in America.* New York: Anchor Books, 1965.

ROTH, CECIL. *Short History of the Jewish People.* London: East and West Library, 1963.

SKLARE, MARSHALL. *America's Jews.* New York: Random House, 1971.

ZBOROWSKI, MARK, and ZBOROWSKI, ELIZABETH. *Life is with People.* New York: International Universities Press, 1952.

JUDAIC AND JEWISH EDUCATION

ACKERMAN, WALTER I. "Jewish Education—For What?," in *American and Jewish Year Book,* Vol. 70, 1969.

ACKERMAN, WALTER I. "The Present Moment in Jewish Education," *Midstream: A Monthly Jewish Review,* Dec., 1972, pp. 3–24.

BEN-HORIN, MEIR. "Major Writings in American Jewish Education, 1924–1959," *Jewish Education,* Vol. 30, No. 2, Winter, 1960.

BEN-HORIN, MEIR. "The Reschooling of American Jewry," *Journal of Jewish Communal Service,* pp. 278–80.

BOCK, GEOFFREY E. "Does Jewish Schooling Matter?," Colloquium Papers, Published by The American-Jewish Committee, January 1977.

CHAZAN, BARRY, "The Crisis of Contemporary Philosophy of Jewish Education," *Jewish Education,* Vol. 42, No. 4, Summer 1973.

COHEN, STEVEN MARTIN, "The Impact of Jewish Education on Religious Identification and Practice," *Jewish Social Studies,* Vol. 36, No. 3–4, July-October, 1974, pp. 316–26.

DORPH, SHELDON ARTHUR, *A Model for Jewish Education in America: Guidelines for the Restructuring of Conservative Congregational Education.* Dissertation for the degree of Doctor of Education, Teachers College, Columbia University, 1976.

KURZWEIL, Z. E., *Modern Trends in Jewish Education.* New York: Thomas Yoseloff, 1964.

MALLER, JULIUS B. "The Role of Education in Jewish History," in Finkelstein, Louis, ed., *The Jews: Their History, Culture and Religion,* 3rd ed. Vol. 2. The Jewish Publication Society of America, 1960.

NEUSNER, JACOB, "Seven Settings for Jewish Learning," *Synagogue School,* Vol. 32, No. 1–2, Winter, 1973–1974, pp. 1–18.

PILCH, JUDAH, ed. *A History of Jewish Education in the United States.* New York: The National Curriculum Research Institute of the American Association for Jewish Education, 1969.

PILCH, JUDAH, and BEN-HORIN, MEIR, eds. *Judaism and the Jewish School: Selected Essays on the Direction and Purpose of Jewish Education.* New York: Block Publishing Co., 1966.

SCHWAB, JOSEPH, "The Religiously Oriented School in the United States: A Memorandum on Policy," *Conservative Judaism,* Spring, 1964, pp. 1–14.

SCHIFF, ALVIN IRWIN. *The Jewish Day School in America.* New York: Jewish Education Committee Press, 1966.

Manual for the Educational Ideologies Profile

Information about obtaining additional copies of the Educational Ideologies Inventory can be obtained from the publisher at the following address:

> Nina James
> Goodyear Publishing Company, Inc.
> 1640 Fifth Street
> Santa Monica, CA 90401

An anthology of selected readings illustrating and exemplifying the major educational ideologies *(Educational Ideologies: Selected Readings),* as well as an educational game designed for classroom use that employs the educational ideologies model *(Controversy and Compromise: A Game for Educators)* are also available. Enquiries should be forwarded to the author at the address listed below:

> Dr. William F. O'Neill
> School of Education (Foundations)
> University of Southern California
> University Park
> Los Angeles, CA 90007

AN INTRODUCTION TO THE MANUAL

The *Educational Ideologies Inventory (EII)* is founded upon the theoretical model that was developed by the author in this book. The Inventory is designed primarily for use by educators, potential educators, and those significantly concerned with education and educational matters.

The EII consists of 104 discriminative ideological statements pertaining to different positions within educational philosophy. It takes approximately thirty minutes to administer, while scoring and determining the Educational Ideologies Profile at the end of the Inventory ordinarily takes about twenty additional minutes.

The EII yields eight specific scores and an overall ideological profile (the Educational Ideologies Profile). More specifically, each person makes a score on the basis of his response to the items pertaining to each of the six educational ideologies: *Educational Fundamentalism, Educational Intellectualism, Educational Conservatism, Educational Liberalism, Educational Liberationism,* and *Educational Anarchism.*

In addition to these six specific ideological positions, the Inventory offers two more generalized indications of a person's overall inclinations in the area of educational philosophy. These are a *General Conservatism* score and a *General Liberalism* score. The items that the Conservative or Liberal ideological proponents (as these terms are used in the book) would agree on, comprise the basis for the *General Conservatism* and *General Liberalism* scores. The *General Conservatism* score is, for example, the score that the individual receives on the basis of his response to those items upon which all of the proponents of the "Conservative" educational ideologies (educational fundamentalism, educational intellectualism, and educational conservatism) concur regardless of their more specific differences with respect to other matters. The *General Liberalism* score is, accordingly, the score obtained on all of those items on which there is a consensus between all of those educational ideologies ordinarily viewed as "Liberal" (that is, educational liberalism, educational liberationism, and educational anarchism).

Finally, a test profile (the Educational Ideologies Profile) is provided in order to give each person an opportunity to visualize his total educational orientation in simple graphic form. It allows each individual to observe the relative intensity of his ideological commitments on a comparative scale and also to see how these commitments are interrelated. The Profile does not include the overall ideological orientations of *General Conservatism* and *General Liberalism,* which are sufficiently broad to incorporate all six of the more specific educational ideologies. These are presented only in the form of numerical scores.

The various educational ideologies employed in the Inventory are explained and exemplified in the foregoing pages, but, for present purposes, the rationale behind the theoretical model used, as well as a brief definition of the various educational ideologies, can be summarized as follows.

RATIONALE

Virtually all philosophers agree that the highest good ultimately resides in personal happiness, and that such happiness is primarily a matter of self-realization—the happy man is essentially that man who is able to *be* what he potentially *is*. Beyond this very general point of agreement, however, philosophers tend to fall into disarray, and a whole host of different moral theories have sprung up to explain *how* it is possible to live the good, or self-realized, life. At basis, however, even here, at the beginning of all ethics, it is possible to distinguish between six basic theoretical differences that mark the fundamental points of departure for most subsequent disputes about moral questions. Phrased somewhat differently, there are, at basis, six fundamental points of view about how to live the good life that are dominant in Western culture at the present time. The specific moral philosophies hold that the highest good grows out of:

1. adherence to intuitive and/or revealed standards of belief and behavior;
2. philosophical and/or religious enlightenment based on speculative reason and metaphysical wisdom;
3. adherence to established standards of belief and behavior;
4. practical intelligence (that is, effective problem-solving);
5. development of new and more humanistic social institutions; or
6. elimination of institutional restraints and the fullest realization of personal freedom.

All of the Conservative ideologies share the common assumption that the ultimate value is self-realization and that self-realization is properly attained by identifying and adhering to natural and/or divine law. In regard to this point, all three of the Conservative positions can be subdivided into two basic orientations, one *secular* and one *theistic*. The *secular* point of view, in all three positions, is that which maintains that reality is restricted to natural experience and that, while there are metaphysical principles (that is, extremely abstract and pervasive principles, like the laws of logic or the formal propositions of mathematics) that apply to all natural experience and which therefore defy ordinary explanation in common-sense terms, even these are merely a different dimension of "natural" experience. The *religious* point of view, on the other hand, holds that reality is essentially dual, possessing both natural and supernatural dimensions, and that man must, correspondingly, realize both the natural and supernatural aspects of his nature in obedience to the universal laws that exist on both of these levels.

All of the Liberal persuasions, like the Conservative ones, share an overriding belief that the highest value is some form of self-realization. For the Liberals, however, the *self* to be realized is quite different from that envisioned by the Conservative. Thus, where the Conservative tends to view self-realization as an end to be approached only indirectly through an overriding dedication to some absolute reality—God, natural law, tradition, or whatever—that transcends ordinary human experience, the Liberal sees *man* as primary, the source of all knowledge whatsoever. Phrased somewhat differently, if Conservatism tends to be an *indirect* humanism, seeing self-realization as a by-product of adhering to the dictates of a suprapersonal reality that exists above and beyond individual experience, then Liberalism tends to be a *direct* humanism, which views all reality as rooted in and deriving from personal and/or collective human experience. For the Liberal, virtually all knowledge is rooted in human experience, and there are no absolutes that are not ultimately relative to being known, to emerging out of some sort of human involvement with the world. Thus, if the basic differences among the Conservative positions relate to different ways in which absolute knowledge can and should be known—God or reason; revelation or faith; intuition or authoritative tradition—the basic differences between the Liberals have to do with the relationship between the individual and his society.

The Liberal points of view, like the Conservative ones, encompass both secular and religious positions. In the final analysis, however, the differences between the secular and religious proponents of the Liberal point of view are far less significant than these same differences as they exist within the Conservative orientations. This is true for two basic reasons.

First, in the Liberal persuasions, the social ethic very seldom, if ever, differs significantly at the level of recommended political and educational practices. What differences exist tend to occur almost entirely in the area of theory. Thus, for example, the differences between the Christian socialist and the secular socialist are not readily apparent at the operational level of actual social policy. The differences occur primarily at the explanatory level with respect to different theoretical preconceptions that pertain to philosophical and/or theoretical first principles.

Thus, the religious liberal will *explain* the love-ethic differently than the secular liberal, viewing it as a divine absolute emanating from a personal God. For the religious liberal, love may be viewed as rooted in the brotherhood of man, but the brotherhood of man may, in turn, be explained on the basis of the fatherhood of God. In a similar sense, the religious liberal's view of the ultimate consequences of adhering to the love-ethic will also ordinarily envision a more transcendent or enduring sort of happiness (frequently encompassing some experience in a life after death) than that of the secular liberal. For the religious liberal, then, the love-ethic is both explained differently, and it leads to somewhat different (or, at least, more extended) consequences than those envisioned by the secularist. For the secular liberal, on the other hand, the ethic remains the same, but it is explained on a purely naturalistic level (on the basis of enlightened self-interest), and it is looked upon as leading to purely natural consequences (that is, as generated in the highest degree of self-realization on both the personal and social levels within the confines of the temporal world).

For all practical purposes, however, the fact remains that the ethical, political, and educational programs espoused by both the secular and religious liberals are essentially the same for all apparent purposes. They advocate the same sort of policies for significantly different reasons, but, since these reasons in underlying belief exist on a level of abstraction far beyond that required by practical action, these differences can be effectively ignored for present purposes, and the two different approaches to educational Liberalism (as it applies to education) are treated in this Inventory as essentially one position.

Second, while fundamentally dualistic—assuming the existence of both natural and supernatural dimensions of experience—the religious liberals tend to downplay the supernatural in two respects:

1. They tend to hold that the supernatural is in most respects amenable to partial (if imperfect) verification on the basis of reason and natural evidence. "Altruistic love" is, for example, generally viewed as *both* a divine prescription *and* a rational imperative, which can be defended on either religious or secular grounds. They maintain that the supernatural love-ethic is essentially compatible with natural reason and experiential evidence.

2. They tend to view fewer ethical sanctions as emanating from the divine, and they generally define these less literally, at a higher level of generalization that requires a significant degree of personal interpretation as a basis for application. Phrased differently, they are more disposed to prescribe abstract principles than specific policies and practices. (They tend, for example, to be more inclined to believe that a person should treat other people as *ends* and not *means,* but less inclined to specify how this should be done in a categorical sense—as, for example, by specifying that one should always love one's parents, that one should always tell the truth, or whatever.) Accordingly, they are less inclined toward traditional "code morality" with its definitive and relatively unconditional prescriptions.

Corresponding to these basic differences in the area of moral philosophy, and in large part growing out of these differing moral assessments, there are six basic *political* philosophies. These are the three basic expressions of the Conservative point of view—*reactionary conservatism* (anti-intellectual authoritarianism), *philosophical conservatism* (intellectual absolutism), and *mainstream social conservatism* (traditionalism), and the three basic expressions of the Liberal point of view—*liberalism, liberationism,* and *anarchism.*

From these contrasting systems of social ethics emerge the six basic educational ideologies, and these educational ideologies consist primarily of the applications and implications of these underlying moral and political positions for the conduct of schooling. The six basic educational ideologies may be summarized as follows.

Educational Fundamentalism

Fundamentalism encompasses all of those types of political conservatism that are basically anti-intellectual in the sense that they seek to minimize philosophical and/or intellectual considerations, and tend to ground their contentions upon a relatively uncritical acceptance of either revealed Truth or established social consensus ("common sense"). In its political expression, the reactionary conservative advocates a return to the real or imagined virtues of the past. There are two basic variations of such a point of view when applied to education: *religious* educational fundamentalism, as is found in certain of the more fundamentalist Christian churches that are profoundly committed to a rather rigid and literalistic view of reality as revealed through scriptural authority, and *secular* educational fundamentalism, which characteristically espouses an equally inflexible commitment to the consensual "common sense" worldview of the average man. In contemporary education, religious fundamentalism is perhaps best observed in the educational ideas of certain of the Bible-centered Christian groups that feature a strict adherence to the word of God as presented in the scriptures. The secular fundamentalist point of view within education is perhaps best exemplified by the "common sense" educational fundamentalism of a well-known figure such as Max Rafferty, with his strong emphasis on nationalism and patriotism.

Educational Intellectualism

Intellectualism emerges out of those expressions of political conservatism that are based upon relatively rigid and fundamentally authoritarian philosophical or theological systems of thought. In general, philosophical conservatism seeks to change existing political (including educational) practices in order to make them conform more perfectly to some established and essentially unvarying intellectual or spiritual ideal. It is, for example, intellectual conservatism that is reflected in the writings of Plato and Aristotle, and that is central to the position of Saint Thomas Aquinas (which, in turn, provides the philosophical basis for the mainstream Roman Catholic point of view). In contemporary education, philosophical conservatism expresses itself primarily as *educational intellectualism,* of which there are two basic variations. *Philosophical intellectualism* is essentially secular and can be observed in such contemporary educational theorists as Robert Maynard Hutchins and Mortimer Adler. *Theological intellectualism* is a religious orientation perhaps best reflected in the writings of such Roman Catholic educational philosophers as William McGucken and John Donahue.

Educational Conservatism

Conservatism espouses adherence to time-tested cultural institutions and processes, coupled with a deep respect for law and order, as a basis for any sort of constructive social change. Accordingly, on a political level, the conservative tends to be well represented by the writings of such men as Edmund Burke, James Madison, and the authors of *The Federalist Papers.* In education, he views the central goal of the school as being the preservation and transmission of established social patterns and traditions. Within education, there are two basic expressions of the social conservative point of view. *Religious* educational conservatism stresses the centrality of spiritual training as a basis for proper moral character. *Secular* educational conservatism is concerned with the necessity of preserving and transmitting existing beliefs and practices as a way of ensuring both social survival and personal effectiveness. At the present time, religious conservatism is probably best represented by the educational orientation of the more devout representatives of such mainstream Protestant traditions as the Lutherans or the Southern Baptists, while secular conservatism tends to be best exemplified by many of the more articulate critics of educational progressivism and permissivism, such as James Koerner and Hyman Rickover.

Educational Liberalism

The educational liberal tends to be a product of the empirical tradition in philosophy that subscribes to an open system of truth. This is a tradition that emphasizes, not answers as such, but rather rational-experimental procedures for determining answers. Focused primarily on the present and the immediate future, the educational liberal emphasizes change and techniques for dealing with change. He advocates gradual, small-scale reforms within the framework of the existing political system in order to further individual freedom and to maximize the fullest realization of human potential. Generally favoring rational and evolutionary change within the existing social order over sudden and wholesale changes of the entire system, the liberal believes that schools should cooperate with other social institutions in bringing about necessary social reforms. For the educational liberal, the long-range goal of education is to preserve and improve the existing social order by teaching each child how to deal effectively with his own emerging life-problems, but educational liberalism ranges in intensity from the relatively mild ''method'' liberalism of a theorist like Maria Montessori, through the directive (or structured) liberalism that is perhaps most characteristic of John Dewey's philosophy, to the virtually nondirective, or laissez-faire, liberalism of A. S. Neill or Carl Rogers.

Educational Liberationism

Liberationism is the point of view that maintains that we should seek the immediate large-scale reform of the established political order as a way of furthering individual liberties and promoting the maximum realization of personal potential. Educational liberationism covers a wide spectrum of views, ranging from the relatively conservative ''reform'' liberationism of the civil rights protests during the mid-sixties to the urgent and passionate commitment of the frequently Marxist ''revolutionary'' liberationism, with its call for the active collaboration of the educational system in the immediate overthrow of the existing political order.

For the educational liberationist, the school should be *objective* (rational-scientific) but not *neutral*. It has an ideological function: it exists not only to teach children how to think effectively (rationally and scientifically) but also to help them recognize the superior wisdom inherent within the most convincing intellectual solutions that are currently available with respect to significant human problems. Phrased somewhat differently, educational liberationism is founded on an open system of truth, but it encompasses a particular commitment to whatever course of action is supported by the informed and objective consensus of the intellectual community at any particular time. It is ultimately a problem- or procedure-centered orientation, but it also encompasses a strong secondary commitment to the best *answers* produced by trained intelligence. It maintains that the school is morally obligated to identify and promote constructive social programs and not merely to train the mind, that it should seek to advance the most convincing course of action that is supported by an objective analysis of the available facts.

Educational Anarchism

Anarchism is the point of view that advocates the abolition of virtually all institutional restraints over human freedom as a way of providing the fullest expression of liberated human potentialities. Probably best represented in education through the writings of Ivan Illich and Paul Goodman, the educational anarchist point of view covers a variety of positions, extending from the ''tactical'' anarchist who would dissolve the schools in order to dramatize the need for a new social system, all the way through the "utopian" anarchist who envisions a society indefinitely liberated from virtually all institutional restraints whatsoever.

The educational anarchist, like the educational liberal and the educational liberationist, generally adheres to an open system of experimental inquiry (the rational-scientific verification of knowledge) or to assumptions held to be compatible with such a system of inquiry. In contrast to virtually all of the other educational ideologies, however, the educational anarchist holds that we should emphasize the need for minimizing and/or eliminating institutional restraints on personal behavior, that we should, insofar as possible, *deinstitutionalize society.* Accordingly, he maintains that the best approach to education is one that attempts to precipitate immediate large-scale humanistic reforms within society by eliminating the existing system of schools altogether.

The Educational Questions

Each of the statements contained within the EII represents a position advocated by one or more of the basic educational ideologies as they address themselves to the following fundamental questions relating to the nature and conditions of education:

1. What is the overall goal of education?
2. What are the more immediate objectives of the school as a specific social institution?
3. What are the general characteristics of the teaching-learning situation?
4. What is the general nature of the child as learner?
5. How should education be controlled, organized, and administered?
6. What should be the general nature of the curriculum?
7. What special subject matter should be taught?
8. What instructional methods and evaluation procedures should be employed?
9. How should discipline be maintained?

SOME BASIC CAUTIONS

While a vast number of qualifications could easily be appended to an inventory of this sort, three are perhaps necessary.

1. Certain terminological problems invariably occur in this kind of enterprise. Three of these generate some degree of confusion in this Inventory. First, the terms *liberalism* and *conservatism* tend to be somewhat confusing, because they refer both to overall *political* orientations (as they often do in everyday language) and also to specific *educational* orientations and ideologies within these political orientations. The ideology of *educational conservatism* is, for example, one of three educational positions that are generally characterized as being socially and politically "conservative" in nature. In a similar sense, the

ideology of *educational liberalism* is merely one of three educational positions that are generally viewed as socially and politically "liberal." This confusion is regrettable, but no other terms seemed quite appropriate or less confusing, and every effort was made to avoid coining new and unfamiliar terms if at all possible. The choice was therefore essentially one of comparative evils.

Second, since this model is based largely on underlying political differences, every attempt has been made to use educational labels that accurately represent the ethical and political origins of the positions described. Unfortunately, this has not been possible in two cases. After some experimentation, the term *educational intellectualism* was settled upon as the pedagogical counterpart for philosophical and theological conservatism, because no more satisfactory term could be located. This is unfortunate, because the term *intellectualism* has a history, as well as a host of connotations, that tend to be distracting and somewhat misleading. On the other hand, all of the other terms considered— *rationalism, absolutism, authoritarianism,* and others—were deemed even more defective in one way or another, and no new term seemed quite appropriate. In a similar sense, *educational fundamentalism* leaves a great deal to be desired, but other terms that were considered—*restorationism, revivalism, populism*—were even more inexact or inappropriate.

Every attempt has been made in this Inventory to keep ambiguity to a minimum. This is difficult at best in such a highly abstract realm as educational philosophy, but, whenever possible, the attempt has been made to rely on a sort of tacit consensus about the meaning of such terms as *education, schooling, state* and such, following ordinary language usage wherever possible and avoiding special professional or academic jargon. On occasion this has led to the elimination of a specific item—for example, "Learning ordinarily implies teaching"—which would have been generally satisfactory for a professional audience but which might very well be misconstrued by those less tuned-in to the meanings professional educators generally attach to the terms *teaching* and *learning*.

There is also a certain vagueness inherent in certain philosophical terms— *knowledge, values, absolutes,* and so on—but no attempt has been made to append tedious parenthetical explanations, examples, and lengthy verbal qualifications in order to keep the items as brief and, hopefully, as simple as possible. In a similar sense, qualifications pertaining to such things as the age of the students, the level of schooling, and such, have been avoided wherever possible unless they were absolutely necessary to clarify the meaning of a particular statement.

2. There are significant differences between the secular and religious expressions of the basic social ethics represented in the educational ideologies model. On the other hand, religious and secular approaches within the same ideological tradition tend to converge in their recommendations for social action, and, in most cases, it is possible to disregard abstract explanatory principles pertaining to more profound metaphysical matters if these make no practical difference in applied ethics, political philosophy, and educational theory. In the case of the Liberal ideologies, for example, there are clearly both religious and secular traditions in all three of the basic positions of *liberalism, liberationism,* and *anarchism,* but these differences tend to occur almost entirely at the level of

philosophical explanation, and the religious and secular expressions of each of the Liberal ideologies tend to favor the same educational principles and practices, albeit for somewhat different reasons.

Indeed, while there is a very real difference between the religious and secular traditions within all of the educational ideologies, these differences have more effect upon ideological rhetoric than upon the substance of actual recommendations at the operational level. Accordingly, in formulating the items for the Inventory every attempt has been made to use nonreligious terminology when conveying ideas common to both the secular and religious traditions within a particular ideological position. Terms with religious associations, such as *God, spirit,* and *soul,* have been avoided in virtually all cases.

3. In almost all instances the range of ideological responses to the different topics included in the Inventory represents *continua* and not *dichotomies.* In other words, with certain exceptions, the educational ideologies differ primarily in *degree* and not in *kind.* In most instances, and as indicated earlier, they represent different perceptions of the same or similar problems (such as the objectives of the school or the nature of the curriculum), or they place different priorities and/or degrees of emphasis on shared ideas or approaches.

THE SELECTION OF ITEMS

In general, six principles were employed in selecting items for use in this Inventory.

1. The items included were largely restricted to rather general ideas relating to social ethics and educational policies as these pertain to each of the six ideological positions. In line with the theoretical assumptions discussed above, no attempt was made to extend overall principles and policies into the realm of highly specific educational practices, such as whether or not to sing Christmas carols, to observe religious holidays, to have flag salutes, and so on.

2. In a similar sense, every attempt was made to include only items that appeared to be logically implied on the basis of more fundamental ethical, political, and educational ideas that were central to the ideological position being presented. Where possible, conventional notions that have long been perpetuated on the basis that they are *correlated with* (that is, associated with, but not logically *implied by*) the more basic ideas within the positions in question were kept to a minimum. In line with this, every attempt was made to eliminate stereotypes and caricatures of the different educational positions. For example, the point of view that holds that all traditional philosophies advocate some kind of prescientific and prepsychological "transfer of training" based upon outdated "faculty psychology" was avoided. In a similar sense, such spurious and untenable generalizations as that which holds that all educational intellectualists (who advocate philosophical enlightenment on the basis of perfected reason) maintain that "learning proceeds from the abstract to the concrete" were discarded.

3. Not all of the basic educational topics (such as the nature of the curriculum, classroom methods, discipline, and so on) that were used in the theoretical model (as represented by contrasting items pertaining to all six of the

ideologies) were employed as sources of items in the Inventory, because, in several cases, one or more of the ideological positions represented did not contrast sufficiently with one or more of the others to yield clearcut conceptual differences. In these cases, no attempt was made to *create* significant differences artificially in order to expedite the sort of conceptual organization that might have facilitated test construction. (In relationship to the objectives of the school, for example, both the educational liberal and the educational liberationist would agree—with somewhat different emphases — that the central objective of schooling is to provide students with the information and skills necessary in order to learn effectively for themselves. Such an item is not therefore included in the Inventory, because it is not sufficiently discriminative.)

4. Propositions where all ideologies are (or might conceivably be) in substantial agreement have been eliminated, since they obviously do not discriminate. For example, virtually all of the ideological positions would agree to such statements as: "One of the basic objectives of the school should be to teach the students how to reason effectively." "Education calls for the fullest realization of each person's unique potentiality as a particular human being." "Knowledge should be a means for ensuring survival and for advancing successful behavior."

5. Where there was agreement across general political orientations (that is, for example, between one of the "conservative" ideologies and one of the "liberal" ideologies) with respect to an idea, that idea was also eliminated as an item. Thus, since both the educational conservatives and the educational liberationists tend to agree on the value of using some kind of active dialectical approach in which the student is constantly challenged by the teacher to examine and resolve contradictions or inconsistencies within his own thinking—an approach common to both the Socratic method and the Marxist dialectic—the decision was made to eliminate such a position as a basis for discriminating between ideological positions.

6. Where one or more of the three ideological positions within a general political orientation does not take a position with respect to an idea, that idea has been excluded as a basis for discriminating between positions, and no items relating to it are included in the Inventory. Thus the statement "Educational goals should be adapted to the greatest good for the greatest number" is acceptable to both the educational liberals and to the educational liberationists but it has limited application to the educational anarchists, so the item has been eliminated altogether. An after-the-fact analysis of the conceptual model upon which the EII was constructed indicates that this principle did not lead to any significant sins of omission with respect to the basic convictions of any of the educational ideologies represented.

SCORING

To score the test it is necessary (1) to identify the educational ideologies represented by the various items and (2) to determine the numerical weight of the responses assigned to the various items. (see p. 2).

Scoring Key (Educational Ideologies)

Educational Fundamentalism	F
Educational Intellectualism	I
Educational Conservatism	C
Educational Liberalism	LL
Educational Liberationism	LB
Educational Anarchism	A

General Conservatism	GC
General Liberalism	GL

1. LL	27. LB	53. LL	79. LB
2. I	28. A	54. A	80. A
3. LB	29. GC	55. C	81. C
4. C	30. GC	56. LL	82. GL
5. F	31. LL	57. I	83. C
6. A	32. LB	58. GC	84. LB
7. GC	33. F	59. LB	85. A
8. LL	34. C	60. GL	86. GC
9. GC	35. LL	61. I	87. F
10. I	36. LB	62. F	88. C
11. A	37. I	63. I	89. GL
12. C	38. LL	64. LB	90. F
13. LL	39. A	65. I	91. A
14. I	40. GL	66. A	92. C
15. LB	41. I	67. LL	93. I
16. GL	42. F	68. C	94. GC
17. F	43. LL	69. LB	95. LB
18. GC	44. GC	70. A	96. A
19. F	45. A	71. F	97. F
20. A	46. C	72. C	98. GL
21. LB	47. GL	73. GL	99. LB
22. C	48. I	74. I	100. I
23. I	49. GL	75. LL	101. F
24. LL	50. LL	76. C	102. GL
25. F	51. LB	77. LL	103. A
26. GC	52. F	78. F	104. C

SCORING FORM

Strongly Agree					+2
Agree					+1
Undecided					0
Disagree					−1
Strongly Disagree					−2

F	I	C	LL	LB	A	GC	GL
5. __	2. __	4. __	1. __	3. __	6. __	7. __	16. __
17. __	10. __	12. __	8. __	15. __	11. __	9. __	40. __
19. __	14. __	22. __	13. __	21. __	20. __	18. __	47. __
25. __	23. __	34. __	24. __	27. __	28. __	26. __	49. __
33. __	37. __	46. __	31. __	32. __	39. __	29. __	60. __
42. __	41. __	55. __	35. __	36. __	45. __	30. __	73. __
52. __	48. __	68. __	38. __	51. __	54. __	44. __	82. __
62. __	57. __	72. __	43. __	59. __	66. __	58. __	89. __
71. __	61. __	76. __	50. __	64. __	70. __	86. __	98. __
78. __	63. __	81. __	53. __	69. __	80. __	94. __	102. __
87. __	65. __	83. __	56. __	79. __	85. __		
90. __	74. __	88. __	67. __	84. __	91. __		
97. __	93. __	92. __	75. __	95. __	96. __		
101. __	100. __	104. __	77. __	99. __	103. __		

Score:

F _____ I _____ C _____ LL _____ LB _____ A _____ GC _____ GL _____

CONSTRUCTION AND STANDARDIZATION

This Inventory has gone through a progressive series of modifications and corrections. Starting with a bank of approximately three hundred items, derived from the conceptual model provided in this book, the EII has, at various stages of development, been administered to approximately 1000 students over a period of three years. Comments and criticisms were solicited, and the final revision of the Inventory was prepared on the basis of this feedback.

The revised Inventory was standardized on a group of approximately 400 students at the University of Southern California (including off-campus and overseas graduate centers of the University of Southern California), California State University at Long Beach, and California State University at Fullerton.

The standardization population consisted of approximately 200 pre-service students taking upper-division courses in the undergraduate teacher education sequences at these institutions and an approximately equal number of in-service professional educators, many with years of professional experience, pursuing advanced degrees at the same institutions. Statistical summaries relating to such things as validity, reliability, and averages were obtained from this population.

Validity and Content Analysis

The construct validity of the EII was established by comparing the Inventory items that were assigned to the various educational ideologies with the conceptual schemata included in this book.

Correlation coefficients for the EII categories were computed and subjected to the Guilford scale for interpretation. This indicated that the individual ideologies were factorially "clean." In addition, the inner correlations among the positions of the more Conservative ideologies continuum and the inner correlations among those of the more Liberal ideologies continuum provided validation for the contention that the ideologies do in fact range on a continuum from extreme conservatism (educational fundamentalism) to extreme liberalism (educational anarchism).

Correlations of a moderate degree (according to the Guilford scale) were observed to exist among the Conservative continuum positions (see Table 1), with one paired correlation achieving a high degree of magnitude *(Fundamentalism-General Conservatism)*. In a similar sense, all the correlations achieved among the Liberal ideologies were also observed to be of moderate magnitude as interpreted according to the Guilford scale.

NORMS

The means and standard deviations determined for the standardization population (rounded off to the nearest whole number) were as follows:

	Mean	Standard Deviations
Fundamentalism	−6	8
Intellectualism	−1	6
Conservatism	0	8
Liberalism	12	6
Liberationism	7	6
Anarchism	4	7
General Conservatism	0	6
General Liberalism	7	4

These norms provide the basis for all subsequent interpretations of individual scores. Obviously, group and/or class norms may be established by those using the Inventory, and in some cases it may prove useful to determine local norms for the population at hand.

TABLE I
CORRELATION MATRIX: EDUCATIONAL IDEOLOGIES INVENTORY

	Fundamentalism	Intellectualism	Conservatism	General Conservatism	Liberalism	Liberationism	Anarchism	General Liberalism
Fundamentalism		.55	.64	.71	−.02	−.11	−.17	.12
Intellectualism			.42	.56	.13	.16	.10	.18
Conservatism				.59	.25	.06	−.09	.30
General Conservatism					.05	−.07	−.18	.08
Liberalism						.52	.47	.64
Liberationism							.58	.51
Anarchism								.40
General Liberalism								

Guilford interpretive scale:

$0 \ r \pm .20 \ = $ Slight
$\pm .20 \ r \pm .40 \ = $ Low
$\pm .40 \ r \pm .70 \ = $ Moderate
$\pm .70 \ r \pm .90 \ = $ High
$\pm .90 \ r \pm 1.00 = $ Very High

DETERMINING THE EDUCATIONAL IDEOLOGIES PROFILE

Once the total scores have been obtained for each of the ideological positions, these scores can easily be graphed on the Educational Ideologies Profile form in the manner indicated in the following example:

EDUCATIONAL IDEOLOGIES PROFILE

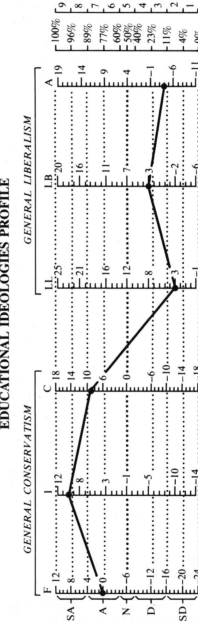

It should be noted that the mean score (or 50th centile) for each of the ideologies is not zero, but rather the mean score obtained from the standardization population. In the prior example, for instance, a person who earns a score of +10 on educational intellectualism would count up 11 intervals above the mean (which is the heavier horizontal dots in the center of the graph). Thus, a score of +10 on intellectualism indicates that the individual has a score that exceeds that earned by approximately 96% of those taking the Inventory. In cases where an individual earns a score that exceeds the range listed on the graph, he should plot his score as if it were the extreme score that corresponds most closely to the score he actually obtained on the Inventory.

Once graphed, the scores will be seen to correspond to approximate centile rankings that are listed on the right-hand side of the Profile. Thus, as on the example, a score of +3 on educational liberationism means that a person has a score which falls at approximately the 23rd centile on a scale ranging from 0 to 100%. Accordingly, if the scores earned by the standardization population are representative of those within the general population, about 75% of those taking the Inventory should be *more* enthusiastic about educational liberationism and about 25% should be *less* so. In terms of the response-categories used in conjunction with the items in the Inventory, a score in the lowest 2 intervals (extending from 0 to 10%), is the equivalent of a generalized response-orientation of *Strongly Disagree,* a score in the next 2 intervals up (extending from roughly 11 to 40%) to *Disagree,* and so on. These intervals, indicating the intensity of agreement/disagreement, are listed in the left-hand column of the Profile.

The stanine scores, which range from 1 to 9 along the extreme right-hand vertical column, are used when the Profile is employed in conjunction with the educational game entitled *Controversy and Compromise*, which uses the same ideological positions identified in the inventory. (See the first page of this appendix for information on availability of the game.) The significance of these numbers is discussed in the scoring procedures for the game, but they can be disregarded by those taking the Inventory solely for diagnostic purposes.

The two scores that are not plotted on the Profile are *General Conservatism* and *General Liberalism.* Since these are more encompassing and generalized ideological *orientations* rather than specific educational *ideologies,* they are not comparable to the more specific ideological positions that are represented on the graph. The appropriate raw scores and norms (means and standard deviation scores) for these two positions should be entered at the appropriate point indicated at the bottom of the profile graph, but these scores must be interpreted differently from the more specific scores for the ideological positions, which are charted on the graph itself.

INTERPRETATION OF SCORES

This taxonomy is an "ideal-type" conceptual model and is not intended to represent a clear-cut separation of actual beliefs and practices. The fact that one subscribes to a particular position does not necessarily restrict one from subscribing to other positions as well, and the degree and combination of a person's convictions are probably much more indicative of his overall orientation than a score in any one area. Some combinations—such as those between liberalism, liberationism, and anarchism—are more likely to occur than others (such as that between fundamentalism and anarchism), because there is a common line of reasoning between some of the ideologies that makes correlations more likely to occur.

Indeed, there are probably underlying philosophical convictions that are capable of yielding certain predictable relationships between different ideological areas. Conjecturally, for example, a strong affinity for both intellectualism and liberationism may be indicative of an underlying commitment to the philosophy of existentialism, and, in a similar sense, a predilection for both anarchism and intellectualism may suggest that the individual is predisposed toward the "libertarian" *Objectivist* philosophy of Ayn Rand or some similar position. On the other hand, particular combinations probably reflect ambivalence, inconsistency, or self-contradiction. A strong tendency toward fundamentalism would ordinarily seem to be inconsistent with a strong affinity for anarchism, and it would seem very difficult to reconcile conservatism with liberationism.*

Scores on General Conservatism and General Liberalism

General Liberalism scores can be interpreted as follows:

Strongly Agree (90% and above)	+13 and above
Agree (60% to 90%)	+ 9 through +12
Neutral (40% to 60%)	+ 6 through + 8
Disagree (10% to 40%)	+ 5 through + 2
Strongly Disagree (10% and below)	+ 1 and below

General Conservatism scores can be interpreted as follows:

Strongly Agree (90% and above)	+8 and above
Agree (60% to 90%)	+2 through +7
Neutral (40% to 60%)	+1 through −1
Disagree (10% to 40%)	−2 through −7
Strongly Disagree (10% and below)	−8 and below

---

*On the other hand, there are positions in Eastern philosophy, such as Zen Buddhism, which *could* be invoked to explain even ostensibly contradictory orientations. In Japan, for example, Zen Buddhists have traditionally subscribed to a very Conservative orientation—which, educationally, might be described as combining elements of fundamentalism, intellectualism, and conservatism—while, at the same time, they advocate that the individual go through a process of enlightenment in which he successfully undergoes a transition from a *cognitive* approach to living to one better characterized as more or less "aesthetic," in which ostensibly anarchistic "spontaneity" and "immediacy" is prized over any sort of self-conscious intellective process whatsoever. In the case of Zen Buddhism, however, the ultimate goal is a psychological transition from self-consciousness to pure (non-self-conscious) consciousness. The important thing is not what the individual *does* but how he *experiences* what he does. In other words, the nature and content of society is fundamentally irrelevant, because the goal of education is to master the imperatives of the particular social order so effectively that they become second-nature and can therefore be dismissed from consciousness, which thereby becomes more available to a much wider range of otherwise inaccessible types of purely *personal* experience.

THE EDUCATIONAL IDEOLOGIES PROFILE

The Profile is, in many respects, more important than the constituent scores. It answers four basic questions:

1. Does a person have a clear-cut educational ideology or ideologies? Does he have a decided tendency in any given ideological direction or directions? Does he significantly exceed the average in either a positive or negative direction on any particular ideology or ideologies?
2. Is his Educational Ideologies Profile consistent? Do his inclinations in any one ideological direction tend to reinforce similar inclinations with respect to other ideological positions in the same general political (liberal or conservative) orientation? Do his inclinations in any particular ideological direction tend to be inconsistent in terms of his performance with respect to other ideological positions?
3. Does he tend to be highly suggestible, agreeing rather uncritically with virtually all positions regardless of consistency or self-contradiction?
4. Does he tend to be negativistic? Does he tend to disagree with, or to be hypercritical of, virtually all of the ideological positions without exception?

Glossary

The following are somewhat abbreviated definitions of key terms that have occurred in the body of the text. In most cases these definitions are significantly less definitive than the explanations provided in the various chapters. For less simplistic considerations, the reader should consult the Index and refer back to the original discussion of the various terms as they occur in context.

Academic learning—has reference both to learning how to learn, and to mastering the sort of technical knowledge and skills that are only indirectly related to more central human problems.

Aesthetics—is one of the central topics traditionally viewed as constituting a necessary aspect of any fully conceived philosophy; specifically, asking the question, "What is *beauty?*"

Apocalypticism (apocalyptic)—has reference to any doctrine concerning the end of the temporal world, but especially one that is based on the supposed prophetic passages in the Revelations of St. John the Divine. Most apocalyptics forecast imminent disaster and total or universal destruction, and most also espouse the millenial doctrine of the Second Advent and personal reign of Jesus Christ on earth.

Augustinian conservatism (in Christian theology)—is a conservative theological position that emphasizes intuition and faith over reason.

Axiological epistemology—has reference to any philosophical speculation about how we come to know about either personal or social values, whether and to what extent values are related to facts, and whether cognition is based upon affective behavior (or vice versa).

Axiology—is one of the central topics traditionally viewed as constituting a necessary aspect of any fully conceived philosophy; specifically, asking the question, "What is ultimately *good?*"

Behaviorism (behavioristic)—is the philosophical position that holds that sense-perceptual experience is a function of psychobiological behavior in the physical world.

Biological (or **qualified**) **empiricism**—holds that only personal experience is knowable, and that all personal experience is based on biological processes, growing out of the sense-perceptual encounter between the physical organism and the material world.

Cause-and-effect-determinism—is the point of view that holds that all events are caused by the prior interaction between immediately preceding objects and events, which were themselves the products of the relationship between prior objects/events, and so on and on, ad infinitum.

Circular processes (in philosophy)—are explanations, such as those that occur in the case of synergism and self-fulfilling prophesies, where one particular sequence of events leads inexorably to a subsequent sequence of events, which inevitably terminates in a recapitulation of either the initial sequence or in some slight modification thereof. Attempts to represent circularity (and, particularly, synergism) through two-dimensional diagrams are generally misleading. What actually occurs in most cases is a spiral progression in which, other things being equal, conditions become either progressively better (in the case of **positive synergism**) or progressively worse (as in the case of **negative synergism**).

In other words, synergism and circularity in philosophy seldom refer to a causal sequence in which there is a sterile and mechanical repetition. Thus, Marx's sociology of knowledge point of view—which is essentially circular, representing a positive synergism when viewed in broad perspective—does not deny novelty or imply the constant recapitulation of the past. Rather, it guarantees novelty and change: physical and social conditions generate personal behavior, which creates personal experience, which provides the basis for organized social existence—which, in turn, generates ideology, which (ultimately) works to modify physical and social conditions (and so on and so on).

Circularity of knowledge—has reference to the idea that holds that belief systems are essentially self-perpetuating and self-reinforcing; what one believes determines what one does, which, in turn, determines what one learns and therefore believes, which (since it is indirectly the product of the individual's initial beliefs in the first place) tends to generate the same and similar sorts of belief as those which the individual began with in the first place.

Civil religion—is the term revived by sociologist Robert Bellah with reference to a general religion (sometimes labeled "the American way of life") in contrast to the far more particular religions usually identified with specific churches, synagogues, revivals, missions, and such. Such a religion has its own set of sacred symbols, rituals and beliefs, and it generally functions as a "religiofication" of the nation, providing an ultimate and overriding goal for the political process.

Classical Protestantism—has reference to groups whose religious convictions are rooted in reformation-based theologies, who align themselves with the point of view that what happened at the Reformation was fundamentally right. Such groups are based upon the notion that ultimate authority is vested in the Scriptures, but they do not assume the verbal inerrancy and historical accuracy of every single statement in the Bible.

Closed-truth approaches to philosophy—consist of those philosophies that begin with specified interpretations of the nature, content, and meaning of reality that go beyond the contention that a particular process or mode of inquiry and/or verification provides the best access to truth.

Collective consciousness—see **Corporate selfhood**.

Common sense knowledge—is that which is known precognitively by the average man as the result of "lived" experience (in contrast to what is understood on the basis of intellectual speculation).

Conative behavior—is presymbolic behavior mediated by tacit motor-emotional response-tendencies that are implicitly purposive (as in the behavior of the newborn infant).

Conservative educational ideologies—are those which share the common assumption that the ultimate value resides in some type of self-realization but which maintain that self-realization is properly attained only indirectly, by identifying and adhering to natural and/or divine law. The three Conservative ideologies are educational fundamentalism, educational intellectualism and educational conservatism (each of which can be subdivided into two or more basic suborientations).

Conservative Judaism—is one of the three major traditions in contemporary Judaism. Less stringent and encompassing than orthodox Judaism, it views "Jewishness" as the ultimate source of "Judaicity." Conservative Judaism generally adheres to traditional beliefs, but accepts some variations from traditional observances and rituals, generally being more traditional in beliefs than in practices.

Continuum (continua)—has reference to a total situation that can be reduced conceptually to a continuous series of differences in degree. Generally speaking, for example, the Liberal educational ideologies tend to represent a continuum, but the Conservative educational ideologies are probably best represented as substantially different kinds of orientations rather than as simply different gradations within a generically similar point of view.

Corporate selfhood—holds that identity is basically a suprapersonal phenomenon located in the historical consciousness of entire cultures or nations; therefore self-actualization is invariably a corollary of participating in some *corporate* (or *collective*) identity far broader than individual personality. This corporate identity is sometimes referred to by the German term *Volksgeist* ("spirit of the people"), or by the term popularized by the sociologist-philosopher Émile Durkheim, *collective consciousness.*

Cultural relativism—maintains that all personal experience is largely relative to (and therefore reliant upon) existing social conditions (the nature of child-rearing patterns; family organization; dominant political, economic and religious institutions; and so on). Human personality is essentially a sociovocal creation, emerging out of man's capacity to construct an indirect, or symbolic, universe through the medium of culture.

Deism—is the point of view that accepts God only as an historical agent, a force that originally created the universe but which no longer intercedes directly in its operations.

Democratic capitalism—has reference to the political philosophy that is staunchly committed to the capitalistic economic system of individualistic free enterprise, and which typically views this system as characterized by private ownership of property, little or no limitation on the accumulation of property, and the absence (or severe restriction) of governmental intervention in the economy.

Democratic socialism—ordinarily favors a limit on the accumulation of private property (including public ownership of all major industries, utilities, and transportation) as well as extensive government regulation of the economy.

Dialectical materialism—has reference to Karl Marx's philosophy that holds that the observable world is real in its own right, neither deriving its reality from any supernatural or transcendental source, nor depending for its existence on the mind of man. The term *dialectical* expresses the dynamic interconnectedness of things, the universality of change and its radical character. Everything possessing any sort of reality is in process of self-transformation, owing to the fact that its content is made up of opposing factors or forces, the internal movement of which interconnects everything, changing each thing into something else. Thus, physical and social conditions generate personal behavior, which creates personal experience, which provides the basis for organized social existence—which, in turn, generates ideology, which (ultimately) works to modify physical and social conditions (and so on and so on, in what is essentially a synergistic process).

Dichotomy (dichotomies)—has reference to the logical classification of phenomena by division into two mutually exclusive and exhaustive groups. Used less rigorously, as it is in this book, it refers to ideas that differ in *kind* and not merely in *degree*. Thus, in the case of the educational ideologies, educational intellectualism is a substantially different kind of theory from educational liberationism; it differs substantially in what it says, why it says it, and how it justifies its contentions, and not merely in the extent to which it emphasizes or develops common themes or ideas.

Directive liberalism—seeks basic reforms in both the means and ends of the schools as they presently exist, maintaining that both the established ends and means (including objectives, content, and methods) need to be radically revised away from their traditional authoritarian orientation, and adapted instead to the more appropriate objectives of teaching every child to think effectively for himself or herself.

Double-truth theory—holds that truth (and value) is both natural and supernatural. Most frequently associated with the theistic intellectualist position, the practical upshot of this is to break the world up into not only two but three basic spheres: (1) the self (the natural subject with supernatural attributes—the supernatural aspect frequently being referred to as the "soul"); (2) the world (the natural object); and (3) God (the supernatural determinative reality that transcends and, in some sense, determines both subject and object).

Eclecticism—is the philosophical approach in which an individual selects ideas from a variety of different philosophical positions in order to synthesize his own particular worldview.

Educational anarchism—is that educational ideology that holds that we should emphasize the need for minimizing and/or eliminating institutional restraints on personal behavior, that we should, insofar as possible, *de-institutionalize society*. Accordingly, the educational anarchist maintains that the best approach to education is one that attempts to precipitate immediate large-scale humanistic reforms within society by eliminating the existing system of schools altogether. In a decentralized, deinstitutionalized society, people would be returned to themselves, to a radically simplified world of I-thou relationships based on significantly fewer needs, significantly greater vitality, enhanced rationality, and the sort of true morality that is based upon enlightened personal responsibility.

Educational conservatism—is fundamentally that educational ideology which espouses adherence to time-tested cultural institutions and processes, coupled with a deep respect for law and order, as a basis for any sort of constructive social change. In education, the educational conservative views the central goal of the school as being the preservation and transmission of established social patterns and traditions. Characteristically present-oriented, the educational conservative has a deep respect for the past, but he is primarily concerned with the usefulness and applicability of learning within the present social context. He seeks to promote the fullest development of the contemporary society by ensuring the sort of slow and organic change that is compatible with preestablished legal and institutional requirements.

Educational essentialism—is the educational philosophy that holds to the central propositions that the universe is governed by encompassing law and preestablished order, and that the chief task of the school is to acquaint students with this law and order so that they may appreciate it and adjust to it.

Educational fundamentalism—is that educational ideology that encompasses all of those types of political conservatism that are basically anti-intellectual in the sense that they seek to minimize philosophical and/or intellectual considerations, tending to ground their contentions upon a relatively uncritical acceptance of either revealed Truth or established social consensus (usually justified as "common sense"). The educational fundamentalist holds that contemporary society is faced with imminent moral collapse, and that the highest imperative is consequently to reform conventional standards of belief and behavior by returning to the morally superior virtues characteristic of an earlier time. Accordingly, the goal of the school is to restore the older and better ways in order to reconstruct the existing social order.

Educational ideologies—are ideologies relating essentially to the nature and conduct of schooling. They differ from the more conventional "educational philosophies" in the sense of being more specific systems of general ideas; they are more oriented to social ethics than to the more abstract systems of philosophy (like realism, idealism, and pragmatism). The ideologies intend primarily to direct social action and not merely to clarify or order knowledge, and they function both as a cause and an effect of fundamental social change. The educational ideologies consist of the six basic systems of social ethics, refracted through their corresponding political philosophies, which emerge as the three Conservative ideologies (educational fundamentalism, educational intellectualism, educational conservatism) and the three Liberal ideologies (educational liberalism, educational liberationism, and educational anarchism). These educational ideologies consist primarily of the applications and implications of these underlying moral and political positions for the conduct of schooling.

Educational intellectualism—is that educational ideology that emerges out of those expressions of political Conservatism that are based upon closed and fundamentally authoritarian philosophical or theological systems of thought. Generally speaking, philosophical Conservatism seeks to change existing political (including educational) practices in order to make them conform more perfectly to some established and essentially unvarying intellectual or spiritual ideal.

Educational liberalism—is that educational ideology that holds that the long-range goal of education is to preserve and improve the existing social order by teaching each child how to deal effectively with his or her own emerging life-problems. In a more specific sense, the educational liberal maintains that the school as a particular educational institution should attempt both to provide students with the information and skills necessary to learn effectively for themselves and to teach students how to solve practical problems through the application of individual and group problem-solving processes based upon rational-scientific procedures for testing and proving ideas.

Educational liberationism—is that educational ideology that maintains that the ultimate goal of education should be to implement the reconstruction of society along truly humanistic lines that emphasize the fullest development of each person's unique potentialities as a human being. More specifically, the school should provide students with the information and skills necessary to learn effectively for themselves; it should teach students how to solve practical problems through the application of individual and group problem-solving techniques based upon the rational-scientific verification of knowledge; and it should help students to recognize and respond to the need for whatever constructive social reforms appear required by the demands of time.

Educational perennialism—is the educational philosophy that posits the existence of changeless, universal patterns that underlie and determine all actual objects and events and that holds that the proper goal of education is to lead the individual toward everlasting, timeless, and spaceless principles of reality, truth, and value.

Educational philosophies (approach to educational philosophy)—is that approach which holds that it is possible to identify and define "educational philosophies" (commonly identified with such terms as *educational essentialism* and *educational perennialism*) that exist substantially apart from other types of philosophy and that can be looked upon as at least conceptually separable from the traditional "formal systems" of philosophical thought, such as realism and idealism.

Educational policies—are ideas pertaining to what sort of knowledge is necessary and how such knowledge should be imparted to others in order to guarantee the success of specified moral and political policies in some particular cultural setting.

Educational progressivism—is the educational philosophy that holds that the central purpose of the school is to improve practical intelligence, to make the child more effective in solving the problems presented within the context of normal, everyday experience.

Educational reconstructionism—is the educational philosophy that holds that the school should lead the way in attempting to create a more humanistic, humanizing, and democratic social order.

Empirical analysis—is the philosophical approach that is essentially directed at determining whether a statement can be proven factual on the basis of some accepted protocol for experimental verification, usually the scientific method.

Empirical logic—is that aspect of epistemology, closely related to formal logic, which deals with the source and nature of truth-propositions (being concerned essentially with *factuality* rather than *validity*).

Empirical philosophies—encompass all of those philosophies that are based upon the primary assumption that existence precedes and determines essence; that personal experience comes before, and gives rise to, all knowledge whatsoever. Empirical philosophies are those systems of philosophy (such as behaviorism and experimentalism) that hold that all knowledge is ultimately personal knowledge, that all knowing is necessarily "evident" and grounded in sense-perceptual encounters with particular objects and events.

Empirical realism—has reference to those philosophies (particularly existentialism) that hold that there is a real world which exists independent of being known but that this world has no meaning—is essentially "absurd"—except as it is encountered and interpreted through personal experience.

Empiricism—holds that all knowledge is the product of personal experience, such experience usually being viewed as emerging out of the individual's sense-perceptual encounter with a world that exists independent of being known.

Epistemological determinism—is the point of view, frequently associated with Einstein, that all objects/events are absolutely determined but that we are (at least temporarily) epistemologically incapable of identifying and defining the determinants beyond a certain (rather crude) level of operations; sometimes referred to as *indeterminable determinism*.

Epistemology—is one of the central topics traditionally viewed as constituting a necessary aspect of any fully conceived philosophy; specifically, asking the question, "What is ultimately *knowable*?"

Establishment conservatives (Tory conservatives)—are frequently associated with the tradition of Edmund Burke. They subscribe to a somewhat pessimistic view of human nature. They reject the idea that individual reason should reign supreme, holding, instead, that the collective wisdom of the group, as this is embodied in established institutions and processes, represents the highest expression of human intelligence at any particular time.

Ethical Judaism—is the point of view that holds that the essence of Judaism/Jewishness is the unique moral vision of a "just society" characterized by the establishment of the Kingdom of Truth, Justice, and Peace among men. The exact nature and varieties of this tradition are open to much dispute, but two basic types of ethical Judaism are generally identified: (1) *supernaturalistic ethical Judaism* ("ethical Judaism"), which holds that the Decalogue is authoritative in the sense of being divinely inspired—that is, the Ten Commandments are the essential spirit of

Judaism, and all other Jewish laws, rituals, and observances are merely secondary considerations; and (2) *naturalistic ethical Judaism* ("ethical Jewishness"), which holds that the Jews are not a "chosen people," but they have been inspired throughout history with a singular sense of moral mission and ethical idealism which, while perhaps best embodied in the Decalogue, is even better summed up in Hillel's words: "What is hateful to yourself do not to your fellow man. That is the whole Torah. All the rest is commentary. Now go and study."

Ethics—is used interchangeably with the term *moral philosophy* to encompass both questions of personal (or psychological) value and questions of social value (or interpersonal obligation), although it is frequently restricted—as it generally tends to be in this book—to the latter topic (that is, goodness and badness with respect to one's relationships with other people).

Ethnic religion (ethnodoxy)—has reference to religious beliefs adapted to the needs and requirements of a special ethnic group that has retained its separate identity within a larger and otherwise dominant culture.

Evangelicalism (or evangelical)—refers, in a broad sense, to any Christian groups that accept the basic authority of the scriptures (the Evangel), although the term is more frequently used in this book with reference to those Christian churches that emphasize the teachings and authority of the Scriptures, especially of the New Testament (usually interpreted quite literally), in contrast to the institutional authority of the church itself. The evangelicals also emphasize both the need for individual spiritual regeneration (salvation) through faith in Jesus Christ, and the action of the Holy Spirit.

Exclusivist-ecumenical gradient—refers to Dean Kelley's theory that existing religious groups in America range from the most exclusive and anti-ecumenical to those typical of the mainstream American religious traditions. traditions.

Existentialism—is an empirical philosophy that subscribes to the overarching idea that existence (personal experience) precedes and determines essence (truth, knowledge, or meaning). The existentialist also subscribes to the basic tenet of traditional realism, the principle of independence—that is, there is a world independent of the personal process of knowing. Unlike the traditional (classical) realist of the Aristotelian sort, however, the existentialist does not accept the idea that this world which is independent of being known (i.e., which constitutes 'Being' as opposed to 'existence,' or 'experienced Being') is both real and meaningful. Rather, this world is fundamentally 'absurd,' that is, 'meaningless' in any transcendent or overarching sense. It is the individual who brings 'meaning' into the world through the continuous process of cognitive *choice* (perceptual selection), which occurs in the course of normal goal-directed intentional behavior. Such choice is free, because it is determined personally. Indeed, man is not free *not to be free*. He cannot reject his goal-oriented intentionality, which generates his particular consciousness-making collision with the world of actual objects and events that have reality outside of himself.

Existentialistic theology—maintains that it is possible to make an existential choice in favor of a nonexistential (metaphysical) worldview that presupposes the reality of a personal God.

Experimentalism (experimentalistic)—is the philosophy based on the assumption that the best pragmatic (practical) test of whether or not an idea is true is one in which one experiences/observes the consequences of discrete (separate and separable) objects or events under the rigorously controlled conditions conventionally described as constituting the "scientific method," or under conditions that best approximate the requirements for such "scientific thinking."

Faith—is, in the religious sense of the term, essentially belief in the authoritative nature of someone else's prior revelation (as well as in the necessary consequences of such belief). Faith necessarily goes beyond reason and natural evidence, and is ultimately grounded in mystical intuition.

Formal logic—is the theory of the structure and relationship of truth-propositions; generally viewed as a subtopic of **epistemology**.

Formal systems (approach to educational philosophy)—is the approach in which traditionally accepted systems of philosophy (such as idealism, realism, existentialism, and pragmatism) are identified and defined, and their implications for the organization and conduct of education are systematically developed.

Free will hypothesis—is the point of view frequently associated in philosophy with David Hume and in science with Werner Heisenberg, which holds that, while reality is generally characterized by constant conjunctions (or correlations) between phenomena, there is no reason to assume that these conjunctions necessarily rest upon necessary causation in which the first element in the series gives rise to the next, which engenders the next, and so on, in a continuous sequence of inevitable determinism.

Fundamentalism (evangelical fundamentalism)—is a movement in American Protestantism that arose in the early part of the twentieth century in reaction to modernism. It stresses the infallibility of the Bible not only in matters of faith and morals but also as a literal historical record, holding belief in such doctrines as atonement by the sacrificial death of Christ, the Second Coming, the virgin birth, and physical resurrection as being essential to Christian faith. The Christian fundamentalists bitterly resist any use of modern historical research and criticism, generally reaffirming the ancient and medieval view of the relation of God to nature.

Gestalt—is a German term having reference to the whole that is greater than the sum of its parts. In holistic philosophy, Being is very often regarded as a Gestalt, which is characterized by a set of interrelated field-properties that cannot be fully understood by any examination of its constituent aspects.

Hasidism—was essentially a mystical pietistic movement within traditional (orthodox) Judaism as it existed in Eastern Europe in the mid-eighteenth century. It stressed the devout heart over the ingenious mind, and, in this sense, ran counter to the prevailing notion that Jewish scholarship and rabbinic learning was the pinnacle of Jewish virtue.

Hedonic behavior—refers to behavior that is directed and regulated by pleasure and/or pain.

Heurism—is a more restricted and specialized idea than **synergism**; in heurism, the individual pursues a line of inquiry that generates new and more productive lines of inquiry.

Holism (holistic philosophy)—is the point of view in philosophy that holds that everything that exists is ultimately encompassed within a totally unified field of forces (a cosmic whole) and that nothing can be truly understood except in its total relationship to all other aspects of Being.

"However-hence" philosophies—are practical philosophies grounded in existing circumstances. They do not reject utopian philosophical ideas; *however,* in our culture and at this time, perfect behavior is impossible; *hence* we should modify existing practices to make them as good as possible in view of the circumstances that prevail.

Humanistic religions (or **naturalistic religions**)—has reference to groups such as the Unitarians or Universalists who tend to combine an essentially naturalistic-rationalistic worldview with a relatively intellectualized concept of God as a "cosmic consciousness" rather than an anthropomorphic presence.

Idealism—is one of the conventional "systems of philosophy," ordinarily defined as encompassing all of those philosophies which accept the first principle that mind (as opposed to matter) is ultimately the only thing that can be known for certain and that it is, therefore, also the first thing to be known and the ultimate basis for all knowing whatsoever.

Ideal-type model—is a theoretical model based on conceptual (ideational) distinctions rather than practical (realistic) differences in the world as it actually exists at any particular time.

Ideology—is a value or belief system that is accepted as a fact or truth by some group, providing the believer with a picture of the world both as it is and as it should be; also frequently used, in the Marxist sense, in reference to interrelated systems of false ideas, false consciousness produced by a person's membership in a particular social class.

"If-then" philosophies—are hypothetical philosophies that assume an utopian stance; holding, in effect, that, *if* we create a perfect society, *then* we should behave in a certain way.

Immanent knowledge—is knowledge (meaning) that exists prior to any sort of purely personal experience whatsoever, and which is therefore independent of any personal act of knowing. Such knowledge (the frequently cited "inherent knowledge" of man's inalienable *free will* might serve as an example) is simply implicit within human nature as such.

Instrumentalism—is the point of view that holds that all thinking is problem solving.

Intellectual learning—refers essentially to the ideational, dealing with broad interpretive theory and abstract reasoning.

Intuitive knowledge (intuition)—is what is known directly and spontaneously, requiring no supportive evidence or proof.

Isness—is used in reference to ideas or theories that purport to *describe* the factual nature of the world, i.e., the way things actually *are* as opposed to the way they *ought to be* (**oughtness**).

Jewish reconstructionism—is the point of view, originally formulated by Mordecai Kaplan, which holds that the Jewish people are the major instrument in bringing about a secular vision of the "just society."

Laissez faire conservatives (Free Marketeers) — are largely associated with the economic doctrines of Adam Smith. They favor individual liberty within a free economic system, tending to be optimistic about human nature, and generally viewing man as naturally active, rational, competitive, acquisitive, and value-maximizing (within the constraints imposed by the objective and impersonal mechanisms of the free market).

Left-wing anarchism—generally envisions a postcollectivist society of freely cooperating individuals coming together on the basis of rational necessity in order to form temporary, *ad hoc* alliances for the solution of common problems. They generally view such a system as emerging out of socialism, which they ordinarily regard as providing a temporary and transitional resocialization of human consciousness to the new and positive kind of social ethic required as one condition for realizing real anarchistic freedom.

Left-wing libertarianism—is founded upon the traditional ethics of altruism, seeking the fullest liberation of the individual within society (based upon the point of view that man is an interdependent social being). It aims at establishing new social institutions that are capable of initiating, supporting, and sustaining the sort of society that guarantees the utilitarian ideal of the maximum realization of happiness for all. It is essentially synonymous with the term *political liberationism* as used in this book.

Liberal educational ideologies—hold that the highest good of self-realization is directly attainable through human experience in the natural world. The Liberal ideologies—educational liberalism, educational liberationism, and educational anarchism—generally hold that all knowledge is rooted in human experience, and there are no absolutes that are not ultimately relative to being known, to emerging out of some sort of human involvement in the world. They view individual experience and judgment—personal problem-solving ability, individual commitment to social liberation, or total and unrestrained self-determination—as taking precedence over all of the more traditional forms of authority and control. They hold that the highest good is to live in such a way as to allow the fullest expression of trained intelligence. Trained intelligence is further defined as critical thinking, the practical application of scientific problem-solving processes through the resolution of personal and social problems. They differ primarily in how they view the conditions necessary for such critical thinking to occur.

Liberal Protestantism—tends to be adapted to modern thought, which is dominated by science. More than any other major Christian persuasion, the liberal Protestants tend to emphasize the right of individuals to decide what is true in religion for themselves.

Logical relationships (in educational philosophy)—occur where there are relatively explicit and necessary relationships implied between moral and political positions or between such positions (generally viewed in combination, as in social ethics) and educational ideology.

Marxism—(see **dialectical materialism**).

Materialism (materialistic)—is the philosophy based upon the assumption that all behavior (and therefore all experience) is elicited by the interaction between physical objects and/or events.

Metaphilosophy (or **metasystem**)—is a philosophical system or set of ideas at a very high level of abstraction that serves as the basic point of departure for the identification and organization of less abstract theories; for example: **empirical philosophy** is a metaphilosophy because it provides the basic philosophical frame of reference that provides the basis for a number of less abstract philosophical systems, such as behaviorism, experimentalism, and Marxism.

Metaphysical (or **essentialistic**) **philosophies**—are those philosophies that hold that some kind of essence (Truth) precedes and determines existence (personal experience). It necessarily therefore stands to reason that this essence must be knowable in some significant sense prior to, and independent of, any personal act of knowing.

Metaphysical nondeterminism—is the idea, frequently associated with Hiesenberg, that holds that cause-and-effect, although presenting a true description of reality at the macroscopic level, does not apply to certain types of subatomic particles at extremely microscopic ranges of behavior.

Metaphysics—is one of the central topics that are traditionally viewed as constituting a necessary aspect of any fully conceived philosophy; specifically, asking the question "What is ultimately *real*?"

Method liberalism—takes the position that, while instructional methods (or means) should be updated to encompass new psychological insights into the nature of human learning, the goals (or ends) of education, including traditional content, are fundamentally sound and do not require significant modification.

Moral policies—are ideas that pertain to determining what course of action a particular system of moral principles implies when it is viewed in the light of specific social conditions.

Moral principles—are ideas, based upon more fundamental **value principles,** pertaining to how value principles apply to the regulation of interpersonal behavior.

Mystical intuition—is actually a sort of crypto-revelation. One knows directly and immediately, and one knows beyond all doubt, but that which is known is in no sense evidential (in the respect that it reflects merely a sudden explicit awareness of the meaning inherent within purely personal experience). As in revelation, one is seized by a nonempirical certitude, but, unlike revelation, this knowledge cannot be traced to an identifiable supernatural source.

Mysticism (in religion)—tends to be the religious counterpart of political anarchism; it is the belief that personal revelation and/or mystical intuition takes precedence over established church authority and accepted theological doctrine (at least with respect to significant aspects of religious practices).

Negative synergism—is the contrary of positive synergism, occurring whenever the synergistic process functions in such a way as to create the ongoing conditions that predispose toward the failure of subsequent phases of the process—which, in turn, creates the conditions necessary to generate even more unsuccessful behavior (in terms of the purpose or goal of the entire course of action) in subsequent phases of the process, and so on.

Neoevangelicalism (or **new evangelism**)—is a post-World War II movement that seeks to retain the religious fervor of evangelical fundamentalism while, at the same time, rejecting its emotionalism, theological legalism, ethical absolutism, and cultural/sectarian separatism.

Neo-orthodoxy—is the Christian position that rejects the characteristic optimism and faith-in-reason characteristic of Christian liberalism, holding that, while man is made in the image of God, he is nevertheless flawed by innate depravity and is therefore subject to a tragic fate.

Neutrality—is the position that refuses to state a preference between conflicting knowledge-claims.

Nihilism—is the political philosophy that actively seeks the destruction of all established laws and institutions; not a synonym for **anarchism.**

Nondirective liberalism (**laissez-faire liberalism**)—consists of those educational liberals who, while agreeing with most of the basic philosophical convictions of the directive liberals, would seek to reduce virtually all constraints within the conventional school situation by eliminating (at least to a very significant degree) such things as compulsory school attendance and compulsory instruction, as well as most prescribed learning experiences.

Nonphilosophical (or **anti-intellectual**) **reactionary conservatism**—is reactionary conservatism that basically rejects philosophical/intellectual justifications for action. This position envisions a return to the intuitive "folk wisdom" of the "common man." It is fundamentally opposed to the complex, the exotic, and the foreign, seeking some clear and simple consensus that is assumed to exist on a more or less intuitive and self-evident basis in the depths of the popular mind.

Nonrational behavior—is behavior that is not directed by conscious reason. Nonrational behavior may or may not be *irrational* behavior—that is, behavior that contradicts the dictates of conscious reason.

Normative behavior—refers to behavior based upon consciously recognized ideas about what is good and bad, right and wrong.

Objectivism—is the philosophy formulated by the contemporary novelist-philosopher Ayn Rand that presents a sort of intellectualistic social Darwinism, subscribing to an ethical system that is very close to unadulterated laissez-faire capitalism. Objectivism posits, among other things, a severe psychological hedonism, which views "selfishness"—in a relatively conventional and common-sense use of this term—as being the highest moral good, and rejecting conventional altruistic ethics as a pernicious lie.

Objectivity—refers to the position that holds that there is one particular point of view that corresponds to things as they really are, and favors ideas that meet this criterion over competing ideas relating to the same problem or issue.

Ontology—encompasses any profound and systematic speculation about first principles relating to knowing (epistemology), the known (metaphysics), and the nature of value (axiology). The term is frequently used to cover any highly abstract philosophical speculation that cuts across two or more of the conventional divisions of formal philosophy (metaphysics, epistemology, axiology, and aesthetics).

Open-truth approaches to philosophy—include all of those philosophical systems that are based upon authoritative procedures for verifying knowledge, such as the scientific method or formal logic, rather than incorporating more specific descriptions of reality (such as descriptions of the nature and conditions of the good life, or theological representations of Being replete with specific codes of conduct governing the regulation of everyday behavior).

Orthodox Judaism—is one of the three major traditions within contemporary Judaism. It looks upon Judaicity as the ultimate source of Jewishness, viewing Judaism as a total and encompassing way of life.

Oughtness—is generally used in reference to statements or theories that admonish a person to behave in a particular manner, that *prescribe* a certain mode of conduct (as opposed to merely *describing* the way things are, i.e., **isness**).

Panentheism—is the position that holds that God is nothing less than the active interrelation of all of the determinative principles (truths, laws, ideas) that shape and control the universe.

Pantheism—is the position that holds that God is to be found in everything, that God is imminent within all Being.

Pentecostalism (pentecostal)—pertains to any of the (generally fundamentalist) Christian groups that emphasize the activity of the Holy Spirit, holiness of living, and expressing their religious feelings very spontaneously, as by speaking in tongues.

Phenomenological demonstration (phenomenological reduction)—is a method by which an individual performs a radical philosophical analysis of his own personal experience, rigorously pursuing the interior meaning of his own subjectivity. It is based upon the assumption that there are objective parameters to subjectivity that can be identified solely through the application of reason.

Phenomenology—holds that all a person can ever know is his own processes of awareness, his own ''subjectivity.'' For the phenomenologist, reality is ultimately personal knowledge, a consciousness of one's own thoughts and feelings. This personal knowledge is fundamental; it is all we know and determines all of our specific beliefs and convictions. Ultimately, it is both *self-evident* in the sense that it *is* experience and therefore constitutes all evidence, and *self-determining,* because it is the primary datum that underlies and gives rise to all more particular conclusions. We only encounter the objective subjectively. At basis, personal experience is irreducible.

Philosophical absolutism (absolute Truth)—has reference to the point of view that holds that the world is inherently meaningful, that there are certain fundamental truths—natural or divine laws—that are authoritative and unchanging, and these truths precede and determine personal experience.

Philosophical behaviorism—holds that personal experience is the product of the behavior (interaction) between the organism and its physical and social environment. It holds that behavior is knowable only *indirectly* on the basis of personal experience but that all personal experience is ultimately explicable only as an expression of personal *behavior.* It differs from **psy-**

chological behaviorism primarily in that it tends to view behavior very broadly, as applying to the responses of all animate beings interrelating to the totality of the objects and events that make up their environment. It also differs in that philosophical behaviorism is *speculative,* being willing to make extended inferences about the existence of apparently prebehavioral conditions that both defy effective scientific verification and that are viewed as fundamental requirements for any sort of personal experience and/or behavior to occur.

Philosophical conservatism—encompasses all of those expressions of political conservatism that are based upon authoritarian (absolute) philosophical or theological systems of thought and that maintain that "right reason" inexorably leads to true conclusions. In general, philosophical conservatism seeks to change existing political (including educational) practices in order to make them conform more perfectly to some established and essentially unvarying intellectual or spiritual ideal. It typically envisions an intellectual and/or moral meritocracy, and provides the political foundation for the ideology of educational intellectualism.

Philosophical experimentalism—maintains that the best way to think is to perfect the natural (instrumental) process of problem-solving by imposing certain controls on inquiry that will give rise to more objective (that is, trustworthy and effective) knowledge. A common-sense adaptation of scientific problem-solving procedures is the best way to think and therefore the best way to live, since effective thinking is the best guide to effective living.

Philosophical intellectualism—is probably best represented in America today by such individuals as Robert Maynard Hutchins and Mortimer Adler, who are both primarily concerned with metaphysical wisdom in the traditional Aristotelian sense and who both tend to place great emphasis on traditional "liberal arts" education in the spirit of the "Great Books."

Philosophical reactionary conservatism—is the intellectual tradition of reactionary conservatism frequently associated with the philosophies of Hegel and Durkheim. It generally expresses itself as a sort of "quasi-mystical nationalism" (as in fascism and naziism, which seek the voluntary subordination of individual reason to the superordinate will of the entire people, which is expressed through the instrumentality of a totalitarian state).

Philosophy—is the attempt to formulate a logical and coherent system of general ideas at the highest level of meaningful abstraction, in terms of which all less general systems of ideas can be related and viewed as a meaningful whole. Philosophy is not necessarily the same as *philosophizing,* which may involve the analysis of general propositions without any corresponding attempt to formulate an overarching intellectual worldview.

Political anarchism—is the political philosophy that advocates deinstitutionalized free cooperation, terminating in direct participational democracy (which usually occurs in a postsocialist era). This position provides the basis for educational anarchism.

Political liberalism—is the political philosophy committed to social democracy (stressing representative democracy in a mixed economy). A rather diffuse orientation that generally advocates gradual, small-scale reforms within the framework of the existing political system in order to further individual freedom and to maximize the fullest realization of human potential, it provides the political basis for educational liberalism.

Political liberationism—is the point of view that maintains that we should seek the immediate, large-scale reform of the established social order as a way of augmenting individual liberties and promoting the maximum realization of personal potential. Advocating democratic socialism (stressing representative democracy in a state-controlled economy), it provides the foundation for educational liberationism.

Political philosophy—is (ideally) applied ethics. It specifically addresses itself to the question of what social conditions—what institutions and what relationship between institutions—are necessary for moral policies to be implemented and sustained. It is primarily concerned with how morality can be institutionalized as a continuing aspect of society at large.

Political policies—are those ideas pertaining to what social conditions—what institutions and what relationship between institutions—are necessary in order for specified moral policies to be implemented and sustained in a particular society.

Positive synergism—exists whenever the synergistic process (viewed as implicitly or explicitly purposive or goal-oriented) functions in such a way as to create the ongoing conditions that predispose toward the success of subsequent phases of the process—which, in turn, create the conditions necessary to generate successful behavior (in terms of the purposive or goal of the entire course of action) in subsequent phases of the process.

Postrevolutionary radical liberationism—is primarily concerned with the sort of educational system that is required in order to construct and consolidate the new, reconstituted socialist state in the era after the required political revolution has occurred.

Practical learning—refers to learning that is immediately useful in the everyday world.

Pragmatism (pragmatic)—holds that an idea is "true" if (and to the extent that) it leads to effective consequences when applied to the solution of a real (practical) problem.

Predeterminism—is closely related to cause-and-effect determinism in that it is based on the idea that anyone who is (hypothetically) possessed of perfect knowledge of the world as it exists at the present (in all of its complexity) would be able both to predict the future without error and to reconstruct the past (by logical implication) on the basis of existing information. (A second point of view about predeterminism, which is not dwelled upon in this book, is the supernaturalistic point of view that holds that God, or some kind of cosmic consciousness, has already designed the future, and that history is merely the evolution of divine will).

Prerevolutionary educational liberationism—advocates the kind of education necessary to create the sort of revolutionary consciousness required to elicit a popular demand for restructuring the existing socioeconomic system.

Priestly mode of civil religion—has reference to theologian Martin Marty's distinction between four basic modes of civil religion in contemporary

America. The priestly mode of civil religion is essentially "celebrative, affirmative, culture-building." It is, in turn, expressed in two different ways: in the *transcendent* mode, which sees the nation "under God," assuming that there is "a transcendent objective reference of a kind that has traditionally been associated with deity"; and in the *immanent* mode, in which the nation displaces God, the nation itself assuming self-transcendence.

Principles—in philosophical discourse, are ordinarily considered to be more abstract and basic than *policies* (which are typically viewed as applications of principles to some specified set of circumstances), and policies are normally viewed as regulating *practices,* the actual behaviors that (ideally) emanate from intellectually derived principles and policies.

Problems analysis (approach to educational philosophy)—is the approach where the emphasis is placed upon "doing philosophy" with respect to some specific educational problem or issue rather than attempting to formulate any particular philosophy of education; usually involving some combination of **semantic analysis, rational analysis** and/or **empirical analysis**.

Process philosophies—are predicated upon the basic assumption that life is ultimately rooted in some relatively indefinable "process" such as *experience* or *behavior* (ordinarily viewed as a transitional phenomenon, the interaction between literally "unknowable" conditions that may hypothetically undergird such a process but which can only be "known" indirectly in and through the process itself).

Prophetic mode of civil religion—is theologian Martin Marty's distinction that holds that there is an expression of civil religion which is essentially dialectical and judgmental. The prophetic mode, like the **priestly mode** (see glossary entry), can be expressed as either a commitment to a transcendent or immanent goal.

Psychological behaviorism—is the psychological theory that holds that only behavior is observable and that therefore no assertions about the conditions that ostensibly underlie behavior as such can be the object of legitimate psychological inquiry. For the "hard behaviorist" (such as B. F. Skinner in his purely psychological works) the object of psychology is to formulate laws about behavior, not to make inferences about the nature of reality above and beyond observable action. For the less rigorous, or "soft," behaviorist (such as Abraham Maslow), the behavior of the organism in specified circumstances remains the basic focus, but certain influences about "why" certain patterns of behavior occur — explanations rather than mere correlations — are also deemed permissible.

Psychological developmentalism—holds that, while responses are basically mediated by personality, an individual's personality is itself primarily contingent upon the development of the first sense of personal identity that emerges during the earliest era of life.

Psychological freedom—is the idea, central to existentialism, that holds that, while man is neither free to choose the objective world as it actually is nor the basic value structure that he assimilates through his earliest childhood conditioning, he is totally free to relate to (and therefore construe) his external circumstances in any manner he prefers. He is not free to interpret the world or himself *de novo,* but he is free to interpret the world—to respond to it—anyway he likes.

Psychological hedonism—holds that the highest good is the experience of pleasure. Pleasure is defined as the expression of natural human potentialities as these relate to natural possibilities in the light of specific situations. The interaction between human potentialities and factual possibilities in the light of perceived problems gives rise to **hedonic behavior,** that is, behavior directed by pleasure and pain.

Psychological relationships—exist where there may be no *logical* necessity between a particular social philosophy and a particular educational theory but where there is a rather obvious correlation between the two. This appears to be more associated with the psychodynamics governing the choice of both (possibly determined by something else altogether, such as character structure) than with any inherent relationship between the two.

Psychological relativism—maintains that all personal knowledge is relative to the nature and content of the personal experience by which it has been confirmed.

Psychological value—refers to that aspect of axiology that enquires into the ultimate nature and conditions of personal value, that is, value for the individual *as an individual* rather than, as in the case of social value (or conventional ethics), the individual in his relationship to other people.

Radical liberationism—would use the schools to criticize and reconstruct the very foundations of our culture. As the radical liberationist sees it, we need to rethink and radically revise certain of the most fundamental institutions upon which our society is founded (for example, traditional religion, capitalism, democracy, sex roles, the family, and so on).

Rational analysis—is the philosophical approach that is primarily directed toward determining whether a particular line of reasoning is logical and coherent.

Rationalism (philosophical rationalism)—holds that there are certain fundamental truths—natural or divine laws—that are absolute and unchanging, and that these truths are apprehensible through the exercise of reason. For the rationalist, intellectual consensus about the nature of Truth is implicit within reason itself. Man is rational (predisposed toward the discovery of ultimate meaning through the application of reason), and he exists in an inherently rational (meaningful) world. When man's reason encounters the Reason inherent within Being, the inevitable result is Truth. Therefore Truth is the inevitable convergence of subjective (personal) reason and objective (universal) reason. In the process of speculative reason the individual distinguishes those things that are metaphysically certain (self-evident) from those that are merely probable (evident) and develops a full and coherent system of general beliefs by logical inference on this basis.

Reactionary conservatism—refers to all of those types of political conservatism that are basically anti-intellectual in the sense that they seek to minimize philosophical (or intellectual) arguments and tend to ground their contentions upon a relatively uncritical acceptance of either revealed Truth or established social consensus (frequently viewed as ''common sense'').

In its political expression, the reactionary conservative generally advocates a return to the real or imagined virtues of the past.

Realism—is one of the conventional "systems of philosophy," ordinarily defined as encompassing all of those philosophical positions that accept the fundamental principle that there is a real world that exists independent of being known, that an objective reality exists independent of subjective processes of consciousness.

Reform Judaism—is one of the three major traditions in contemporary Judaism. It attempts to move toward a contemporary redefinition of *Jewishness* and *Judaism,* as well as to redefine the relationship between the two. It generally favors the adaptation of traditional beliefs and practices in accordance with the "spirit of the age."

Reform liberationism—refers to that branch of educational liberationism that maintains that we should correct basic social inequities both within the educational system itself (as through racial desegregation, compensatory instruction for the educationally disadvantaged, and so on) and also within the overall society (by publicizing sources of social injustice, educating children about the necessity for certain types of social action, and such). In short, the school should actively proselytize for the fullest implementation of democratic principles within the existing social system.

Reinforcement theory—maintains that man learns by the emotional (affective) consequences of his behavior. Other things being equal, he learns only those things that entail emotional consequences, and he retains that knowledge which is confirmed by pleasurable effects.

Relativism—is the idea that holds that all knowledge is fundamentally contingent upon circumstantial considerations (which are themselves dependent upon further considerations, and so on); hence all knowledge is fundamentally indeterminate.

Relativity (relationalism)—is the position that holds that all knowledge is "relative" in the sense of being *relational,* and therefore capable of being determined and defined only within some specified context. Relativity (relationalism) holds that any truth-proposition is inevitably related to a broad field of other interrelated truth-propositions and cannot be *totally* defined and understood in isolation; and that undergirding all particular truth-propositions are highly abstract truth-propositions (or meta-assumptions). These meta-assumptions, although themselves relational (in the final analysis), nevertheless provide an absolute basis (for all practical purposes) when it comes to establishing a foundation for ongoing communication.

Religious educational conservatism—is that expression of educational conservatism that stresses the centrality of spiritual training as a basis for proper moral character. The religious educational conservative is perhaps best represented by certain of the more seriously dedicated members of the established (or mainstream) protestant denominations, such as the Southern Baptist Convention or the Lutheran Church (Missouri Synod), which are primarily concerned with transmitting the established beliefs and practices—the time-tested moral and religious orthodoxies—of their own particular churches or denominations. The religious conservative is less rigid and moralistic than the religious fundamentalist. He is also less concerned with justifying and comprehending the intellectual bases of religion than is the theological intellectualist.

Religious educational fundamentalism—maintains that the ultimate purpose of education—that is, to revive and reaffirm the older and better ways, to reestablish traditional standards of belief and behavior—is always decidedly secondary to the overriding universal goal of working for the salvation of the individual's immortal soul. Such salvation is primarily a matter of recognizing and obeying the will of God as this has been revealed through accepted Scriptures (usually interpreted quite literally).

Religious rationalism—is the position, most frequently associated with the philosophy of Saint Thomas Aquinas, that holds that reason is a necessary but not a sufficient condition for apprehending Truth. Supernatural Truth—that is, knowledge concerning the ultimate nature of the external world, encompassing such things as a knowledge of the existence of God, a belief in the divinity of Christ, and so on—transcends ordinary experience, and does not lend itself to purely natural determination by means of reason and evidence. In order to grasp Truth, it is necessary to supplement reason with faith in the perfect knowledge that derives (directly or indirectly) from direct revelation or from the authority of the Church (which serves as God's agent on earth).

Religious reactionary conservatism—holds that truth is primarily founded upon revelation and faith, centering in a literalistic interpretation of accepted Scriptures. Accordingly, this position advocates a return to Biblical truth, black-and-white moral categories, and the sort of simple Christian living that is generally looked upon as more characteristic of an earlier era. Typically other-worldly in their overall orientation, religious reactionary conservatives vehemently oppose any sort of serious theological speculation that would suggest that essential truth has not already been satisfactorily established.

Revelation—is undeniable truth that is communicated directly through a recognized spiritual source, usually God.

Revolutionary anarchism—holds that the most effective way to further the required social revolution in the cause of social justice is to recognize that our educational institutions themselves are the pathological agents that reproduce the "sick" system, and to rise up and eliminate the schools.

Revolutionary liberationism—feels that the only way in which the schools can effectively counter a dehumanizing social system is by eliminating all pretense of "educating" children who have already been rendered uneducable by more profound social forces. This position advocates using the schools, instead, as the primary agency for the immediate overthrow of the existing social system and for its replacement by a different kind of society founded upon truly humane and rational principles.

Right-wing anarchism (right-wing libertarianism)—envisions a laissez-faire capitalism in which the rational-productive capacity of the individual is freed from gratuitous, and essentially destructive, social restraints. The right-wing anarchist, most frequently associated with the objectivist philosophy of Ayn Rand, tends to be absolutistic in his approach to knowing, "egoistic" in his moral philosophy, and capitalistic in his politics. He frequently tends to disavow the label "anarchist."

Right-wing Christian fundamentalism—is a hybrid blend of nationalism and religion that contends that America is God's country and that a twentieth-century reformation is necessary in order to save it from total destruction by the forces of Satan.

Scientific (qualified) behaviorism—holds that the best way to understand human experience is to study its basis in human behavior, and the best way to conduct such a study is through the application of experimental (and, especially, more exacting scientific-experimental) procedures.

Scientific knowledge—refers to that body of information and ideas that has been confirmed through the scientific process or that, at the very least, appears to be highly probable on the basis of those things that have been verified through such scientific verification procedures.

Scientific paradigm—is a model containing the fundamental substantive and procedural assumptions from which research activities peculiar to science or a particular type of science are based. There is a significant difference of opinion about whether there are a variety of different paradigms that are appropriate for different sorts of scientific activity or whether there is only one scientific paradigm that represents the most exacting statement of the conditions required for defensible scientific activity (generally to be found in the more rigorous natural and physical sciences).

Scientific process—is conventionally understood in terms of controlled variables, public verification, intersubjectivity, quantifiability, observability, and such. It describes the research activities peculiar to science as a particular way of acting and thinking.

Secular conservative ideologies—are those educational ideologies that maintain that reality is restricted to natural experience. They hold that, while there are metaphysical principles (that is, extremely abstract and pervasive propositions, like the laws of logic or the formal propositions of mathematics) that apply to *all* natural experience (and which therefore defy ordinary explanation in common sense terms), even these are merely a different dimension of "natural" experience.

Secular educational conservatism—does not necessarily reject the spiritual aspects of education, but it tends to be much more utilitarian and practical in its approach to schooling than those orientations that hold more decided religious inclinations. The secular educational conservative's primary concern is with the school's role in preserving and transmitting established social institutions and processes. He seeks to propagate the sort of information and skills that are necessary in order to ensure the individual's success within the secular social order as it presently exists.

Secular educational fundamentalism—is that expression of educational fundamentalism which characteristically espouses a rather inflexible commitment to what is deemed to be the consensual "common sense" worldview of the average man.

Secularism (secular)—is the point of view represented by all of those philosophies which hold either that there is no personal God (atheism) or that there is no way to determine the existence or nonexistence of a personal God (agnosticism) even if one exists.

Self-actualization (self-realization or **self-perfection)**—is the idea that holds that the individual naturally seeks to *become* what he potentially *is*, that is, he seeks to exist in such a way as to realize his essential nature as a particular human being.

Self-fulfilling prophecy—is a special sort of **synergism cycle** that occurs when belief creates the sort of behavior that serves to verify the belief that generated the behavior in the first place.

Semantic analysis (in philosophy)—is the attempt to clarify the meaning of certain terms or statements employed in philosophical discourse.

Situational morality (**contextual morality** or **situation ethics**)—holds that the moral act is the intentionally "loving" act that is guided by useful and generally trustworthy religious maxims, but which is ultimately tested by the real or conjectural consequences of acting on such maxims in some specific situation when these consequences are weighed against the overriding "love-ethic" itself.

Social conservatism (in political philosophy)—is essentially that position which espouses adherence to time-tested cultural institutions and processes, coupled with a deep respect for law and order, as a basis for any sort of constructive social change. The social conservative advocates a proper relationship between reasoned change and reasonable conformity, with his enthusiasm for either depending largely on his assessment of existing conditions. Ordinarily expressing itself as a type of authoritarian conventionalism, social conservatism emphasizes democratic capitalism (indirect constitutional democracy, stressing rule by law, due process, and property rights within a relatively uncontrolled economy), and it provides the political basis for educational conservatism.

Social Darwinism (**Spencerian Conservatism**)—is the theory, stemming largely from the thought of Herbert Spencer, that holds that history must be viewed primarily in terms of conflict between nations and between peoples, stressing that the survival of the fittest is true, not only within the species, but also between nations and races.

Sociological epistemology—is a point of view closely related to that which is ordinarily referred to as the *sociology of knowledge,* which holds that a person's understanding of the world is fundamentally determined by the nature and conditions of his social relationships in a particular culture.

Social ethics—is that aspect of philosophy that normally encompasses the areas described as moral and political philosophy. It refers both to ethics, in the sense of general theory of interpersonal responsibility, as well as to the practical implications and/or applications of particular ethical positions for social action in specified cultural settings.

Subjectivism—holds that, after the earliest, purely physical, encounters with the world, a person does not respond to the world *as such,* he responds to his own interior (subjective) *responses* to the world. We know the world only indirectly through the medium of personal experience, refracted through the lens of self.

Subjectivity—has reference to knowledge that is radically affected by the existing personality system, which is, in other words, significantly altered by the nature of existing ego-states.

Substantive philosophies—have reference to those philosophies that maintain that there is some kind of definable "meaning" relating to the nature, identity, and/or purpose of objects and events in the world that can be known directly and independent of any mediating process of personal experience. Usually, contrasted to the so-called **process philosophies.**

Synergism—is the process whereby certain kinds of behavior elicit the sort of conditions that, in turn, generate the subsequent kinds of behaviors (and resulting conditions) that ultimately lead to a repetition of the entire process (in what is essentially a self-sustaining cycle of cause-and-effect).

Systems of philosophy—are actually metaphilosophies (that is, philosophical systems that constitute an ultimate structure or taxonomy by which the philosophies of particular individuals can be classified) rather than representing the particular philosophies of specific philosophers as such. These systems of philosophy are variously defined, but most authorities would include realism, idealism, pragmatism, and existentialism among the basic philosophical systems.

Tactical anarchism—maintains that the most "educational" thing we can do is to eliminate the schools altogether so that we can use the immense wealth we are presently expending on an inefficient and authoritarian system of formal education to correct the more pressing *social* (and therefore educational) injustices that virtually preclude under existing circumstances the possibility of real education for most children.

Teleological nationalism (Hegelian conservatism)—is most closely associated with the thought of the great German philosopher Georg W. F. Hegel. The teleological nationalists need to be distinguished from the far more extreme **teleological totalitarians** (represented by such groups as the Fascists and the Nazis on the extreme "Hegelian right"). For the teleological nationalist, the individual basically discovers his nature and identity as a person in and through his participation in some collective. The individual realizes himself, but only indirectly, through the group. It is ultimately the group that realizes itself, through the teleological unfolding of its inner soul or spirit, and not the individuals that comprise it. Accordingly, the individual realizes his personal destiny by voluntarily subordinating himself to the higher Self of the nation or race.

Teleology—holds that some sort of dynamic design and/or purpose is inherent within nature.

Theism—consists of all of those positions which assume the existence of a personal God who is an active force in the determination of contemporary events, who has personality (in the sense of thinking and feeling in a manner very much like human beings), who can be communicated with, and who can, on occasion, be induced to intercede in human events.

Theistic conservative ideologies—are those educational ideologies that hold that reality is essentially dual, possessing both natural and supernatural dimensions, and that man, correspondingly, must realize both the natural and supernatural aspects of his nature in obedience to the universal laws that exist on both of these levels, as dictated by the will of a personal God.

Theological existentialism—holds that it is possible to be a theist within the overriding context of existential doubt relating to the possibility of any sort of objective knowledge.

Theological intellectualism—is a religious expression of educational intellectualism that is perhaps best reflected in the writings of such contemporary Roman Catholic educational philosophers as Jacques Maritain, William McGucken, and John Donohue. From the point of view of the theological intellectualist, the ultimate purpose of education is always secondary to the ultimate purpose of life itself, which is to bring the individual into a perfect union with God.

Theological liberalism—generally has reference to orthodox religious beliefs made less restrictive by an emphasis on the critical examination of traditional beliefs and practices, generally viewed as a continuing form of spiritual renewal.

Theological liberationism—emphasizes the social interpretation of the Scriptures and church authority (frequently bordering on so-called *liberation theology*) in which the role of the church is seen as encompassing an active commitment to the political and economic reconstruction of society as a way of expediting the fullest realization of man's natural and supernatural potentialities.

Thomism—is the philosophy of Saint Thomas Aquinas, a religious rationalism that attempts to reconcile the philosophy of Aristotle with the teachings of (Roman Catholic) Christianity. Thomism is the official philosophy of the Roman Catholic Church, but Roman Catholicism, like all large and complex religions, encompasses a variety of different points of view that occasionally deviate in significant degree from official policy.

Traditional (metaphysical or **essentialistic) realism**—constitutes all of those philosophies (such as the philosophy of Aristotle) that hold that there is a *real and meaningful* world that exists independent of being known or experienced.

Transcendent knowledge—is knowledge that exists in a metaphysical realm beyond the individual's awareness but which is capable of being communicated directly to him without any sort of personal (empirical) mediation whatsoever. In such cases—revelation, mystical intuition, and so forth—the truths are communicated quite involuntarily by some higher power who speaks *through* the individual. Such truths are beyond doubt, because they signify a direct contact with the realm of essence, which is in no way adulterated by the usual sort of subjective processes.

Truth (absolute or **metaphysical Truth)**—generally has reference to absolute knowledge that transcends mere personal experience. Such Truth is *absolute* and *indubitable* precisely because it is not relative to being known or to being proven in terms of other things that have already been experienced. It is, in this sense, "true," not on the basis of *evidence* (personal experience) but *self-evidently,* in and of itself. Such intrinsic truths—such things as cause-and-effect, free will, or the existence of God are frequently viewed as such—defy either verification or refutation, because they are first principles (primary assumptions) that precede all particular experience whatsoever and which provide the necessary basis for any sort of intelligent behavior. They are *true* by definition, tautologically; they *are* because they *are.* Taken together, such ideas comprise the *essence of Being.*

Truth (philosophical truth)—is a term for which no simple definition is possible. Generally speaking, however, the term is used in this book in three basic ways:

1. to distinguish statements of fact (**isness**) from statements of value (**oughtness**)—*descriptive* statements from *prescriptive* statements;
2. as a synonym for *factuality* (existence or identity), which is the way the term is ordinarily used in the various empirical philosophies; and
3. as a term used in reference to the intrinsic meaningfulness of reality itself (for example, "absolute Truth," "ultimate Truth," "Truth," as the term is frequently used in the metaphysical philosophies).

Generally speaking, when talking about the empirical positions, an idea can be true in the sense of being *factual* and yet "meaningless." For the existentialist, for example, there is a factual world that exists independent of being known, but it exists without meaning until it is actually construed by individuals on the basis of their personal encounters in the world. For the pragmatist, a large number of people may all agree that an event has occurred (that it is factually *true*) but may all disagree significantly about what this event *means* (that is, about its relevance to them and how it relates to other things that they already accept to be true).

In general, however, the term *truth* has been used in contradistinction to the term *value,* or it has been used to distinguish between *metaphysical Truth* (the inherent meaningfulness or significance of reality) as opposed to *empirical truth* (the factuality of a statement with respect to some specific object or event).

Truth via reason—is the philosophical position that subscribes to the notion that the individual is rationally disposed to recognize certain basic truths when they occur either through "reminiscence" in the Platonic sense or because they tend to evoke a sense of aesthetic closure (in the Aristotelian tradition). In the Platonic sense, the truths are inherent within the mind to begin with, and therefore are "matched up" and remembered when such ideas are evoked by some actual experience in the natural world. In the less esoteric and mystical Aristotelian sense, the truths invoke closure (experienced as a sort of intuitive certitude) because of the inherent "match" between the individual's distinctive intelligence and the infinitely rational nature of that which is known.

Uncertainty principle—is Werner Heisenberg's proposition that holds that, in any of the natural sciences—and most particularly in physics—the acts of observation and measurement, being physical acts that insert new quanta of energy into the observational sequence, necessarily interfere with and alter that which is being observed.

Utopian anarchism—holds that conventional schooling is totally obsolete. We live on the brink of a utopian postindustrial society characterized by affluence and leisure for all, the sort of society in which only a small number of trained workers will be necessary in order to maintain an almost entirely automated system of production. Under these conditions, people should be left free to learn for themselves, voluntarily and on the basis of their own spontaneous interests. If we simply leave people alone, a sufficient number will naturally choose to learn those things that society requires and that are not capable of being done better by machines, and those who choose to perform a given job on a voluntary basis are likely to be better and more productive than those who have been "programmed'' to act with little or no consideration for their own natural inclinations.

Value experience—refers to a psychological state (such as pleasure, pain, or happiness) that an individual undergoes. It is frequently contrasted to *value objects* (such as power, position, or wealth) that have reference to specific objects/events that can potentially elicit value experiences, and from *value principles,* abstract ideas about the overall nature and conditions of the entire value process (such as enlightenment or self-actualization).

Value principles—are ideas that pertain to the nature of the good at the very highest level of abstraction—that is, ''What is ultimately good? What is ideally good? What is the *summum bonum?*''

Value theory—is that area of ontology which occurs in the interface between axiology and epistemology; it is primarily a matter of **axiological epistemology,** concerned with the relationship between facts and values in the knowing/learning process.

Volitional behavior—refers to behavior that is consciously willful; explicitly purposeful action.

Volitional evil—holds that a man who *knows* (and therefore really *believes*) that a particular course of action is ''good'' can nevertheless act contrary to this belief; that a conscious awareness of what is truly ''good and proper'' conduct does not necessarily cause an individual to direct his actual behavior in accordance with that understanding.

Volksgeist—see **Corporate selfhood**.

Zionism—is the belief that the Jews are destined to be restored to their homeland in Palestine. Zionism is scarcely a simple movement, however, and it is important to bear in mind that there are at least three basic concepts that are, in some sense, ''Zionist'':

1. political Zionism—either religious or secular in nature—which seeks the restoration (or, as of the present, ''continuation'') of a politically independent Jewish Israel, generally through secular means;

2. supernatural Zionism, which holds to the more traditional belief in a miraculous return to the homeland and the restoration of political sovereignty under the leadership of the prophesied Messiah; and

3. what might be termed ''spiritual Zionism,'' which envisions not a reinstituted Jewish state but the advent of a Messianic age in which the entire world will become spontaneously perfected as a new and universal Zion through the enlightened moral and religious consciousness of a perfected Judaism.

Index

Page numbers in italics refer to illustrations; page numbers in boldface refer to glossary entries. Numbers followed by an ''n'' refer to a footnote.